OCR A LEVEL

1

SOCIOLOGY

Katherine Roberts
Paul Taylor
Sue Brisbane
Nayda Ali
Steve Chapman
Jannine Jacobs-Roth

HODDER
EDUCATION
AN HACHETTE UK COMPANY

Acknowledgements

Kath Roberts: I would like to thank my husband Martin, for his enduring love, support and encouragement during the writing of this book, and always. And to all my Sociology students, past, present and future – thank you for continually inspiring me; **Paul Taylor**: I would like to acknowledge Jo for supporting me with love and cups of tea through writing the book and all my students past and present who have helped to inspire my love of teaching sociology.; **Sue Brisbane**: My thanks and love to Keir and Finlay who always bring humour and balance and especially to Martin – I couldn't have done it without you! In memory of Maggie who was my sociology soul mate. **Steve Chapman**: With love and thanks to Fiona for her eternal patience. **Jannine Jacobs-Roth**: My thanks go to my ever supportive and patient family: Ash, Oz, Fin and Sawyer.

The Publishers would like to thank the following for permission to reproduce copyright material:

Picture credits: P2 tl © Rob Ford / Alamy, bl © roger parkes / Alamy, r © David R. Frazier Photolibrary, Inc. / Alamy; p5 l © Alberto Buzzola/LightRocket via Getty Images, r © Martin Green – Fotolia; p7 © milanmarkovic78 – Fotolia; p8 tl © michaeljung – Fotolia, tr © imageBROKER/REX Shutterstock, b © Andrew Rubtsov / Alamy; p9 © Focus Pocus LTD – Fotolia; p12 © maron – Fotolia; p14 t © David J. Green - Lifestyle / Alamy, b © slava_14 – Fotolia; p20 tl © Simon Bellis/LANDOV/ Press Association Images, tr © Cameron Spencer/Getty Images, b © ERIC FEFERBERG/AFP/GettyImages; p25 l © Matt Crossick/ EMPICS Entertainment/Press Association Images, r © David Bagnall / Alamy; p30 l © Alexander Hassenstein/Getty Images, r © Chris Rout / Alamy; p32 l © Page Images/REX Shutterstock, r © Mark Robert Milan/GC Images / Getty Images; p35 l © moodboard / Alamy, r © Cultura Creative (RF) / Alamy; p36 l © Steve Parsons/AFP/Getty Images, r © Press Eye Ltd/REX Shutterstock; p40 © Mark Pain/REX Shutterstock; p46 © Tim Graham/Getty Images; bl © Charlie Condou / The Guardian Syndication, t © JHP Child / Alamy, br © Lynn Hilton/REX Shutterstock; p52 © News Pictures/REX Shutterstock; p54 t © TopFoto, b © M Y Agency Ltd/REX Shutterstock; p56 t © Everett/REX Shutterstock, b © Dudarev Mikhail – Fotolia; p59 © kichigin19 – Fotolia; p62 © Office for National Statistics; p63 l © Old Paper Studios / Alamy, r © doble.d – Fotolia; p67 t © michaeljung – Fotolia, b © Office for National Statistics; p70 © REX Shutterstock; p73 t © Olesia Bilkei – Fotolia, b © Robert Harding/REX Shutterstock; p76 © Creatas/Thinkstock; p78 © Photofusion/REX Shutterstock; p83 t © GraphicaArtis/Getty Images, b © Peter Macdiarmid/Getty Images; p86 l © Joanna Kearney / Alamy, r © BananaStock/Thinkstock; p88 © WENN Ltd / Alamy; p92 © ABC Inc/Everett/REX Shutterstock; p94 © michaeljung – Fotolia; p97 l © ClassicStock / Alamy, r © Moof/ Cultura/Getty Images; p101 © Thodoris Tibilis – Fotolia; p104 l Luit Chaliha / Demotix / Corbis, r © Frank Trimbos / Gallo Images / Getty Images; p107 t © Chris Hondros/Getty Images, c © John Powell/REX Shutterstock, b © Geoff Swaine/Photosho; p110 t © Katrin_Timoff/iStock/Thinkstock, b © DragonImages – Fotolia; p112 © Monkey Business Images/Stockbroker/Thinkstock; p113 t © The Daily Ma/REX Shutterstock, b © Majority World/REX Shutterstock; tl © Brent Stirton/Edit by Getty Images for Discovery Communications, tr © Matt Cardy/Getty Images, bl © Kumar Sriskandan / Alamy; p116 tl © Brent Stirton/Edit by Getty Images for Discovery Communications, tr © Matt Cardy/Getty Images, bl © Kumar Sriskandan / Alamy; p120 © ANL/REX Shutterstock; p121 © Virginia Turbett/Redferns/Getty Images; p123 © Moore/Evening Standard/Getty Images; p125 © zea_ lenanet – Fotolia; p126 © Tim Coleman/REX Shutterstock; p137 l © razorpix / Alamy, r © Photofusion Picture Library / Alamy; p148 l © ZoomTeam – Fotolia, c © WavebreakmediaMicro – Fotolia, r © katie_martynova – Fotolia; p149 l © Most Wanted/REX Shutterstock, r © REX Shutterstock; p151 l © Richard Saker/REX Shutterstock, c © Neil P. Mockford/GC Images/Getty Images, r © Zak Waters / Alamy; p155 © vadimguzhva/iStock/Thinkstock; p156 © benlister.com; p166 l © Roberto Herrett / Alamy, r © Slava_Vladzimirskaya/iStock/Thinkstock; p169 t © Keiichi Matsuda, b © REX Shutterstock; p175 © Photographee.eu – Fotolia; p177 © Ken McKay/ITV/REX Shutterstock; p180 l © John Powell/REX Shutterstock, r © Matt Cardy/Getty Images; p185 l © Michele Burgess / Alamy, tr © Popescu Iacob Emanuel – Fotolia, br © science photo – Fotolia; p187 l © tadeas – Fotolia, r © COUPLE by VISION / Alamy; p194 © REX Shutterstock, tl © Olesia Bilkei – Fotolia; p222 tl © Jacob Wackerhausen/iStock/ Thinkstock, bl © Blend Images / Alamy, tr © dalekhelen / Alamy, br © Monkey Business – Fotolia; p227 b © Mark Draisey / Alamy, t © REX Shutterstock; p231 t © Ray Tang/REX Shutterstock, b © Dave M. Benett/Getty Images; p252 © Sipa Press/REX Shutterstock; p254 tl © REX Shutterstock, bl © Jonathan Hordle/REX Shutterstock, r © WENN UK / Alamy; p255 l © Kadmy – Fotolia, r © Monkey Business – Fotolia; p287 © Christopher Furlong/Getty Images; p296 t © Ute Grabowsky/Photothek via Getty Images, b © MediaPunch/REX Shutterstock; p300 © oneinchpunch – Fotolia; p305 tl © David Fisher/REX Shutterstock, tc © Franck Leguet/REX Shutterstock, tr © Matt Baron/BEI/REX Shutterstock, bl © Daniel Berehulak/Getty Images, br © Ingram Publishing Limited; p307 © Kevin Peterson/Photodisc/Getty Images; p315 © Paul Maguire – Fotolia.

Every effort has been made to trace all copyright holders, but if any have been inadvertently overlooked the Publishers will be pleased to make the necessary arrangements at the first opportunity.

Although every effort has been made to ensure that website addresses are correct at time of going to press, Hodder Education cannot be held responsible for the content of any website mentioned in this book. It is sometimes possible to find a relocated web page by typing in the address of the home page for a website in the URL window of your browser.

Hachette UK's policy is to use papers that are natural, renewable and recyclable products and made from wood grown in sustainable forests. The logging and manufacturing processes are expected to conform to the environmental regulations of the country of origin.

Orders: please contact Bookpoint Ltd, 130 Milton Park, Abingdon, Oxon OX14 4SB. Telephone: +44 (0)1235 827720. Fax: +44 (0)1235 400454. Lines are open 9.00a.m.–5.00p.m., Monday to Saturday, with a 24-hour message answering service. Visit our website at www.hoddereducation.co.uk

© Katherine Roberts, Paul Taylor, Sue Brisbane, Nayda Ali, Steve Chapman and Jannine Jacobs-Roth, 2015

First published in 2015 by

Hodder Education

An Hachette UK Company

Carmelite House

50 Victoria Embankment

London EC4Y 0DZ

Impression number   10 9 8 7 6 5 4 3 2 1

Year   2019 2018 2017 2016 2015

Cover photo © iStockphoto/Nomadsoul1

Illustrations by Peter Lubach

Typeset in 10.75/13.5 pt Bliss Light by Integra Software Services Pvt. Ltd., Pondicherry, India

Printed in Italy

A catalogue record for this title is available from the British Library

ISBN 9781471839481

Contents

PART 2 Researching and understanding social inequalities

D Age

How to use this book

This book has been written and designed specifically for the new OCR Sociology specifications introduced for first teaching in September 2015.

OCR Sociology for A Level 1 covers the content required for:
- OCR AS Sociology (H180)
- Components 01 and 02 of OCR A Level Sociology (H580).

Component 03 is covered in **OCR Sociology for A Level 2**.

Please note that the following aspects of Component 02, Section B: Understanding social inequalities, are for A Level study only:
- Social inequality and difference in relation to ethnicity
- Social inequality and difference in relation to age
- Weberian and New Right sociological explanations of social inequality and difference.

To view the full specifications, and examples of assessment material, for OCR AS or OCR A Level Sociology, please visit OCR's website: www.ocr.org.uk.

The content of this book, as well as **OCR Sociology for A Level 2**, covers all topic options in the new specification. Each chapter has a range of features which have been designed to present the course content in a clear and accessible way, to give you confidence and to support you in your revision and assessment preparation.

Getting you thinking

Each section starts with an activity that has been designed to get you thinking about the topic.

Activity

Activities appear throughout the book and have been designed to help you develop your understanding and sociological skills.

Study

Sociological studies are summarised in these boxes. The studies included are not required by OCR but have been added to help develop understanding and support further discussion.

Quick question

Quick questions are exactly that – questions to answer quickly that will help you think about, and understand, different topics in the book.

Check your understanding

These questions have been designed specifically to help to check that you have understood different topics.

Section summary

These boxes contain summaries of what you have learned in each section but we have left some blanks for you to fill in!

Practice questions

These have been designed to offer study practice.

Glossary

Key terms in **bold** in the text are defined in the glossary at the end of the book.

Chapter 1

Introducing socialisation, culture and identity

Introduction

What is sociology?

Sociology, put very simply, is the study of society. Sociologists are interested in how societies work and the ways in which individuals, groups and institutions are interrelated. In sociology we look at institutions such as the family, the media, religion and the education system and ask questions about their structure, in whose interests they operate, and the effect that they have on individuals and on society as a whole. We are also interested in areas of social concern such as crime, divorce and poverty, and try to explain why these issues occur and how they affect society and individuals. The important issue of inequality is a key focus in sociology, and sociologists look at how factors such as social class, gender, ethnicity and age can affect an individual's chances in life.

Sociological evidence

As a sociology student, you will come across various forms of sociological evidence, which you will use to express and evaluate ideas about different aspects of society. In order to study and understand society, sociologists develop theories about how it works. You will get a brief introduction to theories in Chapter 2, and will come across theories in more detail throughout this textbook.

In Chapter 1, especially Section 1.3, *What is identity?*, references will be made to some of these sociological theories, so you may need to familiarise yourself with these theories, using Chapter 2, before or during your reading of this section.

Sociologists also carry out research on aspects of society to help them understand what is happening and why. Research methods used by sociologists are relevant throughout your course, but will be considered in detail and assessed in Component 2 of your A Level or AS Level.

In this book, you will come across lots of different sociologists who have developed ideas and carried out research. The use of these sociological studies is important in supporting or challenging different ideas. Sociologists also often develop concepts – these are terms that sociologists use to express particular ideas about society. Finally, because sociology is about the society in which we all live, examples are useful to illustrate sociological points, and also to evaluate ideas. You will come across lots of examples throughout your study of sociology, and you can also think of and apply your own.

You are encouraged to use various types of sociological evidence to understand and explain various social issues, and to think critically about different explanations. No previous knowledge is required, but an open and enquiring attitude is essential.

1.1 What is culture?

Bradford: curry capital

Notting Hill Carnival

Rugby rivalry

Consider the images above. What do they tell you about UK culture?

Culture

The concept of culture is central to sociology. But what does it mean? The word 'culture' is used in different ways in society. For example, it is often used in a narrow way to refer to artistic and intellectual activities; e.g., theatre and art are seen as examples of 'culture', and if you enjoy such things, you are seen as 'cultured'. However, sociologists tend to use the term 'culture' in a much broader way, to refer to the entire way of life of a particular society.

When considering culture, as sociologists, we are considering the whole system of behaviour and beliefs of a society or group, which includes knowledge, language, faith, art, music, fashion, morals, laws, customs, traditions, lifestyle and more.

Cultures vary hugely across the world – there is a diversity (variety) of cultures.

Activity

The Hamar tribe

The Hamar tribe lives in Ethiopia, and has a culture rich in ceremony and ritual. To reach adulthood, Hamar males must perform a ceremony where they leap onto the backs of cattle and run across them. The women are whipped before this ceremony to prove their devotion to men.

1 You can see clips of these ceremonies and find out more about the tribe by searching for 'the Hamar tribe' on YouTube.

2 Contrast this tribe's culture with your own. Identify five features that are different.

Norms and values

What makes each culture distinctive are the norms and values associated with it.

Values are beliefs and ideas that society sees as important, and that are accepted by the majority of society. Values are things that we believe in, strive to achieve, and that guide our behaviour. For example, in the UK we value life, success, honesty, loyalty, hygiene, family … and more!

Quick question

Can you think of any more typical UK values?

Norms are expected patterns of behaviour that are based on the values of a culture. For example, in the UK it is a norm to wear clothes when in public (based on the value of modesty), to eat food with a knife and fork (based on the values of hygiene and manners), to join the back of a queue (based on the values of order, politeness and fairness), and to obey laws or rules (based on the values of order, respect and obedience). In UK culture, there are certain norms and values that most people follow. These may be different from the norms and values in other cultures.

Within any culture, everyday events have certain norms and values associated with them which we all know about and follow – for example, being at school.

Values:
- educational achievement
- obedience
- respect
- conformity
- knowledge.

Norms:
- Wear the uniform.
- Sit down.
- Obey the teacher.
- Listen.
- Be punctual.
- Ask and answer questions.
- Try your best.
- Do homework.

Study

Sex and Temperament in Three Primitive Societies – Mead (1935)

Margaret Mead was an American anthropologist who studied several tribal cultures in Samoa and New Guinea in the first half of the twentieth century. One area that Mead studied was male and female behaviour and gender role expectations in different tribes. She found that these were very different from the gender role expectations in the US at the time. For example, in the Arapesh tribe, both males and females were gentle and cooperative. In contrast, both genders in the Mundugumor tribe were violent and aggressive. Perhaps the most remarkable tribe she studied was the Tchambuli (now spelled Chambri), where males and females were different from each other, but roles were almost the opposite of those expected in the US and the UK. The women were dominant and aggressive and not much involved in childrearing, whereas the men were timid, emotionally dependent and spent their time decorating themselves. Aggressive men were considered 'abnormal'.

Point to discuss and research

How do you think Mead might have gathered this information?

3

Norms are linked to values – the reason we perform certain behaviour is because we hold certain beliefs. For example, from the above list, the value of 'respect' may underlie some of the norms, such as listening and obeying the teacher. However, these may also be influenced by other values such as obedience and educational achievement.

Activity

Norms and values
1 Make similar lists of norms and values for one of the following activities, or one of your own, in a pair/small group:
  ● going food shopping
  ● going on a first date
  ● going out for a meal
  ● going to the cinema.
2 Try to link your norms and values. Which values are being shown by each norm?

The norms and values of any culture are relative. This means they are not fixed, and are not the same for all people and in all situations. For example, wearing clothes is a norm in UK culture when you are in public. However, it would not be a norm if you are in the shower!

Norms and values can also change over time. For example, smoking used to be the norm in pubs and many other social situations, whereas it is becoming more and more deviant to smoke.

Most people in a society follow the norms most of the time – they conform. Those who do not follow the norms of society are considered deviant. Deviance is behaviour that goes against the norms of a group or a society. Deviance will often lead to consequences or sanctions. We will look more at ways in which we are socially controlled in Section 1.2, *What is socialisation?* (page 15).

Cultures also differ enormously from one another. What is seen as normal in one culture may be seen as deviant or offensive in another. This is one aspect of cultural diversity.

Cultural diversity

Diversity refers to variety or difference. Cultural diversity refers to the differences and variety found in societies. Cultural diversity can be seen both between cultures (intercultural diversity) and within cultures (intracultural diversity).

Activity

Intercultural diversity
1 Write down some examples of ways in which other cultures have alternative ideas of what is normal and acceptable.
Hint: Consider examples related to eating, greeting, clothing, food, living arrangements, language, leisure, activities, behaviour, and so on. You could use comparisons with other cultures you have visited on holiday, or seen through the media, and also link back to the examples you looked at from the Hamar tribe and the tribes studied by Margaret Mead.

The UK is culturally diverse. By this, we mean that there is a diversity or variety of norms and values within UK culture: 'intracultural diversity'. This may include the cultures of different ethnic groups, but there is also a diversity of regional cultures (Welsh, Scottish, English, Northern Irish) and diversity within these (North vs South), a diversity of age cultures, class cultures, sexual cultures, and so on. This diversity impacts on the overall UK culture, adding to the range of things that become 'normal'.

Quick question

Can you think of some examples of cultural diversity within the UK? Consider examples such as faith, food, clothing, music and language, linked to some of the diversity of cultures within the UK, as mentioned above.

Subcultures

A subculture is often defined as 'a culture within a culture' – a smaller grouping of people who share distinctive norms and values within a wider culture. For example, within UK culture, there are subcultures based on age (e.g., youth subcultures such as punks or emos), ethnicity, music/fashion, political beliefs, and so on. All of these groups are part of the wider UK culture, but also part of distinctive subcultures. This concept clearly links to cultural diversity – a society with many subcultures will be culturally diverse.

Cultural hybridity

A hybrid is a cross between or merging of two or more things. When cultures merge, it is referred to as cultural hybridity. UK culture is often described as hybrid, because it contains aspects of English, Scottish, Welsh and Irish culture, but also influences from Asian culture, Caribbean culture, US culture, European culture, and so on. In a global society, hybridity becomes more common. Cultural hybridity can best be seen in aspects such as music, fashion and food.

Cultural hybridity in the UK is often considered in relation to second- or third-generation immigrants who adopt hybrid identities, mixing aspects of their parents' culture with aspects of British culture. One example of a hybrid culture is 'Brasians', which is a mixing of British and Asian culture. Traditional aspects of South Asian culture, such as religion, Bhangra music or henna tattoos, may be mixed with British values, music and fashion to create a fusion or hybrid.

We will explore the impact of hybridity on ethnic identities more in Section 1.3, *What is identity?* (page 17).

Types of 'culture' in our society

Different types of 'culture' have been identified in our society, and sociologists use terms like 'high culture', 'popular culture' and 'consumer culture' to identify them.

Activity: Cultural hybridity

Item A

Item B

1 How do the images above illustrate cultural hybridity?

5

High culture

This refers to cultural products and activities that are seen to have a very high status. What is considered 'cultured' in this sense is based on those cultural products that represent the highest achievements in humanity. Examples may be Shakespeare's plays, classical music, opera, ballet and art. High culture is seen as superior to other forms of culture by some, and is often appreciated by those with a high level of education and social upbringing – those who are 'cultured'.

Popular culture

This refers to cultural products and activities that are enjoyed by the majority of a population – such as watching television, going to the cinema, playing or watching football, and reading magazines and tabloid newspapers. Some would argue these are more shallow activities, and so inferior to high culture, but not everyone would agree. Another more negative term, 'mass culture', is sometimes used to represent this perceived shallowness and inferiority.

Some feel that popular culture is manufactured and fake and even that it is a form of brainwashing or 'dumbing down' of the masses (the majority of the general population). However, some writers, such as Bourdieu (1984), argue that the distinction between high culture and popular culture (and how 'worthy' they are) lies in the power of the group who support and access them. So high culture is simply the culture of the higher economic classes – this does not necessarily make it better! The media is usually credited with partially creating and spreading popular culture, providing mass access to things such as music, films and sport, which form the basis of popular culture.

Read more about Bourdieu in Section 1.3, *What is identity?* (page 26).

It is also argued that the distinction between popular and high culture is gradually breaking down – the media gives everyone access to activities previously seen as 'high culture', such as turning Shakespeare plays into movies and using classical musicians in pop songs, but also raising the status of previously working-class pursuits, such as football.

Activity

High and popular culture

1 Fill in the blanks in the following table to give the high culture or popular culture equivalents of the examples given, and add in some examples of your own at the bottom if you can think of any more comparisons.

High culture	Popular culture
Listening to classical music	
	Going to rock/pop concerts
	Going to a football match
Watching intellectual foreign films	
Watching arts documentaries	
	Reading a tabloid newspaper
Reading classic novels, e.g., Dickens, Hardy	

2 Is high culture superior to popular culture? Why/why not? Do you agree with Bourdieu?

3 Are there any examples from your above list that make you question whether these two forms of culture are really that distinct?

Consumer culture

It is argued that we have a consumer culture today as a result of the increasing availability of, and emphasis on, the consumption of goods and services. In a consumer culture, consumer goods are widely available, and excessive consumption and the debt associated with it are regarded as acceptable and 'normal'. Shopping – the focus of consumption – is a leisure pursuit in its own right, and 'conspicuous consumption' – where individuals consume branded goods in a blatant attempt to construct an identity and gain status in the eyes of others – is the norm. This is all encouraged and reinforced by the media, especially the advertising industry and celebrity culture.

Global culture

This refers to the growing trend of cultural products and activities becoming 'universal' – where brands, food, films and other cultural products are identical across many different countries, and national cultures lose their distinctiveness. This is linked to the trend of globalisation – the process by which the world becomes more interconnected, and activities in different countries influence each other. McDonald's, Microsoft, Nike and Coca-Cola are all examples of global brands, instantly recognisable around the world, and thus part of a global culture. McLuhan (1964) argued even in the 1960s that the world had become a smaller place – we now live in a 'global village'. This has been driven by industry (multinational companies), travel, a globally accessible media and the internet in particular.

Globalisation and culture

A number of sociologists have noticed the emergence of global culture, a product of the process of globalisation – which implies that cultures can no longer be seen as separate from each other. What happens in one society is increasingly connected to others. Even in remote parts of the world, people can be found drinking Coca-Cola, eating McDonald's food and watching Western TV sitcoms, dubbed into their own language.

Activity

Consumer and global culture

1 Do you agree that our culture is based around consumption today? How important are the things that you buy to your life?
2 Suggest examples of globalisation in action, i.e., things that have become cross-cultural. Which technological developments have added to the process of globalisation?
3 Consider the positive and negative effects on individual cultures of such developments.

Check your understanding

Briefly define the following terms and give an example of each:

1 culture
2 subculture
3 values
4 norms
5 cultural diversity
6 cultural hybridity
7 high culture
8 popular culture
9 consumer culture
10 global culture.

Section summary

Fill in the blanks, using the words given below.

Culture refers to a way of _____. It includes _____ and values. Norms are agreed ways of behaving, and they are usually related to _____, which are shared beliefs about what's important. There is a huge variety both between cultures and within cultures – this is known as _____. A diverse culture will contain many different _____ with distinct norms and values. Cultures also show _____, as they merge together. We can also identity certain types of culture, such as high culture and _____culture. These are often related to _____. Due to the influence of the media and the pressure to buy things, some say we are living in a _____ today. All cultures are becoming more interconnected through globalisation, and due to many shared experiences, the world could be seen as one _____.

consumer culture, cultural diversity, global culture, hybridity, life, norms, popular, social class, subcultures, values

1.2 What is socialisation?

Getting you thinking ...

(Posed by models)

What do the images above tell you about how children become members of their society?

Culture (and therefore norms and values associated with culture) is learned.

The process of learning the norms and values of society is called 'socialisation'.

One example to consider is how we expect men and women to behave in our culture. We are socialised into our gender roles – this means they are learned.

Activity: Gender role socialisation

Item A: Images of changing gender roles in the UK

Item B: Reconsider the Tchambuli tribe, studied by Margaret Mead
(On page 3.)

1 How do these examples show that gender roles must be learned?

This idea of socialisation – learning how to fit into culture – is explored throughout sociology. It can be linked to the 'nature/nurture' debate.

The nature/nurture debate

What has made you the person you are? Is it your genes (nature) or your upbringing (nurture)?

This has been debated for many years – most sociologists would argue that nurture is more important than nature. Some aspects of culture are clearly learned – we are not born knowing norms and values.

As we have seen, norms and values vary between and within different societies, and they also change over time. However:

- What about other 'human' characteristics, such as walking upright, chewing food and being social with others?
- What about personality traits, such as intelligence, aggression and kindness?
- What about gender differences, such as males being more aggressive and competitive, and females being more emotional?

Are these things natural, or are they learned?

It is very hard to prove how much of your behaviour is innate or biological and how much is learned, because most people are brought up by their biological parents.

So how could we research this?

Item A: Twin studies

Bouchard researched identical twins who had been separated at birth and raised separately. When these twins were reunited as adults, Bouchard found that the similarities were striking.

For example, Oskar and Jack were identical twin boys. Oskar was raised by his grandmother in Germany, in the Catholic faith and as part of the Hitler youth. Jack was raised in the Caribbean by his father as part of the Jewish faith, and spent some of his youth on an Israeli kibbutz.

Bouchard documented the many similarities in their behaviour, likes and dislikes and personalities, despite such different upbringings. For example, their mannerisms, temperament, favourite foods, choice in clothes were all strikingly similar (Holden 1980).

Item B: Feral (wild) children/children without human contact

Isabel the 'chicken girl'

Isabel was found when she was ten years old in Portugal. It seemed that since she was born, she had been left in the chicken coop with the hens by her mother, who worked in the fields. Isabel could not speak, was not toilet trained, and expressed emotion by beating her arms and drumming her feet – probably imitating the behaviour of the hens. She was physically malformed, probably due to malnutrition.

Kamala & Amala – wolf children

These two girls were discovered living with wolves in India. It was assumed that they must have been lost in the jungle or even snatched by the wolves as babies. There was no evidence they were related – one was around eight years old and one was only eighteen months old. Their behaviour was seen to be 'wolf-like' – they howled, walked on all fours and ate directly from a bowl with their mouths, rather than using their hands.

Oxana Malaya

This story was widely reported some years ago, but later evidence casts doubt on its credibility. The original story was that Oxana had been left in the kennel with the family dogs since she was very young. Footage of her in a children's home in the Ukraine was released, and she was barking and running on all fours. Her parents were blamed for abuse. However, later evidence suggests that actually some of this behaviour may have been learned in the children's home itself, where care was allegedly very poor. It is also alleged that the dog-like behaviour seen had already been 'unlearned' by the time the famous footage was shot, and that Oxana was asked to put it on for the cameras. Clearly some time in Oxana's childhood was spent with dogs, but the true sequence of events may never be known. Oxana can now walk and talk normally.

Genie

Genie is one of the most famous cases of privation, a child who had almost no human contact at all until the age of thirteen. She, unlike the other examples here, was not 'raised' by animals, but rather just shut in a room on her own, strapped to a 'potty chair' and given virtually no human interaction or stimulation at all for over ten years. Her father claimed he was protecting her because she was mentally retarded, but it is unclear whether this was actually a result of the isolation. Genie was studied endlessly when she was discovered, but though she made some progress at forming human attachments, she never learned to speak fluently, and spent her life in institutional care.

You can find clips on Oxana, Genie and other 'feral children' on YouTube.

Item C: Experiments

Bruce Reimer

Bruce and Brian Reimer were twin boys born in Canada. When he was seven months old, Bruce's penis was destroyed in a circumcision operation. Over a year later, his parents saw psychologist Dr John Money on television and contacted him for help. Dr Money argued that nurture is more important than nature, and suggested that Bruce could be raised as a girl. He used this as an experiment to test his belief that gender identity is a product of nurture rather than nature. The Reimers changed Bruce's name to Brenda and brought her up to be feminine, wearing dresses and playing with dolls. For a time, Money's experiment seemed to have worked, and he used this case to argue that nurture was more important than nature. However, Brenda was so unhappy at around the age of 13 that she attempted suicide. The Reimers told her the truth, and Brenda decided to live again as a male and called himself David. For a time, David was much

Activity: Different types of evidence used in the nature/nurture debate (continued)

happier and got married. He claimed in interviews that he had always known something was not right. Tragically, the experience took its toll and David eventually took his own life.

You can find out more about this example on the internet, including two detailed BBC *Horizon* documentaries which you may be able to access.

Item D: Cross-cultural studies

These include studies of tribal cultures such as the Hamar tribe and the Tchambuli tribe – look back at these examples from Section 1.1, *What is culture?* (see page 3).

1 Briefly explain what each piece of evidence shows and why – does it support nature or nurture?
2 Which side of the debate do you find most convincing – or is it a bit of both?

Activity

Nature/nurture – what do you think?

1 Prepare for a class debate, with some presenting the evidence and arguments for nature, and some presenting the evidence and arguments for nurture. The rest of the class could ask questions, add comments and then vote on which they find the most convincing.
2 Mini-essay: Outline and assess the view that human behaviour is shaped more by nurture than nature.

Try to create a debate, in which you use some of the evidence you have considered above to support and refute the view in the question. Aim to write approximately 500 words.

Socialisation

Socialisation is the process by which an individual learns the norms and values of society. In other words, socialisation is the way in which we learn to be members of society.

It can be divided into:

- primary socialisation – the first and most important stage of learning.
- secondary socialisation – the continuation.

Socialisation continues throughout an individual's lifetime.

Agencies of socialisation

These are the groups or institutions that play a part in our socialisation – through which we learn the norms and values of society.

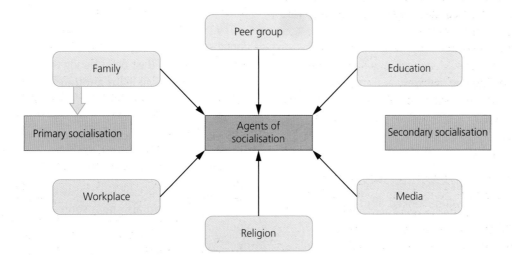

Primary socialisation

- The early years of life (ages 0–5) are very important in the learning process.
- This is the stage of primary socialisation when we are normally in intimate and prolonged contact with our family.
- Our family play a key part in teaching us basic norms and values.
- It is primary socialisation that the feral children like Oxana and Genie did not experience.

Learning from parents

One way children learn from their parents is through imitation. For example, they may copy the way their parents talk or their table manners.

They will see their parents as role models and model their behaviour on that of their parents.

Children also learn what is acceptable and unacceptable by a process of trial and error. Parents will apply sanctions to behaviour to show whether it is desirable or not – positive sanctions (such as praise) or negative sanctions (such as a telling-off). This is a form of social control.

As well as teaching us basic norms and values, the family also make an important contribution to our identity. Examples relating to how we learn our gender, social class and ethnic identities, and links to the family, will be looked at in more detail in the next section.

Quick questions

1 What is 'socialisation'?
2 Name all of the agents of socialisation.
3 What is primary socialisation, and where does it take place?
4 Give three examples of things that children learn through primary socialisation.

Secondary socialisation

Though the family is obviously important, the other agents of socialisation also have an important impact on our norms and values.

Activity

Agents of socialisation

1 In small groups, identify some specific examples of norms and values that may be taught by each of the following agents of socialisation.

Consider exactly how they may socialise the individual into these norms and values:

- family
- peer group
- education
- media
- religion
- workplace.

1. Peer group

Peers are those of a similar age group.

They will include friends, but your peer group is wider than just your friends.

The peer group is a very important agent of socialisation during school years (ages 5–18) since an individual spends a lot of time with their peers during this time.

An individual will learn a lot about acceptable behaviour from peers, because of the desire to 'fit in' – known as conformity.

It may be that peers become more influential than parents during these school years. Within peer groups there are often hierarchies – some individuals will be 'leaders' and have higher status than the 'followers'.

Peer groups can also be a source of rebellion – youth subcultures such as goths, emos and punks are peers who share norms and values and influence each other to resist the norms and values of wider society.

Activity

Looking at research ...

Skelton and Francis (2003) looked at peer groups in primary schools – for example, in the classrooms and in the playground. Play was very gendered, with boys dominating the space and girls taking part is separate activities, such as skipping.

Sue Lees (1983, 1997) looked at the pressure put on teenage girls by peers – for example, how double standards are applied to girls' and boys' sexual behaviour, such as how the term 'slag' is used to control girls' behaviour.

Judith Harris (1998) looked at the comparative influence of parents and peer groups, concluding that the peer group can be more influential than the family in shaping children's identities.

Peer pressure is an important influence on behaviour – though as Harris points out, peer groups don't push, they pull. She means that an individual's desire to conform is a stronger influence than the peer group's overt pressure/bullying.

Tony Sewell (2000) uses the concept of 'cultural comfort zones' to describe the way in which we like to associate with those who are similar to ourselves – to stay in our comfort zone. He links this particularly to African-Caribbean boys, preferring to hang around in gangs with peers than to be in the white middle-class world of teachers and school, which is an alien environment.

1 Pick one of these studies to consider in more depth – do some internet research and see if you can find out more about what was said. Consider whether you agree with their ideas from your own experience.
2 Conduct your own research among your friends to see if they support the study's finding. (For guidance on the research methods you could use, see Chapter 6).

This rebellion was studied by a group of sociologists from the Centre for Contemporary Cultural Studies at Birmingham University, and is considered further in the chapter on youth subcultures (see page 112).

2. Education

Though this clearly overlaps with peer groups, the education system itself is an agent of secondary socialisation.

At school, everyone learns the formal curriculum (maths, French, history, science, and so on). This will be based on the language and culture of society, and reflect its values. For example, maths, English and science are highly valued, history is mostly from a British perspective and child development is usually taught by and taken by females.

However, sociologists argue we also learn the informal curriculum or 'hidden curriculum'. This is all the other norms and values you are learning at school outside of your formal lessons.

Quick question

Can you think of some examples of things you learn at school that are part of the 'hidden curriculum'?

For example, you learn:
● that there are sanctions for those who disobey, such as detention.
● that society values achievement, and you learn how that is measured.
● about the school structure itself – e.g., the genders of the teachers at different levels of authority in the school.

Teachers are the main people who pass on these norms and values, and you will also learn about your own place in society by the way they interact with you.

Study

Schooling in Capitalist America–Bowles and Gintis (1976)

Some Bowles and Herb Gintis were American Marxists (you'll find out more about Marxism and other theories in Chapter 2–see page 36).

They agreed that the hidden curriculum exists, but did not think that that it was just about learning shared norms and values.

They argued that the education system was a 'giant myth-making machine' which brainwashed children through the hidden curriculum into the obedience and unquestioning attitude that they would need in the world of work.

Pupils are taught to accept their place in society, believe that their achievements and failures are of their own making, and that everything is fair and based on merit.

So Bowles and Gintis see the hidden curriculum and the socialisation that takes place in the education system as very significant, but not good for the majority.

Points to discuss and research

1 What kinds of things are children taught through the hidden curriculum which will prepare them for their role in the workforce?
2 Do you think this is a good or bad thing?
3 Who benefits from children learning the hidden curriculum?

3. Media

The influence of the media is growing all the time, and it is arguably the most important source of secondary socialisation. Use of the media has exploded, with new forms of media such as the internet, mobile phones and games as well TV, films and magazines.

Many of us like to claim that we are not influenced by the media, and that we just use it to communicate or to find out things, but most sociologists would disagree.

One way we may be socialised by the media is through its representation of different social groups, which may influence our views. For example, women are represented in very stereotypical ways, according to feminist sociologists. This may affect the way we judge women, or affect women themselves and their own self-image. Mulvey (1975) uses the concept of the 'male gaze' to describe how the camera in films 'eyes up' female characters, encouraging viewers to assess their bodies and their attractiveness, from a male perspective.

An area of concern often expressed is media influence on violence in society – various films and games have been blamed for 'copycat' acts of violence, as viewers were apparently influenced by them.

More widely, the media is seen to influence culture. Some argue it has created a consumer culture where we are encouraged to buy products based on celebrity endorsements or association with a particular lifestyle or image.

Activity: Media and socialisation

Item A: Media representations

Item B: A 'bulimic society'

British criminologist Jock Young (2007) argues that the media is partly responsible for criminality. Young argues that the media has created a 'bulimic society' – one with constant hunger and desire to binge on everything and anything. The bulimic society is one in which even those with little money are 'hooked on Gucci, BMW, Nike, watching television 11 hours per day ... worshipping success, money, wealth and status' but at the same time are 'systematically excluded from its realisation'. It is a culture of 'get rich or die trying', when too often only the latter alternative is available. Young argues that this can explain criminality among youths from deprived backgrounds.

1 What impact may each of the images in Item A have on an individual's views and behaviour?
2 Do you agree with Jock Young that the media has created a 'bulimic society'?
3 How might the media's obsession with 'money, wealth and status' explain why youths from deprived backgrounds may be more likely to turn to criminality?

4. Religion

The importance of religion as an agent of socialisation is in decline for many of us, according to some sociologists who argue that UK society is becoming more secular – which means less religious.

However, it could be argued that many of our norms and values in the UK, including laws, morals and customs, are based on the Christian religion, so we are all influenced by religion more than we realise. Attitudes towards, and laws relating to, issues such as divorce, homosexuality, abortion, euthanasia and even murder are all influenced to an extent by religious views.

In a multi-faith society, religion may influence some groups more than others. For example, Modood and Berthoud (1997) surveyed young people and found that 67 per cent of Pakistanis and Bangladeshis saw religion as 'very important', compared to 5 per cent of white British youths. So individuals brought up in a Muslim, Hindu or Sikh family, for example, may feel that religion is a very important influence on their norms and values. Additionally, many Christian congregations in the UK are now made up of many people of African-Caribbean and also Eastern European descent. So the decline of religion's influence in the UK is not universal.

5. Workplace

The workplace will be a key agent of socialisation for adults, rather than children, and the concept of 'resocialisation' has been used to refer to the new set of norms and values an individuals will learn when they start a new job.

In a similar way to education, the socialisation could be split into formal and informal.

Formal socialisation in the workplace will be in the form of learning the code of conduct, acceptable dress codes, behaviour and other expectations. This will be enforced by formal sanctions such as a formal warning or even being fired, but also positive sanctions such as 'employee of the month' or a promotion or pay rise.

Informally, colleagues will help to resocialise an individual in a similar way to peer groups at school, by making clear what is expected and by sanctioning unacceptable behaviour. For example, if a new employee is 'sucking up' to the boss too much, or informing on his colleagues, it will be made clear to him by informal sanctions such as 'the silent treatment' that this is not acceptable.

The term 'canteen culture' has been used (for example, by Waddington 1999) to describe the set of norms and values that people who work in a particular organisation will be socialised to accept, so that certain language, behaviour and attitudes become the norm.

This has been used in a critical way to describe the culture of racism within the police, whereby even individual police officers who are not racist will start

thinking and behaving in ways that are, as they are socialised into the canteen culture of the police force.

Quick questions

1 What was the name of the researcher who argued that peers are more important than parents?
2 What is the other name for the 'informal curriculum' in school?
3 What is the concept used by Laura Mulvey relating to the way women are viewed in films?
4 What is meant by 'resocialisation'?
5 What is meant by 'canteen culture'?

Social control

The agencies of socialisation can also be seen as mechanisms of social control: ways through which our behaviour is controlled. Behaviour is controlled and reinforced by sanctions. These are used to either positively reinforce a behaviour in order to encourage it or to negatively reinforce a behaviour in order to discourage it.

Formal mechanisms of social control

Examples of formal mechanisms of social control are the police, the courts and criminal justice system, the government and the military. Via the passing and enforcement of laws, these institutions directly and explicitly control the behaviour of the population. In the UK it is rare that the military is used to control UK citizens, though it has been known, for example in Northern Ireland, and is more common in some other countries. The police have also used 'military-style' tactics, such as mounted police charges, 'kettling', and even plastic bullets and water cannons, to control sections of the UK population in times of civil unrest.

Though not traditionally seen as a formal agency of social control, education also has a formal element to its control, with legal requirements in terms of attendance and behaviour codes. Similarly, the workplace can be a mechanism of formal control, in terms of official disciplinary procedures and codes of conduct. Religion may also operate in a more formal way within some families and communities. Sanctions imposed by a religious organisation (such as expulsion or public condemnation) may operate to formally control behaviour.

Sanctions used by formal mechanisms of social control would include:

● warnings from the police
● sentences from the court
● dismissal from work
● exclusion from school.

Formal social control is explicit and obvious – people are aware it is happening.

Informal mechanisms of social control

These control our behaviour more subtly – they would include peer group, education, religion, family, workplace and media.

Different types of sanction used may include:
- socially excluding a person from a peer group
- disappointed reactions from parents
- being passed over for promotion at work
- celebrities being criticised in magazines.

Informal control may be less obvious, but it is just as powerful in influencing our behaviour as formal control, and even more so in some cases.

Activity

Social control

Below is a table showing examples of sanctions.

	Formal sanctions	Informal sanctions
Positive	Pay rise Awards/certificates	Saying 'thank you' Applause
Negative	Exclusion from school Formal warning from work	Stopping pocket money Gossiping or spreading rumours about someone

1 Write down some more examples for each type of sanction.

Check your understanding

Briefly define the following terms and give an example of each:
1 the nature/nurture debate
2 socialisation
3 primary socialisation
4 secondary socialisation
5 cultural comfort zones
6 hidden curriculum
7 resocialisation
8 social control
9 sanctions.

1.3 What is identity?

Getting you thinking ...

Who am I?
Write down a list of ways in which you would answer this question.

The concept of identity

Identity is often defined as how you see yourself. Other related terms include self-concept or self-identity, both referring to your idea of yourself. However, consider where your 'self-concept' or 'sense of identity' comes from. It is clearly affected by how others see you, sometimes referred to as 'social identity'. So identity is both personal and social, and it marks us out as different to others, but also emphasises our similarities.

When you answered the question 'Who am I?', you probably identified yourself as a member of various social groups, perhaps defined by gender or age, but also selected things that are personal to you, such as your name, accomplishments and personality traits.

Your identity is also a product of all of the experiences you have had through socialisation. It is formed by your family, but also by peers, education, media, religion and the workplace. Positive and negative experiences will all have an impact on your identity, and it will change as you go through life.

Some argue that your identity is imposed onto you and fairly fixed in relation to your gender, class, age and ethnicity, for example, but others say it is more fluid and can be an active process. These days we construct our own identities, using the media for ideas and deciding who we want to be. What we choose to buy and wear, how we choose to look and these are all ways in which we are constructing our identities and making a statement to others about who we are.

Section summary

Fill in the blanks, using the words given below.

Socialisation is the _____ by which an individual learns the norms and _____ of society. There is a debate about whether most aspects of human behaviour are learned through socialisation or whether they are _____ or biological. This is known as the _____ debate. _____ socialisation takes place in the family and, as well as teaching very basic norms and values, the family will also socialise a child into its _____, ethnicity and social class. Agents of secondary socialisation include education, the media, the _____, religion and the workplace. They each perform a crucial role in continuing the process of _____. They also help to control our behaviour, imposing positive _____ to reward conformity and negative sanctions to punish _____. In this way individuals are taught to become part of society.

deviance, gender, innate, nature/nurture, peer group, primary, process, sanctions, socialisation, values

Quick question

Which of the agents of socialisation have had the biggest impact on your identity? Rank them in order of importance.

media, work, family, peer group, education, religion

Aspects of identity

Any individual's identity is made up of key aspects about them, which will have a crucial effect on how they see themselves and how others see them. These aspects of identity will vary in importance for different individuals. For example, sexuality may be a more significant part of the identity of someone who is homosexual than someone who is heterosexual, and ethnicity may be more important to someone from an ethnic minority. These aspects of identity may also intersect in different ways. For example, age identity may have more significance for women than men, as looking attractive (and/or youthful) is arguably a more significant aspect of female identity than male identity. National and ethnic identity will clearly overlap for some individuals, and social class may have more significance for someone from an ethnic minority, as they experience additional discrimination. As you consider each aspect, consider the ways in which it may intersect with other aspects to create an individual's identity.

Hybrid identities

As we have seen previously, a hybrid is a cross between two or more things. So when we consider a hybrid identity, we mean that someone's sense of who they are is a mixture of two or more influences. This can be seen most clearly within ethnicity, nationality and identity. An individual may have an identity as a British person, but also a Muslim and a Pakistani. Thus their ethnic identity is a hybrid of both British and Asian ethnicity. This is very common for second- and third-generation immigrants who grow up in one culture but retain influences on their identity from their culture of origin.

Labels to describe such hybrid identities have been developed, such as 'Brasian' (British and Asian) and 'Blasian' (black and Asian). Hybrid identities can also be found in the white British population, due to the influence of immigration and global culture. For example, 'white wannabes' is a term used by Nayak (2003) to describe white British males who dress, act and speak in a way that is influenced by black hip-hop culture. A famous parody example of this would be Ali G, the character created by Sacha Baron Cohen. Another example is 'Multicultural London English', often called 'Jafaican', referring to a style of speech and accent used in particular areas of London by young white people, which is influenced by African-Caribbean speech and accent. This is not necessarily an attempt to imitate Jamaican speech, but a product of the multicultural nature of certain parts of London, where mixed groups of white and black young people influence each other, creating a hybrid dialect.

Ethnicity and identity

Getting you thinking ...

'On a recent train journey into central London, I heard a middle-class white woman admonishing an Eastern European woman for speaking loudly on her mobile phone. Shortly after, a black woman angrily pushed past the Eastern European woman, muttering something under her breath. I was reminded of another journey in the early 1980s. Another middle-class-sounding white woman complained to other passengers about a young black man listening to loud music on his Walkman. She said ... "I am fed up with being a second-class citizen in my own country". Her words exposed her categorisation of him ... as "different", and encircled her in an exclusionary zone of bounded white Britishness and implied superiority. Jump forward ... and my train "drama" has the same plot and dialogue – ethnicity, racism, class, culture and hierarchy – although the parts are taken by different (ethnic) actors. ... However, there is also evidence of shifting identity dynamics in late modern Britain. The Eastern European woman was "racially" white, and the indignation shown by the black woman was indicative of a shared hostility between white and black residents towards the newer white and minority ethnic groups in Britain.'

Source: Phillips (2008)

What does this experience tell you about the changing relationships between different ethnic groups in the contemporary UK?

Ethnicity relates to culture, so we all have an ethnic identity – made up of our religion, language, where we live, our ethnic origin, skin colour, and so on. These cultural characteristics all affect who we are and how we see ourselves.

In the UK we tend to identify certain ethnic groups by their shared cultural characteristics, such as religion, language and lifestyle, though this is often problematic (see *Who are British Asians?*, below). Additionally, second-, third- and fourth-generation migrants and those of mixed race will also have a range of cultural characteristics that make their ethnic identity more complex. It is also important to recognise that ethnic identity intersects with other aspects of identity, such as nationality, gender, social class and age, making everyone's experience slightly different.

Who are British Asians?

'Asians' are often identified as an ethnic group in the UK, but those who may fall into this category do not necessarily share the same cultural characteristics. Modood (1997) points out, for example, that the category 'Asians' includes different nationalities such as Pakistanis, Bangladeshis and Indians; different religious groups such as Sikhs, Muslims and Hindus; and several language groups, including Gujarati, Punjabi, Urdu and Bengali. Asia is a whole continent!

In the US, when the term 'Asian-Americans' is used, it is usually referring to those of Chinese or possibly Japanese origin. Increasingly, probably due to the influence of the US media, younger people in the UK may consider British Asians to include those of Chinese origin. Though China is clearly in Asia, the majority of Asian immigrants in the UK originate from the Indian subcontinent due to our colonial history, and the small Chinese population is usually discussed separately. So when sociologists discuss British Asians they are usually referring to those with origins in India, Pakistan or Bangladesh.

Most studies relating to ethnic identity in the UK have researched its importance for those in ethnic minorities. For example, in researching British-Asian identities, Ghumann (1999) found that tradition, religion and family values played an important part in the upbringing of second-generation Asians in the UK, and that Asian children tend to be socialised into the extended family, with the emphasis on duty, loyalty, honour and religious commitment.

Gilroy (1993) looked at the identity of young black people, arguing for the use of the term 'Black Atlantic' to describe an identity that was not specifically rooted in the UK or in their country of origin (often a part of the Caribbean that they may have had little association with), and was shared with young black people in the US. He argued that the shared experience of racism and powerlessness can transcend differences in background and history to create a 'black' identity.

Derrington and Kendall (2004) have researched ethnic identity in the traveller community, and studies by Song (1997) and by Francis and Archer (2005) have looked at different aspects of identity in British-Chinese families. All of these studies consider the challenges of growing up within a minority ethnic group in the UK and the influences this has on an individual's identity.

There have also been studies on the white British ethnic identity. For example, Hewitt (2005) considers the white 'backlash' against **multiculturalism**. Policies designed to achieve equality have been perceived as unfair to the white community, and a white working-class person under pressure economically has often reacted with anger at perceived 'positive discrimination' in favour of ethnic minorities, feeling the need to defend their ethnic identity – as Hewitt puts it, '[C]omplaints by the white "have-nots" about the impact on them of the black "have-nots" … '. (2005: 2).

In contemporary UK society, due to the expansion of the European Union, growing numbers of ethnic minorities are white, with an ethnic origin from Central or Eastern Europe. There is evidence that they may face similar issues relating to resentment, racism and discrimination that immigrants from parts of Asia and the Caribbean faced in previous decades, as was illustrated in the Activity at the beginning of this section. For example, Spencer *et al.* (2007) suggest that Eastern European migrants spent relatively little time socialising with British people. In their research, one Ukrainian waitress commented that '[T]hey [British people] do not let you into their circles'. Dawney (2008) also found evidence of racism against European migrants in the rural community she studied, which largely came from a perceived threat and fear of numbers that did not necessarily have a basis in reality.

Resistance or hybridity?

The response of those from ethnic minorities to racism may be to find ways in which their ethnicity can be used as a form of protection. Cashmore and Troyna (1990) argue that there will be a tendency for ethnic minorities to 'turn inwards', to seek support from within their own ethnic community as a response to the racism that they experience. Thus religion and culture may be strengthened, as they become key sources of identity and support.

Winston James (1993) suggests that the experience of racism unified the culture and identity of African-Caribbeans in the UK. Black people from the Caribbean had cultural differences based on their island of origin, and may also have been divided based on the darkness of skin, a hierarchy of colour imposed by colonialism. However, in the UK, the common experience of racism had the effect of drawing African-Caribbeans together. A shared oppositional culture grew, organised around the label 'black', as a resistance to racism.

Jacobson (1997) argues that many young Pakistanis are adopting a strong Islamic identity as a response to social exclusion from white British society. She found that young British Muslims face difficulties and problems, and a strong Muslim identity gives them a sense of stability and security. This positive embracing of an Islamic identity in terms of diet, dress and other religious practices is a form of defence and resistance to marginalisation and racism, and is not just absorbed through the family, but consciously constructed.

However, as we have previously considered, ethnic identities may be becoming more hybrid, as those from ethnic minorities and those of white British origin are all influenced by each other's cultures and by the media. Ethnic hybridity is not simply a mix between two cultures, however, and many studies have suggested it is a much more complex process.

Changing ethnic identities

Modood (1997) found a number of generational differences over the issue of identity, suggesting that second-generation ethnic minorities from both African-Caribbean and Asian backgrounds felt much more British than their parents, while still seeing their ethnic origin as a key part of their ethnic identity.

Postmodernists may argue that in a globalised and media-saturated society such as the contemporary UK today, identity is all about choice – everyone can create their own identity, and the hybridity we have discussed in this section means that ethnicity is becoming less clear-cut and less significant. However, some would disagree, arguing that ethnicity and race are still sources of discrimination and hugely affect identity.

Activity: Considering hybridity

'Neighbourhood nationalism' and cultural hybridity–Back (1996)

From his ethnographic study of two council estates in London, Les Back did find cultural hybridity, but it was not just black youths who developed hybrid identities. White youths were attracted to aspects of black culture, and local youths from all ethnic backgrounds developed a sort of shared identity based on mixed ethnicity and 'neighbourhood nationalism' – a feeling of solidarity and common identity with people from the same area.

Cultural code-switching–Brah (1996)

Avtar Brah argues that young British Asians are very skilled cultural **code-switchers**, and that this is a more appropriate way to see their identities than as a hybrid or a cross between two cultures. She suggests that the idea of two cultures is misleading, since neither white British culture nor Asian culture are clear-cut and homogeneous anyway. The idea that young British Asians experience conflict or culture-clash is not backed up by evidence, and most will find ways to successfully negotiate their own identity, as will any young person living in a globalised and hybrid culture such as the contemporary UK.

1 Consider some of the ways in which your own ethnic identity is hybrid in the contemporary and global UK, and examples of code-switching that you may experience. For example, consider areas such as fashion, music, food and language.

2 You may wish to research into other studies on hybrid and negotiated ethnic identities, such as those by Butler (1995), Johal (1998) and Burdsey (2004).

Nationality and identity

Images of national identities

Welsh rugby fan

2014 Commonwealth Games hosted in Scotland

British success at the London Olympics 2012

How would you describe your national identity?

National identity is often considered in a wider context – as the identity of a whole country. However, an individual also has a national identity that may affect how they see themselves. National identity is often expressed through supporting your national team in sport, but also through pride in the anthem and flag, and through language.

Anderson (1983) argues that a 'nation' is an 'imagined community', in that members of a nation will never meet most of their fellow members, and so a national identity is socially constructed through symbols such as the flag and the anthem, and rituals such as national holidays and festivals. Anderson argues that the social construction of national identities was facilitated by developments in printing technology leading to the mass circulation of newspapers and books, which created a 'national' language. Contemporary examples of this can be seen in media coverage of international sporting events, but also conflicts and disasters, where the fate of British people involved is given a higher status than that of others and we are encouraged to get behind our nation's interests.

National identity for British people is often quite confused. English and British are sometimes seen as synonymous, but for someone who is Welsh, Scottish or Northern Irish, there is a clear distinction. This could be because Wales, Scotland and Northern Ireland have historically been in a position of subordination to England, leading the people in these countries to seek to distinguish themselves from the dominant English identity and assert their differences. The distinction may have seemed less important for English people, as part of the majority nation within Britain.

Kumar (2003) has discussed the fact that, unlike the Scots, the Welsh and the Irish, the English find it difficult to say who they are, and that English national identity is elusive. He argues that the long history of the English as an imperial people has developed a sense of 'missionary nationalism', which, in the interests of unity and empire, has necessitated the repression of ordinary expressions of nationalism. So, he argues, the quest to expand 'Britishness' may have diluted 'Englishness'.

Changing national identities

Sardar (2002) suggests that the world is in the middle of a global identity crisis, in which many of the old divides such as *East versus West* and *capitalists versus communists*, by which we had defined ourselves, have broken down. Britain, having lost its empire and feeling very small in a global world, is unsure about whether it should become more American or more European. 'Englishness' was based on historical traditions that are meaningless to the vast majority living there today, so there is a struggle to find an 'English' identity. Sardar argues that to develop a more confident identity, we must embrace diversity but also focus on what makes us the same – our common humanity.

Activity

Scottish identity and the future of 'Britishness'

The 2014 campaign and vote for Scottish independence from the UK raised many issues of national identity. Though many of the political arguments were related to economic issues, for many ordinary Scottish people it was a question of identity. The majority of Scottish people voted to stay as part of the UK, but the whole campaign demonstrated key differences in the identity of those in Scotland and those in other parts of the UK.

Opinion polls showed roughly equal numbers of Scottish people (around 25 per cent each) describing their identity as 'more Scottish than British' and 'Scottish not British', but slightly more choosing 'equally Scottish and British' (around 30 per cent).

However, this suggests that roughly half of Scottish people do put their Scottish identity first (source: **www.whatscotlandthinks.org**).

During the campaign and following the result, there was also a renewed interest in English identity. One commentator argued that the campaign has awakened the 'sleeping giant of English nationalism'. Changes promised for Scotland may also affect the national identity for those in Wales and Northern Ireland, and it could be argued that 'British' identity has been changed forever.

1 Consider which country of the UK you live in or identify most with.
2 Is this more part of your national identity than being British?
3 Do you think it is a good or a bad thing that the UK remains together as one nation?

However, in more recent times, in the face of devolution, economic crises and increasing immigration, English national identity appears to have strengthened. As we have seen previously with ethnicity, any aspect of identity becomes more significant to an individual if it is a perceived source of conflict or oppression. Some would argue that this new English identity is negative and exclusive, with the growth in popularity of groups such as the English Defence League (EDL).

The broadcaster and writer Darcus Howe argued in his Channel 4 documentary series *White Tribe* (2000) that, as someone who grew up in the Caribbean as part of the British Empire, he can comfortably see himself as Black and British, but that a growth of English nationalism seems much more exclusive and 'white', leading him to question where he would fit in a new nationalistic England.

However, others would argue that national identity will become less and less significant in today's globalised society. Young people are arguably 'citizens of the world', and national boundaries and cultures are less significant. The internet and social media have contributed to this breaking down of boundaries.

Responses to globalisation

Stuart Hall (1991) suggested that countries may display three different reactions to globalisation:

1 They may accept a global culture, and all countries will become more similar, which he referred to as **'cultural homogenisation'**.
2 They may take in some parts of global culture alongside their more traditional culture, and develop a new but still individual culture, which he called **'cultural hybridity'**.
3 They may resist global culture and fiercely protect their cultural heritage, becoming more traditional and nationalistic, which he called **'cultural resistance'**.

Arguably, there is evidence that all three of these responses are happening in different countries around the world, and in the UK.

Quick question

Can you think of examples of each of cultural homogenisation, cultural hybridity and cultural resistance? Your examples could come from the UK, or you could use international examples.

Activity: The disappearance of Britishness?

Our lives are becoming hopelessly Americanised, says Professor Halsey

Life in Britain can no longer be said to be uniquely British, a leading social scientist declares.

Growing international homogeneity and the dominance of American culture mean that it is increasingly difficult to pinpoint Britishness, according to the sociologist A.H. Halsey. He suggests that Britain has lost the distinctiveness it had when he was a child, and that our lives are becoming Americanised to the point that life in Britain can no longer be said to be uniquely British.

Source: Adapted from Brindle (2000)

1 What is meant by the term 'homogeneity' (second paragraph)?
2 Which of the three responses to globalisation put forward by Stuart Hall is being supported by the views of A.H. Halsey?
3 Do you agree that our lives have become 'Americanised'? Is this a good or a bad thing, in your opinion?

Gender and identity

Getting you thinking ...

1 What are some of the cultural characteristics associated with male and female gender identities in the UK?
2 Write down three ways in which your gender has affected/will affect your life.

Many would argue that gender is one of the most significant aspects of an individual's identity. Whether you are male or female will have a huge effect on how you see yourself and how others see and relate to you.

Gender identity is something that is fluid and changing. The way that women are seen and the expectations surrounding their appearance, behaviour and roles have all changed in the last hundred years. However, male identity is also changing, and expectations of masculinity are also different in today's society. Traditionally there were clear ideas of what was meant by femininity and masculinity, but today many would argue that there are many ways to be a woman or be a man, and it may make more sense to discuss 'femininities' and 'masculinities'.

Gender as a social construct

This idea relates back to the nature/nurture debate we have considered previously (see page 9). Though some argue that gender is based on biological differences between males and females, most sociologists argue that it is socially constructed.

The biological view

Sociobiologist Wilson (1975) argues that the need to reproduce requires men to be more promiscuous – literally 'spreading the seed'. Women, on the other hand, need to nurture one child and stay faithful to the father of their child to ensure his help in its upbringing.

The functionalist view

According to Parsons (1955), females have an 'expressive role' in the family. This is natural, and based on their childbearing role, but it is reinforced by socialisation.

Males have an 'instrumental role' in the family, that of breadwinner and protector. This is also natural, based on their physical strength, but also reinforced through socialisation. These roles are functional for the family and society.

However, most sociologists argue that gender, and thus gender identities, are socially constructed, learned through socialisation, but also changeable.

Earlier in the chapter we saw the different gender roles in the Tchambuli tribe studied by Mead (see page 3), which suggests that gender identity, what it means to be male or female, is learned rather than biologically determined.

The social construction of gender identities

Feminists argue that gender identity is socially constructed by patriarchal society. By this, they mean that male-dominated society creates and reinforces stereotypes of how males and females should be.

It is not only the family that contributes to the social construction of gender. The other agencies of socialisation may also reinforce stereotypical expectations of gender roles.

For example, the peer group monitors and regulates acceptable behaviour for girls and boys from an early age. Hey (1997) studied friendship groups among teenage girls and looked at the power the female peer group has over girls' behaviour, and how the norms of the female peer group are deeply rooted in **patriarchy** and expectations of how girls should be. Mac an Ghaill (1994) explored how boys learn to be men in their peer groups at school, policing their own and others' sexuality. Gender power, based on '**hyper-masculinity**', was the main source of identity for the 'macho lads' identified by Mac an Ghaill, who valued the '3Fs' – 'fighting, football and f***ing'.

Femininities: Is there only one way of being 'feminine'?

Arguably, there are a range of feminine identities available in the contemporary UK, including the traditional and the less traditional – for example, housewife and mother, but also breadwinner, career woman and single mother. However, even today, feminine identity is often related to a submissive or passive role, and associated with a lack of self-confidence and ambition. Feminists argue that this is learned through socialisation, and there is evidence to suggest that this may be changing, albeit slowly.

Study

Gender role socialisation in the family – Oakley (1981)

Ann Oakley is a feminist who argues that gender roles are socially constructed through socialisation. She explains how children are socialised into their gender roles by their families in four ways:

1 **Manipulation** – This consists of encouraging behaviour that is seen as stereotypically acceptable for the child's gender and discouraging behaviour that is not considered the norm. Examples could include laughing if a boy gets muddy, or congratulating him for attempting something adventurous, but discouraging a girl from doing anything that would involve getting muddy or dirty, or from even attempting adventurous activities.

2 **Canalisation** – This involves parents channelling their child's interests into toys, games and activities that are considered the norm for their gender, such as encouraging girls to play with dolls and to go to ballet class and encouraging boys to play football.

3 **Verbal appellation** – This refers to giving children nicknames or pet names that reinforce gender expectations, such as 'little angel' or 'princess' for girls, and 'little monster' or 'soldier' for boys.

4 **Different activities** – Parents or family members may encourage children to participate in activities around the home that reinforce stereotypes, such as a girl helping her mother with baking, and a boy helping his father to clean the car.

Point to discuss and research

Can you think of examples of each of these four processes from your own upbringing?

Item A: 'Run like a girl'

If you think of the phrases 'You run like a girl' and 'You throw like a girl', you will probably know they are not usually meant as compliments. Procter & Gamble's Always brand has produced a campaign that aims to turn these phrases into positive ones and challenge the stereotypes underpinning them. Their research showed that more than half of girls experience a drop in confidence around puberty and that most consider 'like a girl' to be an insult.

Watch the Always #runlikeagirl video on YouTube.

Item B: Ban Bossy

This is an American campaign recognising the knock to girls' confidence based around the word 'bossy'.

'When a little boy asserts himself, he's called a "leader". Yet when a little girl does the same, she risks being branded "bossy". Words like bossy send a message: don't raise your hand or speak up. By middle school, girls are less interested in leading than boys—a trend that continues into adulthood.'

Source: **www.banbossy.com**

This campaign has developed the slogan 'I'm not bossy, I'm the boss' to encourage leadership qualities in young girls, and has had support from Beyoncé and Sinead O'Connor, among others.

1 Watch the video clip 'I'm not bossy, I'm the boss' on the Ban Bossy website.
2 Do you think campaigns such as the ones discussed in Items A and B are important?
3 Think of some reasons why phrases such as 'run like a girl' and 'bossy' are used as insults.

Changing female identities: The rise of the 'ladette'?

'Laddishness' refers to a specific form of masculine behaviour, typically involving sportiness, hardness, hanging out and not being seen to be making an effort at school. Jackson (2006) found that some girls, or 'ladettes', also spent time drinking and smoking, swearing and disrupting lessons, for fear of doing otherwise and being considered unpopular and 'uncool'. Similarly, Denscombe (2001) looked at the increase in female risk-taking behaviour, particularly smoking, as being related to a 'ladette' culture, where young women want to be seen as anything but the stereotype of a woman.

Masculinities: Is there only one way of being 'masculine'?

Connell (1995) has argued that there are a range of masculine identities available today, but that **hegemonic masculinity** (macho, dominant, aggressive, breadwinner) is the most common and the one that is still reinforced most strongly. Other forms of masculinity he identifies, such as **subordinate masculinity,** which he links to homosexual males, and **marginalised masculinity**, which he links to unemployed men, are present but not fully accepted as 'real' masculinity.

Changing male identities: The 'crisis of masculinity'?

Mac an Ghaill (1994) used this term to refer to the insecurity felt by working-class men today. There has been a loss of the 'breadwinner' identity with the decline of traditional male industries (mining, steel, shipbuilding, manufacturing, and so on).

Canaan (1996) researched working-class men in Wolverhampton. She questioned both those who were employed, and those who were long-term unemployed and found interesting differences in their views of masculinity. When she asked them 'What is the most important thing about being a man?', the men who had jobs gave fairly predictable responses relating to fighting, drinking and sexual conquests. However, the men who were unemployed said that having a job was the most important thing, and that they felt emasculated due to their unemployment.

A crisis for female and male identity? – Faludi (1993, 1999)

In *Backlash: The Undeclared War against American Women* (1993), Susan Faludi discussed the reaction of patriarchal society, particularly led by media campaigns about the family, which aim to undermine the successes of feminism. Independent and successful women were judged and blamed for a range of social problems.

In *Stiffed: The Betrayal of American Man* (1999), Faludi developed this theme by looking at the reaction of men, particularly working-class males, to the successes of feminism, coupled with the crisis of masculinity, particularly the decline in male jobs and breadwinner roles.

One example she looks at is the Spur Posse, a group of young males who gained brief notoriety in the US. Their 'game' of sleeping with as many girls as they could to gain 'points', and get that number printed on a T-shirt, came to light when one was charged with the rape of a 12-year-old girl. His response to Faludi when asked about it was 'Well, she had a body'.

Faludi argues that their attitude towards women, and increases in domestic and sexual violence against women, can be seen as part of this masculinity issue – it is their one remaining source of power.

Points to discuss and research

These books were both based on American society.

1 Do you think there is a backlash against successful women in the UK?
2 Is there a difference in how they are portrayed compared to successful men? Are they celebrated or undermined?
3 Do you agree that there is a crisis for men in today's society?
4 Do you recognise the attitude of the Spur Posse in young males you know?
5 Conduct some internet research on the recent rise of 'lad culture' in the UK – for example, the 'UniLad' and 'LAD Bible' websites. Can this recent trend be explained as evidence of a 'crisis of masculinity', or as a 'backlash' against female success?

Social class and identity

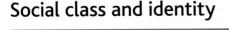

1 What do we mean by social class? Can you come up with a definition?
2 How is class measured/judged? Write down all the things by which you would judge someone's social class.

There are several ways to define class – one definition is a group who share a similar economic and social situation.

Though it may seem less significant to some people today, and despite arguments from some people that 'class is dead', social class is arguably a very significant aspect of identity. It will clearly affect the economic circumstances of an individual's upbringing, and related issues such as housing, health and schooling.

However, it is argued that this will also lead to a social class developing similar norms and values, cultures and lifestyles. This may affect an individual's identity: how they see themselves and how others see them. Class identity can be seen as a product of socialisation, started in the family, and related to cultural characteristics such as education, occupation, lifestyle and taste.

Studies

Distinction: A Social Critique of the Judgment of Taste and The Forms of Capital – Bourdieu (1984, 1986)

According to Pierre Bourdieu, 'class fractions' are determined by varying degrees of social, economic and cultural capital. The dominant (ruling) class has the power to shape which attributes are valued, and are in a position to acquire and pass on capital to their children.

- **Cultural capital**: the knowledge, attitudes, skills, education and advantages that a person has, which give them a higher status in society.
- **Economic capital**: economic resources (cash, assets).
- **Social capital**: resources based on group membership, relationships, networks of influence and support.

All of these types of capital are interrelated, and someone with high levels of one type of capital is more likely to be able to attain the others as well. However, **cultural capital** is the most significant for Bourdieu. Parents provide their children with cultural capital by transmitting the attitudes and knowledge needed to succeed in the current educational system. So it may include the right ways of speaking and behaving in different circumstances, knowledge of 'high culture', etiquette, confidence in different social situations, and so on. Those with high levels of cultural capital will be in a position to accumulate the other forms of capital as well.

Bourdieu, as a Marxist, argued that it is the power of the ruling class that allows them to define the knowledge and skills that are valued, and to ensure that they, and their children, are in the best position to acquire them, giving them an unfair advantage.

Judging social class

These are some of the things you may have thought of when you considered how you would judge someone's social class:

- money/income
- possessions – car, gadgets
- house – type, size, area
- lifestyle/leisure/hobbies
- holidays
- television viewing habits
- dress/style
- accent/speech
- norms/values
- occupation – the traditional way to measure/assess social class.

The main classes in the UK are traditionally identified as the upper class, the middle class and the working class. However, defining these three classes is not easy, and not everyone will identify themselves as belonging to one of them. More recently, sociologists have identified other groups such as the super-rich and the underclass.

Who are the upper class?

Traditionally, the upper class are those with inherited wealth, often in the form of land. Mackintosh and Mooney (2004) have pointed out that a key feature of the upper class is their invisibility. The upper class operate '**social closure**', meaning that their education, leisure time and daily lives are separated from and partially invisible to the rest of the population. They may send their children to boarding schools, socialise in exclusive clubs and participate in leisure activities that are largely unknown or inaccessible to the majority, such as hunting, polo and opera. However, it could be argued that this group is waning in numbers and power, and that the new 'super-rich', based on achieved rather than ascribed (inherited) status, are now much more significant.

Who are the middle class?

The middle class are now seen as the majority of the population by many. Tony Blair famously said, 'We are all middle class now'. Traditionally, the middle class is associated with those who have professional or managerial careers. They are likely to have been university-educated and to own their own homes. However, these features now apply to more and more of the population as access to home ownership and university education has spread, more people are self-employed, and there are fewer people working in manual jobs or trades.

Chapter 1 Introducing socialisation, culture and identity

Because of this, the middle class is a very diverse group, containing a wide variety of people with very different incomes, attitudes and lifestyles. Fox (2004) discusses 'upper middles', 'middle middles' and 'lower middles' to highlight these differences within the middle class. There is also likely to be a big difference between public-sector professionals, such as teachers and nurses, and private-sector professionals, such as lawyers and bankers. Thus, it is unlikely that everyone who sees themselves as middle class shares a common experience or identity.

Who are the working class?

The working class used to form the majority of the population, though it is shrinking. It was traditionally made up of manual workers and those with trades. However, Hutton (1995) has argued that the decline in trade union memberships and the manufacturing sector, and the dispersal of working-class communities, has eroded working-class identity.

Unlike the **underclass**, the working class are often romanticised as a hard-working, straight-talking, 'salt-of-the-earth' identity, which many, who are clearly middle class in terms of education, career or income, still clamour to claim as their identity. However, Skeggs (1997) studied working-class women who felt humiliated by the ways in which others, such as teachers and doctors, judged and dismissed them due to their working-class background. As a result, the women made a strenuous effort to show they were 'respectable', taking care in how they dressed ('Do I look common in this?'), their leisure pursuits and home decorations.

Who are the underclass?

This is a controversial term and it is unlikely that many would consciously identify themselves as a member of the underclass. The term was originally used by sociologists from conflict perspectives who wanted to draw attention to the social exclusion experienced by those who were at the very bottom of society, and who lacked opportunities in terms of education, health and earning potential. However, the term is now often used in a negative way to describe those who rely on benefits and are blamed for their own situation due to the choices they have made. It is particularly associated with Murray (1984), who argues that over-generous benefits encourage some people to develop a culture, or set of norms and values, in which they do not take responsibility for their own actions and have an expectation that they will be looked after by the state.

Governments are unsurprisingly concerned about this group, and groups such as NEETs – young people who are not in education, employment or training – have been targeted by various policies, such as the raising of the school-leaving age. This group are also often portrayed in very negative ways in the media, through shows such as *The Jeremy Kyle Show* and fictional and non-fictional portrayals such as *Shameless* and *Benefits Street*.

Changing class identities: Does class still matter?

Postmodernists such as Pakulski and Waters (1996) suggest that there has been a shift from production to consumption in the definition of identities – we are now defined by what we buy, not what we do.

Offe (1985) argues that in today's society, fewer and fewer individuals share a common, unifying experience of full-time work – the experience that used to shape the culture of social classes. The days when people had a job for life have gone, and we are all able to create our own identities regardless of the social class of our families and the particular level of qualifications or job we may have at any one time.

Additionally, the contemporary UK gives choices and opportunities to everyone, which may have been limited to the privileged few in the past, such as the possibility of going to university, travelling, starting your own business and owning your own home. The media also gives access to an endless range of information and cultural experiences, and has broken down many social and class-based barriers that may have existed even 30 years ago.

However, not everyone would agree that today's society is as class-free as it seems. Social-class background remains the most significant indicator of outcomes such as education, health and life expectancy, and there is still a lot of evidence suggesting a difference in culture and lifestyle between people from different social and economic backgrounds. It is also important to recognise that the ability to make choices and take opportunities depends on money, and some sections of the UK population do not even have access to the internet, and are more concerned with struggling to feed their family.

Activity: Does class still matter?

Item A: Strong class identities – Marshall et al. (1988)

- 60 per cent of their sample thought of themselves as belonging to a particular social class; 90 per cent could place themselves in a class if prompted.
- 75 per cent agreed that people are born into a social class and it is difficult to move from one class to another.

Item B: Weak class identities – Savage et al. (2001)

- Few of their sample thought Britain was a classless society; most of them were well aware of the strong influence of class in the wider society.
- However, most saw themselves as 'outside' classes and just 'ordinary' individuals.
- Savage et al. described a paradox – class is an important structural force in people's lives, yet class identities are generally weak.

Item C: Social Mobility and Child Poverty Commission 2014

This detailed study found that those who had attended fee-paying schools included:

- 71 per cent of senior judges
- 62 per cent of senior armed forces officers
- 45 per cent of chairs of public bodies
- 44 per cent of the Sunday Times Rich List
- 43 per cent of newspaper columnists and 26 per cent of BBC executives
- 50 per cent of the House of Lords
- 33 per cent of MPs, 36 per cent of the cabinet and 22 per cent of the shadow cabinet.

However, they make up just 7 per cent of the UK population as a whole.

1 Is social class still significant in the UK? Is this the same as class identity?
2 Why do you think that people may recognise class divisions, and yet have a weak class identity themselves, as Savage discovered?
3 How might a Marxist answer this question?
4 How might a postmodernist answer this question?
5 What does the evidence in Item C suggest about access to positions of power in the UK?

Sexuality and identity

Getting you thinking ...

Sexuality around the world

Quinn (2001) studied the same-sex relationships of some tribal people. Many Native American Tribes celebrated same-sex marriage between two males, with the 'wife' being a feminine-acting 'berdache' who dressed in female clothing, and between two females, where the 'husband' was a dominant 'amazon' who participated in male activities and was often a female warrior.

Quinn also noted that some sub-Saharan African peoples have man–boy marriage ceremonies. These African 'boy-wives' are between 12 and 20 years of age and the boy-wife is treated in the same way as a female wife. When he becomes a man, he becomes a warrior, and takes a boy-wife of his own.

The Kinsey Reports (1948, 1953) in the US found that homosexual encounters among both men and women were much more common than many people would have imagined, at a time when homosexuality was still classified as a mental illness in the US. For example, 37 per cent of men had had a homosexual experience to the point of orgasm, but less than 4 per cent were exclusively homosexual.

What do these cross-cultural examples tell you about sexuality, and about ideas about what is 'natural' and 'unnatural'?

Sex and sexuality is an area of social life that society, and especially the media, seems obsessed with – images relating to sexuality are everywhere you look. Feminists in particular have been concerned to point out the way in which women are often portrayed through their sexuality – as sexual objects for men to fantasise about. However, though sexual identity is a significant issue for many, as with other aspects of identity, it tends to be more significant for those who are not heterosexual. As Weeks (1987) points out, not many would say 'I am heterosexual' in relation to their identity, but to say, 'I am gay' or 'I am a lesbian' makes a statement about belonging and your relationship to dominant sexual codes.

'The homosexual role' – McIntosh (1996)

Mary McIntosh argued that in Western cultures, the role of homosexual male involves certain expectations or cultural characteristics. For example, the homosexual role may include effeminate mannerisms, a higher voice and attention to appearance. McIntosh argued that once a male has accepted the label or identity of 'homosexual', he will start to fulfil these expectations, so the label actually creates the behaviour.

McIntosh supported her argument by citing evidence of married men who see themselves as 'straight', but still admit to attractions to males, but do not exhibit any other 'signs' of homosexuality. Conversely, males she studied who were 'out' did fulfil all of the expectations of the homosexual role.

Points to discuss and research

1 Do you agree with McIntosh that we sometimes change our behaviour to live up to the identity we have adopted?

2 What cultural characteristics would be associated with the 'lesbian role' or the heterosexual male or female roles?

Historically, homosexuality was considered a perversion, a mental illness that needed to be cured and even a criminal offence in the UK. Attitudes towards homosexuality have changed significantly in British society over the last 50 years, but in some parts of the world, such as Uganda and Nigeria, homosexuality is still illegal, and homosexuals are still denied basic human rights in many counties.

The process of developing and accepting a homosexual identity has been referred to as 'coming out'. Studies suggest that homosexual behaviour does not automatically lead to a homosexual identity. Weeks (1991) argues that 'sexual identification is a strange thing', and more complex than other aspects of identity. He points out that there are people who identify themselves as gay and participate in the gay community, but do not participate in same-sex sexual activity, but there are also people who do have same-sex sexual encounters, but do not identify themselves as gay. For example, in Reiss' 1961 study, he found that young male prostitutes, or 'rent boys', regarded themselves as heterosexual, despite having sex with men for money, and they actively despised the men as a way of neutralising their behaviour.

Plummer (1996) partially supports McIntosh's ideas (see above), seeing homosexuality as a process and discussing the 'homosexual career', where a male who has accepted the label of homosexual will seek out others and join a subculture in which stereotypical homosexual characteristics become the norm.

These studies suggest that it is not actually sexual attraction that creates the 'homosexual', but the acceptance and internalisation of the identity of 'homosexual'. In a society where homosexuality is still not accepted by many, this is not an inevitable or easy process: 'Becoming a homosexual' is a difficult process of 'becoming the other', or 'becoming what one has learned to despise' (Gay Left Collective 1980: 80).

Rich (1980) argues that women's sexuality is oppressed by men in patriarchal society, through institutions such as marriage, through sexual violence and rape and through the sexual objectification of women. Taking a feminist perspective, she uses the term 'compulsory heterosexuality' to describe the way women are socialised into a subordinate and heterosexual role, ensuring their availability to men. Rich believes that most women are not necessarily inherently heterosexual, but that this is forced upon them, and that lesbian existence is quite distinct from homosexuality in men, with little evidence of anonymous promiscuity and more focus on empowerment and joy. She argues that lesbian identity has been written out of existence or constructed as abnormal, since it is a threat to male dominance and power over women.

As the examples given above show, cross-cultural evidence suggests that a distinct homosexual identity is not apparent in all cultures, and that a sexual encounter between two people of the same sex is not uncommon, but also not necessarily defined as 'homosexual'.

Changing sexual identities

In the UK, attitudes towards homosexuality have, at least publicly, changed enormously in the last 30 years, which is likely to have a big impact on sexuality and identity. Homosexuality is no longer classified as a 'condition'; the age of consent for sexual intercourse was equalised in 2000, and the Equality Act 2010 makes it unlawful to discriminate against any individual on the grounds of sexuality.

Activity: Changing views on homosexuality

Item A: Same-sex marriage

In March 2014, a change in the law meant that same-sex couples could legally marry for the first time. Politicians of all parties welcomed this change and many ceremonies have taken place across the UK. However, some surveys suggest that around one-fifth of people would refuse an invitation to a same-sex wedding and some religious groups remain deeply opposed, though the Church of England has dropped its opposition since the change in the law. Prior to the change in the law, over 60,000 civil partnerships had taken place in the UK since these were legalised in December 2005, and more than 1,400 same-sex marriages took place in the first three months after they were made legal, with government predictions that approximately 6,000 civil partnerships and same-sex marriages will take place each year.

Item B: The 2014 Commonwealth Games

The opening ceremony of the 2014 Commonwealth Games in Glasgow was led by John Barrowman and Karen Dunbar, who are both openly gay. Barrowman then kissed his male 'bride' in a mock-up Gretna Green marriage ceremony. This has been seen by some as a deliberate statement aimed at the 42 countries who attend the games in which homosexuality is still illegal.

1 What do Items A and B tell you about homosexual identity in the UK today?

Age and identity

Getting you thinking ...

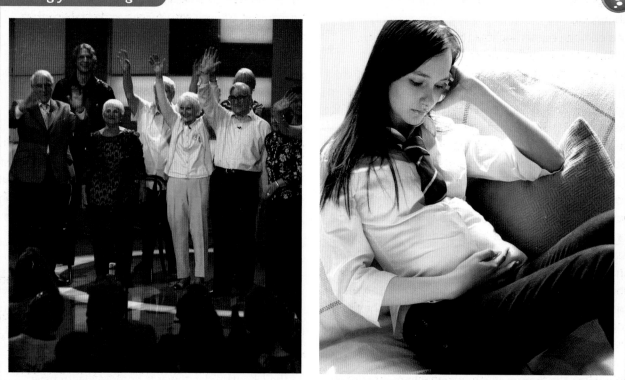

What does age actually mean – is it a number, a lifestyle or an attitude?

Age is probably the only aspect of identity for which we will all experience the changing effects. As children, young people, adults and eventually older people, we will all find our identity affected by how our age makes us feel and how other people relate to us. The world is run by adults, and it is often young people and older people whose identities are the most negatively affected by their age, often due to lack of status and power.

Quick questions

1 How is your identity influenced by your age?
2 Are you the same person you were when you were 10?
3 Will you be the same when you are 45?
4 What about when you are 70?

Age is sometimes looked at chronologically – as in your actual age (e.g., 17). Alternatively, age is often looked at as a stage in the **life course**: childhood, youth, adulthood, and so on.

The problem with looking at stages in the life course is that the ages at which they start and end vary – they can be seen as socially constructed. For example, when does childhood, end? When does middle age start? Individuals will also differ; some keep their 'youth' going for longer, others seem 'old before their time'.

Stages in the life course

Childhood

This can be seen as socially constructed. In some cultures, 'childhood' is not seen as a period of innocence, dependence or vulnerability, as in the UK. For example, children will be working, and even fighting as armed soldiers, in some countries. Marriage may be considered at the age of 12 or 13, especially for girls. Even in the UK children were working in factories until the mid-nineteenth century.

Today, it is argued that we have a contradictory view with childhood in the UK. Children are either portrayed in the media as little angels and vulnerable victims or as little devils (delinquent or shocking).

There is a generally held view that children 'grow up' more quickly today than previously, but actually, until the mid-twentieth century, childhood lasted for a shorter time, and people were usually working and even having families of their own before their eighteenth birthday.

Postman (1982) argues that childhood emerged only when the spread of literacy enabled adults to better shield children from various aspects of adult life – particularly certain aspects of sexuality and certain horrors associated with death and disease – so the 'innocent' child was created. He suggests that the emergence and spread of the media and visual culture in the twentieth century has brought about a decline in childhood and threatens, ultimately, to bring about its disappearance.

Youth

This tends to be associated with those between the ages of 12 and 25. In our culture, youth is socially constructed as a period of transition from childhood to adulthood and a time of rebellion/resistance. However, some cultures have no concept of 'youth' as a stage in the life course. Through initiation ceremonies, such as the one seen in the Hamar tribe earlier in this chapter (see page 3), childhood ends one day and adulthood begins. Margaret Mead (1928) also argued that the 'storm and stress' associated with youth is culturally specific and not found in all cultures, though her findings and methodology have been questioned.

See Chapter 4 on youth subcultures for more examples of youth identity and the social construction of youth.

Young adulthood and middle age

Very little is said about normal 'adulthood' by researchers. Young adulthood is normally characterised by career and family. Most people form relationships, have children and establish their careers during this time, often moving into their own home and becoming independent from their parents.

Middle age tends to be associated with those in their forties and fifties. Bradley (1996) argues it has a higher status than youth or old age – middle-aged people are running the country and hold power at work. However, middle age is also seen as a negative time, as 'youth' is lost and old age comes closer. It is sometimes associated with negative ideas, such as a 'mid-life crisis' and 'empty nest syndrome'.

Old age

When does old age start? Some say it starts at retirement age, but there is a lot of difference between a 65-year-old and an 85-year-old.

UK culture admires youth and the beauty of youthful bodies. In contrast, ageing bodies represent ugliness and degeneration. Older people have been socialised into this view themselves. The language used by older participants about their own identity in Corner's (1999) study was mostly negative, reflecting that used by the media and popular culture. Participants described the problems of old age for society and the 'burden' of the ageing population. Participants were concerned with becoming a 'burden' themselves and the dominant stereotype they presented was of later life being a time of ill-health and dependency.

Growing Up and Growing Old – Hockey and James (1993)

Jenay Hockey and Allison James say that children are seen to lack the status of personhood, and are separated and excluded from the public, adult world, largely confined to 'specialist places' for children such as schools, nurseries and the family. They are seen as the opposite of adults – dependent, innocent, vulnerable – and needing care and control.

Hockey and James link old age and childhood, and argue that they are socially constructed in a similar way, having lost their 'personhood' status. Terms such as 'gaga' are used, relating to baby noises, and the elderly are also seen as helpless and vulnerable, dependent and needing care. They use the concept '**infantilisation**' to describe this. In their research in a retirement home, they report that the clients were treated like children: they weren't allowed to keep

their own money, but were given 'pocket money'; they had their privacy taken away – being bathed, dressed and having to ask to be taken to the toilet; their daily routine was decided for them; and they were assumed to be quite innocent, and definitely not sexually active. Such practices will create a self-fulfilling prophecy, but Hockey and James argued that in most cases it was not based on medical needs.

They do argue that such an identity is possible to resist. Alternative sources of status may be used to retain some power. For example, male residents in the home exerted some power over female staff. Also, it is possible to resist the status by assuming a different one, such as children who pretend to be older to gain more status, and older people who act younger. Hockey and James give accounts of residents in the home who mocked the care staff by deliberately behaving in a childlike way, or even poking their tongues out at the staff!

Changing age identities

Postmodernists would look at trends such as living and working for longer, anti-ageing products and procedures, and the extension of 'youth' and childhood to show how age is fluid and becoming less significant today.

Featherstone and Hepworth (2005) argue that media images of ageing, which have been a source of negative stereotypes and identities, can also create new identities, and suggest that as the population ages, more positive images may emerge. The popularity of 'retro' fashions and comeback tours from bands from the 1970s and 1980s are also trends that help blur the boundaries of the life course.

Disability and identity

Images of disability – disabled or differently able?

David Weir winning Gold

Warwick Davies – film star

For those who are not living with any impairment, disability may not seem a significant aspect of identity. However, those living with a physical or mental impairment may often find it is the most significant aspect, especially in terms of how they are seen by others. The profile of those with disabilities has arguably improved significantly in recent years, with events such as the Paralympics raising awareness of positive achievements and images in relation to disabled people. In 1995, the Disability Discrimination Act was passed, giving legal protection and enforceable rights to disabled people. However, despite such positive developments, a lot of discrimination and social and physical barriers to full inclusion remain, which have a significant impact on a disabled person's identity and experience.

There are two broad approaches to understanding disability in society.

The **medical model** sees disability as a medical problem, focusing on the limitations caused by the impairment, and this has long been the prevalent approach taken by society. This approach leads to the defining of a disabled person by their disability or impairment. The problem is that this leads to a 'victim-blaming' mentality, where the problem lies with the disabled individual, rather than with a society that has not met their needs.

Shakespeare (1996) argues that disabled people are often socialised into this way of seeing themselves as victims, and that '[T]he person with impairment may have an investment in their own incapacity, because it can become the rationale for their own failure', thus creating a 'victim mentality'.

The **social model**, by contrast, focuses on the social and physical barriers to inclusion that may exist, such as the design of buildings and public spaces that deny access to those with mobility problems, or discriminatory attitudes and practices against those with disabilities. Society is therefore the disabling factor. This approach can lead to the view that disability is socially constructed, since it rests on assumptions of what is 'normal' or 'abnormal'. Some campaigners have argued against the use of the term 'disabled' at all and prefer 'differently able'.

Shakespeare argues that there are major obstacles to forming a positive disabled identity. Disabled people are often socialised to see themselves as inferior. He also points out that disabled people are often isolated from one another, so forming a strong, collective identity is difficult. There is also a lack of positive role models in public life and the media, and often even within the immediate family. Additionally, disability or impairment in a largely able-bodied society often leads to reactions of pity, avoidance and awkwardness.

Activity

Does disability make you feel awkward?

Lee Ridley is a comedian who suffers from cerebral palsy. This means that he communicates with an aid, rather like Stephen Hawking does, and when he walks he moves slowly, 'like a zombie', due to one side of his body being weaker than the other. He has often pondered the question, 'Does disability make you feel awkward?' Does it?

The disability charity Scope UK conducted a study that found that two-thirds of people felt awkward talking to a disabled person, and so they launched a campaign to highlight and attempt to remedy this: **www.scope.org.uk/awkward**.

This survey also suggested that 43 per cent of people don't know anyone who is disabled, which is statistically unlikely – it's just that some disabilities are more visible than others. Not all disabled people require a wheelchair, and even those who do don't always need them.

Less than a fifth of people have disabilities that are congenital – that is, there from birth. Ridley calls the other four-fifths 'not yet disabled', because being able-bodied is not a lifetime guarantee. This, Ridley says, *is* awkward.

The consequences of being disabled are serious. Ridley cites being overlooked for jobs as just one injustice, and wonders why he wasn't asked by his potential employers how he intended to carry out his job to reassure them he could do it; did they simply feel too uncomfortable to ask?

That, in short, is what Ridley and the Scope UK campaign are trying to eradicate: not the disability itself, but the uneasiness, embarrassment and awkwardness that surrounds it.

Source: Adapted from Ridley (2014)

1 Did the article make you feel awkward? If so, consider why.
2 Have you experienced a situation involving someone with a disability where awkwardness was a factor?
3 Visit the Scope website (or search for 'Scope end the awkward' on YouTube) and view the films they have made to highlight this issue.

The label 'disabled' carries with it a **stigma** (negative label) that affects all interactions between the disabled person and others, creating what interactionists (see page 43) would call a '**master status**'. This means that it transcends all other aspects of identity and becomes the defining characteristic by which the individual is judged. A key issue for many disabled people is that their disability becomes the defining aspect of their identity for others, who only see them in relation to their disability and not as a man or a woman, gay or straight, young or old, and so on.

The issue of disability becoming a master status may also be true for the individual themselves, as they learn to see themselves first and foremost in terms of their impairment. According to disability psychologist Carol Gill (1997), a polio survivor who became disabled later in life, reconciling your identity as a disabled person with previously held notions about what being disabled means is a common hurdle: 'When you become a member of the group that you have previously felt fear or pity for, you can't help but turn those feelings on yourself.'

Zola (1982), a sociologist also disabled through polio, writes that '[T]he very vocabulary we use to describe ourselves is borrowed from [discriminatory able-bodied] society. We are de-formed, dis-eased, dis-abled, dis-ordered, ab-normal, and, most telling of all, called an in-valid' (1982: 206).

This could lead to a form of '**learned helplessness**', a concept that originates in psychology, describing the way that some disabled people may internalise the idea that they are incapable of changing a situation, and thus fail to take action to help themselves. Low self-esteem and a highly structured life in which decisions are often made for disabled people can contribute to this. It has been argued that policies such as segregated schooling actually encouraged learned helplessness, even if the intentions were well-meaning.

However, Murugami (2009) argues that a disabled person has the ability to construct a self-identity that accepts their impairment but is independent of it. So they see themselves as a person first, and see their disability as just one of their characteristics.

Activity

A person first?

Murugami discusses the way in which many disabled people form their self-identity based on what they are able to do, rather than in terms of their disability. If their abilities are blocked by societal and environmental barriers, such as poor access or lack of awareness, then the blame is directed at society rather than the impairment. Watson (2002: 509) illustrates this point, quoting a person with a disability who said: 'I know this is going to sound very strange to you, but I do not see myself as a disabled person.'

Source: Muragami (2009)

1 Why do you think that as a society we tend to define people by their disability first, and as a person second?
2 What could be done to try to change this in the future?

Check your understanding

Briefly define the following terms and give an example of each:

1 identity
2 (ethnic) hybridity
3 hegemonic masculinity
4 cultural capital
5 social closure
6 social construct
7 infantilisation
8 learned helplessness.

Select one sociologist for each of the seven aspects of identity we have looked at (ethnicity, nationality, social class, gender, sexuality, age and disability) and summarise his or her ideas.

Section summary

Fill in the blanks, using the words given below.

Identity is about how you see _____ but also relates to how you are seen by _____. Most sociologists see identity as _____ and ever-changing, as an individual moves through life. Those aspects of an individual's identity that lead to _____ or inequality are likely to be more significant. Thus _____ is often more significant for those from ethnic minorities, and _____ may seem more important to those from Scotland, Wales or Northern Ireland than it does to those from _____. Similarly, sexuality and _____ tend to be significant aspects of identity for those most affected by the issues they raise. _____ means a mixture of two or more things, so ethnic identities are often said to be hybrid. _____ tend to argue that identity is more fluid today, and aspects such as_____, gender and even age are less significant for individuals, though Marxists and _____ would disagree.

active, disability, England, ethnic identity, feminists, hybridity, national identity, others, postmodernists, social class, subordination, yourself

Practice questions

Identify and briefly explain two examples of cultural hybridity. [6]

Practice questions

Source A

Source B

Almost $270 billion was spent worldwide on anti-ageing products and services in 2013. Meanwhile, in the UK, young adults in their mid- to late twenties and early thirties are more likely to be living with their parents than they were 30 years ago, and one in ten will still be living with parents when they are 40.

Using Sources A and B and your wider sociological knowledge, outline and briefly evaluate the view that age identities are changing in the contemporary UK. [20]

Chapter 2

Introduction to sociological theory

Getting you thinking ...

Thousands of people celebrating the Queen's Diamond Jubilee in front of Buckingham Palace in 2012

A protest by the anti-capitalist movement

A. Society works best when people follow the same religion, speak the same language and respect the same values and beliefs.

B. The government in Britain is too influenced by wealthy people such as financiers and businesspeople and doesn't really understand the lives of ordinary working people.

C. Women have only gained most of the rights they have in the UK today – for example, the right to vote and equal pay – by fighting for them.

D. Though the British monarchy is not democratically elected like the US president, the monarch plays a valuable role as a symbolic figurehead which helps to unite the whole country.

E. School rules benefit everyone because if they did not exist, schools would be chaotic and no learning could take place.

F. The government should tax rich people and big businesses more heavily and increase the minimum wage so all workers can earn enough to live on.

Points to discuss and research

1 In small groups, discuss the six statements on the previous page and decide which you agree with and which you disagree with. How far do you and the others in your group agree?

2 Some of the statements suggest that society works best when people agree on how things are organised and have shared values whereas others suggest that society works for the benefit of some people more than others. Decide in which category each statement belongs.

3 Decide which group of statements you agree with most. If you agree most with the first category, you are likely to have more sympathy with a consensus view of society, but if you agree with the second category, you perhaps lean more towards a conflict view.

2.1 Consensus theories

Many sociologists see themselves as social scientists systematically collecting data (or information) about society in order to understand it. However, sociologists have to make sense of their data and put it into some kind of framework and this is where theories come in. Sociological theories help make sense of how society works and what causes societies to change. Theories are often built around important concepts (or ideas) – for example, in the first chapter of this book you will have encountered important concepts such as norms, values, socialisation and identities which are used by most sociologists.

Consensus theories are one group of theories in sociology. They emphasise the idea that human societies work best when their members agree on fundamental principles of how society should be organised and share common **norms**, **values** and **beliefs**. This makes social life more predictable and means that there is a social order in society. For example, in schools and colleges, teachers and students know what to expect of one another in their roles and have a shared understanding that they have come together so that students can learn.

Consensus theories also examine how different social institutions in society work together to ensure that members of society get the things they need. For example, schools and colleges exist to educate their students but they also serve the needs of businesses and the economy by ensuring future workers are suitably socialised and have the skills needed by employers.

Functionalism

Functionalism is the most influential consensus theory in sociology and has its origins in the work of early sociologists such as Emile Durkheim (1858–1917). Durkheim argued that members of societies need to feel a sense of **social solidarity**, a feeling of belonging to a larger community and a shared identity. Durkheim was concerned that in large modern societies, people would lose their sense of belonging and become anonymous individuals uncertain about how to behave or what their roles are in society; Durkheim described this as a sense of '**anomie**', or normlessness.

Another functionalist sociologist, Talcott Parsons (1902–79), emphasised the important role of **socialisation** in creating value consensus in society. Parsons saw key institutions such as families, the education system, mass media, peer groups and religious organisations as working together to transmit shared norms and values to each new generation ensuring stability and continuity in society. Parsons saw such institutions of society as working together in harmony, with each institution depending on the others and contributing to maintaining society as a whole. Functionalists sometimes use an **organic analogy**, seeing society as like a human body with different organs contributing to the whole. For example, our lungs provide oxygen for the blood, which is pumped around the body by the heart; the kidneys remove waste matter from the blood. In the same way, in society, families and educational institutions socialise future workers, so they can play a role in the economic system, which in turn provides us with the consumer goods and services that we need. Functionalism is often referred to as a **structural theory** because of the way it sees parts of society as linked together in a structure.

Functionalism is so-called because functionalists tend to analyse social institutions in terms of the **functions** (roles or purpose) they perform for society. For example, Parsons saw the functions of families in industrial societies in terms of socialising children and providing psychological security for adults (see page 79). Durkheim saw the function of religion as creating a sense of social solidarity through individuals participating in acts of collective worship and focusing on shared symbols.

Parsons' model of the social system

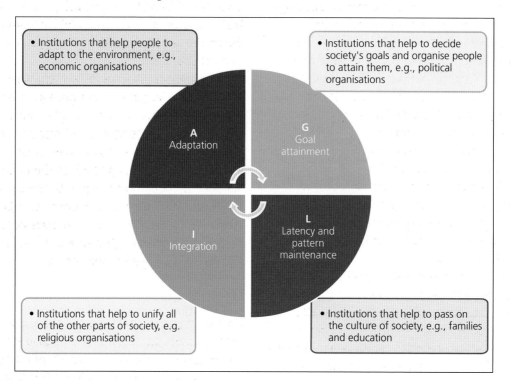

- Institutions that help people to adapt to the environment, e.g., economic organisations

- Institutions that help to decide society's goals and organise people to attain them, e.g., political organisations

A
Adaptation

G
Goal attainment

I
Integration

L
Latency and pattern maintenance

- Institutions that help to unify all of the other parts of society, e.g. religious organisations

- Institutions that help to pass on the culture of society, e.g., families and education

Parsons saw society as a **social system** and argued that all societies must fulfil four functional prerequisites (or functions that must be performed to keep the society going). These are summarised above and are often abbreviated to AGIL.

Evaluation of functionalism

Functionalism was probably the most influential theory in sociology up to the 1950s. It is particularly effective at analysing how different parts of a society work together to provide for its members' needs. Functionalism also highlights how societies tend to operate more effectively when people can agree and cooperate.

However, since the 1960s, functionalism has come under strong criticism from other theories and only a few sociologists today would describe themselves as functionalists. In particular, functionalism fails to explain conflicts in society and tends to assume that society operates for everyone's benefit equally. In a multicultural society like the UK, there may be conflicts between different religious, ethnic and cultural groups over, for example, the role of women, the acceptability of homosexuality or the teaching of religion in schools. It could also be argued that where conflicts exist, it is the ideas and beliefs of more powerful groups that tend to dominate.

The New Right

A political stance rather than a sociological theory the origins of New Right ideas lie in the theories of liberal economists such as Adam Smith (1723-1790) who argued that capitalist societies work best when there is a free market. In other words the state should avoid interfering in the economy, for example by restricting trade or setting the price of goods or wages. Smith argued that this should be left to the **hidden hand of the market** and determined by the law of supply and demand. If lots of people want something (demand) the price will rise and this will encourage more producers to supply it bringing the price back down to a reasonable level as there will be more competition.

Smith's ideas were revived by neo-liberals in the twentieth century such as Friedrich Hayek (1944) who argued that individuals had the greatest freedom in a free market capitalist society. Although state intervention to control the economy and reduce problems like poverty and unemployment might be well meaning, it ultimately created more problems. For Hayek the policies pursued by Labour governments in Britain such as nationalising key industries and introducing a welfare state represented the beginning of a 'road to serfdom' whereby the state would run people's lives and take away the freedom of the individual. Hayek's ideas were an importance influence on the Conservative Prime Minister Margaret Thatcher (1979-90) who tried to cut back on state welfare expenditure and privatised many of the government owned industries such as coal, gas and the railways.

Perhaps the most influential New Right thinker in terms of sociological debates has been the American political scientist Charles Murray. Murray (1984) argued that in both Britain and the USA excessive government intervention to try and alleviate poverty by providing the poor with benefits had led to a **dependency culture** whereby groups such as the unemployed and lone parents were rewarded for irresponsible behaviour (for example failing to look for work or having children outside marriage when unable to support them). Murray argued that this had led to the emergence of an **underclass** of people separated from the rest of society and lacking a commitment to the norms of the wider society such as hard work, self-discipline and bringing children up within marriage. Murray (1990) later blamed rising levels of crime in Britain and the USA on the underclass suggesting that the growth of lone parent families meant that an increasing number of poor children were growing up without a father figure or discipline in the home and were consequently turning to crime.

Evaluation of the New Right

New Right ideas have some similarities to functionalism offering a politically conservative viewpoint which supports the capitalist economic system. British sociologist, David Marsland (1988) argues that most British sociologists are influenced by Marxism and fail to teach students about the potential benefits of capitalism instead focusing on the alleged problems of living in an unequal society. Arguably New Right ideas provide a useful counter-balance to the predominantly left wing or anti-capitalist stance of most sociology.

However, critics of the New Right argue that many of their arguments are not based on clear sociological evidence. For example, Murray's view that the poor are reckless and irresponsible is contradicted by numerous studies of poor people which reveal that groups such as the unemployed and lone parents mostly aspire to the same things as other people such as economic security and stable family life and find themselves dependent on benefits not through choice but because of circumstances beyond their control.

2.2 Conflict theories

Conflict theories start from the observation that in most societies there are social inequalities between different social groups. Conflict theorists argue that in these circumstances it is difficult to achieve consensus in society, as what serves the interests of the powerful or dominant groups may go directly against the interests of subordinate groups lower down in society.

Conflict theorists do not deny that on the surface some societies may appear to be based on consensus, but argue that this is only because subordinate groups have been socialised into accepting their inferiority within the prevailing system. Conflict theorists use the concept of **ideology** to describe how powerful groups put across ideas that justify their own position and help to make the existing social system appear to be fair and legitimate. For example, when slavery operated in the southern states of the US, slave owners used a variety of arguments to justify why black people of African origin were socially and intellectually inferior to whites. Many slaves, outwardly at least, accepted their place within this hierarchy even though most people today would see this as an exploitative and unjust system. Conflict theorists argue that in societies where there is inequality, conflicts will always exist, though they may only erupt openly from time to time.

The 2012 Olympic Games and shared values

In 2012, British people had a lot to be proud of. The nation's monarch, the Queen, celebrated her 60th year on the throne and Brits threw parties on the street to celebrate her Diamond Jubilee. Union Jacks were waved as people rejoiced.

The summer after that momentous Jubilee, the 2012 Olympics arrived in London. People were showcasing their Britishness for the first time in many years and the nation seemed united. Fears that the British national identity was dying out were extinguished.

The Union Jack was reclaimed. Having been used in the recent past by far-right groups preaching racism and **xenophobia**, many Brits felt ashamed of what the national flag had come to represent. But now it was displayed with pride, fluttering at our monarch and our Olympians, adorning faces, clothing, kitchenalia and many souvenirs.

We may all be European now, but fears of national allegiances counting for nothing were allayed. Jessica Ennis, Greg Rutherford, Victoria Pendleton and Jason Kenny made us swell with pride.

But surely the moment to make us all proud was the British-spirited Mo Farah's post-race press conference, when an African journalist asked Somalia-born Farah if he would have rather represented the country of his birth. Farah replied: 'Look, mate, this is my country. When I put on the Great Britain vest, I feel proud. Very proud.' The 10,000-metre champion, if it were possible, bolsters our sense of patriotism even more.

1 In what ways might events such as the 2012 Olympics in London help to create a sense of social solidarity and reinforce shared values in British society?

2 Suggest other ways in which individual members of British society are socialised to believe in similar values to other British people.

3 How could the idea that British society is based on shared values be criticised? You could start answering this question by thinking about any areas of disagreement or conflict between groups or sections within British society.

Mo Farah after winning the 10,000 metres

Marxism

Marxism is probably the most influential conflict theory in sociology and derives from the ideas of the German writer and political revolutionary Karl Marx (1818–83). Marx argued that historically all societies, apart from the most simple hunting and gathering societies, are based on **class divisions** between those who benefit from the economic system and those who do not. Marx described the economic system of modern industrial societies, such as the UK and the US, as **capitalist societies**. They are based on a **ruling class** of capitalists, people who own capital or wealth and invest it in running businesses to make a profit, and a **working class** comprising the majority of people who have little or no wealth and who therefore have to work for wages. Marx argued that this is an unequal and exploitative system in which most of the profits created by businesses go to the owners (or capitalists) while the labour (or work) to create this wealth is performed by the workers.

Marx argued that eventually the working class would become aware of their exploited position and would overthrow capitalism and create a **communist society** where the means of production (such as farms, factories and other businesses) would be taken over by the workers and run for the benefit of everyone.

The role of ideology

Marxists today see capitalist societies as being just as unequal and exploitative as they were in the nineteenth century; however, they would accept that in most Western societies there is little sign of the communist revolution that Marx foresaw as inevitable. Modern Marxists such as Louis Althusser (1971) argue that capitalist societies have survived not simply by forcing workers to accept the system but by developing **ideological state apparatuses** (ISAs), which transmit ideas that legitimate or justify the capitalist system and its class inequalities. Ideological state apparatuses include the education system, mass media, families and even religious organisations. For example, the media in the form of television, newspapers, cinema and pop music helps to entertain the workers and make their lives more bearable and also encourage them to see the consumption of goods created by capitalist businesses as a priority. All of this diverts attention away from the real inequalities in society and creates what Marx called '**false consciousness**', whereby the working class cannot see any alternative to the existing system.

Though Marxism is a conflict theory, it is similar to functionalism in that it also focuses on structures in society, particularly the way in which the economic system shapes other aspects of society, such as families, schools and the mass media.

The structure of society according to Marxism

The **superstructure** includes all of the cultural institutions of society (e.g., families and the education system) and is shaped by the requirements of the **infrastructure**, the economic system that provides for people's material needs.

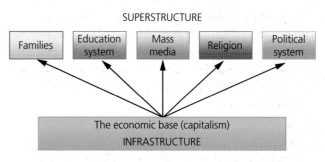

Evaluation of Marxism

Marxism became one of the most influential approaches to sociology from the 1960s onwards and Marx's ideas have been interpreted in a number of different ways by different groups of sociologists. Many sociologists are attracted to Marxism because it offers a more critical view of capitalist societies than theories such as functionalism. Since the 1980s social inequalities have widened in many Western societies. Marxism, with its focus on the way the capitalist system benefits the wealthiest groups, offers a plausible explanation of this.

However, Marxists have also faced criticism from other sociologists. For example, the idea that the working class are 'brainwashed' into a false consciousness by capitalist ideology has been attacked for suggesting that people are not conscious of their own interests. It could be argued that though capitalist societies are very unequal, most of the working class still enjoy a much higher standard of living under capitalism than in the societies that preceded it – or indeed in communist societies, supposedly based on Marxism, such as the former Soviet Union. Marxism also mainly focuses on divisions and inequalities of class; other sociologists have argued that other forms of inequality may also create significant divisions and conflicts in society, such as those based on gender, nationalism, ethnicity and religion.

Other conflict theories

Weberian theories

Marxism is not the only conflict theory in sociology. The German sociologist Max Weber (1864–1920) disagreed with the way Marx analysed social inequalities. He argued that differences of **status** and **power** were important and were not always linked to economic or class inequalities. A good example of this is ethnic inequalities; minority ethnic groups – for example, black and Asian people in the UK – may be treated less favourably in the workplace, for example, because of skin colour and appearance, even when they come from relatively well-off backgrounds. Thus ethnicity can be seen to be linked to status rather than social class. (Weberian theories of social inequality are discussed in more detail on page 278).

Activity: Class divisions in twenty-first-century Britain

Item A: Bankers' bonuses

Bankers bonuses have long been a cause of controversy but this has intensified since the financial crisis struck in 2008. There has been mounting public anger that investment or 'casino' bankers, whose reckless risk-taking helped to bring the global financial system to the brink of collapse, are still taking bonus payments while the majority are suffering in the recession. The anger, at least in the UK, is directed particularly at bailed-out banks such as Royal Bank of Scotland (RBS), which has received £45bn of taxpayers' cash, but all banks paying bonuses have come under increasing fire. In 2014 RBS defended plans to pay £588m in staff bonuses despite suffering an £8.24bn loss in 2013 as it slumped for the sixth successive year.

The fact that payments continued to be made, even as taxpayers bailed out the banks, enraged the public. Politicians railed against the payments but seemed unable – or unwilling – to curb them. The anger over excessive salaries and bonus payments in the banking sector was a factor in the founding of the Occupy protest movement in 2011.

In Britain, Fred Goodwin of the Royal Bank of Scotland became the focus of the mounting backlash, as it emerged that he had a pension pot worth £16m. He quit the group just weeks before it reported the largest loss in British corporate history, £24bn. He was stripped of his knighthood – for 'services to banking' – in 2012. The European Union has promised legislation to limit bankers' bonuses but banks have suggested they will simply increase bankers' basic salaries to compensate them.

Source: Adapted from Bowers et al. (2013)

Item B: Food poverty in the UK

NUMBER OF PEOPLE GIVEN EMERGENCY FOOD
FROM TRUSSELL TRUST FOODBANKS

Year	Number
2012–13	346,992
2011–12	128,697
2010–11	61,468
2009–10	40,898
2008–09	25,899
2007–08	13,849
2006–07	9,174
2005–06	2,814

At least **4.7 million** people live in food poverty in the UK

The shocking scale of food poverty in Britain is exposed today by new figures showing record numbers of people are reliant on handouts because of punitive benefits cuts. More than 900,000 people were given emergency food in the past year, an increase of 163 per cent, according to figures from the Trussell Trust, the biggest food bank charity. The explosion in demand has coincided with an increase in those seeking help following a benefit reduction. A coalition of anti-poverty charities, including the Trussell Trust, claims the figures show that the UK is breaching international law by violating the human right to food.

Source: Adapted from Dugan (2014)

1 How could the examples in Items A and B be used to support the Marxist view that capitalist societies such as the UK are characterised by huge class inequalities?
2 Why might Marxists argue that there is a conflict of interest between rich people, such as bankers, and poor people, such as those receiving assistance from food banks?
3 In what ways might critics of Marxism argue that inequalities between rich and poor people are necessary for the good of society as a whole?
4 How far would you agree with this view?

Feminist theories

Feminist ideas have a long history but began to influence sociology most strongly from the 1970s onwards, following the 'second wave' of feminism. Feminists argue that in most societies, women have been disadvantaged compared to men. Men often control the key institutions in society, such as businesses and political institutions. They also tend to be more dominant in personal relationships, family life and intimate relationships. Feminism has encouraged sociologists to focus much more on **gender inequalities** and women's experiences of the social world. Like Marxists, feminists use the concept of ideology but refer to **patriarchal ideologies**, ideas that help to justify men's dominance and women's subordinate place in society. See page 266 for further detail on the different strands of feminism and discussion of feminist explanations of gender inequality, and page 294 for details on Black feminism.

2.3 Social action theories

Both consensus and conflict approaches are what sociologists call **structural** theories. These see society as something external to individuals which influences or even constrains them to behave and think in certain ways. For example, our socialisation encourages us to follow certain norms of behaviour which are likely to be similar to other members of our social groups. Structural theories are often described as **macro** (or large-scale) theories because they try to give us the big picture by looking at society as a whole or how particular parts of society relate to others. Structural theories are sometimes seen as 'top-down' theories because they examine how individuals behave by reference to the wider society and its institutions.

Social action theories, in contrast, are **micro** (or small-scale) theories that tend to focus on individuals within small groups. They are also often referred to as **interpretivist** theories, because they are concerned with how individuals interpret the social world around them to make it meaningful. Social action theories offer a 'bottom-up' approach as they try to view the wider social world through the eyes of individuals.

Interactionism

Interactionism (or symbolic interactionism) is one of the main social action theories in sociology. Interactionists argue not only that people interpret the social world around them but also that how they do so is influenced by the way they **interact** with other people. In these interactions individuals use **symbols** such as words and gestures to communicate meaning and then react to other people's actions in terms of how this is interpreted. Social life is a constant series of actions and reactions whereby we come to shared understandings of the social world. For interactionists, norms, values and identities are not handed down to individuals through a process of socialisation, but are constantly redefined and renegotiated by individuals in their interactions with others.

Labelling theory

Labelling theory is a theory based on interactionism which was developed by the American sociologist Howard Becker (1963). Interactionists are interested in the notion of the **self**. The self is our unique identity based on how we see ourselves; however, our sense of self is also influenced by how we interact with others. Becker developed this by arguing that our sense of self is affected by the process of labelling whereby other people categorise us and attach identities to us. For example, a teacher may constantly label a child negatively – for example, as 'lazy' or 'lower ability'. In this situation children may seek out other children who have been similarly labelled and become part of an anti-school subculture. The original label placed on the child has thus become part of the way they see themselves – what interactionists call a **self-fulfilling** prophecy. A label can also become a **master status** overriding other aspects of a person's self. Thus labelling someone as a criminal may mean that everyone treats them as a criminal even though there may be many other more positive aspects to their self. Labelling a person as disabled may obscure the many things the person is actually able to do.

Evaluation of social action theories

Social action and interactionist approaches have produced some fascinating sociological research which is often very rich in detail, focusing on the lives on small groups of people. Such approaches also offer us an insight into the social world through the eyes of people themselves. Rather than seeing people as puppets controlled by structures and institutions, they see people as skilled actors, acting out their roles but actually capable of writing their own scripts and negotiating who they want to be in interactions with others.

However, critics argue that social action approaches can be too microsociological and fail to give us the big picture of society as a whole and how individuals are part of larger patterns and trends in society; these can only be understood by a more structural approach. Social action theories also tend to accept the viewpoint of the people they are studying; this has the merit of not judging them but also means that sociologists may fail to consider influences on people's behaviour and attitudes that they themselves are not even aware of.

In response to this, some sociologists have combined the insights of structural and social action approaches. For example, in Item B in the Activity below Paul Willis looks at the viewpoint of working-class boys about to leave school. However, later in his book Willis also examines this small group of boys in the context of the wider education system, arguing that they are part of a larger pattern or structure whereby the working-class pupils are systematically failed by the system. In this respect Willis draws on both interactionist and Marxist approaches in his study.

Many feminists also combine structural and social action approaches. For example, in her study of housework Ann Oakley (1974) examined how forces in the wider society encouraged the idea that the normal role for married women was as a housewife, making it difficult for women who wanted careers. However, she also carried out detailed research on a small sample of women who were housewives to explore their experiences of the role.

Activity: Structural and social action approaches in education

Item A: The influence of class and gender on educational achievement

The graph below is taken from national statistics published by the Department for Education. It shows differences in the proportion of pupils achieving five or more GCSEs both by gender and comparing pupils eligible for free school meals (i.e., from low-income families) with other children.

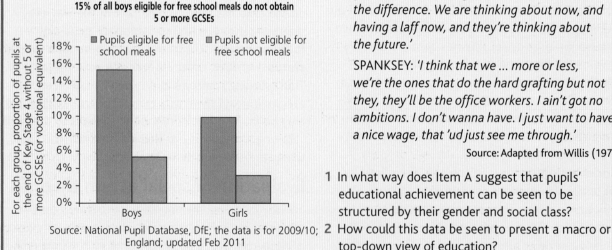

15% of all boys eligible for free school meals do not obtain 5 or more GCSEs

Legend: ■ Pupils eligible for free school meals ■ Pupils not eligible for free school meals

For each group, proportion of pupils at the end of Key Stage 4 without 5 or more GCSEs (or vocational equivalent)

Source: National Pupil Database, DfE; the data is for 2009/10; England; updated Feb 2011

Item B: The meaning of education for working-class boys

The extracts below are taken from informal interviews conducted by Paul Willis with a group of eight working-class boys whom he calls 'the lads'. The boys were in their last year at secondary school and saw school as a waste of time, often getting in trouble with teachers and disrupting lessons.

JOEY: 'We wanna live for now, wanna live while we're young, want money to go out with, wanna go with women now, wanna have cars now, and er'm think about five, ten, fifteen years' time when it comes. But other people, they'm getting their exams, they'm working, having no social life, having no fun, and they're waiting for fifteen years' time when they're people, when they've got married and things like that. I think that's the difference. We are thinking about now, and having a laff now, and they're thinking about the future.'

SPANKSEY: 'I think that we ... more or less, we're the ones that do the hard grafting but not they, they'll be the office workers. I ain't got no ambitions. I don't wanna have. I just want to have a nice wage, that 'ud just see me through.'

Source: Adapted from Willis (1977)

1 In what way does Item A suggest that pupils' educational achievement can be seen to be structured by their gender and social class?

2 How could this data be seen to present a macro or top-down view of education?

3 In what ways does Item B help us to understand the meanings or interpretations that some working-class boys give to education?

4 How could Item B be seen to present a micro or bottom-up view of education?

5 What are the advantages and disadvantages to each approach to studying society?

2.4 Postmodernism

Postmodernism cannot be described as a sociological theory, partly because postmodernists present a variety of ideas about the social world which do not always agree with one another. Moreover, some postmodernists such as Jean-François Lyotard (1984) argue that we should abandon the attempt to explain the social world using what he calls '**metanarratives**' or grand theories, which might include sociological theories such as functionalism and Marxism. Instead, most postmodernists would argue that we should focus on small parts of the social world and try and understand them from a variety of viewpoints. Postmodernists reject the idea that any one theory can be correct or proven and thus undermine the whole idea that sociology is a social science that can provide theories about the social world that are superior to common sense or opinion. Despite this, postmodernism has had considerable influence on sociology and has encouraged sociologists to ask some important questions about how they approach studying society.

Postmodernists start from the assumption that the era of **modernity** started to come to an end in the late twentieth century and we are now moving into a new kind of social world variously described as **postmodernity** or the **postmodern condition**. Modernity was the kind of society that emerged with the Industrial Revolution, modern machine technology and mass production of goods. It is associated with a move from religious and traditional ways of thinking to scientific and rational thinking. It also resulted in larger more complex societies usually organised around nation states rather than smaller tribal societies.

Postmodernists argue that the age of mass production is giving way to an age of knowledge production in which computers, digital communications and mass media are much more significant, both culturally and economically. People's identities are increasingly defined by personal choice and individualism rather than by their place in social structures such as genders, classes or business organisations. There is also a distrust of experts such as scientists, priests and political leaders. All of this means we increasingly choose our own identities, rather than following identities and norms laid down by society or by leaders in social groups. Postmodernists therefore question the assumptions made by structural theories such as functionalism and Marxism because they suggest that structures such as nuclear families, traditional gender roles and social classes, which guided our lives in modernity, are now breaking down and fragmenting, leaving individuals free to choose who they want to be.

Evaluation of postmodernism

Postmodernism helps sociologists to focus on many of the changes taking place in the world today – for example, the process of **globalisation** whereby boundaries between societies based on nation states are being broken down. Postmodernists also highlight the complexity of personal identities, showing that we are not defined simply by being male/female, black/white or rich/poor, but by a complex set of factors, the importance of which varies between individuals and in different social contexts.

Many sociologists, however, are reluctant to fully accept the ideas of postmodernism because of the way it tends to undermine the view that through sociology and science more generally we can understand the world around us in a logical and rational manner. Most sociologists would argue that while their theories cannot be said to be 'true' or 'fact', they are usually based on systematic research and carefully collected data and thus present a better understanding of the social world than ideas that are based purely on opinions. Many sociologists would also reject the idea that social structures no longer matter, pointing out that identities are not simply freely chosen. There are still things that are difficult for women (or men) to do simply because of their gender and the choices of the poorest members of society may be very limited simply because they lack the resources to do anything they choose.

Postmodernity and 'the dissolution of life into TV'

One of the most important theorists of postmodernity is the French author Jean Baudrillard (1988). He believes that electronic media (such as TV, the internet and computer games) have destroyed our relationship to our past and created a chaotic empty world. He was strongly influenced by Marxism in his early years. However, he argues, the spread of electronic communications and the mass media have reversed the Marxist theory that economic forces shape society. Instead, social life is influenced above all by signs and images.

In a media-dominated age, Baudrillard says, meaning is created by the flow of images, as in TV programmes. Much of our world has become a sort of make-believe universe in which we are responding to media images rather than to real persons or places. Thus when Diana, Princess of Wales, died in 1997, there was an enormous outpouring of grief, not only in Britain but all over the world. Yet were people mourning a real person? Baudrillard would say not. Princess Diana existed for most people only through the media. Diana's death was more like an event in a soap opera than a real event in the way in which people experienced it. Baudrillard speaks of 'the dissolution of life into TV'.

Source: Adapted from Giddens p. 115.

1 Why does Baudrillard argue that most people's experience of Princess Diana, both as a living person and after her death, was based on media signs and images rather than real life?

2 Think of an example of a recent event that has been featured in the news media. How far do you think Baudrillard's idea that we now experience life through the media is relevant to your example?

3 Can you think of any criticisms of Baudrillard's argument? For example, can you think of any areas where your understanding of the world is not influenced by media signs and images?

The death of Princess Diana provoked a huge outpouring of public grief as seen in hundreds of bouquets and messages left outside Kensington Palace by members of the public, most of whom had only seen her on TV

Section summary

Fill in the blanks, using the words given below.

Consensus theories see society as based on shared _____ and _____.

Functionalism is one form of consensus theory and examines how different parts of society carry out important _____ that help to ensure the smooth running of society.

_____ theories argue that different groups in society are often socially unequal – for example, there are divisions of class, gender and ethnicity.

Marxist theories argue that the _____ system is the most important part of society as it influences the organisation of other parts of society such as family life or the education system.

Weber agreed that society was based on conflict but argued that conflicts could be about differences in _____ or _____, rather than just class.

Feminists see the most important inequalities in society as those based on _____ and argue that most societies are based on male dominance or _____.

_____ theories focus on how individuals interpret the social world around them to make it meaningful.

Labelling theories focus on how, in interacting with others, people frequently put _____ on one another which may involve categorising others negatively. This can lead to a _____ whereby the person so categorised starts to live up to their reputation.

Postmodernists argue that in the era of _____ science and modern technology became more important in society; however, in the twenty-first century they argue we are moving into the era of _____ where electronic images and digital media are defining our lives.

conflict, economic, functions, gender, labels, modernity, norms, patriarchy, postmodernity, power, self-fulfilling prophecy, social action, status, values

Chapter 3

Families and relationships

Activity

Types of families

1 Explain in your own words what Murdock means when he suggests that families are characterised by:
   a) common residence
   b) economic co-operation
   c) reproduction.
2 Look at the examples of families today shown in Items B–F.
   a) To what extent do these fit Murdock's definition of a family?
   b) To what extent do you think that each of these examples should be seen as a family? Give reasons for your answer.
3 Write your own definition of the family so that it includes all of the different groups that you would regard as a family. Compare your definition with others in your class.

3.1 How diverse are modern families?

Fifty years ago many people would have seen a family as comprising a father and mother who were married, and their biological children. Fathers were usually seen as the main wage-earners and many women gave up paid work when they married to become full-time housewives. Most couples stayed married for life and, particularly in traditional working-class communities, most families maintained strong relationships with other relatives. Even in the 1960s, not all families fitted this image and in recent decades sociologists have observed a variety of changes in society that have meant that we are witnessing a growth in what is called **family diversity**. Some sociologists have suggested this means that there is no such thing as a normal or typical family in the UK, and instead people have much greater choice and flexibility in their personal lives and intimate relationships, meaning there are many social groupings that could be called families.

Family and household types in the contemporary UK

Families and households

Sociologists make a distinction between families and households. A family is generally regarded by sociologists as based on relationships of blood, marriage or adoption. However, some sociologists would now point to the emergence of **families of choice**, whereby individuals choose to include people as family members who are not traditionally related. For example, a cohabiting couple may see one another as family, though not formally married, and some same-sex parents may adopt close friends as honorary aunts and uncles to ensure their children have adult role models of both sexes.

A **household** is simply a group of people who live at the same address. The majority of households in the UK are still made up of different kinds of families but an increasing proportion of the population now live alone or with people who are unrelated.

Item A: The universal family?

The American social anthropologist George Murdock (1949) compared research on 250 societies ranging from small hunting and gathering bands to large-scale industrial societies. He concluded that some form of family could be found in every society. He suggested that all families correspond to the following definition:

'The family is a social group characterised by common residence, economic co-operation and reproduction. It includes adults of both sexes, at least two of whom maintain a socially approved sexual relationship, and one or more children, own or adopted of the sexually co-habiting adults.'

Murdock argued that in all societies the nuclear family (father, mother and one or more children) is the basis of the family unit, though in many societies it can include other relatives (**extended family**) while in **polygamous** societies it may be acceptable for a man to have more than one wife (**polygyny**) or for a woman to have more than one husband (**polyandry**).

Item B: Co-parenting

Coronation Street star Charlie Condou (left) lives with his male partner Cameron and son Hal, but had a daughter, Georgia, with a female friend, Catherine, by IVF. Georgia spends time at both her mum's house and at the home of her two dads. All three share parental responsibilities.

Item C: Lone-parent families

Over half of African-Caribbean families in the UK are lone parents, in most cases with the mother as the head of the family.

Item D: Living apart together

A growing number of couples have long-term relationships but do not live together, sometimes even raising children together in separate households. Until their recent separation, actress Helena Bonham Carter and film director Tim Burton were LATs (people who live apart together) and lived in adjoining houses in London with their children.

Item E: Same-sex families

Barrie and Tony Drewitt-Barlow made history in 1999 when they brought home Saffron and her twin brother Aspen, who they had fathered with a surrogate mum in California and fought for the right to legally adopt the children in the UK. The millionaire Drewitt-Barlows now want to extend their family, which now numbers four boys and one girl (pictured above), so that daughter Saffron, 12, doesn't feel outnumbered.

Item F: *Friends*

The American sitcom *Friends* focused on six young people living in New York. Young people in the UK often choose to live with friends once they leave their parents' home.

Nuclear families

A nuclear family consists of a father, a mother and one or more children who could be their biological or adopted children. Up to the 1970s, many sociologists saw the nuclear family as the typical family of Western industrial societies (see the section on functionalism on page 37).

Figures from the Office for National Statistics (ONS) (2013a) data reveal that the most common type of family with children in 2013 was a married or civil partner couple family with dependent children (essentially a nuclear family), of which there were 4.7 million. However, this was the only family type to decrease in number since 1996 with an increase in other types such as cohabiting-couple families and lone-parent families over the last decade.

Extended families

Extended families are families that include **kin** (or relatives) beyond the nuclear family. A family can be extended vertically, meaning that it comprises not just two generations (parents and children) but three or more (grandparents). Families can also be extended horizontally, meaning that relatives from the same generation live together; for example, two brothers and their wives and children may form a family unit.

There is a lot of evidence that extended families were important, especially in working-class communities in Britain up until the 1950s. However, by the 1970s, many sociologists believed that the extended family was in decline. Young and Willmott (1973) argued that a new type of family – the **symmetrical family** – had spread to all social classes. This was based on a nuclear family and centred on the relationship between husband and wife.

More recently, sociologists such as Ulrich Beck and Elisabeth Beck-Gernsheim (1995) have argued that we are undergoing a process of **individualisation**, whereby individuals choose their own lifestyles and identities rather than following norms laid down by tradition. Part of this entails individuals choosing whether to maintain ties with extended families or to lead more independent lives.

In recent years, a number of sociologists have argued that the extended family continues to be important to many people. According to the ONS (2013a), less than 1 per cent of households in the UK are multi-family households (which would include extended families), but they are the fastest-growing type of household. Today, most extended families are what Peter Willmott calls **dispersed extended families**, which means that kin do not live together in the same household; nuclear families are the main living unit but can rely on a network of extended family members who offer one another support and come together for special occasions. Better transport and modern communications technology – for example, the internet and mobile phones – mean that extended families that are quite widely dispersed, even across different countries, can continue to support one another.

Lone-parent families

Lone-parent families are families where at least one child lives with just one parent. In 91 per cent of lone-parent families the parent is the mother, reflecting the fact that women are more likely to take the main caring responsibilities for children when relationships break down.

In 2013 there were nearly 1.9 million lone parents with dependent children in the UK, a figure that has grown from 1.8 million in 2003. Lone parents with dependent children represented 25 per cent of all families with dependent children in 2013 (ONS 2013a).

For many individuals, being part of a lone-parent family is a stage in the life course. Many children will spend part of their childhood in a lone-parent family, but most lone parents remain alone for only an average of about five years. The Millennium Cohort Study (Panico *et al.* 2010) was a longitudinal study following families of children born in 2000. Seven per cent of the families remained lone parents throughout the five years of the study, but a further 3.9 per cent went from being lone parents to cohabiting and 1.9 per cent went from lone parenthood to marriage. On the other hand, 7.9 per cent of those who had started the study as married or cohabiting had become lone parents after five years.

Reconstituted families

A **reconstituted family** is created where a couple come together and form a family including at least one child from a previous relationship of one of the couple. In other words, it includes a step-parent and one step-child or more. Reconstituted families are also sometimes called **step-families** or **blended families**.

In 2011 there were 544,000 reconstituted families with dependent children in England and Wales, in which 340,000 couples were married and 203,000 were cohabiting. Eleven per cent of couple families with dependent children were reconstituted families. Due to the fact that the majority of children stay with their mother following a divorce or separation, most

Activity: Lone-parent families

Item A: Official statistics on lone-parent incomes and employment

According to government statistics, children in lone-parent families are twice as likely as children in couple families to live in relative poverty. Over four in every ten (43 per cent) children in lone-parent families are poor, compared to just over two in ten (22 per cent) of children in couple families (DWP 2014). It is a myth that all lone parents are dependent on state benefits. Once their children are aged 12 or over, single parents' employment rate is similar to, or higher than, the employment rate for those in couples – 71 per cent of single parents whose child is 11–15 are in work (DWP 2010).

Item B: Disadvantage in lone-parent families

A study by Nick Spencer (2005) of over 15,000 children examined whether living in lone-parent families accounted for poorer health, lower educational achievement and increased risk of children becoming involved in anti-social behaviour. Spencer found that children from lone-parent families were at more risk of these outcomes but mainly because of material disadvantages – for example, low incomes and poor housing. Spencer argues that government policies should focus on reducing inequality and tackling material disadvantage rather than stigmatising lone parents.

1 Suggest reasons why lone-parent families are more likely to be in poverty than other types of families.
2 To what extent does Item A support the idea that the low incomes of lone-parent families are due them being unwilling to work and claiming state benefits?
3 How does Item B suggest that children in lone-parent families may be disadvantaged by growing up in poverty?
4 Assess Spencer's views on how government policy should aim to help lone-parent families.

---

reconstituted families have a stepfather as opposed to a stepmother. It has been suggested that men are increasingly likely to be living with other men's children while their own grow up elsewhere (Grant 2006).

Reconstituted families are a diverse category of families. Parentline Plus, an organisation for step-families, suggests there are 72 ways in which step-families can be formed. Step-families can include children from one or both parents' previous relationships and may or may not include children of both parents. Children may also have strong relationships with their absent biological parents or have little or no contact.

Same-sex families

Lesbian, gay, bisexual and transgender (LGBT) people have achieved considerable advances in terms of equality in society since 1967, when homosexual relationships between men over 21 were legalised for the first time in England and Wales. Since then, same-sex couples have gained the right to legally adopt children, and in 2005 were able to form civil partnerships which gave them most of the same rights as married couples. In 2013, legislation to allow same-sex marriage came into force.

Families based on same-sex couples remain a tiny minority of families in the UK. There were only 8,000 civil partnerships and 5,000 cohabiting same-sex couples with children (compared to 5.7 million opposite-sex couples with children) recorded in 2013 (ONS 2013a). However, given that such families were almost non-existent until recently, this is a significant change and a further extension of the diversity of families in the UK.

Non-family households

Not all households in the UK are made up of families. In 2013 there were 7.8 million households in the UK consisting of one person living alone (an increase from 7.2 million in 2003). There were also 800,000 households containing two or more unrelated adults – for example, friends sharing accommodation (this figure is unchanged since 2003).

Living alone

American sociologist Eric Klinenberg (2013) argues that in western European and North American societies, people are living alone in large numbers for the first time in history. He suggests there are three reasons for this:

1 **The cult of the individual.** Klinenberg uses this term, originally coined by the sociologist Emile Durkheim, to describe the idea that with the emergence of modern industrial societies, individuals are more focused on their own needs rather than on their role in larger social structures such as families, as in pre-industrial and tribal societies. The cultural pressure today is to be 'good to oneself', so more individuals choose to opt out of living with others or as part of a family.

Item A: Gay marriage

Peter McGraith and David Cabreza, who had been partners for 17 years, were the first gay couple to marry in the UK in March 2013

Item B: Children in same-sex families

In 2010, the Centre for Family Research at the University of Cambridge conducted interviews for Stonewall with 82 children and young people who have lesbian, gay or bisexual parents to learn more about their experiences both at home and at school. The study *Different Families* (Guasp 2010) found that very young children with gay parents tend not to see their families as being any different to those of their peers. Many of the older children said they saw their families as special and different, but only because all families are special and different – though some felt that their families were a lot closer than other people's families. The report found that children with gay parents like having gay parents and would not want things to change, but that sometimes they wish that other people were more accepting.

The research revealed problems faced by some children of gay parents at school – such as widespread use of **homophobic** language, homophobic bullying and the exclusion of their families and **LGBT** people in school. But the children interviewed had very clear recommendations for schools in how to tackle these issues.

Source: Adapted from Guasp (2010)

1 In what ways might same-sex families be:
   a) similar to other families?
   b) different to other families?
2 Why does the Centre for Family Research study suggest many of the problems faced by children in same-sex families have more to do with the attitudes of people outside their families than the nature of the families to which they belong?

2 **The communications revolution.** Individuals can achieve the pleasures of a social life even when they are living alone, thanks to new technologies such as email, mobile phones and digital social networks.

3 **The ageing population.** Because people are living longer, it is likely they will be divorced or widowed in old age. Elderly women are particularly likely to live alone as they have a longer life expectancy than men.

While Klineberg sees the popularity of living alone as a significant change in society, a study by Adam Smith and his colleagues (2005) found that over a ten-year period between 1991 and 2002, only 7 per cent of those studied remained living alone throughout that period. They also found, using data from the Scottish Household Survey, that of those who lived alone, 59 per cent had been to visit relatives in the last fortnight, meaning that many of those who live alone are still part of family networks.

Living apart together

The fact that individuals live alone does not mean that they are not part of families or other intimate relationships. Many elderly people have regular contact with their children and other family members. Some individuals choose to live alone but maintain long-standing intimate relationships with a partner who lives elsewhere. Levin (2004) has identified what are called **LATs** (living apart together) as a newly emergent form of family which allows individuals to enjoy the intimacy of being part of a couple with the autonomy of living alone. However, Haskey and Lewis (2006) point out that for many, living apart together is simply a prelude to cohabitation and possibly marriage, so many LATs may aspire to relatively conventional relationships in the long run.

Rejecting the heteronorm – Roseneil and Budgeon (2004)

Sasha Roseneil and Shelley Budgeon suggest that aspects of intimacy and emotional relationships are increasingly taking place outside the family. Their study was based on small-scale research on individuals who lived without partners. They focus on two key changes:

1 **Friends are taking the place of family.** For such individuals, their personal relationships were fluid, with a range of lovers, friends, work colleagues and extended family members offering an often changing set of personal relationships in place of a traditional family.

2 **The decentering of conjugal relationships.** Such individuals no longer build their lives and identities around a marriage partnership and a shared home, meaning that the nuclear family is no longer central to some people's lives. A person's significant other may not in fact be someone with whom she or he has a sexual relationship.

Roseneil and Budgeon see these changes as part of the breakdown of what they refer to as the 'heteronorm', the idea that intimate relationships between heterosexual couples are the normal form of intimate relationship.

This research was based on small number of case studies, so may not be generalisable to the wider population, but it certainly points to another way in which some individuals are diverging from traditional notions of family life.

Source: Adapted from Roseneil and Budgeon (2004)

Points to discuss and research

1 What do Roseneil and Budgeon mean by the breakdown of the 'heteronorm'?

2 What evidence do they offer to support this idea?

3 To what extent do you agree that this is a significant change in people's personal lives and family relationships?

3.2 Aspects of and reasons for family and household diversity in the contemporary UK

Getting you thinking ...

Number of marriages and divorces, 1932–2012, England and Wales

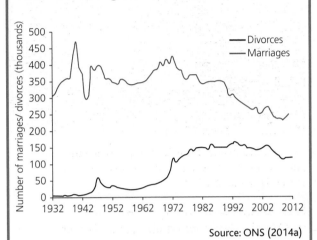

Source: ONS (2014a)

1 Summarise the trends shown above in:
- marriages
- divorces.

2 What explanations would you give for these trends?

3 To what extent can we draw any conclusions about the state of family life in the UK from these statistics?

Trends in marriage

The UK government has collected national statistics on marriages since 1838 and the overall trend up until the 1940s was that the number of marriages increased, though there were major fluctuations around the two world wars. Since the early 1970s the number of marriages has declined, the average age at which couples marry has increased and an increasing proportion of marriages are remarriages. Traditionally, marriage in Western societies has been based on monogamy, a lifelong union between one man and one woman. However, some sociologists have suggested that we are moving to a practice of serial monogamy whereby the norm is to have only one partner at a time but individuals may have a series of marriages or long-term relationships during their lifetimes.

Facts and figures about marriage in England and Wales

According to the Office for National Statistics (ONS 2014b), marriage appears to be declining in popularity. The number of marriages in England and Wales peaked in 1940 at 470,549, while in 2012, 262,240 took place, even though the population is now much larger.

A growing proportion of marriages are remarriages. In 1940 in only 9 per cent of marriages had one or both partners been married before, while in 2012, 34 per cent of marriages were remarriages. The majority of these involved people who had been divorced rather than widowed.

Civil ceremonies have outnumbered religious ceremonies since 1976; in 2012, 70 per cent of marriages were civil ceremonies. There is a growing trend for couples to marry in approved premises such as hotels, stately homes and historic buildings rather than registry offices, and 60 per cent of marriages took place in approved premises in 2012.

The proportion of men and women who have ever married has been declining over recent decades. Of those born in 1930, 90 per cent of men and 94 per cent of women had married by age 40. In contrast, of those born in 1970, only 63 per cent of men and 71 per cent of women had married by the same age.

The mean age at marriage for men in 1972 was 28.8 years, compared with 36.5 years in 2012. For women, the mean age at marriage in 1972 was 26.2 years, compared with 34.0 years in 2012. These increases result from people delaying entering into a first marriage and, to a lesser extent, increases in the proportion of marriages involving divorced men and women where the mean age of marriage has risen.

Activity: Changing patterns of marriage

Item A: A traditional wedding in the 1950s

Item B: A twenty-first century Star Wars-themed wedding

Item C: Changing attitudes towards marriage

The British Social Attitudes Survey has asked a large national sample of people to respond to the following statement in a number of surveys since 1989:

'People who want children ought to get married.'

	1989 %	1994 %	2000 %	2002 %	2010 %	2012 %
Agree strongly	25	18	21	14	13	9
Agree	46	39	33	37	29	33
Neither agree nor disagree	10	14	19	17	23	23
Disagree	14	21	20	22	25	27
Disagree strongly	3	6	6	8	8	7

Source: Adapted from Park *et al.* (2013) These figures are approximate.

1 What do Items A and B suggest about changes in attitudes to marriage in the last 60 years?
2 What changes in attitudes towards marriage since 1989 are shown in Item C?
3 How would you explain both sets of changes sociologically?

Cohabitation

Historical evidence suggests that cohabitation was by no means uncommon in past centuries, particularly among the lower classes for when marriage was less important as a mechanism of inheritance of property. While the number of people marrying in the UK has declined since the 1970s, the number cohabiting or living together as couples outside marriage has increased.

Facts and figures about cohabitation in the UK

According to the Office for National Statistics (ONS) (2012a), the percentage of people aged 16 or over who were cohabiting steadily increased from 6.5 per cent in 1996 to 11.7 per cent in 2012. This makes cohabitation the fastest-growing family type in the UK.

39 per cent of opposite-sex cohabiting couples had dependent children, compared with 38 per cent of married couples, though married couples were more likely to have two or more children.

The average age of people cohabiting has increased in recent years, partly because younger people and are delaying marriage for longer and partly because the number of older people who have been divorced and are cohabiting has increased. Between 1996 and 2012, the over-65s had the largest percentage increase in cohabitation of all age groups, despite the small percentage of people who do cohabit in this age group.

In 2012 there were 2,893,000 cohabiting opposite-sex couples in the UK and 69,000 same-sex couples, though cohabitation has been increasing in popularity fastest among same-sex couples since 1996.

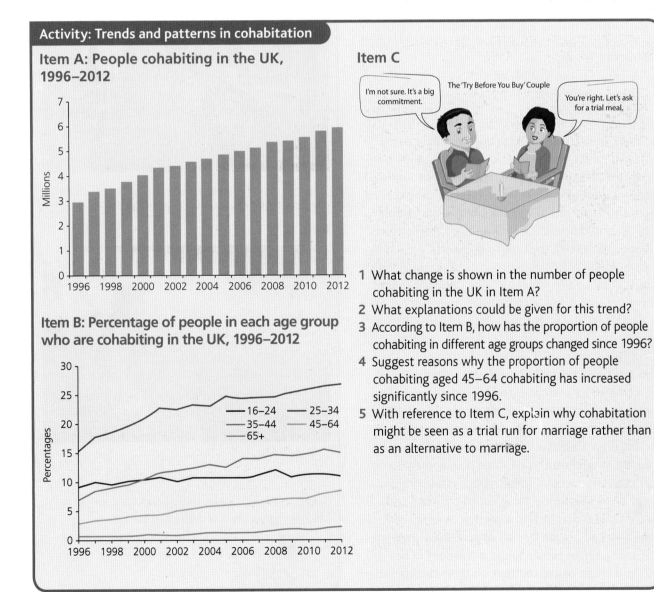

Activity: Trends and patterns in cohabitation

Item A: People cohabiting in the UK, 1996–2012

Item C

The 'Try Before You Buy' Couple

I'm not sure. It's a big commitment.

You're right. Let's ask for a trial meal.

Item B: Percentage of people in each age group who are cohabiting in the UK, 1996–2012

16–24   25–34
35–44   45–64
65+

1 What change is shown in the number of people cohabiting in the UK in Item A?
2 What explanations could be given for this trend?
3 According to Item B, how has the proportion of people cohabiting in different age groups changed since 1996?
4 Suggest reasons why the proportion of people cohabiting aged 45–64 cohabiting has increased significantly since 1996.
5 With reference to Item C, explain why cohabitation might be seen as a trial run for marriage rather than as an alternative to marriage.

Éva Beaujouan and Márie Ní Bhrolcháin (2011) used data from the General Household Survey to analyse patterns of cohabitation. Some of their key findings were as follows:

- Cohabitation before marriage has become the norm with 80 per cent of couples who marry having previously cohabited in 2004–7, compared to around 30 per cent in 1980–4.
- Couples now tend to live together longer before getting married. In the 1980s, most cohabitation before marriage lasted less than two years, whereas by 2004–7 most cohabiting couples spent around four years living together before marriage.
- While the popularity of marriage has declined, the proportion of people reaching their early 40s who have entered into some kind of long-term relationship is similar to the mid-twentieth century, when marriage was at its most popular. There does not appear to have been a long-term flight from partnership, merely a greater proportion of those who do find partners now choosing to cohabitate rather than marry.

Singlehood

While cohabitation represents one alternative to marriage, an increasing proportion of people are remaining single. In the section on non-family households (see page 51), we have already considered reasons for the growth in the number of people living alone and some of the ways in which single people may develop different kinds of intimate relationships with people outside their own households.

One significant change noted by some sociologists is in attitudes to remaining single. Until relatively recently, being single was regarded by many people as a negative status in comparison to being part of a couple, and terms such as 'old maid', 'spinster' and being 'left on the shelf' were applied to older women who remained single. In recent years, being single has come to be seen as more glamorous, assisted by media representations of young single people leading fulfilling lives in TV series such as *Friends* and *Sex and the City*. Some sociologists have used the term **creative singlehood** to describe how some people now choose to remain single as a lifestyle option, rather than singlehood being an unfortunate state for those who do not find a partner. A study of never-married people by Hall *et al.* (1999) suggested that many single people found a freedom in being solo and chose to concentrate on their careers rather than establishing a long-term relationship.

Not all single people live alone; Heath (2004) notes the rise of the **'kippers'** (kids in parents' pockets) – young people who continue to live with their parents after they have completed their education, often as a way to save money, though they may be eroding their parents' retirement savings. In 2011, one in three men and one in six women aged 20 to 34 were still living with their parents, a 20 per cent increase in 15 years. There is some evidence that increases in rents and house prices in recent years have meant that many young people are delaying setting up their own homes and fully entering the adult world, remaining in an ambiguous state of being 'adult-kids'.

Activity: Singletons

Item A

The portrayal of Bridget Jones in *Bridget Jones's Diary* suggests that single people are lonely and miserable

Item B

The freedom of being single, not tied down to anyone else and being able to do whatever you want

1 Suggest reasons why more people are remaining single today than in the recent past.
2 Discuss which image, Item A or Item B, is a more realistic representation of life as a young single person today.

Explanations of changing patterns of marriage and cohabitation

Changing social attitudes

Up until the 1960s there was strong social pressure on most couples to marry before setting up home together and, in cases of pregnancy outside marriage, young women would be expected to marry the father or give the child up for adoption. Many sociologists argue that cohabitation and sexual relationships outside marriage generally have become more socially acceptable. This is supported by the British Social Attitudes Survey (Park *et al*. 2013); while the 1989 survey found that 71 per cent of people agreed or strongly agreed with the statement 'People who want children ought to get married', the comparable figure for the 2012 survey was 42 per cent. Views on sex before marriage were even more liberal, with 75 per cent in 2012 believing it was 'rarely wrong' or 'not wrong at all'.

The decline of family values

For New Right thinkers (see page 81), the declining popularity of marriage is seen as part of a more general weakening of what they refer to as **traditional family values**. From this perspective, marriage is the bedrock of stable family life and alternatives such as cohabitation are no substitute, as cohabiting relationships are more likely to break up than marriages. Patricia Morgan (2000) argues that in recent years, governments have given insufficient support to marriage both through public support for marriage as an institution and in terms of financial support through the tax and benefit system for married couples bringing up children.

Individualisation

For sociologists such as Ulrich Beck and Elisabeth Beck-Gernsheim (1995), these changes reflect the growing trend towards **individualisation** in late modernity. Individuals are no longer bound by traditional social norms and loyalty to families and instead seek a lifestyle and relationships that fulfil their needs as individuals. Many therefore see alternatives to marriage such as cohabitation, living apart together or staying single as offering more freedom and less risk than conventional marriage.

Anthony Giddens (1992) presents a similar perspective, arguing that in late modernity there has been a transformation of intimacy. Individuals no

longer seek the kind of romantic love associated with traditional marriage, based on the idea of lifelong commitment to a partner. Instead, there has been a growth of **confluent love**, where individuals enter into more temporary and fragile intimate relationships where the expectation of each partner is that the relationship will continue only so long as what they invest emotionally is returned. However, many individuals feel they can find this kind of love outside marriage and those who do marry are more likely to break up when they feel they can no longer find confluent love. Giddens is less pessimistic than Morgan and feels that the quality of intimate relationships is improving, especially for women who are no longer trapped in unhappy marriages by a lack of alternative choices, as they often were in the past.

Study

Cohabitation as an alternative form of commitment – Jamieson *et al*. (2002)

A study by Lynn Jamieson and her colleagues questions the view put forward by individualisation theorists that couples living together without marrying represent a reduced willingness to create and honour lifelong partnerships. They carried out a survey and in-depth interviews with samples of 20–29-year-olds living in an urban area of Scotland and found that most of the cohabiting couples strongly stressed their 'commitment'. Many respondents questioned the idea that they would gain any added value in marriage. However, some respondents also perceived cohabitation as a 'try-and-see' strategy, part-way to the perceived full commitment of marriage. The notion that 'marriage is better for children' also continued to have support among respondents. Jamieson *et al*. therefore suggested that the rise of cohabitation does not represent a turning away from committed relationships, rather it offers an alternative choice to marriage – albeit one that in some cases may precede marriage.

The changing role of women

Feminists have often seen traditional marriage as a patriarchal institution. In past centuries, a marriage involved a woman passing from the control of her father to the control of her husband. Radical feminists such as Germaine Greer (2000) therefore see the decline in the popularity of marriage as a positive development resulting from women's unwillingness to accept oppression by their husbands.

Women today also have more options than in the early twentieth century because they are better educated and have much better job opportunities. Sue Sharpe carried out two studies of working-class girls in the 1970s and 1990s in London. In her first study (1976), girls' priorities for the future tended to be love, marriage, husbands and children. However, when she repeated the research 20 years later in the same schools (1994), girls were more confident and ambitious and put more priority on education, careers and financial independence from men.

Some feminists, however, argue that the search for love and finding Mr Right still continues to act as a powerful influence on many women. In a small-scale study based on in-depth interviews with 15 women, Wendy Langford (1999) found that many women still fear being alone and report wanting to be wanted for themselves. Langford suggestsed that love is still seen as the natural basis for relationships and a way in which individuals can transcend a meaningless, harsh and alienating world. On the other hand, she argued that this is an illusion and in reality love ends up concealing the way in which men exercise power and control women in many relationships. Her study did, however, suggest that women have not given up the search for love, though this may be in the context of other kinds of relationships as well as marriage.

The continuing importance of marriage

While the popularity of marriage can be seen to be declining, there is evidence that for many people it is still important. People may be delaying marriage rather than rejecting it as an institution. Women in particular have become more career-oriented and are typically waiting until their 30s before they first embark on marriage. Many people who cohabitate subsequently go on to marry.

In 2012, around a third of marriages were remarriages for one or both partners (ONS 2014b). The high level of divorce has clearly not deterred many people from trying marriage again.

Families headed by married couples remain by far the most common type. In 2013, there were around 18.2 million families in the UK, of which over 12.2 million were married-couple families (ONS 2013a).

Marital breakdown and divorce

Types of marital breakdown

Divorce is the legal ending of a marriage. However, marriages can break down without resulting in divorce. It is not possible to know how many marriages in the past broke down because up until the mid-nineteenth century, for most people, divorce was virtually impossible to obtain. For example, many unhappily married couples would have remained in 'empty shell' marriages, staying together to maintain outward appearances.

While there was a dramatic increase in the number of divorces in the late twentieth century in Britain, we must be cautious about assuming that this indicates an increase in the number of marital breakdowns. What is more likely is that today couples are much more likely to turn to divorce as the preferred solution when their marriages do break down.

Trends in divorce

Divorce can be measured statistically in different ways. The simplest measure is the number of divorces, which is based on records from the courts compiled in official statistics. An alternative is to calculate some kind of divorce rate. The most widely used in the UK is the number of divorces per 1,000 of the married population. Eurostat, which collects data from EU countries, uses a measure of divorces per 1,000 of all adults, married or unmarried. Divorce rates are more useful for comparing different countries, as countries have different-sized populations. In 2011, the UK had a divorce rate of 2.1 per 1,000 of all adults, considerably lower than Latvia, which had a divorce rate of 4.0, but much higher than Ireland, which had a divorce rate of 0.5 – Ireland did not legalise divorce until 1995 (Eurostat 2014).

In 1960 there were 23,868 divorces in England and Wales. Over the next three decades the number of divorces increased dramatically, reaching a peak in 1993 at 165,018. Since then, the overall trend has been for the number of divorces to decline and there were 118,140 divorces in 2012 (ONS 2014a). The ONS estimates that 42 per cent of current marriages will end in divorce. For some sociologists, these changes represent the most significant change in family life of the last 100 years.

Divorce legislation in England and Wales

1857 Matrimonial Causes Act

This set up civil divorce courts. Grounds for divorce were adultery, cruelty and desertion and one partner had to prove the other guilty of one of these matrimonial offences. Divorce was still beyond the means of most people and was particularly difficult for women who, unlike men, could not gain a divorce on the grounds of adultery alone. Women did not gain this right until 1923.

Activity: Changing attitudes to marriage

Item A: Are traditional marriages such as this on the way out?

Item B: Trends in marriage

Number of marriages in the UK

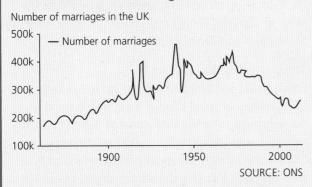

SOURCE: ONS

Item C: Government policies on marriage

For a long time the government discouraged sex outside marriage and encouraged marriage. Children were taught at school about the problems sex before marriage might bring and the tax system offered lower taxes for married couples. In 1986 married men claimed £4.5 billion in additional tax allowances to what they would have received if they had remained single.

The Conservatives replaced the married man's tax allowance with a married couple's allowance after objections that it was sexist. Gordon Brown then abolished that in 2000 and replaced it with a child tax allowance, arguing that the government's job was to prevent children growing up in poverty, rather than to judge the lifestyle of parents.

The emphasis in sex education in schools has also changed towards a focus on ways to avoid unwanted pregnancy and sexually transmitted diseases rather than insisting on abstinence.

There have always been some politicians, especially among the Conservative Party, who argue that the government should intervene more in marriage and family life. Interestingly it is often the same politicians who are most opposed to state intervention in the economy who are keenest on intervention in the bedroom.

When Gordon Brown abolished the married couple's tax allowance it was roundly condemned by many Conservatives, who claimed there is now an 'anti-marriage bias' in the tax and benefits system. In 2013, the coalition government announced it would offer a small financial incentive to some married couples by allowing one member of a married couple who earns under the £10,000 income tax threshold to transfer £1,000 of their allowance to their spouse, reducing their tax bill by up to £200 a year.

Source: Adapted from Andy McSmith (2009)

Item D: Should the government reward marriage?

Speaking in January 2015, a senior judge, Sir Paul Coleridge, suggested that that married couples should get milestone tax breaks. This would mean that the longer they stayed together the less tax they would pay. At a debate organised by the pro-marriage think tank Marriage Foundation, he said the allowances would encourage families facing a break-up to try and stay together and financially reward families that remain stable. His suggestion would of course mean that families who break up – often at a high cost to the tax payer – would pay more tax.

Sir Paul described the tax allowance of £212 that David Cameron gave to some couples in spring 2015 as 'ridiculous', and asked: 'Where is the incentive for people to stay together?' He suggested a milestone tax break could increase in stages so newlyweds would have a small tax advantage over unmarried couples. There would then be increases to the tax allowances at five and ten years, possibly linked to the arrival of children. After 25 years of marriage, a married couple could expect to enjoy a considerable income boost compared to people their age who had never married.

Source: Adapted from Doughty (2015)

1 Using data from Item B, summarise the trends in marriage since the 1970s.
2 What evidence is there in Items C and D to suggest that government policies towards marriage have changed in recent years?
3 With reference to Item D, evaluate the arguments for and against the government offering financial incentives for being married.

1937 Matrimonial Causes Act

This extended the grounds for divorce (to include, for example, drunkenness, insanity and desertion) but spouses still had to prove an offence to get a divorce.

1949 Legal Aid and Advice Act

This provided financial help for legal fees in divorce for those who could not afford them.

1969 Divorce Reform Act (became effective in 1971)

This removed the need to prove matrimonial offences, such as adultery, as the basis for divorce. Instead, couples only had to show that the marriage had 'irretrievably broken down'. No-fault divorce became possible where a couple had been separated for two years and both agreed to a divorce (or five years if one objected). This made divorce accessible to nearly everyone for the first time. In the 1970s, a special procedure was introduced that allowed judges to deal with divorce cases without the couple even attending court. The vast majority of divorces are dealt with using this 'quickie divorce' procedure today.

1984 Matrimonial Proceedings Act (became effective in 1985)

This reduced the time for which a couple had to be married before they could petition for divorce from three years to one year.

1996 Family Law Act (became effective in 1999)

This increased the amount of time a couple had to be married before petitioning for divorce from one year to 18 months, introduced a 'period of reflection' with compulsory marriage counselling, and required children's wishes and financial arrangements for children to be agreed before a divorce was granted. This was an attempt by the government to reduce the number of couples applying for divorce, but the compulsory counselling sessions were later abandoned as they appeared to encourage more people to go through with a divorce.

2011 Practice Direction 3A

This directed divorcing couples to undertake mediation (where a solicitor attempts to resolve disputes between them) before they were permitted to go to court. This was an attempt to reduce the amount of time cases took in the over-worked family courts.

Explanations for changing divorce rates

Changing divorce rates can be explained by changes in the law. Before 1857, the only way to obtain a divorce was by a private Act of Parliament. This was expensive and complicated and required friends in parliament, and so was only available to a small number of wealthy people. Over the next 150 years, divorce became simpler, cheaper and available to many more people (see the section on divorce legislation in England and Wales on page 58). Changes in the law have allowed many more people the option of escaping from unhappy marriages via divorce, but these changes do not in themselves explain why so many more people are choosing this option. Moreover, changes in divorce rates have not always coincided with changes in the law; for example, though the number of divorces doubled in 1971 after the Divorce Reform Act, divorce levels were already rising in the 1960s, so the change in legislation may have simply reflected growing public demand for easier divorce. Most sociologists would therefore suggest that we need to consider changes in society in any explanation of why the popularity of divorce has increased.

The privatised nuclear family

Functionalist sociologists have tended to see high divorce rates as going hand in hand with a trend towards nuclear families. Parsons and Bales (1955), for example, argue that the modern American family has become structurally isolated from extended family with the main focus on the relationship between the husband, wife and children. This means there is less pressure from extended family for a couple to stay together and greater demands are placed on the couple's relationship, which becomes central to the working of the nuclear family (see page 50). For functionalists, this is not a problem; high divorce rates are simply the price we have to pay for living in nuclear families.

Some critics, however, argue that the nuclear family is far from perfect. For example, the social anthropologist Edmund Leach (1967) argued that the nuclear family was the 'source of all our discontents'. He portrayed the relationship between husband and wife as like an over-loaded circuit, having to fulfil all of the emotional needs of a couple. Leach argued that it was no surprise that nuclear families were a source of conflict for many, with divorce one possible outcome.

Higher expectations of marriage

Another functionalist, Ronald Fletcher (1966), argued that higher divorce rates were linked to a higher value being placed on marriage as couples came to expect a more companionate relationship based on love and mutual support rather than one based on the economic and practical reasons that kept couples together in more traditional family systems.

Changing social attitudes

Up until the 1960s there was a strong stigma attached to divorce, but more recently most people in Britain (apart from some with strong religious or moral views) appear to view divorce as normal and acceptable. The British Social Attitudes Survey 2006 (Duncan and Phillips 2008) found that 63 per cent of respondents agreed that 'Divorce can be a positive step towards a new life' and only 7 per cent disagreed. Seventy-eight per cent also agreed that 'It is not divorce that harms children, but conflict between their parents', with again only 7 per cent disagreeing.

The decline of religious beliefs may also have contributed to the greater social acceptability of divorce. Colin Gibson (1994) argues that Britain has undergone a process of **secularisation**, whereby religious values have weakened in society, including the influence of the traditional teaching of the church about the value of lifelong marriage.

Though divorce appears to have become normalised in Britain and other Western societies, Deborah Chambers (2012) highlights a range of evidence that 'divorce, cohabitation and lone parenthood are still viewed within dominant public discourses as signs of moral decline, despite being widespread'. For example, lone parents are often defined by the tabloid press as 'undeserving scroungers', and there is still a widespread belief that divorce leads to bad parenting. This would suggest that the stigma attached to divorce has not entirely disappeared.

Individualisation and reflexivity

Ulrich Beck and Elisabeth Beck-Gernsheim (1995), like Fletcher, focus on changing expectations of marriage but, rather than seeing these as based on shared values, like functionalists, they argue that in late modernity there is less agreement over what marriage should be like. Instead, there is growing individualisation and uncertainty, meaning that the nature of relationships is open to negotiation and choice in what they describe as the normal **chaos of love**. This means that traditional norms and values about marriage and family life no longer constrain people, and where individuals feel that a relationship no longer serves their personal interests, they are less likely to maintain it purely because of a sense of commitment to others.

Anthony Giddens (1992) reflects a similar viewpoint, arguing that there has been a growth in **reflexivity** in late modernity. By this, he means that individuals reflect on their personal lives and constantly question whether they are getting the best out of life. Giddens also argues that individuals seek **confluent love**, by which he means a form of love based on deep intimacy where each partner gains emotional fulfillment from the other. However, such relationships are not based on a permanent commitment; partners only maintain the relationship as long as both are fulfilled. Giddens argues that women in particular (but also men) have gained from this as they are no longer trapped in unsatisfactory relationships because they have no alternatives, but he acknowledges that the consequence has been greater insecurity for individuals and higher rates of divorce and family break-up.

The changing role of women

Graham Allan and Graham Crowe (2001) argue that the changing position of women in society has been one of the main factors influencing a rise in the number of divorces. In the 1940s, around two-thirds of divorce petitions were initiated by men. Women often did not have the financial resources to fund divorce cases and were likely to find themselves much worse off without the economic support of a husband. In 2012, 65 per cent of divorces were initiated by women (ONS 2014a). Since the 1970s, far more married women are employed, giving them a degree of financial independence, and welfare benefits for women with dependent children have improved. However, most women still find themselves financially worse off after divorce. Moreover, research by Lynn Prince Cooke and Vanessa Gash (2010) found no clear relationship between women's employment and earnings and their likelihood of divorcing.

For some feminists, the large number of women seeking to escape from marriage reflects the problematic nature of traditional marriage more than the fact that life as a lone parent is easier for women than it was in the past. This is supported by a small-scale study by Duncombe and Marsden (1995), which found that many of the women they interviewed who had been married for some years became increasingly dissatisfied with their husbands' inability to take on

Trends in divorce

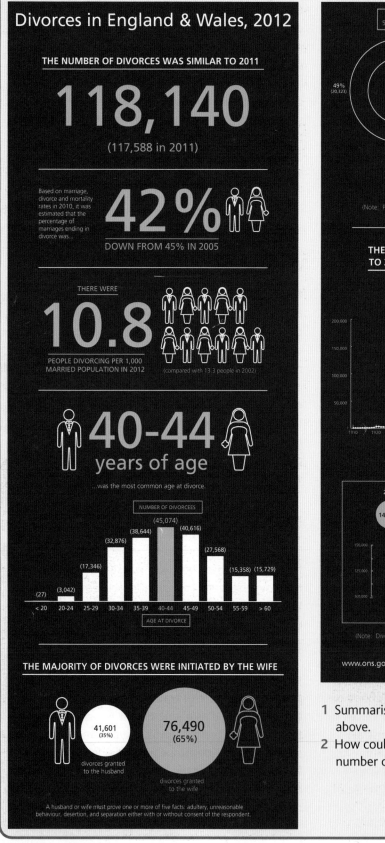

Divorces in England & Wales, 2012

THE NUMBER OF DIVORCES WAS SIMILAR TO 2011

118,140

(117,588 in 2011)

Based on marriage, divorce and mortality rates in 2010, it was estimated that the percentage of marriages ending in divorce was...

42%

DOWN FROM 45% IN 2005

THERE WERE

10.8

PEOPLE DIVORCING PER 1,000 MARRIED POPULATION IN 2012

(compared with 13.3 people in 2002)

40-44 years of age

...was the most common age at divorce.

NUMBER OF DIVORCEES

Age at divorce	Number
< 20	(27)
20-24	(3,042)
25-29	(17,346)
30-34	(32,876)
35-39	(38,644)
40-44	(45,074)
45-49	(40,616)
50-54	(27,568)
55-59	(15,358)
> 60	(15,729)

AGE AT DIVORCE

THE MAJORITY OF DIVORCES WERE INITIATED BY THE WIFE

41,601 (35%)
divorces granted to the husband

76,490 (65%)
divorces granted to the wife

A husband or wife must prove one or more of five facts: adultery, unreasonable behaviour, desertion, and separation either with or without consent of the respondent.

When women were granted the divorce, 54% of the time the fact proven was the man's behaviour

GRANTED TO MEN
49% (20,323)
37% (15,210)
14% (5,675)
1% (334)

GRANTED TO WOMEN
54% (41,248)
32% (24,447)
14% (10,320)
1% (385)

Behaviour Adultery Desertion Separation/Other

(Note: Percentages shown above do not sum to 100% due to rounding.)

THE NUMBER OF DIVORCES FELL FROM 2003 TO 2009, BUT HAS REMAINED STEADY SINCE

1945: End of World War 2 — 15,634
1971: Divorce Reform Act — 74,437
1993: Record High — 165,018
2012: Similar to 2011 — 118,140

THE TREND OVER THE LAST 10 YEARS

2002 — 147,735
2012 — 118,140

(Note: Divorce figures include both decree absolutes and decrees of nullity.)

www.ons.gov.uk

Office for National Statistics

1 Summarise the trends in divorce shown in the graph above.
2 How could both increases and decreases in the number of divorces be explained?

responsibilities in marriage, leaving them to not only perform housework but also to care for the family's emotional needs.

Trends in divorce since the 1990s

Since the 1990s, the overall number of divorces has declined. A number of explanations can be offered for this:

- The number of marriages has declined, meaning that there are fewer potential marriages that can end in divorce. Though this would explain the decline in the total number of divorces, it would not explain the decline in the divorce rate per 1,000 married couples.
- People are waiting longer to marry. Research suggests that couples who marry young have a much higher chance of divorce, so the increase in the average age of marriage may have reduced some of the risks of divorce.
- Most couples now have a trial period of cohabitation before marrying; in many cases these relationships will break up but will not be recorded as divorces. It also seems likely that couples who do go on to marry are likely to be more committed and attach a greater value to traditional ideas of marriage than those who remain cohabiting, meaning that they have a better chance of staying together.

3.3 Demographic changes

Demography is the study of population. This includes studying how factors such as **fertility** (the rate at which children are being born) and **mortality** (the rate at which people are dying) affect the size and make-up of the population. This section considers some of the key demographic changes in the UK population and how they have affected family life.

Births and fertility

Though immigration can add to the size of the population of a country, in most countries the main reason for population increase is births. Demographers use a number of ways of measuring births and fertility.

Number of births

This is simply the number of births in the country in a year. When the number of deaths is subtracted from this, we can calculate what is called the **natural increase** in the population.

Crude birth rate

This is the number of births per 1,000 of the population per year and gives us a measure of how fast the population is producing children. The crude birth rate is useful for comparing the rate of growth

Getting you thinking ...

Changing family size

In the nineteenth century, families were often large, though the one on the left with 16 children was large even by Victorian standards. In the twenty-first century, families are typically smaller, with an average of about two children. More women wait until their 30s or 40s to start a family and an increasing number of women in recent years never have children at all.

1 Discuss possible reasons why:
   a) British families in the early twenty-first century are on average smaller than those of the nineteenth century;
   b) women today tend to delay having children for longer than in the past.
2 Summarise your ideas in a mind map.

of different countries' populations. In general, more developed industrial countries have lower birth rates than poorer less developed countries but in recent years many developing countries across the world have started to experience a decline in birth rates.

Total fertility rate

The total fertility rate (TFR) is the average number of children a woman would have in her lifetime. It is a more useful measure than the crude birth rate as it gives us a measure of the typical size of families. It is estimated that the TFR in 1900 was 3.5 and reached a record low of 1.63 in 2001, while in 2012 it was 1.94.

Trends in births and fertility

Whatever measure of fertility is used, there has been a significant decline since the late nineteenth century. For example, in 1901 there were nearly 1.1 million births, whereas in 2012 there were 812,970 from a much larger population.

This decline in fertility has been a feature of most societies that have undergone industrialisation. Demographers have put forward the following explanations for this.

Declining mortality

From around 1830 onwards, the death rate in the UK decreased and life expectancy increased. Infant mortality (the number of babies dying in their first year per 1,000 live births) in particular declined; in 1901, 25 per cent of all deaths were babies under one year whereas in 2005 they accounted for less than 1 per cent of deaths. This means that families no longer need to have large numbers of children to ensure that some of them survive until adulthood.

Economic factors

In the nineteenth century, children were regarded as an economic asset by many working-class parents, as they could go out to work to bring in money for the family and provide support for parents in old age. Children have arguably become a financial burden on parents as they have been excluded from paid work and the period in which children are financially dependent on parents has been extended as the school-leaving age has increased and more and more young people go on to further and higher education.

According to the annual Cost of a Child Report sponsored by the insurer LV, the cost of raising a child from birth to 21 in 2013 was £227,266. It also suggested that one in five parents are delaying having another child due to cuts to child benefit and the increasing cost of parenting.

Women's opportunities

Over the last century, and especially since the 1970s, there has been a huge expansion in opportunities for women, both in education and employment. Women have many other options apart from marriage and child bearing, and are therefore tending to delay having children until they have completed their education and become established in their careers, meaning that they are likely to have fewer children or in some cases remain childless.

Changing social attitudes

Up until the late nineteenth century, large families were seen as desirable, but from the 1870s onwards, first middle-class and later working-class families began to see smaller families as a way of improving their living standards. By the mid-twentieth century, small families of up to three children became the social norm. While the status of 'childlessness' was seen as unfortunate in the past, many couples now describe themselves as 'child-free', emphasising their lack of children as a freely chosen lifestyle option.

Individualisation

A number of these factors, such as women's desire for careers over children and the notion of being child-free, link in with the individualisation thesis of writers such as Beck and Beck-Gernsheim (1995) (see page 90). Individuals increasingly seek a life of their own in which they can construct their own lifestyle and relationships and are no longer tied to traditional social norms that, for example, might dictate that at a particular stage in life a person should get married and then start a family. Beck and Beck-Gernsheim also refer to the importance of risk in modern society, suggesting individuals seek to control and avoid risk. Just as more people now avoid the risks of commitment and possible divorce by cohabitating or even staying single, so some people feel children are an added risk factor, both to their relationship and to their economic wellbeing. They seek to minimise these risks by delaying or avoiding having children.

Contraception and abortion

Most demographers suggest that the decline in birth rates in the late nineteenth century was attributable more to couples abstaining from sex than to the use of contraception, which was disapproved of in many sections of society. However, in the twentieth century, contraception became more socially acceptable and the introduction of the birth control pill and other more reliable contraceptive methods meant that, for the first time, couples could plan when they wanted children and could engage in sexual relationships without risking pregnancy. In 1968 abortion was legalised for the first time in England and Wales under the 1967 Abortion Act. Though there were a significant number of illegal abortions before this, it seems likely that far more pregnancies are terminated by abortion than in the past; a total of 185,331 were recorded in 2013.

Fluctuations in birth rates

The fall in births over the last century has not been continuous and the number of births, along with the birth rate, has fluctuated considerably. For example, the number of births fell during both world wars and then there were baby booms after the wars and again in the late 1950s and early 1960s with smaller booms in the late 1980s and early 1990s. One explanation is that there is usually a baby boom about 25 years after the previous baby boom as there are more young people of childbearing age in the population. Similarly, there was a drop in the number of births in the later 1990s because the birth rate a generation earlier had a reached an all-time low in the 1970s. Baby booms also tend to coincide with periods of economic prosperity; for example, the rise in the number of births in the late 1950s coincided with a period of full employment and rising wages, encouraging more people to start families.

The number of births and the TFR have been climbing since 2001. Several reasons have been offered for this:
- Children of the last baby boom in the late 1980s are beginning families themselves.
- More women went to university in the 1990s and delayed having children until the 2000s.

- Immigration levels have risen in recent years. Immigrants tend on average to be younger than the UK population as a whole and therefore more fertile, plus larger families are more commonplace among certain immigrant groups.

Family size

In Victorian England, families were much larger than today, with families of up to ten children not uncommon. There was a decline in birth rates in England from around 1870 to 1920. In 1871 the average woman had 5.5 children, but by 1921 this had fallen to 2.4 children (Woods and Smith 1983); families today are even smaller, with an average of 1.71 dependent children in 2012. Married or civil-partnered couples had a higher average number of dependent children in their families than other family types, at 1.79 dependent children per family, meanwhile lone-parent families had 1.59 dependent children on average and cohabiting couples had an average of 1.62 (ONS 2012b). These patterns reflect the fact that married couples tend to be older and are more likely to have completed childbearing.

According to a report by the ONS (2013b), the main reason that the average family size has got smaller in recent decades is that more women are remaining childless. By their 30th birthday, almost half of all women born in 1982 were childless. In contrast, less than a third of their mothers' generation (born in 1955) were childless by their 30th birthday, and just over a quarter of their grandmothers' generation (born in 1927) were childless by their 30th birthday. Possible reasons for this include:
- increased participation in higher education
- delayed marriage and partnership formation
- establishing a career
- getting on the housing ladder
- ensuring financial stability before starting a family.

According to Susanne Whiting (2012), there are only small social class differences in family size today, unlike the early twentieth century, when working-class families were generally larger than those of the middle class. However, ethnicity does impact on family size, with black and Asian ethnic groups (especially Pakistanis and Bangladeshis) having larger families than white and Chinese ones.

Item A: The number of live births and TFR, 1942–2012, England and Wales

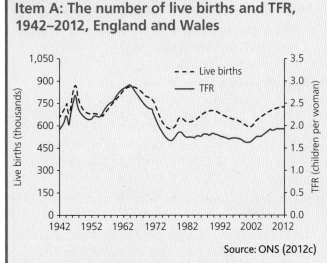

Source: ONS (2012c)

Item B: The end of the baby boom?

Is Britain's baby boom finally coming to an end? While birth rates have climbed almost non-stop throughout the last decade or so, the latest data published by the Office for National Statistics (ONS) today showed that in 2013, just 698,512 babies were born, down from 729,674 the year before. This is the first fall in birth rates since 2001 and the biggest since the 1970s.

The ONS suggests three possible explanations. The first is that welfare benefits for families have been reduced and some have been restricted, putting off some women from having children. The second explanation is that employment has also become less stable and less well-paid so people may feel they can't afford children. Both are sort of plausible. Another explanation is the housing market. The cost of housing is riding and fewer people under 35 can afford to buy their own homes.

A different kind of explanation is offered by Danny Dorling, a geographer at the University of Oxford. He suggests that the baby boom was never all that to begin with and that a large part of the increase in births in the 2000s was simply a result of women delaying having children in the 1990s and early 2000s. If so, then much of the baby boom may be a temporary feature, likely to tail off as the effect works its way through – especially if the squeeze on housing, benefits and the rest of it keeps meaning that economic factors will still discourage childbearing.

All this could lead to a range of problems. The baby boom prior to 2013 meant that primary schools were put under enormous pressure to cope with a massive expansion in their intake. It is, however, difficult for the government to predict in which local areas changes in birth rates will take place. If benefit cuts are the main reason for a decline in births, then we might expect the change to be sharpest in relatively poorer, younger areas such as inner-city Birmingham and Manchester and London boroughs such as Newham. If it is an effect of the increase in students studying at universities in the 1990s, then the decline in births will more likely be among middle class women in the suburbs. If the cost of housing is to blame, the effect could be a mix of both. The government have to not only guess where children might be born, they also have to guess where they will live when they reach primary- and secondary-school age. Suburbs or city centres.

Source: Adapted from *The Economist* (2014)

1 Summarise the changes in the birth rate and the total fertility rate shown in Item A.
2 How can the fluctuations in the birth rate be explained?
3 How can the fall in the birth rate after 2012 be explained?
4 With reference to Item B, discuss what problems fluctuating birth rates might create for both national and local government organisations?

Activity: Childlessness among women in the UK

Item A: Female graduates

Young women today are staying on longer in education than their mother's generation

1 Examine the data from the ONS in Item B. What does it reveal about how levels of childlessness have changed among the three generations of women shown?

2 Using Item A and the section of Item B 'Why the delay?', explain in your own words why women born since 1982 may be waiting longer to have children or not having them at all.

3 How might the sociological concept of individualisation explain the changing patterns of fertility shown?

Item B: Childlessness in three generations of women

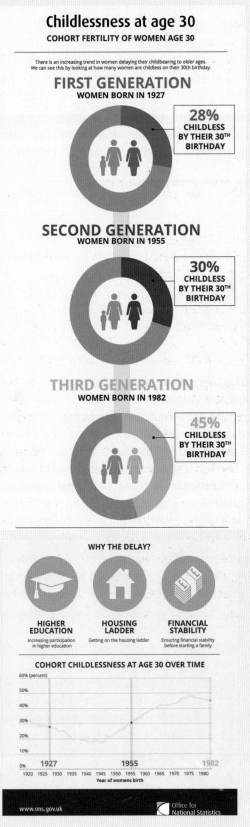

Childlessness at age 30

COHORT FERTILITY OF WOMEN AGE 30

There is an increasing trend in women delaying their childbearing to older ages. We can see this by looking at how many women are childless on their 30th birthday.

FIRST GENERATION
WOMEN BORN IN 1927

28% CHILDLESS BY THEIR 30TH BIRTHDAY

SECOND GENERATION
WOMEN BORN IN 1955

30% CHILDLESS BY THEIR 30TH BIRTHDAY

THIRD GENERATION
WOMEN BORN IN 1982

45% CHILDLESS BY THEIR 30TH BIRTHDAY

WHY THE DELAY?

HIGHER EDUCATION
Increasing participation in higher education

HOUSING LADDER
Getting on the housing ladder

FINANCIAL STABILITY
Ensuring financial stability before starting a family

COHORT CHILDLESSNESS AT AGE 30 OVER TIME

www.ons.gov.uk — Office for National Statistics

Source: ONS (2013c)

Births outside marriage

Up until the mid-twentieth century, having children outside marriage was still considered shameful and unmarried mothers were often encouraged to have their babies adopted. In 1971 only 8 per cent of children were born outside marriage. The percentage has risen steadily since then, reflecting the rise in lone parenthood and also in cohabiting couples having children. In 2012 nearly half of all babies were born outside marriage or civil partnership (47.5 per cent), compared with 40.6 per cent in 2002. This continues the long-term rise in the percentage of births outside marriage and civil partnership, which is consistent with increases in the number of couples cohabiting rather than being married or in a civil partnership (ONS 2012c).

Activity: The consequences of rising births outside marriage

Item A: A longitudinal study of children

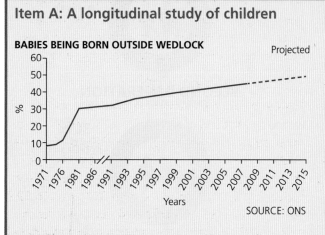

BABIES BEING BORN OUTSIDE WEDLOCK

SOURCE: ONS

Item B: Births outside marriage – a real cause for concern

Soon most babies in Britain will be born outside marriage. Does this matter? In an article entitled 'Births outside marriage: the real story', Professor John Ermisch assessed the evidence and concluded that 'the rise in births outside marriage is a real cause for concern'.

Using 17 years of detailed longitudinal data from the British Household Panel Survey (BHPS), a huge study of 10,000 British adults interviewed every year since 1991, Professor Ermisch has been able to follow the stories of hundreds of real babies and calculate how much time they have spent living with just one parent. He suggests there is powerful evidence that children growing-up without two parents have worse outcomes as young adults.

A baby born to married parents, on average, spends 1.6 years of their first 16 years with a lone parent. A child born to cohabiting parents spends 4.7 years with just one parents and an infant born into a single mother household spends 7.8 years. The experiences of the babies in the survey indicates that being brought up by a lone parent, particularly before they start school, results in lower qualifications in education, worse job prospects and poorer health.

The reason that having married parents makes such as difference is that only 35 per cent of children brought up by unmarried parents will live with both parents throughout their childhood compared to 70 per cent of those with married parents. As Professor Ermisch puts it: 'Having a child in a cohabiting union is often not indicative of a long-term partnership'. Moreover, if an unmarried mother breaks up with her partner, it can take a long time to find a new relationship. More than half are still without a partner five years after the break up. The conclusion, according to Professor Ermisch, is that 'non-marital childbearing in cohabiting unions tends to create lone mother families'.

So what the British Household Panel Survey appears to demonstrate is that in terms of outcomes for children, the traditional nuclear family is most likely to work best.

Source: Adapted from Easton (2008)

1 Summarise the trends on births outside marriage shown in Item A.
2 Why does Professor Ermisch's study quoted in Item B suggest that we should be concerned about the rise in the number of children being born outside marriage?
3 What criticisms could be made of this argument?

Changes in the age of marriage and childbearing

Age of marriage

In the section on marriage, we considered how fewer people are getting married, and how there has been an increase in the popularity of cohabitation and singlehood in Britain. Those who do marry are also getting married later. In 1970 in England and Wales, on average women married at the age of 22.0, and men at 24.1. According to the Office for National Statistics, in 2012 the average age at which men get married was 30.8 years, while women were typically aged 28.9 years when they tie the knot.

The age of marriage has increased for several reasons:
- more couples cohabiting before marriage
- changing social norms and attitudes meaning there is less social pressure to marry young
- extension of education, particularly for women
- the cost of weddings; according to a survey by *You and Your Wedding* magazine, the average cost of a wedding in 2013 was just under £22,000, so many couples are waiting until they have saved up enough to marry.

Age of childbearing

As the section on family size shows, an increasing proportion of women in each generation born since the 1920s have remained childless until the age of 30. The result of this is that the age at which women start bearing children has been increasing for decades. More recent data shows that fertility levels are rising fastest among older women. Since 2001, when the total fertility rate was at a record low, fertility levels have risen for women in all age groups with the exception of those aged under 20. The largest percentage increase in fertility rates was for women aged 40 and over, followed by women aged 35–39, with increases of 66 per cent and 53 per cent respectively. This continues the trend of rising fertility among women aged 35 and over recorded during the 1980s and 1990s. The number of live births to mothers aged 40 and over has more than quadrupled over the last three decades from 6,519 in 1982 to 29,994 in 2012 (ONS 2012c).

This changing pattern of fertility has been linked by some sociologists to the cultural changes associated with individualisation discussed earlier in this chapter (see page 61). This would suggest that women have more freedom of choice in late modernity and many are exercising this by choosing to remain childless or

at least to delay having children. However, a study by Máire Ní Bhrolcháin and Éva Beaujouan (2012) suggests a more straightforward explanation based on the rising levels of educational attainment among women. More and more women are staying on longer in education and are therefore not ready to start having children until later. This is especially so as the most educated women are also likely to be those who will seek to establish themselves in careers once they have completed their studies. This also explains why there is a noticeable class difference in age of childbearing, with professional middle-class women (who tend to spend longer in education) tending to start families much later than working-class women (who are less likely to postpone childbearing to build a career).

The ageing population

The UK, in common with other Western societies, has an ageing population. This means the average age of the population is increasing. From 1985 to 2010, the median age of the UK population (that is, the age at which half the population is younger and half the population is older) increased from 35.4 years to 39.7 years (ONS 2012e). It is predicted that it will reach 42.2 by 2035. An ageing population is also associated with an increase in the proportion of the population who are elderly and a decline in the proportion of young people (see Item B on page 70).

The ageing of the population can be seen most clearly when the age structure of the population is represented in population pyramids like those in Item A on page 70. In 1911, the age structure actually looked like a pyramid as there were generally fewer people in each age group rising up in age. This reflected the fact that there was a high birth rate so there were large numbers of infants at the base of the pyramid but death rates at all ages were high so people died off in every age group, meaning that relatively few people survived to old age. In the 2011 pyramid, there is much less tapering until the population is over 65, reflecting the fact that infant mortality and death rates among younger age groups are relatively low; people only start dying off in larger numbers once they reach pensionable age. The female side, of the graph also tapers off more slowly than the male side, reflecting the fact that women generally live longer than men so there are more elderly females in the population.

The 2011 pyramid also has rather ragged edges, which reflects fluctuations in the number of births; for example, there were fewer ten-year-olds than twenty-year-olds, reflecting the fact that the birth

Item A

Catherine Middleton was 29 when she married Prince William in 2011, just below the average age at marriage for women in England and Wales

Item B: Mean age at marriage for men and women, 1972–2012, England and Wales

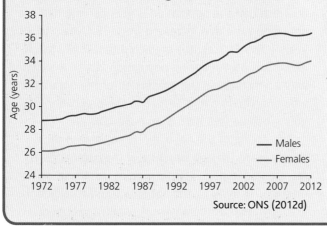

Source: ONS (2012d)

Item C: Age-specific fertility rates, 1982–2012, England and Wales

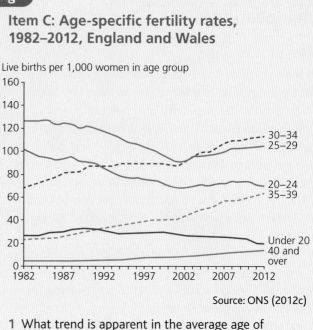

Source: ONS (2012c)

1 What trend is apparent in the average age of marriage of men and women in Item B?
2 How could this be explained?
3 In Item C, in which age groups is the fertility rate increasing fastest and in which age groups is it decreasing fastest?
4 What does this suggest about how patterns of childbearing are changing among women in England and Wales?

---

rate slumped around 2001, whereas it was relatively high in 1991. There are a particularly large number of people in the 40–50-year-old age group, the so-called 'baby boomers', who will enter the retired population in the next 20–30 years, causing a further ageing of the population.

Causes of an ageing population

The ageing population has come about for two main reasons:

1 Lower birth rates. This means that fewer people are being born in the younger generations than in previous generations, reducing the size of the youthful population.
2 Increased life expectancy. In 1951, life expectancy at birth in the UK was 66.1 years for men and 70.9 years for women; by 2010–12 it had increased

to 78.7 for men and 82.6 for women (ONS 2014c). As more people live into old age, the proportion of the population who are elderly is increasing. Mortality rates at older ages have improved due to a combination of factors such as improved medical treatments, housing and living standards, nutrition and changes in the population's smoking habits.

Problems of an ageing population

An increasing age dependency ratio

The age dependency ratio is the ratio of dependents – people younger than 15 or older than 64 – to the working-age population – those aged 15–64. The proportion of dependents per 100 of the working-age population has increased from 51 per cent to 54 per cent between 1994 and 2013.

Activity: The ageing population

Item A: Age structure of the UK population: 1911 and 2011

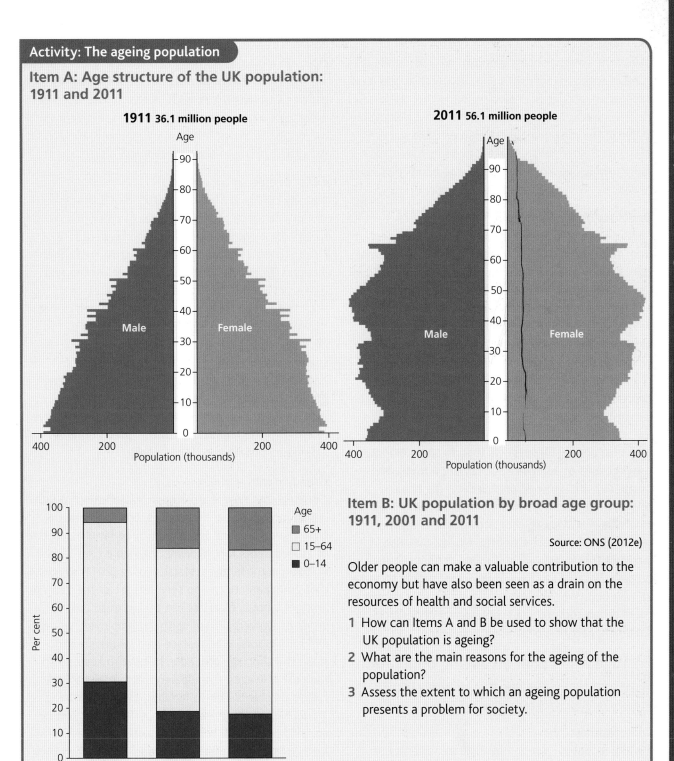

1911 36.1 million people

2011 56.1 million people

Item B: UK population by broad age group: 1911, 2001 and 2011

Source: ONS (2012e)

Older people can make a valuable contribution to the economy but have also been seen as a drain on the resources of health and social services.

1 How can Items A and B be used to show that the UK population is ageing?
2 What are the main reasons for the ageing of the population?
3 Assess the extent to which an ageing population presents a problem for society.

Source: ONS (2011)

Increased public spending

Not all elderly people are a financial drain on the working population but older people, especially the very old, are much more likely to require health services and social services than younger people, while taxes paid by the working population also pay for a variety of financial benefits for the elderly such as state pensions.

Loneliness and isolation for older people

In 2014 the government announced it would be commissioning research into the extent of loneliness among older people after research showed that loneliness could have long-term effects on their health. However, research for the GO programme by Christina Victor and her colleagues (2003) found that the percentage of older people reporting that they were lonely – 7 per cent – is relatively low. The majority of older people demonstrated high levels of contact with family, friends and neighbours and do not experience loneliness. They also found that the extent of loneliness among older people has been remarkably stable in the post-war period. However, the number of isolated older people is likely to be increasing as more people live alone and a growing number of older people are likely to be divorced or single.

Demands on family members

Older people who are cared for by family members may make considerable demands in terms of informal care. Grundy and Henrietta (2006) have identified the emergence of a 'sandwich' generation. These are older middle aged people, especially women, who have taken on the responsibility for caring for older relatives (usually parents or parents-in-law), while still having some responsibility for adult children who might be living at home and partially dependent on their parents. This could be argued to be feminist perspective.

Sarah Harper (2013) suggests that, to some extent, the problems of an ageing society are a myth. She points out that growing pressures on the health service are more to do with rising expectations of what the health service can provide for everyone rather than the demands of the elderly. She also suggests that a high age dependency ratio is only a problem because we force many older people to retire at an arbitrary age, when in fact many older people could go on contributing economically rather than becoming part of a dependent population.

Positive aspects of an ageing population

Some commentators argue that an ageing population offers a number of advantages and opportunities.

Older workers

Most older people remain healthy until towards the end of their lives and increasingly people are working beyond official retirement age. A report for the WRVS, *Gold Age Pensioners* (2011), found that in 2010, over-65s, through taxes, spending power, provision of social care and the value of their volunteering, made an astonishing net contribution of £40 billion to the UK economy.

The voluntary sector

Retired people have time to contribute unpaid work – for example, volunteering for charities or organising local community events. The WRVS study (2011) suggested that 'more than any other group in society, older people are the social glue of most communities'. Their research showed that every year, each older volunteer spends an average of over 100 hours 'informally' volunteering and more than 55 hours in formal volunteering roles. This is worth £10 billion to the UK economy.

Older people as consumers

A study by David Kingman (2012) found that in recent years, the spending power of older people has increased while that of younger generations has declined. He found that mean gross pensioner incomes grew by an estimated 50 per cent in real terms between 1994/5 and 2010/1. For example, spending on overseas travel and theatre and cinema tickets has increased among the over-50s and declined among the under-30s. Older people also spend more on eating out than younger people, and while car and petrol sales have fallen in all age groups, this seems to have affected 65–74-year-olds least. In view of this, some commentators have referred to the importance of the 'grey pound' in helping to sustain the UK economy.

Grandparents

Grandparents now make a huge contribution to family life. In most two-parent families, both parents are now in employment and one in three families depend of grandparents for childcare; the figure rises to half in lone-parent families. Marsha Jones (2011) suggests that grandparents can be seen as part of the 'reserve army of labour'. Marxists use this term to describe a group of workers (including the unemployed, women and immigrants) who replace paid workers when there is a shortage of labour, helping to keep down the cost of wages. Grandparents also make a large financial contribution to families, including helping grandchildren to get on the property ladder, setting up child trust funds for grandchildren and passing on their assets to children and grandchildren when they die. (The role of grandparents in discussed further on page 107.)

Beanpole families

According to Julia Brannen (2003), we are witnessing the emergence of 'beanpole families'. These are extended families of three, four or even five generations. However, unlike traditional extended families, members may not necessarily all live in the same households, but may live close together and see one another regularly. Such families are like beanpoles because they are tall and thin; low birth rates mean only one or two children may be born in each generation so children may have few brothers and sisters or cousins in their own generation. This means intragenerational ties (between family members in the same generation) are weak but individuals tend to have more intergenerational relationships, such as with grandparents and great-grandparents, who are more likely to be alive today because of longer life expectancy. According to Brannen, such relationships can offer valuable support to families going through divorce or to lone parents.

3.4 Family diversity

In the first section of this chapter we explored the range of different families and households that can be found in the UK today. The existence of different forms of families such as nuclear, lone-parent and reconstituted families is referred to as structural diversity as each of these family types has a different structure.

There are other forms of diversity related to cultural differences in ideas about how families should be organised.

Social class and family diversity

For many postmodernist sociologists, social class no longer shapes family life and personal relationships; instead, individuals now have much greater freedom of choice about how they organise their personal lives (see page 27). However, other sociologists argue that social class continues to influence a whole range of aspects of life, including families.

According to Rosemary Crompton (2005), the family still plays a part in ensuring the process of what Marxists refer to as class reproduction. This is the idea that most children will follow their parents into a similar class position in society; most working-class children will go into working-class positions and most middle-class children into middle-class positions. Families play a considerable part in equipping their children for their future roles in society, whether as business leaders, doctors, plumbers or factory workers. This is partly for economic reasons. Wealthier parents can pass on money, family businesses or other financial assets to their children, giving them an obvious advantage. They may also invest in their children's education, such as by paying for private education or assisting with paying for university fees. However, cultural differences are also important as middle-class parents often possess what Pierre Bourdieu (1973) calls 'cultural capital' – forms of

cultural knowledge that can help their children to do well in education and fit in better in the higher levels of society (see also page 26). This can be seen in the study by Val Gillies in the Study box on page 74.

Children from families living in poverty are particularly likely to be disadvantaged. This may simply be due to lack of resources – for example, insufficient income to ensure a decent standard of housing, diet and access to leisure activities. According to Ilan Katz and his colleagues (2007), the stress of living in poverty may make it more difficult for parents living in poverty to bring up their children effectively. However, they also point out that there is equally good evidence to show that most parents living in poverty are remarkably resilient and possess strong coping skills in the face of the adversity in their lives.

Activity: Social class and parenting

Item A

Growing up in poverty can disadvantage children in a number of ways

Item B

Pupils at Eton, one of the UK's top fee-paying schools. Eton old boys are disproportionately successful in gaining places at Oxford and Cambridge Universities and in finding top jobs

Differences in parenting – Gillies (2005)

Val Gillies carried out a survey of 1,112 parents together with more in-depth interviews of 25 mothers and 11 fathers. She found significant class differences in parenting, demonstrating that class is still significant in family life as well as other areas of British society. Some key findings were as follows:

- Middle-class parents used a range of resources to support their children, especially in developing social skills and success in education. Working-class parents, by contrast, tended to help their children develop strategies to cope with poverty, often developing the emotional strength in their children to deal with the injustice and hardship they faced in their lives.
- Middle-class parents emphasised their children's individuality and their right to be respected, often seeing their own children as outstanding and exceptional. On the other hand, working-class parents did not wish their children to be seen as special and were often more concerned that they should stay out of trouble.
- Middle-class parents felt confident in dealing with teachers, and could draw on a range of expensive specialists (for example, doctors and psychologists) to produce reports on their children when they caused concern. However, working-class parents were reluctant to have their children clinically diagnosed with a problem.

Source: Adapted from Gillies (2005)

Points to discuss and research

1 Using Items A and B from the Activity box on page 71 and any other information, suggest ways in which the social class of a child's family may affect their opportunities in the UK today.
2 What differences did Gillies discover between middle-class and working-class approaches to parenting?
3 Suggest possible reasons why social class might affect parenting in this way.
4 What effect might class differences in parenting have on children's opportunities later in life?

Ethnicity and family diversity

Like social class, ethnicity can be seen as another way in which family life is structured by individuals belonging to social groups. Again, this can be used to call into question the view that personal relationships have been individualised and are based on total freedom of choice. People's family life is not determined by their ethnicity and there is significant diversity within ethnic groups; however, there is also considerable evidence that the cultural values associated with different ethnic minorities in the UK influence the way people within them organise their families.

South Asian families

The term 'South Asian' is usually applied to people originating from India, Pakistan and Bangladesh. This comprises a diverse set of ethnic groups with most Indians being Hindu or Sikh and the overwhelming majority of Pakistanis and Bangladeshis identifying themselves as Muslims in the 2011 Census. Language differences are also important, with languages such as Urdu and Punjabi being spoken in many British Pakistani homes and Gujarati and Hindi in British Indian homes.

According to Roger Ballard (1982, 1990), when South Asian migrants first settled in the UK in large numbers from the 1950s onwards, they tended to bring the traditions of family life from their countries of origin. These included:

- a preference for large multi-generational households based around a man and his sons and grandsons together with wives and unmarried daughters (i.e., a form of extended family)
- traditional gender roles, with men being the main wage-earners and women focusing mainly on work in the domestic sphere
- a strong sense of obligation towards other family members, which should override the personal needs of individuals
- a sense of family honour (referred to as *izzat* in many South Asian communities), whereby the behaviour of individuals reflects on the family as a whole
- a preference for marriages to be arranged or at least approved by parents, as marriage involves not just a relationship between two individuals but between two families.

More recently there is evidence of change among South Asian families; for example, younger generations expect more choice in their marriage partners and most South Asian households are now based around nuclear rather than extended families. There is also evidence that levels of divorce and lone parenthood are starting to increase in Asian communities. Nevertheless, research by Richard Berthoud (2001) suggests that South Asians remain in many ways more traditional than white people, with couples being more likely to marry and to marry earlier and less likely to cohabit, divorce or live alone. According to Lucinda Platt (2009), family size also remains larger among South Asians; while only 16 per cent of white households contain four or more people, 43 per cent of Pakistani households and 49 per cent of Bangladeshi households are this size.

African-Caribbean families

Caribbean immigrants brought very different traditions of family life when they migrated to Britain from the 1950s onwards. In some of the Caribbean islands, such as Jamaica, the nuclear family is the norm but there is also a strong tradition of matrifocal or mother-centred families. These are often lone-parent families headed by women, but they also often entail mothers bringing up children with assistance from grandmothers and aunts. While cohabitation has become more acceptable in the British white population in recent decades, common-law families that involve couples cohabiting and bringing up children who may or may not be their own biological offspring have been a long-established pattern in many parts of the Caribbean.

These patterns are reflected in African-Caribbean families and households in the UK. For example, Richard Berthoud and Sharon Beishon (1997) found much lower rates of formal marriage among British African-Caribbeans and higher rates of divorce and separation. This means that lone-parent families are more common among African-Caribbeans than other ethnic groups. Also, while rates of employment are lower among Pakistani and Asian mothers than whites,

they are higher among African-Caribbean mothers, reflecting a tradition of female independence in the black community.

While lone parenthood is common among British African-Caribbean families, this can be misleading. Mary Chamberlain (1999) found that extended family members, especially brothers and sisters, often provide support to lone parents. Tracey Reynolds (2002) noted the existence of visiting relationships where lone mothers would have a male partner who visited them frequently, sometimes playing an active role as a parent.

Patterns of ethnicity

While there are noticeable differences between ethnic groups, there is also diversity within them. We have focused on the two largest groups of ethnic minorities, but there are many other ethnic groups in the UK, particularly White European groups such as Poles, Lithuanians, Slovaks and Portuguese who have migrated in the last twenty years; there is little sociological research on family patterns in these groups.

Richard Berthoud (2001) suggests that families in the UK can be placed on a scale ranging from old-fashioned values (exemplified by the traditional nuclear family) to modern individualism (represented by acceptance of diverse forms of families and households such as lone-parent and reconstituted families). Berthoud argues that when considering the main ethnic groups in the UK African-Caribbean communities are furthest along the road to individualism, even more so than whites, while South Asian communities – especially Pakistanis and Bangladeshis – tend to maintain more traditional family values.

Robin Mann (2009), however, criticises this argument, arguing that aspects of British African-Caribbean family life such as lone parenthood, cohabitation and childbearing outside marriage actually reflect patterns that are traditional in many parts of the Caribbean. This tends to question the idea that African-Caribbean families represent a form of modern individualism.

Activity: Ethnicity and family life

Item A: A traditional Indian wedding

British Asians appear to favour traditional marriage and having children more than most other ethnic groups in the UK

Item C: Changing attitudes to the elderly among British Asians

In 2009 Manjula Shah moved into Aashna House, a residential care home for elderly Asians, in South London. At Aashan House there are 34 residents supported by a team of 30 people also of Asian origin. When Manjula was widowed in 1995 she felt extremely lonely, especially when her daughters subsequently married, so she was pleased when her daughter said she had found a place where she would not be alone.

Aashna House is unusual as it offers care tailored to the needs of people from Indian backgrounds. All those who work with the residents are fluent in Gujarati and Hindi and the food is prepared according to religious requirements; even the television is tuned to Asian channels.

Item B: Family types and size by ethnicity

Ethnic group	Family type, row percentages				Family size	
	Single person	Couple, no dependent children	Couple, dependent children	Lone parent, dependent children	Average family size	% families 4+ people
White British	36	35	20	9	2.2	16
Other white	45	30	18	7	2.0	13
Mixed white and Caribbean	42	8	21	29	2.2	17
Mixed white and African	44	12	23	21	2.2	21
Mixed white and Asian	43	21	22	14	2.2	19
Other mixed	48	18	19	15	2.0	12
Indian	30	30	33	7	2.6	28
Pakistani	24	19	45	11	3.2	43
Bangladeshi	20	14	52	14	3.6	49
Other Asian	40	21	32	7	2.3	23
Black Caribbean	41	14	16	28	2.1	16
Black African	44	9	25	22	2.4	24
Other Black	43	13	23	21	2.3	21
Chinese	56	21	17	6	1.9	13
Other	43	18	28	11	2.3	22
All groups	37	33	20	10	2.2	17

Source: Platt (2009)

Activity: Ethnicity and family life (Continued)

The tradition of elderly relatives being cared for by their families is something in which Asians have taken great pride, unlike the supposedly heartless western custom of throwing parents into a home. To the generation of South Asians who migrated to the UK after the war, care homes were nothing less than a moral obscenity. From their viewpoint, Aashna House should not exist. However, times are changing. Some British Asian children are reluctantly admitting that they can no longer care for their parents at home.

Most residents of Aashna House originate from the western Indian state of Gujarat. Unlike the Indian community, British Pakistanis are far more traditional. To send their parents into places such as Aashna House would still be largely unthinkable for most Pakistanis.

Source: Adapted from Manzoor (2011)

1 With reference to Item A and any other data, discuss possible reasons why British Asians may follow more traditional patterns of marriage and family life.
2 Using the data in Item B identify which ethnic groups are most likely and least likely to:
   a) live alone
   b) live in a couple with no dependent children
   c) live in a two-parent family with dependent children
   d) live in a lone-parent family with dependent children
   e) live in large families.
3 How could these patterns be explained?
4 How does Item C suggest that attitudes to family life may be changing in some minority ethnic groups in the UK?

Sexuality and family diversity

In the section on same-sex families (see page 51), we noted how greater acceptance of same-sex relationships has led to the emergence of new types of families and intimate relationships. Writers such as Giddens (1992) see this as part of a transformation of intimacy whereby individuals have much greater freedom to choose what kinds of intimate relationships they engage in.

Jeffrey Weeks, Catherine Donovan and Brian Heaphy (1999) observe that many gay and lesbian people describe their households and even friendship networks as chosen families because, rather than following traditional heterosexual norms, they are able to choose who to include in their families and negotiate much more egalitarian relationships.

The feminist sociologist Cheshire Calhoun (1997) argues that gay men and lesbians have traditionally been treated as family outlaws who threaten family life; however, she argues that as modern life has come to be characterised by greater choice, so gay and lesbian lifestyles have become more accepted. In fact, she goes further and suggests that lesbian marriage and mothering avoids the exploitative relationships typical of heterosexual marriage. In developing new forms of chosen and egalitarian domestic relationships, lesbian families may be pointing the way for other types of families in the future.

The importance of same-sex relationships should not, however, be exaggerated. In 2012 there were 2,893,000 opposite-sex couples in the UK and 69,000 same-sex couples (ONS 2012a), so though gay and lesbian partnerships contribute to family diversity, they remain a relatively small minority. Furthermore, while there is greater social acceptance of same-sex relationships, the British Social Attitudes Survey 2012 (see Activity on page 76) found that 28 per cent of respondents still thought that sexual relations between two adults of the same sex were 'always wrong' or 'mostly wrong' (Park et al. 2013).

Item A: Demonstration in favour of gay marriage

Lesbian, gay, bisexual and transgender people have had to fight hard to be treated as equal in British society. However, same-sex marriages became legal in the UK in 2013

Item B: Views on homosexuality, 1983–2012

The data below is from selected years of the British Social Attitudes Survey, a large-scale statistical survey based on a representative sample of 1,000 or more British people.

Sexual relations between two adults of the same sex	1983	1987	1990	1995	1999	2003	2007	2012
Always wrong	50	64	58	44	38	31	26	22
Mostly wrong	12	11	11	11	11	9	10	6
Some-times wrong	8	8	8	10	9	9	7	7
Rarely wrong	4	2	4	7	7	7	10	10
Not wrong at all	17	11	15	22	27	37	39	47

Source: Adapted from Park *et al.* (2013)

1 What changes in attitudes towards same-sex relationships are suggested by Items A and B?
2 How might such changes be leading to greater family and household diversity in the UK?
3 Why does Item B suggest that lesbians and gay men may still face hostility in some sections of society?

3.5 The nuclear family in contemporary society

In the 1940s and 1950s, the dominant perspective on sociology was functionalism (see page 37). Functionalists argued that there was a fit between the needs of industrial societies like the US and the UK and the institution of the nuclear family. For example, the American sociologist William Goode (1963) argued that as societies went through a process of industrialisation, they tended to adopt the nuclear family pattern.

While functionalists portrayed the nuclear family in favourable terms, much more critical approaches based on Marxism and feminism began to influence the way sociologists looked at the nuclear family from the 1970s onwards. Since the 1990s, many sociologists have criticised all these approaches for focusing too much on the nuclear family, pointing out that there is increasing family diversity. Theorists of late modernity and postmodernity argue that such approaches fail to take account of the extent to which family life and personal relationships have moved beyond the nuclear family in the late twentieth and early twenty-first century.

Functionalism

Functionalist theories analyse the family in two ways. Firstly, they are interested in family structures, which means the way individuals are linked to one another in particular roles and relationships. For many functionalists, the nuclear family is the basic building block of society, based on the key relationships between husband and wife, and parents and children. Nuclear families may of course be part of larger structures in many societies, such as different types of extended families. Functionalists also examine families in terms of their functions, by which they mean the ways in that families provide things that are needed by their members as well as serving the needs of society as a whole.

Murdock: The universal functions of the family

The social anthropologist George Murdock (1949) carried out a survey of 250 societies (see Item A, page 48) from which he concluded that some kind of family was found in every human society. Murdock argued that this was based on two opposite-sex parents and their own or adopted children – in other words, a nuclear family. However, he acknowledged that in many societies family units included other kin, such as vertically extended families, including grandparents, and horizontally extended families, where brothers (or less frequently sisters) formed households with their partners and children.

Murdock suggested the universal nature of the nuclear family (or units based on it) was for good reasons. He argued that the family performs four essential functions in all societies and the nuclear family is best equipped to carry these out.

Study

The specialisation of family functions – Parsons (1951; Parsons and Bales 1955)

While Murdock suggests that his arguments about the nuclear family are applicable to all human societies, the American functionalist Talcott Parsons focused on the structure and functions of the family in modern industrial societies such as the US.

Parsons argues that in pre-industrial societies, the family carries out a whole variety of functions. For example, in many tribal societies, nuclear families are part of a larger kinship system and extended family members cooperate to carry out a wide range of tasks, such as hunting or farming, educating children, defence against enemies, carrying out religious rituals and looking after members who are sick or elderly.

As societies industrialise, they become more complex and there is a process of structural differentiation whereby specialised institutions develop to perform functions formerly carried out by families. For example, business organisations produce food and other products people need, the welfare state and social services look after those in need and schools take over the education of children. Because the family has fewer functions to perform, it no longer requires a large extended family structure and the nuclear family alone can perform the remaining essential family functions. In Parsons' terms, the nuclear family has become structurally isolated from the wider kinship network in industrial societies. This does not mean that individuals no longer have any contact with extended family members, but that such relationships are no longer an essential part of social life and have become an optional extra.

Parsons argues that in industrial societies the nuclear family only has two essential functions to perform. These are:

1 **Socialisation of children.** It remains essential that children receive their primary socialisation from their parents. Parsons likens the family to a personality factory, where children are moulded by their parents so they learn to adapt to the norms and values of the society they are growing up in. Parsons argues that children need to internalise their society's culture so that the norms and values agreed in their society come to seem natural and they learn to integrate or fit into society. While the family is important in primary socialisation, Parsons sees it as having a reduced role in secondary socialisation where other agencies of socialisation such as schools and peer groups have a greater responsibility.

2 **Stabilisation of adult personalities.** Parsons argues that without the support of wider kin, married couples in industrial societies increasingly rely on one another for emotional support; without this, the stresses of daily life could lead to emotional instability. Parents also benefit from their relationships with their children, such as being able to act out childish aspects of their personalities when playing with their children. The nuclear family therefore provides a safe haven for adults and children from the pressures of the wider society. For Parsons, there seems little prospect that any other social unit could perform this function as effectively.

Apart from still being important in carrying out these two essential functions, Parsons also argues that nuclear families are an ideal fit with the needs of industrial societies for other reasons:

- In a nuclear family, there is one adult of each sex. This allows husbands and wives to perform equal and complementary roles. The father performs the instrumental role of the wage-earner who provides for the family's physical needs, while the mother performs the expressive role of the carer and nurturer who provides for the family's emotional and psychological needs.

- In industrial societies, workers need to be geographically mobile or able to move to wherever jobs are available. Nuclear families are not tied down by obligations to or dependency on extended family and can more easily move from place to place.

- In pre-industrial societies, an individual's status in society is ascribed; in other words, your position or rank is determined by birth often deriving from the status of your family in the community. In industrial societies, status is increasingly achieved, individuals earn their positions through proving their abilities and extended families are no longer important in providing individuals with status.

Sexual function

Most societies encourage people to channel their sex drives into socially acceptable relationships such as marriage. This helps society by minimising conflict but provides individuals with opportunities for satisfying long-term relationships.

Economic function

In many societies, the family acts as a unit of production; the whole family may work together to provide themselves with food and other requirements. In Western societies such as Britain, most families act as units of consumption, buying goods and services for their members. Individuals benefit by having their needs looked after and society benefits from the economic contribution made by families.

Reproduction

The family is the main unit within which children are reproduced; without this, society would cease to exist.

Education

Murdock sees the educational function of the family as going beyond formal schooling; rather, the family is the main agency of primary socialisation (see page 12). Individuals benefit by growing up to be well-balanced individuals who can fit into society, which helps to ensure a society where there is consensus about social norms, creating a stable social system.

Popenoe: A neo-functionalist view of the family

While few sociologists today would describe themselves as functionalists, American sociologist David Popenoe's (1996) approach has been described as neo-functionalist. Popenoe, like Murdock, argues that there are biological imperatives (or necessities) that underlie the way families are organised. For example, he suggests that men and women are biologically different so that women are better suited to nurturing children, especially in their early years. Popenoe argues that we need a new cultural script, a set of guidelines for what families should be like, based on what he calls 'biosocial reality'. Like other functionalists, he therefore implies that some types of family are less functional than others, as they are not based on the biological abilities and needs of human beings. Thus, children brought up in some kinds of alternative families are more likely to be damaged by their early childhood experiences.

Evaluation of the functionalist view

Functionalism is what sociologists would call a 'grand theory'; it makes broad generalisations about the family in all societies. As such, it has helped to identify broad trends in how families and kinship systems develop as societies industrialise. Functionalists try to answer important questions about why most human beings tend to live in families and how families help to ensure the smooth running of society.

However, functionalist views of the family have received extensive criticism from a range of other sociological perspectives.

Functionalism presents a largely positive and optimistic view of the nuclear family. Critics argue that this ignores the dark side or negative aspects of families, such as child abuse, domestic violence and conflict between family members.

Focusing on the functions of the family ignores the fact that many families are dysfunctional. For example, psychologist Oliver James, in *They F*** You Up: How to Survive Family Life* (2003), argues that many of the problems we face in adult life can be traced back to early childhood. For example, if we are over-competitive, lacking in confidence or constantly jealous of other people, these problems can be traced back to the way we were socialised by our parents in our early years.

In focusing on the nuclear family, functionalists ignore the diversity of families in modern society. Even in the 1950s, lone-parent families and reconstituted families existed and the growth in the number of other forms of family such as cohabiting families, same-sex families and families of choice means that functionalism is seen as very out-of-date by many sociologists today. Parsons seems to assume that only the nuclear family can carry out the essential functions of the family effectively, while critics argue that individuals are increasingly inventing a whole variety of other relationships and living arrangements that can effectively socialise children and provide adults with emotional intimacy.

For feminists, Parsons' view of the family is sexist. He assumes that men and women will naturally perform separate roles and that these roles have equal status. Feminists argue that in reality, traditional nuclear families are based on male power and dominance; for example, the responsibilities for emotional support entailed in the stabilisation of adult personalities largely fall on women but receive little recognition or social status while women themselves receive little emotional support from their male partners. Parsons largely dismisses the idea of women playing a significant instrumental role, arguing that in the US in the 1950s, most women were only in part-time jobs or were full-time housewives, whereas today, women make up 47 per cent of the UK workforce and make a significant economic contribution to most families.

For interactionist sociologists, Parsons' view of socialisation can be seen as a top-down process whereby parents instil the norms and values of society into children who are waiting to be 'filled' with culture. In reality, socialisation can be seen as a two-way process where children socialise their parents as much as they are socialised by them.

Parsons seems to see the nuclear family as an ideal institution that modern industrial societies require. For theorists of late modernity and postmodernity, this ignores the degree of choice available in contemporary societies about family structures and relationships. Rather than one dominant family form – the nuclear family – we are seeing increasingly diverse and fluid families and households which provide for the diverse needs of different individuals.

The New Right

Few sociologists today would describe themselves as functionalists; however, support for the functionalist argument that the nuclear family is essential to a healthy society comes from a group of writers usually referred to as the New Right. Most New Right thinkers are politicians, journalists, religious leaders and political scientists rather than sociologists; however, their views stirred up considerable controversy among sociologists from the 1980s onwards. New Right thinkers see traditional marriage and family life as breaking down and argue that a consequence of this has been poorly socialised children who tend to underachieve at school, a rise in crime and an increasing number of lone mothers who depend on the welfare state rather than being supported by the fathers of their children.

The New Right call for a return to what they refer to as traditional family values, including couples waiting to marry before they have children, fathers taking responsibility for economically supporting their wives and children through paid employment, and women focusing on their traditional role of raising children rather than their careers.

Activity

The kibbutz – an alternative to the nuclear family?

The kibbutz (plural kibbutzim) is a form of communal living pioneered by early Jewish settlers in Israel from the 1900s onwards. Kibbutz members wanted to create a community based on equality, where individuals put the needs of the community above their own personal needs. Everyone, both male and female, shared in the work; there was no private property and members simply received what they needed from the kibbutz, including a place to live, food and clothing.

Up until the 1970s, most kibbutzim adopted a form of collective childrearing where children lived in a separate children's house and were looked after by specially trained caregivers or 'metaplets'. Children were separated from their mothers soon after birth and while they had a relationship with their parents, they would typically only see them for a couple of hours a day and would not sleep or eat with their parents. Supporters of the kibbutz lifestyle argue that this allowed women freedom to participate in the community on equal terms with men as they were freed from childcare responsibilities. Children also learned to be independent of their parents and to fit in to the communal lifestyle required by the kibbutz, by growing up in a group of other children of their own age.

Studies of the psychological effects of kibbutz life have tended to conclude that people who have grown up in kibbutzim usually grow up into well-balanced adults. However, some have concluded that a kibbutz upbringing leads to individuals having greater difficulty in making strong emotional commitments thereafter, such as falling in love or forming a lasting friendship. On the other hand, they appear to find it easier to have a large number of less involved friendships, and a more active social life.

From the 1970s onwards, some kibbutzim gradually abandoned aspects of collective childrearing, and most kibbutzim children now sleep in their parents' apartment until they are high-school age, though they still spend most of their day in the company of other children. In this sense, the nuclear family has re-emerged within many kibbutzim.

Source: Adapted from Spiro (1966), Bettelheim (1969) and **http://www.jewishvirtuallibrary.org**

1 In what ways did the original kibbutzim try to abolish the nuclear family?
2 What are the advantages and disadvantages of the form of communal childrearing adopted by traditional kibbutzim?
3 To what extent does the case study of the kibbutzim disprove the functionalist view that some kind of family based on the nuclear family is essential for the smooth running of society?

More recently, some supporters of the New Right have attacked the government's decision to legalise same-sex marriage, arguing that children need a parent of each sex and that allowing gay marriage undermines the traditional basis of marriage as a union between a man and a woman.

Studies

The underclass and the disintegration of family life – Murray (1990, 1994, 2001)

American political scientist Charles Murray is one of the leading New Right thinkers. He argues that in both Britain and the US, an underclass has emerged made up of the poorest people at the bottom of society who are dependent on welfare benefits rather than work. Murray argues that lone-parent families, mostly headed by women, form a significant section of this underclass and that children, especially boys, growing up without a father figure are likely to fare worse at school and are more likely to turn to crime.

Murray lays the blame for this situation squarely on successive governments, which he argues have rewarded irresponsible behaviour in the form of having children outside marriage by giving over-generous welfare benefits to lone mothers, creating what he calls welfare dependency. He also argues that politicians and other leading figures in society have not done enough to support the institution of marriage, and as a result cohabitation, having children outside marriage and divorce have all become far too socially acceptable. Murray has even gone so far as to suggest that children born outside marriage would be better off being adopted than being brought up by lone mothers.

Families without Fatherhood – Dennis and Erdos (2000)

Few sociologists have given much support to New Right views of the family (see *Evaluation of the New Right view*, right). However, some support for their approach was offered by sociologists Norman Dennis and George Erdos. While describing themselves as 'ethical socialists' and rejecting the label of New Right, they argued that children raised by single mothers on average have lower educational attainment and poorer health than children from two-parent families. Boys in particular grow up without learning that adulthood involves taking responsibility for a wife and children, and so develop into immature, irresponsible and anti-social young men.

Evaluation of the New Right view

New Right arguments reflect the concerns of more conservative groups in British society about changes in family life. Few sociologists would dispute the evidence that fewer people are living in nuclear families, divorce levels are much higher than they were up to the 1970s, and more people are living together and having children outside marriage. Where the New Right have caused controversy is in portraying these trends as representing the undermining of family life and the source of social problems.

Opponents of the New Right would put forward the following criticisms:

- New Right thinkers have been accused of looking back to a 'golden age' of family life from the mid-nineteenth century to the mid-twentieth century, where marriage was respected and where the nuclear family was overwhelmingly the norm. In reality, lone-parent families, cohabitation and sexual relationships outside marriage have always existed but were often concealed in the past. Moreover, people who did not fit into conventional families, such as lone mothers and gay people, often received harsh treatment which most people would find unacceptable today.

- The New Right make value judgements about different types of families, making no secret of the fact that they view nuclear families based on marriage as superior to other types of families. Critics have argued that individuals should be free to choose what kind of family works best for them; for some people, the traditional nuclear family does not suit their needs. Jon Bernardes (1997) reflects this view when he argues that governments need to recognise the diversity of families and government policy should support all families equally.

- The New Right place much of the blame for the alleged 'decline of family life' on government policies, which in their view have given insufficient support to married two-parent families. However, they also tend to portray lone parents and poor families in a very negative light. For example, Charles Murray describes the underclass as the 'new rabble'. Critics argue that this is a 'victim-blaming' approach where people are blamed for their own poverty, which is arguably created by an unfair and unequal society. For example, lone parents may find themselves in poverty because of low wages, inadequate state benefits and lack of jobs rather than a wish to live off the state.

- Deborah Chambers (2001) argues that many of the fears about lone-parent families and the decline of marriage and family life are a moral panic (see page 141), an over-reaction to supposed social problems. This moral panic was whipped up by sections of the media and right-wing politicians in the 1990s in a bid to justify cuts in government spending on benefits and to blame groups such as lone parents for a variety of problems. Similar stories have started to emerge again in some parts of the tabloid press more recently.

Activity: Returning to traditional family values

Item A: The Coalition government and traditional family values

In order to slow the process of social breakdown the Conservative government is set to prioritise the ideals of marriage and families. In announcing an increase in government expenditure to assist households that are troubled, Ian Duncan Smith, the Work and Pensions Secretary argued that, previously, government policies had used a neutral stance to hide neglect of the family, and thereby shrugged off responsibility.

In a recent report entitled *Social Justice: Transforming Lives* the government states its aim of eliminating the 'couple penalty' currently existing in the welfare system (this being the fact that married couples get less in benefits than do lone parents). Another goal is to offer support to relationships in an attempt to 'keep families together'. What comes out of the report is the finding that childen are likely to have better lives when supported and protected by the same two parents, with statistics showing that 28% of children from single parent families live in worse relative poverty than 17% in couple families. In the report the government states its belief that putting funds into supporting vulnerable families is the best way to begin dealing with poverty and disadvantage. Future goals will be to assist, look after and promote families in all their varied size and shape and to highlight how important the family is to community life and society as a whole.

By aiming to help reduce the rate of divorce and separation, the government will seek to ensure that families (particularly those with children) continue to stay together. This objective makes clear the government's desire to use its policies to promote and maintain the idea of the traditional household. Duncan Smith observes that there are severe consequences when families fall apart and that the government needs to back up stable families and not just ignore them when they do break down. The government needs to proactive in showing that stable families matters to it. The key message, he believes, is to underline the Government's support for marriage and to make it clear that it is adopting a strategy of actively encouraging and supporting marriage.

Source: adapted from Manzoor (2011)

Item B: The nuclear family, 1950s-style

Item C: Young men looting a shop during the 2011 London riots

1 In what ways do the arguments of government minister Iain Duncan Smith in Item A reflect the ideas of the New Right about family life?

2 Why might it be argued that the type of family illustrated in Item B provides the best environment for bringing up children?

3 Why might New Right thinkers blame the behaviour of the young men in Item C on recent changes in family life?

4 In a group, discuss arguments for and against the New Right's views on family life. Issues to consider might include:
  ● to what extent recent changes in family life confirm the New Right view that traditional family life is declining;
  ● whether these changes are a problem for society or whether they should be celebrated as offering freedom and choice;
  ● whether the government should be trying to influence how people live their family lives, and if so, in what way.

5 Summarise the arguments you have considered and your conclusions as a series of bullet points.

Marxism

Functionalist theories analyse the family in terms of a consensus view of society (see page 37). They assume that society is based on shared values, such as what kind of families are regarded as normal. The family is also essential as an agent of socialisation as this ensures that each new generation accepts the shared values of the society they are joining. New Right theories also assume that society works best when based on consensus; however, they argue that this consensus is breaking down as more individuals diverge from agreed norms of family life, creating a range of problems for society.

Marxists reject this consensus view, arguing that capitalist societies like the UK are based on conflict due to class divisions (see page 41). Marxists therefore dispute the idea that the way families are organised benefits everyone equally; rather, they argue that the family, like many other institutions in capitalist societies, serves to maintain the power of those with wealth and preserve the existing economic system.

Evaluation of the Marxist view

Marxism has helped sociologists to explore how the kind of economic system we live in – capitalism – shapes our families and personal lives. Many people's lives are dominated by the need to earn a living, sometimes working long hours allowing little time for family life. We are also increasingly a consumer society, and family life tends to revolve around consuming the products of capitalism, whether it be the food we buy from supermarkets, electrical goods to help with housework or entertain us, or leisure pursuits such as holidays or days out. In this sense, we do not freely choose how to live our family lives but are encouraged to follow certain patterns of family life. The nuclear family is in many ways ideally suited to capitalism, so for Marxists it is no surprise that it gains considerable support from other institutions of capitalism – for example, the mass media with positive images of happy smiling nuclear families in advertisements and politicians who speak of the need to return to traditional family values.

Critics of Marxism, however, would offer the following arguments:

- Marxism tends to suggest that individuals' personal lives are largely shaped or even determined by economic forces such as the needs of capitalism. Social action theorists (see page 43) argue that this ignores the extent to which we have the capacity to make choices about our own lives; for example, some individuals increasingly choose to reject the traditional nuclear family model in favour of a diverse range of alternatives.
- Marxism can also be seen as outdated as functionalism since, like functionalism, it tends to focus on the nuclear family rather than its alternatives. Though Marxists are far more critical of the nature of family life than functionalists, they have little to say about the diverse range of families and intimate relationships in contemporary society.
- Marxism highlights the extent of class inequalities in family life but fails to fully consider the importance of other kinds of social divisions such as gender, ethnicity and sexuality and their importance in personal relationships.
- Marxism mainly focuses on family life in Western capitalist societies, and has little to say about the nature of families in other parts of the world.

Feminism

Feminists, like Marxists, offer a conflict perspective on society; however, they focus on gender divisions and conflicts, arguing that society is patriarchal and this is reflected in patterns of family life. Like Marxism, feminism is also the basis for social and political movements that seek to change society, such as the women's liberation movement in the 1970s which sought to challenge patriarchal aspects of society including the subordinate (or inferior) role played by women in traditional families. There are a variety of strands of feminism which offer differing analyses of family life.

Delphy and Leonard: Radical feminism

Radical feminists argue that traditional forms of the family, especially the nuclear family favoured by functionalists and the New Right, represent a form of patriarchal control, whereby women's opportunities are limited by the restrictive roles they are expected play in the domestic sphere as wives and mothers. For radical feminists, it is men, rather than the capitalist system, who are the main beneficiaries of women's performing unpaid domestic labour such as housework and childcare.

Christine Delphy and Diana Leonard (1992), for example, point to the way in which men are still usually regarded as the heads of households, often making key decisions. Men also tend to control the finances and property in most families. Women, on the other hand, are expected to perform unpaid domestic work and also undertake reproductive and sexual work (having babies and servicing men's sexual needs). Though women contribute far more to families both in practical tasks and looking after others' emotional needs, Delphy and Leonard argue they receive less in return as men often control the finances, have more leisure time and even have more access to the family car or the best car if there is more than one.

The Origins of the Family, Private Property and the State – Engels (1972, orig. 1844)

Karl Marx, the founder of Marxism, had little to say about families, but his friend and collaborator Frederick Engels was one of the first writers to apply Marxist ideas to studying the family in 1884. Engels argued that the family had developed in an evolutionary way. In the earliest societies, he suggested, there had been no restrictions on sexual behaviour. As societies became more complex, more restrictions were placed on sexuality, first in the form of polygyny (one man with several female partners), until societies reached their most advanced stage with the development of monogamy (marriage between one husband and one wife). Engels linked the evolution of monogamy with the development of the idea of private property. Historically, property in most societies was held by males and passed down to their male heirs, usually their sons. Monogamy ensured that any children born were the legitimate heirs of the father and avoided the complications associated with polygyny about which wife's children should inherit.

Engels argued that in the earliest societies women held power, but as humans learned to herd animals, men took control of the livestock and thus became the first property owners. Engels argued that the result of this was to make women mere chattels (or possessions) of their husbands, another form of private property. With the rise of monogamy, women's role, especially in wealthy bourgeois (or middle-class) families, was simply to provide their husbands with heirs and raise those children to adulthood.

Engels did not wish to see the family abolished, but he argued that in a communist society, the functions of the family such as caring for children and providing people with food would be socialised – in other words, provided by the community as a whole rather than by individual families. The Israeli kibbutz is perhaps a modern example of this idea (see page 81).

Engels' ideas of the evolution of families have been criticised for being based on very weak evidence; for example, many simple hunting-and-gathering societies that attach little importance to private property still practise monogamous relationships. However, Engels was one of the first writers to elaborate the Marxist view that families are shaped by the economic system. He also provided a starting point for feminist theories that point to the way in which women are oppressed by traditional family structures.

Capitalism, the Family and Personal Life – Zaretsky (1976)

Eli Zaretsky offers one of the best-developed modern approaches to the family based on a Marxist perspective.

Zaretsky argues that with the rise of capitalist industrial production in the nineteenth century, work and family life became separated. Under capitalism, work became an alienating experience, meaning that workers had little control over work and were unable to achieve real satisfaction from it. Family life came to be seen as important as a refuge from the pressure of work and somewhere workers could have control over their lives. However, Zaretsky argues that this is only an illusion, as the family is unable to overcome the alienating and brutalising effects of capitalism. Individuals can only achieve really satisfying family relationships when capitalism is abolished so that families are organised around the needs of their members rather than the needs of the economic system.

Zaretsky argues that the family supports the capitalist system in two ways. Firstly, women in the family reproduce and bring up children. Capitalist employers benefit from this unpaid domestic labour as the next generation of workers are reared at no expense to them. Secondly, the family acts as a unit of consumption, buying the products of capitalism and allowing capitalists to continue to make profits from their businesses.

The Death of the Family – Cooper (1972)

David Cooper is not strictly a Marxist, but some of his ideas are influenced by Marxism. His work focuses on the internal relationships of families and how these affect the psychology of family members. For example, Cooper argues that family relationships reflect the property relationships of capitalism in that individuals develop a sense that they own their partners and children, which in his view restricts the ability of people to develop as individuals.

Cooper, like many Marxists, also sees the family as an ideological conditioning device. By this, he means that we live in a hierarchical and unequal society where those higher up control those below them. The family is a miniature version of this and is the first situation where children learn to submit to the capitalist ideology which teaches those at the bottom that they must accept their position and be obedient to those above them – in the family to parents, and as adults to employers.

While for functionalists the process of socialisation is a beneficial process, allowing children to fit into the existing society, for Cooper and many Marxists, children are simply socialised to accept their place in society. This is also reflected in Rosemary Crompton's arguments about how families ensure a process of class reproduction whereby most children end up in a similar class position to their parents (see page 73).

Activity: Capitalism and family life

Item A: The 'commercialisation of intimate life'

American sociologist Arlie Hochschild argues that there has been a 'commercialisation of intimate life'. By this, she means that many services that were provided by families for their members have been taken over by commercial organisations, meaning that these services are provided for money rather than out of love. Hochschild argues that we pay others to care for our children, to clean our homes, to salve our consciences, to ease our fears, to organise our social lives. In short, as the title of her recent collection of essays has it, we have commercialised our intimate lives. Hochschild argues that as women have increasingly moved into the world of paid work, they have been forced to hire other people to do the jobs that they formerly performed unpaid. While this has liberated women, it has also meant that something has been lost in family life.

Hochschild provides some examples:

'There's a new service available that provides a "friendly" visitor to your elderly mother. Someone who'll be like a good daughter to your mother. Well, if you don't get to live in the same town with your mother, and especially if she's a difficult person, this would be a very attractive service. But just to give another example, there are now people who will come into your house and arrange your family photograph album for you – "Oh, there's uncle Fred on the left," you tell them. There are people called "life coaches" who will meet you once a week for $150 at a coffee shop, or have a telephone date with you, and help you achieve your goals.'

In one of Hochschild's essays, 'The Nanny Chain', she looks at the concept of care chains, using the example of Filipino women coming to the US to act as nannies, and leaving their own children behind. She writes that 'the ultimate beneficiaries of these various care changes might actually be large multinational companies ... The care in the chain may begin with that which a rural third-world mother gives (as a nanny) the urban child she cares for, and it may end with the care a working mother gives her employees as vice president of publicity at your company.'

Hochschild is concerned, like many critics, about global capitalism's turning everything in human life into a commodity, something that can be bought or sold. The problem, as she sees it, is that 'Capitalism ... competes with the family'. What she calls the 'time bind' is at the heart of the problem. 'Americans are putting in longer hours than workers of any other industrialized nation,' she says. 'That means less time for raising children, less time for homemaking.'

Source: Adapted from Sutherland (2005) and Hochschild (2003)

Item B: Examples of the 'commercialisation of intimate life'

A Filipino nanny looking after a child (left) and a life coach, someone who provides advice and guidance in how to deal with problems and reach your goals in life (right): examples of the commercialisation of intimate life?

1 Explain what Hochschild means by the 'commercialisation of intimate life', using examples from Items A and B and elsewhere.

2 How could Hochschild's arguments be used to support the Marxist view that family life is shaped by the needs of capitalism?

3 Hochschild's evidence is largely based on family life in the US. To what extent are her arguments applicable to the UK?

Benston: Marxist feminism

While Marxists tend to ignore gender inequality, radical feminists have been accused of ignoring the links between capitalism and gender inequalities. Marxist feminists attempt to combine these two approaches. Margaret Benston (1972), for example, analyses the way in which the unpaid domestic work of women helps to support the capitalist system. She argues that women help to reproduce labour power for capitalism in two ways:

1 On a daily basis, women renew men's ability to go out to work and create profits for the capitalist class by cooking meals, washing clothes and attending to their emotional and sexual needs.
2 On a generational basis, they socialise and care for children, reproducing the next generation of workers at no cost to capitalist employers.

Marxist feminists thus see women as being particularly exploited in family life, not simply for the benefit of men but also because the profitability of the whole capitalist system depends on their unpaid work.

Somerville: Liberal feminism

Both radical and Marxist feminists wish to transform society in a revolutionary way. Liberal feminists, however, argue that a process of gradual reform of society is more effective – for example, working within established institutions such as parliament, schools, businesses and media to change them from within. Liberal feminists would point to the extent to which their approach has achieved a range of legal rights for women such as equal pay, laws against sex discrimination, access to abortion and contraception, and equal opportunities in education.

Jennifer Somerville (2000) has been labelled by some as a liberal feminist because of her sympathy with this argument. Somerville argues that the picture of the family painted by some feminists of women being exploited by men in families is outdated and points to the progress women have made in achieving equality in family life and personal relationships. For example, women have much more choice today about whether to marry or cohabit, to become single mothers or engage in lesbian relationships, than they did in the past.

Somerville acknowledges that many women remain dissatisfied with many men's refusal to take on a full share of family responsibilities but points out that women at least have more freedom to escape from unsatisfactory relationships. Unlike the New Right who call for a return to traditional family values, Somerville argues that the government needs to give more support to working parents by, for example, encouraging flexible working hours, enabling both partners to participate in paid work and to contribute to childcare.

Evaluation of the feminist view

Feminism has played a valuable role in challenging many of the dominant assumptions about families made by more traditional sociological theories such as functionalism. In particular, feminists have highlighted the dark side of family life – for example, domestic violence, child abuse and the inequalities between men and women. In many respects, feminism has gone from an outsider position in sociology attacking what has been described as 'malestream' sociology (studying society from a male viewpoint) to becoming part of the established assumptions of sociology. Thanks to feminism, few sociologists today would ignore issues of gender and power in family life, as was common up until the 1970s. This can be seen in the array of research into gender inequalities in family life discussed in later in the chapter (page 94), much of it inspired by feminist approaches.

Critics of traditional forms of feminism would, however, offer the following arguments:

- Feminists have tended to emphasise the negative aspects of the traditional nuclear family, particularly for women, and have ignored positive aspects of family life. Many women gain real satisfaction from performing traditional roles in the family such as bringing up children.
- Some feminist approaches can be seen as outdated since they seem to portray families as they were 50 years ago; they ignore the very real changes in the roles of women and men in families and the wider society. Post-feminists, such as Catherine Hakim (2000), argue that women can now make free and rational choices about their lives; for example, many women choose to only work part-time and take on a greater share of domestic responsibilities than their partners because that is what they want, not because they have been forced into these roles by the power of patriarchy.
- Some feminists, particularly radical feminists, have been accused of focusing exclusively on gender inequalities and patriarchy. Marxist feminists to some extent overcome this problem by considering capitalism and inequalities of class. However, black feminists such as bell hooks (1981) and Patricia Hill Collins (1990) would argue that many feminists have

focused specifically on white women's experiences and ignored the experiences of family life of women from ethnic minorities. For example, for many ethnic minority women, racism may be experienced as being just as oppressive as sexism, and in many cases such women's families represent their main refuge and protection from racism in the wider society.

- Difference feminists who are influenced by postmodernism (see page 45) take this argument even further. They argue that feminists have tended to lump all women together as a single category of people who are equally oppressed by patriarchy in nuclear families. In reality, women are extremely diverse, coming from different situations in terms of working or not working, age, social class, ethnicity and cultural backgrounds. Women are therefore likely to experience family life in different ways and this may change over a woman's lifetime.

Activity: Domestic violence

Item A: A poster encouraging people to report domestic violence

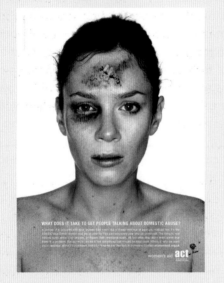

Item B: A survey of the extent of domestic violence

Professor Betsy Stanko, director of the violence research programme at the University of London carried out a snapshot survey of domestic violence in the UK. She based her findings on phones calls to police forces across the country together with referrals to organisations like Victim Support, Relate, Refuge and the Women's Aid Federation during the course of a single day, September 28 2000.

Stanko's data suggested that acts of domestic violence are committed every six seconds and 999 calls reporting attacks are made every minute. The study revealed that a quarter of all violent crimes in London are 'domestics' and more than half of incidents are witnessed by children. One victim who reported an attack was slashed across the throat with a razor blade while a pregnant woman reported bleeding after she was kicked. Rapes and stabbings were also common.

Commenting on the findings, Deputy Assistant Commissioner John Grieve, head of Scotland Yard's Race and Violent Crimes Task Force, said the study was a 'shocking reminder of the scale of domestic violence ... which disregards gender, race, religion and age'.

The police received more than 1,300 crisis calls during the snapshot day, while Stanko estimated 570,000 cases are reported each year — most attacks take place at the weekend, rather than on weekdays. However, she commented that these figures were almost certainly an underestimate because domestic violence is significantly under-reported. Victims were overwhelmingly female; more than 80 per cent of victims were women attacked by men. Eight per cent of incidents involved men being assaulted by women, and 4 per cent were women targeted by other women.

Stanko compared her survey of reported domestic violence with figures from the British Crime Survey. The BCS is based on a confidential survey of the extent to which people are victims of crime and includes many crimes which have not been reported. The Professor suggested that this showed an even grimmer picture and suggested that 'using the BCS to gauge the truer proportion of domestic violence, we could say that an incident of domestic violence occurs in the UK every six to 20 seconds'.

Source: Adapted from Hopkins (2000)

1 What did Stanko's survey (Item B) reveal about:
  a) the extent of domestic violence by men against women?
  b) the extent of domestic violence by women against men?
2 How might feminists explain the gender difference in patterns of domestic violence?
3 How might the evidence from this survey be used to criticise the functionalist view that the family serves to stabilise adult personalities?
4 What problems might there be in accurately estimating the extent of domestic violence in this kind of survey?

Individualisation and postmodernism

All of the theories of family life considered so far – functionalism, the New Right, Marxism and feminism – focus on the nuclear family as the dominant form of family in modern industrial societies. They also tend to emphasise the way the family serves the needs of the wider society. More recently, sociologists have questioned these approaches, arguing that the diversity of families and personal relationships in society today mean that we need to be talking about families and intimate relationships rather than just the family. Sociologists also focus more on what families and intimate relationships offer to individuals and how these are worked out and negotiated in daily life, rather than seeing family roles and structures as based on the needs of industrial society or capitalism.

Family practices and family displays

This type of approach can be seen in the work of David Morgan (1996). He argues that we should focus on family practices rather than the family. By this, he means that individuals create families and other networks of intimate relationships by their daily activities, such as talking to one another, cooking meals for them, sharing leisure activities or buying gifts. From this perspective we should be less concerned about what the family is (its structure) or what it is for (its functions) but rather what it means to individuals themselves and how they work together to sustain the idea of a family.

Janet Finch (2007) has developed this further with the concept of 'family display'. She states that 'display is the process by which individuals, and groups of individuals, convey to each other and to relevant audiences that certain of their actions do constitute "doing family things"', and thereby confirm that these relationships are 'family' relationships. Finch sees rituals such as family meals, family photographs, weddings and funerals as examples of family displays that reinforce people's sense of togetherness and family identity.

Studies

Reflexive modernisation – Giddens (1991, 1992)

Anthony Giddens argues that the modern world brought into being by the rise of industrialisation has not come to an end but has developed and moved forward since the late twentieth century. We are now in the era of late modernity where traditional norms and structures that constrained individuals to fit into certain structures and roles have started to dissolve. This can be seen most clearly in the role of women in society where traditional norms that limited women's opportunities and dictated that married women's place was in the home have become less restricting. Giddens argues that life in late modernity is characterised by reflexivity, by which he means that individuals constantly question what they are doing in life and reflect on possible alternatives. They create their own lifescripts rather than following a script laid down by society based on their gender, social class or other characteristics. This means that individuals have much greater choice about their lives in general and more specifically about how they construct their own domestic arrangements. The nuclear family has therefore become simply another option rather than the social norm. Increasingly, we are seeing more people choosing other options such as singlehood, cohabitation, lone parenting, reconstituted families and gay and lesbian relationships.

Giddens also sees intimate relationships as more fluid and open to change as people pass through their life course. He suggests that the idea of romantic love, which emphasised finding a special person, falling in love and spending the rest of your life with them, has been replaced by confluent love. Confluent love is based on a deep emotional intimacy in which partners reveal their needs and concerns to each other. Giddens argues that couples today seek what he calls a 'pure' relationship. By this he means a relationship that is pursued for its own sake, especially for the emotional fulfillment it offers. In the past, husbands and wives often stayed together for practical reasons; women needed men to support them financially, and men needed women to run the home and look after children. Today these concerns are less important. This means that when relationships work, they are potentially much more fulfilling, especially for women who were often expected to provide emotional support in traditional marriages while receiving little in return from their husbands. However, confluent love is also far more fragile as individuals only stay in relationships while their emotional needs are being fulfilled and are likely to look for love elsewhere when they are no longer satisfied.

Giddens' arguments certainly help to explain the high rates of separation and divorce that we are witnessing in the UK today. They also help to explain the growth of family diversity as reflexive individuals choose to look for confluent love in a whole range of relationships outside traditional marriage and the nuclear family.

Beck and Beck-Gernsheim: Risk society and individualisation

The ideas of German sociologists Ulrich Beck and his wife Elisabeth Beck-Gernsheim share some similarities with Giddens. Beck (1992) sees the contemporary social world as an extension of modernity but refers to it as 'high modernity'. In the earlier stages of modernity there was much more confidence that humans could make the world a better place through, for example, scientific discoveries. This was also reflected in a belief in a particular type of family – the nuclear family – as serving the needs of modern society. In high modernity there is much less confidence; we are much more aware of the risks posed by science and technology, such as global warming, nuclear waste and environmental pollution.

Beck argues that we now live in a risk society where social life is based on the construction of lifestyles and identities, which are based on the avoidance of risks. This is also reflected in personal relationships. For some people, the commitment of marriage or having children presents too much risk and so they prefer to opt for less risky relationships; such as cohabiting, living apart together or simply staying single. Long-term relationships, however, also offer a way of avoiding risks, for example, of loneliness, loss of contact with one's children or the pain of relationship break-up. Like Giddens, Beck argues that in society today we have to constantly make choices.

In *The Normal Chaos of Love* (1995), Beck and Beck-Gernsheim argue that a process of individualisation is occurring in high modernity. This means that individuals are no longer tied to fixed roles or identities as they were in the past. For example, women are no longer expected to necessarily marry, have children and run a home, and similarly, heterosexuality and lifelong marriage are no longer the norm. This again helps to explain the diversity of families and relationships; it also explains the fluid nature of contemporary life as individuals move in and out of relationships and family groupings in search of what suits them best as an individual rather than following traditional patterns laid down by society.

Giddens' work on intimate relationships is relatively optimistic, seeing pure relationships as offering the potential for much greater fulfillment and equality between men and women. By contrast, Beck and Beck-Gernsheim are more pessimistic. They acknowledge the freedom and choice offered by relationships in high modernity but are concerned that families are becoming fragmented and atomised as self-absorbed individuals seek their own fulfilment.

Postmodernism

While Giddens, Beck and Beck-Gernsheim see society as in a later stage of modernity, some sociologists have argued that the society we now live in is so different from the modern world of the nineteenth and early twentieth century that it should be described as postmodern. This is reflected in the work of the French writer Jean-François Lyotard (1984), who argues that today we are living under the 'postmodern condition'. A key aspect of this is that knowledge has become relative – in other words, we can no longer be certain what is true and what is false. In modernity, there was greater certainty, for example that science provided us with answers and solutions and that politicians could create a better society for all. In postmodernity, there is a questioning of such experts and their claims to truth. Instead, individuals have to work out their own truths from experience and find out what is real and what works for them as individuals.

Postmodernist sociologists have applied this to family life, pointing out that traditional forms of family life such as the nuclear family and lifelong marriage were seen by experts as the ideal way to bring up children and organise personal life. In postmodernity, it is argued that there is less certainty about how we should live our lives. Jon Bernardes (1997) argues that as a result, contemporary postmodern families have a number of characteristics:

- choice – individuals can choose from a variety of family types and forms of personal relationships
- freedom – individuals are no longer constrained by traditional norms, for example about gender roles or sexuality
- diversity – families no longer conform to a single type
- ambivalence – there is no longer any certainty about what is normal or correct
- fluidity – families and relationships are not fixed but rather constantly changing as individuals move in and out of different sets of relationships.

Some postmodernists are largely optimistic about family life in postmodernity. Judith Stacey (1996) sees the diversity and fluidity of postmodern families as allowing individuals to develop lifestyles and relationships that suit their changing circumstances as they move through their life course (see the Activity on page 90). Others, like Zygmunt Bauman in *Liquid Love* (2003), see many of these changes as negative. Bauman argues that contemporary family bonds have been weakened and there is a lack of certainty about roles and responsibilities in families, which is jeopardising the family as an institution.

Evaluation of individualisation and postmodern theories

The work of theorists of late modernity and postmodernity has been valuable in helping to explain many of the changes occurring in family life in the UK since around the 1970s. The greater social acceptance of diverse families, cohabitation, same-sex relationships and divorce seems to fit with the argument that something fundamental has changed in family life. This has led sociologists to re-evaluate how they look at families with far less focus on the nuclear family alone and greater interest in new forms of families and relationships. Postmodernists in particular are far more cautious than conventional sociologists about making generalisations about family life such as 'all women are oppressed by patriarchy' or 'the nuclear family is functional for society', and instead reveal how for different individuals family life may be lived and interpreted in very different ways.

Critics, however, would make a number of criticisms of such theories:

- **Continuities in family life.** In emphasising changes in family life, postmodernists and individualisation theories have neglected the extent to which there are still continuities in family. This makes the concept of postmodernity particularly problematic as it suggests a radical break with modernity and the kind of families people lived in the recent past. For example, even though there is greater family diversity, two-parent families remain the norm and appear to be what most people aspire towards (see also the next section).
- **Neglecting social structures.** A number of sociologists have argued that class, gender and ethnicity and other inequalities continue to structure the lives of individuals and in some cases limit their choices. This is at odds with the view that we all enjoy much greater freedom of choice. For example, Yvette Taylor (2007), in a study of working-class lesbians, found that not only sexuality but also class affected the lives of her respondents. For example, working-class lesbian mothers often found it more difficult to negotiate with professionals such as doctors and teachers over their children and also found that the kinds of places working-class parents would take children were less welcoming to lesbian mothers.
- **Ethnicity.** The idea of choice and individualism also seems more applicable to certain groups in the white population than to some ethnic minorities. Tony Chapman (2004) observes that South Asian families still tend to hold to traditional values concerning marriage and follow a much stricter segregation of gender roles than most white families. Moreover, some of the alternative family practices found in South Asian societies are still not accepted in the UK. Sultana Mustafa Khanum (2001), in a study of Bangladeshis in Manchester, found that many men who had migrated from Bangladesh had two wives but were unable to bring their second wife to the UK as this relationship was not recognised under UK law.
- **Gender.** Writers such as Giddens argue that there has been a democratisation of family life, as women can now choose to leave relationships that are unfulfilling. However, feminists have criticised him for ignoring the persistence of patriarchal aspects of family life. Other examples of how contemporary sociologists have highlighted gender inequalities in family life can be seen on pages 94–101.

Activity

Comparing theories about the family

	Functionalism	New Right	Marxism	Feminism	Individualisation theories	Postmodernism
Key writers						
Key concepts						
Views on the nuclear family						
Views on family diversity						
Evaluation						

1 Copy the grid above onto a large sheet of paper (A3 or larger if possible).
2 Write a few key words or bullet points in each box to help you to summarise each theory.
3 In the evaluation boxes, try to summarise both positive and critical points about each theory.
4 Use the grid to help you to write essays and revise for your exam.

Activity: Postmodern families

Item A: *Modern Family* – a representation of postmodern families?

TV sitcoms have traditionally often focused on nuclear family units. The series *Modern Family* focuses on a three related households: the grandfather and his younger second wife and stepson (left), the married daughter and her nuclear family (centre) and the gay son, his partner and their adopted Asian daughter

Item B: Pam and Dotty's postmodern families

Judith Stacey's work on postmodern families was based on detailed ethnographic research focusing mainly on two extended family networks in Silicon Valley, California, headed by two women she calls Pam and Dotty. Stacey points out that the traditional nuclear family only really became dominant in the American working class in the 1960s and 1970s, as men began to earn enough to keep a whole family.

Both Pam and Dotty had married in the 1950s but had to work in order to supplement their husbands' incomes. Both women took college courses in the 1970s and were exposed to feminist ideas, which led them to question their husbands' limited involvement in family life. In Dotty's case, she was physically abused by her husband, and both women eventually left their husbands.

Pam remarried and enjoyed a more egalitarian second marriage but had a close relationship with her first husband's new partner, and they supported one another in different ways.

Dotty took her first husband back after he had a heart attack, but only on condition that he did most of the housework. He eventually died and she also lost two of her adult children. She successfully fought for custody of one of her deceased daughter's children against the wishes of their abusive father, and then formed a household with one of her surviving daughters, who was a single mother. Interestingly, none of Pam's or Dotty's daughters lived in a conventional nuclear family.

Stacey celebrates the decline of the traditional nuclear family, arguing that it was always a myth that distorts and devalues the 'rich variety of kinship stories'. She sees postmodern families, of which Pam and Dotty's are examples, as representing a democratic opportunity whereby individuals can expand and redefine what families are and create the kind of families that work best for them in their personal circumstances.

Source: Adapted from Stacey (1996)

1 Why might the TV series *Modern Family* (Item A) be a better representation of families in postmodern society than conventional sitcoms that tended to focus on a nuclear family?
2 Why does Stacey in Item B describe Pam and Dotty's network of relationships as examples of postmodern families?
3 Using evidence from Item B and elsewhere, assess the view that families in contemporary society are characterised by the following:
   a) choice
   b) freedom
   c) diversity
   d) ambivalence
   e) fluidity.

3.6 Debates about family diversity

Up until the 1980s, most sociological approaches to family life focused on the nuclear family. The key debates among sociologists revolved around whether the nuclear family was a largely beneficial institution – as claimed by the functionalists – or whether it served some sections of society more than others –

the capitalist class according to the Marxists and men according to radical feminists. In the 1980s, a number of studies, such as *Families in Britain* by Robert and Rhona Rapoport and others (1982), began to examine the idea that we were witnessing a growth in family diversity.

Debates about family diversity have mainly centred on two issues:

1 whether family diversity is a good thing
2 the extent to which families are actually diversifying.

Perspectives on family diversity

Concerns about diversity

The strongest concerns about family diversity have come from the New Right (see page 81), who see diversity as destroying traditional family values. They call for social policies that strengthen marriage and encourage raising children in traditional nuclear families. From their perspective, lone-parent, reconstituted, cohabiting and same-sex families do not function as effectively in socialising children and providing a stable family life. While not agreeing with the New Right, some other sociologists have also expressed concern about the trend towards individualisation in personal relationships. For example, Beck and Beck-Gernsheim do not advocate the nuclear family as an ideal form but have expressed concern at the way in which individuals' concerns about the risks of commitment have undermined family life.

Support for diversity

Against these concerns, other sociologists have celebrated the freedom offered by family diversity. Giddens argues that there has been a 'democratisation of intimate relationships', meaning that individuals are not forced into relationships but only engage with them when they find them fulfilling, meaning that there is more equality between partners. Feminists have also welcomed many aspects of family diversity, arguing that the traditional nuclear family was patriarchal. The fact that women can opt out of marriage, bring up children without a male partner or engage in lesbian relationships are all seen as extending socially acceptable lifestyles for women.

The persistence of patriarchy

Some feminists, however, argue that aspects of patriarchy persist even within new forms of families and intimate relationships. Wendy Langford (1999) agrees with Giddens, in that love has the potential to be a liberating and transforming experience, but suggests that all too often women end up feeling alienated because they are the ones who invest emotionally in relationships and do not receive in return the deep emotional intimacy that supposedly characterises confluent love. Deborah Chambers (2012) points out that women who reject traditional family forms, such as single mothers and lesbians, often still face condemnation from more traditional sections of society and mass media.

Study

The neo-conventional family – Chester (1985)

Robert Chester was one of the first sociologists to question the extent to which families were becoming diverse. He argued that families that did not fit the nuclear model were a minority that 'excited disproportionate attention' from sociologists and that most people still aspired to bring up children in a two-parent family. Chester argued that many families that are not strictly nuclear families are based on the nuclear model, and he described them as **neo-conventional families.** Parents may be cohabiting rather than marrying and may be same-sex rather than both sexes, couples may both pursue careers and share domestic roles, and in some cases there may be step-parents and stepchildren in families. However, all of these can be seen as variations of the theme of the nuclear family.

Chester also pointed out that statistics – such as those from the Census or other surveys – are misleading, because they are based on a snapshot. They only show how many households are based on different types of families at a single point in time. In reality, individuals move in and out of different households and families at different stages in their life course. While only a minority of people live in nuclear families at any one time, being part of a nuclear family will be part of the experience of the vast majority of people whether as children or as parents. For example, many of the increasing proportion of people who live alone are either young people who have left their parents' family and who will eventually settle down and create their own family, or they are elderly people who have completed raising a family and are now widowed.

Chester's study was based on data from the 1981 Census and can be criticised for being out of date. Arguably, families and households have become even more diverse in the last twenty years (see data in Item B in the Activity on page 92). However, some support for his arguments is offered by Jennifer Somerville (2000). She acknowledges that there have been major changes in family life – for example, pre-marital sex and cohabitation have become much more the norm than in the past and childlessness, lone parenthood and divorce have all increased – but she claims that only about 5 per cent of people will never marry in their lives. Moreover, comparisons of rates of marriage with the 1960s and 1970s are misleading, as rates of marriage in this period were at their highest since national statistics were first compiled in 1837. Somerville concludes by suggesting that most people in the UK are still committed to family life and that we need to be cautious about exaggerating the extent of change.

Continuities in family life

While some sociologists have debated the reasons for family diversity and its impact on society, others have questioned whether there has been such a radical transformation of family life and have argued that there are important continuities in family life between the past and the present.

Gittins: Family ideology

Chester's arguments echo the functionalist view that there is still a degree of consensus in the UK, meaning that the nuclear family is regarded by many as the normal family type. However, Diana Gittins (1993), drawing on Marxist and feminist approaches, argues that this consensus is only maintained because there is a powerful **ideology** of the nuclear family. An ideology is a misleading view, based on value judgements, defining what is normal and desirable and, in this case, labelling alternative family forms as undesirable. In the last thirty years, politicians have frequently attacked those who deviate from the conventional nuclear family (see, for example, the article on Iain Duncan Smith's views on marriage and lone-parent families in the Activity on page 81).

The mass media also tends to portray nuclear families as the norm, such as in advertising. Edmund Leach (1967) called this kind of image the **cereal packet family**; it portrays happy smiling families, where mothers typically cook and perform domestic chores for husbands and children, in advertisements for everything from cornflakes to washing-up liquid. Such families are not real but create an image of what family life should be like, to which everyone is encouraged to aspire. From this perspective, the reality of family life may have changed, but the ideology that supports the nuclear family as normal is still very powerful.

Smart: Personal life

Carol Smart (2007) does not dispute the evidence that people now live in more diverse families and

---

Activity: Trends in families and households in the UK

Item A: Is the traditional nuclear family in decline?

1 Which types of households have increased in number the most and which have decreased in number the most since 1961?
2 What explanations could be offered for these trends?
3 How could these statistics be used to support the view that there has been a trend towards greater family and household diversity since the 1960s?
4 How could these statistics be used to support the view that the nuclear family remains the dominant family form in the UK?

Item B: Households by type of household and family

	% 1961	% 1971	% 1981	% 1991	% 2001	% 2006	% 2013
One person							
Under state pension age	4	6	8	11	14	14	16
Over state pension age	7	12	14	16	15	14	13
Two or more unrelated adults	5	4	5	3	3	3	3
One-family households							
Couple							
No children	26	27	26	28	29	28	28
1–2 dependent children	30	26	25	20	19	18	18

Source: Adapted from *Social Trends*, 2002, 2007 and ONS Families and Households 2013 Release

intimate relationships. However, she does take issue with the arguments of theorists such as Giddens, Beck and Beck-Gernsheim, which suggest that we have become so individualised and focused on our own personal needs and interests that this has led to a decline in commitment and perhaps even of family life itself. Smart argues that it is more useful to think in terms of **personal life** rather than family life. Many people now exist in a network of relationships, which may include people who are related by blood or marriage, but which may also include other people such as friends with whom we enjoy family-like relationships. Smart argues that individuals are still bonded into such networks and share things like family secrets, memories, homes and possessions. Who we think of as family may no longer just include the nuclear family or even the traditional extended family, but individuals are still embedded in networks of personal relationships that in many respects fulfil the functions of more traditional families.

Section summary

Complete the summary below. Use the words and phrases from the list to fill the dotted spaces and fill the boxes with your own examples.

Many sociologists argue that the most significant change in family life in the UK over the last 50 years has been the growth of _____, meaning that fewer families are _____ and there has been a growth in the number of other types of families and households, such as:

| |
| |

More people also now live in non-family households, such as:

| |
| |

Some sociologists have also noted that patterns of family life and intimate relationships differ in different social groups. There is diversity between social classes, such as:

| |
| |

There is also diversity between ethnic groups, such as:

| |
| |

Finally, there is diversity in terms of people's sexual orientation, such as:

| |
| |

There have been significant changes in patterns of marriage and divorce, such as a rise in _____, meaning that many people have several partners during their lifetime, though it is still customary to have only one partner at a time. The number of people marrying is _____, while the average age at which people marry is _____. This is partly because alternatives to marriage are now more popular and socially acceptable, such as _____ and _____.

The number of divorces has also increased, partly because of changes in divorce laws, such as the 1969 Divorce Reform Act which changed the basis for divorce from _____, such as adultery, to _____. However, many sociologists would argue that changes in society have been more important in encouraging more people to turn to divorce; examples of these are:

| |
| |

Sociologists disagree over what the implications of changing patterns of divorce and marriage are for society. For example, New Right thinkers argue that the decline of marriage has undermined _____ while other sociologists such as Giddens argue that we are seeing the emergence of new types of relationships based on _____, which offer couples more freedom and equality.

Family life has been affected by changing population trends or what sociologists call _____. For example, there have been changes in patterns of _____ relating to how many children are born.

There has also been a reduction in _____, reflected in lower death rates particularly among younger age groups and an increase in _____. One consequence of all this is that there is an _____, meaning that there are proportionately fewer young people and more older people in the population. This may have a number of consequences for family life, such as an increase in _____.

Sociologists disagree over the importance of the traditional two-parent family or _____. For functionalists, this type of family fulfils essential functions that no other family type can perform as effectively; for example, Parsons suggests that the two key functions are _____ and _____. The New Right agree with this view but argue that there has been a breakdown in family life; for example, Murray argues that an _____ has emerged made up of people such as lone parents and the unemployed who fail to adequately socialise their children. Other sociologists argue that traditional families do not work in everyone's interests. Marxists argue the family is mainly organised to serve the needs of _____. Many feminists, however, argue that the family is _____, meaning that it serves the needs of men.

Some contemporary sociologists argue that all of these theories are outdated. Giddens argues that in late modernity people are becoming more _____ and making more conscious choices about what kind of families and relationships they seek. Postmodernists argue that it is increasingly difficult to generalise about what a family is but argue that families are characterised by _____, _____ and _____.

ageing population, ambivalence, beanpole families, capitalism, choice, cohabitation, confluent love, creative singlehood, decreasing, demographic factors, family diversity, fertility, fluidity, increasing, irretrievable breakdown of marriage, life expectancy, matrimonial offence, mortality, nuclear families, nuclear family, patriarchal, primary socialisation, reflexive, serial monogamy, stabilisation of adult personalities, traditional family values, underclass

3.7 To what extent are roles and relationships within families and households changing?

Roles and relationships between partners

A number of sociologists have observed significant changes in **conjugal** roles, the roles of men and women within marriage over the last 50 years. In particular, it has been argued that there has been a shift from **segregated conjugal roles**, where husbands and wives performed separate kinds of work and often had separate leisure activities as well, to **joint conjugal roles**, where husbands and wives both perform paid work, share the unpaid work in the home and have shared leisure and social activities. More recently, sociologists have begun to explore other kinds of intimate relationships, such as cohabiting couples and same-sex couples, in order to discover how roles are organised in these relationships.

Not all sociologists agree that roles and relationships in the family have changed significantly; for example,

many feminists have pointed to the extent to which heterosexual relationships are still patriarchal, with men continuing to play a more dominant role and traditional female responsibilities, such as housework and childcare, still being assigned to women.

Perspectives on gender roles in families

Functionalism

For functionalists such as Talcott Parsons (Parsons and Bales 1955), a division of roles between men and women in families is a functional necessity that ensures that each partner specialises in the role that they are most suited to:

- The expressive role usually performed by mothers is primarily about ensuring that the psychological and emotional needs of the husband and children are provided for. This would include performing the functions of socialising the children and stabilising adult personalities by offering emotional support to her husband.
- The instrumental role is more suited to men and involves providing an income for the family. The husband's occupation also provides the family with its status in society.

Getting you thinking ...

Item A

Item B

1 Which image best represents the kind of roles played by men and women in families in the UK today?

2 What kind of evidence can you use to support your answer?

Parsons suggests that to some extent these roles are based in biology. He points out that as women bear children and nurse them as babies, it is natural that they should also play a bigger role in their socialisation. However, Parsons sees humans as products of the socialisation process but suggests that socialising males and females into different roles simply trains each sex to fulfil the role to which they are naturally suited. Critics would point to evidence that gender roles are socially constructed (see page 23) and would question the idea that men and women's roles in families are biologically determined.

Symmetry and the democratisation of gender roles

From the 1960s onwards, a number of sociologists noted a trend towards the breakdown of segregated conjugal roles and a shift towards more joint roles. Michael Young and Peter Willmott (1973) argued that from the late nineteenth century, a new form of family that they called the symmetrical family had emerged in Britain, first in the higher social classes and spreading to the working class from the 1950s onwards. According to Young and Willmott, the symmetrical family has three main characteristics:

1 **Conjugal roles are joint.** The roles of husband and wife are more symmetrical, because both paid work and unpaid domestic tasks are shared by both partners.

2 **The family is nuclear.** The focus of the family is on the relationship between husband, wife and children, and extended family ties have weakened.

3 **The family is privatised.** Husbands and wives spend more time in the privacy of their home together, rather than with other extended family members or in community activities (such as men going to the pub or a football match). This means that husbands are more involved in domestic life and more likely to share responsibilities with wives and spend time with their children.

Young and Willmott's study contradicted the functionalist view that segregated conjugal roles are necessary and functional. They implied that there has been a historical march towards greater equality in men and women's roles in the family, though this has progressed further in some sections of society than others.

More recently, theorists of late modernity such as Anthony Giddens (1992) have argued that there has been a 'transformation of intimate relationships', meaning that women no longer need to accept male dominance as they have a much wider range of choices in societies like the UK. Giddens argues that this has led to a democratisation of family life, with men in particular becoming more willing to reveal their emotions and engage with women and children in an intimate way (see also page 87).

Feminism

Feminists have questioned Parsons' view that segregated roles are functional for both men and women; however, they have also criticised Young and Willmott's argument that more equal and symmetrical roles have become more characteristic of nuclear families in the UK. Writing in the 1970s, Ann Oakley (1974) argued that the housewife role remained the primary role for married women and showed in her own small-scale study that only a minority of men could be classified as having a high level of participation in housework and childcare. Feminists have also attacked Giddens' notion of democratisation, arguing that women still carry the main responsibility for maintaining family relationships and looking after members' emotional needs.

For radical feminists, the way gender roles are organised in families reflects the patriarchal nature of traditional families and the fact that men still exercise more power than women. Marxist feminists, however, would argue that by undertaking unpaid work in the family, women not only look after men's needs but also serve the needs of capitalism.

Feminists argue that the family has a dark side that is ignored by functionalists and in the idea of the symmetrical family. This dark side can be seen at its most extreme in the form of domestic violence and child abuse, which feminists argue are most commonly committed by men (see, for example, Stanko's study on page 86). Feminists also argue that families are patriarchal in more mundane ways, for example, women still perform most of the work in many families, and men often still control areas such as decision-making and finances. Evidence of these types of inequalities is discussed further below.

Marxism

Marxists have done little detailed research on gender roles and relationships in families but see these as shaped by the needs of capitalism. For Marxists, really fulfilling personal relationships are impossible in a capitalist society because of materialism, consumption and the need for workers to earn a living through wage labour. Marxists argue that the unpaid labour such as housework and childcare performed by family members, especially women, benefits the capitalist class as much as family members, for example, by ensuring that workers are fit to return to work each day. (For further coverage of Marxist theories, see pages 84–86).

Postmodernism

For postmodernists, all of the theories considered above tend to make sweeping generalisations about the nature of roles and relationships in families. They would point to the much more diverse nature of families and relationships in the twenty-first century. This means, for example, that sociologists cannot state that families are either symmetrical or patriarchal. Postmodernists would point to the extent to which family members now create their own family practices (see page 89), such as negotiating what roles work best for them in their own circumstances. Roles and relationships may also change over time (see for example how Pam and Dotty's roles and relationships changed during their lifetimes in Stacey's study on page 92). Postmodernists would also argue that conventional sociological research has focused too much on roles and relationships in traditional nuclear families and point out that these cannot be generalised to other types of families, such as lone parents, cohabiting couples or same-sex relationships.

The domestic division of labour

One contribution made by feminists to sociology has been an understanding that work includes not only paid work but also a variety of forms of unpaid work such as housework, childcare and caring for extended family members. Feminists have pointed to the way in which work is gendered. Women increasingly participate in paid employment but often earn less than men and may work part-time in order to allow them time for family responsibilities. Similarly, in the home it is women who undertake the majority of unpaid domestic tasks. Men tend to undertake more occasional tasks such as DIY or gardening but the tasks that have to be undertaken on a daily basis such as cooking, cleaning, washing, ironing and looking after children are more commonly allocated to women, though men may help out. This division of tasks within the home between family members is what sociologists refer to as the domestic division of labour.

Many feminists have argued that the rise in paid employment of women, especially women with children, has not liberated women. Women are now faced with a **dual burden** where in many cases they are working full-time like men but also undertaking a second burden where they undertake the majority of housework and childcare.

Activity: Choices and gender roles in the family

Item A: Househusbands

Stay-at-home dads or househusbands are still relatively rare in the UK. The Office for National Statistics estimated that there were 200,000 in 2007.

Item B: Constraints on women's choices

Women have won the right to work, to vote and supposedly to be paid equally with men. To accommodate this new influx of women in the work place, society has made a few adjustments: maternity leave, some part-time jobs, flexible working, parental leave. However, the world of work is still largely designed by and for men, with the expectation that they will work full-time to support the family, and that women will maybe work or maybe stay at home. It is not based on true equality. It is in this world that the decision has to be taken as to how to divide up the new responsibilities of caring for a baby and the additional household chores that this brings.

Let's examine this decision from the point of view of a young couple. It is likely that when a new baby is born, the man (let's call him Peter) will be earning more than the woman (Jane) – men working full-time without children are paid 6.3 per cent more than women. Jane is given the right to six months or longer off work, which then not only places her squarely in the role of key childcare provider and household manager, but also often serves to increase any gap in pay that may have existed.

Now cleverly positioned as the one who is best placed to look after the baby, and the one with the deepest emotional attachment to the baby, she is likely to request flexible working or a part-time role. This then reduces significantly her chances of promotion, it reduces the amount of time she spends on the job and

on training, and in many cases it reduces the likelihood of her being able to achieve a positive rating or ranking on her performance appraisals.

As a result of all of this, Jane is likely to downgrade her career aspirations, and may find her interest and satisfaction with the job decrease as well. A second and third child may well follow, and by now the cycle is well set up: further maternity leave, further household duties. For Jane now, life is now pretty tough. For Peter, he certainly has less sleep than before, and finds his weekends less flexible, but he has worked full-time throughout (except a week's extra paternity leave for each baby) and is now earning considerably more than Jane.

So this is the situation. At this point, Peter and Jane are quite likely to weigh up their financial position, the level of stress in the household and the emotional feelings involved and make a sensible and well-thought-through decision for Jane to give up work.

Source: Adapted from Smith (2010)

1 Study Items A and B. Suggest reasons why it is much more common for women to give up paid work or reduce their working hours to look after children than men.

2 Some sociologists have argued that both men and women have become individualised and have much greater choices in relation to their lives today. How does the article suggest that couples do not simply freely choose their roles in families but are constrained by factors in the wider society?

3 The author of the article presents a feminist perspective. How would you evaluate her argument?

Survey research

There has been considerable quantitative research in recent years that has tried to measure the extent of women's and men's participation in domestic labour. While estimates of how much work each sex performs vary, most surveys tend to agree that women do considerably more hours of unpaid work than men. The 2012 British Social Attitudes Survey (Park *et al.* 2013) suggested that men spend an average of eight hours a week doing domestic labour, while women spend an average of 13 hours (see also the Activity on page 99). Such estimates have been criticised, as they rely on respondents to surveys accurately reporting how much time they spend on household tasks. Some studies have suggested that men tend

to overestimate their own participation while women tend to underestimate.

Time budget research

A more reliable method of estimation involves time budget diaries, where respondents complete a daily record of how much time they have spent on different activities. For example, Jonathan Gershuny (1999) compared data collected in this way in the 1970s and in 1997. He found that in 1997 women still did more than 60 per cent of domestic work but there had been a gradual increase in men's participation. However, women had increased their participation in paid work over the same period, meaning that their overall time spent on all work had increased slightly. Gershuny suggested that there has been a process of **lagged adaptation** whereby women's roles have changed more quickly than men's. Women have entered the workforce in large numbers but men have been slow to adapt to this situation. However, Gershuny suggested that in the next generation we are likely to see men taking a bigger share of housework and childcare, giving some support to Young and Willmott's view that families will slowly become more symmetrical.

Interestingly in a more recent study, comparing data from 2005 with data from 2000, Gershuny and his colleagues (Lader *et al.* 2006) found that, overall, both men and women were less likely to spend time on housework in 2005 than in 2000. This may reflect the fact that labour-saving devices and convenience foods mean that both sexes need to spend less time on household tasks. However, women continue to spend more time on housework than men.

Hakim: An alternative perspective on domestic labour

Catherine Hakim (2010) criticised feminists for constantly complaining that men are not doing their fair share of domestic work. She analysed data from time budget studies across Europe and argued that the reality is that most men already do more than their fair share. Hakim argued we need to add all types of work together in comparing what men and women do. She states that 'on average, women and men across Europe do the same total number of productive work hours, once paid jobs and unpaid household work are added together – roughly eight hours a day. Men do substantially more hours of paid work. Women's time is divided more evenly between paid and unpaid work'. She also found that the pattern of equality in total productive work hours is found among couples aged 20–40 and those aged 40–60, so is reasonably constant across the lifecycle. In fact, an analysis by Susan Harkness shows that British men work longer hours in total than women do when there are children in the home, largely because men often work more overtime to boost family income at this stage, while wives switch to part-time jobs, or drop out of employment (Harkness 2008). Couples with no children at home and both in full-time jobs emerge as the only group where women work more hours in total than men, once paid and unpaid work hours are added together.

Diversity in domestic division of labour

Studies based on national statistics, such as those described, tend to be based on large samples and can track changes over time. They therefore have the merit of both representativeness and reliability. However, statistical averages tend to conceal wide variations in how roles and relationships are organised in contemporary families and households.

Social class

An analysis of secondary data by Man Yee Kan (2008) suggests that middle-class women do less housework than their working-class counterparts. She suggested that every £10,000 increase in a woman's annual income reduces the time she spends on chores every week by nearly two hours and educated women tend to do less housework than women who left school at 16. This is mainly explained by the fact that well-off women can afford to employ others (usually women) to do their housework for them, rather than because middle-class men contribute more to domestic work.

Ethnicity

Richard Berthoud's (2001) study of ethnicity and family life suggests that South Asian families are far more likely to adopt more traditional gender roles than whites. On the other hand, a high proportion of African-Caribbean families are headed by lone mothers, meaning that in these households, mothers often combine paid work with complete responsibility for housework and childcare, though in some cases with support from extended family members.

Sexuality

Studies of gay and lesbian couples suggest that they are far more likely to have shared roles and responsibilities, often consciously rejecting the heterosexual norms of traditional nuclear families. Jeffrey Weeks and his colleagues (1999) found that same-sex couples saw issues such as the division of domestic labour as a matter for discussion and negotiation rather than making assumptions about who does what based on tradition. Gillian Dunne (1997) carried out a study of 37 lesbian couples and similarly found that in most cases housework and childcare were equally shared, though in some cases one partner was only employed part-time and couples had agreed that she should therefore undertake more of the domestic work.

Age and life course

Divisions of labour vary between generations. Most research suggests that younger couples are more likely to adopt more equal roles. However, it also appears that when couples settle down and have children, women start to take on a greater burden of childcare and domestic work.

'Emotion work' and the triple shift – Duncombe and Marsden (1995)

Jean Duncombe and Dennis Marsden argued that simply studying activities such as housework and childcare does not fully measure the contribution made by partners to the work undertaken in families and personal relationships. Duncombe and Marsden suggested that in addition to these practical tasks, members of households carry out 'emotion work'. **Emotion work** refers to people giving love, understanding, praise, reassurance and attention, all of which are required to maintain successful relationships.

Duncombe and Marsden interviewed 40 established white couples both separately and together and found that many of the women felt that it was their emotion work that kept their relationships together. This might include, for example, opening up discussion about personal issues, organising events where the couples could experience intimacy, or simply expressing love and care. Women were also frequently dissatisfied with the limited contribution men made in terms of sustaining their relationships through emotion work and often engaged in a kind of acting in order to give an illusion of happy family life. Most of the men denied there was any problem and felt their contribution to the family lay in their paid jobs and ability to earn money.

Duncombe and Marsden's study suggests that emotion work can be seen as a further dimension to the unequal nature of couple relationships highlighted by feminists. While many feminists argue that in taking up paid employment women have taken on a dual burden, Duncombe and Marsden suggested that many women in fact end up performing a **triple shift**. Having finished their shift of paid work, women come home to complete the housework and then have to undertake emotion work as well.

Activity: Domestic division of labour

Most surveys suggest that women do far more domestic work than men

Item A: Household tasks undertaken by men and women, 1994–2012

Individuals reported as always/usually undertaking task *in percentages*	1994	2002	2006	2012
Does the laundry				
Always/usually man	1	6	5	6
Both equally	18	15	17	20
Always/usually woman	79	78	74	70

Individuals reported as always/usually undertaking task *in percentages*	1994	2002	2006	2012
Makes small repairs around the house				
Always/usually man	75	71	73	75
Both equally	18	17	14	10
Always/usually woman	5	7	8	7
Cares for sick family members				
Always/usually man	1	3	3	5
Both equally	45	36	44	38
Always/usually woman	48	48	43	36
Shops for groceries				
Always/usually man	6	8	8	10
Both equally	52	45	47	43
Always/usually woman	41	45	41	44
Does the household cleaning				
Always/usually man	n/a	5	6	8
Both equally	n/a	29	30	29
Always/usually woman	n/a	58	58	55
Prepares the meals				
Always/usually man	n/a	11	11	16
Both equally	n/a	29	27	27
Always/usually woman	n/a	58	58	55

Source: Adapted from Park *et al.* (2013)

101

Activity: Domestic division of labour (continued)

Item B: Perceptions of who does a fair share of household tasks

The British Social Attitudes Survey in 2002 and 2012 asked men and women for their views about the extent to which they felt they were taking a fair share of household tasks. The results highlighted substantial differences in the perceptions of men and women – and revealed that these views have not changed much over the past decade.

Around six in ten women in 2002 and 2012 considered that they did more than their fair share of the household work. However, only around four in ten men in both years thought that they did less than their fair share. Men were unlikely to say they did more than their fair share, as were women to say that they did less than their fair share. Just under half of men and around a third of women thought that they did roughly their fair share.

Source: Adapted from Park *et al.* (2013)

1 Study Item A. Which tasks are mostly likely to be:
   a) performed by men?
   b) performed by women?
   c) equally shared?
2 What does Item B reveal about men and women's perceptions of how far they do a fair share of housework?
3 To what extent has there been a shift towards more symmetrical roles according to the data in Items A and B?
4 What other data might be useful in addition to Items A and B in evaluating whether men and women in families each do a fair share of work?

Power in family relationships

Functionalists do not see the division of roles in families as based on inequality. Parsons' work suggests that men and women play equal and complimentary roles. Feminists, however, argue that men actually exercise power in most heterosexual family relationships and that traditionally gendered roles are a major form of social inequality. The fact that women appear to perform the majority of domestic labour and receive no financial reward and little social status can be seen as one form of power difference. In this section, we consider research on who makes decisions in families as another dimension of power.

Study

Decision-making within marriages – Hardhill, Green, Dudleston and Owen (1997)

Irene Hardhill, Anne Green, Anna Dudleston and David Owen carried out a study of middle-class dual-career households in Nottingham. These might be expected to be relatively egalitarian (equal) families, as both husbands and wives had well-paid jobs. However, using semi-structured interviews, the authors discovered that in 19 out of 30 couples the man's career came first, in five the woman's took precedence, and in six neither career was given more importance. Men also tended to make decisions about where the couple were to live and about cars. However, both partners usually made joint decisions about buying or renting a house.

In a more recent study, Hardhill (2002) points to the contradiction between the rise of individualism (highlighted by writers such as Beck and Beck-Gernsheim) and the need for couples to come to joint decisions that are of mutual benefit. She argues that in dual-career families, couples are often both individually pursuing their careers but this may still mean an inegalitarian partnership, with the male partner prioritising his career while the female partner has to 'juggle' work and home, often by working part-time or taking a career break while she has children.

Hardhill and her colleagues' study is only small-scale and possibly unrepresentative; however, it tends to support feminist arguments that decisions in families favour the interests of men. However, the authors also point to the existence of a minority of households where there appears to be a degree of equality. Critics of this kind of approach have also argued that the fact that women allow men to progress further in their careers does not necessarily mean that men have more power.

Catherine Hakim (2004) argues that many women work part-time not because they are forced to by the patriarchal power of men but through choice. Hakim suggest that based on her own research in Spain and Britain, only about 20 per cent of women are 'work-centred' (meaning that work is their main priority). For other women, family is equally or more important than work and so these women may choose to work part-time or take less demanding careers.

Family finances and money management

Another aspect of power relations in families is how couples manage their finances, an area Jan Pahl has been researching since the 1980s. In her more recent work (2005, 2008), she notes a growing individualisation in couples' finances, especially in younger couples where both partners have paid jobs. Men and women are likely to each have their own bank accounts and take responsibility for paying for different things. On the face of it, this represents a shift towards greater equality, especially when compared with the 'allowance system' that Pahl (1989) found among some older working-class couples in one of her earlier studies. This involved men controlling the majority of the finances and simply giving their wives an allowance to cover housekeeping.

Pahl, however, points out that individualised finances can put women at a disadvantage if they work part-time, are not in paid work or are retired – a significant proportion of women. In these cases women are disadvantaged as men earn more, and therefore have more spending power. If couples share the household expenses but women earn less, then men are likely to have more surplus income, giving them greater control of the purse strings of the family. Pahl's research suggests that women will only enjoy real equality in relation to financial decision-making when they also enjoy equality in relation to earnings.

3.8 Roles and relationships between parents and children

Most people take for granted the idea that children are different from adults. In most Western societies, children are considered undeveloped, immature, vulnerable and in need of special protection. Many sociologists have argued that the idea of childhood as a separate phase of life when children should be separated from adults is very much a modern invention and is still not accepted in many societies around the world. Childhood can therefore be seen as a **social construction**, as something that is created by society's attitudes and the assumptions we make about children in our culture.

Changes in childhood

Cross-cultural and historical differences in childhood

In the UK today, the social status of childhood extends well beyond the age when most children reach physical maturity. Many sociologists would argue that we have extended childhood far longer than most other societies in history. For example, the historian Lawrence Stone (1990) argues that up until the eighteenth century, children were regarded as extra workers to help their parents or to be hired out for wages by poorer families. In richer families, sons were there to inherit titles and property and daughters to be married off in order to create useful alliances with other powerful families. It has only been in modern times that the notion that children need to be loved and protected has emerged.

Activity: The sociology of food

A study of 'food practices'

Nickie Charles and Marion Kerr (1986) carried out interviews with 200 mothers with young children in the North of England. They found that cooking a 'proper meal' each day for their husbands' return from work was seen as a central part of women's domestic routines. They also observed that 'women cook for men, they cook to please men and to show affection for men'. Women made great efforts to ensure that they cooked food that fitted in with their husbands' likes and dislikes and some reported that their husband even reacted violently when they produced certain foods, meaning that they avoided cooking these again. Charles and Kerr's study suggests that women's domestic routines are controlled in subtle ways by men's likes and dislikes in food and drink. Women would try to serve meals to fit in with their husbands' work routines and attempted to maintain domestic harmony by serving food to please their husbands.

Source: Adapted from Charles and Kerr (1988)

1 How could Charles and Kerr's study be used to support feminist views about the nature of power in traditional nuclear families?
2 Charles and Kerr's study was carried out in the 1980s and focused on married women with children. Assess how far their research is representative of families in the UK today.

Childhood in other cultures

In many parts of the world children are not regarded as in need of protection or special treatment. Left: children working alongside adults in an Indian brickyard. Right: South African youths preparing for their initiation ceremony. In many African tribes, teenage boys are expected to undergo an initiation ceremony before entering adulthood, usually involving physical hardships, including being circumcised.

1 In what ways might the images of childhood shown here be seen as going against social norms about how children should be treated in Britain today?

2 How could the examples shown above be used to support the idea that childhood is socially constructed?

The emergence of modern childhood

Many sociologists and historians argue that it has only been in modern times and in Western societies that children have become separated from the adult world; for example, children have been excluded from the world of work and confined to educational institutions. There are also specific foods, clothes and leisure activities aimed at children. Families have become more **child-centred**. Instead of children being regarded as there to serve the needs of adults, families revolve around children's needs. A far greater proportion of family income is now spent on children, to the extent that many parents will make considerable sacrifices for their children's welfare. Parents, especially fathers, also spend more time in actively parenting children than they did in the past.

A number of changes in society have been identified by sociologists as contributing to the emergence of this modern attitude to childhood:

- **Smaller families.** More love, attention and financial resources can be lavished on each individual child.

- **Shorter working hours.** Parents, especially fathers, have more time to spend with their children.
- **Greater affluence.** Improved living standards and higher wages mean that there is more disposable income to spend on children.
- **The extension of education.** Education only became compulsory in England in the 1880s; before that, many working-class children were sent out to work from an early age. Since then, the school-leaving age has risen from 10 to 16 and young people are now obliged by law to continue in some kind of education or training until 18. This extends the period of children being dependent on parents for much longer and also further separates children from the adult world.
- **Social policy.** Successive governments have given ever greater emphasis to child welfare. This can be seen in the range of benefits designed to assist parents in maintaining and caring for children. It can also be seen in greater emphasis on child protection, as is evident in the willingness of social workers to remove children from families where they are abused or neglected.

- **Children's rights.** The United Nations Convention on the Rights of the Child (1989) extended the idea of human rights to suggest that children had specific rights in addition to those of adults. In the UK, the 1989 and 2004 Children Acts established legal rights for children in the UK. For example, in divorce cases, courts must give priority to the needs and wishes of children in making decisions about where they will live and access to each parent.

- **Child experts.** Since the nineteenth century, a range of medical, psychological and educational experts have put forward scientific theories about how children should be brought up. Children are no longer seen as simply naturally developing into adults, but as having special needs, and parenting is seen as a skill that parents must learn. Parents are increasingly turning to childcare books written by such specialists as well as websites where they can exchange ideas and experiences with other parents. There are also TV programmes such as *Supernanny* that offer role models and guidance to parents.

- **Concerns about children.** Parents (and society more generally) have become much more concerned about threats to children due to risks of accidents but also because of fears about 'stranger danger' and paedophiles. Some sociologists, such as Frank Furedi (2001) (see also the Activity in page 105), have argued that this is largely a moral panic encouraged by the media, and that parents' fears are largely unjustified. However, one consequence is that children have become more closely supervised by parents and are less likely to have the freedom to play outside without restrictions. Hugh Cunningham (2007) suggests that the 'home habitat' of typical eight-year-olds (the area in which they are able to travel on their own) has shrunk to one-ninth of its previous size in the last 25 years.

- **Children as consumers.** Big business has created a consumer market targeted at children. Not only toys and games but also foods, clothes and leisure activities aimed at children have become important. Children play a big role in families' spending decisions, using 'pester power' to encourage parents to buy them sweets, toys, computer games and mobile phones. According to an article in the *Telegraph* (17 October 2013), parents spend around £460 a year on average on things they do not need after giving in to the pestering of their children. Sweets, snacks and junk food were among the most popular items, with four in ten pestering their parents for treats.

Power relations between parents and children

Because of such changes, it can be argued that the balance of power between parents and children has shifted. Families have become more democratic not only in relationships between women and men, but also in relationships between parents and children; for example, children have more rights and are given greater protection by the law. Children have also become the centre of family life, having more money spent on them than ever before.

Against this, it could be argued that in a number of respects children are still far from equal with adults in most families. Some sociologists even refer to the idea of **age patriarchy** to describe the idea that adults are more powerful than children and young people:

- Children are still financially dependent on parents as they cannot enter full-time work until at least 16 and usually do not earn an adult wage until even later.
- While the law offers rights and protection to children, it also gives parents authority over their children; for example, parents are given the responsibility for ensuring their children attend school.
- Children still do not receive full adult rights until they are 18; for example, they cannot vote in elections and the world they inhabit (for example, in schools) is largely one created by adults over which they have little control.
- Children can be seen to have more influence over decision-making in families, such as in relation to consumer spending. However, many parents make major decisions such as moving house or separating from one another with little reference to their children.
- Many children also suffer abuse at the hands of family members or other adults (see the Study on page 106).

For some commentators, the idea that the experience of childhood has improved for most children over the last 100 years is a myth. According to Sue Palmer (2007), many children now experience what she calls **toxic childhood** because children are being damaged by a diet of junk food, excessive exposure to computer games and a lack of love or discipline from parents forced to work long hours outside the home.

Child Abuse and Neglect in the UK today – Radford *et al.* (2011)

The following are the main findings of a report for the NSPCC based on a survey of around 6,000 children.

- Children can experience a range of forms of abuse, including physical, emotional and sexual abuse, as well as neglect of their basic needs such as adequate food, clothing and warmth.
- One in five children have experienced severe maltreatment.
- Children abused by parents or carers are almost three times more likely to also witness family violence.
- One in 20 children have been sexually abused and one in three children sexually abused by an adult did not tell anyone at the time.
- All types of abuse and neglect are associated with poorer mental health.
- Strong associations were found between maltreatment, sexual abuse, physical violence and poorer emotional wellbeing, including self-harm and suicidal thoughts.

Diversity in childhood experiences

It is important to note that the changes summarised above are broad trends. There is also considerable diversity is the experiences of children:

- **Social class.** According to official government statistics, there are 3.5 million children (27 per cent of children) living in poverty in the UK today (DWP 2013). According to Julia Margo and Mike Dixon (2006), wealthier parents often spend considerable amounts of their income on activities such as dance or music lessons for their children and emphasise the need for children to attend organised activities such as sports clubs or Scouts and Guides. Poorer children are likely to have a much more restricted range of activities and may be forced to take part-time jobs to pay for the things they want.
- **Gender.** Childhood, like other areas of society, remains heavily gendered. Parents still tend to socialise children very differently in terms of gender, such as the toys that children are given, expectations about girls' and boys' contribution to household chores and the greater protectiveness and restriction on freedom that many parents show towards girls compared to boys.
- **Ethnicity.** Ghazala Bhatti (1999) observed that Asian children are generally more strictly brought up than most other ethnic groups. In most Asian families there is a strong emphasis on *izzat*, or family honour, and bad behaviour by children is seen as reflecting on the whole family. Asian girls in particular are likely to be more closely supervised by parents and brothers. According to Ravinder Barn

(2006), black, Pakistani and Bangladeshi families in the UK are also likely to be associated with low incomes, unemployment and poor housing, which often leads to difficulties in raising children. However, among all minority ethnic groups, extended families appear to be an important source of support.

Changes in parenting

According to Deborah Chambers (2012), ideas about 'good parenting' began to change in the period after the 1970s for two reasons: firstly, the growth of employment of women with children and secondly, the rise in divorce rates. She suggests that this has led to a good deal of public debate about parenting. However, at the same time, roles of men and women in two-parent families remain strongly gendered, meaning that couples often still fall into traditional roles as mothers and fathers.

Motherhood

Jane Ribbens McCarthy and her colleagues (2003) argue that women still feel that they need to conform to traditional norms about what constitutes a 'good mother', and this includes making sure that children also receive 'good fathering'. Mothers are still perceived as the ones who have the ultimate responsibility for emotionally stabilising families and keeping the whole family together. When families do break up and mothers try to bring children up alone, it is they who are often branded by the media as 'scroungers' and 'bad parents'.

Activity: Changing childhoods

Item A: The commercialisation of childhood

Item B: Pester power

Item C: The rise of the child expert

Item D: Fears over children

IN THE NEWS

HUNDREDS OF CHILD ABUSERS ARRESTED IN POLICE SWOOP

- SUSPECTS HELD IN RAIDS ACROSS UK

Item E: Paranoid parents

'Back in my childhood, the expression "over-protective parent' was used as a criticism, but today it's seen as a responsibility', says Frank Furedi, Professor of Sociology at Kent University. He wrote *Paranoid Parenting* in 2001, prompted by the countless warnings of risk he received from health and local authorities as soon as Jacob, his only child, was born. But the risk of abduction or harm is tiny, he says – certainly less than that of taking a child on a car trip.

Since he first wrote the book, the 'idiotic' has become the norm; safety measures preventing parents from taking photographs of their children at school, or stopping them from playing conkers, or from going anywhere near a public bonfire on 5 November, are common.

'All these things that are important aspects of kids' lives are being gradually undermined. There's also an increasing mistrust of adults, where they are no longer allies but potential enemies.' Furedi points to our automatic assumption that adult interest in children is suspicious or sexually motivated, something that research has indicated does not exist to the same extent in other countries. It's so pervasive that sometimes he can't help feeling it, too.

> *'I remember going to the gym with my son when he was six or seven and there was this guy taking a lot of interest in him. I remember saying to myself, "What the hell's going on here?" But then I had a reality check and realised that he was behaving normally, and if I'd been my father, in his time, he'd have just viewed it as a friendly gesture and welcomed the interest that was being shown.'*

What we need, he says, is a cultural change where we regard childhood differently, where adults are allowed to hug children, but also to have responsibility for them; looking after them if they look in trouble, telling them off if they're behaving antisocially. That way, children would be less fearful and become more engaged in adult ideas of social responsibility, and adults would tune their emotional radar to real sources of concern, rather than having to rely on criminal record checks.

Child safety in numbers

- 11.7m under 16s in England and Wales
- 68 children were abducted by strangers in 2002–03
- 166 children are killed on the road every year
- 96 children drowned in 2002
- 917,498 children were injured in falls in 2002

Source: Adapted from Crompton (2008)

1 Examine Items A–D. What changes in childhood does each image suggest?
2 How might each of these changes affect the way parents treat their children?
3 Study Item E. Why does Frank Furedi argue that many parents have become 'paranoid'?
4 To what extent do you agree with Furedi? Refer to the statistics quoted in the article in your answer.

Shelley Park, in *Mothering Queerly, Queering Motherhood* (2014), points out that a significant minority of children are now raised by more than one mother figure. However, she criticises what she calls the **ideology of monomaternalism**, the dominant view in society that children can have one – and only one – 'real mother'. Park points out that many contemporary families do not fit this view:

- Children may be raised by a foster or adoptive mother while also having a biological mother.
- Children may have a biological mother and a step-mother if they are part of a reconstituted family.
- They may be brought up by two mothers in a same-sex relationship.
- They may be brought up in a polygamous family, where mothering is shared between two or more wives of the same husband.

In all of these cases, monomaternalism tends to undermine the ability of other women to share in mothering children because one mother tends to be portrayed as not a real mother. In criticism of Park, it could be argued that it is still comparatively rare for children in the UK to have two mothers due to same-sex parenting or polygamy; monomaternalism may therefore simply reflect the reality of the majority of families.

Fatherhood

Linked to ideas about good mothers are ideas about 'good fathers'. Traditionally, fatherhood has been strongly linked to the role of the male breadwinner. However, a number of changes have also brought this into question:

- **Higher divorce rates.** Men often have more limited contact with their children following divorce, and sometimes lose contact altogether. It is estimated that as many as a quarter of divorced fathers have not seen their children in the previous year and just under half have not paid any child maintenance in the previous year.
- **New concepts of masculinity.** Some sociologists have referred to the rise of the 'new man', often seen to be exemplified by celebrities like David Beckham. New men are seen to be more willing to display their emotions and take an equal responsibility for childcare.
- **Changing patterns of male employment.** There has been a decline in jobs involving heavy physical labour in industries such as manufacturing and mining. As a result, in some parts of the UK there have been high levels of long-term male unemployment. In other instances men have moved into what were traditionally perceived as feminine jobs in the service sector, such as offices and call centres.

A study by Anne Gray (2006) found that many fathers emphasised the need to spend quality time with their children. Fathers viewed time spent with their children on outings, sport, play and conversation as expressions of fatherhood rather than as domestic work. However, many fathers also felt the pressure of long hours at work meant that they were not able to be involved with their children as much as they would have liked. Similarly, Esther Dermott (2003) carried out in-depth interviews with 25 fathers and commented on how many of the men insisted that they wanted a closer and more intimate relationship with their children than they had had with their own fathers.

Study

Time budget diaries – Sevilla (2014)

In 2014 Dr Almudena Sevilla announced the findings of her research based on time budget diaries, showing that fathers spend seven times as much time interacting with their children than their own fathers did with them 40 years ago (McVeigh and Finch, 15 June 2014). The average is fairly low at 35 minutes a day for working fathers, but it is far higher than the five minutes registered in 1974. Mothers' quality time with their children has also risen over the same period, from 15 minutes a day to an hour. Sevilla did, however, note that well-educated middle-class parents were much more likely spend time with their children.

Fathers are now legally entitled to two weeks' paid paternity leave and up to four weeks' unpaid paternity leave. Fathers and mothers can also now share parental leave of up to 52 weeks. A study by Michael Thompson and his colleagues (2005) on 1,200 working fathers of infants aged between 3 and 15 months concluded that new dads are more willing than ever to combine work with staying at home looking after the children. Almost eight out of ten working fathers revealed that they would be happy to stay at home and look after their baby, while nine in ten felt as confident as their partner when caring for their child. Overall, the average amount of leave taken by fathers was slightly more than the statutory paternity leave entitlement – two-thirds of fathers take paternity leave.

There is therefore a range of evidence to suggest that important changes are taking place in ideas of fatherhood with many fathers becoming more involved with their children. However, there is still some way to go before fathers can be said to be taking an equal share in parenting. There are several reasons for this:

- Fathers still spend considerably less time on parenting than mothers.
- There is considerable diversity in the involvement of fathers, as the study carried out by Hatter *et al.* (2002) for the EOC shows (see Item B in the Activity on page 108).
- Many fathers are still constrained by long working hours and limited access to parental leave and flexible working, meaning that they may not be able to spend more time on parenting even if they wish to.
- High rates of separation and divorce mean that many fathers lose contact with their children or only have relatively restricted access to them.

Grandparents

According to June Statham (2011), grandparent care can take many forms, from occasional babysitting through regular help with childcare, to being the sole or main provider of childcare while parents work, or living with their grandchildren in multi-generation households. Grandparents may also care for grandchildren whose parents are unable or unwilling to do so. An HSBC report (2007) costed the amount that parents would spend on childcare (allowing for a proportion who would otherwise use nannies and other more expensive forms of childcare) if they did not use grandparents at a staggering £50 billion. According to Grandparentsplus (2009), grandparents also tend to be more flexible. They are often asked to fill the gaps between formal childcare and parental care. They will also care for a child who is sick when a nursery would refuse to have them. Nurseries, extended schools and childminders tend not to work beyond 6pm. For parents who work shifts or irregular hours, formal childcare simply is not enough. Grandparents also provide an important source of support to parents and grandchildren at times of family break-up.

Though grandparents play a significant role in many children's lives, Deborah Chambers (2013) highlights some issues in relation to this:

- Grandparenting is still very gendered, with grandmothers generally playing a larger role than grandfathers in line with the gendered nature of other aspects of family life. This would support the feminist view of other aspects of family life.

- Many grandparents today are still in employment or, if retired, may have active social lives and are not always able or willing to play an active part in their grandchildren's lives.
- Extended families are now often dispersed over geographical distances, meaning that grandparents are not always in a position to give regular practical help.
- Rising rates of divorce and relationship breakdown mean that grandparents may lose contact with grandchildren. As most children tend to live with mothers after a family break-up, it is usually paternal grandparents who are most affected by this. Maternal grandparents are more likely to be involved in offering support to their daughter and grandchildren following separation or divorce.

Activity: Changing fatherhood

Item A: Different styles of fatherhood

Modern dads range from the 'Enforcer Dad' to the 'Fully Involved Dad'.

Item B: The 'Dads on Dads' study

It's official: there are four types of father. Modern dads range from a dying breed of older disciplinarians, to classic 'new men' who will happily share household chores with their partners, according to the government body set up to promote gender equality.

The four categories of father are identified in a revealing study of the changing patterns of family life in modern Britain by the Equal Opportunities Commission (Hatter *et al.* 2002). First up is the 'Enforcer Dad': the traditionalist with a penchant for strict rules and pocket-money rations who believes his purpose is to provide a stern role model.

'Entertainer Dads' see themselves as the clowns of the family, with a duty to keep their children amused while their mothers do the cleaning and ironing.

Then come the 'Useful Dads' who, while they seldom take the initiative when it comes to domestic tasks, are at least willing to pitch in.

Finally, there are the growing number of 'Fully Involved Dads': progressives who share responsibility for mundane chores on an equal basis with their partners.

The study, which involved in-depth interviews with 60 fathers and their partners, suggests that British men have undergone a profound shift over the past 40 years away from the traditional role of the 'head of the family'. However, it stresses that, in practice, most modern men still see themselves as breadwinners, because the pace of reform has not caught up with the change in their attitudes and behaviour.

Source: Adapted from Morrison (2002)

1. How does Item B suggest:
   a) that there is diversity in patterns of fatherhood as in other aspects of family life?
   b) that traditional attitudes to fatherhood remain dominant in many families?
2. What sociological explanations could be given for the fact that only a minority of fathers appear to be 'fully involved dads'?

Section summary

Fill in the blanks, using the words given below.

Functionalist sociologists see the roles played by men and women in families as naturally different and complementary. Parsons argues that nuclear families work best when women perform the _____ role and men perform the _____ role. However, some sociologists have argued that we are seeing a shift from _____ to _____ as men and women start to share childrearing and domestic responsibilities. Young and Willmott described such families where couples share their work as _____ families.

For feminists, both of these perspectives present too positive a view of the family and they point to the _____ of the family whereby women are often oppressed by men and even subjected to violence and abuse. Some feminists argue that the growing employment of women has simply created a _____, whereby women still have to carry out most of the unpaid domestic work alongside their paid work. Duncombe and Marsden take this even further, arguing that women perform a _____ of paid work, housework and _____. Jonathan Gershuny, however, argues that couples are going through a process of _____ whereby it will take a generation for men to change their roles and work patterns in order to catch up with the changes in women's roles. _____ surveys based on couples keeping diaries of their daily activities also reveal that when hours of paid and unpaid work are added together, there is little difference between the sexes.

Some sociologists have also examined other aspects of gender inequalities in family life. For example, Hardhill *et al.* found that among dual-career families the needs of men often took precedence over those of women in _____. Pahl's research into _____ similarly found that it was often men who controlled the financial decisions of couples.

Some sociologists studying childhood have argued that families have become more _____; for example, more of the money in families is spent on children's needs. It has also been argued that children increasingly use _____ in order to persuade parents to give them the things that they want. However, other sociologists argue that our society is still based on _____, whereby adults have power over children. Sue Palmer also argues that children suffer from _____ because they are overdosed on junk food and computer games.

The role of parents has changed too according to some sociologists; fathers in particular can be seen to play a bigger part in the lives of their children, partly because of _____. Many children also have close relationships with grandparents but grandparenting, like many aspects of family life, can be seen to be very _____, with grandmothers often taking on much more responsibility than grandfathers.

age patriarchy, child-centred, decision-making, dual burden, emotion work, expressive, gendered, instrumental, joint conjugal roles, lagged adaptation, money management, new forms of masculinity, patriarchal nature, pester power, segregated conjugal roles, symmetrical, time budget, toxic childhood, triple shift

Practice questions

1 Outline and explain two reasons for the increase in the number of divorces in the UK since the 1960s. [12]

2 Explain and briefly evaluate the view that the nuclear family serves the needs of capitalism. [16]

3 Assess the view that the nuclear family can no longer be seen as the normal family in UK society. [24]

4 Outline and explain two reasons why the role of grandparents in families may have become more significant in recent years. [12]

5 Explain and briefly evaluate the view that the role of fathers in families has changed in recent years. [16]

6 Assess the view that the family remains a patriarchal institution. [24]

Chapter 4

Youth subcultures

4.1 How and why are youth culture and subcultures formed?

Getting you thinking ...

1 What do you understand by the term 'youth'? Write a definition of 'youth'.
2 Write a description of a 'typical youth'. What characteristics do they have?
3 Are you a 'typical youth'?

Introducing youth subcultures: What do we mean by 'youth'?

Biological changes happen during teenage years, which start to change us from children into adults. Some argue that these changes, with all the hormones related to them, affect the period known as 'youth'. So the biological changes can explain any rebellious behaviour and conflict.

However, sociologists do not agree that biology has much to do with our ideas of youth; they point out that 'youth' varies between cultures and time periods. Thus, according to sociologists, 'youth' is socially constructed. This means that it does not exist in an objective way; it is created by society. Different societies construct 'youth' differently, as with all age-related categories.

Quick question

When do you think youth starts and ends in UK culture?

It is very hard to give an accurate or definitive answer to the above question, as ideas about youth in the UK are constantly shifting. Youth is often seen to correspond to teenage years, but some argue it begins earlier than this, and possibly extends into the early twenties. The term 'tweenagers' is used to describe children of about 7–12. They have already started to focus on pop culture and imitating adult celebrities. Postman (1982) discusses the 'disappearance of childhood', and blames the media for exposing children to the adult world too young and sexualising them.

So 'youth' is beginning earlier and earlier, but is also being stretched at the other end. Nowadays people are staying in education for longer and marrying and starting families later, so 'youth' could be said to continue well into the twenties.

Activity: Youth as a social construct

Item A: Initiation rites

In some societies, the transition from childhood to adulthood is almost instantaneous, often marked by a ritual of some kind. This may involve a 'test', such as proving 'manhood' in a battle or surviving in the wilderness alone. In such cultures, there is usually no concept of 'youth' as an interim phase.

Item B: Inevitable trouble?

The idea of 'youth' as a separate age group is a relatively new one in the UK, which has developed since the Second World War. It can be partly linked to the development and extension of compulsory education. Previously, many of those in their teenage years would have left school at 14 and be working to bring money in to the family.

The youth phase is often also characterised by conflict with adults, particularly parents, and this is often seen as a 'normal' part of growing up. However, other cultures challenge the idea that the emotional turmoil associated with youth is 'natural'. Margaret Mead's study (1928) of Samoan culture suggested that very little trauma is associated with adolescence, and the transition to adulthood is unremarkable.

1 How do Items A and B back up the view that youth is socially constructed?

Item C

Despite the difficulties in clearly defining the period of 'youth', it is argued that there is a 'youth culture' in the UK. The concept of youth culture suggests that all youths share a particular set of norms and values that are distinct from those of adults or children.

Activity

Considering youth culture in the UK

1 Do you think that 'youth culture' exists? Do youths in the UK share distinct norms and values that are different from children and adults?

2 Using the categories below, give some specific examples of norms and values that are specific to youth culture in the UK (i.e., different to other age groups):

a) dress/fashion
b) music
c) speech/slang ('argot')
d) interests
e) consumption patterns.

Other specific features that distinguish youth include:

- their involvement in education rather than work
- their lack of responsibilities (for bills, rent, children, and so on)
- the importance of the peer group.

What do we mean by 'youth subcultures'?

Quick question

Do you remember what a subculture is? (Clue: think back to Chapter 1.)

A subculture is often defined as a culture within a culture, which has its own distinct norms and values, as well as being part of the wider culture.

Youth subcultures are distinctive groups of youths, within the wider youth culture, who stand out in terms of their style, dress, music taste and attitudes. Many distinct youth subcultures have been identified.

Quick question

Can you name any distinct youth subcultures, from the present day or from the past?

'Spectacular' youth subcultures

This is a term that has been used by sociologists to describe some of the highly visible subcultures of the 1950s–1970s, such as Teddy Boys, mods, punks and skinheads. These subcultures had very flamboyant and instantly recognisable styles, and often had confrontational attitudes. They have particularly been studied by the Centre for Contemporary Cultural Studies (CCCS) at Birmingham University.

Theoretical views of the role and formation of youth culture and subcultures

Functionalism

For functionalists, as sociologists who see society as being based on consensus, it is very important that individuals feel integrated into society; they must feel that they belong to communities and social groups within society, so they feel social solidarity with others and learn to share the value consensus. If people are not socially integrated, they will be isolated, and anomie will result – where people have no sense of belonging and lack shared norms and values.

Functionalists see youth as a transitional stage from childhood to adulthood. Children experience social integration through their families, and adults create their own families when they have children and also experience integration through their work. As they seek independence from their families, youths get their sense of belonging from their peers.

Talcott Parsons (1962) argued that 'youth' as a social category only emerged due to changes in the family associated with the development of capitalism. In pre-capitalist societies, the transition from childhood to adulthood is/was marked by an initiation or rite of passage of some kind, as we have seen with the Hamar tribe in Chapter 1 (see page 3). Other less dramatic examples would have existed even in Western societies in the period before capitalism, such as marriage and childbearing. Thus, an extended period of 'youth' did not occur.

Activity

Researching youth subcultures

1 Conduct some research on a particular 'spectacular subculture'. Possible subcultures to research are:
Teddy Boys, mods, rockers, skinheads, hippies, punks, goths, ravers, emos, grungers, new romantics, heavy metal/metal heads
or any others you can think of.

Use the internet, but also consider asking friends or family who may have belonged to, or may still belong to, one of these subcultures. Try to find pictures or even video clips of your chosen subcultures.

Areas to focus on:
- time period
- style/fashion
- music
- gender issues
- class issues
- drugs
- attitudes/views.

Present your findings to your class or group.

However, the development of capitalism created a divide between the role of the family, as a purely nurturing environment, and the specialised requirements of the workplace. This required a period of training and socialisation for young people not previously required – when they could learn the skills required of them as adults, which would not have been taught to them in the family itself. The expansion of compulsory education and training filled this gap, but the period of time this covered included the age when previously people would have already embarked upon their 'adult' lives. Parsons (1942) saw youth as an important transitional stage during a potentially stressful time where an individual must learn to leave the security of the family and become an independent person in terms of occupational status and marriage. It is important that individuals break the ties with their parents (childhood) and develop the independence to start their own families (adulthood). Youths start to become independent from their parents, often getting part-time jobs and spending more and more time away from their family. This gives them experience of independence, and develops skills such as responsibility and money management. So Parsons sees youth culture as a 'rite of passage' that individuals must go through between childhood and adulthood.

Similarly, Eisenstadt (1956) saw youth culture as a way of bringing young people into society. During this isolated phase between childhood and adulthood, there could be a risk of feelings of stress and anomie. This is where youth culture becomes very important, providing a shared set of norms and values with peers, and a sense of belonging. Youth culture can also provide a safe outlet for the tensions that the transition from childhood to adulthood might bring, allowing young people to 'let off steam', find their own opinions and get any frustrations 'out of their system' in an acceptable way. This period of rebellion is accepted and tolerated as a 'normal' and essential part of growing up, and is usually just put down to 'high spirits' or 'hormones'. However, for functionalists, it is also a way of testing boundaries, experimentation and reinforcing acceptable norms and values, and thus will ultimately contribute to social order.

Most functionalists were writing in the 1950s, when a distinct youth culture had just started to emerge. They recognised that the particular social conditions of that time made the transition from childhood to adulthood particularly noticeable. The media was developing, young people had more job opportunities and money in their pockets, and consumerism was taking off. Thus a highly visible youth culture emerged. Abrams argued in *The Teenage Consumer* (1959) that the emergence of youth culture was linked to their emergence as a distinct group with spending power who started to be targeted by businesses and the media. So Abrams believed that youth culture was actually created by the media.

Evaluation of the functionalist view

Functionalists were generalising about youth culture as a whole, and did not account for individual subcultural differences between youths. Some key distinctions that other sociologists have found within youth culture, or between youth subcultures, on grounds of social class, race and gender, were not considered by functionalists. For example, neo-Marxists focused on the impact of social class on the development of distinct youth subcultures, and feminists consider gender differences in expectations relating to youth.

Most of the evidence used by functionalists for their arguments came from white, middle-class American males – much like the sociologists themselves. It is questionable whether the same transitional issues apply to youths in all Western cultures, so their analysis can be considered to be ethnocentric.

Marxism/neo-Marxism

Marxism, a theory that sees society as based on conflict rather than consensus, tends to focus more on youth subcultures than youth culture as a whole, unlike functionalism, and particularly looked at 'spectacular youth subcultures' and their reaction to and conflict with wider society.

The CCCS based at Birmingham University produced much influential work on youth subcultures in the 1960s and 1970s. Influenced by Marxism, but developing slightly different ideas, the CCCS could be seen as 'neo-Marxists' – new Marxists who took their influences from more recent Marxist thinkers such as Gramsci and his concept of 'hegemony'. By hegemony, Gramsci meant the ideological dominance or social authority that the ruling class has over the subordinate classes.

These sociologists tended to focus on social class and the economic situation faced by young people as their explanations for the formation of youth subcultures. They explained the differences between subcultures by looking at the different class and economic situations of those who joined them.

Item A: A rite of passage – the Hamar tribe initiation

Item B: A rite of passage – high-school prom

Item C: Letting off steam – binge-drinking youth

1 Do you agree that youth is a period of transition? Give examples of things experienced during 'youth' that may prepare you for adulthood and independence.
2 Is it a good thing that youths often indulge in extremes of behaviour, such as binge-drinking? How would functionalists view this?

They recognised that, despite looking and dressing differently from their parents or other youths, the members of these subcultures still faced the same experiences and social conditions facing their social class as a whole. Thus, their style could be understood as their response and solution to being part of the working class.

At times during the 1960s and 1970s, there were many social issues facing working-class youths: high unemployment, inner-city decay, racial tensions and strikes. At other times, there were much higher levels of work and disposable income available for young people. Members of the CCCS considered different subcultures and how each could be seen as a form of resistance against the ruling class and reaction to the economic situation working-class youths found themselves in.

So the neo-Marxists challenge the functionalist view of youth culture, which takes no account of the social situation and class issues facing young people. We will examine CCCS studies of subcultures in more detail in the section on social class below.

Evaluation of the Marxist/neo-Marxist view

The main criticism is that neo-Marxists were finding meanings that did not actually exist. Because they were looking for examples relating to class, they interpreted the subcultures in this way. However, to the youths themselves, their fashion and behaviour did not necessarily have this meaning. They may just have been having fun, or wanted to be like their mates.

Feminists challenge the CCCS for ignoring girls in their subcultural analyses. McRobbie and Garber were part of the CCCS, but as feminists they challenged most of the studies and produced their own analysis of female subcultures, which we will look at below.

The middle class also had subcultures – for example, hippies – and these were largely ignored by the CCCS, who saw youth subculture as working class. It could be argued that they picked subcultures to fit their analysis rather than the other way around. However, research on subcultures such as hippies and beatniks was carried out by Brake, who was part of the CCCS (Brake 1977, 1985).

Another criticism of the CCCS and other sociologists who focus on these 'spectacular youth subcultures' is that the majority of youth do not belong to a subculture at all, so they were only studying a visible minority.

The work of the CCCS, though very influential, is seen as dated now. The youth of today inhabit a very different world to that of the 1960s and 1970s and youth subcultures, if they even still exist, look very different. Some newer ideas on youth subculture have been developed by postmodernists, which we will look at below.

Feminism

Feminists argue that the role of girls in subcultures has been ignored by the other theories on youth subcultures.

McRobbie and Garber (1976) argued that girls were conspicuously absent from most research on youth subcultures. When they did appear, it was fleeting, or it reinforced stereotypical views of girls, often just presenting them as the passive 'girlfriends' of the male subculture members, or commenting on their attractiveness. The argument sometimes presented is

that studying girls was not seen as interesting, since girls did not do interesting things. Researchers at this time were also mostly male, thus it is suggested that they may have developed a rapport with their male subjects and found it much more problematic to relate to the teenage girls who were around. McRobbie and Garber argued that girls negotiate different spaces to those inhabited by boys and their friendship groups are often very close-knit. Thus, girls are important, if difficult, to study in their own right. Previous theories of 'youth' were developed to understand male subcultures, but were then presented as theories of all youth. However, such theories do not necessarily apply to girls.

> **Quick question**
>
> Do you agree that peer groups of girls and boys are different, and socialise differently?

In the decades since McRobbie and Garber's work, more feminist researchers have studied young females and their subcultures. We will look in more detail at some feminist studies of youth subcultures in the section on gender below.

Evaluation of the feminist view

Recent developments (e.g., postmodernism) may mean that gender is less significant, and that current subcultures do not have any clear gender distinctions, so feminist analysis is less relevant.

Postmodernism

Since the 1990s, most sociological studies on youth subcultures have been based on postmodern ideas, arguing that youth culture has become increasingly fragmented and diverse.

Youth styles are now much more fluid and changeable, and are eclectic – mixing things from many different sources, and crossing over ethnic, gender and class divides.

One example is research into 'club cultures' of the late 1980s and 1990s, largely carried out by the MIPS (Manchester Institute of Popular Culture). Though not necessarily defined as postmodernist, the MIPS research on club cultures links to postmodernism, because among the clubbers, no clear gender, class or ethnic distinctions could be found; they were very diverse. The MIPS research also emphasises the role of the media as an integral part of club cultures.

'The social logic of subcultural capital' – Thornton (1995b)

Sarah Thornton, in defining club culture, argues that it is not a single culture, but a cluster of subcultures related to dance and rave. She says that club cultures are 'taste cultures', with the key definer being a shared taste in music style and the dance culture surrounding it.

Thornton is influenced by Bourdieu (see page 26), and coins the term 'subcultural capital', as a variation on 'cultural capital'. Having subcultural capital is about 'being in the know about what is "in" or "out" on the subcultural scene' (1995b: 11). She argues that clubbers use this subcultural capital to gain status and distinguish themselves from those who are just mainstream followers, defining themselves as more 'authentic'. The media can be seen as a source of subcultural capital, so plays a more significant role in the development of these club cultures.

Like Thornton, Redhead (1990) argues that the idea of authentic subcultures that develop outside of media influence could no longer be sustained from the 1980s onwards, and that subcultures, or 'club cultures', are formed within and through the media.

Today, young people can be seen as being immersed in a media-driven reality. Researchers studying the impact of 'new media' are just starting to consider the role that social media play in the lives of young people. However, it seems likely that these developments make the ideas of Thornton and Redhead (that the media drives subcultures rather than the other way around, as the CCCS argued) even more true today than when they were writing in the 1990s.

'Neo-tribes'

Maffesoli (1996) uses the term 'neo-tribe' instead of subculture. 'Neo-tribe' refers to a much more loosely organised grouping with no fixed membership or deep commitment. He argues that group identities are no longer formed along traditional social lines such as gender or class, but that young people 'flit' from tribe to tribe, dabbling in different aspects of clothing or music and then moving on. These tribes are not exclusive and the group itself is not the priority; it is used to satisfy individual needs. So a young person can be part of more than one tribe simultaneously.

Bennett (1999) supports this through his research in nightclubs in Newcastle. He found neo-tribes based around fashion, music and lifestyle, but with no shared values. Individuals mixed and matched influences and did not define themselves as members of any particular group. He argues that the idea of 'subculture' rigidly links musical and stylistic preferences, whereas neo-tribalism recognises the shifting nature and fluidity of such preferences. For example, clubbing is multidimensional, involving a series of diverse experiences for clubbers as they move between rooms or floors of clubs and engage with different crowds and music.

'Supermarket of style'

Polhemus (1994) also develops this 'fluidity' idea and writes about the 'supermarket of style', in which youths can create identities by picking and mixing from various cultures, fashions, lifestyles and music. Polhemus argues that all of the choices available today mean that commitment to any one style is less common, and young people are reluctant to give themselves labels and restrict their choices (though some individuals may still choose to do so to create a more distinct identity). Retro fashions, which plunder aspects of subcultures from the past, are common, but the entire subculture is not recreated, just parts of its fashions or music styles, mixed in with other things.

So for postmodernists, style is more important than substance, and fluidity and choice are central for today's youth.

Evaluation of the postmodernist view

There are still some distinct youth subcultures, with clear style and music allegiances – for example, goths and emos – so not everyone mixes styles.

The idea of 'ordinary youth' with which we criticised the CCCS could also be applied to postmodern views – are most young people members, however loosely, of neo-tribes? Or do they just get on with their lives and have a laugh with their friends? Also consider the work of Hollands and Chatterton in the Activity on page 117; they argue that youth culture today is largely 'mainstream' and corporate.

Postmodernists accept the key role that the media has in driving subcultures, but within this, are individuals really exercising choice? Or are these 'neo-tribes' and 'club cultures' actually artificial and media-driven?

The mixed-up, fluid world of neo-tribes in which everyone is equal is not true for many groups of young people, who may still divide themselves clearly on gender or ethnic lines.

Activity: Subcultural capital and corporate youth culture

Item A: Subcultural capital

'Just as cultural capital is personified in "good" manners and urbane conversation, so subcultural capital is embodied in the form of being "in the know", using (but not overusing) current slang and looking as if you were born to perform the latest dance styles. ... Nothing depletes (subcultural) capital more than the sight of someone trying too hard. For example, fledgling clubbers ... will often reveal their inexperience by overdressing ...'

Thornton (1995a)

Item B: Corporate youth culture

Hollands and Chatterton (2002) challenge the prevalence of 'neo-tribes'. They argue that rather than 'a free-floating "pick and mix" story of youth consumption in the night-time economy' (2002: 9), the majority of youth activity is characterised by commercial chart music, a drinking culture and pleasure-seeking behaviour, which are addressed by corporately owned chains of bars, pubs and clubs in town and city centres. They recognised that 'alternative' cultures did exist, with independently run venues catering for less mainstream tastes, but these tended to be on the outskirts of towns and cities.

1 Do you recognise Thornton's concept of 'subcultural capital' (Item A) within your own social group? Are some of your peers more 'in the know' and do some 'try too hard'? Is it valued, or seen as important?

2 Are you part of a 'neo-tribe' or does Hollands and Chatterton's description of the night-time culture in your local town or city (Item B) sound more relevant to your social life? Is it 'cool' to be mainstream?

The political motivation behind youth subcultures that the CCCS presented has been lost in the postmodern analyses, in which youth are presented as individualistic and motivated by pleasure. However, there are still oppositional and protest-driven subcultures today, some much more overt than the subcultures of the 1960s – for example, eco and anti-capitalist groups. St John (2003) discusses 'post-rave technotribes', groups of young people often brought together through music festivals and social media, committed to dance music and hedonism but incorporating resistant ideals such as social justice, green politics and human rights, thus showing commitment to pleasure and politics.

Subcultures as related to social class

In the very influential publication called *Resistance through Rituals* (1976), and then in several follow-up studies, such as Hebdige's *Subculture: The Meaning of Style* (1979), several neo-Marxist sociologists from the CCCS analysed various 'spectacular youth subcultures' in terms of their social class situation.

Study

Resistance through Rituals – Hall and Jefferson (eds) (1976)

Within this collection from the CCCS, several 'spectacular subcultures' were separately analysed.

John Clarke: Skinheads

Clarke argued that skinhead culture represented an exaggerated version of working-class masculinity. They wore an extreme form of manual workers' clothes, consisting of rolled-up jeans, braces and big boots, often with steel toe-caps. Their attitude was macho, aggressive and often racist. Clarke argued that these youths felt that their working-class identity was under threat due to the economic conditions, so were over-exaggerating it as a form of resistance.

Phil Cohen also looked at skinheads. He argued that as a result of their feelings of being threatened (for example, by the decline of working-class industries and increasing immigration), skinheads often focused on reclaiming territory. This was often shown through football hooliganism, as an expression of ownership of the ground and the surrounding area.

Tony Jefferson: Teddy Boys

The Teddy Boys, by contrast, emerged at a time in the 1950s of high employment and relative affluence. However, they had often been excluded from this general affluence, not having done well at school, and with only dead-end futures to look forward to. They had nowhere to go, so used to hang around in large groups in local cafés. They wore Edwardian-style, brightly coloured jackets, suede shoes and bootlace ties. Jefferson argued that the jackets symbolised that they were trying to be like their middle-class superiors, and the ties were like those worn by cowboys in Western films, who represented cool role models.

Dick Hebdige: Mods

Though mods were working class, they were a more affluent group, who used their money to create a style that was a resistance against the middle class, showing that they too could be smart and cool with their Italian suits and scooters.

In a later work, Hebdige (1979) used the term 'bricolage' to describe some of punk culture, referring to punks' reuse of ordinary objects, putting them together in a new way – for example, wearing ripped clothes and piercing their bodies and clothing with safety pins. Bin liners became tops, bondage and fetish clothes were worn as everyday items, and hair was coloured and shaped in extreme ways. Punk emerged as a resistance against the dominance of the mainstream media and fashion industries, which were telling youth how to be. It attracted working-class, disaffected youth, and also college students who were attracted to its energy. Punk also had clear political elements, with bands like The Sex Pistols and The Clash singing about poverty and smashing the system.

So overall, the CCCS analyses suggested that social class and feelings of deprivation and frustration are what lead young people to form subcultures, and that slightly different economic situations can explain the differences between them. They saw youth subcultures as a form of 'resistance' to the capitalist system, and against their social class deprivation, and saw their rituals of fashion, music and attitude as the way in which they expressed this resistance.

The CCCS were not that positive about the outcome, though. Brake (1980) argued that these solutions were 'magical', symbolic solutions, rather than practical, concrete solutions, to the problems faced by the working-class youths. Being in the subculture may have given youths a collective identity and feelings of strength and power, and even made them feel like they were fighting back, but eventually most would end up conforming to the adult world as they submitted to society's social control.

Hebdige (1979) used the concept 'incorporation' to describe how these subversive styles are often taken over by the media and fashion industries, and 'incorporated' into the mainstream, so lose their edge and element of rebellion. So 'punk' clothes find their way into high-street stores, and the styles lose their edge and distinctiveness, eventually fading away.

Activity: Resistance through rituals

Item A: Cultural responses of the Teds

'Despite periodic unemployment, despite the unskilled jobs, Teds, in common with other teenagers at work during this period, were relatively affluent. ... Teds thus certainly had money to spend and, because it was practically all they had, it assumed a crucial importance. Much of the money went on clothes: the Teddy boy "uniform". I see this choice of uniform as, initially, an attempt to buy status (since the clothes chosen were originally worn by upper-class dandies).'

Jefferson (1976: 83–4)

Activity: Resistance through rituals (continued)

Item B: The skinheads and the 'magical recovery of community'

'The preoccupation in skinhead culture with territory, with football and "fanship", and with a particular kind of masculinity thus represents what Clarke calls their "magical recovery of community".'

Clarke (1976: 99)

1 Can you apply the ideas of Jefferson about the Teds' choice of clothes, and of Clarke about the skinheads' preoccupation with territory, to any youth subcultures today?

However, Thornton (1995a) appears to challenge the ideas of the CCCS and the significance of social class as an element of youth subcultures. In her work on club cultures, she argues that because youth are largely exempt from adult financial commitments, such as bills and mortgages or rent, that the vast majority, from whatever class background, do enjoy disposable income, and a short period of freedom from those adult responsibilities to enjoy it. So though she accepts that youth unemployment and poverty are widespread, she argues that all but the very poorest can partake in club culture.

Subcultures as related to gender

Most theories of youth, and examples of youth subcultures, focus on males.

Thornton (1995b) points out that because girls had less disposable income, marrying earlier and earning less than their male counterparts, the 'teenage market' was dominated by boys, particularly in the days of the spectacular subcultures studied by the CCCS. Thornton argues that girls invested more of their time and energy into doing well at school, while boys were investing time and money in music magazines and going out, leading to a difference in their 'subcultural capital'. She argues that girls accept their lack of subcultural capital, defending their taste

in pop music 'with expressions like "I know it's crap but I like it"' (Thornton 1995b: 204). 'Mainstream' culture is often looked down on by those with subcultural capital, and when a style moves from being underground and 'hip' to being mainstream, it becomes 'feminised'. Thornton gives the example of the acid house/rave culture of the late 1980s and early 1990s, which lost its underground status as legal raves sprung up and the scene was characterised by 'techno Traceys', dancing around their handbags. This links with the feminist argument that things associated with females are often characterised as somehow less important or acceptable than things associated with males.

Active girls?

In her later work, McRobbie (1991) accepts that girls have become more active in relation to consumer culture than she had previously given them credit for. For example, she considers the change in the focus of magazines for teenage girls, which shifted from the focus on romance, which she had noted in the 1970s and 1980s, to a more self-confident sexuality. She also recognises the way that girls are active in using magazines, critiquing or even laughing at them, rather than passively accepting their content.

'Girls and subcultures' – McRobbie and Garber (1976)

Angela McRobbie and Jenny Garber were critical of the CCCS for ignoring girls, though their work was published as part of the original *Resistance through Rituals* collection.

They looked at subcultures where girls were present – for example, the 'mod girl', who, similar to her male counterpart, paid much attention to appearance and smartness. Male mods were not overtly macho, and it was a fairly androgynous subculture anyway, so female mods were more visible than in other subcultures of the time.

However, McRobbie and Garber point out that girls at this time (the 1950s) were still restricted by expectations of early marriage, had less freedom than their male counterparts and experienced stricter social control. They identified the 'teenybopper' subculture among girls in the early 1970s, and argued that this culture centred around the girls' bedrooms. McRobbie and Garber used the concept 'bedroom culture' to describe this; girls would get together and experiment with make-up, hairstyles and fashion, gossip with friends about boys and read and discuss teenage magazines. They argued that this could also be seen as a form of 'resistance', as the girls' anxieties about teenage sexual interaction led them to forming very tight-knit friendship groups, giving them a private and inaccessible space that protected them from the scrutiny of parents but also of boys. The implication of this is that one reason for the 'invisibility' of girls in work about subcultures is that they tend to spend time in their houses with their friends, rather than being very visible on street corners, so do not draw as much attention.

Point to discuss and research

1 This study is from the 1970s. Do you think it is true that girls have a 'bedroom culture' today?

Quick question

Do you agree that magazines aimed at teenage girls today encourage more self-confidence?

McRobbie (1994) also considers the intersection of gender with ethnicity, when she discusses black 'ragga' girls, who use music to dance in a sexually explicit way, ridiculing male sexism and opening up their own cultural space. This is ironic in a way, since the music they dance to is very sexist in terms of lyrics. However, the girls are able to challenge the message of the music, reclaim their sexuality and use it to assert their own identities.

Reddington (2003) argues that there have been very active female members of some of the 'spectacular subcultures', such as Vivienne Westwood, who was very influential in the punk subculture. She also points out that the punk subculture involved females from its very inception, being based on a very egalitarian ethos that anybody could do it. Punk also offered an outlet, a form of resistance, for many young women who were appalled at the idea of secretarial college or getting married. However, even within punk, female performers were often not taken seriously by reviewers, being referred to, for example, as 'punkettes', and judged on their physical appearance much more than male punk performers.

Changing roles for females in subcultures

In the more recent subcultures (1980s and 1990s), the role of girls is much more obvious. New Romantics, ravers and goths were more unisex subcultures, as are chavs and emos, even though some of the clothes may vary between the sexes. In the US and Canada, all-female subcultures were identified in the 1990s, such as the riot grrrls in the US (associated with all-female punk bands such as L7 and Bikini Kill) and the sk8er girls in Canada (associated with Avril Lavigne). Both groups had very strong and powerful female identities. These have been seen as a form of resistance against patriarchy and the all-male exclusiveness of other music subcultures. Additionally, as Bennett (1999) has argued, postmodern-style 'neo-tribes' are less gendered, and the loosening of the boundaries within and between contemporary youth subcultures has opened up space for girls to developed their own identities.

Other recent work argues that girls today are much less restricted and controlled, and spend more time out in public spaces, perhaps contributing to a greater presence in more recent subcultures. The 'binge-drinking' and pub/club culture seen among young people in many towns today includes equal amounts of males and females. This is supported by Hollands' study of nightlife in Newcastle (1995), which appears to show that 'bedroom culture' may be a thing of the past – though the young women studied by Hollands were older than the young teenagers associated with bedroom culture by McRobbie and Garber.

Subcultures as related to ethnicity and hybridity

Since the 1950s, youth culture and subcultures have had many ethnic influences, particularly in terms of music. For example, early rock 'n' roll music listened to by the Teddy Boys and the rockers was influenced by black rhythm and blues music in the US. Similarly, Caribbean music, particularly reggae and ska, was favoured by both white skinheads and black 'rude boys' in the UK. Additionally, the influence of Asian Bhangra music can be heard in some modern dance music.

The spectacular subcultures studied by the CCCS were looked at in terms of the way they responded to the presence of black people and their subculture in the UK. Hebdige (1979) argued that British youth subcultures can be read as 'a succession of differential responses to the black immigrant presence in Britain' (1979: 29). Examples include the mods, who were seen as imitating the 'cool' styles of West Indians and their influence from soul music, and the skinheads, who gained a reputation for racism and resistance to immigration, while at the same time themselves taking on some fashion and music from West Indian culture.

More recently, black music and fashion have influenced white working-class subcultures. An example is the 'white wannabes' identified by Nayak (2003) (see page 125). Similarly, examples of white rap stars such as Eminem in the US and Professor Green in the UK illustrate this 'cultural hybridity'.

Quick question

Consider your favourite musicians. Have any of them been influenced by music from other cultures?

Ethnic minority subcultures in the UK

Rastafarians and reggae culture

Rastafarians could be seen as an example of a youth subculture – though they are less exclusive to 'youth' than most of the youth subcultures we consider. Rastas are associated with Jamaican/Caribbean culture, reggae music (e.g., Bob Marley), dreadlocks and often clothes in the colours of red, gold and green. These colours come from the flag of Ethiopia, and Rastafarians have religious beliefs associated with their African roots in Ethiopia. Smoking marijuana is strongly associated with Rastafarians; it is actually seen as part of their religion, as they believe it helps them to reach a higher level of spirituality. Hebdige (1976) saw Rastafarianism and reggae culture as forms of resistance to white culture and racism with roots in the relations of slavery. Thus, Rastafarianism as a political and spiritual movement attracted many Caribbean migrants to Britain, offering a positive identity and source of opposition to the racism and subordination they were experiencing.

Brasian culture

This refers to the subculture of some young British Asians, which is a fusion between Asian and British culture. For example, Bhangra music is often mixed with rap, dance and pop music, to create a hybrid or 'fusion'. Cornershop, The Rishi Rich Project, Jazzy B, Jay Sean and M.I.A. are all Asian or mixed-race performers who have had mainstream chart success with such fusion music. Apache Indian also illustrates the Brasian style and his fans are often known as 'Bhangramuffins'. Young British Asians refuse to accept a subordinate place in society and wish to celebrate their culture by making it more contemporary and fashionable. Johal (1998) suggests that some British Asians adopted a 'hyper-ethnic style', an exaggerated form of their parent culture, including watching Indian or Hindi films and listening to music from the Asian sub-continent. He argues that this can provide a kind of 'empowerment through difference'. However, issues such as religion, choice of marriage partner and diet may lead to a position of selective cultural preference; a kind of 'code-switching' in which young Asians move between one cultural form and another, depending on context and whether overt 'Britishness' or pronounced 'Asianness' is most appropriate.

Resistance or hybridity?

Though Rastafarianism can easily be seen as an example of 'resistance' against white racism, the Brasian subculture shows more hybridity, with young British Asians blending aspects of their parents' Asian culture with aspects of British popular culture. However, by hanging onto some of their traditional culture, this could be seen as a form of resistance – resisting complete assimilation into white British culture, and celebrating their heritage.

Mercer (1987) discusses the styling of hair within the black culture, and its symbolic meaning. For example, the afro and dreadlock hairstyles are seen as emphasising identification with black identity – and so could be a form of resistance – and straightened black hairstyles are seen as imitative of white culture – assimilation. However, Mercer dismisses these interpretations as simplistic, and sees all of these hairstyles as forms of hybridity, making statements about the black individual's place within British culture.

Ethnocentric sociologists

A criticism of functionalists, the CCCS and feminists is that they do not consider the impact of race and ethnicity on youth subcultures. As we have seen, Hebdige (CCCS) argued there is a clear relationship between black styles of dress, music and dance, and urban subcultures, but this was not explored further. These sociologists are often accused of being ethnocentric for this reason. Some studies in the US have been less 'white-focused' and considered hip hop and 'gangsta rap' as subcultures – though these studies have often been carried out by black sociologists.

> ### Activity
>
> #### Rap – hybridity in action
>
> Cashmore's 1997 study of gangsta rap argues that rap can be seen as the ultimate hybrid music form, which has many styles and no obvious point of origin. Cashmore charts the 'rap' culture through Jamaica in the 1960s to New York in the 1970s, LA in the 1980s, and then worldwide. He shows how it evolved and changed, and how local artists in different countries modified the style and sound of rap to adapt it to their own culture. British rap music sounds different to US rap music or to that of other countries. Also, when rap has crossed over into white cultures, it has changed again, as it has when it has been performed by female artists. This changeability and hybridity support postmodernist ideas of the fluidity of recent subcultures.
>
> 1 Think of as many different rap artists as you can. Do they vary in style based on gender, ethnicity, nationality, and so on?

Chapter 4 Youth subcultures

124

Examples of hybrid subcultures

'White wannabes'

'White wannabes' were identified by Nayak (2003) as young white working-class males who adopt the style and language of 'black culture'. Others terms, such as 'wangstas' and 'wiggers', have also been used. They may listen to music such as hip hop or gangsta rap, wear lots of 'bling' and dress in a style similar to that stereotypically associated with young black males. A good example of a parody of a stereotypical 'white wannabe' is Ali G, famous in the late 1990s for his catchphrase 'Is it because I is black?', even though he clearly wasn't black.

'Modern primitives'

'Modern primitives' are a subculture found in the US and in parts of western Europe. Possibly more accurately described as a 'neo-tribe' rather than a subculture, they have a very wide but loose membership, with the focus on individuality and self-expression. Modern primitives are characterised particularly by body modifications, especially tattoos and piercings, which are seen as a form of self-expression, linked to a less complicated way of life. The symbolism is drawn from non-Western ethnic groups, colloquially referred to as 'primitive tribes', thus they can be seen as a hybrid subculture, mixing the modern with the 'primitive' and taking inspiration from many cultures. Vale and Juno (1989) argue that the body modification undertaken by modern primitives is a reaction to the sense of powerlessness created by living in a fast-changing world, through which some sense of power and control can be regained.

Hybridity: Cultural exchange and cultural appropriation

Ever since Elvis Presley was criticised for 'stealing' black music, ethnic hybridity in youth subcultures has been controversial. Hybridity in youth subcultures could be seen as positive, leading to more mixing and understanding between different groups and has been seen as a form of 'cultural exchange'. However, it has also been viewed as negative. Some argue that taking aspects of other ethnic cultures into white subcultures is a form of 'cultural appropriation'. The use of tattoos and piercings seen in the modern primitives' subculture could be seen as an example of this. The popularity of Chinese letters and tribal artwork as tattoos, henna tattoos, bindis, dreadlocks and even the sampling of traditional music have all been criticised as forms of exploitation and disrespect. Hutnyk (2000) argues, for example, that there are power differentials at work, within which Western subcultures may strip the meaning from symbols and use them in a superficial way. Additionally, the idea of 'cultural exchange' suggests a two-way, equal process, which is often not true in reality. For example, it could be argued that aspects of British culture have been imposed on other cultures as part of Britain's imperial past, whereas aspects of other cultures have been taken and used by British subcultures without any 'exchange' taking place.

Activity: Hybridity in youth subcultures – cultural exchange or cultural appropriation?

Item A: A white person with dreadlocks

Item B: The symbolism of dreadlocks

'Dreadlocks are a symbol of Black/African pride and resistance to white supremacist beauty standards and are rooted in Black/African struggles for survival and liberation.

Dreadlocks are rooted in Rastafarianism, a pan-African spiritual/religious movement for healing and decolonization for Africa and African people worldwide. Rastafarianism is a form of resistance to a history of white racism, slavery, colonization and genocide.

Activity (Continued)

The traditions of people of color/non-white people are still under attack across the planet. Appropriating our traditions and ways of dressing/presenting is a further attack on our communities.'

Source: Donovan and Driskill, (n.d.)

Item C: Fakir Musafar, considered the 'father' of the modern primitive movement

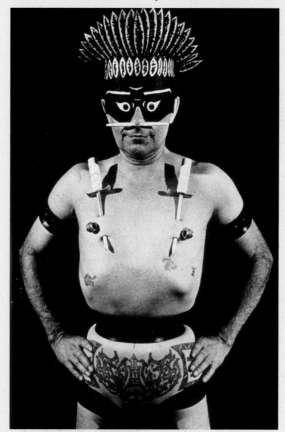

1 Is cultural mixing positive? Or is it 'stealing' culture that belongs to others?
2 Does culture 'belong' to a particular national or ethnic group? Can it be 'appropriated'?

Check your understanding ✓

Briefly define the following terms and give an example of each:

1 youth culture
2 youth subcultures
3 social construct
4 anomie
5 rite of passage
6 resistance
7 hegemony
8 bricolage
9 bedroom culture
10 neo-tribes
11 ethnocentric
12 assimilation
13 cultural appropriation.

Section summary ✎

Fill in the blanks, using the words given below.

Youth is socially _____, but in this culture is usually seen to cover the teenage years. It is recognised that there is a separate youth culture, with different norms and values to those of adults or children. Functionalists, such as _____, see youth as a functional, transitional period, when youths can learn to become independent and prepare for adult life.

Youth _____ are distinct groups of youths with their own norms and values. Those who adopt highly visible styles, such as punks, are known as _____ youth subcultures. _____ argue that youths may adopt these styles as a form of _____ against their class position. _____ would say that this research is dated, and that, these days, youths form much looser '_____', with less distinct styles and rules.

_____ are interested in how female subcultures differ from those of males, and look at ways in which young girls are _____ more. Subcultures are also formed by ethnic minority youths. This could be seen as a form of resistance against _____, and may also give a sense of identity and belonging. Some youth subcultures show _____, incorporating aspects from more than one culture. An example could be _____.

Brasians, constructed, controlled, feminists, hybridity, neo-Marxists, neo-tribes, Parsons, postmodernists, racism, resistance, spectacular, subcultures

4.2 Why do young people participate in deviant subcultures?

Deviant subcultures: Definitions

The terms 'delinquent subcultures', 'criminal subcultures' and 'gangs' are often used interchangeably, and though they do have distinct definitions, explanations relating to them will often apply to all three. The main differences are in the levels of deviance and of organisation found within the subculture.

Getting you thinking ...

In the headlines

- 'Soaring youth crime is linked to rising inner-city gang culture' (*Daily Mail*)
- 'Yob crime blights life in Britain once every second' (*Daily Mail*)
- 'Yobs allowed to run free as police "retreat from streets"' (*Yorkshire Post*)
- 'Teenage knife crime "is one of biggest threats to London"' (*The Times*)

- 'We're plagued by yob gangs, say Bristol shopkeepers' (*Bristol Evening Post*).

This one is more accurate:

- 'Youth crime down, but public think it's rising' (*Western Mail – Wales*).

1 Look at the *Western Mail – Wales* headline. Why would this be?
2 Why do you think such headlines are produced in the press?

1. Delinquent subcultures

'Delinquency' is a slightly old-fashioned term used to refer to youth deviance. A delinquent subculture is a subculture involved in deviant behaviour, such as joyriding, vandalism and other anti-social behaviour, which may not necessarily be criminal.

2. Criminal subcultures

This refers to subcultures that are actively involved in criminal behaviour, which may be quite organised, such as drug-dealing, protection rackets or dealing in stolen goods. Cloward and Ohlin (see page 130) argued that not everyone will have access to such criminal subcultures.

3. Gangs

A group of people, especially young people, who regularly associate together is often referred to as a 'gang', but this term is more commonly used by the media and the police to refer to a group who cause harm to the community and are involved in persistent criminality, often with violence a key element of group identity and solidarity. A gang will often have a name, a territory, a leader, a hierarchy and a set of rules relating to membership.

Some gangs may be delinquent subcultures and some may be criminal subcultures, depending on the level of their criminal activity. However, not all delinquent subcultures or criminal subcultures will be gangs; it will depend on their structure and identity.

The other two types of deviant subcultures are less related to criminality and are more about attitudes.

4. Spectacular youth subcultures

This is a term that has been used by sociologists specifically to describe some of the highly visible subcultures of the 1950s–1970s such as Teddy Boys, mods, punks and skinheads.

These subcultures had very flamboyant and instantly recognisable styles, and often had confrontational attitudes. They have particularly been studied by the Centre for Contemporary Cultural Studies (CCCS) at Birmingham University (neo-Marxists). Because of this Marxist influence, their analysis tended to focus on social class issues, and this form of deviant subculture does not feature so much in studies on ethnicity and gender in relation to deviant subcultures.

5. Anti-school subcultures

The term 'anti-school subculture' is used to refer to groups of pupils who reject the norms and values of school and reverse them. So it will be seen as negative to do well academically, receive praise from the teacher, receive good marks, complete homework, do what the teacher tells you, and so on. Instead, they will value trouble-making, disrupting the class and being cheeky to teachers, and truanting. Academic failure or poor grades may become a positive thing. Sociologists sometimes distinguish anti-school and anti-education subcultures. The former reject the values of school, whereas the latter reject the values of education more widely, and do not value academic success. Thus it is possible for a group of pupils to be anti-school, rejecting particular rules and what teachers expect from them, and yet still be pro-education and recognise the value of qualifications.

Newer/emerging types of deviant subcultures

The nature of subcultures means that they come and go, and new types of deviant subcultures continually emerge. The internet has significantly influenced the development of subcultures, including deviant subcultures.

Whether online communities can be seen as subcultures is debatable, but they do represent spaces where groups of (mainly) youths interact and share experiences, finding a common set of norms and values which may differ from those of the mainstream. Because of the anonymity of the online community, some young people may share deviant sentiments and express resistance and rebellion in a way they may not do among peers in real-life situations. Online communities will often be focused on a particular gender, ethnicity, religion or political view, or may be based on tastes and interests in music, gaming or film. Examples include 'pro-ana' (anorexic) online communities, 'lad' sites such as UNILAD and the LAD Bible, fan-based subcultures/communities such as Little Monsters (Lady Gaga fans), and style-/self-expression- based communities such as modern primitives (see page 125).

Quick questions

1 Are you a member of any online communities?
2 Do you see them as subcultures? Are they deviant?

As discussed earlier in this chapter, postmodernists suggest that subcultures are no longer as distinct and clear-cut as they used to be, instead using the terms 'club cultures' and 'neo-tribes'. However, in his analysis of 'post-rave technotribes', St John (2003) challenges part of this notion, that youth today lack the identity and resistance of previous generations. Technotribes are groups of young people brought together through music festivals and social media. These groups demonstrate resistant ideals such as social justice, green politics and human rights.

Patterns and trends in youth deviance

Patterns and trends in youth deviance are not easy to measure, since much deviance is low-level and does not appear in official statistics. Anti-Social Behaviour Orders (ASBOs) are issued for a number of petty offences, such as spraying graffiti, drinking in the streets and threatening behaviour, and are often associated with youth deviance. Young people aged 10–17 years accounted for 37 per cent of Anti-Social Behaviour Orders issued in 2012, though their rate of breaching ASBOs is much higher than for adults. Since 2005, there have been year-on-year falls in

the number of ASBOs issued, with 1,329 issued in 2012 – a decrease of 6 per cent from the 1,414 issued in 2001. The number of young people entering the criminal justice system is also at its lowest for over a decade, according to a consultation paper issued by the Ministry of Justice in 2013. However, clear patterns can be identified in relation to social class, gender and ethnicity when considering young people within the criminal justice system.

Social class

Official measures of crime, such as the police-recorded rates of crime, suggest that youths from working-class backgrounds are much more likely to become involved in deviance and criminality than those from wealthier backgrounds. According to the youth charity Barnado's, children in the youth justice system are predominantly drawn from the poorest and most disadvantaged families. Jacobson et al. (2010) found multiple disadvantages and complex backgrounds in the majority of the 200 children and young people in custody they sampled. For example, around three-quarters were known to have had absent fathers, around half to have lived in a deprived household and/or unsuitable accommodation, and just under half to have run away or absconded at some point in their lives. More than a quarter had witnessed domestic violence, with a similar proportion having had experience of local authority care. The research found that another common aspect of their lives was disrupted education with, for example, over half known to have truanted or regularly failed to attend school for other reasons, and around half to have been excluded from school. The Cambridge Study in Delinquent Development, a longitudinal self-report study on a sample of over 400 young males, suggested that socio-economic deprivation was a key predictor of future criminality (Farrington 1989).

However, though youths from working-class backgrounds are clearly more likely to find themselves involved with the criminal justice system, it is a matter of debate as to whether working-class youths actually commit more crime and deviance. It may be that the deviance and criminality working-class youths become involved in is more likely to be visible and targeted by the police and criminal justice institutions, whereas deviance and criminality among middle-class youths may be hidden, tolerated as 'high spirits' or negotiated away. Sociological views on this are discussed below.

Gender

Criminality and deviance are overwhelmingly male activities according to evidence from the police, victim surveys and most self-report studies. In particular, females tend to commit the most serious crimes at a much lower rate than males. Home Office data shows that young men aged 10 – 17 years were found to be responsible for 20 per cent of all police-recorded crime in 2009/10 and young women responsible for only 4 per cent. However, some self-report studies filled in by young people themselves about the activities they have been involved in suggest that the difference is not as great as for adults, or as great as the official statistics suggest (for example, Campbell 1981). Official crime data suggests that the peak age for female offending is 15, younger than the peak age for males, which is 18. Though girls may continue to offend in their teens, offending drops markedly after this – they seem to 'grow out of it' – whereas offending rates for males do not decline significantly until well into their 20s.

Some evidence does suggest that female crime is increasing in comparison to male crime. Between 1994 and 2004 the numbers of women in prison in England and Wales increased by 150 per cent. However, Muncie (1999) argues that small rises in recorded crime created a moral panic about female offending and 'girl gangs', suggesting that the rise in the imprisonment of young women has been an over-reaction.

Ethnicity

The overwhelming majority of crime and deviance is committed by youths from white British backgrounds, since these make up the majority of the population. However, a disproportionate number of African-Caribbean youths are processed by the criminal justice system. Home Office statistics show that young people from a black ethnic background accounted for 21 per cent of young people in custody in 2012/13, though this ethnic background accounts for less than 3 per cent of the population. Young black males are also much more likely to be stopped and searched by the police than their white counterparts. For example, black people were stopped and searched 7 times more than white people in 2009/10, and 6 times more in 2006/07, according to Home Office figures. Additionally, black people were arrested 3.3 times more than white people in 2009/10.

Home Office statistics also suggest an increase in crime rates among Asians in Britain. In 2009/10, Asians made up 5.6 per cent of the population, but accounted for 9.6 per cent of stop and searches and 7.1 per cent of the prison population. Arrest rates for Asians rose by 13 per cent between 2005/6 and 2009/10, the largest rise for any ethnic group. Arrest rates for whites decreased over the same period.

These patterns and trends shown in the official statistics raise several issues. There is a discrepancy in the way black and white young offenders are dealt with within the criminal justice system, which may not be solely based on offending behaviour (see Activity below). Lea and Young (1993) argue that the statistics often miss out the important point that most UK crime is 'intra-racial', meaning that it takes place within ethnic communities. Thus most crime committed by young black males is against other young black males. Racially motivated crime against other ethnic groups is much rarer. Lea and Young argue that once this is understood, explanations for the high rates of black criminality can be sought from within the black community, and issues such as street culture, poverty and deprivation must be considered as explanations.

Explanations for young people participating in deviant subcultures

Functionalist-based explanations

Functionalist-based views on subcultures tend to focus on the norms and values found in subcultures, which some argue are shared with the mainstream or parent culture, but which may be fulfilled in deviant ways. These ideas were originally presented by Merton (1938), who recognised that individuals may experience a strain between the goals or values of society and what they are able to achieve, which may lead to deviant responses to this problem, such as innovation, ritualism or retreatism. Merton did not consider this as a collective response or apply it specifically to youth. However, other subcultural theorists such as A. Cohen and Cloward and Ohlin developed these ideas to recognise that within a subculture, the deviant means of achieving society's goals often become the accepted means. These views can be related to both deviant subcultures within schools and also delinquent or criminal subcultures, since a lack of educational opportunity or success is a key factor leading to the delinquent behaviour according to these theorists.

Cohen (1955) argued that teenage boys desire status. By status, he meant 'respect in the eyes of one's fellows' (1995: 65). Cohen claimed that working-class boys are aware of mainstream values,

Item A: Trends in recorded crime and CSEW, 1981 to 2011/12

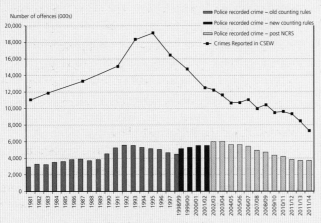

Number of offences (000s)

Legend:
- Police recorded crime – old counting rules
- Police recorded crime – new counting rules
- Police recorded crime – post NCRS
- Crimes Reported in CSEW

- The Crime Survey for England and Wales (CSEW) is a victim survey, asking people about the crimes they have been a victim of during the last year.
- Recorded crime refers to crimes recorded by the police.

NB. It is not possible to make accurate long-term comparisons in police-recorded crime due to fundamental changes in the recording of crimes introduced in 1998 and April 2002.

Source: Crime Survey for England and Wales – Office for National Statistics, Home Office.

Item B: Statistics on youth crime

Ministry of Justice figures show that there has been a steady decline in youth crime, despite public perceptions to the contrary. For example, there were 98,837 proven offences by young people (under 18) in 2012/13, down by 28 per cent from 2011/12 and down by 63 per cent since 2002/03.

Males accounted for 82 per cent of proven offences by young people in 2012/13. This proportion has risen slightly from 78 per cent in 2009/10. The proportion of proven offences committed by females was 18 per cent in 2012/13; this proportion has fluctuated between 16 per cent and 22 per cent over the last decade. In 2012/13, 95 per cent of the young people held in the secure estate were male.

In 2012/13, 59 per cent of the young people held in custody were from a white ethnic background, despite the fact that young people from a white ethnic background accounted for 82 per cent of the proven offences by young people. Young people from a black ethnic background accounted for 21 per cent of young people in custody.

In 2012/13, 18 per cent of young people from a white ethnic background in custody were held on remand (kept in custody prior to their trial), compared to 28 per cent of young people from a black ethnic background and 19 per cent from an Asian background.

Source: Youth justice annual statistics: 2012 to 2013 – Ministry of Justice and Youth Justice Board for England and Wales.

1 Consider Item A. Using both measures of crime shown, summarise the trends in crime over the 30-year period.
2 Why do you think the two measures show different figures?
3 Consider Item B. What do these statistics tell us about the relationship between gender and youth crime?
4 What do they tell us about the relationship between ethnicity and youth crime?
5 How might the differences in sentencing and remand between ethnic groups be explained?

---

such as success at school, good qualifications, a good job and financial success. A boy would get status if he achieved these things, but a working-class boy who clings to this value system will recognise himself as inferior compared to middle-class college (academically successful) boys. This creates a feeling of 'status frustration'.

A delinquent subculture, with values such as aggression and being good in a fight, may form as a way of dealing with status frustration, since this can still lead to the overall value of status. Those who perform successfully in terms of delinquent values within their subculture can gain status in the eyes of their peers. This can explain why more working-class boys get involved in crime and deviance.

Cloward and Ohlin (1961) also saw deviance as a reaction to problems in achieving the values of mainstream culture. The deviant is unable to achieve valued goals (like success, money and possessions) through legitimate means, and thus innovates, using illegitimate or deviant means to attain them.

An important point made by Cloward and Ohlin is that just as some people experience 'blocked opportunities' to attain valued goals through legitimate means (not everyone has equal educational opportunities and so on), similarly the routes to these goals through illegitimate means are differently available; not everyone can use the same deviant means to achieve these goals.

They argued that the 'type' of deviant subculture that develops will depend on the illegitimate means available. They outlined three types of deviant subculture that may result:

1 **Criminal subcultures.** These develop in stable slum areas in which there is hierarchy of criminal opportunity. A boy will learn to steal from his older peers.
2 **Conflict subcultures.** These tend to be formed in unstable disorganised areas with high mobility (people moving in and out). There is no access to an organised hierarchy of criminal opportunity, so youths in such areas turn to violence, and gangs are formed to defend areas.
3 **Retreatist subcultures.** These are formed by youths who fail to achieve in legitimate or illegitimate terms, unable to access success through mainstream values or through joining criminal subcultures or gangs. They will retreat from society's values altogether, and often descend into addiction and petty crime.

Miller (1958) argues slightly differently. Though he is often considered as part of the functionalist view, he challenges the core idea of a value consensus shared by all, because he says that working-class boys do not even try to gain academic success – that is a middle-class value. Working-class values are simply different. Miller calls these 'focal concerns'. Young working-class boys share focal concerns such as being in trouble, being tough and macho, and being smart and 'streetwise'. They will value freedom and excitement.

Evaluating the functionalist view

The main criticism is that functionalists present a view of working-class culture that is a sweeping generalisation. In reality, working-class subcultures are subject to regional, ethnic and individual variations, and not all working-class youths are the same.

Cohen assumes that working-class boys are reacting to their failure to achieve mainstream values, but Miller disagrees, saying it is just to achieve their own values, so they disagree with each other.

Activity: Reasons for youth crime

Item A: Violent street crime

A study carried out by researchers from the University of Glamorgan's Centre for Criminology interviewed 120 offenders in England and Wales. The report said that previous attempts to explain violent street crime put too much focus on the desire for gain, and not enough on the aspect of 'pleasure'. Five of the main reasons given for committing street robbery include 'good times', 'keeping up appearances', 'excitement', 'desire to fight' and 'righting wrongs'.

Some offenders wanted to be able to show off expensive items, such as cars, but this was related to status rather than need. Sometimes street robbery was about the excitement of the fight or the fun of overpowering someone else. 'It wasn't like, for money – I was more addicted to robbing than I was to drugs', said one offender. Another said, 'It weren't even for money. I had money. It was more like the buzz you get from doing things.'

Source: Adapted from Bennett *et al.* (2006).

Item B: Gang violence

Following police raids on gangs where the 'elders' or leaders were arrested, there is concern about a lack of follow-up work with the younger, junior gang members

who remain. This has resulted in a vacuum in which the younger, and often more volatile, gang members have suddenly ascended into senior gang positions. The upshot of this is not only the continuation of gang violence, but its escalation as 'youngers' vie for status and respect using the currency of violence. This is a dangerous turn of events …

Unemployment is a key reason for the increase in youth gangs; as it becomes harder for young people to get employment, a growing number of disadvantaged young people are being drawn into gangs. One voluntary sector organisation stated that:

'Things have been getting tougher. We're in a tug of war with our clients against what their peers are doing. Gangs have upped the "ante" in terms of recruitment. As it becomes harder to get into employment, young people are turning to gangs as an alternative.'

Source: Adapted from Centre for Social Justice (2012).

1 Identify any aspects from Items A and B that support the ideas of A. Cohen, Cloward and Ohlin, or Miller in terms of the reasons why young people may become involved in delinquent or gang activities.
2 What other explanations do these items suggest?

They all accept the official picture, based on police statistics, of the 'typical criminal' being young, male and working class, and so this is what their explanations are based on. However, other sociologists (for example, interactionists) may challenge these statistics by, for example, looking at labelling by the police to explain them, and the idea that youth crime is just more visible.

New Right explanation

Based on the ideas of Murray (1984), the New Right view is that youths in deviant subcultures have not received the appropriate socialisation into the value consensus held by the rest of society. They have a different, deviant set of norms and values, based on dependency, criminality and laziness. Murray's argument is that the underclass do not want to work and see dependency on welfare as a positive lifestyle choice. The entire underclass could be seen as a deviant subculture in Murray's analysis, but it is particularly among youth, through gangs and anti-school subcultures, where this alternative culture would be highlighted. Murray particularly condemns the increase in single mothers raising young boys with no father in their lives. He suggests that this can explain the high rates of crime among male youths from deprived social backgrounds.

In an article for the *Sunday Times* in 2005, 'The Advantages of Social Apartheid', Murray argues that growing up in a single-parent family is more damaging and a greater indicator of criminality that poverty is. He suggests that girls without fathers may be emotionally damaged by this and search for a father substitute, often getting pregnant at an early age themselves. Even more concerning for Murray is boys growing up without fathers: 'Boys without fathers tend to grow up unsocialised. They tend to have poor impulse control, to be sexual predators, to be unable to get up at the same time every morning and go to a job. They tend to disappear shortly after the baby is born.'

Murray's conclusion is that these trends will be disastrous for Britain: 'Over the last two decades, larger and larger numbers of British children have not been socialised to norms of self-control, consideration for others, and the concept that actions have consequences' (2001: 9).

He argues though that, as in the US, the British public will become less tolerant of the underclass, and that politicians, seeking votes, will become more willing to toughen up on them – perhaps cutting benefits and using the criminal justice system more harshly.

Activity

Evaluating the New Right view

MacDonald (2008) summarised several studies of youth undertaken by the University of Teesside which sought to test Murray's idea of a dependency culture among deprived young people. This is an extract from their findings:

Malcolm, 19, had earlier been excluded from school, had no academic qualifications, had been frequently unemployed and had convictions for house burglary. We suspect he is exactly the sort of young man that Murray would elect for underclass membership ... [H]is views were common ones:

'I would hate being on the dole ... I won't do it. It's embarrassing going to the Post Office with your giro. You just become lazy, have a lazy life ... I just don't wanna sign on the dole. I wanna work ... It's a weekly wage for a start, instead of a daft £78 per fortnight. It's just part of life. To have a job and support your family. So instead of him [his son] growing up and when his friends' mams or teachers say 'What does your dad do?' – 'Oh, he's on the dole'. I don't want none of that. I want him to grow up and say 'Oh, our dad's working at summat'. So he can feel proud and have nice things when he gets older.'

1 How do Malcolm's comments challenge Murray's arguments about the underclass?

2 Murray predicted a harshening in the UK's attitude towards the underclass in 10–15 years – he made these predictions in 2005. Has he been proved right?

Marxist/neo-Marxist explanations

Neo-Marxists from the CCCS saw deviant behaviour by young males in subcultures as being a form of resistance against society's control, and a reaction to their identity being threatened. It relates to territory, identity and control. Examples of studies from the CCCS have been discussed in the previous section, including the ideas of Clarke and Hebdige.

Another view on youth crime also influenced by Marxists comes from Left Realists, who could be seen as a type of neo-Marxists.

Lea and Young (1993) say that there are three main explanations for crime and deviance that may particularly apply to youth deviance. These are:

1 **Relative deprivation.** People tend to feel more deprived when they compare themselves to others. The media is a key source of information about what other people seem to have, so the rise of the media has led to an increase of feelings of relative deprivation

in the UK. This can link to youths in particular, because they will often feel deprived compared to adults; they have less freedom, and are more influenced by the media and impressions of what they should have.

2 **Marginalisation.** This means when people feel pushed to the edges of society. They feel excluded, powerless and lack any organised means to voice their frustrations. Young people are particularly likely to be marginalised in society, since they lack power, rights and respect, which can lead to feelings of frustration.

3 **Subculture.** The experience of relative deprivation and marginalisation may lead young people in particular to form subcultures to help them to deal with their feelings of frustration, developing lifestyles involving shared norms and values, which may become deviant.

Evaluating the Marxist/neo-Marxist view

- The CCCS were accused of ignoring gender by the feminists. They also generalised about youth; not all youths were members of spectacular subcultures, and not all youth deviance is part of the rituals of a subculture.
- The CCCS ideas are also outdated; there are few spectacular subcultures today – reconsider postmodernist ideas on neo-tribes, discussed in the previous section (see page 118).
- The Left Realist ideas are more up to date, and they can help to explain youth crime of various types – material crime (such as theft), explained by relative deprivation, violent crime, explained by marginalisation, and risk-taking crime (such as joyriding), explained by subculture.

Interactionist explanations

Interactionists see deviance as a social construct; mainstream society has defined certain behaviour as deviant and identified the kind of people they see as the deviants. Young working-class males get labelled by the police, the public and the media. This affects how they are seen and how they are treated by others.

Becker (1963) argues that labelling relates to power; we may all label each other, but some people are in a position to make their label stick. For example, young people may label the police, which will have no effect. If the police (who have power) label young people, it may have an effect; they may stop and search them more, caution and arrest them more, and so on. This may then lead to a 'self-fulfilling prophecy'. This means that the labelled person accepts and internalises the label and starts to change their behaviour and live up

to the label. For example, if a young male is labelled as 'trouble' and is continually questioned or stopped and searched by the local police, he may start accepting the label, believing he is 'trouble', and will be more likely to make choices that will get him into trouble, thus living up to the deviant label.

Working-class males may also interact differently with the police, perhaps because of past experiences, which may escalate the situation. An example of this can be seen in Cicourel's study (1968).

Study

The Social Organisation of Juvenile Justice – Cicourel (1968)

Aaron Cicourel carried out observations with the police and criminal justice services in two US cities. He found that the process of dealing with potential deviants involves three stages:

- **Stage 1.** The police stop/interrogate/search an individual, based on their interpretations of behaviour as 'suspicious' or 'unusual'.
- **Stage 2.** The police arrest the individual – this may depend on the suspect's appearance and manner and the replies the suspect gives to the police.
- **Stage 3.** Probation officer – he/she has a picture of a 'typical delinquent' and assesses the suspect to see if they fit the profile.

At each stage, the behaviour of the individual has an effect. Cicourel linked this to social class. If the individual is very apologetic and polite, no further action may be taken. At the point of arrest, if the parents come to the station and convince the police that it will not happen again, and show themselves to be a 'good' family, the individual may not be charged. Cicourel thus described how justice can be 'negotiated'.

He also found substantial differences between the two cities he studied, though they were similar in size and socio-economic background of population. One city had constantly high rates of juvenile delinquency. It employed more probation officers and kept more detailed records on offenders. The other city fluctuated depending on media publicity and public concern. Thus Cicourel concluded that 'delinquents' are constructed by the agencies of control and their policies.

Evaluating the interactionist view

By using labelling and the concept of the self-fulfilling prophecy to explain youth deviance, interactionists assume that the label comes first, so they do not explain why some youth actually commit deviant acts before they have been labelled and others do not.

Culture- and identity-based explanations

The theoretical explanations explored above all highlight social class and its related lack of opportunities as a key issue in explaining subcultural deviance. However, explanations based on culture and identity, including social class, ethnicity and gender, can be seen as additional or alternative explanations for youths participating in deviant subcultures.

Social class and deviant subcultures
Criminal/delinquent subcultures and gangs

The theories considered above can be used to explain working-class youths' participation in delinquent subcultures. As A. Cohen argued, the desire for status may be harder to achieve through legitimate means for those from working-class backgrounds, and they may experience 'blocked opportunities', as suggested by Cloward and Ohlin.

Study

The sociology of vindictiveness and the criminology of transgression – Young (2003)

Jock Young has developed ideas from functionalists and subcultural studies to explain underclass youth criminality. The New Right view of the underclass, as a poorly socialised, lawless group who take no responsibility for their actions, is challenged as a 'sociology of vindictiveness' by Young. He argues that we live in a 'bulimic society', a contradictory culture in which citizens are encouraged to worship money, status and success but in which many are excluded from achieving these things. He discusses the 'intensity of exclusion' felt by the underclass, incorporating feelings of resentment, humiliation and anger fuelled by economic insecurity and deprivation. Thus he sees working-class youth deviance as an emotional response to social exclusion, which is about rebellion, risk-taking, anger, frustration and exclusion, but which is also driven by a strong desire for inclusion.

Study

The Street Casino: Survival in Violent Street Gangs – Harding (2014)

Simon Harding conducted an extensive ethnographic study of local residents, professionals and gang members in south London. Using the analogy of the casino, Harding saw gangs as a social arena of competition where members struggle for distinction, status, position and survival. Success is determined by accruing and retaining 'street capital', which Harding adapted from Bourdieu's ideas of cultural capital and social capital, and which is like accumulating lots of chips in a casino.

Harding saw the gang as a dangerous place, a 'game of high stakes' for young people:

> 'It is a world of winners and losers, where everyone in the field must play, where rules change and incumbents strive to maintain their privilege. It is a world where players are encouraged to continue playing even though the returns are meagre. It is a world where the players believe they will be able to stop their risky behaviour while still engaging in it (the gambler's conceit) and where players believe they must continue to play because their bad luck must end sometime (the gambler's fallacy). Mostly they play because it is the only game in town for many, the only game they know.'

(Harding 2014: 267)

Points to discuss and research

1 Consider how aspects of Harding's 'casino' analogy of gangs supports the views of some of the other sociologists we have considered, such as:
- A. Cohen
- Cloward and Ohlin
- Miller
- Young
- Decker and Van Winkle
- White.

The links between gang membership and social deprivation

Decker and Van Winkle (1996) argue that reasons for joining youth gangs consist of both 'pulls' and 'pushes'. The 'pulls' are about the attractiveness of the gang. Gang membership can give status and excitement and provide money-making opportunities for working-class youths. The 'pushes' may come from social, economic, and cultural disadvantages. Feelings of exclusion and marginalisation may push youths from the underclass towards the status and identity that gangs can provide. For youths from dysfunctional families, the clear hierarchy and closeness of relationships that a gang may offer may provide the sense of safety and support that is missing from a young person's life. Fear of violence and a desire for protection may also push youths from deprived neighbourhoods towards a gang, which can provide protection to its members by sheer weight of numbers.

Similarly, White (2002) observes that gangs tend to be linked to 'underclass' conditions, of poverty and social exclusion, and that they arise wherever and whenever these become evident. He notes that gangs provide a sense of social inclusion, support and security for vulnerable groups of young people, providing a mechanism for deprived young people to cope with their oppressive environments and chronic marginalisation.

Anti-school subcultures and social class

It is argued that anti-school subcultures form among working-class pupils in schools as a way of protecting their self-esteem, enabling them to get respect and status from others, and protecting them from the fear of failure. Such subcultures may also be a form of resistance against the school's authority and/or the middle-class education system – though the outcome may actually be to have a negative effect on their academic achievement.

Not all sociologists agree that such distinct anti-school subcultures exist. Brown (1987) identified three possible responses to education among working class youths:

- 'getting in' – from the low achievers who wanted to join manual occupations
- 'getting out' – from the high achievers who wanted to use education to improve their social position
- 'getting on' – the 'ordinary' working-class youths, who just got on with it and complied with the demands and rules of school.

So he suggested that there were quite subtle differences between these groups based on academic ability rather than social class.

Mac an Ghaill (1994) found in his study of 'Parnell School' that there were a number of 'fluid' groups with different responses to school:

- the 'ordinary lads' who were not academic and were indifferent to school
- the 'academic achievers' who were pro-school and who worked hard
- the 'macho lads' who formed an anti-school subculture where they valued 'acting tough', saw academic work as effeminate and referred to the academic pupils as 'dickhead achievers'

Willis' study has been dismissed as outdated due to its focus on boys who had an assured route into manual work, which is rarely the case in today's UK. For example, O'Donnell and Sharpe (2000) predicted the disappearance of the 'cocksure' attitude towards employment prospects that the lads in Willis' study showed. However, MacDonald and Marsh (2005) supported Willis in their findings that the young working-class people they studied in Teesside still rejected academic success, believed that teachers were not bothered about them, and felt it was not good to be seen to be trying hard or doing well at school, due to peer pressure and anti-school subcultures. Many resigned themselves to resitting GCSEs at the local college.

Study

Learning to Labour – Willis (1977)

A famous study showing a working-class anti-school subculture was conducted by Paul Willis in the 1970s. He studied an all-boys school in Birmingham, and particularly focused on working-class lads. He found that the 'lads' saw themselves as school failures, but had turned this round to be a good thing. They disliked and even bullied the 'ear'oles', who they saw as weak and not 'macho'. These boys spent most of their time at school 'havin' a laff' – mucking around and being cheeky. They all knew that they would be getting jobs in the local factory like their dads, so did not share the school's value on education, since they did not see it as necessary. Willis did a follow-up study when they were in the factory and found very little had changed; they still spent their time messing around, finding ways to entertain themselves and get one over on the supervisor in their boring jobs. In this way, Willis said, the school had prepared them perfectly for work.

From an interactionist perspective, labelling and social class can also be seen as a factor in explaining membership of anti-school subcultures. Lacey's 1970 study of a secondary school found that pupils arrived with pro-school norms and values. However, setting pupils in terms of ability and an ethos emphasising competition between pupils led to demoralisation among those identified as having lower ability, who tended to come from lower-class backgrounds. They became disenchanted with the whole experience, and started to develop anti-school subcultures as a response to this.

Reay (2009) argues that it is understandable when confronted with a high risk of educational failure, and in a context in which they are seen to have little value, that anti-school and oppositional attitudes develop within white working-class peer groups. She argues that education is seen as a competition they cannot win, but within their subculture they can create their own competitions, based on macho and deviant behaviour, where some of them can and do win.

> ### Quick question
>
> Were you aware of anti-school subcultures in your school when you were younger? Was it seen by some pupils to be 'cool' to fail and get into trouble?

Gender and deviant subcultures
Delinquent boys

Criminal and delinquent behaviour has long been associated with young males in particular. From the 'ruffians', 'rowdies' and 'Hooligans' of the nineteenth century to the Teds, mods and rockers of the 1950s and 1960s to the 'yobs' of the 1990s and the 'hoodies' of the 2000s, young males have been feared and demonised by society and the media.

Many of the explanations for deviant subcultures considered above, such as those by the functionalists A. Cohen (status frustration) and Miller (focal concerns), and those by the neo-Marxist CCCS (resistance) have been particularly applied to males. Criminal and deviant behaviour could be seen as an extension of desirable masculine traits such as toughness and physical power, and thus could be seen as a 'natural' progression for young males to be attracted to delinquent, criminal and risk-taking behaviour.

Messerschmidt (1993) argues that the gang acts as a location for 'doing masculinity', which has to be 'accomplished' and proved. Harding (2014) develops these ideas, suggesting that how masculinity is made or accomplished depends on the social field a young male finds himself in. Those without access to paid employment, a traditional source of hegemonic masculinity, will find other ways to achieve their masculinity. Similarly, Campbell (1993) argues that by the abandonment of certain communities, the state has unleashed the most extreme forms of masculinity, denying men access to legitimate masculine status through academic success or employment and the breadwinner role. Thus deviance, particularly violence and anti-social behaviour, have become the key means by which young men in such areas could express their masculinity. These ideas can also be linked to the findings of Faludi (1999), which were considered in Chapter 1 (see page 25). In this context, young males committing criminal behaviour is not 'deviant' at all, but an expression of the qualities we admire in males as a society: toughness, bravery and strength.

However, any notion that masculinity can be seen as an 'excuse' for criminality is strongly challenged. The focus on 'masculinity', and this particular form of hegemonic masculinity, ignores the many other forms of masculinity that exist (Connell 1995) and also ignores female violence. Additionally, a Marxist analysis may argue that this focus places the blame on the powerless working-class male, while ignoring the 'symbolic violence' (Bourdieu) perpetrated by more powerful, older males in society through their ideological dominance.

There was a media outcry in Sydney after mixed martial arts fighter Shaun McNeil was accused of killing Sydney teenager Daniel Christie with a single punch in Kings Cross, Sydney. The case sparked a debate about male violence in which alcohol was being blamed. Connell (2014), in response, raises and rejects several 'common-sense' explanations for male violence. She argues that the circumstances surrounding drinking alcohol need to be examined, rather than the drink itself. She also rejects psychological and biological explanations (hormones, 'cave-man' instincts) as 'bedtime stories' and considers the relentless images of violence in the media as a possible explanation, but questions what makes some men take them up.

Activity: Masculinity and violence

Item A: Violent video games

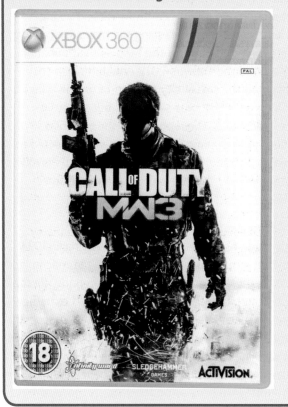

Item B: Young men 'acting tough'

1 Is there pressure on young males to 'accomplish' their masculinity?
2 Does the media encourage violence as an expression of masculinity? Think of some examples that may demonstrate this.
3 Using some of the ideas discussed in this section, explain why male violence is more commonly found in working-class areas, and at times of high unemployment.

She concludes: 'If we want to know why some young men get into zones of exception, confrontations and episodes of violence, we might ask what else is happening in their lives. Is our society giving them secure jobs? Worthwhile work to do? Models of positive relations with women? Occasions for care and creativity?'

She suspects the answer is 'no', but argues that more research into these issues, rather than a 'knee-jerk' blaming of alcohol, is what is really needed.

Delinquent girls

Despite the initial 'invisibility' of girls in subcultures previously discussed, there has been an increasing fascination with deviant girls. Evidence from official statistics and from self-report studies (e.g., Campbell 1981, Graham and Bowling 1995) suggests that female deviance and offending peaks earlier than for boys, but recedes earlier and more significantly. So at ages 14–17 the male:female ratio of offending may be just 4:1, but by the ages of 22–25 it is 11:1.

Heidensohn (1989), presenting a feminist explanation for the lower incidence of female deviance, focuses on social control. Girls are subject to much more control in terms of their behaviour – for example, control by the peer group in terms of 'reputation' (Lees 1983), and control by the family in terms of how much and for how long they are allowed out of the house. Women are also controlled by the idea that their place is in the domestic sphere, and by the fear of being out alone after dark. Such control may discourage and even prevent girls from engaging in delinquent activity. The lure of criminality as a way to demonstrate masculinity discussed above clearly does not apply to girls, and they risk more by becoming deviant, in that it will be seen as 'double deviance' (Heidensohn 1985), going against the femininity into which they have been socialised as well as against laws or norms.

Studies of females in gangs in the US suggest a significant involvement of female youths in gangs, both in female-only gangs and mixed-sex gangs. For example, Klein (1995) suggests that female gang members commit equally violent acts as their male counterparts.

The incidence of gangs in the US is very different to that in the UK, and there is less evidence regarding females in gangs in the UK. However, Pearce and Pitts (2011) estimated that 12,500 young women and girls have close involvement with gangs. Harding (2014) argues that girls in a gang use their social skills to carve out a role. They will never become leaders, but can become 'fixers' (for example, hiding weapons and drugs and trading information with rival gangs). He argues that boys will tend to leave this role to girls, seeing it as 'girls' business', but that girls and young women can become an important part of a gang's operation, and social skills are a source of 'street capital', essential to survival. Violence, including sexual violence, against young female gang members is common as a way of 'keeping them in line'.

Recent research does suggest that girls are increasingly involved in gangs in the UK; however, it is wrong to assume that this suggests increasing numbers of gangs of aggressive females – most research suggests that young female members of street gangs are victims of sexual exploitation. For example, the Centre for Social Justice's research (2014) found that gangs are commonly using sexual exploitation and rape to control girls and young women. Sometimes male gang members as young as 10 are forced to perform the rape as their initiation. This echoed the Centre's 2012 research when they highlighted the sexual exploitation of girls in gangs as a hidden issue that was significant but seriously under-addressed. The report cites the case of a 13-year-old gang-involved girl who was subjected to sexual exploitation and who was found to be involved in grooming her 10-year-old sister for the same purpose.

Anti-school subcultures and gender

In his study of 'Parnell School', Mac an Ghaill (1994) identified a male subculture he called 'the macho lads'. What they valued most was the 3Fs (fighting, football and f***ing). He argued that they showed extreme forms of 'macho behaviour' – 'hegemonic masculinity' – perhaps as a form of resistance to a perceived threat to masculine identity. He found evidence that they bullied academic achievers and had a clear 'anti-school subculture'.

Archer and Yamashita (2003) studied boys in inner-city London who showed norms and values that were anti-school and anti-education.

Activity

Girl gangs – menace or myth?

Burman *et al.* (2000) conducted research into violent behaviour among girls in Scotland in the late 1990s, concluding that female violence was not a major social issue. However, when the study was published, it generated much media interest and Batchelor claims that the media coverage characterised it as relating to 'girl gangs' and some newspapers even suggested that violence among girls was on the increase, which was not true. Their original research found no evidence of girl gangs; not one of the 800 girls they studied was in a gang, and none of them knew of any girls who were. Physical violence perpetrated by the girls was very rare, though most had witnessed male violence. Only 5 per cent of the sample reported being routinely physically violent towards others. However, the press took some of the findings out of context to make more sensationalised headlines, linking violence and girls without making clear what the findings had actually shown. One headline read, 'Deadly as the males – experts probe explosion of violence by girl gangs' (*Daily Record*, 30 September 2000), giving a false impression that the research had discovered widespread female violence and girl gangs (Batchelor 2001).

1 Why might the media have presented the findings of Batchelor *et al.*'s original research in a misleading way?

2 After reading the section on media and crime and the creation of moral panics at the end of this chapter (see page 141), consider whether girl gangs are an example of a moral panic, and whether this coverage could lead to deviance amplification.

They were attached to a 'bad boy' image, related to 'hyper-heterosexuality', and saw reading and academic achievement as 'soft'. They were committed to staying local, with limited aspirations. They saw their local area as 'unsafe' and recognised you had to be tough to survive, but felt vulnerable to attack if they strayed from its boundaries. Their subculture or 'gang' was their 'backup' and being a member and conforming was a key part of 'doing masculinity' within the male peer group.

So these studies suggest that deviant subcultures can have a great effect on male students' attitudes towards school, and the effort they make. The same 'anti-school subcultures' are not so apparent within female subcultures, though some working-class girls have been found to also display such attitudes. For example, Jackson (2006) studied 'laddishness' in schools, and found evidence of this from both boys and girls. It was cool to be clever, but not to work hard. They would hide the fact that they had revised or tried from their friends to avoid the appearance of weakness or failure if they did badly; they would be able to say they did not try or care. The ladette culture included smoking, swearing, acting 'hard' and being loud and open about their sex lives. These were white working-class girls who were underachieving as a result.

Blackman (1998) conducted a detailed study on a female anti-education subculture. The New Wave Girls were a high-profile, academic and resistant youth subculture. They were defined by their music tastes (new wave, punk, ska) and their appearance (Doc Marten boots, big jumpers, some punk fashions, unconventional hair and make-up). Blackman argued that their subculture was based on resistance, and it was largely related to their gender and others' expectations of it. They resisted the regime of the school, for example by skiving lessons that they felt did not enhance their education and by adapting the school uniform and challenging the rules. However, they were academic and did value education, so were not anti-education, merely anti-school.

Quick question

Suggest reasons for the differences between male and female anti-school subcultures.

Ethnicity and deviant subcultures
Criminal/delinquent subcultures and gangs

As we have seen above, criminality is often linked to ethnicity, and much evidence shows that those from certain ethnic backgrounds, particularly those of African-Caribbean origin, are significantly over-represented in the official crime statistics. The social disadvantages imposed by social class and race combine to explain why young black youths may be likely to join deviant subcultures.

Carl Nightingale (1993) studied young black males in Philadelphia. He argued that they consumed the mainstream US culture through the media like everyone else, sharing values like consumerism and money. However, they were excluded, both racially and economically, from fully participating in the mainstream means of achieving society's goals. Thus, they turned to illegitimate means, such as violence and crime, to achieve these goals.

Philip Bourgois (1995) had similar findings when he studied Latino and African-American drug dealers in New York's El Barrio area. He discussed the 'anguish of growing up poor' in the richest city in the world, arguing that this creates an inner-city street culture in which deviant practices become the norm. The world these ethnic minority youths operated in was complex but structured, and they were highly ambitious and motivated (like Merton's 'innovators'). Drug-dealing was their way of surviving and achieving respect. Bourgois saw it as understandable that they might ask why they should take the subway to work a minimum-wage job in the city, when a million-dollar industry – drug-dealing – was on their doorstep.

These two studies both illustrate what Nightingale referred to as 'the paradox of inclusion'. The desire to be included drives the desire for success, designer labels and the American lifestyle, and yet to achieve this for those suffering from poverty and racism means deviance and criminal behaviour, which ensures exclusion.

The link between gangs and ethnicity may be exaggerated, and social class could actually be the key factor in determining youth deviance. The Centre for Social Justice's 2009 report on gangs challenged the popular misconception that gangs in the UK are particularly associated with those from African-Caribbean backgrounds. They found that the ethnicity

Deviant subcultures? Alexander (2000, 1996a)

In the Asian Gang (2000), Claire Alexander studied a group of Bengali youths (aged 14–16) in inner-city London, in the wake of a moral panic about 'the Asian gang', particularly following the riots in Northern England in the late 1990s. She found that they often did get involved in fighting, among themselves and against other ethnic groups. Membership and allegiances within these groups were constantly shifting and evolving, encompassing often contradictory generational, familial, cultural and geographical loyalties, and so the 'gang' was often tenuous and fragile.

However, she argued that the myth of the 'Asian gang' was created through the media after the riots and it was fuelled by general Islamophobia. These stereotypes were also picked up on by teachers, who projected the 'gang' label onto groups of friends who shared an ethnicity and common identity, and chose to stick together, even if they were not part of a gang.

Summarising an earlier study, *The Art of Being Black* (1996), Alexander wrote:

'That the boys were … aware of … tension between themselves as individuals and what society expected of them became clear to me early on in my fieldwork.

One night, outside a pub in Covent Garden, I was introduced to two new members of the group, Nathan and Arif: "This is Claire. She's an anthropologist and she's studying black men. She wants to know why we all stand around on street corners with ghetto blasters, mugging old white women". Nathan glared at me: "We don't all do that you know". After a dramatic pause, he added: "Any white woman will do". Their awareness of the gap between these representations and who they were as individuals was something that the boys confronted, negotiated and played with constantly; the images structured their lives, yet were never allowed to determine them … If the thing that the boys shared was "being black", what this actually meant was always open to new interpretations, new challenges, and new identities … the boys were merely making themselves up like everyone else does.'

(Alexander 1996b)

Points to discuss and research

1 In what ways do each of Alexander's pieces of research suggest that ethnic minority subcultures are not that different to any others? Give examples from each.

2 Why might a group of Asian youths or black youths be more likely to be labelled as a deviant subculture or gang than a group of white youths?

---

of gang members tends to reflect the ethnicity of the local population; thus, in Scotland gang members are mostly white, whereas gang members in London and Manchester are more likely to be black. The report also suggested that the high proportion of black gang members in the UK overall also reflects the disproportionately high presence of black communities in deprived inner-city neighbourhoods, where gangs are most likely to form.

Anti-school subcultures and ethnicity

Research suggests that certain ethnic groups are more likely to develop anti-school or anti-education attitudes as part of their culture. Many studies suggest that forming anti-school subcultures is a response to a perception young people from ethnic minorities have about racism from the education system and from specific teachers. The manner of this response differs for different ethnic groups, and there appears to be a gender divide, with males being more likely to adopt a confrontational response.

For black males, the culture of the streets is anti-education: valuing style and instant gratification and seeing educational success as feminine, according to Sewell (1997). A successful black male would be a target for bullying, whereas educational failure becomes a badge to wear with pride. Sewell identified four visible groupings or reactions to school among African-Caribbean boys, borrowing the responses Merton used to explain deviance and applying them to education: conformists (pro-education, pro-school), innovators (pro-education but anti-school – seeking alternative ways to achieve), retreatists (those who rejected the goals of education/schooling and the means of achieving them – drop-outs) and rebels (those who formed their own alternative subcultures – a posse, often focused on rap music). Sewell argued that the majority of black boys were actually conformists, but it was the minority, the rebels, which accounted for only 18 per cent, that got all the attention and created the negative stereotype.

Young, Gifted and Black – Mac an Ghaill (1988)

Mairtin Mac an Ghaill, in his study of black youth in inner-city schools, suggested that social class and gender intersect with racism and racial stereotypes, creating different responses among groups of young people.

He found that young African-Caribbean males developed subcultures based on very masculine images as a response to perceived teacher labelling and racism. He identified a subculture referred to as the Rasta Heads, whose resistance involved open confrontation with teachers. In the same school were the Warriors, an Asian male subculture. They were also anti-school and showed resistance; however, it was more covert and went largely unnoticed by the teachers, who had a different perception of Asian boys, and did not see them as troublemakers in the same way as the Rasta Heads. The third subculture Mac an Ghaill identified was the Black Sisters, a group of Asian and African-Caribbean girls who were pro-education, and just saw school as a means to an end to achieve what they knew they needed, despite perceiving racism from the teachers. Thus they confused their teachers by showing open defiance in some lessons, but by still working hard.

A more pro-education attitude among African-Caribbean girls was also identified by Mirza (2009). The girls she studied resented teacher labels, racism and the expectation of failure; however, they adopted a 'strategic rationalisation' of what they perceived to be wasteful and unproductive lesson time. They adopted strategies to maximise their chances of educational success, often keeping their heads down, sitting at the back of classrooms and getting on with other work, avoiding confrontation. When teachers used patronising strategies to give inappropriate career advice or enter girls for fewer subjects, the girls would seek advice from other sources, avoid subjects where they perceived the teacher to be racist and support each other academically, resigning themselves to staying on at college to supplement their qualifications if necessary. Mirza did not see this as a form of resistance, but as a rational response to their negative school experience.

Archer (2003) considered Muslim boys and how they demonstrated their masculine and religious identity in peer groups, against a backdrop of Islamophobia and the demonisation of young Muslim males in the media. They saw their identity as Muslim rather than Pakistani, but were also conscious of the protection that being a member of their subculture gave them against other racial groups and the potential for racist bullying.

Distinct differences in the reaction to underachievement between different ethnic groups were highlighted by Strand and Winston (2008), with only one group they studied being particularly affected by anti-school subcultures. They found that negative peer relationships were a particularly significant issue in the underachievement of African-Caribbean boys, whereas for white boys, underachievement was more related to low self-esteem and lack of parental aspirations. They also found that Asian and African boys tended to have positive peer support, and some seemed genuinely surprised when asked whether their friends would laugh at them for working hard or doing well in lessons. Thus, anti-school attitudes seem to develop more among some ethnic groups than others, and intersect with other factors in contributing to underachievement in school.

The media and youth deviance

Note: More on this issue can be found in Chapter 5 on page 180.

Newspaper reports and television coverage exaggerate stories to make them more interesting. Interactionists argue that the media often does this with youth deviance. It exaggerates and over-reports it (a form of labelling), which can then lead to deviance amplification. This means that deviance actually increases as more people are aware of it, and more young people are encouraged to behave in this way, due to labelling and the self-fulfilling prophecy.

You may think that media representations of troublesome youths are a new thing, as the media continually despairs of the 'out-of-control' youth. However, media outcries about youths date back longer than you may imagine, and not just to the 1960s – though this is when media coverage of fights between mods and rockers became the first identified 'moral panic'.

Pearson's research (1983) shows that even in the nineteenth century, social concern about rowdy youths, or 'Hooligans' as they became known, led to sensationalist newspaper headlines and campaigns, denouncing the behaviour as 'alien' and 'un-British' and even blaming it on the hot weather of the August Bank Holiday in 1898 when the trouble first flared up, claiming they were behaving like 'hot-blooded foreigners' due to the heat! Stories continued to appear in the following years, some related to new incidents, but others seemingly just to fill space and keep the outrage alive, with articles asking 'What are we to do with the Hooligan?' (*The Times*, 30 October 1900). Some incidents that now seem fairly minor, such as the knocking over of an ice-cream vendor's barrow, made the newspapers, and it was reported that the boys left the scene shouting 'look out for the Hooligan gang'. Additionally, many crimes related to violence were subsequently reported with the 'Hooligan' tag, whether or not they were actually youth- or gang-related.

Study

Folk Devils and Moral Panics – Cohen (1972)

Stanley Cohen examined media coverage of the mod and rocker clashes in the 1960s. Following an initial altercation between youths styling themselves as mods and rockers on a bank holiday in Clacton in 1964, the media predicted more at other resorts during that summer, and went to these resorts in force to cover the anticipated trouble. Cohen argued that the subsequent coverage was out of proportion to the incidents themselves. He interviewed magistrates, police officers, and the mods and rockers themselves and studied media coverage of the incidents, and found very different views of the same events. According to Cohen, the fights between mods and rockers were no different to the evening brawls that occurred between youths throughout the 1950s and early 1960s, both at seaside resorts and after football games, but due to the media coverage, the public developed an exaggerated concern about the 'problem'. Cohen argued that the media had created a moral panic about young people at this time, and had turned the mods and rockers into 'folk devils'.

A moral panic is an over-exaggerated reaction among the public to a social issue, which has been created and encouraged by the media. This often centres around a particular group of people, frequently youths, who are blamed for the social issue, and thus turned into 'folk devils', or scapegoats. Language and images used in media coverage, as well as the frequency of stories, can contribute to the development of a moral panic. For example, newspapers at the time of the mods and rockers clashes used terms such as 'vermin' and 'louts', and raised concerns about the future of the nation, contributing to a public over-reaction.

Activity

Newspaper coverage of the clashes between mods and rockers in 1964

The clashes at seaside towns during the spring and summer of 1964 became headline news. On 30 March, after clashes in Clacton, the *Daily Mirror* ran the headline 'Wild Ones invade seaside – 97 arrests'. The term 'wild ones' was a reference to a film starring Marlon Brando, *The Wild One*, released in the US in 1953, but banned in Britain for 14 years. Many had seen it despite the ban, and Brando's character had become a cult hero, especially to the rockers. The front-page *Mirror* article began:

> 'The wild ones invaded a seaside town yesterday – 1,000 fighting, drinking, roaring, rampaging teenagers on scooters and motor-cycles. By last night, after a day of riots and battles with the police, ninety seven of them had been arrested.'

On 8 April 1964, the *Daily Star* had the headline 'Mods and wreckers'. On the same day, in an 'Express Special on the lunacy that scarred Easter', the *Daily Express* led with the headline 'Beasts! Boot gang savages victim'. The *Daily Mirror*, on 18 May 1964, led with 'Wild ones "beat up" Margate', stating that after Clacton, there was 'a new battlefield'. The *Daily Sketch* continued the theme the following day with the headline 'Wildest ones yet'.

1 Identify the words and phrases in the newspaper coverage that could contribute to causing a moral panic about the mods and rockers.

2 What similarities can you see between this and the coverage of the Hooligans studied by Pearson in the late nineteenth century?

Cohen showed how agents of social control, particularly the police, 'amplified' deviance. Similarly, Young (1971) looked at the meanings attached to interactions by police and hippies. The police tended to see the hippies as dirty, scruffy, idle 'pot-heads' (constantly smoking marijuana). They brought these meanings to any interaction they had with the hippies. The result was that drug-taking, which Young argued had been a peripheral activity, started to become a central part of the hippies' identity. The police actions led the hippies to form a more cohesive group and identity and exaggerate the original deviant traits perceived by the police. Young argued that there are three stages of deviancy amplification:

1 translation of fantasy (police are susceptible to accepting media stereotypes because they are isolated)
2 negotiation of reality (police negotiate the evidence they find to fit the preconceived stereotypes)
3 amplification (labelling of hippies as 'drug-takers', leading to a self-fulfilling prophecy that may amplify deviance).

Activity: Moral panics in the 1980s and 2000s

Item A: Rave – a moral panic for the 1980s
Following its emergence in the late 1980s, media reports of rave culture often involved stories about drug consumption, particularly ecstasy. Brown (2012) points out that the behaviour of people involved was often distorted and exaggerated, and rave culture was connected to wider concerns about 'youth' and cultural decline in the UK. Tabloid newspapers often ran stories about the perils of taking ecstasy, which were accompanied by photographs of 'writhing masses of sweaty teenagers'. One *Sun* headline entitled 'Spaced out!' was accompanied by such a photo, along with a caption saying, 'Night of ecstasy ... thrill-seeking youngsters in dance frenzy at the secret party attended by more than 11,000' (Fantazia n.d.). It can be argued that this media attention led to deviance amplification since it raised awareness of rave culture and the number of people attending raves escalated.

Item B: Hoodies – a moral panic for the 2000s
Fawbert (2008) looked at the coverage of hoodies in the media. Though some shopping centres had already banned them, it was in May 2005, when the Bluewater shopping centre banned hoodies, that a moral panic began, driven by the tabloid press. The term 'hoodie' became a stigmatising label and the media vocabulary was sensationalised as journalists attempted to outdo each other. Statements about how to deal with 'hoodies' became more and more extreme, with even the former Metropolitan Police Commissioner Sir John Stevens calling for longer prison sentences for 'thugs wearing hoods'. Public opinion was also affected; most of the public thought youth crime was increasing, which was not true.

1 Write a summary of how 'rave' or 'hoodies' can illustrate folk devils and moral panics, in the same way that Hooligans and mods and rockers did. You could do an internet search for newspaper headlines or articles and see if the language used is similar to that found by Cohen in the 1960s.
2 Can you think of another moral panic involving youth and apply this analysis?

Check your understanding

Briefly define the following terms and give an example of each:

1 delinquent subcultures
2 spectacular subcultures
3 anti-school subcultures
4 status frustration
5 focal concerns
6 relative deprivation
7 paradox of inclusion
8 moral panic
9 folk devil
10 deviance amplification.

Fill in the blanks, using the words given below.

Young people are often associated with _____, and sociologists try to explain their reasons for joining deviant subcultures. _____ explanations focus on norms and values, and the responses that working-class youths may have to experiencing _____. Similar ideas have been applied to youths from ethnic minorities, who may experience a _____ according to Nightingale; the strong desire to belong is what leads to deviant choices. _____ also consider exclusion and relative deprivation, but tend to focus more on the _____ response that this may create among youths. Deviant subcultures tend to be associated with males, and the pressure to prove their _____ is an explanation suggested by _____. Interactionists argue that the process of _____ by both teachers and the police may explain youth involvement in _____ as well as criminal activities.

Youth deviance is often exaggerated in the media, and youth are turned into _____. This can create a _____ about youth and even lead to _____ in some circumstances, where the deviance is increased due to the media coverage.

anti-school subcultures, blocked opportunities, deviance, deviance amplification, folk devils, functionalist, labelling, Marxists, masculinity, Messerschmidt, moral panic, paradox of inclusion, resistant

Practice questions

1 Define and briefly explain the concept of anti-school subcultures. [5]
2 Evaluate Marxist and/or neo-Marxist views on the formation of youth subcultures. [20]

Practice questions

1 Outline two ways in which ethnicity influences youth subcultures. [12]
2 Assess the view that gender is a significant reason for young people participating in deviant subcultures. [24]

Chapter 5

The media

Component 1, Section B, Option 3

The media

Content:

1 How are different social groups represented in the media?
2 Theoretical views of media representations
3 What effect does the media have on audiences?

Getting you thinking ...

1 What should be the role of the media in a multicultural society?
2 In what ways are minority ethnic groups represented in the mainstream media? Give both positive and negative examples.
3 Do you think that the mainstream media uses stereotypes when representing minority ethnic groups? Do you consider this to be a good thing or a bad thing? Give reasons for your answer.

5.1 How are different social groups represented in the media?

Ethnicity

According to the 2011 UK Census, minority ethnic groups represent 12.9 per cent of the UK population and the majority of the main minority ethnic groups are British-born and British citizens. The UK is regarded as a multicultural society, i.e. a society within which great differences of language, religion and lifestyle co-exist. It is argued that media representations of majority and minority ethnic groups ought to reflect the diversity of a multicultural society. However, there are those who would contend that the media should help immigrants to assimilate to British culture.

Research finds evidence of continuity and change in media representations of majority and minority ethnic groups. Some research uncovers evidence that media representations of minority ethnic groups are shaped by what media professionals believe the majority white British audience want to see, hear and read, and, as a result, ethnic minorities are generally under-represented or are represented in negative or stereotyped ways. This finding is not completely uniform. Some groups are represented more negatively than others and the representations vary across the media. In addition, representations vary across different ethnic groups and can also be seen to respond to wider social factors. Much of the research into media representations finds that minority ethnic groups are presented in limited, stereotyped ways or are marginalised and excluded from representation in the media.

Media representations of minority and majority ethnic groups – Van Dijk (1991)

One study of media representations of minority and majority ethnic groups was Van Dijk's (1991) content analysis of news reports in the UK (and the Netherlands) over a ten-year period. His research highlighted a number of stereotypes that are used to portray black people in the media. Van Dijk's ideas have been summarised under five categories (Moore *et al.* 2005); members of minority ethnic groups are portrayed:

1 as criminals – the word 'black' is often used in descriptions of criminals but 'white' is not generally used in this way. The study *Policing the Crisis* (Hall *et al.* 1978) discusses the use of this stereotype. In addition, Hall *et al.* argue that characterisations of patterns of crime around the term 'mugger' represent an example of a moral panic (see page 180) with the stereotypical portrayal of the 'black mugger' as an example of a 'folk devil'.

2 as abnormal – media representation of the cultural practices of minority ethnic groups (such as arranged marriages) as odd or abnormal (Ethnic Focus 2004). There is evidence that members of such communities object to homogeneous terms such as 'Asian culture' which conceal a diversity of cultural traditions with developing practices and values. Media representations of cultural values and practices among minority ethnic groups are often portrayed as contrasting with the 'normal' values and practices of the 'host' community.

3 as a threat – tabloid scares about immigrants and asylum-seekers taking jobs and using the resources of the welfare state. In particular, mainstream media representations of Islam have been described as a mixture of some fair-minded portrayals alongside widespread stereotypical portrayals of Muslims as 'intolerant, misogynistic, violent or cruel, and finally, strange or different' (Nahdi 2003).

4 as dependent – images of less developed countries tend to focus on what has been described as 'coup-war-famine-starvation syndrome' with little discussion of their exploitation by Western countries. Critics of representations that centre on high-profile celebrity endorsement of campaigns such as Make Poverty History and Live 8 suggest that there is an absence of balance in such portrayals. Critics also argue that the perspective of developing nations themselves is often neglected, as is the perspective of minority ethnic groups within the contemporary UK.

5 As unimportant – the way in which priority is given to the reporting of issues affecting white people. This is seen as evident in the reporting of crimes against black and Asian people compared with the reporting of crimes against white people. Sir Ian Blair, a former Metropolitan Police Commissioner, spoke of 'institutional racism' among the British media in the pattern of reporting of murders. He cited the way in which newspapers devote less attention to the murders of people from minority ethnic backgrounds compared to the murders of those from the majority ethnic population (Ligali 2006).

Van Dijk argued that the negative language used and lack of reference to quotations from minority ethnic sources resulted in biased reporting that gave a white perspective on news stories.

Point to discuss and research

1 One part of Van Dijk's content analysis entailed identification of key words that featured in headlines about race in national newspapers. For example, he discovered that the most frequent words seen over a five-year period were 'police', 'riot', 'black' and 'race' (Van Dijk 1991: 54). Conduct a similar content analysis of three newspaper headlines over a week and present your findings as a chart. Explain what you think your findings demonstrate about representations of ethnicity.

Malik (2002b) expressed concern that the contemporary media does not accurately reflect the ethnic reality of the contemporary UK. Her research suggested that there are changes in media use among minority ethnic groups. In increasing numbers, members of minority ethnic communities are declining to watch mainstream TV channels (20 per cent less in 1996) and, when they are financially able, switching to new cable and satellite networks that are specifically designed for minority ethnic audiences. This change in media use means that media representation of minority ethnic communities has changed. Malik later highlighted research commissioned by Channel 4 (2008) that found that while most white viewers felt broadcasters were doing a satisfactory job in representing multicultural Britain, all other ethnic

The British media

'The reality of a lived multiculturalism is not represented on British television and the media in general can by no means be seen as ethnically neutral. Although it is now common to see black and Asian people on British television who do not necessarily function to solely "carry" the race theme, the repertoire of imagery still remains limited. We rarely see strong Asian women or black factual commentators outside sports programmes and there are still too few black people actually reaching the industry's boardrooms. Television is still far too "white"; an admission made by the BBC's newly appointed Director General, Greg Dyke, following his visit around BBC departments.'

Source: Malik (2000: 366)

1 List the concerns expressed by Malik about the British media.
2 What do you think Malik means by 'a lived multiculturalism'? Can you think of examples of films or television programmes that represent the reality of 'a lived multiculturalism'?
3 Do you agree with Greg Dyke that television is still far too 'white'? Write a paragraph giving arguments for and against this view.

groups felt their performance was 'very poor'. The research found accusations that mainstream broadcasters were guilty of tokenism and stereotyping, screening exaggerated and extreme representations of minority communities and failing to reflect modern minority ethnic culture, and were responsible for a lack of black and Asian people in positions of power within the media.

Malik noted that change in representations is evident within the genre of reality TV, stating that 'viewers interviewed for the research praised programmes such as Strictly Come Dancing, The Apprentice and X Factor for reflecting diversity' and commenting that 'It has become one of the most racially varied forms of programming today' (Malik 2008).

Malik argued that there has also been a change in representations within alternative media (i.e. media that presents an alternative to the mainstream media) that portrays the experience of minority ethnic communities from their perspective. However, she also noted that there are continuing concerns that representations of minority ethnic groups have not changed in the mainstream media in ways that accurately reflect the ethnic diversity of the multicultural UK.

Chris Barker (1999) studied representations of minority ethnic groups in the soap opera *EastEnders* alongside other examples. This programme is seen as reflecting changes in representations of minority ethnic groups in that it contains a range of black and Asian characters with significant roles and the community that is portrayed in the show can be described as multi-ethnic. On the other hand, he noted that the series has been criticised for using stereotypes since black and Asian characters have been cast as doctors and shopkeepers. Barker argued that the programme fails to engage with wider structural forms of racism and portrays black and Asian characters' experience as the product of individual character traits. He also argued that black and Asian characters occupy more marginal roles within the drama and that the central characters remain white. Barker's research identified both continuity and change in the representation of minority ethnic communities in the mainstream media.

Minority ethnic backgrounds

1 Identify the characters in *EastEnders* or another soap opera/sitcom who come from a minority ethnic background.
2 How far do these characters from minority ethnic backgrounds conform to ethnic stereotypes?
3 Are they central characters in the programme?
4 Are issues of ethnicity and racism considered? If so, how are they dealt with?
5 How far would you say the situation has changed since Barker wrote in 1999? Write a paragraph to explain your view.

It has been argued that some changes in representations of minority ethnic groups entail a shift from a type of overt racism in the portrayal of minority ethnic groups towards a type of 'inferential' racism (Hall 1995). Overt racism is apparent when racist arguments are presented favourably. It is argued that overt racism does occur in media representations but that inferential racism is more evident in recent media portrayals. Inferential racism occurs when coverage seems balanced but is based on racist assumptions. TV news and current affairs programmes make an effort to be balanced, yet debates are often based on the assumptions that black people are the 'source of the problem' (Hall 1995).

Hall (1995) has also argued that it is still rare for black and Asian actors to receive star billing but that this has become more common and in some cases has resulted in the production of positive images of minority communities.

The development of hybrid identities (see page 17) among minority ethnic groups has contributed to change in media representations and makes the overall picture more complex and challenging. The term 'hybridisation' describes a process of blending of cultures which is seen as occurring when different cultures come into close contact with each other or when a culture is strongly influenced by the more dominant culture of the US or Europe. This process of blending means that new cultures are constantly evolving. Styles of cooking can reflect such a process of hybridisation, as can many forms of popular music. Hybrid identities occur when people's social identity does not reflect a specific ethnic category but comes to reflect the diversity and complexity of the different cultures within their society. Hybridity means that media representations have to constantly evolve in order to take account of this diversity if they are to accurately reflect society. Media representations of hybrid identities constitute a change in the portrayal of minority and majority ethnic groups.

Overall, some sociological research suggests that contemporary media representations of ethnic groups incorporate a greater diversity of roles and more positive images are portrayed. However, evidence for these changes is not accepted uncritically and there are concerns that minority ethnic groups continue to be represented in stereotyped and marginalised ways. It is also important to be aware that representations vary across different ethnic groups and can also be seen to respond to wider social factors; for example, it is argued that the impact of the events of 9/11 has changed representations of some Asian groups.

A significant change in the media representations is the development of satellite channels devoted to specific minority ethnic groups (such as 'Asian TV') and these offer media representations that differ from mainstream media sources.

You will find more evidence related to the above debate in the later section on theoretical views of media representations.

Check your understanding

- Explain why the contemporary UK would be described as a multicultural society.
- Describe ways in which minority ethnic groups are stereotyped in the mainstream media.
- Evaluate the argument that the mainstream media is institutionally racist.
- Identify and evaluate evidence that media representations of minority ethnic groups have improved.

Gender

Getting you thinking ...

Which of these media representations offer a stereotyped portrayal of women and men and which portray an accurate picture of how women and men actually are in the contemporary UK?

Sociological research into representations of gender in the media from the 1960s to the 1980s showed that men and women were portrayed in very different ways. Women tended to occupy a limited number of roles as mothers, housewives and sex objects and men were seen as taking leading roles and embodying a wider range of stronger, more dominant characters. Tuchman (1978) argued that the narrow range of roles for women amounted to their 'symbolic annihilation'. Ferguson, in her study *Forever Feminine* (1983), argued that women's magazines promoted traditional ideals of femininity. As part of her research she conducted interviews with magazine editors who claimed that many media items were produced in response to readers' letters. Their view supports the pluralist argument that the content of magazines reflects the tastes and wishes of their audience and that changes will always occur to take account of these tastes. This debate still continues and there is evidence to support and challenge the view that media representations of gender change to reflect developments in society.

Ongoing sociological research points to a number of enduring representations of femininity and masculinity that reflect traditional stereotypes. Women are:
- relatively invisible in parts of the media. For example, a 2008 analysis by the Bristol Fawcett Society found that only 30 per cent of the main characters in a day's output from CBeebies were women. Also, prime-time dramas retained a 60/40 ratio of men to women in speaking parts. This pattern is also evident in sports coverage where women and men can be portrayed in very different ways. There is much greater coverage of men in sport and a strong tendency for women in sport to be portrayed in more sexualised or trivialised ways. Sociological research also suggests that there is a relative invisibility of women within mainstream news coverage.
- portrayed through an image or ideal of the feminine, including traditional ideals of women with a focus on 'him, home and looking good (for him)' (Ferguson 1983), as well as women as sex objects or beauty ideals, entailing distorted objectifications of the female form in terms of exaggerated slimness and emphases on beauty products and techniques to achieve the ideal. Some research has indicated links between these portrayals and instances of eating disorders and other mental health issues among women and girls.

Media representations of masculinity can be described:
- via a myth of men as possessing strength, competitive spirit and aggression and violence on the basis of some sort of biological predisposition. This is seen as evident in Hollywood films and in computer games (Easthorpe 1990).
- as portraying ideals such as that of the new man or the metrosexual man in which men are pictured as expressing their emotions, taking an interest in toiletries and designer label clothing and undertaking new roles within the home and family.
- as portraying a type of retributive masculinity in which traditional masculine virtues and attitudes towards women are aggressively re-asserted. This representation is often associated with some men's magazines. Whannel (2002) analysed media images of David Beckham as an example of both metrosexual and retributive masculinity.

Activity

Media representations of masculinity

1 Study the images of David Beckham and write a paragraph on the underlying messages they may be trying to convey, explaining your analysis.

2 Use the internet to find out more about Whannel's (2002) research and write a summary of his findings, showing how media representations of masculinity can contain conflicting views.

Some research provides evidence of an increasing number of positive female roles emerging, especially in television drama and films. Glascock (2001) describe portrayals of strong independent women such as the female lead in the TV drama *Prime Suspect* or the computer game character Lara Croft. Westwood (1999) offers a similar argument for change in representations of gender and uses the concept of transgressive female roles to describe portrayals that have gone beyond gendered expectations. Programmes such as *The X-Files* (shown in the UK 1994–2003), which starred Gillian Anderson as Agent Dana Scully, are seen as examples of media where a lead character takes a transgressive female role. Gill (2008) argues that there has been a change from passive to active in media representations of women in advertising. She contends that recent media representations within advertising portray powerful women who are not passive recipients of the 'male gaze'. However, she also argues that such portrayals often conform to the 'beauty myth' (see page 167) and cannot therefore be seen as evidence of a fundamental change in representations.

Activity

The 'beauty myth'

1 Using websites such as theguardian.com and goodreads.com, find out more about Naomi Wolf's (1991) concept of the 'beauty myth' and write a paragraph summarising her views.
2 Find examples to support the view that females take a more active and transgressive role in contemporary media representations.
3 In what way might these representations also conform to the 'beauty myth'?

Gauntlett (2008) notes evidence of a shift from the 1990s onwards away from more traditional gender roles across a range of media. His research into prime-time television in this period found that gender roles 'seemed to become increasingly equal and non-stereotyped' (2008: 63). Using the example of the sitcom *Friends*, Gauntlett argues that the characters were equal but different, with males and females adopting more modern characteristics that moved beyond traditional roles.

Activity

Content analysis of *Friends*

1 Watch an episode of *Friends* and conduct a content analysis of the main male and female characters.
2 Identify ways in which the main male and female characters may be seen to be equal but different.
3 Is there evidence of equality and inequality in their roles and the way they are presented? List the evidence.
4 Are there ways in which the characters conform to more traditional gender stereotypes? Explain your views.
5 Discuss your views in class.

Gauntlett's (2008) analysis of gender representations in films since the 1990s shows men and women as having similar skills and talents to each other. He refers to films like *Spiderman 3*, *Knocked Up* and *Fantastic Four: Rise of the Silver Surfer* as examples of modern films that present a challenge to conventional masculinity by showing more traditional masculine behaviour to be fundamentally flawed. Females in these films are more assertive.

However, Gauntlett notes that men still tend to take the leading roles, act as the hero to save a woman and are more likely than women to be lead characters as they get older (for example, Sean Connery, Harrison Ford and Bruce Willis).

Activity

Content analysis of films

1 Use content analysis to consider three contemporary films that you have seen recently.
2 What roles did the males and females take, including lead characters?
3 What skills and talents did they have in the films?
4 Compare the differences and similarities between the male and female characters and list these.
5 Present your findings in the form of a film review comparing the three films.

While Gauntlett believes that representations of gender on television have 'turned a corner' (2008: 63ff), he also suggests that trends towards equality may have reached a plateau as evidence shows that the ratio of men to women on television has hardly changed in a decade. Leading roles in dramas still tend to be played by men, many series on television centre on male characters and discussions about politics continue to be dominated by men.

In addition to the variety and ambiguity noted in portrayal of gender roles in TV and film over a long period, a more complicated picture arises from the vast contemporary range of media products that can be examined for their representations of gender roles. Media products include:

- newspapers of varied kinds
- online news forums, blogs and discussions
- TV programmes
- films.

This variety contains a huge range of images of gender and a large diversity of masculinities and femininities. Overall, there would appear to be a change from the findings of earlier sociological research but no simple line of development or improvement.

In addition, it is argued that media products examined by earlier researchers remain available on satellite and cable networks and via internet-based media outlets. It can be argued, therefore, that audiences are exposed to a more varied (and realistic) representation of gender roles alongside many traditional stereotypes.

You will find more evidence related to the above debate in the later section on theoretical views of media representations.

> **Check your understanding**
>
> 1 Describe traditional media representations of women and men.
> 2 Identify ways in which media representations of women and men have changed.
> 3 Evaluate the extent to which media representations of women and men reflect the actual experience of women and men in the contemporary UK.

Social class

> **Getting you thinking ...**
>
>
>
> 1 How easy is it to identify the social class background of characters portrayed in the mainstream media?
> 2 What factors indicate a person's social class?
> 3 To what extent do media representations of social class reflect the reality of people's lives in the contemporary UK?

Sociological research into media representations of social class has identified different trends in the portrayal of different social classes.

Media representations of the middle classes

There is little empirical evidence of media representations of the middle classes. It is argued that this social group are over-represented numerically in TV soap operas, dramas and sitcoms. In a similar way, many newspapers are aimed at a predominantly middle-class audience. For example, the *Daily Telegraph* and the *Daily Mail* newspapers are seen as focusing on the tastes, ideas and concerns of the middle classes (sometimes termed 'Middle England'). Middle-class people are portrayed in the entertainment media as educated and successful and able to cope with life's problems. It is argued that they also tend to be presented as representing the norm for society. Marxists argue that these characterisations serve to promote ruling-class ideology. For example, the British middle classes are often portrayed as products of a 'meritocracy' in which people who are successful are seen as deserving their success due to their hard work or their talents. Marxists believe that such media representations of the middle classes reinforce a type of 'false class consciousness' in which working-class people are deceived into believing that social inequality is a result of the middle classes deserving their success rather than as a result of unequal life chances. Pluralists, on the other hand, argue that media representations of the middle classes accurately reflect the way that media consumers perceive their society. Research into media portrayals of the middle classes finds little evidence of changing representations. This may be because media professionals themselves tend to come from the middle classes and also because this social class group is often regarded as stable and relatively conservative.

Activity

Media representations of the middle classes

1 Make a list of five films and/or television programmes that portray the middle classes.
2 Identify whether these portrayals are positive or negative.
3 Conduct a content analysis of the *Daily Mail* and write a report outlining what it content tells us about the tastes and concerns of the middle classes.

Media representations of the working classes

Research into media representations of the working classes has included consideration of the portrayal of traditional working-class communities such as those depicted in *EastEnders* and *Coronation Street*. It is argued that these representations tend to embrace a somewhat nostalgic perspective on working-class community life that is no longer experienced by most working-class people.

Dodd and Dodd (1992) present evidence for both continuity and change in media representations of working-class characters in *EastEnders*. They argue that the show has managed to introduce elements of realism that would not have seemed possible in earlier working-class soap operas such as *Coronation Street* in the 1960s. *EastEnders* has included issues such as 'unemployment, imprisonment, rape, drugs, alcoholism, attempted suicide, crime, murder, homosexuality, infidelity, divorce, AIDS, abortion, ageing and death' (1992: 128). Dodd and Dodd suggest that these aspects combine with a nostalgic portrayal of a working-class community as a relatively distinct, supportive communal environment that does not reflect contemporary working-class culture.

On the other hand, Newman (2006) argues that there are very few sitcoms, films or television dramas that concentrate realistically on the everyday lives of working-class people. This is in spite of the fact that this group comprises a numerically significant and important section of society. Newman points out that when working-class people are portrayed, they are often cast in an unflattering or pitying light.

Devereux (2008) argues that working-class people are seen as falling into two main categories. There are positive portrayals of 'happy' and 'deserving' poor that contrast with the negative images of those on welfare benefits.

Activity

Media representations of the working classes

1 Identify three news stories involving the working classes. Try to include at least one story where there are representations of 'deserving poor' and 'undeserving poor'.
2 Using content analysis or semiology, analyse these stories and the representations of those from the working classes.
3 Use your results to make a poster illustrating your key findings.

The Royle Family is often cited as an example of a sitcom known for its realistic portrayal of working-class family life at the turn of the millennium (running from 1998 to 2000). The scripts often contain conversations about the boring details of everyday life and episodes commonly revolve around a family occasion, such as the marriage of the family's daughter Denise, the birth of her first child and the child's christening. All of the episodes take place in the Royles' home, which appears to be a typical British council house or similar; most centre on the telly-centric living room. The speech, actions, jobs (or lack thereof), opinions and behaviours have all been praised as realistic. Noteworthy, perhaps, is the inclusion of the actor Ricky Tomlinson who, as a young man, was heavily involved in trades unions and working-class politics. This representation has been seen by some commentators as an example of a portrayal of working-class culture that is not simply a negative stereotype or nostalgia but is an attempt at a more realistic viewpoint.

Owen Jones, in his book *Chavs: The Demonization of the Working Class* (2012), argues that media use of the term 'chav' has come to represent a way of condemning working-class people and working-class culture. Jones uses the term 'chavtainment' to refer to 'reality TV shows, sketch shows, talk shows, even films ... dedicated to working-class Britain' that portray working-class individuals as 'bigoted, slothful, aggressive people who cannot look after themselves, let alone their children' (2012: 122). Jones criticises a number of successful TV shows, such as *Wife Swap* and *The Jeremy Kyle Show*, which he sees as deliberately portraying working-class people in a negative way. Jones contends that such representations seek to construct a type of underclass that contrasts with earlier ideas about working-class culture; he explores how the working classes have gone from being portrayed as 'the salt of the earth' to being portrayed as 'the scum of the earth'.

Some media representations of the working classes concentrate on social issues associated with extreme poverty. Such portrayals focus on themes such as 'scrounging' from the welfare state and living on the edges of criminality. Media representations of the underclass do this in a more overt way and reflect New Right views of underclass lifestyle.

Media representations of the 'underclass'

Bearing in mind that the 'underclass' is a contested concept, media representations of the underclass are almost universally negative and portray a social group that is seen as a threat to society's norms and values. Golding and Middleton (1982) examined media-generated moral panics about alleged welfare abuse. During their six-month content analysis-based study, they found that welfare issues, as such, did not make the news. Welfare was only seen as newsworthy when it was connected with other issues such as crime, fraud or sex. A key finding from their analysis was that the poor are constructed in the media as either deserving or undeserving. Golding and Middleton argued that the media demonises certain sections of the underclass and that this has contributed towards legitimising welfare cutbacks by the state.

On a similar theme, more recently, Price (2014) has labelled TV programmes that examine the life of the poorest in society, such as the Channel 4 series *Benefits Street* and the BBC two-part series *Famous, Rich and Hungry*, as 'poverty porn'. The phrase 'poverty porn' refers to media representations that are intended to exploit a programme's content in order to have a particular shocking effect on the audience and to shape people's response to the content of the programme. Price used discourse analysis and the ideas of sociologist Stuart Hall to argue that *Benefits Street* is intended to be 'decoded' by its audience as a portrayal of those aspects of lower-class culture that ought to be condemned by hard-working families (as well as middle- and upper-class people). He also argued that the 'the narratives in *Benefits Street* have a human and poignant quality, often presenting decent and compassionate people disenfranchised by an unfair society'. Price argues that these more empathic aspects of the representation are frequently missed by viewers and political commentators.

Chapter 5 The media

Activity

Media representations of the underclass

1 Identify and list at least five television programmes and characters from programmes that represent social class in the ways described above.
2 In groups, discuss how realistic you believe these representations to be.

Media representations of the upper classes

Media representations of the upper classes include the portrayal of the monarchy. Sociological research has produced evidence that large parts of the media appear to support the Royal Family. According to Nairn (1988), media representations of the Queen and other members of her family constitute something of a 'soap opera' in the attention that is given to all of their activities, including relatively trivial events. Media support for the Royal Family is seen as linked to the reinforcement of a sense of national identity. For example, royal events such as weddings and funerals are represented in the media as national events and may be public holidays. In addition, though negative or controversial actions by members of the Royal Family are reported in the news media, they are typically forgotten quickly and replaced by positive portrayals.

Nairn found that:

- The Royal Family as a concept equates to niceness, decency and ordinariness.
- The Royal Family are deemed to be 'like us, but not like us'; the Queen is seen as an ordinary working mother doing extraordinary things. An example might include the difficulties she has experienced with her children which ordinary people can relate to, such as divorce.
- An obsession with the Royal Family developed through British society following the Second World War.

On the other hand, there is evidence of change in media representations of the Royal Family, such as the media criticism of Prince Charles' lobbying of government ministers and civil servants in which he was reported as having met with government ministers 36 times since 2010. This was described by some journalists as inappropriate and unwise since the Prince is supposed to adopt a neutral attitude towards government policy. His meetings were assumed to have involved giving advice to government or questioning of government ideas. Other evidence suggests that such criticism is not sustained but is 'balanced' by positive portrayal of Prince Charles' charitable works. Overall, evidence indicates that little long-term attention is given to criticism of the Royal Family or to questioning of their role. Research into media representations of the Royal Family would seem to provide evidence of both continuity and some change.

Activity

Media representations of the upper classes

1 Find five different media products such as newspapers, TV programmes and film portrayals of the Royal Family and critically examine their intended meaning.
2 Does the media represent the Royal family in a positive or critical way?

The upper classes are an under-studied area of research, perhaps because they are an elite group that practise social closure, which makes it difficult for sociologists to gain access to them. It is often argued that upper-class or wealthy people are seldom represented in a critical light or their role in society scrutinised or questioned. They tend to be portrayed positively and as deserving of their position of wealth, power and celebrity. Traditional members of the upper classes are represented in either an eccentric or nostalgic light such as in television costume dramas such as *Downton Abbey* or films such as *The King's Speech*.

According to Reiner (2010), contemporary representations of people with wealth show them as examples of success within a meritocratic society. This means that when people are shown as having enormous wealth, their achievements are celebrated and the audience is encouraged to identify with the culture of consumption and materialism that is portrayed in the lifestyle of the wealthy.

The portrayal of meritocracy is seen by neo-Marxists as evidence that such media representations are part of an effort to maintain 'false class consciousness' that discourages critical examination of why some people have enormous wealth and others remain poor, and why some people in society seem more able to access private schools and elite universities such as Oxford and Cambridge and others seem unable to thrive in education in spite of their own intelligence and ability. Media representations of wealth tend to focus on 'celebrity culture'. TV programmes, magazines and internet-based media devote large amounts of time and attention to the deeds and lifestyles of celebrities with very little attention being paid to the appropriateness or otherwise of such enormous wealth and prestige in a society where many people doing 'worthwhile' work receive minimal pay and recognition.

Activity

Celebrity culture
1 Collect information from magazines, such as *Hello!*, about the way that the media represents celebrity culture. Give at least four examples.
2 Critically examine any messages contained in these sources.
3 What lifestyle is being portrayed?
4 What norms and values are being promoted?

You will find more evidence related to the above debate in the later section on theoretical views of media representations.

Check your understanding ✓

- Explain media representations of celebrity culture.
- Describe media representations of the Royal Family.
- Explain how media representations of the middle classes might be seen as a form of 'false class consciousness'.
- Identify different ways in which working-class culture is portrayed in the mainstream media.

Age

Getting you thinking ②

1 Draw up a list of the stereotypes that you think are most likely to be used to represent young people and older people.
2 Discuss which group is most likely to be negatively represented and the reasons why this might be the case.

Sociological research into media representations of age tends to concentrate on presentations of the young and old. Research into age has identified the use of stereotypes across a range of media.

Media representations of Childhood
Media representations of children show a varied picture. Some research points to media representations that offer stereotypical portrayals of children's lives.

Study

Children and television – Heintz-Knowles (2002)
Katharine Heintz-Knowles conducted a content analysis of ways in which children are portrayed in entertainment television. This entailed closely examining children's entertainment programmes portraying child characters (i.e. not child news, talk or reality shows). From her analysis, a number of somewhat contradictory findings emerged:

- Children shown on entertainment television are motivated most often by peer relationships and romance, and least often by school-related or religious issues.
- Entertainment television almost never shows children grappling with important issues.
- On commercial broadcast networks, a majority of the child characters engage in anti-social behaviours, and those behaviours often yield positive results for the characters.
- Children from minority ethnic backgrounds are under-represented on entertainment television.

- Girls and boys are almost equally well represented on entertainment television, but there are important differences in the ways that girls and boys are portrayed; for example, girls are twice as likely as boys to show affection and boys are 60 per cent more likely to use physical aggression to achieve their goals.

It is suggested that these representations contain a number of stereotypes and that the programming reflects an adult perspective on children and on their interests and concerns.

Some have argued that this picture has changed since Heintz-Knowles did her research (which was published in 2002 but was actually conducted a number of years before). TV drama is regarded as a medium in which there has been a gradual move towards more realistic portrayal of issues from a child's point of view rather than the adult's point of view.

Points to discuss and research

1 Identify examples of current children's TV programmes that you are familiar with. Does Heintz-Knowles' finding that children's TV programmes contain various stereotypes about children's lives and attitudes apply to your examples?

2 Discuss the programmes that you have selected and consider whether mainstream programmes produced since 2002 offer a more balanced and/or realistic representation of children.

Children are frequently portrayed as more effective and skilled users and consumers of the media than their adult carers. This can lead to a situation in which 'faith in technology' is seen as replacing 'faith in adults'. Adult concerns over the safety of children in their use of the internet are the source of a number of moral panics related to child access to internet chatrooms.

Another concern about children in their use of the media is the increasing media representation of children as consumers. It is argued that the advertising industry's targeting of children and the influence of what has been termed children's 'pester power' to persuade parents and carers to finance the purchase of consumer goods targeted at children (including products such as games consoles, computers, phones, and so on) can lead to financial strains for parents and families.

Postman's research into childhood (1982) suggested that the development of entertainment media from the 1950s has had an effect on 'childhood' as a stage in life. Postman argued that childhood had not existed as a concept in earlier historical eras (children in medieval times, for example, were seen simply as younger adults and were not excluded from the realities of the adult 'world') and that the modern idea of childhood has begun to disappear as children interact more and more with the media. Postman was writing before the invention of the internet and the large-scale development of information technology, but his study of the effects of TV on children nevertheless illustrated sociological ideas about media representations of children. He described ways in which children are prematurely sexualised in media portrayals and the ways in which the media creates a world in which adults and children share the same music, sports, language, literature and films. One illustration of the effects of this lies in the lack of differentiated clothing styles (little girls in high heels, adult men wearing trainers) and the effects of this on young people's self-concept. Postman's ideas can be seen as examples of changes in media representations of children.

Activity

Children's clothing

1 Use semiology to analyse the meanings of these types of children's clothing.
2 How would different feminist perspectives respond to this photograph?

Media representations of youth

Sociological research has identified a phase in media representations of youth that celebrated the relative freedom and prosperity of young people during the 1950s and 1960s. More recent representations of youth culture emphasise youth as a problem for society. Younger people are seen as a social threat in that they deviate from society's norms and values. These more recent media representations of young people make frequent links between younger people and binge-drinking, drug-taking, knife crime and other violent incidents.

For example, Osgerby (2002) studied the shifts in media representations of youth in the second half of the twentieth century. He noted a recurring theme of 'youth-as-trouble', a phrase coined by Hebdige (1988). Osgerby asserted that shifts in media representations of youth reflect wider cultural developments and mirror the spirit of the times. He illustrated this view by referring to the way in which the media represented youth positively in the 1950s and early 1960s in a post-war mood of hope and prosperity. This contrasted with darker images of teenage violence in the 1970s and 1980s which seemed to reflect concerns about growing lawlessness and social breakdown. Moral panics, including Cohen's classic study *Folk Devils and Moral Panics* (1972) (see page 181), provide illustrations of such media representations of youth as dangerous and deviant.

Study

Television news and young people – Wayne (2007)

Mike Wayne (2007) and a team of researchers at Brunel University examined ways in which young people are portrayed on television news. Their analysis covered 2,130 news items across all the main television channels during May 2006. They found 286 stories in which young people were the main subject of the news item. Of these stories, 28 per cent focused on young celebrities, such as footballers Wayne Rooney and Theo Walcott. Wayne comments that this 'mirrored the wider role that young people play in commercial culture'. 82 per cent of the stories focused on young people as either perpetrators or victims of crime. Violent crime made up 90 per cent of these crime-related stories. Wayne argued that this pattern of representation of youth ignores 'stories about how young people are affected by problems in housing, education, health, unemployment, parental abuse, politics and so forth' (Wayne 2007). In addition, young people accounted for only 1 per cent of all of the sources for interviews and opinions that were on offer over the sample. In other words, news reporters did not ask young people for interviews even though the stories related to them.

A study commissioned by the organisation Women in Journalism called *Hoodies or Altar Boys?* (2009) examined national and regional newspaper content, looking at how stories on teenage boys were covered. The results found:

- Terms used in newspaper stories about teen boys included 'thugs', 'yobs', 'hoodies', 'feral', 'evil', 'lout', 'monsters', 'brutes', 'scum', 'menace', 'heartless', 'sick', 'menacing' and 'inhuman'.
- There were more newspaper stories about teens and crime (as victims or offenders) than about teens and all other subjects put together.
- Even on subjects other than crime, few newspaper stories showed teen boys in a good light. Only 24 per cent of stories about teens and sport

were positive about teen boys and only 16 per cent of stories about teens and entertainment were positive.

The researchers also conducted a survey of a representative sample of 1,000 teenage boys aged 13–19.

Findings for this part of the research showed that:

- 85 per cent of teen boys said newspapers portray them in a bad light.
- Reality TV was seen as portraying teen boys most fairly.
- Media stories about yobs and hoodies were the main reason why teen boys were wary of other teenagers.
- 80 per cent of teen boys thought that adults were more wary of them than they were a year previously.

Activity

Hoodies or Altar Boys?

1 Does the Women in Journalism study indicate that media representations of youth are changing?
2 Conduct an analysis of two types of media product:
   a) two newspapers containing news stories about young people
   b) two magazines devoted to young readers.
3 Decide what image of youth is being portrayed in these media representations and draw a poster to illustrate your conclusions.

Media representations of older people

Research into media representations of older people reveals a pattern of portrayal that, in some respects, mirrors the experience of other social groups – in other words, a mixture of relative invisibility and of stereotyping.

Landis (2002) identified a number of stereotypes in representations of older people in TV and film. She described typical portrayals as 'one-dimensional' and identified certain types:

- grumpy old man
- feisty old woman
- sickly old person
- mentally deficient
- depressed or lonely
- having wisdom
- busybody
- having a second childhood.

She contended that such one-dimensional representations ignore the complexity of real characters. In support of this view, Cuddy and Fiske

(2004) showed that in the US, TV programmes portrayed just 1.5 per cent of their characters as elderly. Most of them appeared in minor roles, and usually as figures of fun to provide comic relief, often based on ineffective mental, physical and sexual capacities.

This view is supported in a recent study by Milner, Van Norman and Milner (2012). They report that '[too] often missing from media portrayals is a balanced view of ageing; one that reflects the challenges of getting older, while embracing the opportunities associated with ageing.'

On the other hand, Carrigan and Szmigin (2000) showed the effect of an older audience on advertisers' representations of age. They referred to the 'grey pound', i.e. more older people with money to spend. This has led to an increase in positive images of ageing and positive roles for older people and shows the way in which large conglomerates target the older people's market.

Biggs (1993) argued that there is evidence of change and continuity in representations of older people. He identified contrasting trends in the representations of ageing, including:

- older people appearing in considerable numbers in soap operas
- negative portrayals of old age in sitcoms
- a move towards a more active view of older people.

Activity

Representations of older people

1 Construct a chart listing the research from the section above on representations of older people. List the name of study and three key points in summary of its findings.
2 Add in contemporary examples in support of each study, such as from television shows.
3 Does the evidence indicate a change in representations of older people?

You will find more evidence related to the above debate in the later section on theoretical views of media representations.

Check your understanding

- Describe ways in which children are stereotyped in the media.
- Explain how media representations of youth have changed since the 1950s.
- Evaluate the evidence of changing representations of older people in the media.
- Identify common patterns in media representations of age across the age groups.

5.2 Theoretical views of media representations

Marxism

Marxists believe that the media is part of the superstructure of society and that it supports the economic base, which is controlled by the bourgeoisie.

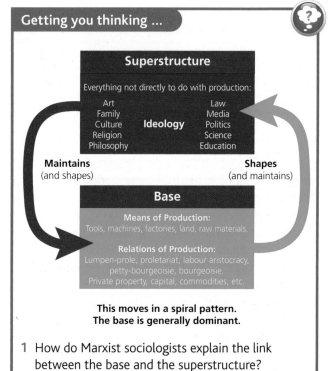

Getting you thinking ...

This moves in a spiral pattern.
The base is generally dominant.

1 How do Marxist sociologists explain the link between the base and the superstructure?
2 Explain how Marxist sociologists might see the role of the media as part of the superstructure.

The media and the role of ideology

Marxists believe that, as a part of the superstructure, the media helps the ruling class because it transmits ideology; it puts across ideas that make the existing unequal social system appear to be natural, fair and legitimate when, in fact, inequalities in society come from the way that capitalism functions. The media is seen as helping to create false class consciousness amongst the working class, which stops them from challenging this unequal, exploitative system. Therefore, Marxists are opposed to the mainstream media as they believe it helps to maintain an unfair society and stops people from thinking critically.

Key Marxist theorist Ralph Miliband, in his book *The State in a Capitalist Society* (1969), argued that the ruling class use the media to control society by creating a false picture of reality that presents capitalism in a positive way. He argued that the media presents the inequalities created by the capitalist system in such a way as to make them appear inevitable, justifiable and effective for society. As a result, the proletariat accept the values of the capitalist system even though these values are not in the interests of their class. Miliband was concerned about the impact of the media on society and referred to it as the 'new opium of the people'. This drew on a reference from Marx in 1844 about religion being the 'opium of the people'. Miliband believed that the media has replaced religion as the institution that acts like a drug to numb the senses and produce an illusion of happiness that is not real. In other words, the media takes the proletariat's attention away from the exploitation and oppression of the capitalist system and allows the ruling class to control and dominate the working class. One way that the media does this is in the way that it represents certain social groups in society.

Activity

Ideology in the media

1 Make a list of at least five examples of media products, such as TV programmes or films, that may be seen as transmitting ideology and explain how they do this.

2 Investigate the concept of 'dumbing down' and write a sentence to explain how it links to the Marxist views on the media.

3 In groups, discuss how the concepts of 'ideology', 'false consciousness' and 'dumbing down' might have an effect on the way in which different social classes are represented in the media.

4 Write a paragraph using these three concepts to support the Marxist view on the media.

Both traditional Marxists and neo-Marxists agree that media representations of social groups are constructed in such a way as to support the interests of the ruling class and to maintain their power and control over the rest of society. However, traditional Marxists focus on social class in particular, as they see this as the fundamental inequality in society. Traditional Marxists also believe that power and control in the media lies with the ruling class, including the state and the owners of the media, and that they shape the way that social groups are represented. Marxists place considerable emphasis on the role of media owners and the power that they exercise to shape the ways in which different social groups are represented and the way in which society as a whole is understood. They argue that the ruling class are presented as trustworthy and deserving of their position in society. The poor are presented as feckless, ignorant and undeserving.

Marxists view society as engaged in a perpetual conflict between social classes – for example, the conflict between the bourgeoisie and the proletariat – but the media is seen as portraying society as characterised by consensus. This means that legitimate points of conflict in society are obscured when these realities are represented within the media. Media owners such as Rupert Murdoch are, therefore, seen as important factors in the ruling class's controlling influence within society. Different media owners are seen as part of the ruling class and as sharing the interests of the ruling class as a whole.

Marxists believe that the media uses particular representations of social class for the benefit of the ruling class. One way this happens is that the social class system is presented as fair and natural. Marxists see such representations as seeking to manipulate the working class into believing that they live in a meritocracy, which refers to a system where success is achieved through talent and ability rather than privilege or wealth, when in reality the rich do not deserve the wealth and power they have, as it is inherited.

Evaluation of Marxism

- Traditional Marxists have been criticised for focusing on social class and ignoring other forms of inequality such as ethnicity and gender in media representations. This criticism would be supported by neo-Marxists and feminists in particular.
- Traditional Marxists are seen to present an overly conspiratorial view of the role of media owners as a united group when, in reality, they are in competition with other.
- Traditional Marxists are criticised for failing to take account of the role of media professionals in constructing representations of social groups. For example, there are increasing numbers of female and minority ethnic journalists who construct positive representations. This is a criticism that would be supported by liberal feminists and pluralists.
- Pluralists would argue that traditional Marxists ignore the wide and varied range of representations in the media, including those that are critical of powerful groups in society. Pluralists would point to the increasing diversity and choice of forms of media and media products as evidence that media representations do not just conform to narrow stereotypes.
- Postmodernists believe that it is increasingly difficult to identify specific social groups in society as boundaries between them have become blurred. They argue that social class is no longer an important source of identity and so there is no clear way of identifying members of different social classes.

Neo-Marxism

Neo-Marxists see the media as playing a key role in strengthening ruling-class hegemony since the media has such a wide reach in society. Journalists and broadcasters tend to be white, middle class and male and more than 50 per cent have attended independent schools (Sutton Trust 2006), which only 7 per cent of the population as a whole attend. The neo-Marxist argument is that such media professionals promote ruling-class hegemonic ideas because they themselves share the norms and values of the dominant culture in society. The idea is that they consciously seek to produce media content that will be popular in the media marketplace but that they unconsciously produce media content that reproduces the norms and values of the ruling class.

Neo-Marxists see this hegemony operating in media representations of social groups. Neo-Marxists argue that social groups who are seen as threatening to white middle-class males are marginalised by being portrayed in negative, stereotyped ways and often subjected to ridicule as a way of neutralising their ideas and removing any threat.

Study

Stereotypes of black people – Hall (1981)

Stuart Hall argued that the media operates with three overriding stereotypes of black people: the native, the clown or entertainer and the slave:

- The native is seen as offering nobility, dignity and savagery. The native always appears in anonymous masses, contrasting with the solitary white hero.
- The clown or entertainer is seen as expressive, emotional and stupid.
- The slave figure is seen as devoted and childlike but also cunning, untrustworthy and maybe mocking.

Study (continued)

Such stereotypes were seen as being especially evident in old Hollywood films, but are surprisingly evident in more contemporary representations of black people and other minority ethnic groups. Hall argued that media representations of minority ethnic groups reflect an unconscious racism in that they typically portray black people as the 'source' of the problems that politicians and others are seeking to solve. Hall argued that representations of conflicts between members of minority ethnic groups and the police reflect the dominant ideology – for example, in the ways in which black and Asian people are seen as troublemakers in riots where television coverage defends the law.

Later, Hall identified a development in media representations where a more diverse range of images were presented. However, Hall saw such diversity as existing within a framework that is constructed by the powerful in society and does not present any challenge to their dominance.

Activity

Minority ethnic groups

1 Using examples from contemporary films and television programmes including the news, draw up a list of representations of minority ethnic groups.
2 Assess how diverse the representations are, taking into consideration factors such as status and power and whether the representations are positive or negative.
3 Summarise your findings in a paragraph.

Hall's neo-Marxist perspective on media representations of minority ethnic groups mirrors the findings of the Glasgow Media Group's (GMG) empirical research into the content of the media, including analyses of television news. Such research has focused on media representations of different social groups including working-class activity such as strikes and other industrial action in the 1970s and 1980s and, more recently, media representations of refugees and asylum-seekers (Philo *et al.* 2013). This research into refugees and asylum-seekers points out that media representations of such groups use a number of stereotypes that appear to mirror ideas that are encouraged by major political leaders and that political leaders and mainstream media outlets such as newspapers, TV and radio seem to be working together. The GMG used a mixture of qualitative and quantitative research methods and sought to identify a number of recurring themes within media representations. They noted the following themes:

- The conflation (or mixing together) of forced and economic immigration. Some immigrants are forced to come to the UK and others come to the UK because they have decided that they would be able to have a better standard of living if they did so. When these two types of immigration are conflated or merged together, people can think that all immigrants are here because they want to make money and ignore the fact that many immigrants have been forced to leave their own country due to circumstances beyond their own control.
- Threatening numbers – some media accounts appear to exaggerate the actual numbers of people immigrating to the UK.
- A burden on welfare and the job market – this is a frequent type of media representation, which ignores the possible economic benefits of immigration for the UK in favour of exaggerating the perceived burden that immigrants put on the welfare state and the job market.
- Criminality, threat, deportation and human rights – refugees and asylum-seekers are seen as threats to the UK population, prompting the need for high-profile deportations of particular figures, such as the Muslim cleric Abu Hamza, who was deported to the US in 2012.
- Need for immigration 'control' – this is a key theme in political debate and a frequent topic in newspaper headlines. The GMG pointed out that there is evidence that relaxing such controls would bring net benefits for the UK economy.
- The benefits of immigration receive only limited media coverage in spite of evidence in favour from key sources.
- Problems facing asylum-seekers in the UK are portrayed minimally in major media outlets.
- The role of the West in refugee movements and economic forces in migration – media representations generally ignore reasons why Western nations such as the UK can be held responsible for patterns of migration, for example, because of their role in armed conflict overseas; instead, the migrants themselves are blamed for immigration.

The GMG concluded that 'hysterical and inaccurate media accounts act to legitimise political action which can have terrible consequences both on the lives of refugees and also on established migrant communities' (Philo *et al.* 2013: back cover).

Activity

Content analysis of newspapers

IN THE NEWS

STOP THE MIGRANT INVASION

DAILY NEWS

SPEAK ENGLISH OR GO HOME

THE EXPRESS

ROMA MIGRANTS TERRORISE OUR STREETS

1 Analyse the content of five recent newspapers or other mainstream media to assess the extent to which issues of immigration and asylum correspond to stereotypes such as those identified by the GMG.
2 Write a 400-word report justifying your views.

Neo-Marxists would argue that media representations of social groups reinforce the hegemony that supports the ruling class in society. This analysis can be applied to representations of ethnicity, gender, social class and age where the images used will help to maintain dominant norms and values. Challenges to these norms and values will be presented as a threat or a joke, or will be ignored.

Activity

Media representations challenging norms

1 Working in groups, look at a variety of media representations (such as newspaper stories, characters in soap operas and films) of either gender, ethnicity, age or social class. Construct a list of examples of representations from within that social group that can be seen to present a challenge to social norms and values (for example, an article about female firefighters challenges traditional masculinity).
2 Discuss the ways in which these more alternative representations are presented.
3 Do the representations differ to the findings of the GMG?

Evaluation of neo-Marxism

- Neo-Marxism has been criticised for ignoring the evidence that shows significant improvements in the representations of social groups.
- It is argued that the increasing number of media available means that there is greater opportunity for variations in media representations including access to programmes and channels dedicated to particular social groups.
- Critics also point to the increasing number of media professionals coming from varied social backgrounds who bring a different perspective to the media they are involved with.
- On a positive note, the GMG (a key example of neo-Marxist research on the media) are often praised for their thorough approach to research which combines both qualitative and quantitative methods.

Check your understanding

- Describe the neo-Marxist perspective on cultural hegemony.
- Explain GMG ideas about media representations of refugees and asylum-seekers.
- Evaluate neo-Marxist ideas using postmodernist theories about people's ability to create their own meaning from media products and representations.

Pluralism

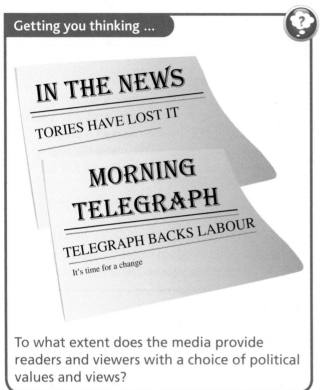

IN THE NEWS

TORIES HAVE LOST IT

MORNING TELEGRAPH

TELEGRAPH BACKS LABOUR

It's time for a change

To what extent does the media provide readers and viewers with a choice of political values and views?

Pluralism is a term that is used to describe theories of the media that were popular in the first 70–80 years of the twentieth century. Pluralist views often represent the perspective of media professionals such as newspaper editors and journalists and there is less empirical evidence to support the approach. Pluralists see media representations as unproblematic and offering a 'window on the world' rather than an unrealistic portrayal. Pluralist ideas centre around a number of key concepts that are useful in helping us to understand pluralists' views on media representations of social groups.

Diversity and choice

Pluralists argue that modern societies such as the UK are democracies in which there is a variety of views. They argue that the media represents the diversity of views and lifestyles that exist in society. People are seen as being able to choose which parts of the media they wish to access and they do this on the basis of their own values, interests and ideas. Pluralists argue that representations of social groups will reflect the diversity of society and, in any case, the audience is active in deciding whether they agree with media representations or not. They would argue that there is a range of ways that different views and representations can be expressed through the media – for example,

Russell Brand's alternative news broadcast *The Trews* on YouTube and his Twitter account, which has a following of 8.8 million. Pluralists would also point to the different TV channels that serve the interests of Asian audiences as an example of the variety of media that can serve a wide and diverse audience.

However, opponents of pluralism would argue that choice is shaped by the media itself and that diversity is limited by the powerful in society, including advertisers, who exercise significant control over media content, including representations.

Marxists would argue that alternative media does not gain a wide audience as they do not have the money to compete with the global capitalist organisations that can afford to spend millions of pounds getting their views across.

Supply and demand

Pluralists argue that media professionals and owners are governed by the markets they serve and that they are in competition for customers. They must compete in the media marketplace and would not be successful if they did not represent different social groups in ways that were fair and balanced. Pluralists argue that the media supplies what the audience demands. According to the pluralist view, media representations will develop to reflect changes in society as the media responds to meet society's needs. Therefore, media representations of social groups both reflect the diversity evident in society and the demands of their audience. According to Whale, a former newspaper reporter and supporter of the pluralist position, 'the broad shape and nature of the press is determined by no-one but its readers' (1980: 85).

> **Activity**
>
> **Media successes and failures**
>
> 1 Use an internet search engine to identify ten examples of media products that have failed due to lack of demand. For example, a search might look for examples of television programmes that failed or were cancelled.
> 2 Write a list of three factors that might influence the success and failure of media products.
> 3 Write an evaluative paragraph assessing the pluralist view that the principle of supply and demand shapes media representations of social groups.

Media workers as skilled professionals

Pluralists argue that media professionals are alert to the responsibility that they have to represent social groups in a fair and balanced way and are guided by professional values. They are also aware of the need to produce successful media that will appeal to the audience. Pluralism suggests that if different social groups were represented unfairly or in a stereotypical way, then people would not continue to use those media products. Pluralists argue that people can see through media representations that contain stereotypes and recognise when they are being manipulated. For example, while feminists argue that many women's magazines portray women in stereotypical and biased ways, pluralists believe that if women did not like these magazines and judged their content negatively, they would not continue to buy them.

Pluralists contend that the self-regulation that operates within the media profession is evidence of its integrity and trustworthiness. The News International phone-hacking scandal, which led to the closure of the *News of the World* in 2011, is seen as supporting the pluralist view. News International is a powerful and influential international media organisation partly owned by Rupert Murdoch and other members of his family. When the phone-hacking scandal came to light, it was realised that News International employees at the *News of the World* had been involved in the practice of 'hacking' (intercepting messages from) the phones of celebrities and members of the Royal Family, as well as people involved in tragic events such as the parents of the abducted child Madeleine McCann. There was a major scandal and the newspaper was closed, with high-profile media professionals being arrested and some jailed. This is seen by pluralists as evidence that media representations that go against professional values will be exposed and dealt with by

the profession. According to pluralists, this shows that the media can control any negative behaviour on the part of their members.

> **Activity**
>
> **The Leveson Report**
>
> 1 Find out about the Leveson Report published in 2012 by using an internet search engine to identify a summary of the Leveson Inquiry's findings.
> 2 Write your own report summarising the findings from the report that shed light on the role of media professionals.
> 3 Does the Leveson Report support or refute the pluralist view?
> 4 Write an evaluative paragraph about the role of media workers as skilled professionals. Include criticisms that Marxists and feminists would make.

The media as the Fourth Estate

The media is known as the Fourth Estate of Democracy because of its role in protecting democracy and freedom. The first three estates date from eighteenth-century French society which was divided into the estates of the clergy, the nobility and the commoners. In the contemporary UK the first three Estates are made up of government, the courts and the church. The media is known as the Fourth Estate because it is claimed that the media gives access to information that is an essential part of a democracy. It is seen as providing information that enables citizens to make responsible, informed choices rather than acting out of ignorance or misinformation. The media also performs a 'checking function' by ensuring that elected representatives uphold their oaths of office and carry out the wishes of those who elected them. The media monitors the political process in order to ensure that politicians do not abuse the democratic process. Williams (2010) argues that journalists provide an essential service in a democratic society in that they offer the information that people need to participate in political and cultural life. In terms of representations of social groups, this means that the media has an important role in ensuring that representations are fair and accurate.

Pluralists would also claim that the notion of a free press is vital within a democracy. If the press were subjected to censorship by government, then they may not be able to criticise political leaders and their policies. It is argued that UK newspapers and other media products frequently pass judgement on political leaders and even newspapers that traditionally support the Conservatives will criticise Conservative governments. Pluralists would cite a range of examples that show the important role of the media in exposing the wrong-doing of the powerful in society, such as MPs' expenses, tax avoidance and sex scandals. This shows that media representations of social groups are subject to scrutiny and should be fair and balanced.

However, it has also been argued that examples such as phone-hacking incidents only serve to demonstrate that the media cannot be trusted to act in a professional way that fairly represents different social groups.

Activity

The Fourth Estate

1 Use an internet search engine to find out about the role of the media as the Fourth Estate. Write a list of three examples of investigations that show the ways in which the media has protected society, and three examples that go against this view.

2 How do these examples help us to understand the role of the media in representing social groups? Write a paragraph to explain your view.

Support for pluralism

It can be argued that indirect theories of media effects, such as the two-step flow model (see page 175), provide empirical support for pluralist ideas about media representations. The argument is that people choose whether to believe media representations of social groups based on their contact with key opinion leaders within their communities. Media professionals are seen as seeking to make contact with their audience and as having to conform to the wishes of their audience. According to this view, 'audiences are seen as capable of manipulating the media in an infinite variety of ways according to their prior needs and dispositions and as having access to what Halloran (1997) calls "the plural values of society" enabling them to "conform, accommodate or reject" (Curran and Gurevitch 1977).

Activity

Political viewpoints

1 Conduct a survey of five different national newspapers to determine the political viewpoint being promoted.

2 Is there a fair spread of views among the papers in your survey?

3 Do people have an adequate degree of choice among print media?

4 Write a newspaper article or blog post to illustrate your findings.

Evaluation of pluralism

- Neo-Marxists, among others, argue that the media meets needs that are created by the media industry itself. Therefore the media does not just respond to people's needs; it can actually shape those needs via articles, advertising, and so on.
- The pluralist view ignores the negative impact that media representations can have on social groups, particularly those that are more marginalised in society.
- Pluralists are accused of ignoring issues of power and control in the way that media representations are constructed.
- Pluralists do not acknowledge that media professionals tend to come from narrow social backgrounds, which mean they may have a narrow world view, which limits the way they represent social groups that they are unfamiliar with.

Check your understanding

- Summarise and explain pluralist ideas about media representations of social groups.
- Identify evidence in support of pluralist ideas.
- Evaluate pluralist ideas on media representations in light of Marxist, neo-Marxist and feminist criticisms.

Feminism

Feminism is a theory that encompasses a number of strands. Feminists are united in opposing patriarchy and sex discrimination but the various strands offer different views on gender inequalities, including those that are identified within different media representations.

It is argued that gender roles in the twentieth-century UK were characterised by distinctively different social roles. Men were seen primarily as breadwinners occupying the public sphere, whereas women were seen as homemakers and as functioning within the private sphere of the family. Women were seen as more emotional and less rational than men. This vision, described as a form of patriarchal ideology by Connell (1995), was seen as being reinforced by the media as a key agency of secondary socialisation within society.

An example of this patriarchal ideology is the concept of the 'male gaze'. This concept was introduced by feminist theorist Laura Mulvey (1975) to characterise cinema as an instrument of male spectatorship. Mulvey used semiology in the analysis of films and the representation of women and her findings can be summarised in the key issues below:

1 Describe the representations of women that are displayed in these images.
2 Do you think that women are portrayed as equal to men?
3 In what ways, if any, do these images represent a change to traditional representations of women?
4 In what ways do these images represent traditional representations of women?

- Film as a form of media manifests the patriarchy of the culture in which it is created.
- Hollywood films are structured around the male gaze.
- The concept of the male gaze implies an active male subject of the gaze and a passive female object of the gaze, which satisfies male fantasies and desires.
- The film experience is one motivated by a patriarchal ideology that seeks to objectify women.
- Mulvey used semiology to analyse Hollywood films including Hitchcock's *Rear Window* and *Vertigo*.

Liberal feminists tend to be cautiously optimistic about the possibility of change and identify evidence of greater equality in media representations of gender. They believe that media representations of women change in accord with women's achievements in securing greater equality in society. However, they argue that changes in media representations tend to lag behind the actual changes that occur in society. They contend that there is a cultural lag as attitudes and ideas change more slowly than social and economic conditions. Liberal feminists note that greater numbers of women are now employed as media professionals and that this has contributed to changes in media representations of gender but that such changes in the gender balance of media professionals remains painfully slow. Research supporting the liberal feminist perspective indicates that there is a wider variety of roles for women in film and TV. These roles include dominant characters such as the female lead Ripley in the *Alien* films, Katniss Everdeen in *The Hunger Games*, Lisbeth Salander in *The Girl with the Dragon Tattoo* and Buffy in *Buffy the Vampire Slayer*. However, other research shows that women remain under-represented in the media industry. Lauzen (2014) found that women accounted for only 16 per cent of all directors, executive producers, producers, writers, cinematographers and editors. This data represents a decrease in numbers of two percentage points since 2012.

Activity

The male gaze

1 Using Mulvey's concept of the male gaze, analyse excerpts from Hitchcock films such as *Rear Window* and identify excerpts that seem to illustrate the male gaze. Identify contemporary films or other media that you have viewed and identify examples that show the male gaze. Identify any points of comparison and contrast and write a review outlining your findings.

2 Can the concept of the male gaze be applied to other forms of media such as video games? Give examples.

3 Using an internet search engine, find out if there is a 'female gaze'. You could also conduct interviews with a sample of people you know to find out their views on the concept of the female gaze. Write a summary of your findings.

4 What criticisms can you think of for the concept of the male gaze?

Radical feminists believe that there is little change in gender representations in the media. They argue that traditional stereotypes remain widespread within advertising and that women are still predominantly portrayed as sex objects for men in a range of media products. They argue that it is in the interests of men that women buy into what Wolf termed the 'beauty myth' – that women should conform to a male image of what women should look like in terms of looks, sexiness, shape, size and weight. Contemporary magazines that present this 'ideal' image are seen as an example of a 'backlash' against the gains that women have made in society. They are seen as intended to instil in women a form of 'false consciousness' that distracts them from seeking to improve their position within the power structures of society and instead focus on pursuing the beauty myth. Radical feminists see the media and other aspects of contemporary culture as controlled by men in a way that reflects the dominance they have in most of the key positions of power in society. Men are seen as setting the agenda within the media. Radical feminists use the term 'malestream' to describe the dominance of men in the mainstream media.

Activity

Symbolic annihilation
1 Use the internet to find out about the concept of 'symbolic annihilation' in media representations (for example, websites such as sociology.org.uk).
2 Write a 400-word article showing how this concept supports radical feminist views.

Marxist feminists view media representations of gender as products of both patriarchy and capitalism. They argue that patriarchy operates within capitalism and together they maintain gender inequality. Marxist feminists describe the media as a capitalist industry controlled by mainly male media owners and dominated by male media professionals. They argue that nothing much will change until both capitalism and the patriarchy that thrives under it are overthrown. Marxist feminists see the media as promoting an ideology of masculinity and femininity that reinforces conventional values and norms that support capitalism. Traditional portrayals of male breadwinners and female housewives mean that women undertake unpaid domestic labour, which keeps the working men in good running order at no cost to the capitalist system. Such representations also mean that women are available as a reserve army of labour when capitalism needs

additional workers. Promoting the 'beauty myth' through the media also supports capitalism as it encourages women to consume beauty and dietary products and the advertising revenues received by media owners boosts their profits. Therefore, according to Marxist feminists, the media in a capitalist society represents men and women in stereotypical ways for both ideological and financial reasons.

Activity

Feminist views
Copy and complete a table like the one below. List as many contemporary examples as you can from a range of media to support each of the different feminist views.

Summary of liberal feminist views on media representations:	Contemporary examples
Summary of radical feminist views on media representations:	Contemporary examples
Summary of Marxist feminist views on media representations:	Contemporary examples

Recent feminist research into the media argues that traditional stereotypes persist and some theorists believe that there is evidence of a backlash against feminism. Imelda Whelehan's (2000) study of men's magazines, like *FHM*, *Maxim* and *Loaded*, argues that they 'are an attempt to override the message of feminism, promoting a laddish world where women are sex objects, and changes in gender roles can be dismissed with an ironic joke' (Whelehan 2000 cited in Gauntlett 2008: 164). Gauntlett criticises Whelehan's analysis as being superficial and he argues that she adopts an overly pessimistic view about the influence such magazines have on men's identities. He believes that men's magazines do not deliver just one message and that often they offer contradictory views that acknowledge changing gender roles and the diversity of masculinities in the contemporary UK.

In a similar vein, Angela McRobbie has conducted a number of studies of girls' and women's magazines. Over the years (her research spans four decades), McRobbie has come to different conclusions about the impact of these magazines on femininity and identity. In her early research she suggested that magazines had a significant influence on their female readers' identity. Later, McRobbie accepted the criticism by Frazer (1987) that her view on the influence of girls' magazines was overly deterministic (i.e. that young women were controlled by the magazine stories and images). Frazer's own research found that girls read the magazines critically and were likely to laugh at their content. In recent times, McRobbie seems to have returned to her earlier concerns about the impact of the media on women's identity. She has expressed worries about the negative effect on young women of celebrity magazines such as *Heat* and *Closer*.

Activity

Women's magazines

'*Such publications trap their readers into cycles of anxiety, self-loathing and misery that have become a standard mark of modern womanhood. "Normative discontent" about body image, about never being beautiful enough, about success and fear of failure, about not finding a husband at just the right moment in the life cycle, about keeping to rules of dating, about the dire cost of breaking the rules: such values become all encompassing, invading the space of other interests and other activities. The girl becomes a harshly self-judging person.*'

Source: McRobbie (2005)

1 What effect does McRobbie see these magazines having on young women?
2 According to McRobbie, what values do magazines such as *Closer* and *Heat* encourage in young women?
3 In groups, design and conduct your own research to find out the attitudes of young women in your class towards the impact of these magazines. You should decide whether to conduct research that is qualitative or quantitative and try to gain views from a variety of people so you should think carefully about who will be in your sample.
4 Discuss your findings in class.
5 Evaluate McRobbie's view expressed above by considering whether you think it is overly deterministic or not. What evidence can you find to show that young women do not take such media products seriously? Write a paragraph evaluating feminist concerns about the impact of the media on women.

Feminist research has analysed a wide range of media products including films, television programmes, magazines, advertising and more recently the internet. Most studies conclude that there is still much to be changed before it can be claimed that there is equality in media representations of gender.

Evaluation of feminism

- Feminist views on the gender representations in the media provide a challenging set of ideas. Liberal feminists produce evidence of change but this is contested by radical and Marxist feminists who regard any change as superficial and lacking in substance.
- Radical and Marxist feminists would argue that while the variety of roles for women may seem greater, the characters often contain aspects associated with traditional femininity. The women in these roles conform to conventional images of attractiveness and aspects of their physical appearance are focused upon.
- Some feminists are criticised for failing to acknowledge the ability of women to resist the ideology of femininity that comes across in the media, such as in women's magazines.

Activity

Changing media representations of gender

1 Using resources including internet sites such as theory.org.uk, and/or *Sociology Review* articles, identify some earlier studies (from around the 1970s or early 1980s) into media representations of gender. Note down the name of the researcher and the key points of the study and then assess whether you think the evidence is still valid today. The results of your research can be used as evidence of change or to support the view of radical and Marxist feminists who believe that traditional gender stereotypes still dominate media representations.
2 Angela McRobbie is an interesting feminist theorist to study, as her views have changed over time to reflect changes she sees in the media and society. Write a 400-word article outlining her views on media representations of women over time. You will find this information on sociology websites such as theory.org.uk.

Check your understanding

1 Explain different feminist ideas about media representations of women and men.
2 List evidence for and against the view that media representations of gender use traditional stereotypes.
3 Decide whether there has been much 'progress' in media representations of women. Offer evidence to support your view.
4 Write an evaluative paragraph summarising feminist views on media representations of gender.

Postmodernism

In what ways does the media affect our understanding of reality?

Postmodernist views within sociology focus on a number of social changes that have occurred in recent years which have had a significant impact on society and, in turn, on media representations of social groups. Postmodernist views can be explained through key concepts that can be applied to media representations.

Diversity and choice

According to postmodernists, social and technological changes have resulted in the media offering a wide variety of images from which people can pick and choose to construct their identity. Similarly this diversity and choice can be seen in media representations, which postmodernists believe show a wide variety of images. Postmodernists believe that this process is also the result of changes in norms and values that have occurred in the twentieth century. They believe that society has moved away from the ideas of collectivism, which emphasises shared norms and values, towards individualism, where there is no fixed ideology or set beliefs shaping representations. If there are no fixed norms and values, then audience members are likely to receive the messages in different ways. Postmodernist sociologists argue that individuals create their own meaning from the media products. Therefore, there are no fixed representations of social groups to be identified; it all depends on the individual interpretations of the media.

Media saturation

Postmodernists see countries like the UK as media-saturated (Strinati 1995). They argue that people interact with the media on a regular basis through a variety of sources and products. As a result, the media is seen as one of the main institutions that have the potential to shape identity. Postmodernist theorists examine the role of media such as lifestyle magazines, TV documentaries, advertising and social networking sites in advising people on how to 'make over' their bodies, their relationships and their lives. Therefore, in terms of media representations of social groups, the media has the potential to have a significant influence, though postmodernists would argue that there is a wide range of representations that reflect the diversity of society.

Globalisation

McLuhan (1964) discussed the concept of the 'global village' as early as the 1960s. He noted that social, economic and technological changes had meant that the world had become much more interconnected. Postmodernists believe that the process of globalisation has had an impact on media representations as it has provided access to a broader range of lifestyles and identities from which people can choose. This, in turn, has had an influence on the range of representations available in the media, including hybrid identities that blend different cultural experiences to create new identities.

Blurred boundaries

Postmodernist perspectives contend that social changes have led to a blurring of boundaries between social groups. The breakdown of shared norms and values and increased individualism have led to less clear divisions between different social groups in society. For example, they would argue that in a postmodernist world, there is no fixed ideology about gender identity, so males and females are not constrained by set roles that they are expected to follow. They argue that the media has been important in the blurring of boundaries because of the wide variety of images portrayed. According to postmodernists, this is reflected in media representations of gender, age, ethnicity and social class.

Activity

Blurring of boundaries

1 Present a scrapbook of evidence showing the blurring of boundaries between different social groups represented in the media – for example, metrosexual men, celebrities whose age is difficult to determine, and so on.

Hyper-reality

Some postmodernist writers take a less optimistic view of the effect of media changes. Theorists such as Baudrillard (1994) believe that the media has altered the nature of reality that the audience experiences. They argue that because of media saturation, what is real and what is fiction are blended together so that there is no clear distinction between them. Baudrillard contends that people are 'engulfed' by communication and this leads to a state of 'hyper-reality'. Turkle (1995) describes a postmodernist perspective on television in which people come to feel that TV is a more real world than the actual world that they inhabit. She also writes of the internet as the main organ of a virtual world, pointing to the popularity of virtual reality sites such as *Second Life*. In a similar vein, Watson (2008) writes of 'superficiality not depth', the loss of authentic community and no true sense of self.

Postmodernist theorists have also examined the ways in which the media encourages consumption of products that create identities such as logos, designer labels and brands and that the 'surface' messages given to these products are seen as being more important than the physical reality of the actual products themselves. Media representations are, therefore, likely to reflect this blurring of the real and the fictional – for example, through the use of air-brushing and other techniques that alter images.

Evaluation of postmodernism

- Critics argue that postmodernism exaggerates the power of media representations to blur boundaries and create choices.
- Postmodernist theorists are accused of ignoring the continuing influence of stereotypes in media representations of social class, gender, age and ethnicity.
- Critics of postmodernism argue that media representations serve the interests of people with wealth and power and are not truly offered as a choice to benefit people.
- It is argued that postmodernist views lack empirical evidence to support them.

Activity

Content analysis of adverts

1 Working in groups, use content analysis to study at least four television adverts portraying gender, ethnicity, age and social class.
2 Each group should analyse one of the social groups and complete the following tasks:
   a) Draw up a chart of products being advertised on a mainstream television channel during one peak-time slot.
   b) Identify and quantify the kind of roles being portrayed.
   c) Assess whether the adverts reflect traditional stereotypes.
   d) Write a report summarising your findings.
3 Compare and discuss findings with other groups.

Check your understanding

- Explain postmodernist ideas on hybrid identities.
- Summarise postmodernist views on media representations.
- Compare and contrast postmodernist views with other perspectives on media representations.
- Evaluate postmodernist approaches to understanding media representations of social groups, including the criticisms that feminists and Marxists might make.

Check your understanding

Briefly define the following terms and give an example of each:

1 stereotypes
2 alternative media
3 tokenism
4 hybrid identities
5 male gaze
6 poverty porn
7 pester power
8 hyper-reality
9 Fourth Estate
10 ideological state apparatus.

Section summary

Fill in the blanks, using the words given below.

The media is seen as an important agent of _____ socialisation with the potential to have a significant influence on the way that society views particular social groups, including those based on ethnicity, gender, _____ and age. The members of these groups exhibit a wide range of characteristics but the media tends to reduce these down to a narrow, manageable set of categories when representing them. It is argued that this results in the creation of _____ which present an oversimplified image that uses generalisations about particular social groups. Though these may include some aspects that are accurate, there is a concern that the media often presents a distorted view that does not reflect _____. Some theorists such as _____ believe that the media creates damaging stereotypes that affect the way that society sees certain groups and that this leads to prejudice and _____. However, _____ argue that, in using stereotypes, the media is simply reflecting the views of society. These theorists believe that the media plays a positive role in society and acts as the _____ to protect democracy. Both traditional Marxists and neo-Marxists are critical of this view and think that media representations of social groups are constructed in such a way as to support the interests of the _____. Postmodernists have an alternative view and some believe that media representations show _____ and choice because there is now a wide range of identities and no _____ shaping the way that different social groups are represented. Other postmodernist thinkers take a more negative view and argue that the media creates a state of _____ where audiences become confused about the boundaries between real-life and media representations. Overall, sociologists tend to engage with two debates about media representations; one discusses whether representations are positive or negative and the other discusses how far media representations are _____.

changing, discrimination, diversity, feminists, fixed ideology, Fourth Estate, hyper-reality, pluralists, reality, ruling class, secondary, social class, stereotypes

5.3 What effect does the media have on audiences?

Getting you thinking ...

1 In what ways might the media influence its audience?
2 Which groups are most likely to be affected by the media?
3 What kind of effect might the media have on individuals and society?

The effect of the media on society is an issue that is debated extensively within the sociology of the media. Researchers and theorists offer different responses that contribute to the discussion. Some argue that the media has a powerful and immediate effect on its audience. Others believe that the effect of the media is gradual and some suggest it occurs because the audience allows the media to influence how they experience the world. Some theorists point to the negative impact of the media and others identify positive and beneficial effects. We will look at sociological theories that examine the direct effect of the media on its audience, theories that identify an indirect effect and theories that emphasise the active role of the audience in using the media products.

Media effects are seen as significant in regard to areas of social life and culture, including:

- violence – concerns have been expressed about the effects of the media on violent behaviour and some seek to protect young people from destructive media effects
- politics – people seek to use the media to have an effect in terms of politics and social change
- health and wellbeing – there are concerns that the right media messages with regard to healthy lifestyle are transmitted in society in view of issues such as diet and alcohol consumption
- body image – there is concern about the effect of the media on body image among both women and men.

Direct effect theories

Getting you thinking ...

How much influence and control does the media have on people's attitudes and behaviour? Write a paragraph to explain your view.

Direct effect theories of the effect of the media are based on the view that the media has an immediate and powerful influence on audiences. Such theories see audiences as being virtually unable to resist media messages and believe that these messages flow from the media directly through to its audience. There is frequent disquiet about the media having a direct effect because of concerns about increasing violence in society and the idea that such violence arises from imitation of images and portrayals seen in media products such as films, computer games and other online resources. Concerns are raised with respect to the effects of the media on children and young people and other more vulnerable members of society, since they may be in an early stage of socialisation and hence more susceptible to the power of the media.

Hypodermic syringe model

A classic direct effect theory is the hypodermic syringe model associated with Vance Packard (1957), also known as the 'magic bullet theory'. Packard argued that the media is like a syringe that injected messages into the audience or, in other words, that it penetrates the audience like a bullet. Packard's work was primarily directed towards the impact of advertising but others have applied it more widely to explain the effect that the media has on its audience. It is argued that some media aim to have such an effect; for example, many newspapers will seek to influence their readers directly to vote for a particular political party during elections. According to direct effect theories, the media's influence is seen as immediate and powerful and the audience is regarded as passive and unable to resist the media's messages. The theory does not acknowledge differences between members of the audience and, therefore, the audience is seen as homogeneous.

A key area of research and reflection has been the effect of violence in the media. The psychologist Elizabeth Newson (1994) argued that children's exposure to media violence has a desensitising effect and that they are more likely to commit acts of violence in reality if they have been exposed to violence in the media. Reference has been made to significant events in which young people have participated in extreme violence and links have been made to media use. For example, following the murder of James Bulger in 1993 by two ten-year-old boys, it was suggested that the perpetrators' viewing of violent videos had influenced their behaviour. A significant media campaign was launched to have so-called 'video nasties' banned because of their immediate and powerful effect in this tragic event.

Packard's theory and Bandura's research mirror wider concerns about the effect of media violence on vulnerable members of society. More recently, scenes from films like *Natural Born Killers*, *Rambo* and

---

Study

Children's imitation of violence – Bandura (1961, 1963)

A classic study into children's imitation of violent media images was conducted by Albert Bandura in 1961 and 1963. Bandura believed that his research demonstrated that children imitated violence shown on television. Bandura's now famous bobo doll experiment involved showing young children a film clip of a large inflated toy, known as a bobo doll, being hit by an adult. The children were then led to a laboratory and on the way shown attractive toys that they were told they were not allowed to play with. The children were left alone in the laboratory with toys including a bobo doll and their behaviour was observed through one-way mirrors. There was also a 'control group' of children who were not shown the film clip. The study showed that the children who had seen the film clip acted aggressively towards the bobo doll. Overall, according to Bandura, the effects of the media were seen as direct and immediate; the children saw the acts of violence towards the bobo doll and then behaved violently towards a bobo doll themselves.

Points to discuss and research

1 Watch the bobo doll experiment (search for 'Bandura' and 'bobo doll' on YouTube).
2 Draw or make your own visual representation of Bandura's bobo doll study and add the key aspects of the experiment and findings to your image.
3 Write a 400-word article about the potential dangers of allowing children to witness violence in the media, citing the Bandura study as evidence.

Child's Play 3 have been associated with acts of violence in society. Similar concerns have been expressed about other forms of media such as video games including *Grand Theft Auto* and *Manhunt*.

In summary, media theorists such as Packard and Bandura argue that there are two main effects:

1 imitation, or 'copycat' violence
2 desensitisation (which we will go into more detail about later in the chapter).

However, such worries are often fuelled by media hype and remain unsubstantiated and unproven. For example, the police produced no evidence that James Bulger's young killers had seen the particular video that was regarded as the key prompt for their violent act.

Anderson *et al.* (2003) conducted research into the direct effect of music on an audience. They studied the effects of violent song lyrics on the attitudes and emotions of 500 college students who were asked to listen to songs with violent, non-violent and 'humorous' violent and non-violent lyrics. Their findings indicated a clear pattern of increased aggressive thoughts and feelings of hostility following on from listening to violent song lyrics. The researchers suggested that this was another form of entertainment media in which violent content appeared to be linked to violent effects.

In a similar vein, Hall *et al.* (2011) conducted research into the direct effects of sexualised song lyrics on young audiences. They studied the content of song lyrics from 1959 to 2009 and found a significant increase in the amount of sexualised content over the years. They argued that such lyrics 'can teach young men to be sexually aggressive and treat women as objects while often teaching young women that their value to society is to provide sexual pleasure for others'. The effects on young women can lead to poor body image, depression, eating disorders and substance abuse.

Other research by Hardcastle *et al.* (2013) into the direct effects of song lyrics examined positive references to alcohol and the use of alcohol in popular music. They contrasted such references with public health messages about the dangers of excessive alcohol use. They argued that 'the exposure of young people to alcohol in the media is a major concern given its potential impact on drinking behaviours'.

Researchers into direct media effects have also examined the effects of media images on eating and dieting behaviour among young women (average age 17 – see Study box).

Study

Effects of TV images on communities in Fiji – Becker *et al.* (2002)

A study by Becker *et al.* considered the effects of TV images on communities on the island of Fiji that had previously had no exposure to TV. Prior to 1995, there were no TVs in the Nagroda region of Fiji and most young women had good appetites and larger body shapes. Following the introduction of TVs, the study showed that girls living in houses with a television set were three times more likely to show symptoms of eating disorders. Girls reported that they compared their own body shape with body images portrayed on TV and dieting had become commonplace. In 1998, 69 per cent of those studied said they had gone on diets to lose weight and 74 per cent said they thought they were 'too big or fat'. The Fiji study was deemed to be significant because of the before and after effect of the introduction of TV media images on young viewers.

Other media theorists utilise the concept of catharsis, which confirms that that the media can have a direct effect but challenges some of the fears that are founded on such theories. Field experiments, such as that conducted by Feshbach and Singer (1971), use real-life situations to research media effects. They used two groups of participants, one exposed to media violence and one not, and found that the group that viewed non-violent images displayed more aggression than the other group. Such findings suggest that watching violence in the media can have a direct effect in providing a safe means of release for aggression, known as catharsis.

It has also been argued that exposure to media violence can have a quite different outcome. The concept of a sensitising effect suggests that viewing graphic violent images makes the audience aware of the real results of violence and puts them off it and therefore acts as a deterrent. Young (2003) argues that the effects of media violence depend on 'the narratives within which violence is seen as permissible and reprehensible and the manner in which heroes and villains are depicted'. If violence is depicted in one way, it can have a sensitising effect; if it is depicted in another way, it can have a desensitising effect.

Overall, direct effect theories tend to reflect early studies into media effects which express concern about exposure to violence. Some concepts explain a more positive direct result of media violence on its audience and demonstrate that it can constrain aggression.

Evaluation of direct effect theories

- Laboratory experiments such as the bobo doll example are criticised on the grounds that they do not reflect real-life situations. Field experiments conducted in real-life settings tend to find a weaker effect than laboratory experiments.
- It is also very difficult to measure direct effects because of the problem of isolating all other influences that can lead to particular kinds of behaviour.
- Critics argue that the research that establishes direct effects is limited because it only measures short-term effects.
- Gauntlett (1995) criticises direct effect theories for blaming television for problems such as crime while ignoring other possible causes, such as social inequality.
- A further contribution to the discussion comes from research by Gamson *et al.* (1992) into the factors involved in shaping people's views on political issues. Using focus groups, they found that, while people draw on the media, they also use their own experiences and understanding, which is shaped by popular knowledge of issues. They concluded that, 'people read messages in complicated and sometimes unpredictable ways' (1992: 6). Direct effect theories do not tend to acknowledge much complexity in the process of media effects.

Activity

Media and effects of behaviour

1 Use an internet search to gather five examples of media products that have been linked to possible effects on behaviour.
2 Make a list and summarise each example.
3 What other factors could explain each case? For example, people might argue that 'violent' children influenced by video games are actually influenced more by their 'violent' peer group.

Check your understanding ✓

- Explain the hypodermic syringe model.
- Summarise the different views on direct effects, including those that suggest a beneficial effect.
- Evaluate direct effect theories.

Indirect effect theories

Indirect effect theories acknowledge that the media has an effect on its audience but see this effect as the product of interaction between different influences alongside the media messages that have been received by the audience. Such theories look beyond a simple one-way effect process that sees the media conveying messages to the audience and looks at the way that audiences receive media messages and the factors shaping this reception. These theories are, therefore, distinctly different to the hypodermic syringe model in which media messages and influences are seen as being directly 'injected' into the audience. Indirect effect theories use different images to convey their ideas.

Getting you thinking ... ?

1 Who influences your response to media messages?
2 Which areas of your life are most influenced by the media?

The two-step flow model

The two-step flow model sees the effect of the media coming through the interaction between people. People experience the media directly but the effect of the media depends on their interaction with other people such as family, friends, teachers, work colleagues, and so on. The perspective of a person of influence may lead a person to accept, modify or reject a media message. Katz and Lazarsfeld (1955) identified the role of opinion leaders in influencing the views of others. An opinion leader is an individual who has more exposure to media views on a particular topic through, for example, reading newspapers or watching television, and she or he comes to be regarded by his or her social contacts as something of an expert on a topic. The influence of the media reaches the audience through two steps:

1 The opinion leader takes in the media messages.
2 The opinion leader transmits these on within the context of social relationships.

In this theory, therefore, the process of social interaction is an important element in media influence. People are seen as choosing to adopt a particular way of thinking or behaving based on discussion and interaction with an opinion leader. The audience is not, therefore, entirely passive in its interaction with media messages.

Two-step flow model

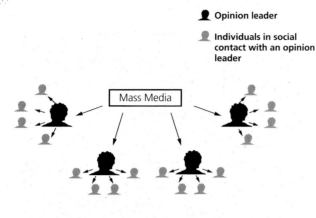

● Opinion leader

● Individuals in social
contact with an opinion
leader

Mass Media

The cultural effects theory

Another 'indirect' approach to understanding the effects of the media on its audience comes through the cultural effects theory. This argues that the media affects the attitudes and behaviour of different social groups in different ways depending on their cultural background. For example, the effect of media messages will vary according to the gender, social class, ethnicity and age of the audience. It is argued that a news report about binge drinking will be viewed differently by younger and older audiences. In a similar way, violent films may not affect men and women in the same way. According to the cultural effects theory, media effects, though significant, are not direct but are shaped by the norms, values and experiences of the audience.

This approach links with the research of some theorists from Marxist, neo-Marxist and interpretivist perspectives. Neo-Marxist research in the cultural effects tradition emphasises ways in which the media reflects the values of rich and powerful members of society, such as those who own, control and produce the media. From this perspective, the audience will interpret media messages differently according to their cultural background and experiences but will tend to adopt a view that is influenced by the dominant perspective or 'preferred reading' of those with power in society because the messages are constructed to be read in this way. Marxist thinker Antonio Gramsci saw certain institutions such as the media as a site of struggle for hearts and minds and argued that the media has to be continuously alert to the need to keep the audience on the side of capitalism. He used the term 'hegemony' to discuss the way in which capitalist ideas were presented as 'common sense' and seen as 'natural' in order to maintain control.

He believed that the audience must consent to these ideas and the media had an important role in gaining this consent. Gramsci emphasised the 'struggle' involved in this process and noted that 'common sense is not something rigid and immobile, but is continually transforming itself' (Gramsci, cited in Hall 1982: 73). Gramsci was aware that the social experience of the proletariat contradicted the ideology being projected by the media and, therefore, there was a constant struggle to maintain hegemony. In this sense, the experience of the audience is an important factor in interaction with the media and has an indirect effect on the way that messages are received.

The cultural effects theory and other indirect effect theories are sometimes described as 'drip-drip' models in their perspective on how the media is seen as shaping the norms and values of the audience. The process is regarded as happening gradually over long-term exposure to the media. This contrasts with more direct effect theories such as the hypodermic syringe model, which tend to have a more short-term immediate perspective on media effects. The concept of desensitisation can also be associated with the drip-drip model. It describes the way that the audience's norms can be altered by viewing particular images, such as those of a violent nature. It is claimed that over time the audience stops finding such images disturbing and violence becomes more acceptable. The concept of desensitisation has also been applied to the effect of media images of famine and poverty in developing countries in that prolonged exposure to distressing images of poverty and famine is associated with 'compassion fatigue', which might be seen as a type of desensitisation. Drip-drip theories do not describe such media effects as being immediate and powerful but as occurring gradually over time and as depending on other influences such as those of opinion leaders and wider cultural norms and social influences.

Evaluation of indirect effect theories

Indirect effect theories share some of the criticisms of direct effect theories:

● It is very difficult to measure the effect that the media alone has on the norms, values and attitudes of the audience. Audiences are likely to be affected by a range of factors and it is almost impossible to isolate the impact of the media in this complex web of influence.

● Individuals who may be most at risk of being influenced by the media may be socially isolated and not members of any social network, and so do not have access to opinion leaders who might help interpret media content in a healthy way.

- While indirect effect theories see greater complexity in the way that the media affects its audience, their analysis tends to look more at the issue from the point of view of the media impacting on the audience. Recent research has shifted focus from the effect of the media on its audience to the way in which the audience receives media messages.

- A criticism of both direct and indirect theories of media effects is implied in the uses and gratifications approach (see below). This model argues that audiences use the media for their own purposes and to satisfy their needs. According to McQuail (1972), individuals are active in their approach to the media and use it in a number of ways including as a form of escape, as a means of gathering information, to form personal relationships and in constructing personal identity.

Activity

Agents of socialisation

1 Conduct a survey within your class to examine the factors that shape people's opinions. For example, you could focus on topics including environmental issues, fashion and style, sports, and so on, and ask respondents to think about where they acquired their knowledge and views about these topics. You will need to make sure that your questions explore the role of opinion leaders and agents of socialisation.
2 Summarise your findings in a 500-word report.

Check your understanding

- Outline the key ideas of each of the indirect effect theories.
- Compare and contrast direct and indirect theories of media effects.
- Make a judgement about which seem to have the strongest supporting evidence.

Active audience approaches

Both direct and indirect theories of media effects argue that the media has a strong influence on its audience. Active audience models suggest that such perspectives ignore the role of the audience in using, interpreting and making sense of media content.

Getting you thinking ...

1 Consider what people 'get out' of media products, such as magazines, video games or TV programmes.
2 Describe a possible range of different responses to a leading storyline from a popular soap opera or sitcom. You might choose a significant event and consider how people's responses might differ according to their gender, age, ethnicity and class.

The uses and gratifications model

The uses and gratifications model serves as a criticism of both direct and indirect theories of media effects. It argues that audiences use the media for their own purposes and to satisfy their needs. In this sense, the audience is an active agent in its use of the media and the effects of the media are seen as depending entirely on the wishes and needs of the audience.

This approach focuses on why people use particular media rather than on media content. In contrast to the concerns of direct and indirect effect theories with 'what the media does to people', uses and gratifications theory can be seen as part of a broader trend among media researchers towards 'what people do with the media', allowing for a variety of responses and interpretations.

Uses and gratifications theorists refer to ways in which people's needs influence how they use and respond to media. Zillmann (cited by McQuail 1987: 236) has shown the influence of mood on media choice; for example, boredom might encourage the choice of exciting content and stress might encourage a choice of relaxing content. The same TV programme may gratify different needs for different individuals. These different needs are associated with individual personalities, stages of maturation, backgrounds and social roles.

Active audience theorists argue that people use the media to meet identified needs, which may be biological, psychological or social. They also suggest that people's needs are relative to various factors that influence their use of the media, such as age, gender, ethnicity and social class. These factors are seen as influencing how people access the media to gratify their needs.

Research in the uses and gratifications tradition can involve audience members completing a questionnaire about, for example, why they watch a particular TV programme. McQuail (1987: 73) offers the following categories of common reasons for media use:

- information – for example, finding out about relevant events, seeking advice on practical matters or opinions and decisions, satisfying curiosity and general interest, learning, gaining a sense of security through knowledge
- personal identity – for example, reinforcement for personal values, finding models of behaviour, identifying with valued others (in the media), gaining insight into one's self
- integration and social interaction – for example, gaining insight into circumstances of others, identifying with others, finding a basis for conversation, having a substitute for real-life companionship, helping to carry out social roles, enabling one to connect with family, friends and society
- entertainment – for example, escaping or being diverted from problems, relaxing, getting cultural or aesthetic enjoyment, filling time, emotional release, sexual arousal.

Activity

People's use of the media
1 Conduct a research study into people's use of the media. Either use questionnaires or interviews or both. You should consult between five and ten people. Seek to uncover people's motivations for their use of the media.
2 Compare your findings with those of McQuail.
3 Decide if your sample of research participants makes use of the media for the reasons identified by uses and gratifications theorists.

Other active audience approaches

Neo-Marxist Hall (1973) offers a more complex set of ideas that nevertheless suggest active involvement from the audience. His coding/decoding model of communication is often cited as an example of an active audience approach to media

effects. Though he argues that media messages, such as television news broadcasts, are coded or constructed by media professionals in ways that support the power structures of society, he also contends that audiences are able to decode these messages in a variety of ways that reflect their social background and ideas. Hall suggests that there are different possible ways of 'reading' a media message:

- the dominant or hegemonic reading, in which the audience takes in the meaning that media professionals intend: they 'believe the message'
- the negotiated reading, in which the audience mixes the dominant reading with alternative ideas and the meaning is slightly altered in relation to that intended by media professionals
- the oppositional reading, in which the audience constructs a meaning that is totally different to the dominant reading intended by media professionals – for example, a person watching a TV programme that supports a political party decides to vote against that party.

Activity

News broadcasts
1 Use semiology to uncover the coding of news broadcasts from different television or internet sources. Select a sample of at least four news broadcasts and analyse the content.
2 Identify examples of coding and explain your analysis.
3 Write a short storyboard or script encoded with a message that you would like to convey and ask a classmate to decode your message.

Klapper's selective filter model is useful in explaining the process that the audience goes through when interacting with the media. Klapper (1960) argued that audiences are not passive receptors of media propaganda but that the media simply reinforces previously held beliefs and attitudes. He contended that there are a variety of ways in which individuals filter such content:

- selective exposure – individuals select which media products they will expose themselves to
- selective perception – individuals choose how they will perceive the message being conveyed
- selective retention – individuals will retain content that accords with their interests and beliefs.

Selective filter model

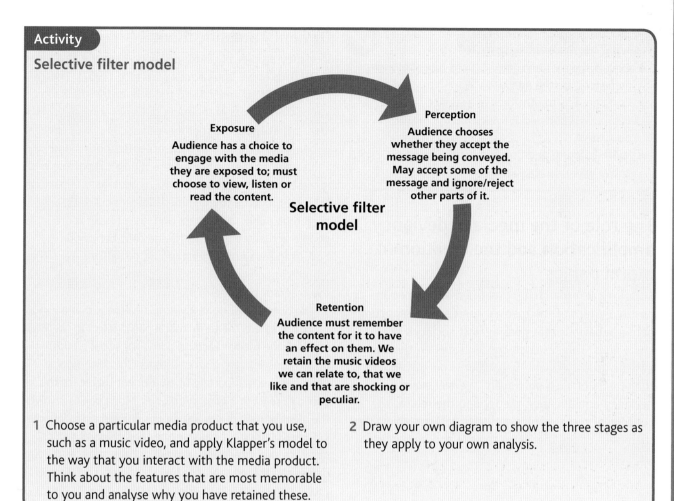

Exposure
Audience has a choice to engage with the media they are exposed to; must choose to view, listen or read the content.

Selective filter model

Perception
Audience chooses whether they accept the message being conveyed. May accept some of the message and ignore/reject other parts of it.

Retention
Audience must remember the content for it to have an effect on them. We retain the music videos we can relate to, that we like and that are shocking or peculiar.

1 Choose a particular media product that you use, such as a music video, and apply Klapper's model to the way that you interact with the media product. Think about the features that are most memorable to you and analyse why you have retained these.

2 Draw your own diagram to show the three stages as they apply to your own analysis.

Evaluation of active audience approaches

- The research methods employed in the uses and gratifications model have been criticised. The use of retrospective 'self-reports' such as questionnaires is limited, as viewers may not know why they chose to watch what they did, or may not be able to fully explain their choices. People may simply offer reasons that they have heard others mention.

- Active audience approaches have been seen as overly individualistic and ignore the socio-cultural context. They emphasise individual psychological and personality factors and de-emphasise sociological interpretations. It is arguable that people's interpretation of media content is shaped by their cultural background and socio-economic status.

- Marxist sociologists suggest that the needs that are met by media content are created by the media. For example, people might argue that they use a media product such as Facebook as it fulfils needs such as those identified by McQuail above. However, these needs were met in entirely different ways prior to the recent invention of Facebook. Marxists argue that the need for such a media product is created by capitalism to make money and to distract people from real issues that affect them, such as issues of social inequality and exploitation.

- While audiences seem to select media and content (for example, choice or avoidance of TV soap operas), often media use is habitual, ritualistic and unselective rather than the product of an active choice (Barwise and Ehrenberg 1988).

- Some neo-Marxists argue that, though the audience has some agency in decoding messages, the media is a powerful and dominant institution that exerts a great deal of control over the production of ideology. Access to alternative ideas is limited and such views are often the subject of informal censorship, criticism or ridicule.

- Explain the uses and gratifications model of how audiences use the media.
- Compare this to other active audience approaches and decide which are the most persuasive.
- Write an exam question and mark scheme on active audience approaches.

The role of the media in deviancy amplification and the creation of moral panics

Sociological research has identified an important possible effect of the media's approach to reporting public behaviour that goes against society's norms and values. This research concentrates on the ways in which such 'deviant' behaviour is portrayed and the effects of such portrayals. We will examine deviancy amplification theory and the related concept of moral panics and their role in explaining the effect of the media on society and on particular social groups.

Deviancy amplification

Deviancy amplification theory was originally developed by Wilkins in his book *Social Deviance* (1967). The theory seeks to understand the role of the media in strengthening and magnifying deviance in society. The idea is that there are members of society who engage in behaviours that go against accepted norms and values and that an effect of the media's reporting and representations of this deviance is that such behaviour is strengthened and magnified. The media's response heightens public awareness and, as a result, more people actually engage in the deviant behaviour.

A useful way of understanding deviancy amplification is to think of the process as a spiral (see the diagram on page 179).

The outcome of deviancy amplification is that a moral panic is created. The term 'moral panic' refers to the way in which the media reacts to particular social groups or activities that are seen as a threat to social order. It describes media reporting of an incident that leads the public to react in a panicky manner. Moral panics involve the identification of deviant groups (known as 'folk devils') who are blamed for causing the threat. Moral panics carry a moral dimension, and are not the same as media panics about food safety or fuel shortages. Therefore, moral panics are panics that threaten society's norms and values rather than being general panics.

Getting you thinking ...

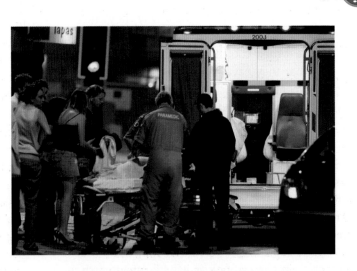

1 What kind of 'deviant' behaviour receives most attention in the media?

2 Which groups tend to be focused on as deviant in the media?

3 What is the result of these sorts of media images?

A 'deviant' act is committed. Such acts are often criminal but may include legal acts that are considered as going against society's norms and values.

A problem group is identified (known as 'folk devils') and sensationalised reports of their deviant behaviour appear in the media. The reports highlight what are often borderline examples but are seen as confirming a pattern. The reports ignore statistics that show that the behaviour is actually not common. The reporting suggests that the examples are 'the tip of the iceberg', which increases public concern.

The media profits more from the whole spiral and continues to report on the deviance.

The deviancy amplification spiral

There is an increased public desire to be kept informed of events, which results in higher audience/readership numbers.

The public feel their fear is justified, which reinforces the moral panic.

A moral panic develops. Public concern is aroused at the real or imaginary threat to society. There are more reports in the media and demands for action to be taken against this perceived threat. Police and other law enforcement agencies focus attention on the deviant act. Judges and magistrates come under public pressure to deal out harsher sentences and politicians pass new laws to show that they are dealing with the perceived threat.

Publicity glamorises the 'deviant' behaviour and makes it attractive to some and therefore more people engage in the deviant behaviour.

Moral panics

Study

Folk Devils and Moral Panics – Cohen (1972)

Cohen popularised the term 'moral panic' in his study of the media's response to youth deviance. Using interactionist methodology, Cohen observed seaside fights between two youth subcultures, the mods and rockers, and he examined the media's response to the event. He argued that the media labelled the mods and rockers in a negative and stereotyped way, and as a result they came to be seen as 'folk devils'. Cohen highlighted the role of the media in defining the situation and argued that they had created a greatly exaggerated picture of the conflict between the mods and rockers. A result of the panic over 'mods and rockers' was the reinforcement of regular police forces with soldiers as though the issue was as serious as an invasion by a foreign power and yet a short time later these social groups were more or less forgotten about; they were remembered as examples of 'folk devils' but people did not worry about them in the same way. Cohen's view is that the earlier reaction was the result of media-created hype. Using the concept of a deviancy amplification spiral, he identified the stages of development of a moral panic:

- Firstly, the media uses sensational, stereotypical and exaggerated language to write stories and headlines about a particular event or group.
- This results in public anxiety, which is fuelled by influential commentators like bishops and politicians.
- This puts pressure on the authorities to intervene and can lead, for example, to greater police involvement.
- The increased social awareness of the problem can also lead more people to participate in the activity.

In a later edition of this classic study, Cohen (2002) makes reference to more recent examples of moral panics. He refers to media responses to issues or events including:

- murders such as the killings of James Bulger and Steven Lawrence
- the death of teenager Leah Betts from ecstasy
- child abuse scandals
- the role of violence in the media
- welfare cheats and single mothers
- refugees and asylum-seekers.

Activity

Moral panics

1 Choose a social group or activity that has been the subject of a moral panic and make a poster to show, step-by-step, the process that creates a moral panic as outlined above.
2 In groups, use the internet to conduct research into recent moral panics and present your findings to the class. These can be used as contemporary evidence to support your arguments in exam questions.

Later research by Goode and Ben-Yehuda (1994) rejected Cohen's view that a moral panic goes through a series of stages that have a beginning, middle and end. Instead, they described five elements present in a moral panic:

1 concern – heightened public concern that the behaviour of a particular group is seen as a threat to social order
2 hostility – an increased hostility in the media towards the group that leads to its members being seen as 'folk devils'
3 consensus – influential people, known as moral entrepreneurs, lead the campaign against the group that leads to general agreement about their behaviour
4 disproportionality – the reaction is out of proportion to the harm caused by the group
5 volatility – moral panics come and go quickly as interest moves on to another issue.

Furedi (1994) argues that moral panics arise when society fails to adapt to dramatic social changes and it is felt that there is a loss of control, especially over powerless groups such as the young. Furedi argues that moral panics reflect wider concerns that the older generation hold about the nature of society. They see themselves (and their families) as being at greater risk from a variety of groups and that things are out of control. They believe, with the media's encouragement, that traditional norms and values are losing relevance in their lives. Furedi contends that people feel a sense of loss, which makes them very susceptible to the anxieties promoted by moral panics.

Angela McRobbie (1994) presents another view of moral panics, which challenges the older models. She still sees moral panic as a means of social control, but believes that there are now so many of them that their effect has changed, 'to the extent that the panics are no longer about social control but rather about the fear of being out of control' (McRobbie 1994: 199). She suggests that older moral panic models assumed a clear distinction between the world of the media and the world of social reality. She points out that 'We do not exist in social unreality while we watch television or read the newspaper, nor are we transported back to reality when we turn the TV off to wash the dishes or discard the paper to go to bed'. She believes that it may not make sense to think of any kind of social reality outside the world of representation, as social reality is always the product of communication and representation and, as a result, is always a partial view. She suggests that sociologists who argue for an account of reality that is not sensationalised and exaggerated are themselves speaking from an account of reality that is partial and selective. So McRobbie is arguing that in our 'postmodern condition', we are more likely to see all representations as simply that – representations – with none being more 'right' than any other.

Sociological perspectives on deviancy amplification and moral panics

Deviancy amplification and moral panics have been studied by a number of sociologists, including those from interactionist and Marxist perspectives.

Marxist sociologists argue that deviancy amplification and moral panics are used as a form of social control to support capitalism. They argue that an effect of the media is to distract people from the real issues that create inequality in society. Deviancy amplification is seen as an example of media strategies that highlight issues that have been exaggerated and have the effect of masking the real problems that affect people on a daily basis. Cohen argues that studying deviancy amplification and moral panics helps people to 'identify and conceptualise the lines of power in any society, the ways we are manipulated into taking some things seriously and other things not seriously enough' (2002: 85). Neo-Marxists see it as important to investigate who has the power to define deviance and to explain why some groups come to be identified as folk devils in the first place. For example, Hall *et al.* (1978), writing from a Marxist perspective, believed that moral panics serve an ideological function to support capitalism. They referred to the emergence of the use of the term 'mugging' in the UK and the way in which it was introduced and used to generate a moral panic. They argued that it was applied to the behaviour of young working-class black men to cause division between the black and white working class. They suggested that the moral panic took attention away from economic problems caused by capitalism and allowed laws to be introduced that could be used to repress other groups that opposed capitalism.

Interactionist sociologists explore the process of defining and labelling deviance. Deviancy amplification is seen as part of the process by which different behaviours are labelled and come to be seen as 'deviant'. Interactionists believe this labelling can lead to certain groups being victimised as criminals and deviants. For example, the police might label black youths as more likely to be criminals, resulting in people from this group being more likely to be charged with a criminal offence. Interactionists contend that labelling can cause an individual to be singled out as deviant, which could result in a self-fulfilling prophecy, where they adopt the behaviour of the deviant label that was applied to them. Interactionists argue that targeting of certain groups by agents of social control can actually lead to deviancy amplification. This means that the some members of the audience are attracted to this victimised group and repeat the deviant behaviour.

Evaluation of sociological perspectives on deviancy amplification and moral panics

- Marxist views are criticised for failing to acknowledge that moral panics can be the product of real concerns in society.

- Marxists are also seen to take an over-conspiratorial view where members of the ruling class get together and decide on a course of action that creates a moral panic, but there is no evidence of this having occurred.
- Interactionists fail to explain why certain people are labelled as deviant and other people are not.
- Critics of interactionism argue that it fails to explore the power relations behind the labelling process.
- Pluralists argue that moral panics occur because the media is reflecting the values and concerns of their audience and that the media cannot create such panics if the stories do not match the perspectives of their audience.

For further examples of research into moral panics, see page 142.

Check your understanding

- Explain how moral panics develop.
- Explain how deviancy amplification theory accounts for increases in deviant behaviour.
- Explain different views on moral panics from different sociological perspectives.
- Decide if the concepts of moral panics and deviancy amplification support direct, indirect or active audience approaches to media effects. Explain your view.

Check your understanding

Briefly define the following terms and give an example of each:

1 desensitisation
2 catharsis
3 opinion leader
4 oppositional reading
5 folk devil
6 moral panic
7 deviancy amplification
8 labelling.

Section summary

Fill in the blanks, using the words given below.

When considering the effects of the media on its audience, some theories suggest that the media has a powerful and immediate effect on its audience; these are known as _____ and include the _____ model. On the other hand, indirect effect theories such as the _____ model have introduced greater complexity into the picture and suggest that the media has a less direct effect. Some theories emphasise the role of the audience in interpreting or making sense of media messages; these are known as _____ theories. For example, _____ model explains the process that the audience goes through when interacting with the media. There are also theories that focus on the specific issue of the effect of the media on its audience's response to _____; these include the idea of deviancy amplification and the related concept of _____. Part of the deviancy amplification _____ involves the identification of deviant groups known as _____, who are blamed for causing social problems. _____ sociologists argue that deviancy amplification and moral panics are used as a form of social _____ to support capitalism. Interactionists focus on the process of defining and _____ deviance. On the other hand, _____ argue that moral panics occur because the media is reflecting the values and concerns of its audience. Overall, sociological explanations of media effects offer a range of views ranging from those who see the audience as _____ to those who believe the audience uses the media for their own _____.

active audience, control, deviance, direct effect theories, folk devils, gratification, hypodermic syringe, Klapper's filter, labelling, Marxist, moral panics, passive, pluralists, spiral, two-step flow

Practice questions

1 Outline two ways that social class is represented in the media. [12]

2 Explain and briefly evaluate the view that the media has a direct effect on their audience. [16]

3 Assess the view that media representations of gender are changing. [24]

Chapter 6

Research methods and researching social inequalities

Component 2, Section A

Research methods and researching social inequalities

Content:

1 What is the relationship between theory and methods?
2 What are the main stages of the research process?
3 Which methods are used in sociological research?

6.1 What is the relationship between theory and methods?

Getting you thinking ...

Bird building a nest

Getting you thinking ... (continued)

A volcano erupting

Scientists watching chemicals in a test tube

1 Why do birds, volcanos and chemicals behave in the way they do?
2 Is their behaviour predictable or unpredictable?
3 What have humans got that is lacking in birds, volcanos and chemicals?
4 Do human beings behave in predictable ways?

Introducing theory

There are two broad theoretical approaches to research within sociology known as positivism and interpretivism. They are based on very different views and understandings about why people behave as they do. Consequently, these beliefs have led to researchers developing and adopting very different approaches to sociological research.

Positivism

Positivism refers to a particular set of assumptions about how the social world or society is organised and the appropriate ways of studying it. Positivists are very influenced by the natural sciences. Scientists such as biologists, physicists and chemists have shown us that plants, animals and chemicals behave in very predictable ways because of the existence of natural laws. For example, birds migrate or build nests in certain ways because of the natural law of instinct. Water obeys certain physical laws when it boils or freezes. The natural law of gravity pulls objects to the Earth's surface.

Positivist sociologists have adapted and applied these ideas to human behaviour. They argue that we should treat people as objects whose behaviour can be directly observed, measured and counted in the same way as natural phenomena such as birds, animals, the weather, volcanos, chemicals and so on. Positivists therefore believe that just as there are natural laws governing the behaviour of these natural phenomena, so there are social forces or laws (Durkheim called these 'social facts') shaping and determining the social actions of people, particularly with regard to our everyday experiences and life chances. Such laws are the product of the organisation of the society in which we live. The organisation of society is called the social structure and the positivist sociologists who study the organisation of society are known as structuralists.

Patterns and trends

Positivists argue that the social structure of particular societies produce social forces or laws over which people have little or no control. From a positivist perspective, free will, individualism and the ability to make choices are less influential than society's ability to shape human behaviour. This is because society exists outside of the individuals who comprise it and consequently society is more important than the individual. For example, positivists point out that individuals are born, take their place in society and then die, but society continues on, largely undisturbed, by the majority of these people's existence.

Individual behaviour, therefore, as far as positivists are concerned, is the product of social forces beyond the individual's control and understanding. All social actions are the outcome of the way that societies are organised. In this sense, positivists regard individuals as the 'puppets of society'. Their behaviour is only important as a part of a wider collective whole. This means that whole groups of people behave in very **patterned** or similar ways as a result of the social structure. **Trends** in human behaviour can clearly be seen and catalogued. Human behaviour, therefore, is consequently very predictable.

Positivists take a 'macro' approach to the study of society in that they are mainly concerned with examining the relationships between different parts of the social structure to work out their 'effects' on the behaviour of members of society. For example, positivist interest in why particular groups are wealthy or poor would probably focus on how structural forces such as social class, patriarchy, racism and so on influence how the wealthy and poor behave and how these forces interact with social structures such as local and global economies, the political system and so on to produce wealth and poverty. It is highly unlikely that positivist research would focus on the 'micro' aspects of wealth and poverty such as how the rich and poor experience and interpret their respective social worlds on a daily basis. This is because positivists are not particularly interested in seeing the world through the eyes of individuals.

Functionalism, Marxism and feminism tend to be positivist theories because they believe that individual behaviour is less important as a subject for study than value consensus, social class and patriarchy respectively – all of which are the product of the social structure.

> ### Quick question
>
> Do you believe you are a puppet of society? List aspects of your experience that support and challenge this idea.

Sociology as a social science

Positivist sociologists see sociology as the 'science of society' – that is, a social science – and believe that the behaviour of human beings can be objectively and scientifically measured in much the same way as the subject matter of the natural sciences. They consequently argue that sociologists should adopt the logic and methods of the natural sciences in their exploration of how the social structure shapes people's behaviour and actions.

Activity: People as the puppets of society?

Item A: Functionalist theory

Functionalists argue that people behave the way that they do because society and its social institutions have socialised them into a very powerful value consensus. It is difficult to behave differently to everyone else because people fear the disapproval and punishment that might result from non-conformity.

Item B: Marxist theory

Marxists believe that behaviour is shaped by the economic organisation of capitalist society, and particularly the social class relationships that result from it. Marxists argue that a person's social class position strongly influences educational achievement, job opportunities, life expectancy and even cause of death.

Item C: A white wedding

Item D: A scantily-clad glamour models

1 How do each of the above sources back up the positivist view that people's behaviour is shaped by factors beyond their control?

This approach, which is known as the hypothetico-deductive approach, suggests that positivist scientists and sociologists begin by making observations about the world. These observations then lead to positivists coming up with hypotheses or conjectures. These are informed guesses about how and why the social situations they have observed have come about.

Positivists may test the hypothesis by collecting data or evidence. Scientists normally do this by carrying out laboratory experiments whereas, as we shall see, positivist sociologists generally go out 'into the field' – that is, into a social context – and conduct a scientific survey.

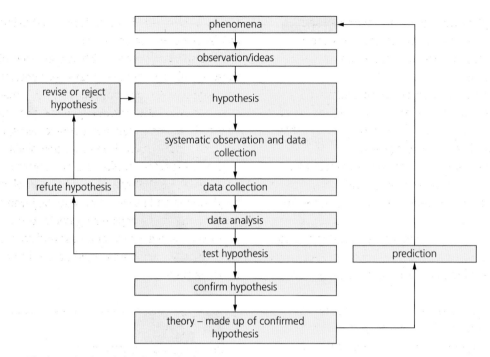

The hypothetico-deductive method

(Source: McNeill and Chapman 2005: 69)

Objectivity, value-freedom, reliability and quantitative data

Sociological positivists argue that the sociological research methods used to test hypotheses should exhibit the following ideal features if they are to qualify as scientific.

- The research method should follow systematic and logical procedures so that other social scientists can replicate the research.
- Replication is important in order to ensure the **reliability** of the research method and process. Positivists argue that if the research process used to test a hypothesis is reliable, another sociologist should be able to repeat the research and consistently obtain the same or very similar results. This repeating of the research, therefore, aims to check and verify the scientific accuracy of the way that evidence or data is gathered.
- Positivists believe that scientific research should be **objective** or **value-free**. In other words, the sociologist should be neutral and not allow their personal or political values or their prejudices to bias any aspect of their research method or their interpretation of the data they collect. The sociologist should be determined to pursue scientific truths with an open mind. This is not really a problem for scientists. They can ensure objectivity

by carrying out their research under controlled conditions such as laboratories. However, sociologists very rarely use laboratory experiments and have had to devise alternative methods to ensure that possible bias in their research is eliminated. As we shall see in Section 6.2, positivists have developed various techniques called sampling that they use to keep their distance from the people they are studying – that is, to maintain neutrality and objectivity.

- **Representativeness** is also important to positivist methodology. It is normally practically impossible and costly to study the whole social group that the sociologist is interested in. Positivists therefore aim to select a representative sample of that group to take part in their research. Representativeness means that the people who take part in the research should have characteristics that are typical of the larger population being studied – that is, they should come from the same or similar socio-economic backgrounds and reflect the same ratio of gender, age and ethnicity.
- This then justifies the sociologists making **generalisations** based on the data that they have collected from the sample. This means that the sociologist can safely conclude that what is true of the sample that was actually studied is probably true of the wider population to which the sample belongs. As we shall see in Section 6.2,

careful sampling methods have been devised to try to ensure that both representativeness and generalisability are possible when designing positivist research.

- Positivists are very keen on **quantitative** data – that is, data that can be expressed in numerical form and presented in the form of graphs, tables, bar-charts and so on. The patterns and trends in human behaviour that are demonstrated by such data can then be observed and compared in order to establish correlations or links between aspects of the social structure such as social class and social behaviour. These correlations can then be used to help to uncover cause-and-effect relationships which can establish 'social facts' or 'laws'.

- All sociologists, whether they are positivists or not, strive to achieve **validity**. Validity is a concept that generally refers to whether the research findings give a true picture of what is being studied – that is, it should reflect the reality of the persons or groups being studied. The research should have achieved what it set out to do. Positivists argue that their approach is the most effective way of achieving such validity because they believe that if the research is well designed, then the data gathered should present an authentic or valid picture of what is being investigated.

Positivist sociologists argue that the scientific approach that they advocate can produce absolute truths or scientific laws of human behaviour that they call 'social laws' or 'social facts'.

Early sociological positivists argued that uncovering these social facts or laws means that predictions can be made about the social world and this makes possible a certain amount of social engineering to modify or change it for the better. For example, using Durkheim's research, positivists believed that any deviations from the expected suicide rate of a society can be investigated so that the cause of the problem can be identified and solved. Positivists believed that this potential for social engineering could lead to a reduction of poverty, crime, or social unrest and so on. In other words, positivist research could be used to create a better society.

Activity

Considering positivism

1 Positivist scientists mainly use laboratory experiments to investigate natural phenomena in a scientific fashion. Why do you think positivist sociologists do not use this method?
2 What is the difference between reliability and validity?
3 What is the difference between objectivity and value-freedom?

Positivism has been extremely influential and consequently positivist research methods have dominated social research for three reasons.

Study

Study of suicide – Durkheim (1897)

Durkheim used the positivist scientific approach to investigate suicide. He examined nineteenth-century suicide statistics across a number of European societies and observed three trends: that suicide rates remain constant and predictable over time, that they remain constant between societies and that they remain constant between social groups within the same society. On the basis of these observations, he concluded that the suicide rate was not the result of individuals using their free will and choosing to kill themselves. Instead, he hypothesised that the suicide rate was a social fact – that is, suicidal behaviour was shaped by the nature of the society to which the individual belonged, and specifically by its level of social integration and moral regulation.

Durkheim argued that the main type of suicide, which he called 'egoistic' suicide, was caused by too much individualism. Society had failed to integrate particular individuals into society. He saw religion as playing a big role in whether individuals were sufficiently integrated or not. For example, he argued that the Catholic sense of community was more powerful than that encouraged by Protestant religions and therefore Catholics had a stronger sense of belonging to society and were subject to stricter community controls. Consequently, he argued that Protestants were more likely to kill themselves than Catholics because Catholic society provided more community protection against suicide. In contrast, the Protestant religion's failure to impose a strong sense of community on its followers led to people believing that they were more important than the group – hence egoism, and suicidal actions.

1 Most sociologists believe that remaining objective and adopting a scientific approach free from one's own values and biases is vital in sociological research. The British Sociological Association's (BSA) ethical guidelines implicitly encourage the type of quantitative research associated with positivism because the BSA stresses that researchers need to obtain the 'informed consent' of those taking part in sociological research and that sociologists need to be clear 'about their detachment from and involvement in their areas of study' (p182). Both of these aims are easier to achieve when using positivist methods.

2 The government, when funding sociological research projects through agencies such as the Economic and Social Research Council tends to favour (and therefore fund) more positivist-style research because it allows generalisations to be made. Governments are also attracted by positivist research because it is less likely to be contaminated by the researcher's own values and is more useful when drawing conclusions for government social policies.

3 Science still has great status in society and is still perceived as a source of much human progress. It is therefore no surprise that techniques that claim to be scientific – such as positivist ones – attract prestige.

As we shall see in Section 6.3, positivist research prefers the extensive use of primary research methods such as the social survey, which incorporates questionnaires and structured interviews and which mainly produces quantitative data. They also prefer to use quantitative forms of secondary data such as official statistics and documents because these are usually the outcome of systematic and standardised procedures. The strengths and weaknesses of both these primary and secondary research tools will be explored in Section 6.3.

> ### Quick question
>
> List some of the reasons why science has great status in society.

Interpretivism

As we have seen, two of the founding fathers of sociology, Durkheim and Marx, were very influenced by the positivist approach to scientific study. However, a third founding father, Max Weber, had huge reservations about positivism.

Weber argued that there is an important difference between the subject matter of sociology and the subject matter of the natural sciences. He rejected the view that human beings can be treated like objects in much the same way as things in the natural world. He noted that people are active, conscious beings with free will who are aware of what is going on in social situations, and therefore capable of making choices about how to behave. In contrast, the subject matter of the natural sciences such as atoms, elements, gravity, plants, animals and so on are not comparable to human beings because they are not conscious or self-aware. They do not act with purpose. They cannot interpret what is happening to them and choose to behave in particular ways.

Meanings and experiences

Weber's ideas led to the development of the anti-positivist approach known as interpretivism. Interpretivist sociologists reject the positivist view that human behaviour is determined and shaped by social structure or social laws over which people have no control. They also reject the idea that human actions are predictable. Interpretivist sociologists argue that people are active creators of their own destinies because they are conscious beings who act with intention and purpose. People's ability to exercise choice and take alternative courses of action means they are not passive victims who are compelled against their will to take certain pre-determined paths because of the way society is organised.

Interpretivists believe that society (sometimes called the social world) is socially constructed in that it is the product of two crucial social processes:

1 First, people choose to come together to interact in social groups. For example, they choose to live in families and choose to work alongside others.

2 However, Weber argued that what makes an interaction or event 'social' is that all those who take part give it the same meaning. They all interpret what is happening – the group interaction or experience – in broadly the same way. They all share the same sense of what is going on. If they do not, social interaction would not be possible. Interpretivist sociologists point out when people interact with each other, they are constantly interpreting (i.e. giving meaning to) their own behaviour and that of others. For example, a family is not just a group of people with a biological relationship but a group of people who interpret themselves as a family and interact accordingly.

The way you interpret your parents' and siblings' behaviour towards you will in turn influence your behaviour, and so on.

Weber, therefore, concluded that if we are to explain some event in the social world, our explanation has to take into account what the people involved feel and think about it – that is, their experiences and the meanings they apply to those experiences. Weber argued that we must not regard people simply as helpless puppets, as positivists do. Instead, we need to acknowledge that society is a social construct in that it is the net sum of all social interactions and the interpretations or meanings that underpin them. In this sense, people are the architects of society.

Study

Coroners and suicide – Atkinson (1978)

J. Maxwell Atkinson's study of the work of coroners and suicide was an interpretivist critique of Durkheim's positivist study of suicide. Atkinson was very critical of Durkheim's use of official suicide statistics because Durkheim failed to appreciate that these are socially constructed. This means that they do not just come about by themselves. They are the end result of an interaction between the victim, their relatives and friends, and most importantly a legal official called a coroner whose function is to interpret how people have died and to officially apply one of five possible labels or categories – natural causes, misadventure, homicide, suicide and the open verdict – on the basis of the evidence available, thereby creating an official death statistic.

With regard to suicide, if a coroner suspects intent to die, he or she will look for various clues such as a suicide note and will look closely at how and where the person died using their previous experience and interpretation of suicidal action. However, most coroners will interact with friends and relatives in order to work out the frame of mind of the deceased person. They will look for clues in the person's biography that might have motivated such action, such as redundancy, death of a loved one and so on. Atkinson notes that it is at this stage that relatives in particular can influence a coroner's final decision by insisting that the victim was not depressed, upset and so on.

Atkinson argues that Durkheim's methodology was crucially flawed because he failed to recognise that suicide statistics are socially constructed by coroners who come to their decision as a result of interacting with the friends and relatives of the deceased and interpreting the dead person's actions and intentions.

Some of Weber's ideas were further developed by Mead, who demonstrated that people's sense of self can only develop in a social context. He argued that an important part of the socialisation of children was learning how to interpret every interaction they found themselves in by learning to put themselves in other people's shoes (or, to put it more vividly, to get inside other people's heads). Mead observed that the central feature of social life is that actions are the result of people's interpretations of the situation that they are in. People interpret the actions of others, and react according to that interpretation. Most of the time, such interpretations are shared by all of those involved and social life proceeds smoothly. However, when interpretations are not shared, social breakdown can occur. Mead therefore concluded that the causes of social action lie in people's 'definition of the situation' – that is, their interpretation of events – rather than as a result of objective laws that govern from outside.

Activity

Considering interpretivism

1 In groups, consider the following list of social interactions. What interpretations or meanings do we share and apply to these interactions and how do these affect our behaviour?
   a) When we are ill and go to the doctor.
   b) When we are stopped and questioned by a police officer.
   c) When we use a public toilet.
   d) When we go to a nightclub.
   e) When we sit an examination.

Verstehen and empathy

Interpretivist sociologists argue that if we want to explain social actions, we have to first understand them in the way that the participants do. We must learn to see the world from their standpoint. We need to develop empathetic understanding, which Weber called 'verstehen'. The job of the sociologist therefore is to uncover the shared interactions and interpretations that make up society.

Researcher imposition

Interpretivists do not believe that a scientific approach is central to good sociological research. They see validity as more important than objectivity and reliability. They even suggest that the positivist emphasis on reliability can result in researcher imposition; they claim that positivist research only focuses on what the sociologist thinks is important and consequently it may neglect what the research subject really thinks. (This idea will be discussed further in Section 6.3.)

Rapport, subjective experience and qualitative data

Interpretivists therefore prefer to highlight the concept of validity (which they define as seeing and documenting the world as it really is) and they claim that their research approach ensures this in a number of ways:

- Interpretivist research methods are ethnographic; they involve trying to understand social behaviour and the organisation of societies and cultures by going out and talking to people wherever they are and while they are doing whatever it is they do. They involve the insertion of the sociologist into the everyday world and natural setting of the research subject with the minimum of fuss and disturbance.
- Interpretivists strongly believe that unique and trusting relationships or rapport should be established with those being studied so that a true picture of their lives is constructed.

Quick question

What does 'verstehen' mean?

- Interpretivist research endeavours to get inside people's heads and to experience the world from the research subject's point of view. It is therefore essential to validity that the sociologist is able to establish 'verstehen' in order to understand how the research subject really feels about his or her subjective experience of social life. The job of the interpretivist sociologist is to objectively uncover the subjective experience of his or her research subjects – that is, how they interact with others and how they interpret the social reality they find themselves in.
- Data collected by interpretivist research is very different to the positivist emphasis on quantitative data. Interpretivists prefer **qualitative** data which presents the quality of the way of life of the research subjects in the form of words rather than numbers. Many of the research reports produced by interpretivist research contain material in which the research subjects 'speak for themselves ' in that they are often verbatim accounts of the social world which are expressed in the actual words of the research subjects.

Quick question

What is the difference between objectivity and subjectivity?

- Interpretivists prefer primary research methods such as unstructured interviews because of their naturalistic conversational style and observation, especially the covert kind in which the subjects of study are unaware that they are being watched. Interpretivists are also keen on secondary data in which the research subjects' interpretation of reality is paramount, such as diaries, letters and autobiographies. The strengths and weaknesses of these methods will be examined in Section 6.3.

Activity

Considering ethnography

1 Which of the following research situations would you consider to be ethnographic? Explain why they qualify or not.
   a) Interviewing a pupil in the head teacher's office.
   b) Asking career women to keep detailed diaries of their daily life at work.
   c) Observing a section of a football crowd via CCTV cameras.
   d) Renting a flat on a deprived council estate and living life as an ordinary resident for six months.
   e) Sitting in the public gallery of a courtroom and observing how a trial is organised.
   f) Carrying out a series of informal interviews with a group of people affected by poverty in their own homes over a period of a year.

The positivist critique of interpretivist research

Positivist analyses of interpretivist research methods are generally not very complimentary. In fact, they suggest that the interpretivist research process is 'bad' science and poor research for the following reasons:

- It is often unsystematic and unstructured because it focuses on naturally occurring behaviour. Positivists are critical of the fact that interpretivists often make no attempt to control possible influential independent variables or causes.
- Interpretivist research requires the researcher to be part of the study, and consequently there is always the possibility that their presence may become obtrusive and influence the behaviour that is being researched.
- It is not possible to judge from ethnographic research whether the social context or the people studied are in any way typical or representative.

- Interpretivist research and data is difficult to replicate and, therefore, verify because much of it is the product of the unique rapport that the researcher has built up with members of the group. It is likely to be the case that another sociologist, even with similar social characteristics, would have a qualitatively different relationship with the research group and consequently produce quite different sets of data. Reliability, then, cannot be guaranteed.

- The qualitative data that interpretivist sociologists use may be biased because it is the result of the researcher's subjective and selective interpretations; the researcher has experienced thousands of social interactions but in practice only a few can be selected for analysis and publication. This data may therefore be unrepresentative. It may have only been selected because it supports the researcher's point of view.

- Ethnography is criticised as a methodological approach because it involves too narrow a view of the group or institution studied. The researcher usually does not study the wider context within which the research setting is located. In other words, he or she often fails to assess the impact of structural influences such as social class or patriarchy on the behaviour of the group being studied.

Quick question

Why is the macro positivist approach particularly critical of the interpretivist's micro focus on interaction and interpretation?

Reflexivity

Some interpretivist sociologists have attempted to counter this type of criticism by keeping research diaries that document the trials and tribulations of every stage of the research. This is known as reflexivity. It is intended as a form of self-evaluation that involves researchers reflecting critically on how they organised the research process, their everyday experience of it and how a range of influences might have positively or negatively affected the validity of their findings. For example, the researcher might consider:

- how power inequalities between the researcher and research subjects affected the quality of the data collected
- the social context of the research – that is, how wider structural forces impacted on the behaviour of those being researched
- mistakes made during the course of the research
- how the researcher's own social background and beliefs influenced how they got on with the research subjects or how they collected the data.

The purpose of reflexivity then, is to document how the researcher's role might undermine the validity of the findings. It is a recognition that the research team might be contributing to the way that the research subjects interpret the problem that the sociologists are investigating. In other words, the researchers who use reflexivity are acknowledging that they may be the cause of some of the data that they have collected.

Quick question

Some sociologists think that too much reflexivity can undermine the research process. Why do you think they believe this?

A third way?

Not all researchers are happy with the positivist/interpretivist divide that is supposed to exist in the world of sociological research. Some critics have even gone as far as suggesting that no such divide actually exists in the real world because many researchers acknowledge that people's social actions are the result of a combination of free will and structural constraints. Moreover, these critics point out that it is rare to find researchers who exclusively use positivist or interpretivist methods. Most researchers use whatever methods work best and this normally means a combination of positivist and interpretivist methodology.

Check your understanding

Briefly define the following terms and give an example of each:

- positivism
- reliability
- social construction
- reflexivity
- validity
- representativeness
- verstehen
- quantitative data
- data that speaks for itself
- value freedom
- qualitative data
- subjectivity
- interpretation
- generalisability
- objectivity.

Fill in the blanks, using the words given below.

_____ see the study of society as more important than the study of individuals. They see human or social behaviour as a product of _____ over which people have little or no influence such as consensus, class, gender and ethnicity. Consequently, social or human behaviour is _____. Positivists believe that sociological research should be _____ in character, (i.e. standardised, _____, and _____) and it should focus on collecting _____ data. Positivists see _____ as the most scientific primary methods of data collection.

On the other hand, the _____ approach is anti-positivist and points out that human beings have _____, which differentiates them from animals and so on. Instead, they see human beings as self-aware individuals who are able to exercise _____ and _____. They see society as the product of people choosing to come together in social groups such as the family, religion, peer group and so on. Society is the net sum of _____ in groups. When people socially interact, they use a set of _____ or _____ to make sense of what is happening around them and to choose how to react. This approach argues that we need to get inside people's heads in order to see the world through their eyes – that is, to document their interpretations of reality. This approach uses methods that produce _____ (e.g. in the research subject's own words) that is collected from a natural or _____ setting and that is high in _____.

choice, consciousness, ethnographic, free will, interpretations, interpretivist, objective, positivists, predictable, qualitative data, quantitative data, reliable, scientific, social forces, social interaction, social meanings, social surveys, validity

6.2 What are the main stages in the research process?

DAILY TABLOID

QUARTER OF BRITISH CHILDREN LIVING IN POVERTY

Consider the approach of these three groups of individuals and organisations to the study of poverty in the UK.

1 What do you think a tabloid newspaper journalist is likely to report about poverty? Where do tabloid newspapers get their information from?

2 How do you think their sources differ from those used by sociologists working for the Economic and Social Research Council?

3 How might the views of David Cameron and Ed Miliband differ on the causes of poverty? Where do you think politicians get their information from about poverty and how does it differ from that generated by sociologists?

A common misconception about sociology is that it is just 'common sense' or, at the very best, not that different from what journalists do in terms of observing and reporting social behaviour. However, it is important to recognise that this view of sociology fails to understand that sociology is empirical or research-driven. This means that the purpose of the subject is to go beyond everyday 'common sense' personal experience and journalistic reporting in order to collect evidence or data that provides objective insight into patterns and aspects of human behaviour and the real social world that would normally remain hidden from sight. For example, sociological research into the everyday behaviour of the poor suggests that they respond to poverty in very different ways compared with the popular stereotypes of the poor reported by some journalists – that is, as worthless, workshy and welfare-dependent.

Factors influencing the choice of research topic

The relationship between sociology and social policy

Two types of social phenomena interest sociologists with regard to choosing topics to research:

1 **Social problems** – these are aspects of social life that cause misery and anxiety to both private individuals and society in general. Crime, child abuse, domestic violence and suicide are examples of social problems. The research of social problems is often sponsored by those in power, particularly governments. Often government social policies aimed at solving or reducing social problems are based on the evidence gathered by sociologists. For example, the poverty surveys of Townsend and the Breadline Britain surveys of Mack and Lansley (1990) influenced the social policies of Labour governments with regard to the benefit system and child poverty respectively. Sociological research is therefore central to social policy because it can provide governments with crucial data about the extent of a problem while sociological explanations can help shape the social policy response. However, governments do not always take action when sociologists identify a social problem or when their empirical research suggests solutions. Politicians may, for example, disagree with sociologists about the cause of a social problem because their ideological position may be different.

For example, a politician might prefer to blame poverty on its victims rather than on government economic policy or the way that capitalist society is organised. Social policymakers may therefore ignore sociological research.

2 **Sociological problems** – a successful society involves a number of social institutions effectively carrying out a range of social processes and functions. Sociologists are interested in how societies and social institutions work and how individuals interact and interpret one another's behaviour. Any aspect of social life – whether it is 'normal' or 'deviant (and therefore a social problem) – is a sociological problem. For example, sociologists are interested in divorce as a social problem because it can have negative effects for individuals and society but they are just as interested in marriage as a sociological problem and ask questions such as 'Why is it important?', 'What makes a good or happy marriage?' and 'Why do some marriages break down?' Consequently, a great deal of sociological research functions to increase knowledge of how society works and to explain why social institutions as well as social groups and individuals tend to behave in patterned and predictable ways. Such research may have side-effects in that it might too encourage politicians and social policy-makers to adjust or change existing laws and policies.

> **Quick question**
>
> Identify three social problems associated with social inequality in the UK.

Much sociological research is therefore focused on social and sociological problems, and their relationship to social policy in three ways:

1 Some sociological research simply aims to be descriptive. Its purpose is to describe a particular situation or set of facts. For example, some sociologists are dedicated to describing the extent of inequality by examining facts and figures relating to wealth, income and poverty.
2 Some sociological research is explanatory. It sets out to explain a particular social phenomenon such as poverty. This might involve some description but the ultimate goal is to suggest reasons why poverty occurs and perhaps to encourage social policy-makers to do something about it.

Some sociological research is evaluative. It sets out to monitor and to assess the effect of a social policy. For example, when the Labour government introduced Sure Start centres into deprived communities to help poorer families, they commissioned sociologists to evaluate whether these were making any difference in terms of educational achievement, getting single mothers back into the workplace, and so on.

In addition to whether a sociologist is interested in pursuing the answers to social or sociological problems, the choice of research topic is dependent on a number of other practical influences.

The interests and values of the researcher

Some sociologists are strongly attracted to the subject of sociology because they strongly feel that some injustice or inequality needs to be corrected. Feminists, for example, may feel that patriarchy is a social problem that needs to be challenged and consequently their research interests may lie in areas in which they feel women are exploited or in which they face particular inequalities. Other sociologists with Marxist or socialist sympathies may feel strongly about inequalities in wealth and income and wish to draw the attention of the general public to the social problems generated by capitalism. The poverty researcher Peter Townsend was committed to eradicating poverty and his studies of the elderly (1957) and the poor (1979) were the result of that commitment.

However, it is important to understand that this does not mean that sociological research by such committed sociologists is biased. A major difference between sociologists and journalists is that the latter often work for newspapers that occupy a particular political position in the world. For example, the *Times* and the *Sun* are right-wing newspapers. Journalists working for these newspapers are aware that if they wish to keep their job, they must write up their stories in ways that support that right-wing perspective. Sociologists, on the other hand, regardless of their commitment, must conduct a fair and balanced enquiry and not allow their personal or political values to affect what is discovered and reported. Values may influence their choice of topic but the methods used to gather evidence should be free of bias.

Current debates in the academic world

Researchers will also be influenced by what is currently fashionable in the academic world. For example, the 1970s saw a 'gold rush' of feminist research into the family, the educational system and so on because large numbers of women had entered education and work. Women's position in society consequently became a hot topic. Similarly, the Conservative government's focus on law and order in the 1980s saw a plethora of studies focusing on criminality, riots, moral panics, prisons and so on. The 1990s saw a rise in the popularity of the theory of postmodernism and a consequent avalanche of studies focusing on identity politics and consumption.

Funding

Sociological research costs money and consequently the values of those providing the financing may also affect the direction and tone of the research. Some funding agencies have no agenda and therefore will judge a research proposal by a sociologist purely on its merits. Most universities and the Economic and Social Research Council (ESRC) are the most likely funders of social research to take this neutral position. A good deal of sociological research is also funded by charities and think tanks that specialise in particular interests and consequently are more likely to sponsor and commission research in those fields. For example, the Joseph Rowntree Foundation supports a lot of research in the field of poverty and inequality, the Runnymede Trust is mainly interested in issues affecting ethnic minorities and the Sutton Trust is interested in educational matters. Some think tanks are politically motivated and consequently only fund research into issues that may support their perspective. For example, the Centre for Social Justice, co-founded by the Conservative minister Iain Duncan-Smith, tends to produce research that supports the New Right perspective that believes that the nuclear family and marriage are under attack and that welfare dependency is a major social problem. Governments and businesses also finance sociological research but they are unlikely to commission research that it is going to bite them by suggesting they are the cause of the very problem under investigation.

Access to research subjects

It is often assumed that once a sociologist has made up his or her mind that they are going to research a particular group, the group will be happy to go along with the research. However, this is a naïve view because it fails to consider how much power the group has to negotiate the terms of the research.

Some groups have the power to resist the attentions of sociologists. It is no coincidence that sociologists have carried out thousands of explanatory surveys of the poor and powerless but there are few sociological studies on the rich and powerful. Moreover, the majority of studies of the rich and powerful are descriptive surveys in which the data has mainly been taken from secondary sources such as official statistics, tax returns and so on. Powerful people can more easily use their authority to deny sociologists access to their world. For example, educational studies of schools are overwhelmingly of comprehensive schools rather than of public or private schools. There are few studies of head teachers or governors but hundreds on pupils. Consequently, the sociological world of research can sometimes feel over-peopled by those who are powerless and who are unable to resist the charms and sweet talk of sociologists. In contrast, the world of the powerful – the economic, political and cultural elites - that run society and benefit from doing so is off-limits to sociologists.

Sociologists are sometimes interested in groups that are in closed institutions such as prisons, mental hospitals, women's refuges and so on which are difficult for sociologists to access.

Quick question

How might a sociologist go about getting access to a closed institution?

Access and gate-keeping

Joining exclusive or deviant groups that tend to shut out 'outsiders' or gaining access to them to conduct questionnaires and interviews is not impossible but needs to be sensitively thought through in terms of both ethics and personal safety. Very often, the sociologist will need to use an intermediary, or 'gate-keeper'– a person who does have contact with a relevant or appropriate set of individuals. For example, access to victims of domestic violence is not easy. An intermediary is crucially important

for the sociologist, since he or she can perhaps vouch for the researcher and help to establish a bond of trust between the sociologist and the group in question. Key professionals can sometimes fill this role; for example, social workers can often introduce a researcher to women who have been abused.

Some sociologists have attempted to use gate-keepers to access the world of crime and deviance. This is because the world of crime not only involves people who are conventionally powerful – judges, police officers and so on – but it also includes people who are powerful in the sense that they are potentially dangerous and can do sociologists physical harm if they discover that they are the unwitting subject of sociological study. Gate-keepers can help sociologists to gain access to the criminal world by negotiating with those whom the sociologist is interested in so that a degree of cooperation is achieved. However, finding such gate-keepers is not easy. Getting criminals to agree to be the subject of sociological research is less easy still. Consequently, there are few studies of working criminals. It is easier for a sociologist to access a prison and to interview convicted criminals than it is to access an organised criminal gang.

The choice of research method

Primary and secondary data

There are two types of data or evidence collected by sociologists. Primary data is that which results when the sociologist gets his or her hands dirty by going into the community with a particular research method and persuading a sample of the group that they are interested in to take part in the research process. Secondary data, on the other hand, has already been collected by others – that is, people who are not sociologists – in the form of secondary sources such as official statistics, state documents, diaries and so on. Most sociological research tends to use a combination of primary and secondary data. However, what specific research methods are adopted may depend on the following theoretical and practical factors.

Theoretical factors

The choice of research method is likely to be influenced by the position that the researcher takes with regard to either positivism or interpretivism (see Section 6.1 above). However, sociological researchers can, of course, choose to ignore this debate altogether and just use those methods that work best, regardless of whether they produce quantitative or qualitative data and whether they are regarded as scientific or not. These sociologists will be more concerned with the following practical factors as far as choosing a research method is concerned.

Practical factors

Cost

The choice of research method and the size of the research team will depend on how much funding the research has managed to secure. Research does not come cheap; salaries, living expenses, travel, computer resources, rent for offices, secretarial help and so on all have to be paid for. If funding is generous, the researcher might decide to employ and train a large interviewing team to carry out a national survey or to carry out a longitudinal study over a number of years. However, if financial resources are low, the researcher might not be able to afford to employ a team of interviewers and may have to adopt the cheaper option of sending out postal questionnaires or conducting a limited number of structured interviews. Secondary sources also cost little or nothing to access, and consequently are very attractive to sociologists as a reliable and cheap source of data.

The time available

This depends to a large extent on funding. Obviously a large budget will extend the time available and give the research team the option of carrying out a survey aimed at a sample of thousands of people from across the UK. The results of such a survey may take months to process and collate. If money is available over a period of years, then the sociologist may be able to carry out a longitudinal study – research that focuses on a particular group over a period of years in order to monitor how much change is taking place in their lives. (This type of survey will be examined in more detail in Section 6.3.)

In contrast, if the researcher lacks time, he or she might choose to save time by constructing a small-scale study focused on collecting qualitative data via unstructured interviews from half-a-dozen individuals, or might decide to focus on the analysis of secondary sources rather than carrying out first-hand research.

The subject matter of the research

Some areas of social life are more accessible to researchers than others. For example, some people may feel comfortable discussing how their health is shaped by exercise or lack of exercise, and therefore may be happy to fill in a questionnaire on this topic

or take part in a group interview. However, some subject matter is extremely sensitive; for example, sexual behaviour is a particularly difficult area for research because people may feel that questions on this subject are unnecessarily intrusive and embarrassing, and refuse to cooperate, even if the questions come in a questionnaire form and can be filled in anonymously.

The nature of the subject matter, therefore, can affect the researcher's choice of method. Some subjects are very problematic; for example, people may not admit willingly to behaviour such as domestic violence, racism, tax avoidance and certain types of violent or sexual behaviour. Consequently, researchers need to think carefully about the reaction of the research subjects to the subject matter and which research tools are going to produce the most valid data.

> **Quick question**
>
> Can you think of any other sensitive subjects that might affect a researcher's choice of method?

The social characteristics of the researchers and those being researched

We shall return to this aspect of research in Section 6.3 but it needs to be acknowledged here that the research method chosen is to some extent dependent upon the social characteristics of both the research team and those being researched – that is, their age profile, their ethnicity, their social class and so on. In particular, the status of the researcher(s) in the eyes of those being researched needs to be thought through if research is to be successful. For example, there may be negative consequences for the validity of the data collected if researchers from ethnic minority backgrounds are collecting data from white employers about discrimination in the workplace, or if white researchers are involved in interviewing black or Asian people about their experience of racism. This aspect of the research design and the recruitment of the research team therefore needs very careful consideration.

Ethics

In addition to theoretical and practical factors, sociologists must also consider the ethical rules laid down by the British Sociological Association (BSA) when they choose what social or sociological problem to pursue and which research method they are going to use. The BSA points out that research subjects are people with rights and it is the responsibility of the researcher(s) to make sure that people who take part in their research are not exploited or harmed. Furthermore, a code of sociological ethics is thought to generate trust; it is argued, then, that following an ethical set of rules is more likely to improve the validity of data because people are more likely to convey what they really think, feel and do to a sociologist who is obviously sensitive to their needs. Consequently, sociologists tend to follow six ethical guidelines:

1 The BSA recommends that research subjects should be fully aware that they are part of a sociological research project. Moreover, they need to be informed what the purpose of the research is so that they can make an informed choice as to whether they want to take part. This is known as 'informed consent'. However, giving such consent is not always a straightforward matter. For example, very young children or the mentally ill may not be able to fully understand what the researcher is doing. Consequently, their parents or carers may have to consent on their behalf.

2 The BSA insists that sociologists should not engage in any form of deception. This means that sociologists should not keep information about the research from those taking part and researchers must never lie about the purpose of the research. In particular, the BSA note that it is especially deceptive to establish friendships with people in order to manipulate data from them. However, not all sociologists agree with this ethical rule. Some argue that deceit can produce data that cannot be produced under more honest circumstances, and the value of such data to policy-makers is well worth the ethical costs.

3 The BSA is keen that the privacy of research subjects should be safeguarded as much as possible. This can be a difficult ethical goal to achieve because sociological research is by its very nature intrusive. However, the BSA suggests that maintaining privacy can be strengthened by keeping the identity of research participants secret. Such anonymity means that the information that an individual gives to the researcher should not be able to be traced back to that individual. Most researchers, therefore, are careful to disguise the identity of individual participants when they write up their research. There is some evidence that a guarantee of confidentiality may result in more validity in that

if people know they cannot be identified, they may be more willing to reveal all sorts of personal and private information to a sociologist.

4 The BSA recommends that research subjects be protected from harm. There are, of course, different types of harm. Some sociological research may harm research subjects emotionally or psychologically by asking questions that trigger memories that people would prefer to forget or that create anxiety or fear. Sociological research may also harm the reputation of people who take part in the research. They may feel that they have been misrepresented and/or exposed to ridicule. There is also a danger that people may face punishment; for example, they may lose their job because a sociologist published an account of their activities.

5 The BSA insists that sociological researchers need to make sure that their behaviour is never illegal or immoral. In particular, sociologists need to avoid being drawn into situations where they may commit crimes or possibly assist or witness deviant acts. Some sociologists argue that if a sociologist comes into possession of 'guilty knowledge' – that is, knowledge of crimes committed in the past or future intentions to commit crime – he or she should inform the relevant authorities.

6 Finally, and very importantly, researchers need to avoid putting themselves in situations in which they or their research team are put at risk of physical harm.

Activity

Research methods and ethics

1 What is wrong with the following research proposal?

I have decided to do my sociology project on people's attitudes towards dying. I work part-time in a hospice and have decided to use conversations that I have overheard between patients and their relatives as my research data.

Aims, hypothesis and research questions

Once the research topic and the research method have been sorted out, then the sociologist can start thinking about the aims and objectives of the research – that is, what their main research questions or hypothesis are going to be and how they are going to incorporate these into their research design.

The hypothesis

Once a topic or issue has been identified as worthy of study, the researcher needs a starting point for the research. The first stage in any research project is to read what others have published on the subject. This has three functions.

1 The researcher can avoid repeating research that has already been done.
2 Reading may provide the researcher with ideas as to the direction their research should take.
3 These ideas can be shaped into a hypothesis that the researcher wishes to test by carrying out sociological research.

A hypothesis is an informed guess or hunch that the researcher thinks might be true and that can be tested by breaking it down into aims and objectives. It is informed because it is based on sociological knowledge. It is essentially a prediction of what the sociologist thinks their research will unearth. However, not all research has a clear hypothesis when it begins. Some researchers prefer to begin with a general aim and to allow the hypothesis to take shape and develop as the research data is collected. This is known as 'grounded theory'.

Operationalisation

The next stage of the research process is to break down the hypothesis or research aim into concrete things that can be observed or measured. This process is known as 'operationalisation'. Precise measurement of social phenomena cannot occur without it.

Activity

Operationalisation

1 Take the hypothesis, 'Middle-class parents provide their children with educational advantages in terms of cultural, economic and social forms of capital'. Identify the six concepts included in the hypothesis that need to be operationalised if this hypothesis is to be effectively tested.

One of the most difficult concepts to define and operationalise is the concept of social class. Most sociologists agree that social class is normally based on the jobs that people do. For example, manual workers – people who generally use their hands or strength in their jobs – have traditionally been perceived by sociologists as working class while white-collar workers, professionals such as teachers, and executives responsible for the day-to-day operational control of companies have traditionally been seen as middle class.

Study

Measuring cultural capital – Noble and Davies (2009)

The authors developed a short questionnaire to measure the cultural capital of students aged 16–17 in their final year of school or college. Parental occupation was measured using the government's social class classification, and where the occupation of both parents was reported, the higher of the two was used.

The researchers operationalised the concept of cultural capital by asking questions based on three key areas.

1 The educational and occupational background of parents.
2 Students' leisure activities such as watching popular entertainment on television, going to art galleries, museums, the theatre and classical concerts, playing an instrument, listening to classical music, reading a 'quality' newspaper and keeping up with current affairs.
3 The extent to which parents encouraged their children to take an interest in cultural pursuits such as reading newspapers and discussing art, books, science, music and current affairs. Questioning also focused on how many books were in the home and parents' cultural activities.

The aim was to see whether there was any correlation between particular cultural activities, social class and higher education correlations.

Occupation is therefore regarded by many sociologists as a good indicator of social class. It also generally indicates other status factors, such as income, level of education (most professionals went to university, whereas many non-skilled labourers did not) and whether people own their home (middle-class people are more likely to be owner-occupiers, whereas most council tenants come from working-class backgrounds).

Quick question

Can you think of any problems with regard to using occupation as the main indicator of social class?

The sampling process

The research population is the group that the sociologist has decided to study. It is important that the research is based on a precise definition of this group. For example, if the research is focused on 'the poor', the researchers would need to identify and justify which specific individuals or groups qualify as 'poor'. Once the researchers have precisely identified the research population that they are going to focus their research on, they then need to think about how they are going to get access to that group.

The term 'research or target population' refers to all those people who could be included in the research. There is a very good chance that this group will be made up of a very large number of people, possibly several million, depending on the subject of the research. It is therefore going to be too expensive, time-consuming and impractical to include the whole research population in the research. Accordingly, a sample has to be chosen.

The concept of sampling is a familiar one. As McNeill and Chapman (2005:46) note: 'When I go to the market to buy fruit, I will usually, despite what the stall-holder says, try to handle an apple or two from the display to see what they are like. If I am happy with their quality, I will ask for the quantity that I want. I assume that the quality of the ones I have handled is typical or representative of the quality of the others. When I dip my toe in the swimming pool before going in, I assume that the temperature of that part of the water is representative of the temperature of the whole pool'.

The same principle applies when sampling for social research. Most researchers, therefore, wish to select a sample that is representative – that is, is a typical cross-section of the population that they are interested in. They want a representative sample because they want to ensure generalisability. If a representative sample is used, it is then possible to generalise to the wider research population – that is, to say with some confidence that what is true of the sample's behaviour or opinion should be true of the research population as a whole, or at least it should be possible to calculate the likelihood of its being true.

Sampling techniques

There are two main sampling techniques that are used by sociologists:
1 random sampling
2 non-random sampling

Random sampling techniques

Random or probability sampling is a type of lottery. In its simplest form, it might involve drawing names or numbers from a hat or a machine respectively. When sociologists use this technique, it normally involves selecting the research subjects randomly from a list of names or addresses called a 'sampling frame'.

The sampling frame is crucial to the process of random sampling. It is a list of the names of the people who make up the research population that the sociologist wishes to research. It is normally organised into 'sampling units'; these may be individuals or households. If the researcher is interested in specific types of individuals, there are various lists that can act as sampling frames. The electoral register or roll is often used by sociologists as a sampling frame; this is a list of people aged over 18 years old who are registered to vote. General practitioners' lists of patients, school registers, the Postcode Address File and telephone directories have been used by some sociologists, though the latter are now problematic because they exclude people who are ex-directory and those who only have mobile phones.

> **Quick question**
>
> What sampling frames might be used to identify A-level sociology students, fitness freaks, old age pensioners and new mothers?

Random sampling means that every member of the research population has an equal chance of being included in the sample. However, a simple random sample does not guarantee what the researcher hopes is the outcome – a representative sample – because this sampling technique may end up selecting a disproportionate number of people from one particular group in the research population. This creates a problem known as 'bias', whereby any data collected is going to be skewed in favour of that group. Consequently, sociologists have developed two variations on the random sample in order to produce proper representative samples:

1 **Systematic random sampling** – involves randomly choosing a number between one and ten, say seven, and then picking out every tenth number from that number – that is, 7, 17, 27, 37 and so on – from the sampling frame until the required number in the sample is reached. This technique does not always guarantee a representative sample. However, the larger the sample, the more likely it is to be reasonably representative and the less likely it is to be biased in favour of any one group.

2 **Stratified random sampling** – involves dividing the research population into a number of different sampling frames and then using systematic random sampling to select the group that will comprise the research sample. For example, if a town has 10,000

residents over the age of 21, of whom exactly half are male and half female, a random sample of one tenth of them is unlikely to produce exactly half men and half women. It might produce a very biased sample of, say, 650 women and 350 men. To avoid this possibility, sociologists often choose to use a stratified random sampling technique that might work as follows. Separate sampling frames are constructed for males and females so that 500 people can be sampled from each group using a systematic random sampling technique. If the researcher wanted to stratify further because the hypothesis included reference to ethnicity and age, more sampling frames could be compiled so that the right proportions of each group could be systematically and randomly sampled.

Non-random sampling techniques

These types of methods deliberately target specific groups rather than randomly selecting a sample from the general population. There are five main types that sociologists might use:

1 Quota sampling is like stratified random sampling, but with an important variation. In this case, the researcher decides how many of each category of person should be included in the sample, but then, instead of selecting them at random from a sampling frame, the researcher goes out looking for the right number of people in each category until the quota is filled. Thus if, in a sample of 500 people, the quota of women aged between 30 and 40 is 22, the researcher will look out for 22 such women and, when they have been found and interviewed, that is the quota filled. This method is most often used by market researchers, and by television news companies and newspapers to find out what people's voting preferences are before an election.

However, because it lacks randomness, there is a danger that bias might creep into the selection of the sample; researchers may only stop and question people who look 'suitable' or 'cooperative' or visit homes that look 'respectable'. Consequently, it is doubtful whether this sampling technique is able to gather a sample that is truly representative of the research population.

2 Purposive sampling involves researchers choosing individuals or cases that fit the nature of the research. Purposive sampling occurs when a researcher chooses a particular group or place to study because it is known to be of the type that is wanted. Goldthorpe and his team (1969) wanted to study manual workers with high incomes to see whether they had developed a middle-class way of life. They purposely decided to study workers employed by a car manufacturer in Luton because these manual workers were known to be well paid.

3 Opportunity sampling is very similar to purposive sampling. It essentially means making the most of situations or opportunities in which the research population is likely to be found. For example, if the researcher is interested in researching if African people in the UK experience racism, there is little point in the researchers standing around city centres hoping that some African people might come along and fulfil their quota. It is also very unlikely that a sampling frame of African people is available to researchers. A better alternative would be to identify opportunities in which there is more chance of coming into contact with African people. Researchers might therefore head down to community centres or churches that cater for African people and purposely ask all of those present to take part in the research.

4 Snowball sampling is mainly used when researchers experience difficulty in gaining access to a particular group of people whom they wish to study because there is no sampling frame available or because the research population engage in deviant or illegal activities that are normally carried out in isolation or in secret. This sampling technique involves finding and interviewing a person who fits the research needs and then asking them to suggest someone else who might be willing to be interviewed. In this way, the original small nucleus of people grows by adding people to it in stages, much as a snowball can be built up by rolling it along the snow on the ground. The sample can grow as large as the researcher wants.

> ### Activity
>
> #### Sampling
> 1 If you were researching the following social groups, which sampling technique would you use and why? Think about whether a sampling frame exists for the group.
> a) A level students in both state and private schools.
> b) Women who work in high-powered jobs.
> c) Elderly people in residential care homes.
> d) Young unemployed people from African-Caribbean backgrounds.
> e) Young people working on zero-hour contracts.
> f) Full-time housewives.

5 Volunteer sampling is a variation on snowball sampling. Sociologists may advertise for research volunteers in magazines and newspapers, on university noticeboards or on the internet. However, both snowball and volunteer sampling may fail to produce representative samples. The people who take part in the research may not be typical of the research population that the sociologist is interested in.

Higher educational opportunities for South Asian Women – Bagguley and Hussain (2007)

The research team interviewed a total of 114 young women. Of these, 51 were Pakistani, 37 Indian and 26 Bangladeshi. Potential respondents were approached in a variety of ways. Purposive sampling was initially used in that undergraduates and current sixth-formers were approached in the public social areas of their institutions. Bangladeshi students and recent graduates were contacted through local community centres. The samples were then further boosted through snowball sampling. A small sample of 'widening participation' and careers-service staff in universities were also interviewed about their policy and practice in relation to South Asian women.

Detecting bias

All sampling techniques are a compromise between representativeness and practicality, and researchers often have to make do with samples that are not fully representative. The most important requirement of any research when it comes to sampling is to be aware of any potential bias caused by the sampling technique used, and to report fully on this in the analysis of the research findings.

Pilot studies

One way in which such bias can be discovered before it seriously undermines the research is through the employment of pilot studies. These are essentially small-scale dress rehearsals for the main research involving a sub-sample of the sample that the main research intends to use. Pilot studies are useful because they act as an early warning system for problems that have arisen out of the operationalisation of the hypothesis or the choice of the sample. A pilot study is useful because it can check:

- whether questions are clearly understood and interpreted in the same way
- that the questions do not upset or lead the participants

- that the sampling technique used is successful in obtaining the 'right' types of people to fill in the questionnaire
- that interviewing teams are well trained
- that the data produced is the kind that is wanted.

Respondent validation and interpretation of data

Another means by which bias or other problems can be spotted is through the use of respondent validation. This is the process by which the sociologist's interpretation of an event or data is checked with that of those who took part in the event. Feedback is obtained from the participants about the accuracy of the data and about whether the researcher has fairly interpreted their behaviour – that is, as Bryman notes, how far the researcher's understanding of what is going on in a social setting corresponds with that of the group who normally occupy such a setting. The point of respondent validation, which tends to be mainly used in interpretivist research, is to reduce the possibility of the researcher exclusively applying their interpretation of the research data to the hypothesis because this might contain bias. However, Bryman argues that respondent validation can be problematic because the research sample might not be able to validate the research findings because they misunderstand it or they might be unwilling to validate it because they misinterpret it as critical of their actions.

Check your understanding

Briefly define the following terms and give an example of each:

- sampling frame
- respondent validation
- operationalisation
- systematic sampling
- research population
- longitudinal study
- social problem
- hypothesis
- primary data
- stratified sampling
- sociological problem
- gate-keeping
- opportunity sampling
- informed consent
- secondary data
- snowball sampling.

Section summary

Fill in the blanks, using the words given below.

_____ factors such as cost, time, access to the subject matter and the social characteristics of the research team are very important when choosing a research method and research topic but so too are ethical influences such as gaining _____ _____ and avoiding _____.

The time and resources needed are important. Questionnaires can be designed, sent out and returned within a month. However, if the researcher is intending to use an _____ method such as participant observation, a great deal of time – even years – might be required. The researchers might even want to do a _____ study and revisit the research subjects every couple of years to document how their situation has changed.

Sampling too is important. Most sociological studies use a _____ sampling technique in order to generate a _____ sample. However, this technique requires a list of people known as a _____ but some sociologists use non-random techniques such as _____ sampling that target particular sections of the population, usually in the street – for example, housewives out shopping. Others use _____ sampling, which involves the researcher being introduced to members of a group by other members one by one; for example, a heroin addict might introduce the researcher to other heroin addicts that they know. However, there is a danger that these techniques might result in a sample that is _____.

biased, deception, ethnographic, informed consent, longitudinal, practical, quota, random, representative, sampling frame, snowball

6.3 Which methods are used in sociological research?

Getting you thinking ...

Item A: Ethnicity and mental health – Nazroo (1997)

James Nazroo used the social survey method, specifically a postal questionnaire composed of closed questions which was sent out to a sample of 8,000 people who were representative of the ethnic minority population of the UK asking them about their experience of the mental health system. Response rates were reasonably high because Nazroo translated his questionnaires into Urdu, Punjabi and so on. His questionnaire was piloted and therefore the questions asked were objective – that is, they were carefully worded, clear and unambiguous, and did not lead the respondents. However, the validity of his findings may have been undermined by the diverse nature of the sample in terms of culture and language. There is no guarantee that everybody who took part interpreted the questions in the same way. For example, Nazroo had difficulties in translating the term 'depression' into Asian languages because different cultures define this concept in different ways.

Item B: Life on a psychiatric ward – Quirk and Lelliott (2002)

Alan Quirk and Paul Lelliott carried out an ethnographic study using participant observation to describe life on acute psychiatric wards from the point of view of patients. They were particularly interested in the nature and use of coercion by medical staff to control patients and how the power of doctors and nurses is viewed and responded to by patients. Their study lasted three years. Three hospitals gave Quirk special ethical permission to conduct the research. The participant observation consisted of three separate three-month periods on three different wards: two in psychiatric units in London and one in a unit in the south-east. Quirk immersed himself in life on each ward as much as was possible. Patients, doctors and nurses knew he was a sociologist. He attended a range of 'events' such as ward rounds and occupational therapy sessions. He 'hung around' in television rooms, dining rooms and corridors in order to observe events and talk to people, and collected a great deal of qualitative data about how patients interacted with one another and with staff, and how patients interpreted their experiences on the ward.

1 Consider each of the studies above in turn and make a list of what you think are their strengths and weaknesses.

2 Which do you think is the most reliable or scientific study and why?

3 Which do you think might produce the most valid results and why?

The social survey

A social survey involves the systematic collection of mainly quantitative data from a fairly large number of people. Social surveys usually obtain this information through questionnaires or, less often, through structured interviews.

Longitudinal surveys

Some surveys are 'longitudinal', i.e. they study the same group of people over a long period of time. Such surveys provide us with a clear image of changes in attitudes and behaviour over a number of years. For example, the National Child Development Study has followed the same 40,000 children all born in one week in March 1958. Follow-up studies have surveyed the group at the ages of 16, 23 and 33 in order to track the influence of class, education and family on their health.

However, such surveys can be problematic for several reasons:

- Respondents may drop out or researchers may lose track of them. This undermines the representativeness of the original sample.
- The views of those who remain in the sample may also be significantly different to those who drop out. This may undermine the validity of the research.
- There is a danger that the research team may get too friendly with members of the group and consequently lose their ability to be objective.
- They are expensive.

> **Quick question**
>
> Use the internet to look up two television programmes, *7 Up* and *Citizen 2000*. In what sense are these longitudinal studies?

Questionnaires

Questionnaires are the main method for gathering data in social surveys. A questionnaire is simply a list of questions written down in advance that are handed or posted to the respondent (the person chosen by the researcher to answer the questions) for self-completion. Sometimes, they are included in mass media publications such as newspapers and magazines or posted on the internet. However, some questionnaires become interview schedules in that they are read out and filled in on behalf of the respondent by trained interviewers. This type of questionnaire is known as a formal or structured interview.

Questionnaire design

Questionnaires use a variety of question types. The most common are 'closed' questions and 'open' questions.

At one extreme, closed questionnaires contain a series of questions accompanied by a choice of answers; all the respondent has to do is tick the box next to the most appropriate answer. Such questionnaires produce quantitative data – that is, statistical data.

At the other extreme are open questionnaires that ask open-ended questions, i.e. the respondent is asked to write down what they feel or what they have experienced. Such questionnaires produce qualitative data – that is, data that is expressed in the respondent's own words, and is concerned with how they see the world in terms of feelings, attitudes, experiences and so on.

However, most researchers tend to use questionnaires that employ a combination of mainly closed questions with occasional open questions – these are sometimes called 'semi-structured' questionnaires – though there are variations on this type. For example:

1. A self-report is a type of questionnaire that lists a number of items or activities and asks respondents to tick those they have experienced. For example, the Breadline Britain poverty survey (2015) asked people to tick a number of items and activities that they believed were 'necessities' in order to measure those who did not have these – that is, those experiencing relative poverty.

2. Attitudinal questionnaires usually ask respondents on a scale of 1–5–1 being 'strongly agree', 3 being 'neutral' and 5 being 'strongly disagree' – whether they subscribe to a particular point of view.

It is important that the questionnaire is as short as possible because people usually cannot be bothered to spend a long time completing a questionnaire. Furthermore, questions need to be asked in a straightforward and simple manner that can be clearly understood in the same way by those completing the questionnaire. Therefore, the researcher must think very carefully about the language used in the question. Ideally, questions should be neutral and objective.

However, a weakness of questionnaires is that they can suffer from poor question design.

- For example, questions can be biased in that they can lead respondents into the answers required by the researcher.

They can sometimes be 'loaded', i.e. written in such a way that the respondent is provoked into an emotional response that seeks to evade the truth.

- Sometimes they contain technical vocabulary that people cannot understand.
- It is also important to ensure that all respondents share the same understanding of questions. This is difficult if vague words like 'few' or 'several', which mean different things to different people, are used.

Activity

Questionnaire design

1 What is wrong with the following set of questions?
   a) Do you believe that your bad habits and immoral behaviour are responsible for you being in poverty?
   b) Have you discriminated against anyone on the basis of their colour?
   c) Don't you think that the way the elderly are treated is shameful?
   d) Do you think an underclass exists in the UK?
   e) Do you think men are superior to women?
2 Can you re-word the above questions to make them more effective?

The strengths of questionnaires

- They can be used for reaching larger and consequently more representative samples of people since the questionnaire can simply be handed or posted out to hundreds or even thousands of people.
- Postal questionnaires can be used if the research population is geographically dispersed across the country or if information is required from different regions for comparative purposes.
- Questionnaires are less time-consuming and cheaper than other methods.
- Questionnaires, especially if they guarantee anonymity, are useful for research that intends to ask embarrassing or sensitive questions such as sexual behaviour.
- A questionnaire ensures that the sociologist has minimum contact with the respondent. The researcher therefore will not directly influence the results by being present when the respondent fills it in.
- Positivist sociologists are very keen on using questionnaires, which they argue are scientific because they are high in reliability. It is argued that if a questionnaire is well designed and questions are neutral and objective (that is, not leading, loaded and so on), another researcher using the same questionnaire should be able to repeat it and

achieve similar results. It is therefore a standardised instrument of measurement.

- Positivists are also keen on this method because it produces lots of statistical data which can be compared, correlated and turned into tables, charts and graphs.

The weaknesses of questionnaires

- Many people cannot be bothered to reply to questionnaires. In other words, questionnaires, especially if postal, suffer from low response rates or even non-response. Response rates of less than 50 per cent can undermine the validity of the research findings because they are unlikely to reflect the social make-up of the research population that the sociologist is investigating.
- Postal questionnaires suffer the worse response rates. It can be difficult to motivate people to return postal questionnaires.

Quick question

How might recipients of postal questionnaires be encouraged to send the questionnaires back?

- Questionnaires have been criticised by interpretivist sociologists for producing data that is low in validity because they argue that real life is too complex to categorise in closed questions and responses. Questionnaires may therefore not be suitable for finding out why people behave the way that they do – that is, for uncovering motives for behaviour.
- Interpretivists suggest that there is a danger with questionnaires that respondents may interpret the question in a different way to that intended by the researcher. The fact that the sociologist is often not present when the questionnaire is filled in to clarify any misunderstandings may mean misinterpretation of questions is likely to occur which may undermine the validity of the data collected.
- There is evidence that people like to manage the impression other people have of them and this can shape their responses to a questionnaire. People may therefore lie or misrepresent themselves. For example, people often respond negatively to questions about depression or mental illness (whether they have experienced it or not) to give an impression of themselves as 'normal' citizens.
- Finally, interpretivist sociologists argue that questionnaires that use closed questions with tick-box responses suffer from the 'imposition

problem'. This means that they measure what the sociologist thinks is important rather than what the person completing the questionnaire experiences. The sociologist, by choosing particular questions and responses, has already mapped out the experiences, interpretations and so on of the respondents. Also, respondents completing questionnaires may be forced to tick boxes that only approximate to their experiences, views and so on. This may also frustrate some respondents and result in non-completion of the questionnaire.

> **Quick question**
>
> What other topics might people respond negatively to if they are asked about them?

Activity

Social class survey

In 2013, sociologists carried out an online survey composed of five questions that they claimed would help people living in the UK to identify their social class. These were as follows:

1 What is your annual household income after taxes? Total income for you/spouse/significant other:

Under £10K   £10K–25K   £25K–50K   £50K–100K Over £100K

2 Do you own or rent a property? Own   Rent

Value of all property owned/mortgaged by you/ spouse/significant other

Under £125K   £125K–250K   £250K–500K Over £500K

3 Do you have any savings? Pensions, shares, ISAs etc

None   £0–10K   £10K–25K   £25K–50K   £50K–100K Over £100K

4 Which of these people do you know socially?

Select all of the people you know:

Secretary   Farm worker   Nurse   Chief executive Teacher   Software designer   Cleaner Call centre worker   University lecturer   Postal worker Artist   Scientist   Electrician   Lorry driver   Solicitor Office manager   Accountant   Shop assistant

5 Which of these cultural activities do you take part in? Select all of the activities you do sometimes or often:

Go to stately homes   Exercise/go to gym   Go to the opera   Use Facebook/Twitter   Listen to jazz   Socialise at home   Listen to rock/indie   Go to museums/art galleries   Go to gigs   Listen to classical music Play video games   Do arts and crafts   Watch sports Watch dance/ballet   Go to the theatre

Listen to hip hop/rap

1 Look closely at the questions. How do you think the sociologists justified this choice of questions?
2 Which responses to Questions 4 and 5 do you think the sociologists were using to indicate whether someone is middle class or working class?
3 It could be argued that this is a poorly designed questionnaire – identify six problems in the wording and categories used that support this argument.

Interviews

Interviews, whatever type are being used by the sociologist, are generally recorded manually (i.e. people's responses are written down by the sociologist) and/or tape-recorded/videoed in order to produce a transcript from which quotes illustrating the point of view of the respondent can be used to support (or to contradict) a particular hypothesis. Interviews can be carried out in a public space – for example, on the street by market researchers, on the telephone or on the internet in chat-rooms. However, the most successful interviews are carried out in private, neutral and unthreatening venues.

Interviews are particularly useful when studying areas that are not accessible to sociological study using other methods; for example, it might not be practical to observe how a family cares for a sick member on a daily basis and a surgeon might not respond to a questionnaire about surgical mistakes.

However, interviewing can be an expensive business especially if a large interviewing team needs to be recruited and trained. Moreover, the success of interviewing often depends on how well the interviewers are trained in interview techniques such as listening skills and observation of body language.

Structured interviews

A structured interview usually involves the researcher reading out a list of closed questions from an interview schedule (a questionnaire) and ticking boxes or writing down answers according to pre-set fixed categories on behalf of the respondent. The interviewer plays a passive and robotic role in that he or she is not normally allowed to deviate from the questions on the interview schedule. There is usually little or no flexibility in the way that questions can be asked. The interviewer is usually not allowed or encouraged to add new questions. He or she merely repeats those on his or her interview schedule.

The responses to these types of interviews are usually converted into a quantitative form, and expressed in statistics, percentages, tables, charts and graphs. In this sense, they are very similar to questionnaires and consequently they share many of the strengths and weaknesses of questionnaires.

The strengths of structured interviews
- Positivists are very keen on structured interviews because they regard the method as scientific.

> **Quick question**
>
> Why do you think positivists regard structured interviews as scientific? Use concepts such as standardised, reliability, objectivity, quantifiability and correlation in your answer.

- The use of closed questions and fixed-choice tick-boxes generates large amounts of quantitative factual data that can be easily converted into tables, charts and graphs for comparison and correlation.
- Structured interviews can be conducted quite quickly because they follow a pre-set range of questions, which means that hundreds and even thousands of people can be interviewed in a relatively short period of time. This increases the possibility of getting a representative sample from which generalisations can be made.
- Interviewers can explain the aims and objectives of the research and clarify instructions. This may reduce potential non-response as well as addressing people's ethical concerns.
- Structured interviews have better response rates than questionnaires because interviewers can return if the respondent is not at home.

The weaknesses of structured interviews
However, compared with other methods, particularly unstructured interviews, there can be problems when using structured interviews:
- Structured interviews, like questionnaires, are artificial devices that are not a normal part of everyday reality; people may therefore respond to them with suspicion and only supply evasive, partial or false information. This is known as 'interview bias' and it can severely undermine the validity of the data collected. For example:
  1 Interviewers can also create the potential for demand characteristics by unconsciously leading respondents into particular responses through the tone of their voice or by the look of approval or disapproval on their face.
  2 Some respondents may react negatively in an interview because of the social characteristics (i.e. the age, gender, social class, ethnicity and so on) of the interviewer, which undermines the possibility of the interviewer building up a relationship of trust and rapport with the interviewee.
- Structured interviews are inflexible because the questionnaire or interview schedule is drawn up in advance and the interviewer must stick to it rigidly. Interpretivists note that this makes it impossible for researchers to pursue any interesting leads that may emerge in the course of the interview.
- Structured interviews are only snapshots taken at one moment in time and they therefore fail to capture the dynamic and changing nature of social life. People's experiences and attitudes may change over time, and structured interviews are unlikely to record this change.
- Interpretivist sociologists argue that interviews, like questionnaires, that use closed questions with category/list responses suffer from the imposition problem, meaning that they measure what the sociologist thinks is important rather than what the interviewee experiences. By choosing particular questions and responses, the researcher has already mapped out the experiences, interpretations and so on of the respondents and consequently the sociologist may fail to ask the really important questions.
- The success of interviewing depends on what people know about their own behaviour. Obviously, this may be affected by faulty or hazy memory but some people may simply not be conscious that

they behave in a particular way or they may be in denial. This obviously reduces their ability to answer questions in a structured interview.

Secondary data

Secondary data refers to any data that the sociologist has used that they did not collect for themselves. There are two types of secondary data that you need to aware of:
1 official and unofficial statistics
2 media products – television and radio programmes, articles from newspapers and magazines and websites on the Internet.

Official and unofficial statistics

Official statistics are the numerical data collected by the government, usually gathered through surveys carried out by state agencies such as the Office for National Statistics. The most commonly available sources of official statistics are those from the Census.

This is a questionnaire survey carried out by the government that has been done every ten years since 1851 (excluding 1941) on the whole population. The last one was in 2011.

Other government surveys include the General Household Survey, the Family Expenditure Survey and the Labour Force Survey. These surveys collect important data about income, wealth, jobs, family life, unemployment, poverty and so on.

Some official statistics are made up of registration data; by law, all births, deaths, marriages and divorces have to be registered and recorded. With regard to death, the registered death certificate gives information about the age, gender, occupation and cause of death, which gives us important insights into the relationship between mortality, life expectancy and inequality.

Unofficial statistics are the quantitative data that is collected by non-government sources such as employers, professional bodies, trades unions, political parties, think tanks, charities and so on.

The strengths of statistics

Both official and unofficial statistics are considered useful by sociologists for the following reasons:

- They are extremely easy and cheap to access; they are often available via the internet and involve little effort on behalf of the sociologist.
- They are usually extremely up-to-date and consequently give sociologists a very contemporary picture of patterns and trends in human behaviour.
- Positivist sociologists see official statistics as 'hard' reliable facts because they have been collected in a standardised, systematic and scientific fashion.
- Statistical relationships can be identified by comparing official statistics from regularly conducted surveys such as the Census. For example, by examining groups of statistics, sociologists might see a relationship between poverty and mortality.
- They are often gathered by surveys that involve large representative samples and therefore their findings can be generalised to similar populations.
- Trends over a period of time can easily be seen too; for example, we might see an improvement in life expectancy for some social groups as they gradually give up smoking.
- They often form the basis of hypotheses that motivate sociological research.

The weaknesses of statistics

However, interpretivists warn that sociologists need to be cautious in their use of such statistics for the following reasons:

- They may not represent a complete picture of whatever social or sociological problem the sociologist is interested in because the definitions used by the data-collecting organisation may be different to those used by sociologists. For example, sociologists prefer to use 'relative' measurements of poverty whereas the British government uses an 'absolute' measurement.
- Official statistics are open to political abuse; statistics can be manipulated or 'massaged' by governments for political advantage. For example, governments frequently change the ways in which unemployment statistics are defined and collected in order to give a positive impression of their economic policies.
- Statistics are socially constructed; this means they do not just appear or happen. They are the end result of someone making a decision or judgement that a particular set of activities needs recording and that statistics need collecting. These decisions are sometimes selective and biased. For example, the government may be happy to produce statistics showing the number of successful prosecutions for benefit fraud but reluctant to publish statistics showing how many wealthy individuals or global corporations are avoiding paying tax.
- Statistics tell us very little about the human stories or interpretations that underpin them. For example, poverty statistics tell us very little about the everyday strains, stresses and humiliations of actually living in poverty.

Activity

Official statistics

1 Official statistics are often divided into 'hard' statistics, which are regarded as highly reliable and accurate, and 'soft' statistics, which are often open to different interpretations. Look at the following list and explain why some of them are 'hard' and some of them are 'soft':
   a) taxation statistics
   b) birth registration statistics
   c) poverty statistics
   d) death statistics
   e) unemployment statistics
   f) suicide statistics
   g) marriage statistics
   h) wealth statistics.

Media products

Media products such as newspapers, magazines, advertisements, radio, music products, posters, films, novels, the internet and computer products, fanzines and so on tell us something about the particular society that we live in. Sociologists will often use media extracts or items such as adverts or television programmes to examine and analyse the values, priorities or concerns of a society at any one point in time.

A technique used by some sociologists to analyse media reports or products is content analysis. Usually, the aim of this type of research is to identify how particular social groups or social situations are portrayed in the product being analysed. Usually, sociologists design a content analysis schedule: a list of things that the sociologist is looking for in the media content on which they record how often the 'thing' occurs. This is normally done by counting the frequency of certain images such as those contained in adverts and photographs or words contained in newspaper/magazine articles or headlines. In this sense, content analysis is mainly a quantitative method.

The strengths of content analysis

As a method, it has a number of strengths:

- It is very cheap. All the sociologist needs to do is buy the magazines or newspapers or watch the television programmes.
- It is a comparative method in that it allows the sociologist to compare media reports and content over a period of time. In other words, content analysis can be longitudinal.
- Quantitative content analysis is regarded as reliable because other sociologists can repeat and cross-check the results by looking at the same media using the same content analysis schedule.

The weaknesses of content analysis

However, researchers using this method need to be aware of the following methodological weaknesses:

- It can be a very time-consuming method because media products might need to be checked over a fairly long period of time.
- It can often be a very subjective method. The categories used by content analysis largely depend on what the researcher interprets as important.
- Sociologists who have used it have been accused of analysing text out of context.
- It cannot be assumed from content analysis that media products and content have an effect upon their audience; this may not be the case. It is not proven or unproven.

- Media products may only tell us about the personal and political beliefs of those who produce media products, i.e. the prejudices of journalists and broadcasters.

Study

A content analysis of the media coverage of Amanda Knox – Freyenberger (2013)

Newspaper coverage can have a positive or negative impact on the image of an individual. This study examined the framing of Amanda Knox in newspapers published worldwide during the four years that Knox was imprisoned in Italy. An American foreign exchange student, Knox was studying in Italy when her roommate was murdered. Content analysis of 500 major world newspapers was conducted. The study's purpose was to determine the tone, story placement and page placement of each mention of Amanda Knox.

The results showed that mentions of Amanda Knox were more negative in the UK and Ireland. On the other hand, stories about Amanda Knox were more likely to be found on the front pages of newspapers in the USA. The general tone of these stories was sympathetic to her plight.

Ethnography

'Ethnography' literally means writing about the way of life, or culture, of social groups. At its simplest, it involves the researcher inserting himself or herself into the natural setting of the social group being studied and participating in and observing their daily activities. Other methods, particularly informal or unstructured interviews, may be used to sketch out a fuller picture of the group's behaviour.

The purpose of such research is to describe the culture and lifestyle of the group of people being studied in a way that is as faithful as possible to the way that they see it themselves and to the social contexts in which their behaviour occurs. The idea is to 'tell it like it is' – that is, to capture ordinary activities and people's interpretations of those activities.

Quick question

What sorts of groups might sociologists choose to study using ethnographic methods and why?

Ethnographic research is preferred by interpretivist sociologists, who argue that only ethnographic methods such as unstructured interviews allow researchers access to the 'lived experience' of particular social groups and to get inside their heads. In this sense, ethnography is about imitating real life. It is about achieving 'verstehen' – being able to empathise with or think like the people who are being studied. This closeness to the research subjects has led interpretivists to claim that ethnography produces the most valid and authentic type of qualitative data of any type of social research method.

Unstructured interviews

An unstructured or informal interview is essentially a guided conversation, where the talk is informal but the interviewer plays an active role in that he or she manages the questions to ensure that the participant keeps to the subject of the research. The interviewer in this situation does not normally have an interview schedule; rather, unstructured interviews are very flexible interviews because though the interviewer has an idea of the topics he or she should be covering, he or she is quite happy to follow the respondent if it is felt that this might produce useful results. A skilful interviewer will follow up ideas, probe responses to previous questions and investigate motives and feelings in ways in which the questionnaire and structured interview can never do.

Interpretivist sociologists argue that this type of interview is ethnographic because it is normally carried out in the natural setting of the respondent in which they feel most comfortable. Moreover, this type of interview is enhanced by the fact that such interviews are often in-depth and carried out over a period of hours rather than minutes. Often more than one interview takes place with a single respondent.

The strengths of unstructured interviews

It is argued that unstructured interviews have the following strengths:

- They allow the researcher to establish a qualitative interaction or relationship with the respondent, which generates trust and rapport and which puts the interviewee at ease. This may mean that interview subjects are more likely to open up and say what they really feel and mean, or give the interviewer information that they would not dream of divulging in a questionnaire or a structured interview. The problem of interview bias is therefore more likely to be avoided and more valid data is likely to be collected as a result.

- The way that an unstructured interview is organised stresses that what the interviewee says or thinks is the central issue; the respondent is placed at the centre of the research. Respondents may be more likely to discuss sensitive and painful experiences if they feel that the interviewer is sympathetic, empathetic and truly interested.
- Unstructured interviews are very flexible. The interviewer is not restricted to a fixed set of questions but can explore and follow up interesting responses from the interviewee. The researcher (who has to be a trained sociologist so they can recognise when the interviewee has made a sociologically important point) can formulate new hypotheses and put them to the test as they arise during the interview.
- Unstructured interviews are seen as particularly suited to researching sensitive groups, such as people who might be suspicious of or hostile to outsiders. Unstructured interviews allow the interviewer to explain the purpose of the research. Anonymity and confidentiality are also usually stressed, which encourages people to open up and give more valid responses.
- Unstructured interviews provide richer, more vivid and more colourful data; the data collected often speaks for itself in the form of extensive quotations from those being interviewed. Data therefore is highly valid.

The weaknesses of unstructured interviews

However, positivists are particularly critical of unstructured interviews for the following reasons:

> **Quick question**
>
> Why might positivists be critical of the relationship between the interviewer and interviewee in unstructured interviews?

- Unstructured interviews gather a fantastic amount of data and consequently the researcher has to be selective in what he or she actually publishes in support of his or her hypothesis. The researcher may end up consciously or unconsciously selecting material that supports his or her views. In other words, the selected material might be biased. What is left out of the final analysis may actually contradict the hypothesis.
- Because there are no pre-coded answers in unstructured interviews, the qualitative data from unstructured interviews is difficult to analyse and categorise because of the sheer volume of material in the respondent's own words. Positivists do not like this sort of data because it is impossible to quantify and turn into graphs, tables and so on.
- Sociological research that uses unstructured interviews tends to use fewer participants than surveys. Positivists claim that unstructured interview participants tend to be less representative of the research population as a result. It is therefore difficult to generalise from them to similar populations in the wider community.

> **Activity**
>
> ### Women, class and reality TV
>
> Research by Helen Wood and Beverly Skeggs (2012) aimed to look at how reality television portrayed working-class people and particularly how programmes such as *Wife Swap* and *The Only Way is Essex* have portrayed working-class people as failing or being out of control in some way.
>
> Research was conducted into how 40 women from four different friendship groups drawn from South London interpreted the behaviour of participants in reality TV shows. There were three stages to the methodology. First, one-to-one unstructured and informal interviews were conducted about lifestyles, home life, leisure activities and media use in order to work out the social class of the women. Second, 23 'text-in-action' sessions were conducted in order to capture people's responses to watching particular reality TV shows. The women
>
> were observed watching particular programmes and their responses were recorded. Third, the women were organised into focus groups in order to understand how friendship groups interpreted the content of the programmes. Focus group interviews usually involve getting a group of people together to discuss an issue, rather than simply giving answers to questions. The researcher relies on the dynamics of the group to keep the discussion going. There is minimal interference from the sociologist. Usually, the interaction between members of the group is recorded on audiotape or video.
>
> 1 What in your opinion are the strengths of this research?
> 2 Why can we safely describe such research as ethnographic?
> 3 Can you see any weaknesses in the design of this research?

- Unstructured interviews are expensive because training needs to be more thorough and specialised. Interviewers need to be trained in inter-personal skills so that they establish good relationships with interviewees. Interviews are exceptionally time-consuming to conduct and transcribe. They often take several hours to complete.
- Like structured interviews, an unstructured interview is highly dependent on what people know about their behaviour. If people are unaware that they behave or think in a particular way, it does not matter how trusting they are; this gap between what people think and what they actually do is not going to be uncovered by any type of interview.

Group interviews

Some unstructured interviews are carried out with groups rather than individuals. These may involve the interviewer talking to a group or panel of respondents. They are often used to interview children, who may feel threatened if interviewed by an adult in one-to-one situations. However, such children may feel reassured if their friends are present.

They may also be used to investigate the dynamics of how particular groups operate, such as a nursing team. The sociologist may believe that a truer and more valid picture of their behaviour will only emerge when the group is interviewed together.

Quick question

Identify two problems that might occur if children are interviewed in groups.

Focus group interviews

Another variation on the unstructured interview is the focus group interview in which participants are encouraged to talk to one other. Focus group interviews usually involve people getting together to discuss an issue, rather than simply giving an answer to a question. This method was first used by market researchers to see how consumers responded to particular products and has since been adopted by media organisations, political parties and sociologists.

Focus group interviews normally involve the sociologist introducing a group of people to an issue; for example, they may be shown an advertisement or public information film or simply asked to discuss particular questions or topics. The researcher relies on the dynamics of the group to keep the discussion going. There is minimal interference from the sociologist.

Usually, the interaction between members of the group is recorded on audiotape or video. However, one danger of these types of interview is that one or two strong personalities can dominate and influence other participants' opinions.

Semi-structured interviews

Many sociological interviews are a mix of the structured and unstructured interview. They usually contain lots of closed questions in order to generate facts but also contain a few open questions. These open questions allow the interviewer some flexibility to ask for clarification of vague answers. They can jog respondents' memories and ask them to give examples. All of these things can add depth and detail to the responses. They can also assess whether the interviewee is telling the truth.

However, the reliability of such interviews has been questioned because an interviewer might find that some interviewees may need more probing than others. This may mean that every interview is different; the data may, therefore, not be strictly comparable since, to some extent, the interviewees are responding to different questions.

Study

Working-class boys and educational success – Ingram (2009)

Two Catholic boys' schools were selected for the study: one secondary school and one grammar school. The research focused on two groups of pupils, those aged 11–12 and 15–16, because these pupils were respectively beginning and coming to the end of compulsory secondary education.

Most of the children in the study lived in a working-class Catholic community in Belfast. The area ranks within the top ten in Northern Ireland in terms of deprivation, measured by income, educational qualifications, skills and training. In 2006, 60 per cent of children were eligible for free school meals compared with 19 per cent of the population of Northern Ireland.

Two types of interview were conducted in order to generate qualitative data. First, group discussions were carried out in each school with eight of the younger and eight of the older pupils. The discussions lasted an hour and the issues raised became the basis of questions used for the second stage of the research. Second, individual semi-structured interviews with open-ended questions that allowed students to digress were carried out with working-class boys in both schools.

Observation

Interpretivist sociologists are interested in understanding how people live their everyday lives and argue that the research method of observation is the best possible ethnographic way of understanding why people behave the way that they do because it gives first-hand insight into how people interpret the social world around them. People can be observed in their natural environment. The sociologist is able to gain insight into normal everyday behaviour as a result of being part and parcel of his or her respondent's social world. If the observation is managed effectively, he or she should see that world in much the same way that the research population do.

Types of observation

There are essentially two different types of observation.

Non-participant or direct observation usually involves the researcher sitting and observing an activity such as a doctor–patient interaction, a school lesson and so on. The observer is a detached and unobtrusive onlooker who plays no active role in the activity being observed.

Usually, this type of observation is structured in that it normally uses a coded observation schedule that directs what is to be observed. The observation is therefore focused on particular types of behaviour or activity; activity that does not fit the schedule is ignored. This type of schedule is especially appealing to positivist sociologists who stress the need for scientific method because it produces 'facts' in the form of quantifiable data.

It is argued by supporters of this type of observation that because the researcher is detached and therefore objective, he or she is less likely to take sides and be biased in the way he or she interprets the group's behaviour. Moreover, because the researcher is not making any decisions or joining in activities, the group itself should not be influenced by the observer.

However, critics disagree and note that the observer is likely to be observing artificial behaviour caused by their actual presence. For example, pupil behaviour may be shaped by their curiosity about the researcher's motives while teachers may feel threatened or compromised by another adult's presence in their classroom. This type of observation also gives us little insight into the reasons why people behave the way that they do. It has also been suggested that objectivity can be difficult to achieve because observers have to make value judgements about whether behaviour or activities fit particular categories on their observation schedule. Other researchers may disagree with the interpretation of what counts as a significant event, which raises the issue of how reliable such recording is.

> **Quick question**
>
> You have probably taken part in a lesson that was observed by an Ofsted inspector or another teacher. In your opinion, in what ways was that lesson different to the norm?

Participant observation is the most common type of observation and involves the sociologist immersing himself or herself in the lifestyle of the group he or she wishes to study. This then is the main method used by ethnographers because it is research driven from the 'inside' rather than research imposed from the 'outside'. Research methods such as questionnaires and interviews involve the sociologist as the 'outsider looking in' and consequently, as we have already seen, run the risk of imposing the sociologist's own values and interpretations on those being studied. Participant observation, on the other hand, involves the sociologist being 'on the inside looking out' because he or she joins in with the activities of those being studied and shares their experiences of social reality.

Sociologists using this method participate in the same activities of the group being researched and observe their everyday lives. Participant observation can be either:

- **overt** – that is, the researcher joins in the activities of a group but some or all of the group know that the researcher is a sociologist and is actively observing them, or
- **covert** or complete – that is, the researcher inserts himself or herself into a group and conceals the fact that he or she is doing research – he or she pretends to be an authentic member of the group.

The aim of participant observation, whether it is overt or covert, is to understand what is happening from the point of view of those involved, to 'get inside their heads' and to understand the meaning that they give to their situation. The research, then, is ethnographic, which means that it is naturalistic, i.e. it is carried out in the environment in which the respondents normally find themselves.

Participant observation, particularly the overt type, is often dependent on a gate-keeper – that is, a person who can smooth the entry of a sociological observer into a social group. Fielding (2001) argues that gate-keepers are 'the unsung heroes of ethnography' because they can speak to a group beforehand and allay their suspicions about the researcher. In essence, they sponsor and validate the researcher and the research. However, Fielding also notes that it is important to also understand that some, especially institutional gate-keepers, may have an agenda of their own – that is, they may wish to control what is observed.

It is also important to understand that the choice of whether to use covert observation is often shaped by the social characteristics of the research team. The social class, gender, age and ethnicity of the researcher may make it impossible to infiltrate particular situations; for example, males are excluded from exclusively female situations or groups and vice versa.

Once inside a group, it is important that the researcher:

- focuses on 'looking and listening', and going with the flow of social life. A participant observer should not try to force the pace of the group activity or interfere with or disrupt 'normality'. A good deal of participant observation, therefore, involves informally 'hanging around'. It is therefore important to be patient but vigilant.
- maintains a delicate balance between being an insider, i.e. getting close to the subjects and establishing a rapport, and being an outsider, i.e. adopting the professional role of detached observer who can avoid getting too emotionally involved with the group. As Brewer notes, 'ethnographers earn people's trust by showing a willingness to learn their language and their ways, to eat like they eat, speak like they speak and do as they do' (2000:85) but that trust takes time, and consequently researchers may have to spend considerable periods of time in the field so that people get used to their presence.

Fielding recommends the role of 'acceptable incompetent', acting in a naïve fashion so that group members feel obliged to explain things to them. Marvasti (2004) suggests that showing interest in the respondents' culture and way of life can help to establish rapport because people are often flattered by the attention. He also suggests self-disclosure – telling people about yourself – is another way in which rapport can be maintained because it can help to establish trust.

Interpretivist sociologists argue that participant observation has a number of distinctive strengths:

- The researcher-observer sees things through the eyes and actions of the people in the group. The researcher is placed in exactly the same situation as the group under study and experiences what the group experiences. Life is therefore seen from the same perspective as the group. As a result of this closeness to the group, the sociologist experiences 'verstehen'; this means that the sociologist can empathise with the group, and understand why members of the group act the way that they do because the sociologist has experienced the same situation. This results in highly valid research data.
- Interpretivist sociologists point out that often what people say and what they actually do are very different. People lie, exaggerate, mislead and so on in questionnaires and interviews. Often people are not aware that they are acting in the way that they do. However, in observation studies, the sociologist can see what people really do and the truth is more likely to be recorded.
- Observation can be supplemented by asking informal questions, though if the researcher is carrying out covert research, this might arouse suspicion and mistrust. Observers sometimes develop special relationships with key people within groups. This acts as a type of respondent validation because the observer can question this person so that he or she can clarify the motives for particular types of behaviour and therefore not misinterpret the behaviour of individuals in the group.

Quick question

Why might observational research generate new ideas and hypotheses?

- Interpretivists like observation because what the researcher observes is first-hand and not the product of what he or she thinks is important, as is often the case with questionnaires and interviews. By watching and listening, a participant observer has the chance to discover the priorities and concerns as well as the meanings and definitions of the people being studied in their everyday natural contexts.

Participant observation takes place over a long period of time and therefore allows an understanding of how changes in attitudes and behaviour take place over months and years.

Observation may be the only practical method available to research hard-to-reach groups such as criminal gangs or religious sects who may be hostile to conventional society or engaged in illegal or deviant behaviour. However, observation of these groups is likely to be covert unless you are sponsored by a trusted member of the group or you can offer the group some sort of service or role.

Observation produces qualitative rather than quantitative data about how people interpret the world around them; the data gathered often 'speaks for itself' and gives real insight into people's feelings, motives, experiences, attitudes etc.

However, not all sociologists marvel at observation. Some, most notably positivists, are very critical of this method for the following reasons:

The biggest problem, especially with overt forms of participant observation, is observer or researcher effect. This means that the presence of the observer may result in the group acting less 'naturally' because they are aware that they are being observed and studied. In Whyte's study, Doc, the leader of the gang, said that he used to do things on instinct but now thought about how he was going to justify his actions to Whyte. Some sociologists recommend a 'settling-in' period, where no notes are taken, to overcome this problem. The sociologists should only begin the observation once they are satisfied that the group takes their presence for granted. However, the overt observer can never be sure that his or her presence is not undermining validity. Covert observation, on the other hand, is less likely to lead to this effect.

Quick question

In your opinion, why is covert observation less likely to lead to this effect?

Some observers can get too close or attached to the group they are observing and consequently their observations become biased. The observer becomes too sympathetic towards the group and 'goes native' – that is, the observer loses detachment and objectivity, and identifies too closely with the group. Paul Rock suggests that if

the group that a sociologist is observing no longer surprises or shocks the observer, the researcher has lost his or her open-mindedness and objectivity and the research should be brought to an end. Rock argues that a good observer should always be critical of the group they are studying (1999).

Observational studies involve too narrow a view of the group or institution studied because the researcher cannot study the wider social context in which the research population finds itself. Observational studies are by their very nature micro-studies and cannot appreciate the influence and impact of structural factors such as social class or patriarchy on the research setting and those being observed.

Activity

Covert observation and ethics

A major problem with observation is that covert observation often infringes ethical rules. For example, some sociologists object to covert observation because it involves lying to people as well as misleading and sometimes emotionally manipulating them. In particular, covert observation, because of its very nature, does not allow people to give their consent to having this type of research conducted on them. Another ethical problem is that the sociologist may choose or be forced to take part in criminal or immoral activities in order to either gain or retain the trust of the group or to protect his or her cover. The publication of the research may also create ethical problems for the group. For example, it might get them into trouble with the police or authorities. It may cause them harm in terms of ridicule or reprisal.

1 Identify four ethical problems that the critics of covert observation highlight.
2 If you were carrying out covert observation on a deviant group, would you feel you had a moral duty to report them to the police if you knew the group had broken or intended to break the law?
3 In your opinion, is it sometimes justified to ignore the ethical rules?
4 Can you think of any research situations in which this may be justified?

Covert observation can sometimes pose great danger to the sociologist. The African-Caribbean sociologist Ken Pryce was actually murdered while attempting to carry out a participant observation study of organised drug crime.

List reasons why covert participant observation might generate more valid data than overt forms of participant observation.

There can also be major practical difficulties with observation:

- These types of studies generally take months and, in some cases, years and, require terrific dedication and, in the case of covert observation, acting ability. They are also consequently very expensive projects.

- Recording the observations and conversations can be a real problem in both overt and covert forms of observation. The researcher needs to write up conversations while they are still fresh in his or her mind but constantly taking notes can be off-putting to those who are being observed. If the researcher is carrying out covert observation of a criminal or deviant group, writing things down or disappearing for periods to do so may arouse suspicion and put the researcher in danger. However, most researchers will keep a research diary documenting the everyday activities of the group and to reflect on problems that they might have experienced.

Positivist sociologists generally disapprove of observation studies for a number of reasons:

- They question the reliability of both overt and covert participant observation because there is no way of knowing whether the findings of the researcher are true or not since it is impossible to repeat the research and verify the data. Often the success of the research is due to the personality of the sociologist and the unique relationships he or she has established with members of the group. Another sociologist who attempted to replicate this may produce quite different results.

- Positivists criticise observation studies for their lack of representativeness either because they are very exotic and therefore not typical of 'average' people (for example, observation studies have tended to focus on people like jazz musicians, members of the National Front, people who believe that the world is about to be destroyed and so on) or because the number of people actually observed at any given time is quite small. The observer cannot be everywhere observing large numbers of people. In view of these small numbers, it is not possible to generalise from the findings of participant observation to members of similar groups.

- Positivists claim that participant observation is often the epitome of 'bad' science, and that its design and data analysis breaches fundamental rules of scientific procedure. Positivists accuse observation studies of being unsystematic, unstructured and unreliable because they focus on naturally occurring behaviour. Positivists despair of the fact that observers make no attempt to control possible influential variables.

- Many ethnographic studies prefer to let their subjects speak for themselves, and observational evidence is often expressed in a qualitative form, such as long quotations, extracts from conversations, field notes and so on which are not quantifiable and can be difficult to compare with each other or with other evidence. Therefore, positivists claim this type of data is too subjective.

Study

Gang leader for a day – Venkatesh (2008)

Between 1989 and 1996 Sudhir Venkatesh spent time with the Black Kings, an organised gang that controlled most of the drugs trade in the public housing projects in Chicago. He managed to get access to the Black Kings via an influential gate-keeper, JT, a local leader of the gang. JT's sponsorship gave Venkatesh access to the gang and various influential individuals who lived in the projects who were not gang members. Venkatesh shadowed JT and therefore was able to observe first-hand the subculture of the gang and how it was responsible for overseeing the day-to-day life of the people in the projects by offering them protection and by organising social activities for the residents. However, Venkatesh's role did create some problems for him. For example, it was dangerous for him to enter some parts of the projects because rival drug gangs associated him with JT and the Black Kings. He has also been criticised for behaving unethically in that criminal behaviour occurred in his presence.

These criticisms have stung some ethnographers into developing scientific procedural rules, especially in regard to reliability. For example, in addition to observation schedules, some studies have used two or more observers in order to verify what is being observed. Unfortunately, this inter-observer verification is really only suitable for very structured forms of observation such as non-participant observation. However, Barker argues that the overt observer should always follow up his or her observations with respondent validation by conducting informal interviews with members of the group (1984). These are useful as a tool of validation in that the observer can ask members of the group how they saw certain events to ensure that the researcher's field notes contain an authentic picture of what went on.

Other sociologists have kept research diaries that document the trials and tribulations of every stage of the field research. This is known as reflexivity and is a form of self-evaluation that involves researchers reflecting critically on how they organised the research process. It involves the researcher thinking about how a range of influences might have impacted on the validity of the findings. This approach has been very influenced by postmodernism, which argues that ethnography should not be concerned with the pursuit of some universal truth because, at best, accounts of social reality can only be relative, partial, partisan and selective truths. Specifically, postmodernists argue that ethnographic accounts are autobiographical – that is, they only tell us about the researcher's version of the observation, and they leave out other participants' experience of it.

Mixed methods

Many sociologists use a combination of multiple research methods which collect both quantitative and qualitative data. There are essentially two ways in which this is done.

Triangulation

This is the combining of research methods in order to check or verify the validity of the research findings. For example, a sociologist using observation to investigate employer–employee relationships in the workplace might check the validity (i.e. truth) of what he or she observed by asking the employees that he or she worked alongside to fill in questionnaires to make sure that the sociologist fully understood what he or she was observing. Such sociologists might also carry out unstructured interviews with managers and employers to compare what the management thought was happening with the sociologist's interpretation of what was going on.

Methodological pluralism

This is the combining of different research methods in order to build up a fuller picture of what is being studied. For example, the following stages might make up a pluralistic approach to doing research on the effects of unemployment:

- Stage 1: Official Department of Employment statistics can be examined to work out how many people in a particular region are unemployed.
- Stage 2: Local newspapers (media reports) can be examined to assess the impact of unemployment on particular regions.
- Stage 3: The sociologist can carry out a questionnaire survey of both the employed and unemployed to assess local experiences of unemployment.
- Stage 4: Unstructured interviews can be carried out with a sub-sample of long-term unemployed people to gather qualitative data about the everyday experience of unemployment.
- Stage 5: The sociologist can carry out direct observation by observing interaction between staff in job centres and unemployed people.

Methodological pluralism, like triangulation, involves the use of primary and secondary methods, and the collection of both quantitative and qualitative data.

The case study

A variation on this pluralistic approach is the case study; this is a detailed and in-depth examination of one particular case or instance of something using methodological pluralism. For example, the case study might focus on one single person's life (life history), or an organisation, or a specific group of people, or a religion, or a specific incident or situation such as a strike. Case studies are useful because by looking at a single thing from several angles using several methods, a sociologist can build up a rich picture of the dynamics that underpin the actions of a particular person, situation or institution.

Quick question

Why might case studies be criticised as limited and unrepresentive?

Conclusion

Today, very few sociologists focus entirely on the use of either quantitative positivist methods or qualitative interpretivist methods. In order to guarantee both reliability and validity, most sociological research will mix and match methods. As C. Wright Mills once argued 'what works best is best' (1959).

Check your understanding

Briefly define the following terms and give an example of each:

- triangulation
- informal interview
- covert observation
- interview schedule
- methodological pluralism
- focus group interview
- demand characteristics
- structured interview
- interview bias
- participant observation
- impression management
- non response
- official statistics
- content analysis.

Section summary

Fill in the blanks, using the words given below.

_____ involve the _____ collection of the same type of data from a fairly large number of people. They usually obtain this information through _____ or, less often, through _____. The information is then analysed using statistical techniques.

_____ are interviews in which the interviewer informally asks _____ questions about a topic and allows the respondent to respond freely and in depth. The interviewer does not have an _____ or questionnaire. They will have some general questions but the interviewer will be _____ and willing to follow the lead of the person who is being interviewed. A good _____ interview will feel like a _____ and the interviewer will have very good inter-personal skills and will be able to encourage people to talk at length.

_____ is a research method that produces _____. It involves a researcher joining a group of people and observing them on a daily basis, usually over a long period of time. The sociologist takes part in the same activities as the group and tries to see and experience the world as they do. This is called empathetic understanding or _____.

conversation, flexible, informal, interview schedules, open-ended, participant observation, qualitative data, questionnaires, social surveys, structured interviews, systematic, unstructured interviews, verstehen

Practice questions

Read the source material and answer all of the questions in Section A.

Source A

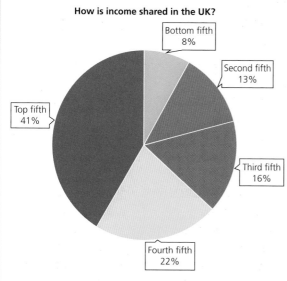

How is income shared in the UK?

- Bottom fifth 8%
- Second fifth 13%
- Top fifth 41%
- Third fifth 16%
- Fourth fifth 22%

Source B

Does unemployment contribute to poor self-esteem?

The purpose of Pia Pettersson's (2012) study was to examine whether self-esteem can be affected by unemployment. The research aimed to show how work gives people the opportunity to participate in society and allows people to be a part of the social structure, which makes them feel content in terms of personal, familial and social aspects of life. Moreover, it is important to a person's health that he or she feels that he or she is involved and has influence in society. The research aimed to show that unemployment can have negative effects in terms of cutting off social contact, undermining one's sense of status and identity, and causing mental health problems.

A manager of a Jobcentre in Leicester was contacted for help in getting volunteers to take part in the study. The city was chosen because of the possibility of getting a large sample of unemployed respondents. The manager was informed about the purpose of the study, and he was also shown the questions that were approved.

A purposive sample was used in the study, which means that the sample was accessed via the manager of the Jobcentre who distributed 70 questionnaires. 64 of these were returned. An information letter was sent out informing the sample about the purpose of the research and respondents were asked to consent to taking part in the study.

(Source: Pettersson 2012)

1 Describe two findings from the data in Source A. [4]

2 With reference to Source B, explain why sampling is used by sociologists. [9]

3 With reference to Source A, explain some of the strengths and weaknesses of using official statistics. [12]

4 Using Source B and your wider sociological knowledge, explain and evaluate the use of questionnaires for researching the effects of unemployment on self-esteem. [20]

Practice questions

Source A

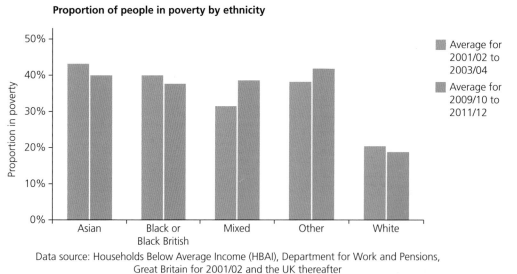

Proportion of people in poverty by ethnicity

Data source: Households Below Average Income (HBAI), Department for Work and Pensions, Great Britain for 2001/02 and the UK thereafter

(Source: Joseph Rowntree Foundation 2014)

Practice questions (continued)

Source B

Class, gender, heterosexuality and schooling

The aim of this research was to explain why a significant number of working-class girls are leaving school at the age of 16 with few or no qualifications. The study intended to explore two possibilities. The first was that underachieving girls were involved in subcultural forms of resistance to schooling expressed by behaving in a hyper-heterosexual manner. It was suggested that this behaviour, which is focused on sexuality, dress and appearance, was leading to teacher–pupil conflict. The study also aimed to explore whether the choices of working-class girls are shaped by traditional expectations that encourage girls to believe that settling down and having children are more important than higher education.

The researchers used a multi-method and mainly qualitative approach. First, data was collected from 89 pupils aged 14 to 16 using semi-structured interviews. Six London comprehensive schools were selected because they served working-class areas suffering from severe economic and social deprivation. The sample of 89 pupils was made up of pupils who had been identified by their schools as being at risk of dropping out of school at 16. The sample included boys and girls from a variety of ethnic backgrounds, though over 50 per cent of the sample was white.

This was also a longitudinal study in that 53 of the pupils were individually tracked for two years across Years 10 and 11 with each pupil interviewed three or four times. Discussion groups were also set up with an additional 36 pupils. Eight female pupils were asked to complete photographic diaries focusing on their everyday interests and activities. Finally, semi-structured interviews were conducted with 19 members of staff.

(Source: Archer *et al.* 2007)

1 Summarise the data found in Source A. [4]

2 With reference to Source B, explain two reasons why some sociologists use a multi-method approach. [6]

3 With reference to Source A, explain one strength and one weakness of using official statistics to study the relationship between poverty and ethnicity. [10]

4 Using Source B and your wider sociological knowledge, assess the usefulness of qualitative data for investigating why working-class girls leave school at the age of 16 with few or no qualifications. [25]

Chapter 7a

Understanding social inequalities: Social class

7a.1 What is social class?

Social class is the term used by sociologists to describe the form of social stratification found in modern industrial societies. Sociologists do not agree on what we mean by social class or on how people should be classified. However, it is generally agreed that members of a social class share a similar economic position – for example, similar levels of income and wealth – as well as similar occupations and levels of education. These economic inequalities can be linked to inequalities of status and power. Some sociologists also link social class to differences in attitudes and culture. For example, working-class and middle-class people have different attitudes to the

Getting you thinking ...

1 Study the four images above. Decide in each case what social class you think the people in the picture might belong to.
2 What factors did you use in putting people into social classes?
3 How far do you think class differences are important in British society today?

importance of education and different tastes in leisure activities and consumer goods.

The ruling class and the subject class

In the nineteenth century, Karl Marx (see page 41) argued that capitalist societies such as Britain were essentially divided into two social classes: the ruling class, or the bourgeoisie, who owned the means of production such as factories and other businesses, and the subject class, or the proletariat, who were employed by the ruling class to produce goods and services.

Manual and non-manual workers

While the Marxist approach has influenced some sociologists, most modern sociologists would argue that the class system is more complex than this. Some sociologists have argued that a middle class exists between the wealthy upper class at the top of society and the working class at the bottom. The middle class were traditionally seen as non-manual workers who depended on educational qualifications and mental skills in order to earn higher incomes than the working class or manual workers who depend on physical strength and skills.

The Hope–Goldthorpe classification

Some sociologists argue that there are divisions even within these broader social classes. For example, John Goldthorpe (1980) developed the Hope–Goldthorpe scale in order to undertake research into social mobility. Goldthorpe distinguished three main classes, which could be further sub-divided into seven occupational classes:

Service class	
1	Higher professionals, high-grade administrators, managers of large companies and large proprietors
2	Lower professionals, higher-grade technicians, supervisors of non-manual workers, administrators, small business managers
Intermediate class	
3	Routine non-manual workers (clerical and sales)
4	Small proprietors and self-employed artisans (craftspersons)
5	Lower-grade technicians and supervisors of manual workers
Working class	
6	Skilled manual workers
7	Semi-skilled and unskilled manual workers

The underclass

Some writers such as Charles Murray (1989) have argued that a new social class, the underclass, has emerged below the working class (see also page 27). This consists of the poorest members of society, such as the unemployed, lone-parent families and chronically sick and disabled people who cannot work. Unlike the working class, who have paid jobs, these groups are largely dependent on state benefits.

The National Statistics Socio-Economic Classification

The National Statistics Socio-Economic Classification (NS-SEC) scale is used to classify people by social class in official statistics such as the Census and government surveys.

Class	Occupational classification	% of working population of England and Wales, 2011	Examples
1	Higher managerial and professional	10.3	Company directors, senior civil servants, doctors, barristers, clergy, architects
2	Lower managerial and professional	20.8	Nurses, journalists, teachers, police officers, musicians
3	Intermediate	12.7	Secretaries, clerks, computer operators, driving instructors
4	Small employers and own account workers	9.4	Taxi drivers, window cleaners, publicans, decorators
5	Lower supervisory, craft and related	6.9	Train drivers, plumbers, printers, TV engineers
6	Semi-routine	14.1	Traffic wardens, shop assistants, hairdressers, call centre workers
7	Routine	11.1	Cleaners, couriers, road sweepers, labourers
8	Long-term unemployed and never worked	5.6	

(Source: ONS 2011)

223

Occupation and social class

Many sociological approaches to class base their classifications on occupations. Occupation is a useful guide to social class because many sociologists would see the class structure of modern industrial societies as based on the occupational structure, the ranking of occupations in terms of income, status and power. A person's occupation not only tells us roughly what their income is, it also gives a good indication of what level of educational qualifications they have, what kind of housing they live in and possibly what kind of lifestyle they have outside work. These are all factors that many sociologists would link to social class.

Occupational classes, however, have their limitations. Some people have no occupation but may be very wealthy or else their occupation is a poor guide to their social position. For example, Prince Harry is a member of the Royal Family but his occupation of army officer would not reveal his true social position. Occupational classes can also contain very diverse occupations; for example,

NS-SEC Class 2 covers teachers, ranging from newly qualified teachers to head teachers who might earn as much as five times as much. Class 1 includes both millionaire businesspeople who would be classified as company directors and clergy who often receive very modest salaries.

Subjective social class

Occupational classifications are objective definitions of class – in other words, based on commonly agreed criteria for classifying people. These do not always coincide with subjective definitions of class. These are based on the social class to which people see themselves as belonging. Gordon Marshall *et al.* (1988) found that many people in their research saw themselves as 'working class' despite the fact that they were in non-manual or white-collar jobs that many sociologists would describe as middle class. Another study by Mike Savage *et al.* (2001), however, found that a significant proportion of their respondents were reluctant to identify themselves with a social class at all and concluded that in general the notion of class identity was 'relatively muted'.

Activity: New forms of social class

Item A: Social classes in the Great British Class Survey

PRECARIAT: THE POOREST AND MOST DEPRIVED CLASS IN BRITAIN. WITH LOW LEVELS OF ECONOMIC, CULTURAL AND SOCIAL CAPITAL, EVERYDAY LIVES OF THIS CLASS ARE PRECARIOUS.

EMERGENT SERVICE WORKERS: YOUNG AND OFTEN FOUND IN URBAN AREAS. THIS NEW CLASS HAS LOW ECONOMIC CAPITAL BUT HAS HIGH LEVELS OF 'EMERGING' CULTURAL CAPITAL AND HIGH SOCIAL CAPITAL.

NEW AFFLUENT WORKERS: GENERALLY YOUNG AND ACTIVE. MEMBERS HAVE MEDIUM LEVELS OF ECONOMIC CAPITALS AND HIGHER LEVELS OF CULTURAL AND SOCIAL CAPITAL.

ELITE: THIS IS THE MOST PRIVILEGED CLASS IN GREAT BRITAIN, WHO HAVE HIGH LEVELS OF ALL THREE CAPITALS. THEIR HIGH AMOUNT OF ECONOMIC CAPITAL SETS THEM APART FROM EVERYBODY ELSE.

TRADITIONAL WORKING CLASS: CONTAINS MORE OLDER MEMBERS THAN OTHER CLASSES BUT ALSO SCORES LOW ON ALL FORMS OF THE THREE CAPITALS. THEY ARE NOT THE POOREST GROUP.

TECHNICAL MIDDLE CLASS: A LESS CULTURALLY ENGAGED NEW CLASS WITH HIGH ECONOMIC CAPITAL. SMALL IN NUMBERS, THEY HAVE RELATIVELY FEW SOCIAL CONTACTS.

ESTABLISHED MIDDLE CLASS: NOT QUITE ELITE BUT MEMBERS OF THIS CLASS HAVE HIGH LEVELS OF ALL THREE CAPITALS. THEY ARE A GREGARIOUS AND CULTURALLY ENGAGED CLASS.

Activity: New forms of social class (continued)

Item B: The Great British Class Survey

The factors traditionally used to define the idea of 'class' have been education, occupation and wealth but recent research by the BBC argues that this is overly simplified. The *Great British Class Survey* surveyed 161,000 people and concluded that class is better measured by three other aspects: economic, social and cultural.

The BBC's study used the ideas originally proposed by a French sociologist, one Pierre Bourdieu, to apportion class by three forms of 'capital'. Bourdieu identified 'economic capital' as being income, savings and house value, 'social capital' as the number of high status people someone knows and 'cultural capital' as the range and type of cultural interests and activities a person has. The survey scored respondents according to the degree they possessed each form of capital and then came up with seven social classes now existing in the UK.

- The **Elite** is the greatest privileged group in the UK, which is distinguished from the other six classes by its wealth. It scores the highest level in each of the three capitals.
- The second wealthiest, still with a high score on all three capitals, is the '**Established middle class**'. This group is the largest and most gregarious and scores second highest in terms of cultural capital.
- The next class group is a new one, the '**Technical middle class**'. Its members are a small group strongly identifiable as prospering but with low levels of social and cultural capital. Identifying features of this group are that they are socially isolated and culturally apathetic.
- Then there are what are referred to as '**New affluent workers**', which describes a young class group with medium levels of economic capital and which is socially and culturally active.

- The **Traditional working class** still exists and is identified as scoring low on all forms of capital though not being totally deprived. Because this group of people has the oldest average age of 66, members of this class have reasonably high house values.
- A new, youngish urban class is the '**Emergent service workers**'. Members of this class are relatively poorly off but they do have a high level of social and cultural capital.
- Finally, there is what is called the '**Precariat**, or precarious proletariat'. These people make up the poorest class, suffering the most from deprivation and with low scores for social and cultural capital.

Source: adapted from BBC News 2013 and Savage et al. (2013)

You can take the test to work out what social class you belong to according to this study by going to www.bbc.co.uk/news/magazine-22000973.

1 In what ways did the Great British Class Survey define social class differently from traditional models of social class such as the three-class model?
2 What are the advantages and disadvantages of this approach to class?
3 How important do you think each of the following are in defining what social class a person belongs to?
   a) occupation
   b) income
   c) ownership of wealth
   d) level of education
   e) leisure and cultural interests
   f) social contacts
   g) the social class to which they feel that they belong
   h) social class background of parents.
4 If you were carrying out a piece of research and wanted to ask one question that would be used to place respondents into a social class, what question would you ask? Give reasons for your answer.

7a.2 Patterns and trends in social class inequality and difference

Social class and life chances

The sociologist Max Weber (1948) first defined the term 'life chances' to describe how some members of society had much better opportunities than others to achieve the things in life that most people would see as desirable. These might include:

- the chance to live a long and healthy life
- the chance to achieve good educational qualifications and to go on to higher education
- the chance to have a fulfilling and well-paid job and avoid being made unemployed
- the chance to own your own home in a desirable area, with a low risk of crime and with access to open spaces and leisure facilities
- the chance to enjoy paid holidays and a range of leisure activities and to appreciate cultural amenities such as art, music and theatre.

Weber saw life chances as closely linked to a person's social class background. The higher a person's social class, the greater their opportunities to achieve desirable things in life, such as those above. Modern sociologists would point out that other kinds of social inequalities also affect life chances; for example, women have traditionally had worse life chances in terms of achieving high-paid and high-status jobs than men.

Activity: Unequal life chances in twenty-first-century Britain

Item A: Findings of the National Equality Panel

People's origins shape their chances throughout their lives, the biggest study of equality and inequality in Britain has demonstrated. In spite of the aspirations of the main political parties since the Second World War, Britain remains anything but a society of equal opportunity, according to the National Equality Panel, an independent body of academic researchers set up by the government.

Social and economic advantages 'reinforce themselves over the life cycle' with 'deep-seated and systematic differences' in outcomes between social groups. Some inequalities have narrowed or stabilised over the past decade, the study found – on measures such as earnings, the gender pay gap and the educational qualifications of ethnic groups. But the large growth in inequality between the late 1970s and early 1990s has not been reversed. Britain has bigger differences of income than most other industrialised countries.

'Inequality in turn then acts as a barrier to social mobility', says the report, adding that 'it matters more in Britain who your parents are than in many other countries'.

'It is not that your origins determine your chances in life', John Hills, the panel's chair and Professor of Social Policy at the London School of Economics, said. 'The children of poor parents can do well and the children of rich parents can do badly'. The differences in outcome within any social group – whether defined by class, gender, disability, sexual orientation or ethnicity – are larger than the differences between each of these groups. 'But your origins and your parents' income provide a series of nudges that tend to push people in a particular direction, from your chances of being read to as a child, whether your parents can buy a house in the catchment area of a good school, educate you privately, pay for a second degree, provide help with a deposit to buy a house, or leave an inheritance'.

(Source: adapted from Timmins 2010)

Item B: Chances of teenage motherhood

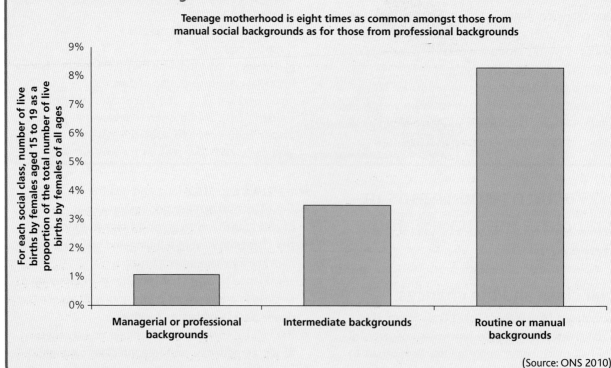

Teenage motherhood is eight times as common amongst those from manual social backgrounds as for those from professional backgrounds

For each social class, number of live births by females aged 15 to 19 as a proportion of the total number of live births by females of all ages

Managerial or professional backgrounds

Intermediate backgrounds

Routine or manual backgrounds

(Source: ONS 2010)

Activity: Unequal life chances in twenty-first-century Britain (continued)

Item C: Social class and early years outcomes

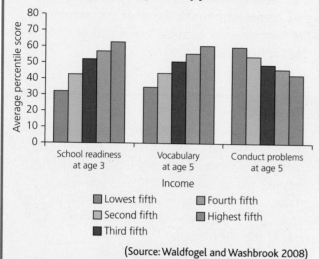

Children from higher income backgrounds do significantly better on a range of early years outcomes

Average percentile score (y-axis: 0 to 80)

Categories (x-axis, Income): School readiness at age 3, Vocabulary at age 5, Conduct problems at age 5

Key:
- Lowest fifth
- Second fifth
- Third fifth
- Fourth fifth
- Highest fifth

(Source: Waldfogel and Washbrook 2008)

Item D: Speech day at Harrow, one of the UK's top private schools

Item E: Young people in one of Glasgow's poorest housing estates

1 According to Item A, which types of inequalities in life chances appear to have narrowed and which have remained as wide as ever?

2 According to Item A, how does the influence of social class on life chances in Britain compare with other European countries?

3 Examine Items B and C. What evidence do they show that social class is still linked to life chances in Britain?

4 Study Items D and E. In what ways might the life chances of the young people in Item D be different from those in Item E? Make a list of different aspects of life chances that might differ between the two groups.

Social class inequalities in income

Income inequalities are the basis of many social class inequalities in a society like the UK. A person's income affects their access to a variety of things that might be regarded as desirable in society, including the kind of food they eat, the value, quality and location of their housing, access to transport such as car ownership, their ability to afford consumer goods such as electrical goods or new furnishings, and leisure activities such as eating out or taking holidays abroad.

Income refers to the flow of money to a person or household over a time period – for example, monthly or annually. The main sources of income for people in the UK include:

- earnings from employment or self-employment
- state benefits
- pensions
- interest and dividends from savings and investments.

Income statistics

Calculating how incomes are distributed is not easy. Official statistics on income are derived from a number of sources, which include the following:

- The Family Resources Survey (FRS) is a government-sponsored survey that provides information about the living conditions and resources of households in the United Kingdom.
- The Annual Survey of Hours and Earnings (ASHE) provides information about the levels, distribution and make-up of earnings and hours worked for employees in all industries and occupations.

The ASHE is based on a 1 per cent sample of employee jobs taken from HM Revenue and Customs' Pay as You Earn (PAYE, or income tax) records.

- The British Household Panel Survey is a form of longitudinal survey. It began in 1991 and follows the same representative sample of individuals – the panel – over a period of years. It is household-based, interviewing every adult member of sampled households.

Surveys rely on their respondents giving accurate data and in the case of incomes there may be reasons why people exaggerate their income. More frequently, people are likely to underestimate their income in official surveys, especially where they do not wish to declare all of their income for tax purposes – for example, where people work for 'cash in hand'.

Activity: Income inequalities between occupations in the UK

Item A: Incomes of selected occupations in the UK, 2012

Chief executives and senior officials	£120,830
Aircraft pilots and flight engineers	£77,906
Financial institution managers and directors	£69,890
Health & social service managers and directors	£48,754
Barristers and judges	£40,242
Pharmacists	£37,379
Teaching and educational professionals	£32,105
Web design and development professionals	£28,291
Office supervisors	£25,054
Roofers, roof tilers and slaters	£22,420
Assemblers and routine operatives	£19,850
Farmworkers	£17,038
Nursing auxiliaries and assistants	£15,474
Childminders and related occupations	£12,593
Fitness instructors	£11,151
Sales and retail assistants	£9,742
Waiters and waitresses	£7,010
School midday crossing patrols	£3,021
Average for all employees	**£26,664**

(Source: ONS 2012a)

The data in the table is published in the ASHE and covers the average pay for workers in more than 400 trades and professions. The data is drawn from HMRC and PAYE tax records. The ASHE does not include groups such as self-employed businesspeople and top earners in sport and entertainment who make up the ranks of the really wealthy.

Item B: Incomes earned by high earners, 2013

- The Queen £36,100,000
- Adele (singer) £27,540,000
- Angela Ahrendts (Burberry CEO 2006–2014) £16,900,000
- Wayne Rooney (footballer) £15,600,000
- Mike Rees (Standard Chartered Bank Boss) £8,986,000
- David Cameron (Prime Minister) £142,500

(Source: *Daily Mirror* 2014)

In 2013, Adele earned about 1,000 times as much as the average UK worker.

1 Briefly summarise what the data in Items A and B reveals about the extent of income inequalities in the UK.
2 What problems might there be in using official statistics such as those above to study income inequality?
3 To what extent are such inequalities in earnings fair and justified?

Trends in income distribution

Britain is one of the most unequal societies in Europe in terms of incomes and has become more unequal in the last 30 years (see graph above). From the 1950s to the 1970s, there was a slight narrowing of income inequalities but during the 1980s, inequalities of income increased sharply during the period that Margaret Thatcher was Prime Minister. The

government during this period cut rates of income tax for the very rich and also cut the link between earnings and many state benefits. This meant that though benefits increased with inflation, they gradually lagged behind the rise in earnings, which has generally increased faster than prices. While the rise in income inequality slowed down in the 1990s, it has increased again in recent years.

Activity

Trends in income inequality
Inequality of household incomes before housing costs, 1961 to 2011/12

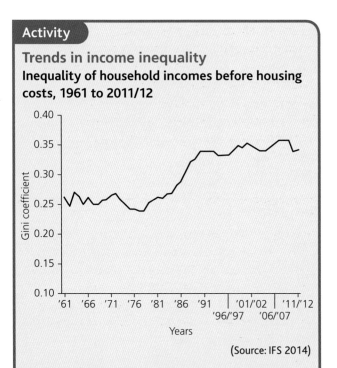

(Source: IFS 2014)

The **Gini coefficient** is often used to represent the income distribution of a nation's residents. This is the most commonly used measure of inequality. The coefficient varies between 0, which reflects complete equality, and 1, which indicates complete inequality (one person has all the income, all others have none).

1 Examine the graph above. What does it suggest about how the extent of income inequality has changed in the UK since the 1970s?
2 When did income inequality increase fastest? Suggest some reasons for this.

The effects of taxes and benefits on income distribution

The government takes more in taxes from the rich than the poor and gives more to the poor in benefits than the rich. However, the tax and benefits system is not as redistributive as many people imagine. In 2013 the poorest fifth of the population paid far less tax in cash terms than the richest fifth, but as a proportion of their income the poorest fifth paid more at 37.4 per cent of their incomes compared to 35.1 per cent of the incomes of the richest fifth. One reason for this is that though direct taxes (such as income tax) fall most heavily on the rich, indirect taxes (such as VAT and duty on tobacco, alcohol and fuel) fall most heavily on the poor. A poor person buying a litre of petrol pays the same duty as a rich person but it represents a much larger share of their income.

Incomes of high earners

In recent years there has been considerable debate about the salaries of bankers and top executives of large companies. Many such high earners receive not only very large basic salaries but also annual bonuses that are often several times their annual salary. Critics would point out that even executives of companies that are performing poorly receive bonuses, which are supposedly a reward for high performance.

In 2012 the High Pay Centre (http://highpaycentre. org/) reported that the total pay of chief executives of the 100 largest companies on the London Stock Exchange had risen by 49 per cent during the previous year alone, compared with average increases of less than 3 per cent for their employees. The rise left the chief executives with average pay of £4.2m. That was 145 times the average pay of their employees and 162 times the British average wage.

Debates about income inequality

Whether income inequalities matter is open to debate. Some sociologists and economists would point to the absolute increase in incomes of almost everyone in UK society over the last 50 years. While the rich have got richer, so poor people are also better off. An alternative view would point to the relative inequality between rich and poor. The incomes of the poor have only risen very slowly since the 1970s, while those on middle incomes have enjoyed much larger increases in real terms (incomes measured in terms of what a person can buy). The richest members of society have seen the biggest increase of incomes overall and critics of the way that income is distributed today would argue that we live in an increasingly unjust society as a result.

Functionalist and New Right thinkers (see pages 246–249) have argued that unequal rewards are actually beneficial for society as they ensure that those with talent are encouraged to work hard and use their abilities. This argument is often used as a justification for the high salaries and bonuses offered to top businesspeople. It is argued that unless companies in the UK offer large salaries, they will not be able to compete for highly skilled staff with companies in other developed countries in a global market.

Against this, sociologists influenced by Marxist and Weberian perspectives (see pages 250–254) would argue that senior managers and company directors are often in a position to determine their own salaries. It is the power that such individuals have within their organisations that allows them to create a culture where huge rewards have become the norm. Ordinary workers, on the other hand, have to bargain for their rewards either individually or through trades unions and may have little option but to accept whatever wages and other rewards employers are willing to offer.

229

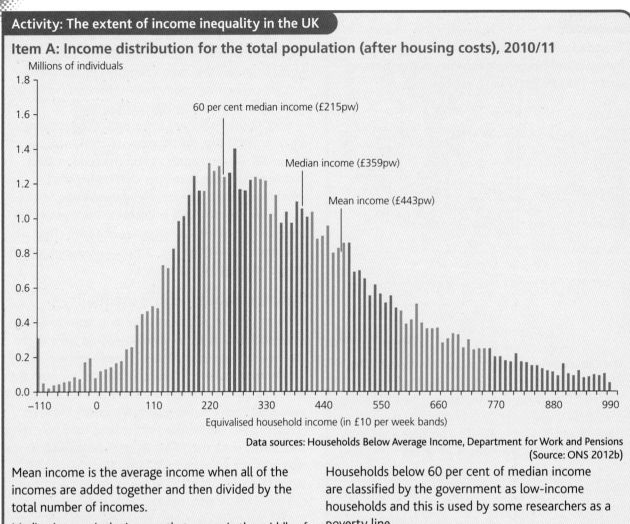

Activity: The extent of income inequality in the UK

Item A: Income distribution for the total population (after housing costs), 2010/11

Millions of individuals

Chart labels:
- 60 per cent median income (£215pw)
- Median income (£359pw)
- Mean income (£443pw)

X-axis: Equivalised household income (in £10 per week bands), ranging from −110 to 990

Data sources: Households Below Average Income, Department for Work and Pensions
(Source: ONS 2012b)

Mean income is the average income when all of the incomes are added together and then divided by the total number of incomes.

Median income is the income that comes in the middle of the income range when all incomes are arranged in order.

Households below 60 per cent of median income are classified by the government as low-income households and this is used by some researchers as a poverty line.

Item B: Taxes paid by the rich and poor

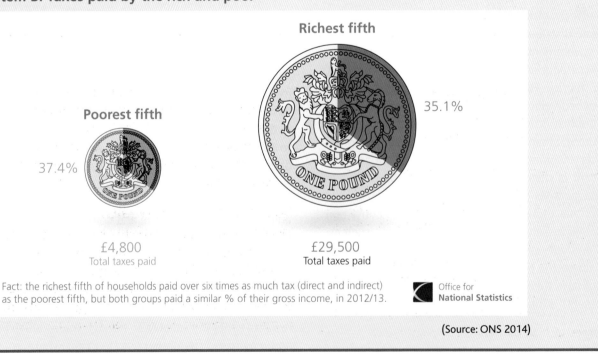

Richest fifth

35.1%

Poorest fifth

37.4%

£4,800
Total taxes paid

£29,500
Total taxes paid

Fact: the richest fifth of households paid over six times as much tax (direct and indirect) as the poorest fifth, but both groups paid a similar % of their gross income, in 2012/13.

Office for
National Statistics

(Source: ONS 2014)

Activity: The extent of income inequality in the UK (continued)

Item C: Reactions to income inequality

Occupy protestors outside St Paul's. The slogan suggests that most of the wealth in the UK is owned by just 1 per cent of the population.

In October 2011 a protest group called Occupy London set up a camp outside St Paul's Cathedral in the City of London. The protestors wanted to highlight a range of issues including social injustice, corporate greed, lack of affordable housing in London and the influence of lobbyists for big business on the government. In February 2012, the protestors were eventually removed by bailiffs and police.

(Source: *Guardian* 2012)

Burberry CEO Christopher Bailey, pictured with models Carla Delevigne and Jourdan Dunn. Bailey's £20m pay deal includes £460,000 for clothes and other items.

In July 2014, 52 per cent of shareholders voted not to support the remuneration report at fashion house Burberry, in a rare stand against large salaries. It is rare that protesting shareholders are in a majority, having happened just six times since 2000. (Remuneration is the amount of pay or reward an employee receives from their company.)

(Sources: BBC News zoika; BBC Democracy Live 2013)

1   Examine Item A. What conclusions can you draw about the extent of income inequality in the UK from this data?
2   Examine Item B. How do the richest 20 per cent of earners compare with the poorest 20 per cent in terms of:
    a) the amount of money they pay in tax?
    b) the proportion of their incomes which is taken in tax?
3   What arguments are there for and against the view that the rich should pay a bigger share of their incomes in tax than the poor?
4   What evidence is there from Item C that different groups in British society are concerned about the extent of income inequality?
5   Why might it be difficult for such groups to bring about any change in the distribution of incomes?

Social class inequalities in wealth

Income is often described as a 'flow' concept because income flows in and out of the pockets of people or households. Wealth, on the other hand, is a 'stock' concept; it measures the economic resources and possessions of a person or household at a fixed point in time. The Office for National Statistics (ONS) defines the following as forms of wealth for compiling official statistics:

- property wealth, such as houses and land – housing accounts for about 81 per cent of total net worth in the UK (Cowell *et al.* 2012)
- physical wealth – this would include any valuable assets such as cars, jewellery, paintings or antiques

- financial wealth – this is wealth in the form of money such as bank accounts, savings and investments, for example in shares
- private pension wealth – this is the cash value of what an individual has accumulated in their pension fund.

Sources of data on wealth

The Office for National Statistics bases its estimates of the distribution of wealth on the Wealth and Asset Survey. This has the merit of being a large-scale national survey backed by the government. In 2012, the annual *Sunday Times* Rich List suggested that the richest 200 families had between them total wealth averaging £225 billion between 2008 and 2010, an average of more than £1 billion each (*Sunday Times* 2012). John Hills (2013) suggests that the *Sunday Times* list is probably better at capturing business assets but the ONS data probably gives better coverage of assets such as pensions.

Problems with measuring wealth

It is not easy to measure wealth for a number of reasons:

- Defining what should be counted as wealth is not straightforward; for example, should state pensions be included as well as private pensions?
- Calculating the value of assets is difficult; for example, the value of a person's home may change rapidly if house prices are rising or falling quickly.
- Obtaining data about wealth is not easy. Wealthy people are often careful to conceal their wealth in order to avoid taxation. Very wealthy people often have assets in different countries so it is difficult to track what they actually own.
- Distinguishing wealth from income can be difficult. One example of this is 'capital gains'. A person may receive a gift of money or property from a relative or friend. This will be taxed as income and subject to capital gains tax but could also be seen as a form of wealth if the person chooses to hold on to the money or other asset that they have acquired.
- Much of the wealth in the form of shares in businesses in the UK is now owned by institutions such as pension funds, banks and insurance companies rather than private individuals. This means that while individuals may indirectly own a share in a company – for example, because their pension fund has invested in it – they may have very little control over how that money is invested.

Evaluation of the distribution of wealth

Wealth is much more unequally distributed than income in the UK. It would be very difficult to survive in the UK today with no income but a large proportion of the population has little or no wealth. The poorest 50 per cent of the population have only 10 per cent of the wealth of the UK between them and the poorest 10 per cent have virtually no wealth at all, with many people being in a state of negative wealth, such as those with debts that are greater than their assets.

Study

The Birmingham Commission Report – Rowlingson and Mullineux (2013)

A recent piece of research was the Birmingham Commission Report (Rowlingson and Mullineux 2013). Some key finding of the report were as follows:

- Wealth inequalities occur in different ways. Some people have higher incomes than others; some choose to accumulate wealth rather than spend; some receive higher levels of inheritance/ lifetime gifts from parents; and some invest in housing or other assets just before they increase substantially in value.
- Wealth affects physical and mental wellbeing, as well as education and employment opportunities. It has also been argued that wealthy people become insulated from the lives of others, leading to a divide between rich and poor. The ability of wealthy people to gain greater political influence is a potential threat to democratic processes.
- Low levels of income reduce the ability to avoid debt and/or accumulate savings. Levels of problem debt have been increasing in recent years and look set to increase still further.
- Those in the middle of the wealth distribution tend to have some housing and pension wealth or the ability to accumulate some. However, there are a number of difficulties facing this group. For example, young people may struggle to get a foot on the housing ladder. Older home owners may find it difficult to access some of their housing wealth to maintain or increase their living standards, particularly in retirement.
- Those at the very top of the income distribution have seen huge increases in their incomes in recent decades, which have subsequently fed through into wealth inequalities. Those on high incomes are also much more likely to receive an inheritance and/or lifetime gift, and much more likely to receive one of high value.

The report concludes by arguing that the government should consider actions to redistribute wealth, including fairer rewards for work, as well as reforms to wealth taxation, including an overhaul of council tax and capital gains tax, while also giving consideration to a mansion tax (on very valuable homes) and a land tax.

Are wealth inequalities based on age or class?

Critics of this kind of analysis argue that inequalities of wealth are more related to age than social class. People tend to accumulate wealth as they get older. For most middle income earners, their major sources of wealth are likely to be their homes and their pensions; in both cases, the value of these tends to increase as people approach retirement.

This is to some extent supported by the Birmingham Commission. They found a clear link between wealth and age, with those in the 55–64 age group having the highest levels of wealth. However, there is considerable inequality within this age group; the poorest tenth have less than £28,000 of wealth on average compared with the top tenth who have more than £1.3 million. This reflects the fact that those on higher and middle incomes have much more chance to accumulate wealth than those on lower incomes.

Are wealth inequalities based on meritocracy?

It can also be argued that inequalities of wealth represent a meritocracy. In other words, people with talent and those who save their money or invest prudently are rewarded by building up more wealth. Entrepreneurs such as Lord Alan Sugar, who came from a working-class background and built up a business empire based on his company Amstrad (see also page 245), are often cited as an example of people who build up considerable wealth based on their own merits.

Research by Tony Atkinson (2013), however, reveals that an increasing proportion of national income now comes from inherited wealth, reversing a long-term decline in the importance of inherited wealth going back at least as far as the nineteenth century. Before the First World War, total transmitted wealth represented some 20 per cent of national income. This gradually fell to around 10 per cent after the Second World War, eventually dipping below 5 per cent in the late 1970s. Since then, the long-term trend has been reversed, with a rise from 4.8 per cent in 1977 to 8.2 per cent in 2006. This suggests that inequalities of wealth do not simply result from differences in talent between individuals, as an increasing proportion of people simply inherit wealth that their parents accumulated.

Activity

The relationship between social class and wealth

	Median financial and physical wealth	Median financial physical and property wealth	Total household wealth		
			10th percentile	Median	90th percentile
Large employers/higher managerial	152	451	326	1,166	2,297
Higher professional	157	441	320	998	2,401
Lower managerial/professional	100	312	179	715	1,638
Intermediate	69	235	82	408	1,015
Small employers/own account work	66	227	44	352	1,240
Lower supervisory/technical	55	182	33	321	886
Semi-routine	42	140	15	229	777
Routine	31	86	8	154	644
Never worked/long-term unemployed	12	15	4	30	356
All	**67**	**231**	**29**	**431**	**1,459**

Household wealth for 55–64-year-olds by household occupational social class, 2008–10 (cash terms, $000s, GB)

(Source: Hills et al. 2013)

1 What relationship between social class and ownership of wealth is suggested by this data?
2 Given that the data is based on people in the same age group (55–64-year-olds), why might it be argued that inequalities of wealth are related to class rather than age?

Activity: The distribution of wealth in the UK

Item A: The distribution of wealth in the UK

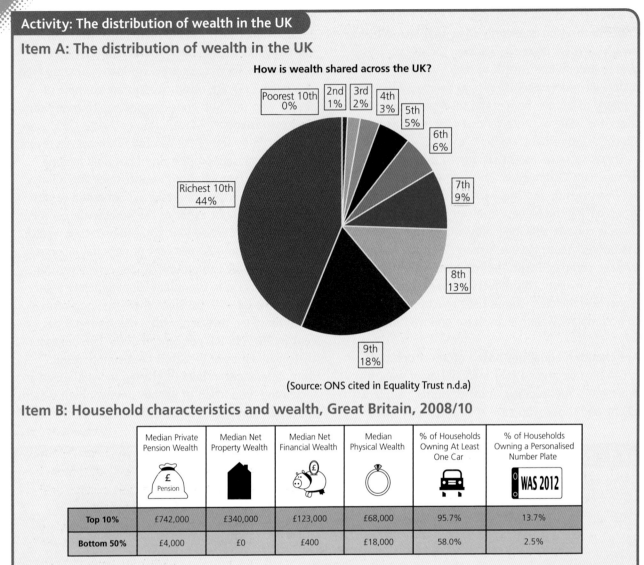

How is wealth shared across the UK?

Poorest 10th 0%
2nd 1%
3rd 2%
4th 3%
5th 5%
6th 6%
7th 9%
Richest 10th 44%
8th 13%
9th 18%

(Source: ONS cited in Equality Trust n.d.a)

Item B: Household characteristics and wealth, Great Britain, 2008/10

	Median Private Pension Wealth	Median Net Property Wealth	Median Net Financial Wealth	Median Physical Wealth	% of Households Owning At Least One Car	% of Households Owning a Personalised Number Plate
Top 10%	£742,000	£340,000	£123,000	£68,000	95.7%	13.7%
Bottom 50%	£4,000	£0	£400	£18,000	58.0%	2.5%

(Source: ONS 2012c)

Item C: The distribution of wealth – what we think, and how it is

Karen Rowlingson and Stephen McKay (2013) analysed research comparing how people thought wealth should be distributed with how they thought it was actually distributed. The research was conducted by Ipsos MORI and surveyed a representative sample of 1,016 adults aged 16–75 across Great Britain. They then compared the public's perceptions of wealth distribution with data from the Wealth and Assets Survey showing how wealth is actually distributed.

Figure 1: How people think wealth *should* be distributed, September 2013 (%)

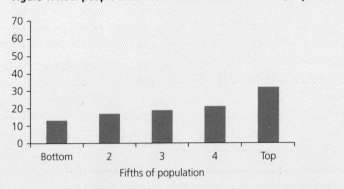

Fifths of population

Source: Ipsos MORI for Birmingham Wealth Commission

Activity: Distribution of wealth in the UK (continued)

Figure 2: How people *think* wealth is actually distributed, September 2013 (%)

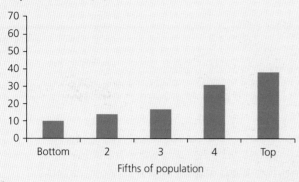

Fifths of population

Source: Ipsos MORI for Birmingham Wealth Commission

Figure 3: How total wealth is actually distributed, 2008–10 (% for each fifth)

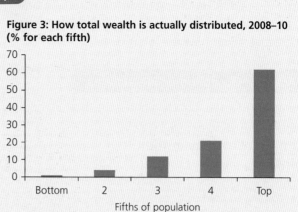

Fifths of population

Source: Wealth and Assets Survey, wave 2, Birmingham Wealth Commission. Total wealth including private pension rights.

1 Study Item A. What proportion of the UK's wealth is owned by:
   a) the richest 10 per cent of the population?
   b) the poorest 50 per cent of the population?
2 Study Item B. Summarise three ways in which people in the wealthiest 10 per cent of the

population are likely to be better off than those in the poorest 50 per cent.
3 Study Item C. What does this data suggest about the difference between people's perceptions of how wealth is distributed and how it is actually distributed? Suggest some possible reasons for this difference.

Social class inequalities in work and employment

In most workplaces there is a hierarchy of occupations with higher-status jobs not only enjoying more pay but also a number of other advantages. Such inequalities are seen by many sociologists as related to the position of individuals in the labour market. For Weberian sociologists (see page 252), more privileged workers tend to be in more skilled and high-status occupations that can command higher levels of pay and other rewards. Workers who are less skilled tend to have significantly less bargaining power, or what Weber referred to as a poorer market situation.

Marxists (see page 250), by contrast, argue that inequalities of income and other rewards derive from the need for capitalist employers to keep wages down and profits up. Marxists also suggest that key workers such as managers who run business enterprises on behalf of their owners are likely to be much more highly rewarded because of the way that they act as the agents of the ruling class ensuring the profitability of businesses for their shareholders.

There are not only social class inequalities in relation to work in terms of basic levels of pay but also in relation to a variety of other types of rewards:

● **Financial rewards.** Compared to senior staff, more routine workers not only earn less pay but are less likely to enjoy other perks such as occupational pensions or longer paid holidays.
● **Status.** In most work, organisations, differences of status reflect differences of income; for example, there may be different uniforms or work dress, canteens and rest facilities for different grades of workers.
● **Power and control.** More senior staff in workplaces often have more autonomy and control in their work; for example, they may be able to set their own working hours and make decisions about how they do their jobs. More routine and lower-paid workers are often more closely supervised and may have to follow set routines or instructions from above about how they perform their jobs.
● **Opportunities for advancement.** In professional and managerial jobs, there is often a career ladder so employees tend to receive training and development and thus move up to positions of higher pay and responsibility over the course of their working lives. In manual and routine jobs, workers often stay at the same level throughout their career.
● **Job satisfaction.** More skilled workers may achieve higher levels of job satisfaction because they exercise a wider range of skills and can make decisions in their jobs. Routine jobs such

235

as working on an assembly line in a factory or on a supermarket checkout are likely to be more repetitive and lack scope to make decisions or be creative about how the job is done.

● **Job security.** Manual workers and other routine workers are much more likely to face job losses and unemployment than more skilled workers.

Activity: Occupational inequalities

Workers in restaurants and hotels are most likely to be paid less than the living wage.

Item A: Low pay in the UK

The living wage is an hourly rate of pay set independently and updated annually. It is calculated according to the basic cost of living in the UK. The Living Wage Foundation encourages employers to voluntarily agree to pay all of their workers at or above the living wage. The company behind Holiday Inn and Intercontinental in May 2012 became the first hotel chain to back the London Living Wage. However, most of the leading supermarkets have so far refused to sign up to the living wage for their workers.

In total 4.8 million Britons – 20 per cent of employees – were paid at a level below the rate deemed necessary for a basic standard of living, an increase from 3.4 million in 2009. Unlike the minimum wage (which is legally enforceable), it is up to employers to decide whether their staff are paid the living wage, which in 2014 was £7.85 an hour or £9.15 in London.

The report by the Resolution Foundation think tank found that 77 per cent of employees aged under 20 earned less than the living wage. The study found that two-thirds of restaurant and hotel workers (67 per cent) were paid below the benchmark and 41 per cent of retail and wholesale workers. The report's author Matthew Whittaker, senior economist at the Resolution Foundation, said: 'For most of the working population, real wages have been flat or declining for many years and as a result more and more people have dipped below the level of the living wage. This means an increasing struggle to keep up with the cost of living.'

(Source: adapted from Channel 4 2013; Living Wage Foundation n.d.)

Item B: Occupation and unemployment

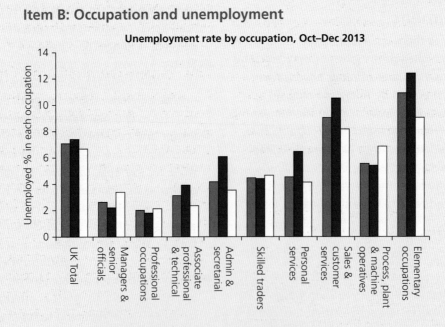

Unemployment rate by occupation, Oct–Dec 2013

ONS cited in (Source: Ripped-off Britons 2014)

1 What evidence is there in Item A that low pay is a feature of many jobs in Britain?

2 Suggest some possible reasons why many British companies have so far failed to sign up to the idea of a living wage for their workers.

3 What relationship is suggested by Item B between social class and the risk of unemployment?

4 How would you explain this relationship?

Social class inequality in poverty

Studying poverty focuses our attention on those at the lower end of the income scale, on people who often own little or no wealth. However, there is no agreement as to what we mean by poverty. This means that there is also considerable controversy over the extent of poverty. Child Poverty Action Group argues that there are 3.5 million children in poverty in the UK (about one in four children); however, some Conservative politicians have denied that poverty still exists in the UK at all.

Definitions of poverty

Absolute poverty

Absolute poverty is a lack of basic essentials needed to survive physically; these include adequate food, clothing, housing and fuel. Working out what essentials a person needs and how much they cost is a complex task and not all researchers would agree where this kind of poverty line should be drawn. Nevertheless, a number of researchers, such as Jonathan Bradshaw and his colleagues (2008), have attempted to develop a budget standard of poverty. This tries to define a minimum acceptable income by calculating what is needed to afford an acceptable living standard based on a costed list of items deemed as essential.

Critics argue that absolute definitions only allow for a person's physical needs and take no account of what is needed to participate fully in society. It could also be argued that in the UK today being able to take part in leisure activities such as holidays and outings, being able to buy presents for friends and family and having access to a TV or mobile phone are seen as socially necessary by most people though none of these are necessary to physical survival.

Relative poverty

Most sociologists today use some form of relative definition of poverty. Relative poverty involves judging whether a person's income is so far below that expected by the majority of people in society that they are excluded from a normal lifestyle. The problem here is agreeing what items should be included as being necessities without which a person should be regarded as being in poverty. Relative definitions of poverty also imply that what we define as poverty is not fixed, and that the poverty line in the UK will be much higher than, say, India because the majority of people have a much higher living standard in the UK. Critics argue that it is impossible to ever eradicate relative poverty as some people will always be worse off than others and therefore arguably in relative poverty.

Households Below Average Income (HBAI)

There are no official statistics of poverty in the UK. However, the government does publish statistics on Households Below Average Income (HBAI), drawing on data from official surveys such as the Family Resources Survey and the British Household Panel Survey. HBAI defines low incomes as being below 60 per cent of the median (the mid-point on the income scale, where half of households fall below and half above – see page 228).

HBAI has been criticised for being an arbitrary cut-off point; for example, why not use 50 per cent or 70 per cent of median income? Some critics would argue that many people just below the 60 per cent cut-off point are not so badly off that they should be defined as poor.

The HBAI statistics for 2012/13 (see the Activity on page 236) show little change in levels of poverty in the UK since around 2003. However, it can be argued that poverty has become more severe since the start of the recession following the banking crisis in 2008. Figures from the Trussell Trust, a charity that provides food banks to help the poorest families, suggest that in 2014, 4.7 million people were in food poverty – in other words, had insufficient income to afford a healthy diet – compared to fever than 26,000 in 2008/9 (see the Activity on page 236-237).

The consensual measure of poverty

Another method of measuring relative poverty was pioneered by Joanna Mack and Stuart Lansley (1985) and involved asking a series of representative focus groups which of a list of items they regarded as 'necessities'. Items that were rated as necessities by 50 per cent or more of respondents were then included in a list (see, for example, see Item B in the Activity on page 41). The researchers then carried out a living standards survey of a sample of the general population, asking them about how many of these necessities they had to go without because they could not afford them (items that people went without out of choice were not counted). Households that lacked three or more necessities were counted as poor and those that went without five items were defined as in severe poverty.

This approach has been repeated in a number of studies, most recently the PSE study *The Impoverishment of the UK* (Gordon *et al.* 2013). Interestingly, respondents in each successive survey have tended to include an ever increasing number of items in the list of necessities, supporting the view behind the relative definition of poverty that we need to constantly revise what we mean by poverty in line with rising expectations in society.

The PSE study carried out in 2012 suggests that there has been a major increase in poverty since Mack and Lansley's original study was published. In 2012, 33 per cent of households were defined as suffering from multiple deprivation because they lacked three or necessities, compared to 14 per cent in 1983.

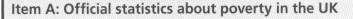

Activity: Measuring poverty in the UK

Item A: Official statistics about poverty in the UK

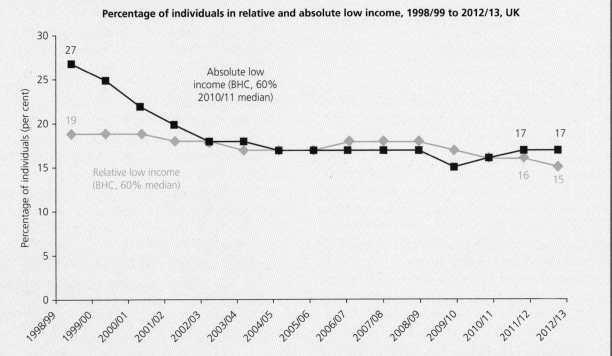

Percentage of individuals in relative and absolute low income, 1998/99 to 2012/13, UK

(Source: HBAI statistics from DWP cited in Tinker 2014)

Item B: Rising child poverty

A recent report warns that there is a risk that the UK will be a permanently divided society if the next government fails to approach the issue of child poverty in a radically new way. Furthermore, the Social Mobility and Child Poverty Commission is predicting that the goal of cutting child poverty in half by the year 2020 will not be achieved. The Commission's Chairman, Alan Milburn, argued that the current government has produced an 'unholy mess' by undermining existing child poverty targets while not managing to instigate new ones. At present the measure of a child being in relative poverty is if the family income is below 60 percent of average earnings. The Commission's findings are that as a result of rising rents and mortgage costs since 2010 there are now 1.4 million children in relative poverty. This is in spite of the fact that in the overall population relative poverty has dropped to its lowest levels since 1984. It is now being predicted by independent experts that there will be a significant increase in child poverty in the coming few years.

Source: adapted from BBC News (2014b)

Item C: Surveys based on the consensual approach to poverty

The table below shows the results of four surveys based on the consensual approach to defining poverty first used in 1983 for the Breadline Britain study. The first three studies did not cover Northern Ireland, while the 2012 survey covered the UK as a whole. The items listed were ones that at least 50 per cent of the public classified as being necessities.

Examples of items defined as necessities by the public	Percentage of households going without			
	1983	1990	1999	2012
Heating to keep home adequately warm	5	3	3	9
Damp-free home	6	2	7	10
Fresh fruit and vegetables	n/a	6	5	7
Meat, fish or vegetarian equivalent every other day	8	3	2	5
Replace or repair broken electrical goods	n/a	n/a	12	26
Household contents insurance	n/a	n/a	10	12
Regular savings for rainy days	n/a	n/a	27	32
Some new (not second-hand) clothes	n/a	n/a	3	4
Hobby or leisure activity for children	n/a	n/a	3	6
Children going away on a school trip at least once a term	n/a	n/a	2	8
A holiday away from home for at least one week a year for children	n/a	n/a	22	26
Percentage lacking three or more necessities (defined as being in poverty)	**14**	**20**	**24**	**33**

(Source: adapted from Gorden *et al.* 2013)

1 What trends are suggested in the percentage of people in relative poverty according to the official HBAI statistics in Item A?

2 Study Item B. Why does the Social Mobility and Child Poverty Commission suggest that child poverty may be more of a problem than is suggested by the statistics in Item A?

3 Suggest reasons why governments should be particularly concerned at high levels of poverty among children.

4 In what ways does Item C present a different picture of how levels of poverty in the UK have changed since the 1990s when compared with Item A?

5 Using material from all of the items, explain how the way in which poverty is defined and measured can affect estimates about how many people are actually poor.

Social class inequalities in social mobility

Social mobility is the movement of individuals up or down the social scale. Sociologists measure social mobility in two main ways:

1 Intergenerational mobility refers to mobility between generations. For example, a man whose father was a coal miner but who ended up becoming a doctor would have undergone upward social mobility from the working class into the middle class.

2 Intragenerational mobility refers to movement between classes by an individual during their working life. For example, a woman might start off as a secretary and end up running the company by the end of her career.

Open and closed societies

Research into social mobility is useful because it can tell sociologists a lot about the nature of the class structure of a society. If there is a great deal of social mobility, it suggests we are an open society – that is, a society where there are few obstacles to those with talent rising out of their social class. This is sometimes referred to as a meritocracy.

A closed society is one where there is little or no social mobility. The feudal system that existed in western Europe in the Middle Ages would be an example of this, as most individuals stayed at the same social rank as their parents – for example, as peasants, knights or lords.

Problems of researching social mobility

Research into social mobility has typically placed people into social classes based on their occupations and, in the case of intergenerational mobility, the occupations of their parents. Researchers can then study a sample of people to see how many of them have changed their class position and by how much. However, there are a number of problems with measuring social mobility:

- **Classifying occupations.** As we noted previously, sociologists do not agree on how people should be classified by occupation. Comparing studies is therefore difficult as different researchers have used different classifications.
- **Studying the mobility of women.** Most older studies of social mobility – for example, the Oxford Mobility Study (Goldthorpe 1980) – focused on the mobility of male heads of households only.
- **Studying the mobility of the very rich and poor.** The very wealthiest people in society are not usually clearly identified in social mobility studies as they are often categorised alongside professional and managerial occupations. Arguably these top positions are much more closed than those below them, as the wealthy often acquire their positions through inheritance. Similarly, the poorest groups often have no occupations, so focusing on the working population may ignore the extent to which they are trapped at the bottom of society.
- **Studying current patterns of social mobility.** Studies of social mobility cannot really draw conclusions about how far people are mobile until they are well established in their careers; this is not usually until they are in their 40s or 50s. This means that researchers are often studying the impact on social mobility of government policies on education or changes in the labour market that took place 30 or more years ago.

Goldthorpe: The Oxford Mobility Study

The Oxford Mobility Study (OMS) undertaken by John Goldthorpe (1980) in 1972 was one of the largest studies of social mobility in the UK and studied a sample of around 10,000 men. Goldthorpe used the Hope–Goldthorpe scale to compare the occupational classes of sons and their fathers (see page 223). Some of his findings are summarised below.

Activity

Absolute and relative social mobility

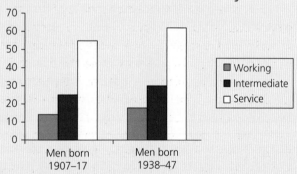

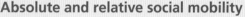

Goldthorpe calculated the odds of men in two generations (those born 1908–17 and those born 1938–47) of ending up in jobs in the service class. He found that the chances had increased for the younger generation who had grown up since the Second World War, i.e. there had been an increase in absolute social

mobility for everyone. However, the relative chances of social mobility when comparing the odds for the three social classes had hardly changed. He expressed this as the 1:2:4 Rule of Relative Hope. Whatever chance a working-class boy had of reaching the service class, an intermediate-class boy had twice the chance and a boy starting off in the service class had four times the chance. This rule applied to both generations.

(Source: adapted from Kellner and Wilby 1980)

1 What is meant by absolute social mobility?
2 Suggest possible reasons why there appeared to be an increase in absolute social mobility in Britain in the second half of the twentieth century.
3 What is meant by relative social mobility?
4 Suggest possible reasons why men born in the service class had a better chance of upward social mobility than those born in the working class.

Goldthorpe's study found that in the period after the Second World War there had been considerable upward social mobility, though much less downward social mobility. In fact, over two-thirds of the service class had started off in either the working class or the service class. One possible explanation for this was the introduction of free secondary education after 1944 and the expansion of opportunities in higher education. However, Goldthorpe suggested

that this was not as important as many people believed. Instead, he argued that changes in the occupational structure were more significant. In the mid-twentieth century there was a reduction in the size of the working class because there were fewer manual jobs and an increase in the size of the intermediate and service classes due to the growth of the service sector – for example, professionals and administrators in fields such as education, welfare, health and financial services. This meant that even if every son of service-class parents had obtained a job in the service class, some sons of intermediate- and working-class parents would have needed to be recruited to fill the growing number of service-class occupations.

Goldthorpe's research points to an increase in absolute social mobility – in other words, an increase in the number of men who ended up in a different class position to their fathers – mainly because there was more room at the top of society. However, when we compare relative mobility rates, based on the chances of different social classes achieving upward mobility, little changed during the period studied by the OMS.

Evaluation of the OMS

Goldthorpe's findings were largely confirmed by later studies. He carried out a follow-up study using 1983 British Election Survey data (Goldthorpe and Payne 1986) which confirmed the continuing expansion of the service class, creating more opportunities for absolute mobility; however, relative mobility remained about the same.

Another study by Gordon Marshall and his colleagues for the Essex University Mobility Study (1988) also found evidence of inequality in relative mobility rates, with someone starting off in the service class having seven times as much chance of ending up in the service class as someone from a working-class background.

Both Goldthorpe's findings and his methodology have been the subject of much criticism from different quarters. Peter Saunders (1990, 1996) argues that we should focus on absolute rather than relative mobility rates. He argues that the increasing number of working-class children who do well in education and go on to service-class jobs should be celebrated. In common with New Right thinkers (see page 247), Saunders argues that Goldthorpe's arguments have a left-wing bias, presenting Britain as a class-ridden closed society, rather than highlighting the opportunities presented by capitalism for everyone to achieve.

Saunders also argues that Goldthorpe makes the mistake of assuming that innate ability in the form of intelligence is evenly distributed throughout the social classes. Saunders argues that children of the service class are likely to inherit higher levels of intelligence

and thus have a better chance of achieving service-class jobs because of their ability rather than because they have more opportunities. This has been hotly disputed by many other sociologists who would question the idea that intelligence is innate or inborn. Saunders' arguments also ignore a range of research pointing to ways in which working-class children are disadvantaged not by lack of intelligence but by their home backgrounds and unequal opportunities within the education system.

Feminists such as Michelle Stanworth (1984) and Pamela Abbott (1990) have criticised studies like the OMS for focusing exclusively on men (see also page 253). Goldthorpe claimed that there was no need for research on female mobility as in most households men were the main wage-earners and most women took their class position from their husband or father. For feminists, this ignores the importance of women as wage-earners. Abbott also argues that women's experiences of mobility are likely to be different from men's; for example, because of the disadvantages faced by women in the workplace, they are less likely to achieve either intergenerational or intragenerational mobility.

Goldthorpe's study focused on mobility into the service class – around 25 per cent of the workforce when he did his research. If we focus on the very top positions in UK society – for example, the richest 5 per cent of the population – it seems likely that the UK appears much more closed. Marxists, for example, would point to the fact that many of the super-rich have achieved their positions through inherited wealth. Similarly, many of the top jobs in UK society are still filled by people who were privately educated, an opportunity usually only available to children of well-off parents (see the table below).

Top jobs	% who attended fee-paying schools
Senior judges	71%
Senior armed forces officers	62%
Permanent secretaries (most senior civil servants)	55%
Senior diplomats	53%
Chairmen/chairwomen of public bodies	45%
Sunday Times Rich List	44%
Newspaper columnists	43%

Top jobs	% who attended fee-paying schools
BBC executives	26%
House of Lords	50%
Cabinet	36%
Shadow Cabinet	22%
MPs	33%
England, Scotland and Wales rugby union teams	35%
England cricket team	33%
UK population as a whole	**7%**

(Source: Social Mobility and Child Poverty Commission cited in Burns 2014)

Savage and Egerton: The NCDS study

A more recent study of social mobility in Britain was undertaken by Mike Savage and Muriel Egerton (1997) and used data from the National Child Development Study (NCDS), a longitudinal survey of people born in 1958. The study was based on the class that people had reached in 1991. Unlike the OMS, it included data on the social mobility of women.

Ken Roberts (2001) adapted data from both the OMS and the NCDS studies in order to analyse changes in social mobility in the twentieth century. Some of his main findings are summarised below:

- The working class continued to contract and the intermediate and service classes to expand. This provided opportunities for upward mobility from the working class.
- The chances of escaping the working class did not, however, increase greatly. 55 per cent of men originating in the working class stayed in that class.
- The chances of working-class men rising to the service class did increase significantly from 16 to 26 per cent.
- In the NCDS study, service-class sons were more than twice as likely to end up with service-class jobs compared to those from the working class.
- In both studies, the service class were recruited from fairly diverse origins, including as many as 40 per cent from working-class backgrounds; however, around three-quarters of the working class in both studies came from working-class backgrounds. This was explainable because there has been more upward than downward mobility.

- Women have different patterns of mobility from men, with more working-class women likely to move up into the intermediate class and more service-class women moving down to the intermediate class compared to men. This reflects the fact that the kind of jobs done by women, such as office work, are concentrated in the intermediate class.

Government policy and the Social Mobility and Child Poverty Commission

The government recognised the issue of barriers to social mobility in the UK by setting up the Social Mobility and Child Poverty Commission in 2010. One example of its success has been the so-called 'London effect', where attempts to improve education for the poorest children in London, particularly focusing on primary schools, have meant that in London as a whole poorer children now perform better than average children in the rest of the country. However, the Commission criticised the government in 2013 for failing to do more to tackle issues such as child poverty that hold back the most disadvantaged children.

As other sections of this part of the book demonstrate, Britain remains a highly unequal society in terms of social class inequalities, such as in the distribution of income and wealth. Research by Richard Wilkinson and Kate Pickett (2009) demonstrates that countries with the highest levels of income inequality also have the lowest levels of social mobility (see Item B in the Activity on page 241). Most wealthy European countries have a much lower degree of income inequality than the UK and also have higher mobility rates. The UK is much closer to the USA in having low rates of social mobility and a high degree of income inequality. If Wilkinson and Pickett are correct, the UK is only likely to become a more open society if the government can reverse the widening social inequalities of recent years.

Social class inequalities in other areas of social life

Elsewhere in this book you will find a range of evidence about social class inequalities in different areas of social life. You can apply evidence from whichever option topics you have studied to answer

Activity: Patterns of social mobility

Item A: An international comparison of social mobility

The relationship between the incomes of parents and their children is stronger in Great Britain than in many other countries

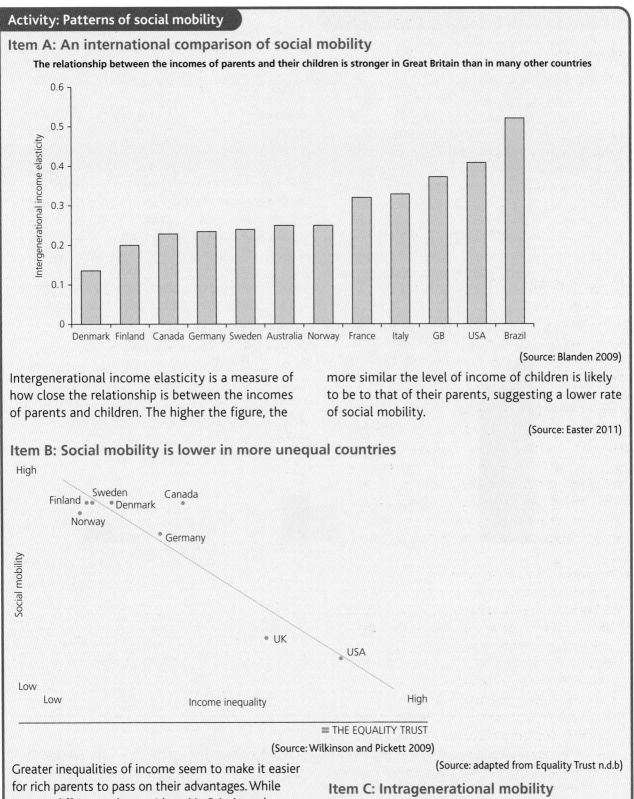

(Source: Blanden 2009)

Intergenerational income elasticity is a measure of how close the relationship is between the incomes of parents and children. The higher the figure, the more similar the level of income of children is likely to be to that of their parents, suggesting a lower rate of social mobility.

(Source: Easter 2011)

Item B: Social mobility is lower in more unequal countries

(Source: Wilkinson and Pickett 2009)

THE EQUALITY TRUST

Greater inequalities of income seem to make it easier for rich parents to pass on their advantages. While income differences have widened in Britain and the USA, social mobility has slowed. Bigger income differences may make it harder to achieve equality of opportunity because they increase social class differentiation and perhaps prejudice.

(Source: adapted from Equality Trust n.d.b)

Item C: Intragenerational mobility

A major new study published by Lee Savage at the Resolution Foundation tells us what changed in intragenerational mobility in the 2000s compared to the 1990s. It tracks a large number of people in their

30s through the 1990s and compares how socially mobile this group was compared to another group in their 30s during the 2000s.

The results are fascinating. The good news is that the chances of someone moving a long way up the earnings distribution increased by over 20 per cent in the 2000s compared to the 1990s. More interesting still is the change in mobility across the earnings distribution. As the chart below shows, when we look at the position of the lowest earners in society we see a small fall in the proportion who stayed at the bottom of the wage pile throughout the 2000s; a sizeable increase (31 per cent) in those who moved up from the bottom to the middle; and a doubling in the proportion who leaped right up to the top.

So much for the good news. Most people looking at this chart will, of course, notice something rather bleaker. The overriding story remains that, regardless of whether you were in the 1990s or 2000s generation, if you started off at the top of the earnings distribution, you were much more likely to stay there than move somewhere else. And if you started off at the bottom, you were likely to stay there too. Mobility may have picked up, but from a very low base. The doubling of the chance of moving from the bottom to the top in the 2000s loses much of its gloss when you realise that the absolute increase was from a measly 3 per cent to 6 per cent. So, all in all, some important if modest gains – certainly enough to confound the story of the social mobility pessimists who say things only ever get worse – but not exactly a revolution in opportunity.

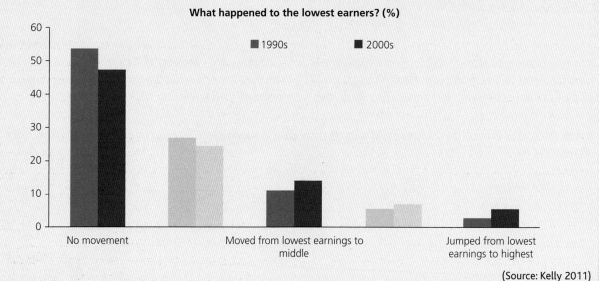

What happened to the lowest earners? (%)

■ 1990s   ■ 2000s

No movement | Moved from lowest earnings to middle | Jumped from lowest earnings to highest

(Source: Kelly 2011)

1 Study Items A and B. What does this data suggest about how levels of social mobility in the UK compare with other countries?
2 What does Item B suggest about the relationship between levels of social mobility and levels of income inequality in different countries?

3 Using data from Item C, assess how far opportunities for intragenerational mobility have improved for the lowest earners since the 1990s.
4 Using data from all of the items, assess how far the successful entrepreneurial businessman Ken Wills shows that the UK is an open society.

questions on social class and other forms of social inequality in the exam.

Some examples of topics from which you could draw evidence are summarised below. You may be able to think of some others for yourself.

Topic	Example of evidence of social class inequalities
Introducing socialisation, culture and identity	The role of social class in creating identities
Families and relationships	The role of families in reproducing social class inequalities
Youth subcultures	Youth subcultures as a response to social class inequalities, such as deviant subcultures
The media	Representations of social class in the mass media
Globalisation and the digital social world	How digital technologies may be affecting social class inequalities
Crime and deviance	Class differences in crime both in offending and victimisation
Education	Class differences in educational achievement
Religion, belief and faith	Patterns of religion in relation to social class, such as new religious movements as a response to social deprivation

Section summary

Fill in the blanks, using the words given below.

Many sociologists use a person's occupation to determine their social class. There are a number of occupational scales including the _____, which was developed for the Oxford Mobility Study, and the _____, which is used by the government for official statistics. Social classifications based on generally agreed criteria such as occupation are known as _____ of social class; however, people's own perceptions of class may not correspond with these and these are known as _____ of social class.

Weber suggested that a person's social class could be linked to their _____ or opportunities to achieve desirable things in life such as _____ or _____. Social class is also linked to other inequalities, such as a person's _____ or how that money they have coming in on a regular basis and their _____ or assets that have a cash value. Social class can be related to a person's _____ or their earning power based on their skills, qualifications or other assets.

Incomes in the UK are very unequally distributed, with workers at the bottom receiving only _____ or the lowest legal wage set by the government. Some campaigners now want more employers to pay _____, which is a more realistic level of income to live on. Those at the lowest end of the income scale can be seen as being in poverty. However, some researchers argue that if we define poverty as _____ or a lack of the basic necessities to stay alive, then few people in the UK are in real poverty. On the other hand, other researchers argue that there is an increasing level of _____ based on people who are excluded from the accepted lifestyle of the majority. The government defines poverty as _____ or less than 60 per cent of median household income.

The movement of people up or down the social scale from one class to another is called _____. Sociologists measure this in two ways: _____, comparing a person's class with their parents, and _____, comparing how far a person has changed their class position since starting their career. Studying social mobility can help to determine how far we are _____ where movement from one class to another is frequent and easy or _____ where most people end up in the same social class as their parents. Determining how much social mobility there is in the UK is not simple. For example, most studies suggest a high level of _____ based on the total number of people who move up or down but continuing inequality in terms of _____, which compares the chances of people from different social classes of achieving social mobility. _____ researchers also point to the fact that most social mobility studies have been done on men and do not represent women.

absolute poverty, absolute social mobility, a closed society, an open society, educational qualifications, feminist, Hope–Goldthorpe scale, households below average income, income, intergenerational, intragenerational, life chances, long life, market situation, NS-SEC scale, objective definitions, relative poverty, relative social mobility, social mobility, subjective definitions, the living wage, the minimum wage, wealth

7a.3 How can patterns and trends in social class inequality and difference be explained?

Functionalism

Parsons: Value consensus and stratification

Functionalism is often described as a consensus theory because it suggests that society works best when there is agreement or consensus over shared values. For the American sociologist Talcott Parsons (1951), different forms of social stratification, including social class, reflect this value consensus. Parsons argued that in all societies some individuals are better than others than at achieving things that are regarded as worthy of reward according to the prevailing value consensus. In the Middle Ages, knights were highly rewarded because being a successful warrior was seen as important. Similarly, he suggests that most people agree that in modern industrial societies, entrepreneurs and executives who successfully run businesses creating wealth and jobs deserve the highest rewards as they contribute most to the smooth running of society.

Davis and Moore: Some principles of social stratification

Perhaps the most famous functionalist theory of stratification was offered by Kingsley Davis and Wilbert Moore (1945). They argued that social stratification of some kind has been a feature of all human society and therefore concluded that stratification is functionally necessary. They argued that the main function of social stratification is to ensure effective role allocation and performance. Social stratification therefore does two things:

1 It allocates the right people to the most important roles. This ensures that the most important positions in society are filled by the most able people by offering them higher rewards, such as in terms of income and status. Thus training to be a doctor requires people with very high educational qualifications and demands a long period of training and a lot of responsibility. To motivate the best people, we need to offer doctors higher rewards than other less demanding jobs.

2 It ensures that people in these roles perform them to the highest standards. People in key positions such as doctors or chief executives of companies have many others depending on them so it is important to motivate them to work to the best of their ability for the good of the whole organisation.

Davis and Moore argue that we can tell which positions are most important by two factors:

1 **Functional uniqueness.** A position is functionally unique if only one person or a small number could carry out the role. Thus only one surgeon in a hospital might be able to lead a team performing a heart transplant, whereas many people (including the surgeon) could, if necessary, do the porter's job and wheel the patient into the operating theatre. So the consultant surgeon is functionally unique and requires a higher reward.

2 **The degree of dependence of others.** Similarly, many other people depend on the consultant surgeon to do their jobs, including more junior doctors and nurses who operate under his or her orders. In the same way, the chief executive of a company is not only functionally unique but makes decisions and gives orders to many employees lower down the organisation and is dependent on nobody else above himself or herself except perhaps the shareholders.

Tumin: A critique of Davis and Moore

Another American sociologist, Melvin Tumin (1953), offered a series of criticisms of Davis and Moore which resulted in a lengthy debate about their theory.

- **Is it possible to determine the functional importance of a position?** After all, the low-paid cleaner who ensures the operating theatre is disinfected is perhaps just as important to the patient's survival as the highly paid heart surgeon. Which positions are most important is perhaps a matter of opinion rather than fact.
- **Is there consensus about rewards?** Arguably there is considerable conflict and resentment about the unequal distribution of rewards such as incomes.
- **Power and rewards.** It can be argued that the high pay of some jobs such as top business executives reflects their power rather than agreement among the rest of society that they deserve it.
- **The pool of talent.** Davis and Moore seem to assume that only a small number of people have the unique talents to perform top jobs. In reality, many more people may have the ability to be doctors or business executives but have simply never been given the opportunity.
- **Is training a sacrifice?** Davis and Moore suggest that higher rewards are needed to motivate people

to undergo the long training needed for top jobs. In reality, going to university has its own rewards, such as freedom and the chance to learn what we are interested in, and most graduates more than make up for lost earnings in their first ten years of work.

- **Motivation.** Davis and Moore seem to assume that only monetary rewards motivate people to do demanding jobs. This does not account for people who may be motivated by altruism or a sense of service; for example, professionals in many public services such as teachers, nurses and social workers earn less than similarly qualified workers in the private sector but often choose these professions out of a desire to serve others.
- **The dysfunctions of stratification.** Tumin points out that, far from stratification helping society to run smoothly, it often creates hostility, suspicion and mistrust between different sections of society.

For both Parsons and Davis and Moore, modern industrial societies are meritocracies. Those who achieve the top positions do so on the basis of merit rather than family background and inheritance. However, as the first part of this chapter demonstrates, not everyone in UK society has the same life chances. Access to the top positions is often denied to those from lower classes as much because of lack of opportunity as because of lack of ability or merit.

By the 1960s, functionalist approaches to stratification became unfashionable among most sociologists, partly because of the issues raised by critics such as Tumin. Many sociologists turned to the ideas of Marx and Weber for inspiration. However, in the 1980s, the rise of neoliberal or New Right approaches in politics and sociology led to a renewal of support for functionalist views.

Activity: Aristocracy versus meritocracy

Item A: The Duke of Westminster

Gerald Grosvenor, Duke of Westminster, is Britain's wealthiest man with wealth estimated at £7.9bn. The Duke was educated at Harrow School where he passed two O levels. He then passed out (graduated from) of Sandhurst and became a Territorial Army officer, rising to the rank of Major General, as well as running the family business. He and his family owe the bulk of their wealth to owning 77 hectares (190 acres) of Mayfair and Belgravia, adjacent to Buckingham Palace. As the value of land rockets in the capital, so too does the personal wealth of Grosvenor. The family also own 39,000 hectares in Scotland and 13,000 hectares in Spain, while their privately owned Grosvenor Estate property group has $20bn (£12bn) worth of assets under management including the Liverpool One shopping mall.

(Source: adapted from Elliott 2014)

Item B: Lord Sugar

Alan Sugar was born in the East End of London, the son of a Jewish tailor. As a child, he lived in a council flat and attended state schools. He left school at 16 and started selling car aerials and electrical goods from the back of a van, which he bought with savings of £50. He started his electronics company, Amstrad, in 1968, and sold it in 2007. In 2011, his estimated fortune was £700m and he was ranked 89th in the *Sunday Times* Rich List. In 1991, Sugar became chairman of Tottenham Hotspur Football Club, but sold his last shares in the club in 2007. Sugar became a life peer in 2009 and is also famous for his appearances on the BBC series *The Apprentice*. He is still involved in a number of business ventures including Amsair, Amsprop and Amscreen.

1 Compare the social background, education and career of the two wealthy men in Items A and B. What differences do you notice?

2 Using the two items and any other evidence, evaluate how far Britain can be seen as a meritocracy.

The New Right

From the 1980s onwards, a new approach to politics and economics emerged in Britain and the USA, often referred to as neo-liberalism or the New Right. This was a revival of nineteenth-century liberalism which believed that the economic system worked best when it was based on a free market. The British Prime Minister Margaret Thatcher and US presidents Ronald Reagan and George Bush have been seen to be strongly influenced by neo-liberalism in their policies.

New Right ideas have generally not been popular with sociologists, partly because they emphasise the importance of the individual and free choice. Sociologists, by contrast, tend to see individuals as always operating in a social context and making choices influenced by their socialisation and the norms of the groups to which they belong. Nevertheless, some sociologists have been influenced by New Right thinking.

Saunders: In defence of inequality

Peter Saunders (1990) draws on New Right ideas in his work on social stratification. Unlike functionalists, Saunders does not see stratification as an inevitable part of all societies. However, he argues that a society based on social equality would only be possible if considerable force were used – for example, the threat of death or imprisonment – to ensure that everyone did their jobs to the best of their abilities because they would not be motivated by economic rewards.

Saunders is not opposed to some forms of equality. He argues that it is right and just that everyone enjoys legal equality (being judged by the same laws and having the same legal rights). He also supports the principle of equality of opportunity (whereby everyone has the same chances to compete for unequal rewards); this is similar to the functionalist idea of meritocracy. It is a third type of equality, equality of outcomes, that Saunders rejects. This would involve everyone being rewarded in the same way whether they deserve it or not. Like the functionalists, Saunders therefore argues that a degree of inequality is desirable and functional in order to motivate people to compete, as long as everyone has an equal opportunity to take part in the competition.

Saunders is critical of attempts by left-wing governments (for example, Labour governments in the UK) to try and equalise society, as he sees them as misguided. For example, taxing the rich to pay for benefits or programmes to help the poor or supposedly disadvantaged simply interferes with market forces and reduces the incentive of the rich to invest in developing businesses. Similarly, in education, attempts to ensure that working-class children do as well as middle-class children are mistaken because he argues that middle-class children are probably more able and intelligent and deserve to do better than working-class children.

Critics of Saunders argue that it is mistaken to assume that capitalist societies based on the free market necessarily offer individuals more freedom than socialist or communist societies which seek to make people equal. After all, the system of slavery in parts of the USA in the early nineteenth century, the apartheid system of South Africa where black people were denied the same opportunities as whites, and military dictatorships such as Chile in the 1980s, were all based on free market capitalism but were extremely oppressive in terms of the treatment of certain social groups. Many of the criticisms made by Tumin of functionalist theories of stratification could also be applied to Saunders and the New Right.

Murray: The underclass

One of the most famous proponents of New Right ideas is the American political scientist Charles Murray. Murray (1984) argued that US government policies of providing welfare benefits for groups such as the unemployed and lone-parent families were creating a dependency culture whereby poor people were given no motivation to better themselves – for example, by trying to find paid work – as they were allowed to remain dependent on the state. The result was the creation of an underclass of people trapped at the bottom of society. The underclass were not only a drain on taxpayers paying for their benefits but also tended to poorly socialise their children, meaning that they generally underachieved at school and turned to crime.

Murray visited Britain and argued that there were signs that Britain too was developing an underclass (1989). He suggested that rising rates of births outside marriage, crime and youth unemployment were all signs that the irresponsible attitudes found in the underclass were infecting certain neighbourhoods in the UK. Murray called for a reduction in welfare benefits and less government intervention to reduce poverty, arguing that this did more harm than good. Like other New Right thinkers, Murray argued that disadvantaged social groups such as lone parents and the unemployed needed to be encouraged to stand on their own feet rather than expecting the state to support them.

Murray's work attracted considerable support from some politicians in the British Conservative party. However, his work is also highly controversial and has been criticised by many British sociologists.

Studies of poor people tend to suggest only a minority have the kind of attitudes described by Murray as typical of the underclass. Most people without jobs and on benefits want to work and earn a decent living.

It is unclear who exactly is responsible for the alleged problems created by the underclass. Sometimes Murray blames groups such as the unemployed and lone parents for behaving irresponsibly – for example, in refusing to work or by having children whom they cannot afford to support. At other times he blames the welfare state for encouraging this kind of behaviour by giving benefits to those who are underserving.

Murray's work only focuses on those at the bottom end of society, the poorest. He makes no connection between the wider pattern of social class inequality and the growing gap between the rich and poor in trying to understand why poverty is a growing problem in both Britain and the USA. Many Marxist and Weberian sociologists would argue that it is the working of the capitalist system that leads to poverty and inequality. Blaming the poor for their own poverty is simply blaming the victims of the system.

Activity

The negative effects of inequality

In their study *The Spirit Level*, Richard Wilkinson and Kate Pickett (2009) carried out an analysis comparing the effects of inequality in a range of societies. They ranked societies in terms of inequality by comparing the income of the richest 20 per cent with the poorest 20 per cent in each country. Thus, Japan proved to be the most equal country, with the richest 20 per cent having only four times the income of the poorest 20 per cent, whereas in Singapore, the richest had nearly ten times the income of the poorest.

Wilkinson and Pickett then devised an index of health and social problems based on measures of the following:

- levels of mental illness
- infant mortality
- life expectancy
- obesity
- teenage births
- homicide
- imprisonment
- educational performance of children
- drug and alcohol addiction
- social mobility.

They found a clear correlation between high levels of inequality and high levels of social and health problems. Wilkinson and Pickett also tested their theory on different US states and found a similar relationship between income inequality and social problems.

Wilkinson and Pickett offered a number of explanations for this relationship:

- High levels of inequality mean low status for those at the bottom, which in turn affects people's mental and physical wellbeing.
- Low status can also lead to a sense of shame, possibly encouraging higher rates of crime, including homicide.
- Countries with greater inequalities also have less social mobility as the poorest groups are likely to be more disadvantaged in competing for top positions.
- High levels of inequality lead to a lack of trust between people. This is dysfunctional for everyone, rich and poor alike.

Wilkinson and Pickett are not Marxists; they did not advocate total equality, but they did argue that societies such as Japan, Norway and Sweden with lesser degrees of inequality have fewer social problems and function more effectively than societies such as the UK, Australia and New Zealand that have wider income inequalities.

Wilkinson and Pickett have in turn been criticised. For example, it has been argued that they were selective in the countries they analysed and including countries such as South Korea, Slovenia and Hong Kong in their study would have produced a much less clear-cut relationship between income inequality and problems such as poor health and crime. Their study also adopts a fairly crude measure of social inequality: simply comparing the income of the richest and poorest 20 per cent in each country.

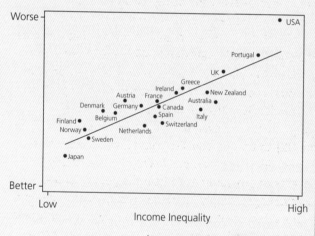

(Source: Wilkinson and Pickett 2009)

1 What relationship did Wilkinson and Pickett find between levels of income inequality and better or worse outcomes in terms of health and social problems?

2 Study the graph above. How does Britain compare with other advanced industrial countries in terms of its level of social inequality and its rating in terms of health and social problems?

3 How could Wilkinson and Pickett's findings be used to criticise functionalist and New Right views of social inequality?

4 What arguments might be put forward in defence of these perspectives?

249

Marxism

Karl Marx (1818–83) saw the economic system as the basis for all societies. Different societies have different kinds of economic systems or modes of production. According to Marx (1844 and Marx and Engels 1848), the earliest human societies were based on primitive communism where all members worked together to obtain what they needed, such as by hunting and gathering. As societies evolved and a more specialised division of labour developed, so class relationships began to emerge. In ancient societies like Greece and Rome, there was a division between masters and slaves and, under feudalism in medieval Europe, between landowners and serfs.

Much of Marx's work focused on capitalist societies like modern Britain. Capitalism emerged from feudalism between the sixteenth and nineteenth centuries as goods began to be mass produced in factories and steam power was used to drive modern machinery. According to Marx, this gave rise to two new classes: the bourgeoisie, or capitalist class, who invested their wealth in financing the new industries of the industrial age, and the proletariat, or working class, the majority of society who owned no wealth and were forced to sell their labour for wages to the capitalists. The bourgeoisie were the ruling class because they owned the means of production: the factories, mines, banks and other businesses that were used to generate wealth. This in turn meant that they controlled the political system and cultural institutions that shaped people's ideas such as the media and the education system.

Class conflict

Marx argued that though the bourgeoisie and the proletariat depend on one another, their relationship is also based on conflict or class struggle. While the workers create the wealth of the bourgeoisie, only a fraction of what Marx called the surplus value that they create comes back to them in wages. For Marx, the workers are exploited by their employers who seek to keep wages low and profits high.

Marx argued that capitalism suffered from a series of inherent contradictions or problems which would eventually leads to its downfall:

- **Polarisation of social classes.** The divide between the working class and capitalists would grow steadily wider as the bourgeoisie tried to drive down wages and increase profits. Intermediate classes such as small business owners would be driven out of business by increasingly powerful big businesses, further widening the divide between the two main classes.
- **Alienation.** Workers would not be able to find any satisfaction or contentment because they would have no control over their own work, simply being used as commodities to increase production and profits. Outside work, people would be encouraged to find satisfaction in consumer goods and materialism rather than in real human relationships.
- **Economic crisis.** Marx argued that capitalist economies tend to suffer from periodic crises. Competition between companies creates boom periods but these are inevitably followed by recessions. Eventually, a crisis would lead to the collapse of the whole capitalist system.

The overthrow of capitalism

Marx argued that the working class had the potential to overthrow capitalism because the workers were in the majority and had only to realise their potential by uniting in a revolution. However, to achieve this, they had to throw off what Marx called 'false class consciousness' and become a class for itself. Marx argued that the capitalist class perpetuated an ideology or series of ideas that justified capitalism and its inequalities through the political system, law, mass media, religious beliefs and the education system.

Once the working class realised the nature of their exploitation, Marx was convinced they would rise up and overthrow capitalism. Marx believed that a new economic system called communism would replace capitalism where the means of production would be shared by the whole community. Everyone would be expected to contribute something to society 'according to their ability' and, instead of wages, would receive what they needed in terms of food, accommodation, health care and so on 'according to their needs'. This would mean that social classes based on economic inequalities would disappear and communism would result in a classless society.

Evaluation of Marxism

Marx's ideas have had a huge influence on political thought and inspired the rise of socialism and communism, leading to revolutions in countries like Russia and China. Marx has also influenced sociologists who have used his ideas to analyse the workings of capitalist societies and the nature of social class inequalities in them. Many sociologists who do not see themselves as Marxists draw on some of his key concepts, often combining them with ideas derived from the work of Weber.

However, Marx has also come in for extensive criticism, especially since the fall of communist regimes in Eastern Europe in the 1990s, which led many critics to argue that communism as it was practiced in such societies was an even more oppressive system than capitalism and simply did not deliver what it promised. Some of the main criticisms of Marxism are summarised below:

- **Economic determinism.** Marx argued that ultimately all societies can be explained in terms of the economic system and economic relationships. However, people may think or behave in certain ways for cultural reasons – for example because of the influence of religious or nationalist beliefs rather than because they are following economic or class interests. Marx's emphasis on economic or social class inequalities also tends to ignore the importance of other types of inequality such as those based on gender or ethnicity.

- **The middle class.** Marx largely dismissed the importance of classes situated between the bourgeoisie and proletariat, such as small business owners, highly paid professionals and managers who run businesses on behalf of the capitalists. However, critics point out that rather than shrinking or being absorbed into the two main classes, these groups have grown in size and importance, meaning that we should be talking about a middle class or middle classes.

- **Class consciousness and revolution.** Marx saw the downfall of capitalism in advanced industrial societies such as Britain, Germany or the USA as inevitable. In reality, communist revolutions have usually occurred in relatively under-developed societies such as Russia, China and Cuba. In Western societies there is little sign of class consciousness; for example, fewer and fewer workers support trades unions or even moderate socialist parties such as the Labour Party and support for revolutionary parties and political movements has waned since the 1980s.

- **The success of capitalism.** Capitalist societies seem to have flourished despite their inherent contradictions. Though capitalist economies tend to go through a cycle of 'boom and bust', in most cases discontent created by economic problems is contained. In most Western societies the working class have enjoyed rising living standards and access to ever wider consumer goods, while the political system of liberal democracy associated with many (though not all) capitalist societies allows everyone to elect their own governments and enjoy political freedoms and human rights.

In defence of Marxism

Modern Marxists have argued that, despite these criticisms, much of Marx's theory is still relevant to understanding social class inequalities in capitalist societies.

The continuing importance of social class inequality

Writing in the 1970s, Marxist sociologists John Westergaard and Henrietta Resler (1976) argued that there was little evidence of class divisions in British society disappearing and suggested that such inequalities could only be understood as the result of the way that the capitalist system operates. Arguably class divisions have actually widened since the 1970s.

The proletarianisation of the middle classes

Some sociologists claim that as the gap between the rich and poor widens, Marx's prediction about polarisation is coming true. American sociologist Harry Braverman (1974) argues that many so-called 'middle-class' workers have in reality been de-skilled. For example, the skills of clerical workers and even professionals have been programmed into machines or broken down into simple tasks that can be performed by less skilled workers. This reduces the control such workers have over work processes and also means that employers can pay them lower wages. The result is a process of proletarianisation, whereby more and more workers who might formerly have been regarded as middle class are reduced to the same class position as the working class or proletariat.

Neo-Marxism

Neo-Marxists have tried to develop and adapt Marx's ideas to deal with some of the criticisms made of Marx's work. For example, the Italian communist leader Antonio Gramsci (1971) developed the concept of hegemony to explain why the working class in western European countries had not risen up in revolution. Gramsci argued that the ruling class rarely need to use force to exert power because they rule through persuasion. Hegemony means using cultural and political means to encourage enough of the working class to side with the ruling class and the capitalist system to ensure the stability of the economic system. This involves using institutions such as the media and education to control people's minds. However, Gramsci argued that this hegemony is never complete; many of the working class have dual consciousness and are to some degree also aware of the inequalities and injustices of capitalism. Gramsci called on left-wing intellectuals to build on this awareness to create a greater class consciousness and ultimately lead the working class to a revolution.

Globalisation and transnational corporations

Some sociologists argue that capitalism has been transformed since Marx was writing in the nineteenth century by the process of globalisation. Increasingly, big businesses such as IBM, BP, Coca-Cola and British American Tobacco operate in a global economy, often controlling assets spread across a number of countries; they are transnational corporations (TNCs). The largest TNCs have annual sales in excess of the gross national income of many of the poorer countries in the world. According to Leslie Sklair (2003), nation states now find it difficult to control the activities of TNCs, giving TNCs greater power than national governments. From this perspective, those who control TNCs have become a global ruling class.

Weberian theory

Weberian theories of social class inequality derive from the work of the German sociologist Max Weber (1864–1920). Weber, like Marx, was a conflict theorist. He saw inequalities in society as based on the struggle between different groups to secure resources such as wealth, but argued that status and power were also resources that could be unequally distributed. Weber was a leading critic of Marx; he was sceptical as to whether a revolution resulting in the overthrow of capitalism would occur in Western societies and suggested that communism might end up being just as oppressive as capitalism.

Stratification

Marx's view of capitalism emphasised economic divisions and the class struggle as the basis for stratification. Weber (1948), however, suggested that there were three dimensions to social stratification – **social class, status** and **party** – and in some societies, economic or class divisions would not necessarily be the most important of these.

Activity: Is Marxism still relevant?

Item A: The fall of communism

Removal of the statue of Lenin (leader of the communist revolution in Russia) in Vilnius, Lithuania in 1991.

Item B: Sweatshop workers in Bangladesh

In Bangladesh, 3.5 million workers in 4,825 garment factories produce goods for export to the global market, principally Europe and North America. The Bangladeshi garment industry generates 80 per cent of the country's total export revenue. However, the wealth generated by this sector has led to few improvements in the lives of garment workers, 85 per cent of whom are women.

The majority of garment workers in Bangladesh earn little more than the minimum wage, set at 3,000 taka a month (approximately £25), far below what is considered a living wage, calculated at 5,000 taka a month (approximately £45), which would be the minimum required to provide a family with shelter, food and education.

As well as earning a pittance, Bangladeshi factory workers face appalling conditions. Many are forced to work 14–16 hours a day, seven days a week, with some workers finishing at 3 a.m. only to start again the same morning at 7.30 a.m. On top of this, workers face unsafe, cramped and hazardous conditions which often lead to work injuries and factory fires.

(Source: War on Want n.d.)

1 How might Item A be used to suggest that Marxism no longer has any relevance in the twenty-first century?
2 How might Item B be used to argue that Marxism is as relevant as ever?

Social class

Weber defined a social class as a group who share a similar **market situation**. By this, he meant that members of a social class receive similar economic rewards. Members of a social class also share similar **life chances** (see page 225). Weber agreed with Marx that there was a basic economic division between the property owners and those who sold their labour for wages; however, he also argued that there was a further division within each of these two groups. For example, owners of big businesses can potentially earn bigger profits than small businesses and so have a better market situation. Similarly, highly qualified white-collar workers can sell their labour at a higher price than manual workers with fewer qualifications. As a result, he suggested that in capitalist societies there are four main social classes.

1 **The propertied upper class** – The wealthy owners of big businesses.
2 **The property-less white-collar workers** – These have a better market situation than manual workers because of their skills and educational qualifications, and thus they form a middle class.
3 **The petty bourgeoisie** – Owners of small businesses. Unlike Marx, Weber did not see this class as disappearing or merging into the working class.
4 **The manual working class** – This class has the poorest market situation as they possess neither wealth nor valuable educational qualifications that could be used to improve their market situation.

Status

Though individuals may identify themselves as part of a social class, or in Marx's terms, develop 'class consciousness', Weber suggested that in some circumstances people with a common status situation may form a stronger group identity. Status refers to the distribution of social honour – in other words, how much respect a person receives from others and whether they are seen as superior or inferior to others. Status may be linked to a person's economic or class position but may also derive from other things such as their ethnicity, religion or lifestyle. For example, members of ethnic minorities may have a relatively low status because they face prejudice and discrimination even though they are wealthy in class terms. On the other hand, someone with a relatively low class position may achieve a high status because of their sporting achievements or through raising money for charity.

Weber argued that while social class may be relatively unimportant for many people as a source of identity, individuals are usually very aware of their status situation and tend to identify with others of a similar status. For example, in the caste system found in the traditional Hindu society in India, individuals are part of a hereditary caste from birth. The highest caste (Brahmins) enjoy their position not so much because of their wealth but because they are regarded as purer in religious terms than the lower castes.

Weber acknowledged that in capitalist societies class and status are closely linked as wealth and income are major sources of status. However, he pointed out that within social classes, status distinctions may be important. For example, in nineteenth-century British society, there was a divide between the landed aristocracy (who had the status of titles and wealthy ancestors) and the *nouveaux riches* (those who had only recently made their fortunes). The *nouveaux riches* were often looked down on, even though they might be incredibly wealthy.

Party

Weber defined parties as groups who were concerned with exercising power or influencing decision-making. In this sense, parties are much broader than conventional political parties. Parties might include groups such as trades unions that seek to improve the wages and conditions of specific groups of workers or pressure groups such as Greenpeace, the RSPCA or CND. Some parties are linked to class interests; for example, many trades unions represent groups within the working class. However, pressure groups often draw their members from all social classes. Some parties may also represent specific status groups; for example, the pressure group Stonewall campaigns for the rights of lesbian, gay and bisexual people.

Evaluation of Weberian theory

Weber's approach to stratification has been adopted by many sociologists as it allows them to create more complex and multi-dimensional models of how society is stratified. Weber points out that people may come together and identify with others not just on the basis of economic interests but also because of a shared status position or shared political goals. While such inequalities are often based on economic factors, it could be argued that they have much more to do with individuals' social status. Moreover, they may also be a basis for forming parties. For example, in the 1960s and 1970s the women's liberation movement tried to bring together women from all social backgrounds to fight for women's rights.

The main criticism of Weber's approach comes from Marxists, who argue that focusing on multiple social classes and different dimensions of inequality obscures the fundamental importance of class divisions in capitalist societies. Marxists argue that status distinctions within the working class are often encouraged as a means of 'divide and rule' by the ruling class, and that the really important political struggles are linked to the class struggle and conflicts over economic interests.

Despite these criticisms, Weber's ideas have had considerable influence on modern sociologists:

- **Multi-class models.** Most sociologists interested in social class today adopt a multi-class model rather than Marx's two-class model. For example, the Hope–Goldthorpe classification and the NS-SEC classification are largely based on Weber's idea of distinguishing occupational classes by their market situation.
- **Social mobility and life chances.** Weber's idea that social class affects life chances has influenced a whole variety of research on the link between social class and educational achievement, health inequalities and opportunities for social mobility.
- **New social movements.** A number of sociologists have argued that in the late twentieth and early twenty-first centuries, social class has become less important in politics. New social movements have arisen such as the women's movement, nationalist movements, peace movements and environmentalism. This could be seen to support Weber's view that parties and political conflicts will not always be based on a class struggle between the owners of property and the property-less, as claimed by Marx.

Activity: Class and status

Item A

Jessica Ennis with her gold medal for winning the heptathlon at the London Olympics in 2012. Jessica's father was a painter and decorator and her mother was a social worker. She graduated in 2007 from Sheffield University with a degree in Psychology.

Item B

Katie Price's father left her mother when Katie was four and so she took the surname Price from her stepfather, who was a builder. She left school at 16 with few qualifications and soon started posing as a topless model using the name Jordan. She has since made numerous TV appearances.

Item C

This photo shows injured war hero Ben Parkinson laying a wreath on Remembrance Sunday. He joined the army in 2000 and was injured by a bomb blast in Afghanistan in 2006. He can now walk on computerised legs that let him stand at nearly his old height.

1 Examine Items A–C. In each case, explain the source of status of the individuals portrayed.
2 Using the items and any other evidence, evaluate how far a person's social status in the UK today is linked to their social class position.

Feminism

Feminist theories have focused primarily on gender inequalities and are discussed further in the next chapter. However, some feminists have also been highly critical of traditional sociological theories of class for neglecting women and gender inequalities. Pamela Abbott (1990) criticises Goldthorpe's (1980) study of social mobility for completely ignoring women. Abbott argues that there is a need to study women's social mobility, as women's experiences of work are different from men. The fact that women actually have lower rates of absolute mobility because they have less chance of reaching top jobs helps to boost men's chances of upward mobility. This has encouraged more recent studies of social mobility to include both women and men in their research.

Some feminists also argue that social classifications such as the Hope–Goldthorpe scale are based around men's occupations and are not well suited to exploring the class situation of women. This has led some researchers to develop new classifications such as the Surrey scale (see below), which differentiates between women and men in different occupational classes more effectively.

Activity: Classifying women

The Surrey Occupational Class Schema

1 Higher professional
2 Employers and managers
3 Lower professional
4 Secretarial and clerical

5 Supervisors and self-employed manual
6a Sales and personal services
6b Skilled manual
7 Unskilled

The Surrey scale reflects the gendered nature of work, such as distinguishing between mainly male skilled manual jobs (left) and mainly female personal service jobs (right).

The Surrey Occupational Class Schema was developed by feminist sociologists Sara Arber, Angela Dale and Nigel Gilbert (1986) as an alternative to existing classifications, which were perceived to have a patriarchal bias. In the Surrey scale women are classified on the basis of their own occupations, whereas in other scales married women are often classified by their husbands' occupations. The Surrey scale reflects the gendered nature of work in society today. For example, Class 6 is divided into two: 6a (sales and personal services) is heavily female-dominated while 6b (skilled manual) is overwhelmingly male.

Critics of the Surrey scale argue that women's occupations are not necessarily a good guide to their class position because many women only work part-time or occupy jobs for short periods because they move in and out of work due to pregnancy or childcare. It can be argued that for many women with male partners, it is their partner's occupation that mainly determines the income and lifestyle of the rest of the household.

Ken Roberts (2011) argues that we can no longer assume that women share a class position with their male partners (if they have one). Today, more women remain single or form partnerships later in life, and divorce is much more common. Men also die earlier than women and women may be left with only limited occupational pensions. In view of this, women's life chances are more likely to depend on their own education and career rather than those of their husband or partner.

1 Compare the Surrey scale with the Hope–Goldthorpe scale (see page 223). What differences do you notice between the two scales?

2 What are the advantages and disadvantages of these methods of putting people into social classes? Consider:
   a) classifying men and women individually according to their own occupation
   b) classifying households according to the occupation of the main wage earner.

Postmodernism

Postmodernist theorists argue that class is losing its significance in contemporary society. They argue that theories of class developed by writers such as Marx and Weber in the nineteenth century to describe modern societies are no longer relevant, and that in the twenty-first century people see themselves much more as individuals than as part of a social class.

Australian sociologists Jan Pakulski and Malcolm Waters (1996) argue that in advanced capitalist societies people are now stratified by cultural rather than economic differences. This means that people now group themselves together according to symbolic values.

German sociologist Ulrich Beck (1992) argues that the class conflicts of early industrial societies concerned the distribution of wealth, reflecting the fact that many people suffered from poverty and lack of job security. Since the 1970s, in economically advanced societies, most people have enough to meet their material needs such as food and housing. This has led to a focus on new problems and conflicts in what Beck terms 'risk society'. By this, Beck means that the central problem of society is no longer creating and distributing wealth but of managing the risks created by science and technology, such as nuclear energy or environmental pollution.

Beck argues that many such risks affect everyone, rich and poor alike, and so people's awareness of social class and willingness to act together based on shared class interests has diminished. Instead, people have become individualised and more concerned with their personal interests. When people do come together to change things politically, it is more likely to be as part of temporary coalitions, as groups who act together because they have a concern about one issue and then break up when they achieve their goals or lose interest. Like Pakulski and Waters, Beck concludes that class is paling into insignificance and people are adopting much more individualised identities.

Section summary

Fill in the blanks, using the words given below.

Functionalist theories argue that stratification is _____ for society. For example, Parsons argues that the way that people are ranked in society reflects a _____ or set of shared beliefs about what is valuable and worthwhile. Similarly, Davis and Moore argue that social stratification helps with _____ because it ensures that the most talented individuals are placed in the most important positions in society. The New Right also agree that inequality in society is necessary and justified, though they argue in favour of _____, the idea that everyone should have the same chances to compete for unequal positions. New Right thinker Murray argues that the _____ or poorest people in society are not trapped in their class position because of lack of opportunities but because of their _____; for example, they lack motivation to better themselves by improving their skills or finding well-paid jobs. Both functionalist and New Right thinkers argue that modern societies are based on _____, meaning that people are recruited for the top positions on the basis of ability and qualifications.

Tumin criticises functionalist theories. He argues that, rather than stratification being based on consensus, it can create _____ between disadvantaged and privileged groups. Wilkinson and Pickett also criticise the idea that inequality is functional for society; they show that in industrial societies there is a _____ between high levels of social inequality and a higher incidence of a variety of social problems. Weber also saw society as based on conflict and argued that class was based on competition for _____ rewards. He argued that the higher social classes were those with the best _____ based on qualifications or other assets that would increase their earning power. Weber also argued that society was not only stratified by class but also by _____ and _____.

Marx argued that all societies have been based on _____ and that in capitalist societies there is a conflict between the _____ who own the means of production and the _____ who sell their labour for wages. Marx argued that eventually capitalism would be overthrown and replaced by _____, but first the working class would need to develop _____ or an awareness of their exploited situation. Some modern Marxists have argued that class divisions are widening as Marx predicted; for example, they claim that the middle class is disappearing as white-collar workers fall into the working class through a process of _____. Critics of Marx

Section summary (continued)

argue that there is little sign of the _____ that he predicted occurring in most capitalist societies, as most of the workers appear to accept their lot.

attitudes, bourgeoisie, class consciousness, class struggle, communism, conflict, correlation, economic, equality of opportunity, functional, market situation, meritocracy, party, proletarianisation, proletariat, revolution, role allocation and performance, status, underclass, value consensus

Practice questions

1 Outline ways in which inequalities of wealth and income are linked to other forms of social class inequality.   [20]

2 Assess the usefulness of Marxist theory for understanding social class inequalities in contemporary British society.   [40]

Understanding social inequalities: Gender

7b.1 Gender and life chances

Getting you thinking ...

1 Write a list of five jobs that you associate with men and a list of five jobs that you associate with women.
2 Use the internet to find out the average wages for these jobs.
3 What do you think are some of the key differences in the work that men and women do?

The concept of life chances was used by Max Weber in relation to social class (see page 225) but it can usefully be applied to a range of social groups. It describes the opportunities (chances) for advancement that an individual or social group possesses. It includes chances for educational attainment, health, material reward and social mobility. Education is often regarded as a key means of improving life chances as well as increasing social mobility. The following data on educational achievement suggests that females do at least as well and often better than males in educational achievement at different levels of qualifications:

- In 2013 universities reported a gender gap in admissions. Data from the Universities and Colleges Admissions Service (UCAS) shows that women are now a third more likely to enter higher education than men. Among UK residents, 134,097 women aged 19 and under were accepted to English universities in 2012, compared with 110,630 men.
- According to the Higher Education Funding Council for England (2014), of students who enter with A Level grades AAB, 79 per cent of female students go on to gain an upper second- or higher-class degree, compared to 70 per cent of male students. This difference is because of the proportion achieving upper seconds. The same proportion (20 per cent) of women and men achieve first-class honours degrees.
- GCSE exam results have consistently shown that girls out-perform boys. In 2014 the A*–C pass rate for girls was 73.1 per cent, compared to 64.3 per cent for boys.

Despite these positive outcomes for females in education, much of the evidence that we will explore in this chapter suggests that women have reduced life chances compared to men in a number of important areas. A key question to consider as we explore this data is why females' educational success does not translate into similar levels of achievement in the workplace.

7b.2 Patterns and trends in gender inequality and difference

Gender is considered to be a major source of inequality both in the contemporary UK and globally. In the public sphere of work and social life and in the private sphere of family life and relationships, males and females often encounter different experiences. These can translate into social inequalities; for example, gender differences in family roles can make it difficult for women to compete equally with men in the public sphere. On the other hand, men have reported wishing to spend more time with their children but being unable to do so because of the expectations that go with their role as main breadwinner. Gender inequalities can be seen in a range of areas.

Gender inequalities in work and employment

Over the past 40 years the number of women in employment has steadily increased, while the number of men in employment has decreased. There are other significant differences in the employment patterns of men and women relating to the type of work they do, how much they work and their pay and conditions of employment.

Facts and figures: Women in the labour market

A study by the Office for National Statistics (2013) gives an overview of some key differences in employment between men and women:

- Men with children are more likely to work than those without – the opposite of the picture for women.
- More men tend to work in the professional occupations, which are associated with higher levels of pay, than women.
- Women dominate employment within the caring and leisure occupations.
- Female graduates are more likely to work in a slightly lower skilled occupation group than men.
- Men make up the majority of workers in the top 10 per cent of earners for all employees, but the gap is lower for those under 30.

Evidence from a range of sources develops the points found by the ONS and indicates that, though here are more women in the labour market, they suffer significant inequalities in their experience compared to men:

- In the private business sector of employment, the gender pay gap is 24.8 per cent compared to the public sector, which is 17.1 per cent (Fawcett Society 2013).
- Self-employed women earn around 40 per cent less than self-employed men (Fawcett Society 2013).
- Women make up 20.4 per cent of directors on FTSE 100 boards and just 11.1 per cent of UK bank CEOs are women (Fawcett Society 2013).
- It will take 70 years at the current rate of progress to see an equal number of female and male directors of FTSE 100 companies (Equality and Human Rights Commission 2011).
- Up to 30,000 women are sacked each year simply for being pregnant (even though this is illegal) and each year an estimated 440,000 women lose out on pay or promotion as a result of pregnancy (UK Feminista n.d.).

- Women who work, with or without children, spend 15 hours a week on average doing chores, while men spend only five (UK Feminista n.d.).

Gender inequalities in income and wealth

There are also significant differences in the pay that women receive and the amount of wealth they hold:

- Cuts to state benefits disproportionately affect women as benefits typically make up a fifth of women's incomes, as opposed to a tenth of men's (UK Feminista n.d.).
- 22 per cent of women, compared to 14 per cent of men, have a persistent low income (Oxfam 2008).
- The income of retired women is less than 40 per cent of that of retired men (Oxfam 2008).
- Approximately 70 per cent of people in national minimum wage jobs are women (Low Pay Commission 2007).
- It is estimated that for each year a mother is absent from the workplace, her future wages will reduce by 5 per cent (UK Feminista n.d.).
- Women comprise more than 50 per cent of the world's population but own only 1 per cent of the world's wealth (United Nations 2014).

Gender inequalities in poverty

A range of evidence suggests that women are more likely than men to experience poverty, both in the UK and globally:

- According to a survey of more than 10,000 adults, one in four women will be living below the poverty line when they retire, compared to 12 per cent of men (Prudential 2011).
- Women make up half of the world's population and yet represent 70 per cent of the world's poor (Global Citizen 2014).
- Chant (2011) of the London School of Economics argues on her blog that women are particularly prone to experience 'time poverty' as a result of the multiple areas of work that they are engaged with, many of which are unpaid or underpaid. These activities make it difficult for them to get out of poverty through engaging in activities that would give them higher returns.
- 2009 figures produced for the Department of Work & Pensions show that 52 per cent of children living in lone-parent families are poor – and 90 per cent of lone-parent families are headed by women.

- According to the Women's Budget Group (2005), mothers frequently go without food, clothing and warmth in order to protect children (and partners) from the full impact of an inadequate income.

- The Trussell Trust (2014) also found that food poverty affects women and men differently, with many women going hungry in order to feed their children.

Women and Poverty: Experiences, Empowerment and Engagement – Joseph Rowntree Foundation (2008)

The Joseph Rowntree Foundation described their study as 'a project to empower women in poverty to take part in the policy-making process'. Their rationale for the study is outlined below:

'*While the Government has developed strategies to combat poverty, especially for children and pensioners, there is no strategy to challenge women's poverty specifically. This project sets out to support women living in poverty so that they could go beyond being "witnesses" to poverty to become actively involved in policy development. It allowed them to develop ideas to improve their lives and better understand how policy is made. The project's aims were:*

- *to encourage participation in and understanding of the policy-making process by women living in poverty, using participatory methods*
- *to help women living in poverty to understand policy debates, explore policy solutions and engage with policy-makers directly*
- *to improve the evidence base that informs policy-makers by enabling direct dialogue with women living in poverty*
- *ultimately, to develop more effective policies as a result.*'

In summarising their findings, they reported the following:

'*The participants were asked to define what poverty meant to them, and their responses reveal a complex and dynamic understanding that went beyond finances. The participants framed poverty as a human rights issue and defined poverty as an experience of social isolation. The impact of their poverty on their children was a central theme and the participants talked about sacrificing their own food, clothing, heat and other basic needs in order to put their families first.*

Their experiences of poverty ranged from pervasive disrespect from other members of their community to feelings of low self-esteem, lack of self-confidence and hopelessness. They felt that poverty affected their ability to be good parents, and expressed anguish at not being able to provide even the smallest of luxuries or treats for their children. Poverty was experienced as a constant sense of financial insecurity and instability and the lack of any real opportunity to improve their situation.'

Points to discuss and research

1 Is the Joseph Rowntree Foundation study an example of qualitative or quantitative research? Explain your answer and make a list of the strengths and weaknesses of using such as approach in this study.
2 In what ways did the women in the study define poverty and how did their experience go beyond financial issues?
3 How would different structural and social action theories explain the situation faced by these women?
4 Choose one of the theories you have discussed above. List some criticisms of your chosen theory.

Gender inequalities in social mobility

Social mobility is the movement of individuals, families or households within or between social strata in a society; for example, moving from the working class to the middle class would be an example of upward social mobility. There are clear variations in the levels of social mobility experienced between men and women and between women from different ethnicities:

- According to Li and Devine (2011), women are still less likely to be upwardly mobile and more likely to be downwardly mobile than men.

- Variations in mobility by gender and ethnicity have been noted by researchers Heath and Li (2014): black Caribbean men (39.3 per cent) and Chinese women (46.8 per cent) were found to experience lower rates of upward mobility than black Caribbean women (67.3 per cent) and Chinese men (56.9 per cent). Their study also showed that for second-generation south-Asian groups in the UK, men had benefited more from upward occupational mobility than women.

- The 2014 Global Gender Gap Report published by the World Economic Forum, which ranks countries according to how well they divide resources and opportunities among male and females, puts Iceland, Finland, Norway and Sweden at the top, with Britain lagging behind in 26th place. Of the four pillars used for assessment, the UK is ranked 33rd for political empowerment, 32nd for educational attainment, 46th for economic participation and opportunity and 94th for health and survival. These figures mark a deterioration in all areas compared to 2013.
- Savage (2011) studied social mobility in the 2000s and found men were 40 per cent more likely to climb the career ladder than women.
- Research conducted by the Equality and Human Rights Commission in 2011 found a decrease in women's participation in ten sectors of employment, most of which related to positions of high reward and/or status, including:
  - members of the Cabinet
  - National Assembly for Wales
  - local authority council leaders
  - public appointments
  - editors of national newspapers
  - chairs of national arts bodies
  - health service chief executives.

Women's average representation since 2003 in selected 'top jobs' across Britain

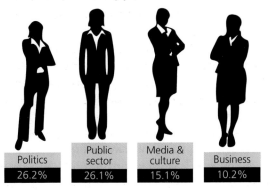

Politics	Public sector	Media & culture	Business
26.2%	26.1%	15.1%	10.2%

(Source: Equality Human Rights Commission 2011)

Contemporary sociologists tend to believe that it is useful to take a multi-dimensional approach when studying the experience of inequality. Doing so allows us to see the interplay between factors such as gender, social class, age and ethnicity to gain a more valid picture. Li and Devine used this approach in their study, 'Is social mobility really declining?' (2011). They used a range of sources including census data, the General Household Survey (GHS), the British Household Panel Survey (BHPS), the UK Longitudinal Household Study, and Health Surveys for England to study trends in social mobility. Key findings from their report showed that:

- Black African and black Caribbean women have experienced a 15–20 per cent fall in full-time employment rates over the past decade, while those for white women have remained stable.
- 39 per cent of Bangladeshi women and 35 per cent of Bangladeshi men work part-time, double the levels of two decades ago.
- The rates of part-time employment for Chinese and Indian men have doubled in the last ten years.
- 53 per cent of self-employed Pakistani men work in the transport industry, compared to 8 per cent of the rest of the population.
- Surveys of young British Muslim women have highlighted how employer discrimination has been a significant barrier to employment for those who wear the hijab and niqab notwithstanding their high levels of graduate and post-graduate qualifications.

Activity

The gender pay gap

1 In 2013 the gender pay gap widened for the first time in five years. In 2014 it stood at 19.1 per cent for all employees. Using the internet, research into the history of the gender pay gap since 1970 and make a diagram, graph or timeline showing how it has changed over time.

2 Using the internet, find the synopsis of the film *Made in Dagenham* and summarise the main concerns of the female Ford workers. Discuss the outcome of their campaign and its impact on equal pay. Why do you think there is still a gender pay gap?

3 Study the data below and the pie charts on page 265 and write a list of the main differences between male and female economic activity. What possible reasons do you think there are for those differences?

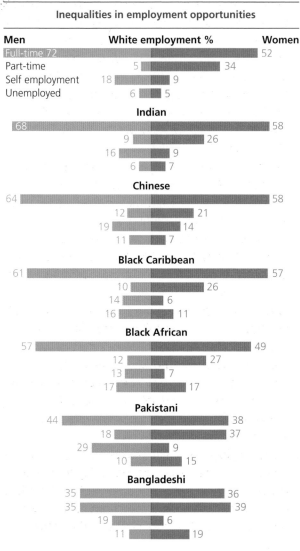

Inequalities in employment opportunities

Men	White employment %	Women
Full-time 72		52
Part-time 5		34
Self employment 18		9
Unemployed 6		5

Indian

68		58
9		26
16		9
6		7

Chinese

64		58
12		21
19		14
11		7

Black Caribbean

61		57
10		26
14		6
16		11

Black African

57		49
12		27
13		7
17		17

Pakistani

44		38
18		37
29		9
10		15

Bangladeshi

35		36
35		39
19		6
11		19

(Source: Sedghi 2014)

Gender inequalities in other areas of social life

Topic	Example of evidence of gender inequalities
Introducing socialisation, culture and identity	The role of gender in creating identities (see page 22)
Families and relationships	The role of families in reproducing gender inequalities (see page 98)
Youth subcultures	Youth subcultures as a response to gender inequalities, such as deviant subcultures (see page 121)
The media	Representations of gender in the media (see page 148)

Males and gender inequalities

As we have seen, much of the evidence on key indicators relating to life chances shows that men do better than women on most measures. Gender inequalities appear to disadvantage women more than men and are a persistent feature of life in the UK. However, as already discussed, good sociology involves taking a multi-dimensional approach to gain a valid picture across different social groups. When applied to the experience of males, there is evidence that working-class men have experienced a change in their circumstances over recent years, and in many cases a decline in their life chances. Mac an Ghaill (1994) referred to a 'crisis in masculinity' brought about by a number of social and economic changes including de-industrialisation and feminisation of the labour market. There is a concern that young men have no clear identity or path in life as a result of the growing equality of women, the lack of traditional male jobs and the expectations placed on men today. This has resulted in many young men displaying their masculinity in anti-social and criminal ways. It is argued that males, particularly from the working class, have become unclear about their identity and role in society. The concept has also been used to explain educational underachievement among working-class boys.

Education

- GCSE results consistently over a number of years show that girls in the UK gain more A*–C grade GCSEs compared to boys.
- Government data shows that boys are twice as likely to have a Special Educational Need and twice as likely to have literacy problems. They are also four times more likely to be excluded from school.
- Department of Education figures since 2008 have shown that white working-class boys are the largest underachieving group in education. The head of Ofsted said in 2012 that this was due to their anti-school subculture.
- Tests conducted in 2009 by the Programme for International Student Assessment, carried out by the Organisation for Economic Co-operation and Development (OECD), showed that boys lag a year behind girls at reading in every industrialised country.

Health

- Department of Health data from 2010 showed that on average females are likely to live four years longer than males.
- The ONS data in 2010 found that on average men develop heart disease ten years earlier than women.
- ONS data in 2011 found the rate of suicide for men is three times that of the number for women.
- Men are more likely than women to have an alcohol or drug problem. 67 per cent of British people who consume alcohol at 'hazardous' levels, and 80 per cent of those dependent on alcohol, are male. Almost three-quarters of people dependent on cannabis and 69 per cent of those dependent on other illegal drugs are male. (ONS 2001).

Work and income

- According to health and safety data collected in the UK, more than 95 per cent of the 200 people killed in the workplace every year are men.
- In 2010 the Office for National Statistics found that men in the UK work an average of 39 hours a week, compared with 34 for women.
- David Benatar, in his book *The Second Sexism* (2012), states that the least desirable and most dangerous jobs, and those with least pay and security, remain largely the domain of men.

Family life

Warin *et al.* (1999) found from their study of 95 families in Rochdale that the majority of fathers, mothers and teenage children believed that the father should be the breadwinner. They found that fathers felt under pressure to provide for their families and this was intensified by demands of teenage children for consumer goods and designer label fashions. Men in low-paid jobs and those who were sick, disabled or unemployed were frustrated and sad that they were unable to supply what their family wanted. The study claimed that the contribution of fathers tends to go unrecognised. According to the study, fathers nowadays are attempting to juggle the role of provider with the emotional support role traditionally provided by mothers. Men are turning into 'all-singing, all-dancing superdads'.

A report published by the Equal Opportunities Commission in 2007 called *The State of the Modern Family*, based on research tracking 19,000 children born in 2000 and 2001, found that:

- fathers are more likely to be employed, and to work longer hours, than men without dependent children
- 89 per cent of fathers are in employment, compared with 74 per cent of men without dependent children
- fathers are less likely to work part-time (4 per cent) than men without children (9 per cent), unlike mothers, who are more likely to work part-time (60 per cent) than women without children (32 per cent)
- UK fathers work the longest hours in Europe – an average 46.9 hours per week, compared with 45.5 hours in Portugal, 41.5 hours in Germany, 40 hours in Ireland and 35.5 hours in France
- around one in eight fathers in Great Britain work excessively long hours of 60 hours a week or more, and almost 40 per cent of fathers work 48 hours or more a week
- fathers working more than 50 hours a week spend less time looking after children than fathers working shorter hours
- the fact that men's earnings are generally a higher proportion of the family income than women's can limit the time men are able to spend with their children (different patterns emerge where women earn more)
- many employers still see flexible working or family-friendly working policies as something for women
- male-dominated workplaces, especially in traditional craft industries and occupations, are less likely to offer flexible working arrangements than other employers
- fathers often feel discouraged by workplace norms and culture from taking time off work for family, or expressing a wish for flexible work
- fathers' expectations about whether they would have access to work–life balance policies are lower than for mothers.

Activity

Men and gender inequality

1 Using the internet, conduct further research into the EOC study and write a summary outlining what it tells us about the role of fathers in UK society.
2 Describe the four types of fathers that were identified in the EOC study.
3 Identify four well-known fathers (for example, David Beckham and Brad Pitt) who correspond to the four types of dad in the EOC study and write a paragraph explaining why you think they fit these categories.

Evaluation of male inequalities

● Feminists tend to agree that male inequalities are minor in scale compared to those faced by women. According to Natasha Walter (2008), 'There is more debate to be had about the sacrifices that men make, but obviously I wouldn't go so far as to say that shows women hold all the cards. You have to look at the structural inequality. Sexism against men doesn't exist in the same way because of the way the system is balanced.'

● It may be argued that evidence shows that the labour market continues to favour men and that this is a crucial way in which inequality is maintained. In 2012 there were still 13,917,000 males in full-time employment, compared to 7,682,000 females, and 3,048,000 males compared to 7,533,000 females in part-time employment.

● Similarly, evidence shows that the gender pay gap persists and in almost every profession men still earn more on average than women.

Activity: Men in crisis?

Item A Warren Farrell

Warren Farrell (2013), men's rights author, refers to the 'glass cellar' when discussing male inequality. He argues that while there may be a glass ceiling for women: 'Of the 25 professions ranked lowest [in the US], 24 of them are 85–100 per cent male. That's things like roofer, welder, garbage collector, sewer maintenance – jobs with very little security, little pay and few people want them.'

Item B Diane Abbott

In 2013 Labour MP Diane Abbott, in a speech to the think tank Demos, warned about the emergence of a '*Fight Club*' generation where young men with reduced employment prospects would increasingly turn to lawlessness and other ways of proving themselves. She argued that 'this generation no longer asks itself what it means to be a man … I'm particularly troubled by a culture of hyper-masculinity – a culture that exaggerates masculinity in the face of a perceived threat to it. We see it in our schools; in the culture of some of our big business financial institutions; in some of our in inner cities; and even on many student campuses. At its worst, it's a celebration of heartlessness; a lack of respect for women's autonomy; and the normalisation of homophobia. I fear it's often crude individualism dressed up as modern manhood'. Abbott added, 'For many, what makes a man in modern Britain is his ability to flaunt consumer power. And for many of our young men, that will simply remain out of reach. What we teach many of our young boys is the price of everything, and the value of nothing.'

To deal with this 'masculinity crisis', Abbott calls for a strengthened role for fathers in family life, with father-friendly parenting classes, meaningful parental leave for men, and more conversations between fathers and sons about manhood.

Item C David Benatar

David Benatar, in his book *The Second Sexism* (2012), claims that sexism against men is a widespread yet unspoken problem. He argues that 'more boys drop out of school, fewer men earn degrees, more men die younger, more are incarcerated' and that the issue is so under-researched that it has become the prejudice that dare not speak its name. Benatar asserts that in most parts of the world, custody rights cases are stacked firmly against men: 'When the man is the primary care-giver of a child, his chances of winning custody are lower than when the woman is the primary care-giver … Even when the case is not contested by the mother, he's still not as likely to get custody as when the woman's claim is uncontested.'

He is also concerned about education as an area where men are falling behind. He cites tests in 2009 by the Programme for International Student Assessment that showed that boys lagged a year behind girls at reading in every industrialised country. Benatar argues that 'When women are underrepresented as CEOs of companies, that is deemed discrimination. But when boys are falling behind at school, when 90 per cent of people in prison are male, there's never any thought given to whether men are discriminated against.'

1 Read Item A and then, using the internet, compile a list of the 25 lowest-paid jobs in the UK and work out whether they are jobs mainly done by men or women to find out if there is a similar situation affecting men in the UK.

2 Read Item B and write a 300-word article in response to Diane Abbott either supporting or challenging her view.

3 Referring to Item C, consider how feminists would respond to David Benatar's views. Write a paragraph of analysis of what liberal, Marxist or radical feminists might say to David Benatar in a debate.

4 Looking across Items A, B and C, summarise the main arguments and identify the similarities and differences between the three views.

5 Make a table showing how you think that Marxism and functionalism would respond to the view that males are experiencing a crisis.

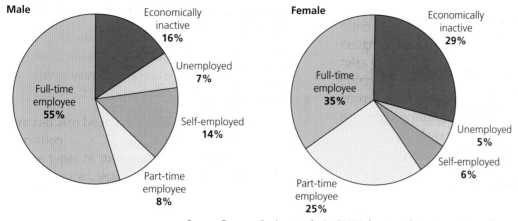

Source: Fawcett Society analysis, ONS Labour Market Statistics, Q3 2012.

Activity

Life chances for males and females

1 Using data from this chapter, make a chart summarising the key areas that show differences in life chances for males and females, such as the impact of gender differences in the workplace on men and women.

2 Consider how age, ethnicity and social class might have an impact on gender inequalities and make a list of key issues.

Check your understanding

Briefly define the following terms and give an example of each:

- public sphere
- private sphere
- multi-dimensional approach
- time poverty
- gender pay gap.

Section summary

Fill in the blanks, using the words given below.

Gender inequality can be seen in a number of areas of social life including work and employment, income and wealth, poverty and _____. Patterns of gender inequality have changed over the past 40 years as women's _____ has steadily increased. Evidence suggests that though there are more women in the _____ they suffer significant inequalities compared to men. There is a gender _____ where men earn more than women in a range of occupations. Approximately _____ of people in national minimum wage jobs are women. Men are more likely to occupy the top jobs in the labour market such as directors of companies. Women are more likely to experience _____ than men and research shows that women go without _____ and _____ to protect their families from the impact of inadequate income. Levels of social mobility between men and women also vary. According to Savage, men are _____ more likely to climb the career ladder than women. Contemporary sociologists believe that it is useful to take a _____ _____ when studying the experience of inequality to take account of other differences such as social class and _____ and the interplay between these factors.

40 per cent, 70 per cent, clothing, employment, ethnicity, food, labour market, multi-dimensional approach, pay gap, poverty, social mobility

7b.3 How can patterns and trends in gender inequality and difference be explained?

There are a number of theories that offer explanations for gender inequalities and difference including functionalism, the New Right, Marxism and Weberian theory. However, it is feminism that has provided the widest range of evidence when explaining gender inequalities.

The development of feminism

The main explanation for gender inequalities comes from feminism, or perhaps – some would argue – more accurately, feminisms. It is important to acknowledge that there are different strands of feminism but that most feminists share some common core beliefs. They generally agree that gender inequalities form the major division in society. Most feminists also see gender relationships as being based on conflict and exploitation of women by men. They share the view that much of culture has been shaped by men and neglects the contribution that women have made in society. Feminist thinkers have, at times, tried to introduce new vocabulary to counter the disregard that women have suffered in culture. The term 'malestream' is used in place of 'mainstream' to describe an approach where the point of view of men is taken as normal and usual. It is also used to describe the type of sociological research that concentrates on men, is usually conducted by men and then assumes that the findings can be generalised to women as well. Feminists believe that the experiences of women have been under-studied because sociology has until recently been dominated by men. A key aim of feminist sociologists is to redress this imbalance by focusing on issues that affect gender relationships and, in particular, the role of women in society. Some feminist sociologists have devised their own approach to carrying out research and most favour qualitative methods because they enable researchers to gain a fuller understanding of women's experiences. Feminist sociologists are also often keen to empower the women taking part in the research process because they believe that women have been oppressed in all areas of social life and they want to treat them as equals when they are doing their research.

It is argued that feminism can be seen as emerging in different phases of history and that each of these phases, known as waves, has focused on particular concerns.

First wave

The first wave of feminism emerged in the mid-1800s with the main aim of reforming the social and legal inequalities affecting women and, in particular, to achieve universal female suffrage (the right to vote for all women). The first wave of feminism was mainly led by middle-class women, often known as suffragettes. As well as campaigning to achieve the right to vote, they were concerned about the poor educational opportunities available to girls and fought for better secondary education and access to higher education. They also wanted to open up entry to the professions for women and to change the law that stated that once women were married, their wealth and income became the property of their husbands. In addition, women at this time could not divorce their husbands unless their husbands agreed and, once divorced, women were forced to give up any contact with their children. First-wave feminism wanted to see these inequalities addressed.

By the early 1900s, the first wave of feminism was seen as having achieved a number of its goals (the right to vote was granted to women in 1928 in the UK). Laws were passed that gave women greater access to higher education. The education system was reformed to give girls more rights; for example, girls were allowed to take part in formal national examinations. In terms of employment, women were granted greater access to some professions, such as medicine, which enabled some women to enter high-status careers. Other achievements included the recognition of married women's property rights and some improvement in divorce and child custody rights. Feminist campaigning subsided in the aftermath of these successes, though significant gender inequalities continued to exist in society and women were still socialised to be housewives and mothers rather than paid employees. These issues gave rise to the development of the next phase of feminist activity, though the tone and focus was very different.

Second wave

The second wave of feminism grew in the 1960s and 1970s and was linked to other campaigns for social change such as the civil rights movement, gay rights and anti-war protests. The focus of the second wave of feminism is summed up by their slogan 'The personal is political'. This refers to the view that many of the personal problems that women experience in their lives are the result of the unequal way that society is organised, which gives men more power over women. This leads to women's oppression in the private sphere of the home and to inequalities in the public sphere of work, politics and so on. Key issues for the second wave centred on achieving anti-discrimination policies and equal rights. Feminists aimed to raise women's consciousness about the problems that they faced in society, often through female-only meetings and groups that would provide support networks. These groups created a sense of 'sisterhood' whereby women felt responsible for each other and worked collectively to bring about social change. In the UK, a significant event in the second wave was the first National Women's Liberation Movement conference, held in 1970, which brought together many such groups.

The outcome was that four demands were established as the focus:
1 equal pay for equal work
2 equal education and job opportunities
3 free contraception and abortion on demand
4 free 24-hour nurseries.

In 1978 further demands were added:
- legal and financial independence for all women
- an end to discrimination against lesbians
- freedom for all women from intimidation by the threat or use of violence or sexual coercion regardless of marital status

- an end to all laws, assumptions and institutions that perpetuate male dominance and men's aggression toward women.

Though there was a clear list of demands that seemed to represent the women's movement at this time, different strands of feminism had emerged during the 1970s. Each had its own views on the causes of female inequalities, the relative importance of the different demands and the methods that should be used to achieve the demands. The main strands were liberal feminism, radical feminism and Marxist feminism and we will discuss these later in the chapter. The second wave of feminism achieved some success but most demands were not met and the divisions between the groups led to a fragmented movement and the second wave seemed to have lost its unity and momentum.

Third wave

The third wave of feminism developed from the mid-1990s onwards and is argued by some to be the current wave of feminism, though there is also a view that a fourth wave of feminism has now begun. Third-wave feminism is seen as a much more diverse and individualistic form of feminism which came into existence in the context of globalisation and an increasingly digital information society. It focuses less on laws and political processes and more on individual identity. It acknowledges that women come from many ethnicities, nationalities, religions and cultural backgrounds so there can be no single approach to feminism. It criticises second-wave feminism for expressing the interests of mainly white middle-class women. Third-wave feminists argue that they want women to define feminism for themselves in a way that reflects their own identities and belief systems. Despite this, third-wave feminists do have distinct goals; they focus on making changes to traditional ideas about sexuality and abolishing gender roles and stereotypes, including those seen in the media.

Fourth wave

The fourth wave of feminism is a contested concept, with some theorists arguing that it is not distinct from previous waves. Fourth-wave feminists claim that it is a movement that is necessary in the twenty-first century to take action against sexism and a range of inequalities facing girls and women across the globe. According to Kira Cochrane (2013), 'It's defined by technology: tools that are allowing women to build a strong, popular, reactive movement online.' Fourth-wave feminists claim that they use the internet to bring about change wherever they see the need by means of online petitions and direct action. They point to a number of examples of new feminist activism to support their claim that they are a powerful force in challenging sexism:

- the success of the Everyday Sexism Project, which began as a social media campaign in 2012 with the aim of 'documenting experiences of sexism, harassment and assault to show how bad the problem is and create solidarity'
- the introduction of an activism badge for Girl Guides under the heading 'Go For it! Be the change'
- the growing influence of online organisations such as Mumsnet – a survey of Mumsnet users in 2013 found that 59 per cent consider themselves to be feminists
- UK Feminista's campaign against supermarkets displaying lads' mags.

> ### Activity
>
> #### The waves of feminism
>
> 1 Using the internet, find the timeline of the Women's Liberation Movement (British Library n.d.). Make a list of ten events from the timeline that you think were the most important in bringing about greater gender equality.
> 2 Make your own timeline showing the development of the four waves of feminism and include the key ideas that characterised each of the four waves.
> 3 How do these ideas link with what was happening more widely in society at each wave such as wars, economic changes and so on? (Internet sources such as BBC History and the British Library website will help you.) You could add these to your timeline.
> 4 Draw a diagram or poster showing the similarities and differences between the first and second waves of feminism.

Different strands of feminism

As mentioned above, the second wave of feminism saw the development of three main strands of feminist theory and these remain a useful way of distinguishing between some of the different viewpoints held by feminists.

Liberal feminism

Liberal feminists are focused on obtaining equal opportunities and equal rights for males and females in society in areas such as the workplace, education and politics. They argue that gender inequalities are mainly a result of gender role socialisation and unfair laws and practices that reinforce discrimination between men and women, rather than innate, biological differences. Liberal feminists believe that changes in the norms and values that reinforce gender divisions in society will bring about equality and they regard legislation as one way of achieving this. They would point to the Equal Pay Act and Sex Discrimination Act as evidence of the success of liberal feminist campaigning.

Oakley (1974) argues that gender role socialisation in the family is an important area where gender inequality takes root from a young age. She believes that this occurs through processes such as manipulation and canalisation which teach children expected norms and values for their sex. Manipulation refers to the encouragement of behaviour that is seen as gender appropriate – for example, girls being dressed in a 'feminine' way and attention being paid to their appearance. Canalisation relates to the 'channelling' of children towards toys and activities seen as appropriate for their gender. This promotes different activities between boys and girls that will teach or reinforce accepted gender behaviour. Children learn their gender identity through internalising behaviour experienced in the family – for example, imitation of parents, parents discouraging gender-inappropriate behaviour such as crying in boys, parents adopting different modes of speech for male and female children and parents assigning gender-specific chores to children. This gender role socialisation is then reinforced and developed by other agents of socialisation such as the education system and the media.

Oakley's work has been praised for its endurance in still being able to provide explanations for gender differences that continue to be evident in society. However, there have been a number of criticisms:

- Postmodernist ideas suggest that gender identities are no longer fixed and that there are a range of masculinities and femininities to choose from; therefore, there is no longer a clear set of gender norms for children to be socialised into. This means that Oakley's views are out of date and, therefore, lack temporal validity.
- Oakley seems to regard children as passive recipients of gender role socialisation. It has been argued that at least there is a process of negotiation between parents and children. Theorists such as Connell go further and contend that there is resistance to gender role socialisation as some children actively go against traditional gender stereotypes.

Liberal feminists believe that equality can be achieved by legal and wider cultural reforms. Most liberal feminists would agree that progress has already been made and they are optimistic about further improvements in the future. Liberal feminists do not see men as oppressors and are usually happy to work with them to bring about change. Sue Sharpe's studies into girls' priorities may be used as evidence of changing gender norms and values and also supports the view that gender roles are socially constructed rather than the product of natural biological factors.

Evaluation of liberal feminism

- Radical and Marxist feminists would argue that liberal feminists fail to explain how males and females come to hold different levels of power in the family and more widely in society. Radical feminists would explain this by referring to patriarchy and Marxist feminists would cite capitalism.
- Some other forms of feminism take issue with liberal feminism's focus on reforming existing structures in society and argue that more revolutionary change is needed to bring about equality.
- It has been argued that liberal feminists are overly optimistic and positive about their achievements. For example, despite the Equal Pay Act of 1970, there has continued to be a significant gender pay gap throughout the years, which in 2014 stood at 10 per cent.
- Critics argue that liberal feminism is a middle-class movement that represents the interests of educated, professional women but fails to address the concerns of a wider range of women such as those from minority ethnic groups or the working class.

Marxist feminism

Marxist feminists believe social class affects the life chances of women and it is a key factor in the relationship between men and women. They are heavily influenced by Marxist theory but believe that it is necessary to combine these views with a feminist approach to highlight the way in which capitalism is an economic system that leads to the oppression of women. They argue that the family is a patriarchal institution and that women's position in the family, as wives and mothers, results in them being exploited by capitalism. Gender inequalities in society are maintained because women are encouraged to accept the dominant ideology that the nuclear family is a natural family form and that any inequalities and differences between men and women in society are fair and legitimate because capitalism is presented as a meritocratic system. Marxist feminists argue that women play a central role in the family through their domestic labour and, in doing so, serve the needs of capitalism in a number of ways:

- They reproduce the next generation of workers and socialise (or, as Marxist feminists would view it, brainwash) them into norms and values that benefit capitalism by encouraging the children to be obedient and hard-working. Boys are brainwashed to believe that their role is to become breadwinners and girls learn that their primary role is as housewives. Feeley (1972) argues that the family teaches children to submit to a form of parental authority that is patriarchal. She claims that they emerge from family life preconditioned to accept their place in the capitalist hierarchy of power and control. She believes that the family is 'designed to teach passivity not rebellion'. The family socialises its members into accepting traditional gender roles and the view that it is 'natural' for men and women to get married and engage in separate roles and jobs in the home – an attitude that is passed down from generation to generation. For Marxist feminists, such a family ideology supports patriarchy since it suggests that men and women should have different roles in the family and society that lead to the subordination of women to men.
- Women's domestic work is unpaid, which benefits capitalism since only one wage has to be paid and the wife is then dependent upon her husband's wage. Benston (1972) argues that a wife keeps her husband in good running order by feeding and caring for him and that this is essential to the smooth running of capitalism. In addition, the fact that a man must provide for his wife and children means that he is less likely to challenge the capitalist system. Benston believes that the unpaid domestic labour of women helps to support the capitalist system. She contends that if women were paid a wage for their work, there would have to be a massive redistribution of wealth. Benston is highly critical of the nuclear family and women's role within it and sees it as a stabilising force in capitalist society.
- Women soothe the stresses and frustrations of proletariat men after a hard day at work. Ansley

Just Like a Girl: How Girls Learn to be Women: from the Seventies to the Nineties – Sharpe (1994)

In this research, Sue Sharpe interviewed young women to find out about their priorities. Her findings are useful when investigating changing gender roles and the extent to which progress has been made in achieving greater equality between men and women.

Sharpe compared the attitudes of working-class girls in London schools in the early 1970s and then again in the 1990s. She found that the girls she studied in the 1990s were more confident, more assertive, more ambitious and more committed to gender equality. Sharpe found that the main priorities of the girls from the 1970s were 'love, marriage, husbands and children'. However, by the 1990s this had changed to 'job, career and being able to support themselves' especially in the event of a breakdown of marriage. They saw education as the main route to a good job. The girls in the 1990s also had less positive attitudes towards marriage. They had witnessed adult relationships breaking up around them, and had seen women coping alone, in a 'man's world'.

The research for *Just Like a Girl* was first conducted in four schools in Ealing in 1972. In 1991 Sharpe revisited the schools and replicated the study with another group of girls. She was interested in finding out about girls' attitudes to education, work and marriage.

Education

In the 1972 study, 67 per cent of girls wanted to leave school at 16 or earlier. In the later study, 67 per cent wanted to stay in education at least until 18. In the earlier study, girls considered it 'unfeminine' to work hard at school. By the 1990s, other studies showed that it was the boys who considered it 'unmasculine' to concentrate on their studies. Since the 1970s, girls' underachievement in schools has reduced and it is now boys who are underachieving. Girls are able to study a greater range of subjects at school, partly as a result of equal opportunities programmes to reduce gendered subject choice.

Work

In 1972, only 37 per cent of the workforce was female; now it is around half. In the 1970s, girls' ambitions were generally limited to office work and other perceived 'women's work'. By the 1990s, there had been a widening of aspirations, though science and technology continues to be male dominated. In the 1972 study, work was seen almost entirely in instrumental terms of increasing the household income. In the 1990s, it was seen more in terms of personal development and achieving independence. For the girls in the 1990s, the expectation or desire to do office work or become a shop assistant had significantly diminished and some girls showed an interest in car mechanics, engineering or firefighting. However, the girls still largely expected to do work that could be described as 'women's work', such as teaching, health and social care work, beauty therapy, working with children and clerical work in banks.

Marriage

The 1990s girls wanted to marry later and fewer of them wanted to have children. A higher number thought work and independence were more important than marriage. The 1990s girls expected that husbands or partners would help with housework and childcare. However, they expressed the feeling that the idea of the 'new man' was a bit of a joke. The young women in the later study anticipated a future in which they were likely to end up juggling work and domestic life like their mothers before them.

Conclusion

In many ways, Sharpe's study can be used as evidence of changing gender roles and so supports liberal feminist views. A comparison of the two studies shows that females' priorities have changed in the twenty years between them. It is likely that this is as a result of a variety of factors including the impact of feminism on attitudes and legislation, changes to the labour market (the feminisation of the labour market) and perhaps a more postmodernist outlook that sees some blurring of the more traditional aspects of gender identities. The 1991 study also revealed that equality between the sexes has not yet been achieved and that men and women still occupy different gender roles in society.

Points to discuss and research

1 Make a poster or chart outlining the main differences in findings between Sharpe's two studies.
2 Make a list of possible reasons for the changes in attitudes between the 1970s and the 1990s.
3 Make a list of strengths and weaknesses of Sharpe's research.
4 In pairs, conduct your own research in your sixth form to find out if girls' attitudes today seem similar or different to those in Sharpe's 1991 study. Use a sample of 10–15 participants to gather your data.
5 What factors might explain continuing gender inequalities in education, work and relationships? List and explain three.

(1976) sees women as acting as a 'safety valve' and talks of women as being 'the takers of shit' as husbands return home having been exploited at work and take their frustrations and anger out on their wives. She contends that, 'When wives play their traditional role as takers of shit, they often absorb their husbands' legitimate anger and frustration at their own powerlessness and oppression. With every worker provided with a sponge to soak up his possibly revolutionary ire, the bosses rest more secure.' Ansley, therefore, demonstrates the important role that women play in maintaining capitalism.

- Because of women's unpaid domestic labour, they are available to work outside the home as a reserve army of labour for capitalism. Bruegel (1979) argues that the family is central to women's oppression and points to the way that the ruling class use women to join the workforce when needed and send them back to the role of full-time housewife when not required. Marxist feminists claim that the situation faced by women in the recent economic recessions experienced in the UK and elsewhere shows that women are the ones most affected by redundancies, low pay and job insecurity.

Study

The Power of Women and the Subversion of the Community–Dalla Costa and James (1972)

Marxist feminists are concerned about the way that the unpaid domestic labour provided by women oppresses and exploits them at the same time as propping up capitalism. They argue that if women were paid for the work they do in the family, there would have to be a massive redistribution of wealth that would greatly reduce the wealth of the capitalist class (see Benston above).

In 1972, Mariarosa Dalla Costa and Selma James published *The Power of Women and the Subversion of the Community*. It launched the 'domestic labour debate' by drawing attention to how the unpaid housework and other caring work women do contributes to the economy. A debate followed about whether full-time caring was 'work' or a 'role', and whether it should be compensated with a wage. In the same year, James founded the International Wages for Housework Campaign with a core demand of money paid from the State for unwaged work in the home and in the community. As well as highlighting the need for wages for domestic work, the campaign also drew attention to the way that capitalist economies rely on the exploitation of women and how this increases their profits.

James has continued the campaign for wages for domestic work and from 1985 she coordinated the International Women Count Network, which was successful in securing the decision from the United Nations that governments should measure and value unwaged work in their national statistics. In 2006, Venezuela amended its constitution with an Article that recognises work in the home as an economic activity. Article 88 declares: 'The State guarantees equality and equity between men and women in the exercise of their right to work. The State recognizes work in the home as an economic activity that creates added values and produces social welfare and wealth. Housewives are entitled to Social Security.'

Points to discuss and research

1 Should domestic work be paid in the UK? Write a list of arguments for and against.
2 Find out about the campaign for a Citizen's Income. Write a 300-word article outlining what it is and either promote it or argue against it.
3 Would a Citizen's Income address the concerns of Marxist feminists about women's unpaid labour? Write a paragraph explaining why/why not.

Evaluation of Marxist feminism
- Marxist feminists tend to be criticised for placing too much emphasis on social class and not paying attention to other factors that may impact on women's lives such as ethnicity or age.
- Postmodernist thinkers are also critical of the focus on class as they believe that it is no longer a significant social division.

- Radical feminists are critical of the emphasis on capitalist exploitation. They argue that patriarchy is a more significant form of exploitation that predates capitalism and has existed in all known societies, not just capitalist ones.
- Some theorists have questioned the usefulness of Marxist feminism as it relies on a revolution to bring about change and that does not seem to be happening.

271

Radical feminism

Radical feminists believe that it is patriarchy not capitalism that is the main source of oppression for women. They argue that society is run by men and in the interests of men. As a result, men are advantaged in every area of society and have no interest in giving up any of their power and control to women. Radical feminists believe that gender inequality is the outcome of the collective efforts of men to dominate, control and exploit women. Radical feminists also tend to believe that only revolutionary change can offer the possibility of female liberation.

Radical feminists see the family as central to the oppression of women. They argue that there has always been a gender division of labour that has served to reinforce male domination, as it is men who define ideas about women's 'natural' roles through establishing a patriarchal ideology. Some radical feminists argue that there is also a biological element to women's oppression because it is women who carry, give birth to and feed a child, and this has contributed to their position in society. However, radical feminists do not accept that biological differences should mean that women are treated unequally. Millett (1970) argues that men originally acquired power over women because of biological factors (i.e. women who were frequently pregnant could not make the same contribution to society as men), but she suggests that modern technology has provided developments such as the contraceptive pill and modern machinery that have meant that men can no longer legitimate their power and domination.

Radical feminists believe that men are prepared to defend their power at all costs and will use violence against women to control them and maintain their domination. Johnson's (1995) concept of patriarchal terrorism can be used to explain violence that is the result of 'patriarchal traditions of men's right to control "their" women'. It is a form of terroristic control of wives by their husbands that involves the systematic use of not only violence but also economic subordination, threats, isolation and other control tactics. Radical feminists point to the level of domestic violence across the world as evidence of the broad nature of patriarchal aggression. The issue has been widely recognised and the World Health Organization reported in 2013 that the incidence of women who had experienced physical or sexual abuse from an intimate partner in their lifetime was 30 per cent globally and 25.4 per cent in Europe.

Some radical feminists believe that men also use patriarchal ideology to enforce compulsory heterosexuality as a way of maintaining their control. Some radical feminists advocate separatism in the form of political lesbianism as a choice that women can make to liberate themselves from men and avoid (literally) sleeping with the enemy. During the second wave of feminism, radical feminist theorist Ti-Grace Atkinson stated that, 'Feminism is the theory; lesbianism is the practice.' This has been a controversial idea among feminists and led to divisions within the movement.

The traditional nuclear family is also viewed as a means to ensure male dominance through female subordination to men in their unpaid domestic labour as housewives and mothers, forcing them to be dependent upon men.

Study

Familiar Exploitation: A New Analysis of Marriage in Contemporary Western Societies–Delphy and Leonard (1992)

Coming from a radical feminist perspective, Delphy and Leonard propose the view that the family is an institution that plays a major part in the oppression of women. They see the family as an economic system in which men benefit from, and exploit, the work of women. The key to this exploitation is that women work for the male head of the household and in this relationship he holds the economic power. In looking at the family as an economic unit, they identify a number of characteristics:

- Family-based households have a social structure that involves two types of roles: head of household and their dependants.
- The male head of household makes the decisions about the allocation of roles and tasks and even where there is negotiation, he has the final say.
- Members of the household work without pay for the head of household and wives also carry out sexual and reproductive work. Domestic work is the responsibility of females even where males help out.
- The economic relationships in the family do not usually involve formal contracts or bargaining but mainly use informal methods of negotiation. For example, 'Wives and children have to study their

Study (continued)

husbands and fathers closely and handle them carefully so as to keep them sweet.'

- Dependants often receive payment in kind from the head of household in the form of clothing and so on rather than money.
- When dependants, particularly wives, have paid employment outside the home, they still have to carry out household tasks, or pay someone else out of their wages to do the housework or childcare for them.

Delphy and Leonard argue that men are the main beneficiaries of the economic arrangements within the family. They accept that most men do some housework, but point out that it is usually women who do such tasks. Delphy and Leonard believe that wives contribute much more work to family life than their husbands but get fewer benefits. Men hold the responsibility for family finances and have the 'decision-making power'. Delphy and Leonard accept

that women can attempt to resist the domination of their husbands, but economic and social factors make it difficult for women to leave such relationships.

Delphy and Leonard support their argument with empirical evidence and this may be seen a strength of their work. They use a number of already existing studies of British factory workers and their families and data from Delphy's own studies of French farming families. This evidence all shows that men hold a dominant position and women undertake a disproportionate share of the work in the family. However, the British studies that they used are dated and focus on working-class families.

Points to discuss and research

1 Identify similarities and differences between Delphy and Leonard's view and that of Marxist feminists.
2 What are the strengths and weaknesses of Delphy and Leonard's research?

Evaluation of radical feminism

- Radical feminists tend to talk about 'the family' without acknowledging variations in family life between social classes and different ethnic groups. For example, many women from matrifocal African-Caribbean family networks regard their experience of family life as supportive and positive.
- Radical feminists see women as sharing common interests because they are female but it has been argued that social class and ethnicity are important sources of inequality and difference between women. For example, the experiences and life chances of upper-class females are significantly different to those of working-class females and it could be argued that working-class women have more in common with working-class men than they do with upper-class women. Similarly, the experience of women in Britain will be very different to the lives of women across the globe.
- Liberal feminists would argue that the position of women in society has changed over time and that this is ignored by radical feminists.
- Radical feminists have been accused of over-emphasising the factors that separate women from men. It is argued that men and women work cooperatively together in a range of ways in society, including campaigning for gender equality.

Men and women also report having very fulfilling family relationships based on more equal division of labour than previous generations so, it is argued, improvements are happening.

Activity

Comparison of feminist theories

1 Make a grid listing the key issues and solutions that concern liberal, Marxist and radical feminists. Add a column to show key criticisms for each.
2 Make a banner for each feminist perspective showing what they believe in and their demands for change.

Intersectionality: Sylvia Walby

Sylvia Walby offers a different and unique set of ideas that combine aspects of both Marxist and radical feminism. Walby has been writing about feminism since the 1980s and continues to write about feminist issues in the twenty-first century.

In the 1980s, Walby wrote about the effect on women of the combined systems of patriarchy and capitalism. Later, she developed the concept of triple systems of oppression, which also included the impact of racism. More recently, Walby has developed her ideas further to embrace the concept of intersectionality, which recognises the complex interplay between different forms of social inequality including class, gender, ethnicity, religion, nationality and so on.

In *Theorizing Patriarchy* (1990), Walby produces a detailed analysis of the concept of patriarchy which moves beyond other feminist views. She is critical of radical feminism for seeing patriarchy as universal and unchanging. She is also concerned that the radical feminist approach ignores the impact of class and ethnicity on gender. Walby believes that Marxist feminism is problematic because it focuses too much on capitalism and fails to explain women's exploitation in non-capitalist societies. Walby is also critical of liberal feminism because it does not consider the way that the structure of society affects gender relations.

Walby sees the concept of patriarchy as important in providing an understanding of gender inequality. She believes that patriarchy is not fixed and changes over time. She argues that it has evolved from 'private patriarchy', where women were limited to the domestic sphere of home and family, to 'public patriarchy', in which women have entered the public sphere of employment, politics and so on, but continue to suffer disadvantage.

According to Walby, this disadvantage happens through six patriarchal structures in society, which restrict women and maintain male domination:

1 **Paid employment**. The patriarchal ideology that 'a woman's place is in the home' means that women face discrimination from employers and restricted access into careers. When women work, they experience horizontal and vertical segregation with low pay and low status.

2 **The household**. Women are exploited in the family and take primary responsibility for housework and childcare even if they are working in full-time paid employment.

3 **The state**. This acts in the interests of men rather than women in terms of taxation, welfare rules, the weakness of laws protecting women, and so on.

4 **Cultural institutions such as the media**. These represent women in a narrow set of social roles, such as sex objects or mothers and housewives. These representations reinforce patriarchal ideology.

5 **Sexuality**. A double standard is applied to men and women. Men are 'applauded' for having many sexual partners, whereas women are condemned for the same behaviour.

6 **Violence against women**. Violence, the threat of violence and sexual assault are used by men to control women.

Walby also points out that in contemporary societies different groups of women may be exploited by different combinations of public and private patriarchy through the intersection of social inequalities. For example, British African-Caribbean women are more likely to experience public patriarchy, and British Muslim women are more likely to experience private patriarchy.

In her study *Gender Transformations* (1997), Walby argues that though there have been numerous social changes affecting gender relations, patriarchy continues to exist in new forms in Britain. Walby believe that young women have made important gains compared to older women. Older women may still experience private patriarchy whereas younger women tend to have better educational qualifications and are less likely to accept gender discrimination at work. They also have greater sexual freedom and are more likely to be involved in environmental and social movements, giving them more involvement in political processes. However, some young women are still poorly qualified and they may be heavily dependent upon a husband or they may be single parents experiencing poverty. Even well-qualified women still find it difficult to reach the highest positions in the occupational structure as vertical segregation continues to have a significant presence in the labour market.

Overall, Walby believes that even though young, well-educated women have made progress in areas of social life, patriarchy continues to have an impact on their lives. In the case of poorly qualified young and older women, the restrictions of patriarchy, she believes, are even greater.

Evaluation of Walby

- A strength of Walby's work is that it can be viewed as improvement on other feminist theory as it incorporates aspects of different feminisms.
- Walby has developed and refined her ideas over time and she has incorporated social changes into her analysis.
- Stacey has criticised Walby for over-emphasising the influence of social structure on behaviour. Instead, she argues that women negotiate such systems and are more active than Walby assumes.

Preference theory: Catherine Hakim

Catherine Hakim (2006) is extremely critical of most feminist theories. She argues that women are not the victims of unfair employment practices but that they have preferences and make rational choices in terms of the type of work they do; for example, they choose part-time work in order to manage childcare and housework because they *choose* to put childcare first. She argues that a lack of affordable and available childcare is not a major barrier to women getting jobs, because mothers prioritise childrearing over employment. In other words, women are not as committed to their careers as men are and inequalities in the workplace are the result of the different behaviour and attitudes of men and women.

Hakim contends that there is solid evidence that men and women continue to differ in their attitudes to work and labour market behaviour, and that these differences relate to broader differences in life goals and the relative importance of family life and careers to men and women. According to Hakim, preference theory is the only theory that can explain patterns and trends such as the glass ceiling, the continuing pay gap and occupational segregation.

Hakim proposes three classifications of women's work–lifestyle preferences in the twenty-first century:

- **Home-centred.** Family life and children are the main priorities throughout life for this group, and they prefer not to work – 20 per cent of women in Britain.
- **Adaptive.** This group is most diverse and includes women who want to combine work and family, plus drifters and those with unplanned careers, who want to work, but are not totally committed to their career – 60 per cent of women in Britain.
- **Work-centred.** Childless women are concentrated here. Their main priority in life is employment or equivalent activities in the public arena: politics, sport, art, and so on – 20 per cent of women in Britain.

According to Hakim, the majority of men are work-centred, compared to only a minority of women. Preference theory suggests that men will retain a dominant position in the labour market, politics and so on because only a minority of women are prepared to prioritise their jobs in the way that men do.

Preference theory supports the functionalist human capital theory (see below) as it suggests that women are not as committed as men to paid work.

Evaluation of Hakim

- Hakim has been heavily criticised by a number of other feminists. For example, Ginn *et al.* (1996) point out that it is often employers' attitudes, rather than women's attitudes, that confine women to the secondary labour market of low-paid, part-time and insecure work.
- Many feminists criticise Hakim for ignoring the power of patriarchy to subordinate and oppress women. It is argued that patriarchal ideology has a powerful effect on shaping women's preferences.

Functionalism

Functionalism is a perspective that is based on the view that society is made up of interdependent parts, each of which contributes to the functioning of society as a whole. Functionalists tend to argue that men and women have separate social roles that are based on biological differences and that these different roles contribute to the smooth running of society. Functionalists suggest that since women give birth and nurse a child, it is natural that they will take care of it. This leads to a division of labour between men and women, in which women are more involved in domestic activities such as preparing meals and maintaining a home. Men, therefore, act as breadwinners and other economically dominant roles. Murdock (1949) studied gender roles in over 200 societies and found that women were located in the home because of their biological function of bearing children and because their physique meant that they were less able than men to perform strenuous tasks. He concluded that this gender division of labour was evident in all of the societies he studied and therefore universal because they were functional. Parsons and Bales (1955) referred to men as having the 'instrumental', practical role while women have the 'expressive' caring role. These separate roles are seen as contributing to the smooth running of society but they also explain why men and women have different experiences in the labour market and elsewhere in the public sphere.

Human capital theory contends that the wage gap and other employment-related differences can be explained by the amount of human capital an individual or group of workers develop through the knowledge and skills they have obtained, often through education and training. It is argued that personal incomes vary according to the amount of investment that is made in developing human capital.

Rastogi (2002) sees human capital as 'knowledge, competency, attitude and behaviour embedded in an individual'.

The theory has been used to support functionalist views on meritocracy with the argument that men and women serve different roles and functions in society and are rewarded in different ways. Men are work-oriented and committed to their jobs whereas women choose to prioritise their roles as homemakers and caring for family over their careers. As a result, gender inequalities in the workplace arise and are a legitimate outcome as women develop lower levels of human capital than men.

Evaluation of functionalism

- Feminists such as Oakley have shown that gender roles are socially constructed rather than based on biological differences.
- Human capital theory ignores the structural constraints in society that may disadvantage women.
- The functionalist perspective is criticised because it has not kept pace with social changes in gender roles.
- Functionalism tends to refer to the experience of white middle-class people and neglects other social groups.

The New Right

New Right theory developed from the 1970s as a political and social movement that sought to influence government policies and public attitudes. It continues to exert power in the British Conservative Party and through the journalism of newspapers such as the *Daily Mail*. There are also a small number of sociologists who align themselves with New Right ideas. New Right thinkers are often regarded as neo-functionalists as they hold a number of similar views to functionalists. In terms of gender relations, both approaches believe that gender roles are biologically determined and that men and women should play different roles in society, and much of their discussion centres on women's roles in the family. Men should take the roles in the public sphere of work and politics and so on, and women should be located within the private domestic sphere. Theorists of both approaches argue that the conventional nuclear family and the gender division of roles within it are desirable and based on human nature. Both functionalists and the New Right believe that the conventional nuclear family is essential to having a stable, ordered society and any move away from it could lead to social breakdown and disorder. Traditional gender roles are important for the wellbeing of individuals and society. The male breadwinner provides for the economic needs of the family and this means that they will not need support from the state. Having a female housewife means that the male breadwinner is supported, and children will not suffer from maternal deprivation which could lead to problems in later life for them and for society.

The main difference between functionalists and New Right theorists is the era in which they were writing. The most prominent period for functionalism was the early to mid-twentieth century, when the nuclear family was seen to be widespread, whereas the New Right approach dates from the more recent period, when the nuclear family was seen as under threat. The focus for the New Right is on achieving a return to traditional family values and the traditional gender roles that accompany this. They are particularly concerned that changes in gender roles have led to social problems such as an increase in lone-parent families headed by women who do not socialise their children appropriately.

New Right thinkers argue that the fundamental differences between men and women mean that men should be the decision-makers and women should take a subordinate role in supporting men. The New Right, therefore, believe that men and women will not have the same experience in the public sphere and this is why there are gender 'inequalities', though the New Right would tend to describe these as natural differences rather than inequalities.

The New Right on gender roles: Schlafly's response to feminism

New Right campaigner Phyllis Schlafly, writing from the 1970s onwards in response to feminist demands, proposes an alternative approach to gender relations that reflects New Right views. She acknowledges that marriage can be difficult but sees it as the most fulfilling role for women and states that 'Marriage and motherhood have their trials and tribulations, but what lifestyle doesn't? ... The flight from home is a flight from self, from responsibility, from the nature of woman, in pursuit of false hopes and fading fantasies' (2003).

The issue	Schlafly's view of the feminist stance	Schlafly's stance
Women's roles	'[T]he women's liberation movement [believes] … that there is no difference between male and female … and that all those physical, cognitive, and emotional differences you think are there, are merely the result of restraints imposed by a male-dominated society … The role imposed on women is … inferior, according to the women's liberationists.' (Schlafly 1977)	'A positive woman cannot defeat a man in a wrestling or boxing match, but she can motivate him, inspire him, encourage him, teach him, restrain him, and reward him, and have power over him that he can never achieve over her with all his muscle'. (Schlafly 1977)
Marriage	'Feminist literature paints marriage as slavery, the home (in Betty Friedan's words) as a "comfortable concentration camp", the husband as the oppressor, the family as an anachronism, and children as the daily drudgery from which the modern woman must be freed in order to pursue more fulfilling careers.' (Schlafly 2003)	'What does a woman want out of life? If you want to love and be loved, marriage offers the best opportunity to achieve your goal … Marriage and motherhood give a woman new identity and the opportunity for all-round fulfilment as a woman.' (Schlafly 2003)
Motherhood	'Feminist ideology teaches that it is demeaning to women to care for their babies, and therefore the role of motherhood should be eliminated … so that women can fulfil themselves in the paid labor force.' (Schlafly 2003)	'[No measure] of career success can compare with the thrill, satisfaction, and fun of having and caring for babies and watching them respond and grow under a mother's loving care.' (Schlafly 2003)
Family	'Except for the unfortunate women who were caught up in the feminist foolishness of the 1970s, most women don't want to be liberated from home, husband, family, and children.' (Schlafly 2003)	'Society simply has not invented a better way of raising children than the traditional family … [The] division of labor is cost efficient, the environment is healthy, and the children thrive on the "object constancy" of the mother.' (Schlafly 2003)
Employment	'[T]he propaganda of the women's liberation movements [states that] motherhood is the least attractive role a woman can choose, and that the work force offers more rewards and more fulfilments.' (Schlafly 1977)	'After twenty years … a mother can see the results of her own handiwork in the good citizen she has produced and trained. After twenty years … in the business world, you are lucky if you have a good watch to show for your efforts.' (Schlafly 1977)
Women and the military	'The push to repeal laws that exempt women from military combat duty must be the strangest of all aberrations indulged in by … the women's liberation or feminist movement. The very idea of women serving in military combat is so unnatural that it almost sounds like a death wish for our species.' (Schlafly 2003)	'There are many cultural, societal, family, pregnancy, and practical reasons why women should not be drafted. Women have more important things to do, such as taking care of their babies and keeping their families together.' (Schlafly 2003)
Gender neutrality	'Operating like a censorship gestapo, the feminist movement has combed primary-grade readers, school textbooks, and career-guidance materials to eliminate any mention of the natural gender traits of youngsters.' (Schlafly 2003)	'[D]espite all the attempts to blur gender identity … and even to pervert the English language by forcing schoolchildren to use such annoying pronouns as he/she or s/he, there is no evidence that human nature is changing. The attempt to change it confuses youth and frustrates adults.' (Schlafly 2003)

Activity

Schlafly

1 Evaluate Schlafly's views in one paragraph.
2 Gather evidence from this textbook, sociology websites such as sociology.org.uk and your own knowledge to support or refute the claims that she puts forwards. (A key criticism could be that she does not back up her conclusions with empirical evidence.)
3 Decide whether you will argue for the New Right or feminism, and prepare for a debate on the role of men and women in society.

Evaluation of Schlafly

- The biological argument for gender-segregated roles has not been proven.
- New Right thinkers tend to ignore the negative effects of the gender roles that they propose, such as the dark side of the family.
- The New Right approach can be seen as dated as it ignores the increasing numbers of people who choose to adopt non-traditional gender roles and report these as positive experiences.
- The New Right is accused of looking to the past for a 'golden age' that never really existed as lone parenting, cohabitation and extra-marital affairs existed then, too.

Marxism

Marx's friend Engels is credited with putting forward the early Marxist view on women's position in society. He suggested that women's subordinate position is a result of the ownership of private property and the development of the nuclear family that went with it. He argued that the rise of a class-based society through capitalism brought with it rising inequality. The exploiter–exploited relationship that occurs between the bourgeoisie and the proletariat is translated into the household in relationships between men and women. Engels argued that under capitalism men gained control over women as they wanted to pass on private property in the form of inheritance from one generation to the next and they wanted to be sure that the heirs were their legitimate offspring. This gave rise to the ideology of the nuclear family, which sought to restrict women's sexuality and enforce monogamy to protect male property rights.

Marxists also share an interest with Marxist feminists in the role of women in supporting capitalism through their unpaid domestic labour and their position in the world of work as a reserve army of labour (see page 269).

Neo-Marxists have developed Marxist theory beyond an analysis of social class. They argue that social structure is based on the dominance of some groups over others and that groups in society share common interests, whether their members are aware of it or not. Conflict is not simply based on class struggle and the tensions between owner and worker or employer and employee; it occurs on a much wider level and among almost all other groups. These include parents and children, husbands and wives, young and old, sick and healthy, people of different ethnicities, heterosexual and homosexual, females and males, and any other groups that can be differentiated as minority or majority according to the level of resources and power that they possess. From the 1960s onwards, neo-Marxists have sought to support all oppressed groups in their struggle for equality, including women. However, much of the research into this area has been conducted by Marxist feminists who have a particular focus on gender inequalities.

Evaluation of Marxism

- Marxists have been criticised for over-emphasising the impact of class and economic factors on gender. Radical feminists argue that the oppression of women by men was the first form of oppression.
- Marxists have been criticised for focusing on macro, structural issues and neglecting the small-scale interactions that provide a more valid understanding of relationships between men and women.
- Marxists have been accused of creating a conspiracy theory that suggests that the bourgeoisie work together to create and enforce dominant ideas such as the ideology of the nuclear family but there is little empirical evidence to support this claim.
- Postmodernists would argue that Marxist views are outdated and fail to recognise the changes to gender roles that have happened over the last 50 years or so.

Weberian theory

Weberian views on social inequalities in general can be applied to a consideration of a range of forms of stratification including gender. Weber identified three dimensions of stratification – class, status and party – and it is the latter two that seem particularly useful when discussing gender inequalities.

When examining the role of status in gender inequalities, it is helpful to look at concepts related to occupational segregation, as they offer some explanation for the inequalities that women face both across and within the labour market. There are two main types of occupational segregation. Horizontal segregation refers to differences in the number of males and females present across occupations. For example, nurses and primary-school teachers are jobs done mainly by women, whereas architects and engineers are jobs usually associated with men. Such occupational segregation is regarded as one of the strongest influences on young people's choice of career, with individuals typically choosing occupations where they see their own gender represented. The Equal Opportunities Commission (2004) identified key explanations for the continued presence of horizontal occupational segregation, including:

- individual differences, including human capital theory
- individuals' career choices based on their perceptions about different careers, also affected by parental influence and the influence of teachers and careers advisors
- discrimination by employers
- barriers within organisations.

Vertical segregation describes men's domination of the highest-ranking jobs in both traditionally male and traditionally female occupations. The concepts of 'glass ceiling', 'concrete ceiling' and 'glass elevator' are also relevant here. The glass ceiling is a concept that may help to explain the difference in social mobility between women and men, since employment is a key means of upward mobility. It refers to an invisible barrier that keeps women from achieving power and success equal to that of men, such as by moving up the career ladder. The concept of the concrete ceiling suggests that the situation has worsened and it is now even more difficult for women to reach higher positions in society. The glass elevator effect refers to how men often rise higher and faster up the career ladder than women, particularly in female-dominated careers such as teaching and nursing. It is argued that this happens because men have 'hidden advantages' that assist them to get promotion, including:

- gender stereotypes that result in men being viewed as more natural leaders than women

- the way that women are often seen as making emotional decisions whereas men are viewed as making rational decisions
- views about women's childbearing and family obligations
- the rarity of men in certain occupations, which makes them stand out and may lead to preferential treatment.

Additionally, Barron and Norris (1976) argue that there is a dual labour market and this concept has also been used to explain women's employment patterns. The primary labour market consists of secure, well-paid jobs that have good promotion prospects. The secondary labour market refers to jobs with low pay and poor security and promotion prospects. The suggestion is that women are concentrated in the secondary labour market and that men dominate the primary labour market. The Weberian concept of status is also useful in helping to explain gender inequalities, as it can be argued that women are more likely than men to work in the low-status jobs found in the secondary labour market. Additionally, it is argued that women's domestic role as housewives and mothers is not held in high esteem in society and carries little status or power.

Weber also used the concept of social closure to describe the exclusion of some people from membership of certain status groups. Feminists would be keen to point out that in contemporary society this is effectively what happens in relation to gender as men reserve and protect top positions in society for themselves and exclude women.

Similarly, in terms of the Weberian concept of party, women tend to participate less than men in groups that exert pressure and power in society.

Study

Political activism gap – Electoral Commission (2004)

According to the Electoral Commission, there is a 'political activism gap' by gender. According to their findings, 'Women are significantly less likely than men to participate in campaign-orientated activities, such as contacting a politician and donating money to, working for, or being a member of, a political party. Women are also less likely than men to join voluntary organisations'. They identified the following explanations for the gap:

- Those in paid employment are more likely to be politically active.

- The activism gap is smaller among better-off households and those who have attended university, and larger among those with the lowest levels of educational qualifications.
- Marital status is also a predictor of activism, with married men significantly more likely to participate than married women.
- The gap is significant among those with children, but closes among those without children living at home.
- Age and ethnicity also have different effects on men and women's levels of activism. Women from ethnic minorities are less active than other women.

- Men and women have different attitudes towards the political process; women have lower confidence that they can influence the political process, express less interest in politics than men and are less likely to trust political institutions.
- Mobilising organisations like trades unions also play a key role in encouraging people to participate in public affairs. Women in the UK are less likely than men to be a member of many kinds of associations.
- The presence of women in representative institutions has an important effect on women's political activism. For example, in 2001, in seats where a woman MP was elected to parliament, women's turnout was 4 per cent higher than men's. Women were also far less interested in the election campaign, and less likely to say that they would volunteer to work for a candidate or party in seats where a male MP was elected.

% reporting having participated in the following activities in the previous 12 months	Women (%)	Men (%)	Activism gap (%)	Sig.
Voting				
Voted in the last national election	68	66	+2	N/s
Campaign-oriented				
Contacted a politician	17	20	−3	*
Donated money to a party	6	9	−3	**
Worked for a party	2	4	−2	**
Been a party member	2	4	−2	**
Worn a campaign badge	10	11	−1	N/s
Cause-oriented				
Signed a petition	42	36	+6	**
Bought a product for a political reason	36	29	+7	***
Boycotted a product	27	25	+1	N/s
Demonstrated legally	5	4	0	N/s
Protested illegally	1	1	0	N/s
Civic-oriented				
Member of a church group	18	10	+7	**
Member of an environmental group	6	6	+1	N/s
Member of a humanitarian group	3	4	−1	N/s
Member of an educational group	6	7	−1	N/s
Member of a trade union	15	16	−1	N/s
Member of a hobby group	14	19	−5	**
Member of a social club	13	19	−6	**
Member of a consumer group	28	35	−7	**
Member of a professional group	9	17	−7	**
Member of a sports club	20	33	−13	**
Total 21-Point Activism Index				
Mean index score	3.58	3.87	−0.29	**

Points to discuss and research

1 Using the table, identify the areas where the political activism gap is greatest.

2 Write a list of reasons to further explain the findings above.

3 Write a 500-word report proposing solutions to close the political activism gap.

Evaluation of Weberian theory

- Though Weberian concepts can be applied to gender inequalities, Weber neglected this area.
- Weberian concepts do not actually explain why some social groups, such as men and women, end up in different sectors of the labour market and why some groups have more status than others.

- Though Weberian explanations look beyond class, the three dimensions that they examine are, in practice, inter-related. Those who have economic power also tend to have a high standing in the community (status) and are able to use these two forms of power to influence the political process.
- Postmodernists would argue that there is no longer a consensus about what constitutes high and low status as norms and values are no longer fixed.

Activity

Theories relating to gender inequality

1 Complete the table below.

A summary of key theories	Consensus or conflict theory	Key theorists/concepts
Liberal feminist		
Radical feminist		
Marxist feminist		
Walby		
Hakim		
Functionalist		
New Right		
Marxist		
Weberian		

Check your understanding

Briefly define the following terms and give an example of each:

1 malestream
2 patriarchy
3 patriarchal terrorism
4 intersectionality
5 occupational segregation
6 human capital theory
7 glass ceiling effect
8 glass elevator effect
9 crisis in masculinity
10 feminisation of the labour market.

Section summary

Fill in the blanks, using the words given below.

Feminism offers the widest range of evidence to explain gender inequalities but explanations are also provided by functionalism, the New Right, Marxism and _____. Feminism developed over time in a number of _____ and each had its own focus; for example, the first aimed to achieve universal female _____ to ensure that all women had the right to vote. The three main strands of feminism are _____, liberal and Marxist and they all have different views on gender inequalities. _____'s work is often used to support _____ feminism as she believes that gender roles have changed over the years and women's priorities have become more _____ -focused. However, Marxist feminists argue that gender equality will only be achieved when _____ is overthrown and radical feminists contend that gender inequalities are caused by _____. Walby, on the other hand, uses the concept of _____ to recognise the complex interplay

281

between different forms of social inequality including class, gender, ethnicity, _____, nationality and so on. Functionalist and _____ thinkers believe that gender roles are _____ and that it is natural that men and women take separate roles in the family and in society. _____ disagreed and argued that under capitalism men gained control over women as they wanted to ensure that they would pass on private property to their rightful heirs. The Weberian concepts of _____ and party are used to explain why men and women achieve different outcomes from the labour market. Both men and women experience gender inequalities and there is evidence to suggest that some males suffer a _____ in _____ because of social changes such as the _____ of the labour market. However, _____ are often sceptical about the extent of male inequalities and argue that these are minor in scale compared to those faced by women.

biologically determined, capitalism, career, crisis, Engels, feminisation, feminists, intersectionality, liberal, masculinity, New Right, patriarchy, radical, religion, Sharpe, status, suffrage, waves, Weberian theory

Practice questions

1 Outline ways that gender may affect life chances. [20]

2 Discuss feminist explanations of gender inequalities. [40]

Chapter 7c

Understanding social inequalities: Ethnicity

> **Component 2, Section B**
>
> Understanding social inequalities
>
> **Content:**
>
> 1 Ethnicity and life chances
> 2 Patterns and trends in ethnic inequality and difference
> 3 How can patterns and trends in ethnic inequality and difference be explained?

7c.1 Ethnicity and life chances

> **Getting you thinking ...**
>
> 1 What is the difference between race and ethnicity?
> 2 Do some ethnic groups experience more inequalities compared to others in the contemporary UK?
> 3 Do these inequalities reflect what is going on globally?
> 4 Which ethnic groups experience most advantage in the contemporary UK? Why?

According to the Office for National Statistics (2014), the White ethnic group accounted for 86 per cent of the UK population in 2011, meaning that ethnic minorities in the UK make up roughly 14 per cent of the total population. However, ethnic minorities are a diverse group of people, with some ethnic groups experiencing more challenges in the form of ethnic inequalities in contemporary society compared to others. In this chapter we examine the patterns and trends of inequality between ethnic groups in Britain and the explanations for their existence. For example, these inequalities may be caused by individual racism, cultural racism or institutional racism. However, more recently some evidence suggests that ethnic minority groups like Indians fare better in the education system and the labour market compared to other ethnic groups, including the White British majority. However, whether this is the result of changes in the law such as the Race Relations Act or Equality Acts is a much debated issue. Despite the existence of these laws, ethnic minorities as a whole still tend to fare less well in education, work, health and housing compared to their White British counterparts which may affect life chances. The concept of life chances was used by Max Weber in relation to social class but it can usefully be applied to a range of social groups (see pages 225 and 292).

7c.2 Patterns and trends in ethnic inequality and difference

Ethnic inequalities in work and employment

According to the Office for National Statistics (2014), in the 2011 Census:

- The proportion of men aged 16 to 64 who were unemployed was highest in the Other Black (17 per cent), White and Black Caribbean (16 per cent) and Caribbean (15 per cent) ethnic groups. For women, it was highest for Black African (12 per cent), White and Black Caribbean (11 per cent) and Other Black (11 per cent) groups.
- The highest rates of unemployment for women were in the Arab (64 per cent), Bangladeshi (61 per cent), Pakistani (60 per cent) and Gypsy or Irish Traveller (60 per cent) ethnic groups.
- Of those in employment, men from the Pakistani (57 per cent), Black African (54 per cent) and Bangladeshi (53 per cent) ethnic groups were most likely to work in low-skilled jobs. For women, the

most likely were Gypsy or Irish Traveller (71 per cent), Bangladeshi (67 per cent) and White and Black Caribbean (66 per cent).

- Bangladeshi (56 per cent) and Gypsy or Irish Traveller (54 per cent) women were the most likely to work part-time (fewer than 30 hours a week). Bangladeshi and Pakistani women had the highest proportion working fewer than 15 hours a week (23 per cent and 20 per cent respectively).

There is evidence of less favourable treatment of people from many ethnic minority backgrounds in recruitment processes from a number of studies. Research by Wood *et al.* (2009) found that discrimination in favour of white names over equivalent applications from candidates from a number of ethnic minority groups was 29 per cent. Standardised application forms were used in 79 per cent of public-sector applications, compared with six per cent in the private sector, which may suggest unfair practices in the private sector.

Heath and Yu (2005) have examined the evolution of ethnic penalties using data from the General Household Survey (GHS) and the Labour Force Survey (LFS). For men, they found that first-generation Black, Indian and Pakistani migrants (born 1940–59 and interviewed in the 1970s) faced significant ethnic penalties in terms of access to professional/managerial jobs. Since then, while subsequent generations have invested heavily in increasing their skills, direct labour market discrimination still exists.

According to the Joseph Rowntree Foundation (2007), there is evidence that some ethnic minority graduates, particularly women, are finding it harder to gain higher-level positions in their occupations.

Battu and Sloane (2004) argue that ethnic minorities in employment are more likely to be overeducated than the White group in the UK; therefore, it follows that employment rates might not give a complete indication of the welfare of particular groups if those groups are doing jobs for which they are overeducated.

Activity

Ethnic minority women in the job market

An article in the *Guardian* by Vikram Dodd (2012) reported that many Muslim women remove hijabs or make names sound more English to beat discrimination in the labour market.

The article reported that prejudice and discrimination explains a quarter of the higher unemployment rate faced by women from Pakistani, Bangladeshi and black communities and that 'Pakistani and Bangladeshi women are particularly affected, with 20.5 per cent being unemployed compared to 6.8 per cent of white women, with 17.7 per cent of black women also being unemployed. The higher unemployment rate covered all ages, dashing hopes that more enlightened attitudes mean the problem is lessening for younger women.'

Dodd's article also cited research by Professor Yaojun Li, who found that 'After 1983 the unemployment rate of Pakistani and Bangladeshi women has remained consistently and substantially higher than the rate for white women', and findings from a report from the all-party parliamentary group on race and community, which highlighted the following:

- Some employers' attitudes worsened when they realised women with European-sounding names were black.

- Some Muslim women were removing their hijab to increase their chance of getting work.
- Black and Asian women complained of being asked during job interviews about their plans for marriage and having children.
- Fewer Pakistani and Bangladeshi women than white women were taking up their children's free nursery places.
- Some ethnic minority women were 'deselecting themselves' from the jobs market and deciding not to apply because of the extra barriers they faced.

Off the back of this report, Labour MP David Lammy, who chairs the all-party group, said: 'It is staggering that in twenty-first-century Britain there are women who felt they had to remove their hijab or change their name just to be able to compete on the same terms as other candidates when looking for jobs.'

1 Summarise some of the obstacles that ethnic minority women may experience when finding employment.
2 How do these experiences differ from the obstacles some ethnic minority men experience when they are finding employment?
3 If you were responsible for developing strategies that were designed to help ethnic minority women to overcome the obstacles they encounter when finding a job, what would they be?

Davidson (1997) used the term 'concrete ceiling' to describe the embedded discrimination that prevents ethnic minority women being promoted. While white women may face a glass ceiling, or an invisible barrier that obstructs their journey to the highest levels of professions, women from ethnic minority groups report that their journey is even more difficult. The obstacles that ethnic minority women face have been called the 'concrete ceiling'; while white women have the opportunity to break through the glass ceiling, the concrete ceiling is impenetrable.

Ethnic inequalities in income and wealth

According to the Office for National Statistics (2014), around two-fifths of people from ethnic minorities live in low-income households, twice the rate than for white people.

The Joseph Rowntree Foundation (2007) also found that all ethnic minorities continue to have lower earnings than comparable White groups, with large earning differentials experienced by the Black African, Pakistani and Bangladeshi groups. Men from each ethnic minority earn at least 10 per cent less than the comparable White group with Black African, Pakistani and Bangladeshi men experiencing more than a 20 per cent earnings deficit. For women, the differentials were around 5 per cent for most. The earnings deficit was highest for Black African women at 18 per cent.

The National Equality Panel (2010) showed that there are considerable differences in median total wealth between different ethnic households. For example, White British households had the greatest level of wealth in 2006/8, on average, at £221,000, but these were followed fairly closely by Indian households. Other ethnic minority groups were much further behind. The group with the least wealth was Bangladeshi households, with only £15,000 total net wealth on average.

Rowlingson and McKay (2012) controlled for differences in occupational class to consider the particular effect of ethnicity on wealth inequality. Their research findings revealed that White British people in managerial occupations had greater wealth than other ethnic groups in the same positions but that White British people in intermediate and routine non-manual positions had less wealth than Asian or Asian British/ Indian groups in these positions. Black or Black British/ Black Caribbean people had considerably lower levels of wealth than other ethnic groups after controlling for occupation.

The Joseph Rowntree Foundation (2007) also found that the Bangladeshi ethnic group experience the significant income inequality and are consistently the worst off. They have the highest poverty rates of all groups and only 25 per cent have incomes that are among the top half of incomes overall.

Ethnic inequalities in poverty

According to the 2011 Census, one in three Bangladeshis and Pakistanis in England and Wales were living 'in deprived neighbourhoods'. In contrast, only one in twelve of the Census's White British group lived in deprived neighbourhoods.

According to the Joseph Rowntree Foundation (2007), living in a deprived area reduced employment prospects. While this is unsurprising, the effect was larger for ethnic minorities.

The Joseph Rowntree Foundation (2007) report *Poverty and Ethnicity in the UK* provided a good snapshot of the weekly household income of different ethnic groups and illustrated the shares that came from earned income and welfare benefits. The largest share of income in White households came from wages and self-employment income (74 per cent). However, as much as 83 per cent of Indian households' income came from wages and self-employment income. For the other groups, income from work made up between 73 per cent and 77 per cent of total income, with the exception of Pakistani and Bangladeshi households, for whom only 67 per cent of income came from these sources. Instead, a relatively large share of their income came from 'other social security benefits', which included Income Support, Housing Benefit and Jobseeker's Allowance among others. Means-tested benefits such as these indicate a lack of alternative resources in terms of both income and savings. They are also much more closely associated with poverty as they are frequently the only source of family income and are paid at rates that frequently put recipients below standard poverty lines.

Using the General Household Survey for 1991–6, Evandrou (2000) explored the poverty of older people and how it varied by ethnicity. She found that the white elderly had the lowest levels of income poverty followed by Irish, then Black Caribbean, then Indian elderly, with up to 60 per cent of the Pakistani and Bangladeshi elderly were in income poverty.

The Runnymede report *Ready for Retirement?* (2010) found that ethnic minority groups are up to three times more likely than white people to experience poverty in retirement. In addition, the report found that any older people from ethnic minority groups, particularly recent migrants, also face language barriers as well as difficulties accessing information and navigating an unfamiliar and complex pensions system.

Flaherty et al (2004) suggest a number of reasons for high rates of poverty among ethnic minority groups, including the following:

- Members of ethnic minority households are more likely to be unemployed compared to whites.
- Many ethnic minorities used to work in the manufacturing sector and these jobs have significantly declined over the last few decades, leading to a great number of ethnic minorities becoming unemployed.
- Many ethnic minorities are concentrated in low-skilled and therefore low-paid work.
- Educational disadvantage is a contributory factor to lower than average pay and could explain why many ethnic minorities remain poor.
- Ethnic minorities may find it difficult to escape

poverty because they tend to live in deprived areas where there is a lack of job opportunities and the quality of schools is less than satisfactory.

- Many ethnic minorities are likely to live in poor-quality, overcrowded and damp housing, which has a negative impact upon their health.
- Many ethnic minorities can end up in poverty as a result of difficulties with the benefits system. For example, first-generation immigrants are unlikely to have the continuous contributions record to be entitled to full benefits. Furthermore, the complexity of applying for such benefits leads to low take-up rates among some ethnic minorities.

Alcock (1997) argues that many ethnic minority groups experience material deprivation and that this can lead to social exclusion. Alcock claims that 'deprivation in housing, health and education adds significantly to the financial inequality of Black people in Britain, and they have remained important despite the introduction in the 1960s of the race relations legislation.' Furthermore, Alcock argues that material

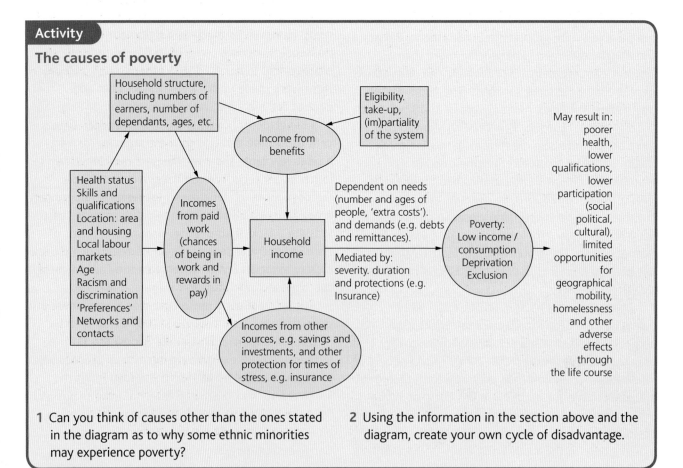

Activity

The causes of poverty

1 Can you think of causes other than the ones stated in the diagram as to why some ethnic minorities may experience poverty?

2 Using the information in the section above and the diagram, create your own cycle of disadvantage.

deprivation maybe further exacerbated by racial harassment, which can have the effect of making ethnic minorities feel even more isolated.

Ethnic inequalities in social mobility

Platt (2005) researched intergenerational social mobility of ethnic minorities over time by examining the Office for National Statistics Longitudinal Study. Her research looked closely at where ethnic minorities were located in the occupational structure in 1971, and then where they were positioned in 1991. In particular, she found that, of those with higher occupational attainment in the first generation, Indians were able to maintain these achievements in the next generation. In contrast, the relative occupational position of Caribbeans had slipped by 1991. Platt also reported that the occupational position of women from the ethnic minority communities was more dependent on their origins than it was for men.

Platt also analysed the 2001 Census to further investigate the evolution of occupational achievement for ethnic minorities and found that Caribbeans, Black Africans, Indians, Chinese and Others experienced upward occupational mobility relative to the White UK-born, after origins had been taken into account. However, the Pakistani and Bangladeshi groups performed less well in terms of occupational achievement.

Platt also examined information on religion from the 2001 Census and reported that some diversity existed within South Asian groups in patterns of educational performance; for example, in the Indian group, Hindus outperformed Sikhs and Muslims.

Guardian journalist Ami Sedghi (2014) reports that, according to findings from a report published by the Centre on Dynamics of Ethnicity at the University of Manchester, despite levels of educational attainment improving significantly for ethnic minorities, they are still facing barriers to social mobility and job opportunities. The report brought together the Centre's research on education and employment, based on census analysis of ethnic groups, and a considerable number of longitudinal surveys of individual experiences of social mobility.

The report findings highlighted that Chinese, Indian, Irish, Bangladeshi and black African students are outperforming their white British peers in obtaining five or more GCSEs at grade A*– C, and ethnic minority groups have seen significant improvement in access to degree-level qualifications. For example, just under 5 per cent of Bangladeshi people were recorded as having a degree-level qualification in the 1991 Census; by 2011, the figure had reached almost 20 per cent.

However, though the increased educational success of ethnic minority groups has translated into the growth in the number of ethnic minorities in clerical, professional and managerial employment, the report indicated that they are still facing 'significant barriers to enjoying the levels of social mobility of their white British peers'.

Key findings from the study are:
- Black African and black Caribbean women have experienced a 15–20 per cent fall in full-time employment rates over the past decade, while those for white women have remained stable.
- 39 per cent of Bangladeshi women and 35 per cent of Bangladeshi men work part-time, double the levels of two decades ago.
- 53 per cent of self-employed Pakistani men work in the transport industry, compared to 8 per cent of the rest of the population.
- The rates of part-time employment for Chinese and Indian men have doubled in the last ten years.
- Surveys of young British Muslim women have highlighted how employer discrimination has been a significant barrier to employment for those who wear the hijab and niqab notwithstanding their high levels of graduate and post-graduate qualifications.

The report also presented new research by Professors Anthony Heath and Yaojun Li, who looked at 40 years of data to define rates of social mobility through identifying the percentage who moved up or down from the occupational class of their father. They found that: '43 per cent of white men and 45.6 per cent of white women moved up to a higher socio-economic class than their father and that in contrast, first-generation black African, Indian and Pakistani and Bangladeshi groups had significantly lower upward mobility rates. Just 34.3 per cent of first-generation Pakistani and Bangladeshi men and 27.6 per cent of Pakistani and Bangladeshi women moved up from the socio-economic class of their father'.

Getting you thinking ...

What strategies do you think need to be put in place to enable ethnic minorities who excel in the education system to become upwardly socially mobile?

Activity

Ethnic inequalities and life chances
The **Weberian** concept of **life chances** refers to the opportunities that a person will have in life.

1 Re-examine the patterns and trends section in relation to ethnicity and write down at least five ways in which ethnic inequalities and difference may affect life chances.

Section summary

Fill in the blanks, using the words given below.

Ethnic minorities are a diverse group of people with some ethnic groups experiencing more _____ in contemporary society compared to others. There is clear evidence of ethnic inequalities in work and employment, as demonstrated by the higher proportion of _____ among Black groups in particular. Even when in work, ethnic groups like Pakistani, Black African and Bangladeshi are most likely to be concentrated in _____. The situation is particularly acute for ethnic minority women who are said to experience the _____. There are also considerable differences in the median _____ between different ethnic households. For example, White British households had the greatest level of wealth in 2006/8, on average, at £221,000. The group with the least wealth was Bangladeshi households with only £15,000 total net wealth on average. According to _____, because ethnic minorities are more likely to experience unemployment and be concentrated in low-skilled and therefore low-paid work, they are more likely to experience higher rates of poverty compared to the rest of the population. Poverty in the form of _____ can be further exacerbated by racial harassment, which can have the effect of making ethnic minorities feel even more isolated from the rest of society. Finally, ethnic inequalities can seriously hinder the _____ of ethnic minority groups, which can create a cycle of disadvantage that is hard to break out of.

Concrete ceiling, ethnic inequalities, Flaherty *et al.* (2004), life chances, low-skilled and low-paid jobs, material deprivation, total wealth, unemployment rates

7c.3 How can patterns and trends in ethnic inequality and difference be explained?

Functionalism

Functionalists argue that the early ethnic inequalities experienced by **immigrants** were the product of their cultural difference and relatively low level of skills.

Functionalists are optimistic that in a **meritocratic society** ethnic inequalities would decline as immigrants adopted the norms and values of mainstream society and climbed their way up the career ladder.

Study

The host – immigration model – Patterson (1965)

Patterson's host immigrant model is a good example of a Functionalist approach. Patterson's theory presented Britain as a stable, **homogeneous** and orderly society with a high degree of **consensus** over norms and values. However, this **equilibrium** was disrupted by the arrival of immigrants in the 1950s, who subscribed to very different sets of norms and values. Patterson argued that this resulted in a culture clash between the immigrants (for example, the West Indians who were considered boisterous, noisy, and not in the habit of queuing at bus stops!) and the host community (who valued privacy, quiet and 'keeping oneself to oneself'). Patterson interpreted these clashes in terms of understandable fears and anxieties on the part of the host community. She claimed that the hosts were not actually **racist**, just very unsure about how to act towards the newcomers.

On the basis of this, Patterson suggested that there were three causes of ethnic inequality. These were:

firstly, the host culture's fear of the cultural difference of the immigrant 'strangers' and the social change they would bring to society; secondly, the host culture's resentment of having to compete with immigrants for scarce resources such as jobs and housing; finally, the failure of immigrants to **assimilate** i.e. to become totally 'British' and integrate.

Patterson's theory cautiously implied that ethnic minorities who continued to practise their native cultural norms and values in the public domain could potentially experience some hostility from their host culture. This is because cultural strangeness had the potential to make the host culture anxious. However, Patterson was reasonably optimistic about the long-term prospects for racial harmony. She thought that Britain's immigrants would eventually move toward full cultural assimilation by shedding their 'old' ethnic values and taking on the values of the host society.

Activity

The host – immigrant model

The host – immigrant model proposed that immigrants would go through three stages before they completely assimilated into the host society. These are as follows:

- **Accommodation:** This involves only minimal adaptation to and acceptance of mainstream culture, such as finding employment and learning the customs of co-workers.
- **Integration:** This occurs when hosts and immigrants socialise with one another outside of work.
- **Assimilation:** This stage signifies the complete assimilation of the immigrants into mainstream society, and complete acceptance of them by the rest of society.

Patterson also argued that assimilation could potentially lead to physical amalgamation, in which interbreeding between the races could lead to a complete disappearance of the distinctive features of the immigrant groups and their hosts.

1 Do (and should) all ethnic minorities go through the above stages?
2 Can ethnic inequality be eradicated if all immigrants assimilate completely into mainstream society?
3 Identify and explain three government policies that have been influenced by this assimilationist model.

Evaluation of Patterson

Though Patterson's theory emphasises the dynamic nature of ethnic relationships, her critics would argue that she is naïve to assume that all ethnic minority groups assimilate into 'British culture'. For example, some postmodernists would argue that Britain is a multicultural society in which different ethnic cultures co-exist side by side and that this diversity should be celebrated. Moreover, some Marxists would criticise Patterson for ignoring the significant role that capitalism plays within society and how

the division of people by race helps to maintain the capitalist structure. This means that assimilation will remain an idealistic goal that is impossible to achieve under capitalism.

Marxism

In comparison to functionalists, Marxists have a rather pessimistic view of race relations that stresses that immigration serves the needs of the capitalist class for labour, and is used to divide workers from each other so that they are easy to control. Therefore, capitalism prefers conflict between ethnic groups as it is beneficial to the ruling class.

Cox (1970)

One Marxist theory of racism was developed by Cox (1970), who stressed that the idea that 'race' is itself a human creation. To Cox, racism is always something that is developed by exploiters against the exploited. In fact, Cox argues that racism has its origins in the development of capitalism, with its need to systematically exploit labour power. Furthermore, Cox argues that early capitalism went hand in hand with colonialism. As European nations conquered other areas of the world, they were able to exploit the workforce in those colonies and they justified their actions through racism, by claiming that white Europeans were superior to other races.

Cox also argues that if racism is developed to justify exploitation, it cannot be developed by those who are exploited. It is not only White people who are capable of racism, but it was White people who developed capitalism, and therefore it was they who first developed racism. According to Cox, if capitalism had not developed, then the world may never have experienced racial prejudice.

Evaluation of Cox

Though Cox's work is useful as it details the economic imperatives of migration for the capitalist class, critics would argue his views are too simplistic. This is because it is difficult to prove that racism is a capitalist ideology; it may benefit capitalism in the long term, but there is no evidence that it functions exclusively as an ideological apparatus, as Cox seems to be suggesting. Furthermore, many critics argue that Cox does not treat race as an important factor in its own right because he is mainly interested in the economic differences caused by capitalism. Therefore, Cox's theory has been labelled 'race blind'.

Castles and Kosack (1973)

In another Marxist study of immigrant workers in Britain, Castles and Kosack (1973) found that most immigrants were concentrated in low-skilled and low-paid manual jobs that were mainly carried out in poor working conditions. Many immigrants were also unemployed. Castles and Kosack claimed that in Britain this treatment of immigrants ultimately derived from the need in capitalist societies for a **reserve army of labour**; it was necessary to have a **surplus of labour power** in order to keep wage costs down, since the greater the overall supply of labour power, the weaker the bargaining position of existing workers became.

Furthermore, Castles and Kosack believed that capitalist economies were inherently unstable. They underwent periods of boom and slump, and a reserve army of labour needed to be available to be hired and fired as the fluctuating fortunes of the economy dictated. After the Second World War, capitalist societies exhausted their indigenous reserve army of labour: women. Therefore, countries in Europe turned to immigrant labour to provide a necessary cheap pool of workers who could be profitably exploited.

Activity

The rise of the English Defence League

The English Defence League (EDL) sees itself as a defender of British values, which includes the army. In its mission statement, the EDL says its first priority is 'protecting and promoting human rights', which it believes are threatened by Muslim extremists. However, a YouGov survey of 1,600 EDL supporters found that this concern extended into the wider issue of immigration. This was the top concern of respondents, followed by the economy, while 'Muslims in Britain' was named as the third most quoted concern.

This research is supported by media reports at the time of EDL protests in Manchester where a number of EDL supporters talked about the fear of losing their jobs or businesses and all of them blamed 'foreign' workers. This is typical of fascist movements. As their world is threatened, their fears and frustrations are directed at a scapegoat. Today this is Muslims.

EDL supporters are likely to be white and working class, and what characterises supporters is a strong disillusionment with politics in this country. The movement around the EDL appears to be escalating. The central question is: what kind of organisation are they? The foot soldiers are clearly drawn from a number of football hooligan gangs of clubs including Chelsea, Queens Park Rangers, Luton, Aston Villa, Bristol Rovers, Wolves and Preston North End. The media likes to portray these hooligans as working-class 'yobs'.

1 Why do groups like the EDL exist?
2 How might such groups benefit the bourgeoisie?

The arrival of immigrants led to the working class being divided into two groups, with the indigenous white population becoming the top layer of the working class and the immigrant workers becoming a distinctive grouping at the bottom – making them the most disadvantaged group within the working class. Castles and Kosack argue this **divide-and-rule** tactic was beneficial to the ruling class as it suppressed the overall wage levels of the working classes and immigrants could be **scapegoated**, i.e. blamed for problems such as unemployment and housing shortages, thus allowing the capitalist class to divert the white working class' attention from the real cause of inequalities: capitalism. Furthermore, this situation also meant that the working class became too divided to unite and overthrow the capitalist system.

Meet the Hindujas: Britain's wealthiest men

In 2014 Gopi Hinduja and his three brothers, known in their native India as the Fab Four, were collectively worth £11.9bn, making Srichand, 78, and Gopi, 74, who live in London, Britain's wealthiest men.

But who are the Hinduja brothers, and where and how did they make their astonishing fortune? The *Sunday Times* claimed the 'Hindujas – all four of whom are teetotal, vegetarian and religious – built their empire from nothing, from humble beginnings in the Indian subcontinent, and are now neighbours to the Queen of England – a classic rags-to-riches story.'

Sri and Gopi moved to London, where they now own a six-storey home in Carlton House Terrace and, like many global businesspeople, have found themselves caught in a number of controversies. For example, it transpired that then Northern Ireland Secretary Peter Mandelson had speeded up Sri's application for a British passport after he had donated £1m to the 'Faith Zone' of the Millennium Dome.

Despite such controversies, the Hinduja brothers remain some of the most powerful people in the world of business. Their friends include former US President Bill Clinton and numerous other UK politicians.

Activity

The Morecambe Bay tragedy

On 5 February 2004, 23 Chinese cockle pickers drowned when they were trapped by sweeping tides while working in Morecambe Bay, Lancashire. Yet, ten years on, campaigners say immigrant workers are still being dangerously exploited in the UK.

21 bodies were recovered from the bay; the victims were aged between 18 and 45. All were working illegally, picking cockles for hours on end to send money back to their families. A skull was washed up six years later, and one other body has never been found.

Mick Gradwell, the detective who led the investigation into the Morecambe Bay tragedy, said: 'Tens of thousands of illegal Chinese workers are living in the country in hidden communities and building a life below official recognition …The main reason 23 people died in Morecambe Bay on this particular night was because of poverty in the Fujian province of China. There is a constant threat and risk of people being abused like this and dying because they're being forced to move to the UK and work in dangerous conditions to earn enough money to send home.'

1 Is there a need for a reserve army of labour in contemporary society?
2 Are all immigrants concentrated in the reserve army of labour?

Evaluation of Castles and Kosack

Though Castles and Kosack offer a good illustration as to how workers are divided from one another through racial divisions, critics would argue that it would be a mistake to think that all ethnic minorities are disadvantaged in the UK. For example, recent statistics suggest that there are currently over 5,000 Muslim millionaires in Britain. Furthermore, de-industrialisation has changed the nature of economic immigrants; historically, the skill level of immigrants was not a concern to the state as manual workers were simply needed to plug the gaps in the workforce, whereas in recent years immigration laws have become a lot tighter. Consequently, many economic immigrants tend to possess higher-level skills and knowledge.

Miles (1989)

Like Cox, neo-Marxist Miles (1989) argues that racism was originally used to justify the exploitation of non-Europeans in various parts of the world. However, Miles then goes on to argue that by the end of colonialism, the type of racism that saw different types of biological grouping as superior or inferior to others was replaced with **nationalism,** in which individuals saw their nation as superior to other nations.

Furthermore, Miles is influenced by Weberian theory as he argues that the concept of status should be used alongside the concept of class to explain racism and racial inequality. Miles argues that the class position of ethnic minorities is complicated by the fact that they are treated by White society as culturally and socially different. Consequently, some ethnic minorities have fallen victim to racism in some domains of society. At the same time, some ethnic minorities themselves may set themselves apart from the White majority by stressing and celebrating their own cultural uniqueness; for example, young African-Caribbeans may stress **Black power** through membership of Rastafarian groups, while Asians may stress the importance of family ties and community through where they choose to live and who they choose to marry. Miles argues that as a result of these two processes, ethnic minority groups become members of '**racialised class fractions**'. These racialised class fractions are then further reinforced when the White working class stress the importance of their ethnicity and nationality through prejudice and discrimination, and when ethnic minorities react to such racism by stressing their own ethnicity even more by observing their cultural and religious traditions overtly.

Miles also argues that there is evidence that increasing numbers of ethnic minorities are entering the ranks of the professional middle class, though this is often into the lower middle-class positions where status and pay are not very high. Miles points out that racism probably means that many White middle-class professionals/managers may not accept the fact that middle-class ethnic minorities have the same status as them. Furthermore, many of the White working class may not perceive middle-class ethnic minorities as having a higher status compared to themselves. This means that even if ethnic minorities do not experience social class inequality, they are not immune to experiencing status inequality and therefore class and status are not inextricably linked.

Evaluation of Miles

Though Miles recognises the importance of status and how it can cut across class lines, which helps to explain some apparent divisions between the White majority and ethnic minorities, he downplays possible cooperation between both groups in trade union movements, where people work together to ensure their rights as workers.

Weberian Theory

Weber recognised the importance in the difference between the bourgeoisie and proletariat, but he argued that differences within the working class (for example, ethnic differences) were also significant. Therefore, Weber had a strong influence on explanations for racial discrimination and inequality. This is because Weber was keen to point out that stratification in modern society could occur on the basis of non-economic factors too, such as status and party.

Weber also defined class in terms of market situation (some workers have more sought-after knowledge and skills compared to others, which consequently affects the wage levels of their jobs) and work situation (some workers have more authority than others, which therefore affects their level of autonomy in jobs). Classes, therefore, are simply groups that share a similar market situation and work situation and it is these situations combined that affect a person's life chances (the opportunities that a person will have in life). When we apply Weber's theory to our understanding of contemporary patterns and trends of inequality and difference related to ethnicity, it becomes clear that most White British people in the UK are more likely to have a superior market and work situation compared to ethnic minorities, which equates to White British people having superior life chances compared to ethnic minorities.

Weberian theorists also argue that modern societies are characterised by status inequality. Status groups can be competitive and aim to achieve 'social closure', which means that they try to monopolise privilege and exclude other groups from their positions of privilege. In terms of ethnicity, this could potentially mean that status and power are in the hands of the majority ethnic group, thereby making it difficult for ethnic minority groups to compete equally for jobs, housing and so on. Weber also observed that status could divide a class group or even cut across class differences; for instance, ethnic minority manual workers may have a lower status than white manual workers and middle-class ethnic minorities doing professional jobs may experience status inequality in the form of prejudicial attitudes held by members of both White middle and working classes. Ethnic minorities, therefore, not only suffer from social class inequality, they also suffer from status inequality too.

Weber also referred to party in his work. This can be defined as a group that forms in order to gain power and in doing so reflects and promotes their own interests. Organisations such as trades unions, professional bodies and groups like Liberty are examples of party. They reflect the idea that status groups, as well as economically based class groups, can form the basis for political action. However, trades unions are dominated by White members, which often leads to ethnic minorities' voices not being heard.

To conclude, Weber's theory shows that structured inequality can occur as a result of cultural differences as well as economic differences.

Evaluation of Weberian theory

Weberian theory is useful because it suggests that there are other sources of power besides economic power, such as status derived from culture. In doing so, it provides some useful insights into the nature of ethnic differences in contemporary society. However, critics may argue that Weberian theory still does not provide any way to distinguish between the relative importance of the different types of inequality.

Study

The dual labour market theory – Barron and Norris (1979)

The dual labour market theory demonstrates how racial prejudice and discrimination can be seen in the distribution of ethnic minorities in the labour force. Barron and Norris distinguished between the primary labour market consisting of well-paid, secure jobs with good promotional prospects and the secondary labour market consisting of the worst jobs, lowest pay, worse conditions, least job security and very few promotional prospects. After detailed analysis of both labour markets, Barron and Norris reported that White men dominated the primary labour market and ethnic minorities were concentrated in the secondary labour market due to their lower cultural status.

Barron and Norris' theory therefore acknowledges that cultural discrimination exists and that stratification is not purely economic; the existence of status groups such as those based on ethnicity shows that stratification can also occur of the basis of cultural factors. Barron and Norris argue that ethnic minorities tend to be concentrated in the secondary labour market because many employers subscribe to racist beliefs about the unsuitability of Black and Asian people and may even practise discrimination against them, either by not employing them or by denying them responsibility and promotion.

Furthermore, the legal and political framework supporting Black and Asian people is weak. Trades unions are generally White dominated and have been accused of favouring White workers and being less interested in protecting the rights of Black workers. Also, the Race Relations Act of 1976, which was supposed to protect Black people from discriminatory practices, has not worked as effectively as it could have.

Activity

The labour market
1 Identify jobs that you think belong to the primary and secondary labour market.
2 Carry out some independent research using labour market survey reports to establish the percentages of ethnic minorities concentrated within each labour market.

Evaluation of Barron and Norris

Barron and Norris' theory is useful as it provides an insight into how the labour market is divided. However, the theory ignores the fact that there are some ethnic minorities in crucial primary labour market positions, as evidenced by Britain's 100 Rich List. The current richest person in the UK, Lakshmi Mittal, comes from an ethnic minority background. Furthermore, Barron and Norris fail to recognise that the situation for ethnic minority women is worse than it is for ethnic minority men as they are not only concentrated into the secondary labour market, but they experience the concrete ceiling too. Davidson (1997) used the term 'concrete ceiling' to describe the embedded discrimination that prevents ethnic minority women being promoted. While white women have the opportunity to break through the glass ceiling, the concrete ceiling is impenetrable.

Rex and Tomlinson (1979)

Rex and Tomlinson (1979) in their Weberian-influenced study in the Handsworth area of Birmingham in the West Midlands revealed that the **material disadvantage** experienced by ethnic minorities in the area was so great that it actually cut them off from the White working-class group. Rex and Tomlinson found that ethnic minorities formed a separate underclass beneath the White working class, where they experienced disadvantage with regard to the labour market, housing and education. Moreover, these disadvantages were worsened by the hostility directed at them by white society. Rex and Tomlinson argued that a Black underclass had been created, consisting of people who felt **marginalised**, **alienated** and **frustrated.** Furthermore, the Black underclass' experience of status inequality was further compounded by them feeling as if they had been socially excluded from the standard of living that most other members of society took for granted, as well as overzealous policing, which they experienced as harassment. Consequently, these feelings had the potential to occasionally erupt in the form of inner-city riots. Therefore, Rex and Tomlinson concluded that in a capitalist society, the underclass are the ultimate victims and ethnic minorities are heavily concentrated within the underclass.

Evaluation of Rex and Tomlinson

Though Rex and Tomlinson's work is useful in explaining some of the experiences of the Black underclass, they may be criticised for over-emphasising ethnic minority groups as passive victims of racism. The position of ethnic minority groups is changing and some groups, particularly Chinese and Indian people, are outperforming all of their other ethnic counterparts at school and are faring very well in the labour market too. Furthermore, New Right commentators would blame the culture of some ethnic minorities for the poverty and unemployment that they experience. Welfare dependency in particular may be an issue for many politicians.

Activity

The portrayal of the underclass

'Smoggy' (real name Stephen Smith) used Twitter to contact members of the *Dragons Den* to ask for assistance with his fledgling business plan. The dad-of-two won over the British public with his heart-warming cameo on the controversial TV documentary *Benefits Street* in which he was shown selling household items like sugar and tea for 50p each. Stephen came up with the 50p idea while serving a two-month term in Winson Green Prison for what he claimed as 'something really petty'. His initiative also impressed employers across the country and landed him several job offers, so he has now started working for a food distribution firm who got in touch after seeing him on the first episode of *Benefits Street*.

1 Can you think of other examples other than the one above that do not portray Black members of the underclass as being marginalised, alienated and frustrated?

Black feminism

Black feminism has developed out of dissatisfaction with other types of feminism. Within the media there has been much celebration of the feminist resurgence in the twenty-first century. White, middle-class young women are often seen as the ones spearheading this new wave of activity. Black feminists argue that the high-profile campaigns, for example, to have women on banknotes, challenge online misogyny and banish Page 3, though necessary, do not reflect the most pressing needs of the majority of women, and ethnic minority women in particular. The problem is not that these 'white feminist' campaigns exist, but that they are given a focus and attention that overshadows the other work that feminists are engaged with.

The majority of women both in the UK and across the globe do not live lives that are negatively impacted by sexism alone. Because of this reality, the black feminist concept of intersectionality – the idea that oppressions criss-cross and compound each other – has been crucial. Through it, black feminists have been able to point out the failings of the wider feminist movement, which lie in its continual failure to capture and reflect the extreme differences in how women live their lives. For example, Abbott *et al.* (2005) argue previous strands of feminism have:

- been ethnocentric, claiming to address issues concerning women in general but actually concentrating on women's experience derived from white middle-class perspectives and priorities
- perpetuated a 'victim ideology', i.e. viewed black women as the helpless victims of racism and sexism and ignored the extent to which black women have resisted oppression and actively shaped their own lives
- practised theoretical racism, i.e. expected black women to write about their own experiences rather than contribute to the development of feminist theory as a whole.

Brewer (1993)

Black feminist Brewer (1993) sees the basis of Black feminist theory as an 'understanding of race, class and gender as simultaneous forces'. Black women suffer from disadvantages because they are black, because they are women and because they are working class, but their problems are more than the sum of these parts; each inequality reinforces and multiplies the other inequalities. The distinctive feature of Black feminism to Brewer is that it studies the 'interplay' of race, class and gender in shaping the lives and restricting the life chances of black women.

Evaluation of Brewer

Black feminism has been useful in introducing the idea that differences between women are as important as similarities and shared interests but, at the same time, it can be accused of emphasising racial difference at the expense of others such as class, age, sexuality and disability. Furthermore, legislation such as the Equal Pay Act (1970), the Sex Discrimination Act (1975) and the Race Relations Act (1976) aim to prevent discrimination on the grounds of class, gender and race. This legislation has particularly helped to empower ethnic minority women, as demonstrated by Youth Cohort Studies that clearly show that Indian and Chinese female pupils outperform all other ethnic groups within the education system, and therefore need to be able to pursue successful careers free from discrimination.

Mirza (1997)

Mirza (1997) supports Brewer by arguing that there is a need for a distinctive Black feminism. She does not claim that Black women have a unique insight into what is true and what is not, but she does believe that this group can make an important contribution to the development of feminist theory. In fact, Black feminists can challenge the distorted assumptions of

dominant groups by drawing on their own experiences, and in doing so can offer other ways of thinking that can 'invoke some measure of critical race/gender reflexivity into mainstream academic thinking'.

In particular, Black feminists have actively challenged the dominant image of Black women as passive victims of racism, patriarchy and social class inequality. Images of the dutiful wife and daughter, the enthusiastic hard worker, the sexually available exotic other, the controlling matriarch and the homogenised 'Third-World' woman have undermined the fact that many Black women are 'brave, proud, strong'. Therefore, Black feminists have struggled in the fight against domestic violence, tried to overcome sexism and racism in school, developed alternative family forms in which women have autonomy and challenged the activities of the police and immigration authorities.

Evaluation of Mirza

Though Mirza offers some useful insight into how Black women can challenge the racism and sexism they experience in contemporary society, the fact that many ethnic minority women continue to experience pressures in the family to conform to traditional gender stereotypes to help to maintain *izaat*, low levels of economic activity particularly in Pakistani and Bangladeshi communities and the concrete ceiling in the workplace means that not all ethnic minority women have developed the confidence to be brave, proud and strong.

Connell (2009)

Connell (2009) stresses the links between Black feminism and postcolonial feminism. Postcolonial feminism is concerned with explaining gender inequalities that were caused by colonialism, particularly in developing countries in Asia, Africa and Latin America. This is because gender inequalities established in colonial times are often embedded in current attitudes towards race, ethnicity and gender. Furthermore, it would be wrong to base theories of gender upon the experiences of a minority of women in the world, such as those who live in the UK. Therefore, Connell stresses the importance of developing feminist perspectives that challenge the dominance of Western feminism; this is because Connell believes most women live in the 'majority world' of the southern continents.

Evaluation of Connell

Postcolonial feminism has been invaluable in helping us to understand the origins of gender inequality, but it sometimes overemphasises the importance of colonialism rather than gender inequalities.

Item A: Hijabi Barbie – growing up Muslim in a world of body image

I was brought up in a model agency. Surrounded by the likes of Naomi Campbell and Sadie Frost, I was all fashioned-out by the age of eight. I immersed myself in discussions of politics and faith; far away from the fashion shows and fashion shoots which I witnessed. Embracing Islam at 16 made sense to me from a theological perspective. Taking on the hijab made sense for a whole host of other reasons. The hijab for me was the antithesis of the beauty fascism that had surrounded me since birth. The hijab represented not just a religious injunction, but a weapon in the war against an industry that demanded women reach unattainable goals of beauty and weight. The hijab was the Muslim equivalent of burning the bra and cutting off the hair.

In 1988 the hijab was rarely seen in the UK, but it was beginning to be worn. The reasons for donning it were varied. In addition to the calling of faith, it stood as a mark of substance over form. For some, it was a search for simplicity; for others a mark of identity. Today it is ubiquitous on the streets of Europe; and indeed in France women have fought to wear it.

Over this time period the extreme demands of body image have also increased, for women and men. The rise and rise of the supermodels, and the decrease in dress size expectations have added to the atmosphere of bodily dissatisfaction. As Nigel says in *The Devil Wears Prada*, 'Size 6 is the new size 14,' and the main character Andy earns Nigel's respect only when she reaches size 4.

Muslims are not immune to all this. The malls of the Arab world are awash with the latest fashions. I have stood stunned in women-only banks as female customers have removed their abayas and scarves to reveal designer clothing complete with belly-button piercings and accompanying jewellery. Iran has become the 'nose job' capital of the world. Incidents of anorexia amongst Muslim girls are on the rise.

Can we lay all of this at the door of the Western world? What role do cultures play in the insecurities of women with the demand for tall, thin, fair brides? How do we help our children, particularly our daughters, to feel confident about their own body images? How can we help them resist the global search for body perfection? How can we stop Muslim women turning into little more than Hijabi Barbies?

(Source: Joseph 2010)

Item B: Malala Yousafzai accepts Nobel peace prize with attack on arms spending

Pakistani education activist Malala Yousafzai was jointly awarded the Nobel peace prize along with Indian child rights campaigner Kailash Satyarthi in 2014.

In fact, she used her Nobel peace prize acceptance speech to launch an attack on 'strong' governments that have the resources to begin wars but not to enable universal education. She said: 'Why is it that countries which we call strong are so powerful in creating wars but are so weak in bringing peace? Why is it that giving guns is so easy, but giving books is so hard? ... We are living in the modern age and we believe that nothing is impossible. We have reached the moon 45 years ago and maybe we will soon land on Mars. Then, in this twenty-first century we must be able to give every child a quality education.'

At the ceremony, attended by dignitaries including the Norwegian royal, Malala was joined by young female activists she had invited from around the world. 'I tell my story, not because it is unique, but because it is not. It is the story of many girls,' she said, pointing to her 'sisters' in the crowd.

In her speech Malala recalled loving school so much as a child that she and her classmates decorated their hands with mathematical formulas and equations instead of flowers. She said: 'We would sit there with big dreams in our eyes. We wanted to make our parents proud and prove that we could also excel in our studies and reach our goals which some people only think boys can'.

She described her 'paradise' home of the Swat valley before the Taliban gained control. 'Education went from being a right to being a crime. Girls were stopped from going to school,' she said. 'When my world suddenly changed, my priorities changed, too. I had two options: one was to remain silent and wait to be killed and the second was to speak up and then be killed. I chose the second one; I decided to speak up.'

Malala was shot by a Taliban gunman in 2012 after drawing attention to her own plight and the plight of girls like her, to get an education. She was airlifted to Queen Elizabeth Hospital in Birmingham, where she was treated for life-threatening injuries. Since her recovery, Malala has become very high profile notably after speaking at the United Nations, meeting Barack Obama, being named one of *Time* magazine's 100 most influential people and publishing the memoir *I Am Malala*.

1 How are the experiences of Muslim women in Western societies different from the experiences Muslim women around the world?

2 What would postcolonial feminists have to say about the plight of Muslim women in different parts of the world?

The New Right

Losing Ground – Murray (1984)

New Right theorist **Charles Murray** published a book called *Losing Ground* in 1984, in which he argued that the USA had a growing underclass that posed a serious threat to American society. He expressed concerns that government policies were encouraging increasing numbers of Americans to become dependent on benefits. Furthermore, he claimed that during the 1960s, welfare reforms led to an increase in the number of never-married black single mothers, and many black youths losing interest in getting a job. Therefore, he argued that increases in the levels of benefits were counterproductive as they discouraged self-sufficiency and were costly to tax payers.

When Murray visited Britain in 1989, he wrote an article for the *Sunday Times* in which he argued that Britain too had developed an underclass. Murray defined the underclass in terms of behaviour. He said that their homes were littered and unkempt. The men in the family were unable to hold down a job for more than a few weeks at a time. Drunkenness was common. The children grew up ill-schooled and ill-behaved and often became local juvenile delinquents.

Murray, who described himself as a visitor from a plagued area coming to see if the disease had spread, found signs that Britain too had been infected. These signs consisted of figures showing rising rates of illegitimacy, a raising crime rate and an alleged unwillingness among many of Britain's youth to take jobs. In certain neighbourhoods, traditional values such as beliefs in honesty, family life and hard work had been seriously undermined. As a consequence, increasing numbers of children were being raised in a situation where they were likely to take on the underclass values of their parents.

Evaluation of Murray

By focusing on the cultural attributes of the working class, Murray ignored economic divisions that lead to the creation of such an underclass, such as racial prejudice and discrimination. Furthermore, rather than taking a sympathetic approach towards the underclass, he blamed them for the predicament they find themselves in, explaining their situation in terms of their own supposed aberrant behaviour.

Sewell (1997)

Sewell (1997) echoes some of the arguments made by Murray in his study as he argues that a high proportion of African-Caribbean boys are raised in lone-parent families (usually headed by women) in the UK. His research highlights that in 2001, 57 per cent of African-Caribbean families with dependent children were headed by lone parents, compared with 25 per cent of white families. As a result, many black boys lacked the male role model and the discipline provided by a father figure.

Sewell argues that the absence of a male role model/disciplinarian within the family makes young African-Caribbean boys more vulnerable to peer pressure. For example, some young boys are drawn into gangs that emphasise an aggressive, macho form of masculinity. Members demand respect, reject authority figures such as teachers and police, and focus on up-to-the minute street fashion and music. This form of black masculinity is then reflected and reinforced by the media, with gangster rap and hip-hop fashions and news reports emphasising black street crime and gun culture.

Evaluation of Sewell

Though Sewell does not label himself as a New Right theorist, his study reinforces some of the points made by New Right theorists. Sewell's study is controversial and has been attacked for what his critics see as blaming African-Caribbeans for the inequalities that they experience. He has been accused of blaming black fathers for deserting their families, blaming black youth for generating a subculture that leads to their own failure and blaming the black community for failing to support its young people. Critics argue that, in the process, Sewell has diverted attention from what they see as the real causes of black underachievement: a racist society, an institutionally racist education system and economic deprivation.

Activity

Independent research

1 Identify and explain two policies devised by the New Right that have a direct impact upon ethnic minorities in the contemporary UK.

Section summary

Fill in the blanks, using the words given below.

Functionalists argue that the early ethnic inequalities experienced by immigrants were the product of their _____ and relatively low level of skills. They were optimistic that in a _____ ethnic inequalities would decline as immigrants adopted the norms and values of mainstream society and climbed their way up the career ladder. In comparison to functionalists, Marxists have a rather _____ view of race relations, which stresses that immigration serves the needs of the capitalist class for labour and is used to divide workers from each other so that they are easy to control. Therefore, capitalism prefers _____ between ethnic groups as it is beneficial to the ruling class. Like Marx, Weber recognised the importance in the difference between the bourgeoisie and proletariat, but he argued that differences within the working class, such as _____, were also significant. This means that Weberian theorists are keen to point out that stratification in modern society can occur on the basis of non-economic factors too, such as status and party. In contrast to the above views, _____ have developed their theory as a result of their dissatisfaction with existing theories on ethnic inequalities. Black feminists argue that the high-profile feminist campaigns, though necessary, do not reflect the most pressing needs of the majority of women, _____ women in particular. Finally, New Right theorists like _____ argued that Britain, like the USA, had a growing underclass that posed a serious threat to society. He expressed concerns that _____ were encouraging increasing numbers of the underclass to become dependent on benefits. However, critics would argue that _____ theories divert everyone's attention from real causes of ethnic inequality- a racist society, an institutionally racist education system and economic deprivation.

black Feminists, conflict, cultural differences, ethnic differences, ethnic minority, government policies, meritocratic society, Murray, New Right, pessimistic

Practice questions

1 Outline ways that work and employment may impact upon ethnic minorities' life chances. [20]

2 'In contemporary society ethnic minorities continue to be disadvantaged compared to their White British counterparts.' Discuss. [40]

Understanding social inequalities: Age

Component 2, section B,

Understanding social inequalities

Content:

1 Age and life chances
2 Patterns and trends in age inequalities and difference
3 How can patterns and trends in age inequality and difference be explained?

Activity

Identity and age (recap)

For this part of the specification there are three main age categories to consider: childhood, youth and old age.

1 In pairs, identify three cultural characteristics (norms and values) attached to each age category and discuss how individuals are socialised into these characteristics.

7d.1 Age and life chances

Before we can begin investigating these issues you need to consider what you have learned about age and identity in Chapter 1. One debate is whether age should be discussed chronologically (in years) or seen as a life course.

Getting you thinking ...

1 Some say youth is the 'time of your life'. What do you think this means, and why do people say it?
2 Why might others think it is a hard age to be?

Laslett (1991) suggested it was better to see age in a three ages of life approach:

- first age: a period of socialisation
- second age: a phase of work and childrearing
- third age: a time of independence.

As life expectancy increases there might now be an argument for adding a fourth age (to be discussed later).

When looking at the elderly, Milne *et al.*'s (1999) study agrees with other sociologists whose research shows that the idea of one homogeneous group – the elderly – masks the reality. There are two distinct groups: those who have just retired and those over 80. When you are 16, 'old' seems to be everyone over 65 and the life experiences are very different. Milne *et al.* use the term 'grey power' to refer to the consumption habits and patterns of those over 65. Pilcher also argued that there should be a division when discussing the 'young old', which she stated was 65 to 74, and the 'middle-aged old', aged between 75 and 84, and the 'old old', which is 85-plus.

The concept of life chances was used by Max Weber in relation to social class but it can usefully be applied to a range of social groups (see page 225) including age groups. Social inequalities experienced by different age groups, for example child poverty, can ultimately affect life chances.

7d.2 Patterns and trends in age inequality and difference

Activity

Discrimination

At the age of 16, your age identity and status are defined by several areas of life: employment, education, media, treatment from professionals such as the police and medical professionals, relationships with family, relationships with peers, and religion.

1 In pairs, discuss how these areas affect a 16-year-old's life.
2 Imagine you are now 70. What will your life be like? Consider the following: employment, media representation, treatment from the health service, treatment by the police, relationships with family, relationship with peers, financial security and religion. Is the future positive or negative looking at your ideas?

Study

Covert participant observation – Moore

Gerontologist (someone who studies the biological, psychological and social process of ageing) Patricia Moore dressed up as an old person over a period of three years to find out what it would be like to be perceived as being old. She used latex wrinkles, make-up, a wig and clothing to disguise herself as a woman aged in her 80s. Her findings were that assumptions were made about her perceived age, such as that she was deaf and would be easily confused. One of Moore's conclusions was that 'perhaps the worst thing about ageing may be the overwhelming sense that everything around you is letting you know that you are not terribly important any more' (Moore and Conn 1985: 76).

Moore's experiment shows that old people are disadvantaged not necessarily by their physical old age but by other (younger) people's stereotypical assumptions based on their appearance of being old.

Point to discuss and research

1 What stereotypes did Moore face when dressed as an old woman?
2 What does that tell you about being old?

Johnson and Bytheway (1993) defined ageism as the offensive exercise of power through reference to age. This can be institutionalised, through organisational and legal practices, or based on stereotypical prejudice or even through well-meaning assumptions. All of these ideas will be discussed below.

Age inequalities in work and employment

Youth

From the Activity above, it should be clear that being young may affect your employment chances. You may have restrictions on when and where you may work, restrictions on the minimum you can be paid and restrictions on your chances of an employer choosing to employ you. If you are 14 or 15 in the UK, you cannot work more than 12 hours during a school week, and if under 13, you are not allowed to do paid work at all. A 16-year-old has a minimum wage of just under £4 per hour, whereas an adult's (over 21) is just over £6.50 per hour. While it may feel that employers are always going to pick someone older for the job as they are likely to have more experience, young people are cheap labour and thus being young may have some advantages in the marketplace of work.

At 16 per cent, the unemployment rate for 16- to 24-year-olds has been largely rising since 2004, but recent reports show a changing picture.

Activity

Youth unemployment

The latest report from the Institute for Public Policy Research (IPPR) says that despite steady falls in unemployment from 20.9 per cent a year ago to 17.8 per cent, there are still 868,000 out-of-work 16- to 24-year-olds and 247,000 of them have been looking for work for more than a year.

About 700,000 young people have never had a job.

The IPPR highlights a striking mismatch between what young people are training for and the types of jobs available. It says that 94,000 people were trained in beauty and hair for just 18,000 jobs, while only 123,000 were trained in the construction and engineering sectors for an advertised 275,000 jobs.

Activity (continued)

The IPPR says that youth unemployment is lower in countries where the vocational route into employment through formal education and training is as clear as the academic route. It says that this helps, as it puts the two on a more equal perceived footing.

Tony Dolphin, IPPR chief economist, said: 'We can learn lots from countries like Germany and the Netherlands. A strong workplace-based vocational education and training system, with high employer involvement, contributes more to a smoother transition from education to work and a low rate of youth unemployment than anything else.'

1 What are currently issues causing youth unemployment?
2 What could be done to help remedy the issue?

The elderly

Elderly life can become difficult once someone leaves work, and can lead to age discrimination and subsequent financial issues. Many media articles discuss people becoming 'too old to employ'. A survey by MORI found that 38 per cent of discrimination cases filed after 2006 (when European legislation made age discrimination illegal) cited age as the reason. There have been many high-profile cases in the media, such as with Arlene Phillips on *Strictly Come Dancing*, where the public have been led to believe that age is the sole reason for someone being made unemployed.

Activity

Age discrimination at work

1 Research another high-profile case where someone has claimed age discrimination.
2 Make notes on the details of the case.
3 Look at how the media presents the story. Are they showing a balanced picture? If not, who do they seem to favour? How can you tell?

Legislation surrounding retirement age is felt by some to be a possible area of prejudice and discrimination. When you retire in the UK, you will receive a state pension subject to having been a working citizen in the UK, paying national insurance for 30 years. The state pension age is currently 65 for men, but slightly younger for women. The female state pension age will keep steadily rising every few months and equalise at 65 for both men and women in 2018. It will then increase every few months, reaching 66 by 2020. The next planned increase, towards 67, will start in 2026 and conclude in 2028. In 2011 the idea of a compulsory retirement age was phased out in the UK, but an employer can still set a compulsory retirement age if they can justify it. Structuralists argue that it is society which determines the age someone is when they retire, rather than the individual's choice. While this structuralist view of retirement seems to set rules for all and thus should not aid inequality, retirement age is far from being the same for everyone in reality. For some an option is early retirement. While a state pension can only be taken at certain times, those who wish to stop working earlier of course may, though for a lot of people this is not financially possible. Research shows that this is an area where there is a great disparity of experience of old age. Those who have financial security will not 'grow old' in the same way as those who have to work until they drop. Debates about retirement age and changes are more important than ever in the UK with its ageing population (by 2021, 33 per cent of the UK population will be aged over 55 years). Some have called this a demographic time-bomb. If there are more people over 65 than under 16, this has repercussions for the UK as a whole. Issues such as dependency and having so many people possibly needing health care, social services and housing mean that there is a potential crisis. However, these risks assume all elderly people will be poor and require a lot of care, but improvements in health care and (for some) financial wealth mean the picture is not that simple and that the impact of the ageing population is not easy to predict. Evidence suggests many older people are working post-retirement, whether it be in voluntary positions or in paid positions because they simply cannot afford to retire, making it a far less homogeneous picture (see page 306 for a further discussion of this).

'The experience of retirement in second modernity: generational habitus among retired senior managers' – Jones *et al.* (2010)

The idea of retirement has changed dramatically over the last quarter of a century. It has transformed from being seen as a time of social redundancy and loneliness to being seen as a potentially positive part of the life course. This change has, in part, been driven by a movement away from fixed retirement ages (65 for men, 60 for women) to a situation where there is now a degree of flexibility about retirement age.

In this research, Jones *et al.* focused on the topic of age identity by examining the ways in which retirement, for some, is actively constructed as a lifestyle and cultural choice. Their study was based on 20 in-depth qualitative interviews with men and women from the UK. Respondents had previously worked in executive and higher management posts and had recently taken early retirement as a matter of choice. The researchers' aims were to explore the experiences of retirement, changes in lifestyle and social roles, and the meanings associated with retirement.

Three main themes emerged. First, the respondents saw the fact that they had more choice in arranging their retirement as an indication of their higher status, compared to other retirees who did not have this choice. Second, the respondents described early retirement very positively as a time of creative renewal and freedom with opportunity to pursue new interests and challenges. Finally, Jones *et al.* found that the respondents were aware that they were fortunate in comparison to both past (their parents) and future (their children) generations who faced more unemployment, reduced pensions and insecurity.

Activity

Later working life and retirement

1 Discuss in small groups anyone you know who is over 65. Are they working or retired? Do they do voluntary work?

Age inequalities in wealth, income and poverty

Middle age is a time associated with independence and financial security. As will be shown below, both childhood and old age can be times of financial uncertainty or even poverty for many. So it seems more appropriate to focus on poverty more when discussing age, over wealth and income.

Child Poverty

There are currently 3.5 million children living in poverty in the UK. That is almost a third of all children. In the UK, 63 per cent of children living in poverty are in a family in which someone works. Child Poverty Action Group (CPAG) notes that child poverty has many effects on life chances. It will affect a child's education, health and the community they live in.

With as many as one in five children in the UK growing up in poverty, campaigns such as End Child Poverty seek to target the areas with children most at risk and offer solutions.

For many, growing up in poverty means being cold, hungry, often ill and struggling with getting to school. Sadly, figures from CPAG predict that the number of children growing up in poverty will only increase. An interesting fact about the UK child poverty is that it is regional; different areas have different levels of child poverty.

According to End Child Poverty, the 20 parliamentary constituencies with the highest levels of child poverty in the UK are as follows:

Constituency (geographical area)	% of children in poverty in 2013 (after housing costs)
1. Bethnal Green and Bow	49
2. Poplar and Limehouse	49
3. Birmingham, Ladywood	47
4. Manchester Central	44
5. Birmingham, Hodge Hill	43

Constituency	% of children in poverty in 2013 (after housing costs)
6. Edmonton	43
7. Westminster North	43
8. Tottenham	42
9. Hackney South and Shoreditch	42
10. Manchester, Gorton	42
11. East Ham	42
12. Birmingham, Hall Green	42
13. Glasgow Central	41
14. Hackney North and Stoke Newington	41
15. West Ham	41
16. Blackley and Broughton	40
17. Bradford West	39
18. Brent Central	39
19. Leeds Central	39
20. Bradford East	39

(Source: End Child Poverty)

Activity

Child poverty

1 Discuss what difference child poverty can make to one's education and health. Why might living in an impoverished community also affect life chances? Draw up a list of possible effects.

The elderly

The risk of poverty among older people in the UK is disproportionately high. Sixteen per cent of pensioners in the UK live in poverty, according to Age UK. Poverty among the elderly has been described as being akin to living in the Dark Ages. Fuel poverty is a concern for Age UK, who state that older people will have to spend more than a tenth of their money on their fuel bill. This can mean that people have to choose whether to eat or heat their house, as fuel is such a financial strain. Statistics from poverty.org show that while some pensioners do live in low-income households, they are not actually the poorest in society or most likely to be in a bad financial position. Those who are of working age, single and with dependants are more likely to suffer the worst of poverty.

Age inequalities in social mobility

The movement of individuals within or between strata in society varies greatly on different variables. It is important to look at social mobility with regards to age in terms of disparity of experience. Being young or being old is not a clear divider of societies; it must be looked at in reference to one's social class, wealth, gender, culture, religion and nationality. A postmodernist view of the subject is required, one that does not look for one theory to explain age inequality.

Age inequalities and disparity of experience

Postmodernists such as Hepworth and Featherstone (1990) would state that all of these discussions on inequality and difference need unpicking. The groups of elderly and youth are far too simplistic. Marsh and Keating (2006) noted that different cultures attach different cultural meanings and values to different age groups. This section will now look at each of the areas mentioned above and question what disparity of experience exists.

All of the information on employment and financial situation give a negative picture of both youth and old age. However, as social action theorists remind us, the statistics are too simple to take at face value.

Clearly gender, social class, nationality, ethnicity, religion and actual age amongst other factors affect one's experience of youth or old age. As age inequality is socially constructed, it changes due to different factors in society.

Age

Judi Dench

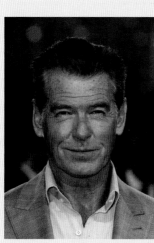

Pierce Brosnan

Oprah Winfrey

1 What connects these three people?
2 All three people are 60 or over. Looking back over the statistics and information in this chapter, how far do you believe they are accurate representations of people of this age?

Age and gender

Youth

Globally, young females suffer specific inequality not suffered by males. According to Advocates for Youth, this includes: 'Harmful practices, including female genital cutting/mutilation, femicide (the killing of females because of their gender), gender-based violence, and early marriage and damage to girls' physical being and self-worth by reinforcing gender-based marginalisation.' While there are cultural differences that preclude these practices, gender is a factor in whether youth suffers inequality. Other areas that create inequality for female youth include employment and education. Often, governments of countries such as Pakistan state that education is the right of all, yet statistics show that there is a huge disparity in gender and schooling. Activists such as Malala Yousafzai continue to fight for females to gain equality in education. Similarly, other rights are gendered according to culture, whether it be the right to work, go out without a chaperone or even drive. Often, the experience of youth is thus affected not just by gender, but by culture, religion and nationality.

1 Choose any two of the areas of inequality discussed above. Research cross-cultural evidence on what they are and why they exist. Be careful to look beyond the first headline you find. It is interesting to see what the government of a country states are the rights of young people and whether those rights are adhered to.
2 The experience of youth is of course also affected greatly by wealth and social class.

What differences are in store for these young people regarding their life chances? Make a spider diagram to brainstorm your ideas. You could consider the following: wealth, education, health and wellbeing, and so on.

The elderly

Statistics show that there is also a disparity of experience among the elderly when looking at gender, wealth, culture, religion and nationality, as there is with youth.

While discussion of old age can show us patterns of inequality and difference, a closer investigation shows that gender is a factor that affects the experience further. As with youth, elderly females are likely to be worse off than elderly males.

Activity

Age, inequality and gender

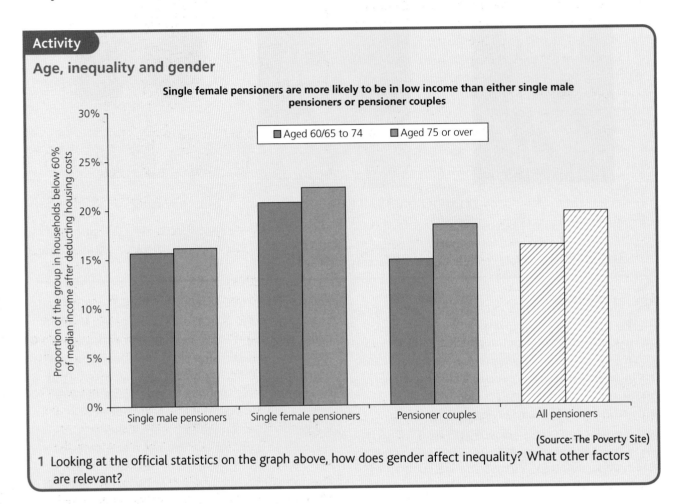

1 Looking at the official statistics on the graph above, how does gender affect inequality? What other factors are relevant?

Age and cultures around the world

Activity

Religion, culture and age

'In the Islamic world, one rarely finds "old people's homes." The strain of caring for one's parents in this most difficult time of their lives is considered an honour and a blessing and an opportunity for great spiritual growth. In Islam, it is not enough that we only pray for our parents, but we should act with limitless compassion, remembering that when we were helpless children, they preferred us to themselves. Mothers are particularly honoured. When Muslim parents reach old age, they are treated mercifully, with kindness and selflessness.

1 How does this quote from the website Islam Guide show how religion can affect the treatment of both young and old?

2 Write a paragraph showing how culture can affect one's experience of old age. Use the two sources above to highlight differences.

The elderly

Globally, the life chances and treatment of the elderly again shows a disparity of experience.

Ideas about getting older vary from culture to culture and over time. This means that ageing is socially constructed. In other words, ideas about age are not based on biology alone, rather age is defined through the culture a person lives in. Historical and cross-cultural evidence reveals to us the richness and disparity of different people's experience of old age. Some societies actually have a system of gerontocracy, which is a form of oligarchical rule in which an entity is ruled by leaders who are significantly older than most of the adult population. While this is often thought to be an ancient form of rule, parts of the world could still be said to be a gerontocracy. In Saudi Arabia, the Saud family have all of the power, largely all being in their 80s and above. The death of their King Abdullah bin Abdulaziz at the age of 90 saw power change hands to his 79-year-old relative, Salman. In Kenya, the Samburu are another example, where the power is with the elders. For instance, the elderly males have priority in choosing wives (as they are polygamous), while those under 30 have to wait, prolonging their adolescent status.

Kagan, in the study 'Activity and aging in a Colombian peasant village' (1980), observed that the old tended to remain socially and economically active, as far as physically possible, throughout old age. They did not constitute a gerontocracy, but were nevertheless seen as valued and respected members of their communities. This is similar to the position of at least some of the elderly in pre-industrial Britain. Every society creates its own definitions of 'old people'.

In nomadic societies, the elderly are a burden to the rest of society when they are unable to follow the nomadic lifestyle. In these societies, the old are frequently neglected or even killed once they start to become a hindrance. While clearly some societies give the elderly higher status and they have better life chances, this example shows that this is not always the case! Geronticide, or senicide as it is also known (abandonment to death, suicide or killing of the elderly), is not widely practised in the contemporary world. While it is illegal, some parts of Tamil Nadu in southern India are said to still practise it. Descriptions are closer to euthanasia than abandonment.

Activity

The experience of an elderly person

1 Who has the oldest living relative in the class? How old are they?
2 Where do they live, and who do they live with?

Gentleman (2009) outlines a day in a care home in Ipswich. She shows how, even with good care and a safe environment, the lack of visits from relatives and the monotony make it an unpleasant experience. The day of a resident is marked by getting up, eating or taking medicine. Gentleman states: 'The scene of torpid, joyless inertia is very dispiriting – but it isn't really the fault of the nursing home managers. The staff here are kind, the rooms are bright, the care is thoughtful and attentive – and yet none of this compensates for the home's unspoken function: a place where elderly people are left by their families to die'. A young Iraqi nurse who was interviewed explained that this was a new cultural experience to him as in Iraq families look after their elderly.

Activity

The treatment of the elderly around the world

In groups, research a global community and their treatment of the elderly. Make a poster showing differences to the UK. This will make good evidence for both evaluating patterns in Britain and your work on other units that look at global experience.

Youth

It is difficult to summarise any global picture of the status of youth. As the discussions on the elderly show, different communities have very different socially constructed ideas. A comparison of a tribe where a boy of three is given a knife and allowed to hunt with a child in the UK who cannot be convicted of a crime until the age of ten show that there are huge differences. What is evident is that religion and culture dictate the treatment of youth. Some differences are merely differences in culture, such as rites and responsibilities, while other differences are more about poverty, war and exploitation of the weak, rather than age discrimination.

Activity: Experiences of children around the world

Item A: Canada
According to Jean Brigg, among the Inuit, adulthood is the point of gaining an inquiring mind capable of reasoning. Until that point, children are treated with tolerance and leniency as they are seen as not being able to understand certain situations.

Item B: Tonga
According to Helen Morton, children in Tonga are seen as those without social competence. This needs instilling through discipline and punishment. Children aged between three and five are often seen as wilful, and therefore face a lot of beatings.

Item C: The Beng in West Africa
According to Alma Gottlieb, the Beng beleive that children are brought out of a spirit world to live on earth. This makes them special and the Beng even think that children can understand any language when born. Children are treated reverently.

Item D: The Fulani in West Africa
According to Michelle Johnson, by the age of four, Fulani girls are expected to be able to care for their younger siblings and fetch water and firewood, and by the age of six will be pounding grain, producing milk and butter and selling these alongside their mothers in the market.

1 Look at Items A–D, the cross-cultural findings from studies by various writers on the global experiences of childhood. Write a paragraph outlining how they are different to that of a child born in the UK.

The digital generational gap

Consideration of a growing gap between young and old must include a discussion of the 'digital divide'. While this term is commonly used to discuss financial divides born out of differential access to technology, there is a clear gap between young and old due to the ability to use technology. This causes problems for employment, as older people may be less comfortable using technology than the young who have grown up with it. It can also hinder the young and old understanding each other, as so much of youth culture is linked to new technology (Facebook, Twitter and so on), and even causes some elderly to feel they are becoming 'strangers in their own land' (Dowd 1986). Examples of this include feeling unable to cope with changes such as paperless banking (all statements being online), a lack of understanding of popular conversations and activities (social media) or even just the difficulty of answering a text message. This marks a cultural separation of young and old. However, a growing phenomenon of 'silver surfers' seems to show two things: that there are those who are post-65 accessing and using digital technology and that as new generations grow up with technological skills, the digital gap may change and the population as a whole will be more technologically informed.

Activity

The elderly and technology
1 Research websites specifically for 'silver surfers' such as www.silversurfers.com. What do they show about the digital gap?
2 Why might the elderly feel like 'strangers in their own land'?

A complex picture

So when looking at the main patterns and trends in social inequality and difference in reference to age, you need to be able to see that it is a complex picture. In its simplest form, age inequality is clearly evidenced within employment and patterns of wealth and poverty. However, a closer look at the statistics show that age may be a correlation rather than a cause, as other factors become increasingly important in causing a disparity of experience.

7d.3 How can patterns and trends in age inequality and difference be explained?

Sociologists discuss inequality in several ways but eventually it can be looked at from either a conflict, consensus or social action perspective. While age inequality exists, as has been proven through the patterns of inequality above, not all of the traditional sociologists explicitly discuss it. Discussions of why age causes inequality often require an application of theoretical views; that is, taking traditional explanations of inequality and applying them to research on age inequality. For example, Bengston

_et al._ (1997) stated that theoretical developments in gerontology (the study of the biological, psychological and social process of ageing) lag behind other fields of research and thus the study of ageing is not clearly directed by social theory. Due to this, Bengston _et al._ felt social gerontology has been 'itty-bitty' in its development of theoretical frameworks for research findings. When discussing age inequality, it is important to recognise that not all writers come from specific schools of sociological thought like functionalism or Marxism. It is more accurate when using the empirical data and evidence to discuss perspectives such as consensus, conflict and social action ideas rather than only looking at traditional theory e.g. marxism and functionalism.

Getting you thinking ...

A. Society's pity and negative treatment of the elderly causes them to become dependent and helpless.

B. Old people should not be allowed to take jobs from young people as they are less able.

C. Old people are less important as they have no money to spend and are just a drain on society's resources.

D. You cannot judge someone by their age; you need to look at factors such as wealth and market position to understand their life chances.

E. Young people should not get jobs when there is someone more experienced who could do it.

F. Young people have more energy and thus should get jobs over old people.

G. The elderly are not useless; their age and time of life just allows them to move on to other roles such as helping with childcare of grandchildren.

Which of the above statements do you believe, and why? Discuss this with a partner.

Consensus vs conflict vs social action theories

Consensus theorists such as functionalists believe that maintaining social order is important for society. Thus, looking at inequality, they will try and find a

reason for inequality that often focuses on a cause that is cultural – the fault of the individual or group's norms and values. Alternatively they will focus on the needs of the majority over the minority of society, sometimes even stating that inequality is functional. Conflict theorists such as Marxists and feminists will always focus on the structural causes such as the needs of capitalism or the needs of patriarchy and find these as the cause for inequality. Social action theorists will not look for macro reasons for inequality but take a more micro approach, looking at fragmented inequality and trying to locate the many variables that affect life chances. From the activity above, the differing views on age inequality can be seen. The study of gerontology looks at many explanations for the varying views on age and ageing.

Consensus theories

Consensus theorists focus on how inequality can be the 'victim's fault'. Put simply, the elderly and the young may face inequality because they do not have the necessary skills that others have. For example, young people are less likely to be paid highly. They deserve less money due to having fewer skills and less experience. This view would be agreed by New Right theorists, who claim that inequality is a product of cultural causes; for example, they blame youth unemployment on a generation by calling them lazy and unskilled.

Functionalism

Functionalist Talcott Parsons (1977), when stating that society can be understood through the organic analogy, was making clear the importance of society's stability. Through interconnected roles, the importance of institutions in society is to maintain social stability. Certain age groups have norms and values that could threaten social stability – for example, rebellious youth or dependent elderly. Functionalists such as Parsons focus on society's role in managing these issues as well as the cause of inequality at these times. For example, youth culture is often associated with a time of turmoil and rebellion. Parsons and also Eisenstadt (1956) focused on youth being a time for individuals to grow up and learn their new adult roles, which are imperative for society's stability. Parsons' work is often remembered by the analogy of a bridge, youth culture being a bridge from childhood to adulthood. This explains that while some youth behave in a way that seems dysfunctional to society, it can actually allow for a more integrated society later. For example, young people may experiment with deviant activities. Institutions in society such as the formal and informal agents of social control are set up to then deal with these actions, to show young people how to behave

and thus grow into functional adults. This stage of life allows for mistakes to be made and lessons to be learnt. For example, a young person will be sanctioned for truanting school; this then allows them to become a member of society who understands the importance of attending work on a daily basis.

Similarly, some elderly people become less physically able to maintain their roles in society specifically in the world of work. Functionalists such as Parsons would view this in terms of social roles and social stability. As the elderly may need to change roles that they can no longer fulfill, new roles are to be acquired. Currently in the UK, the elderly have become an invaluable source of free childcare for many families, with grandparents caring for their children's children. Again, Eisenstadt agreed, writing that differential age groups learn new roles that lead to further cohesion and solidarity in society. In her briefing paper *Grandparents Providing Child Care*, Statham (2011) was commissioned by the Department of Education to look into this role that so many do take up.

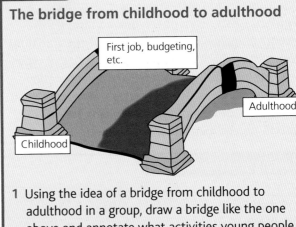

Activity

The bridge from childhood to adulthood

First job, budgeting, etc.

Adulthood

Childhood

1 Using the idea of a bridge from childhood to adulthood in a group, draw a bridge like the one above and annotate what activities young people might try while learning lessons for adulthood.

Disengagement theory

Cummings and Henry (1961) also take a similarly consensus approach to explaining age inequality, looking specifically at the elderly. The disengagement theory that they use to explain age inequality starts with the idea that all people will die. With ageing, a person's abilities are likely to deteriorate. As this process happens, there is a mutual need (both for the individual and for society) for the individual to be relieved of some of their responsibilities and roles. A functionalist would recognise that people leaving their role in society causes a gap that must be filled for social stability to be maintained. A process of disengagement helps to manage that possible social instability. For example, having a retirement age allows a managed disengagement, allowing others to take on the roles that the elderly can no longer fulfil.

Evaluation of consensus theories

As with all functionalist or consensus views, a common critique is their assumption of homogeneity when looking at society and inequality. Not all elderly people deteriorate at the same age, or at all. Others claim that these views always look at the bright side, largely ignoring the negative experience of ageing; not all elderly people are able to take on a new role and stay happy and fulfilled, and not all youth will be successfully guided by the agents of socialisation and may not leave deviant behaviour behind.

Activity

New roles in older age

Interview a person over 65. Consider which type of interview you would rather use: structured, semi-structured or unstructured. Find out whether Parsons is right and that they are finding that they acquire new roles.

Conflict theories

Marxism

Marxists focus on the needs of capitalism when trying to explain inequality. Youth are both an asset and an issue to the needs of capitalism. They are an asset due to the energy and new skills that they can provide, such as technological skills. Even if they lack skills and experience, they can also be a cheap source of labour due to lower minimum wages, which is beneficial to the bourgeoisie and the capitalist system. Similarly, the elderly providing free childcare is good for capitalism as it means that the young and able will be able to work. While Marx and other Marxist sociologists may not have discussed age inequality in great depth, their ideas can be applied to explaining age inequality.

Reserve army of labour

This phrase has been used by many, and some claim that Engels used it first in 1845. Marx stated that a reserve army of labour was a necessary part of capitalism. The basis of the idea is that some members of society are a secondary source of labour. Marx stated that this was either the unemployed or the under-employed; however, it can be applied to other groups such as the young and the elderly. These groups can be used at boom times as temporary or flexible labour. As many media discussions show, there is a growing market of 'zero-hours contracts', where employees are only given work when work is available, but have to be free to work regardless. Other benefits, such as pensions and sick pay, are not given. Clearly, those in the reserve for work are more likely to take up these contracts, such as unemployed youth or elderly people looking to continue bring in some income post-retirement. Phillipson (1982) claimed that the elderly have historically been used as a reserve army of labour, but that this role has grown in recent years. So, clearly, age inequality can be seen as a social construction used to benefit the bourgeoisie.

Quick question

Why would the young or the elderly be more likely to take a zero-hours contract?

Legitimation of authority

Neo-Marxists such as Gramsci (1971) discuss the importance of how the bourgeoisie maintain authority. His work on political society (rule through force) and civil society (rule though consent) can be applied to understanding the inequality faced by different age groups. False consciousness explains that people do not realise their exploitation often through concessions that they receive. It could be argued that small measures, such as child benefit and pensions, act as a form of this. This then creates a form of dependency, legitimating the need for the powers of authority. Thus, the elderly and youth do not question their exploitation through the labour market, accepting things such as zero-hours contracts.

Political economy theory

These ideas focus on inequality as meeting the needs of the economy. Townsend (1981) and Phillipson (1982) use these ideas to explain the inequality faced by the elderly. Phillipson argues that this places the elderly in a negative position as a burden on the economy. Capitalism needs to continually renew its workforce to ensure greater profit by using young workers who may be more productive. To serve the needs of capitalism, this means having a system where the elderly are institutionally marginalised. This happens through a process of institutionalised dependency; for example, through the elderly being made to retire, the needs of the economy are then met as younger, more productive employees take their place. In reality, a forced dependency then takes place, whereby the elderly become dependent on society as they are denied access to work. This then lowers their status, especially in a society where status is dependent on relationships with the means of production. So, in essence, it can be argued that the inequality faced by the elderly meet the needs of capitalism.

Activity

Age inequality

1 Write a paragraph to explain Marxist ideas on why age inequality exists. Ensure you use the following words or phrases:
- means of production
- capitalism
- political economy theory
- institutionalised/forced dependency
- reserve army of labour.

Evaluation of Marxism and neo-Marxism

Similarly to criticisms of the consensus and specifically functionalist approach, critics claim that Marxist and neo-Marxist theorists and research ignore the lack of a homogeneous experience of age. The studies seem to take a macro approach, ignoring factors such as class, gender, nationality, disability and wealth, which all affect one's experience. For example, in many industries and jobs, the elderly are not systematically marginalised and are able to work into their old age – for example, high court judges or political ministers. Moreover, with an ageing population, there has been a growth of the 'grey pound'. With the elderly as consumers, they can become an asset to the bourgeoisie and the economy.

Feminism

Another conflict approach that seeks to explain age inequality is feminism. Recent work looking at the unequal position of women has tried to see the relationship between age and gender and inequality. Arber and Ginn (1991) wrote that when looking at women and inequality, factors such as age will affect their power and status. As discussed in the first half of this chapter, older women face inequalities that older men do not. Itzin (1990) claimed that women face a double standard. Men's status is directly related to employment, whereas women's status is linked to their reproductive cycle. In a patriarchal society, women's status devalues after childbearing age. Put simply, older women, regardless of wealth and background, have a lower status. Owing to this, older women feel immense pressure to fight the signs of ageing (this is known as cosmeticisation, whereby women are encouraged to improve their appearance), which is capitalised on by many industries. Ageing men do not necessarily find the same pressures. Daly (1979) wrote that this had similarities to many global practices that women are made to comply with, such as genital mutilation, in that women are expected to confirm to certain physical standards, but no such expectations are placed on men.

Activity

Cosmeticisation

1 Watch an advert break between television programmes and record any examples of cosmeticisation. Be sure to note who the product is being aimed at (gender, age group) and what the product will help the consumer to achieve.

Evaluation of feminism

Some feel that feminist work on explaining age inequality is always going to begin from the perspective that patriarchy is the cause of the inequality. This may lead to feminist explanations missing the true cause of the inequality, e.g. poverty. A second critique is again to state that the structuralist, macro nature of much of the feminists' work ignores that fact that females, whether old or young, are not a homogeneous group and factors such as wealth and social class greatly fragment females' life chances. There are examples of both young and older females that show that not all face discrimination, and that it is possible to transcend the discrimination. Another criticism is that males are also going through a pressure to cosmeticise. Magazines such as *FHM* encourage males to stay looking young and fight the ageing process (Currie 1990) (the last activity may have shown you that!). Finally, there is an argument that cosmeticisation is not a forced process but one that people choose to take part in willingly, believing that they control the ageing process for their own subjective reasons, not due to the stigma of getting old.

Explanations for age inequality

1 Draw up a table to help to organise the conflict and consensus explanations for age inequality.

Idea	Perspective and source	Main points	Examples in contemporary society
Acquisition of new roles	Consensus: functionalist Parsons (1977)	As they age, people acquire new roles	Statham (2011) research: huge amount of childcare through grandparents

From your table, you should be able to see where ideas are similar and where they are different, which should help you to organise your ideas.

Social action theories

As social action theories include many views – that is, they are micro in their perspective, not macro – it is best to organise your explanations around the cause of the inequality. Some social action theorists, similarly to Marxists, look at economic and social capital as the cause, while others are more interested in the cause of a loss of social interaction or use in society.

Weberian theory

Weber's (1864–1920) work looked at inequality and while he was regarded as a disciple of Marx, he felt that to understand someone's social position and the complex nature of inequality, you need to look at three parts of their life: class, party and status. As Weber looked at the importance of one's market position, this could be used to explain the low status of both the elderly and the young. If someone does not have the skills required in the marketplace, such as the elderly, who do not have necessary technological skills, then they will suffer low status. However, if someone is upper class and becomes elderly, this will explain why they will not suffer the same loss of status, as their financial resources mean that they can continue to live a comfortable life regardless of their skills. For example, the Queen is elderly and female, yet the fact that she hasn't lost status is related to her social position and wealth.

High status and market position

1 Discuss examples of young or old people who have high status due to their market position, regardless of their age.

Negatively privileged status groups

Parkin (1968), when writing about ethnic minorities and inequality, discussed the idea that some suffer in negatively privileged status groups. This means that ethnic minorities can be kept out of high-status privileged groups due to social segregation. The elderly are often socially, segregated: in the media, through invisibility from positive portrayal; in employment, through retirement and even in living arrangements, often in care homes. Alongside other structurally caused inequalities, it is easy to find examples of how this theory can relate to age as well as ethinicity.

Activity theory

In comparison with explanations of inequality using disengagement theory, some interactionists believe that staying mentally and physically active will increase one's happiness. Similar to Parsons' (1977) and Eisenstadt's (1956) ideas, this looks at what happens when social norms withdraw social interaction from individuals. Maintaining these social interactions reduces the negative experience of ageing. Havinghurst (1961) published this theory in critique of disengagement theory, arguing the inequality is more about social interaction than just age. Statham's (2011) research on grandparents providing childcare may mean that continued social interaction may change the inequalities faced by some elderly who are isolated.

Exchange theory

Turner (1989) argues that age discrimination is actually best understood in terms of status. In Western societies, both the elderly and the young become stigmatised due to not having what it takes to gain high status; i.e. they do not control social resources and thus suffer low status. In a society based on consumption, high status is given to those who have material goods. If in Western society both the young and the elderly are least likely to have material goods, they will have low status. By using what Turner calls a 'reciprocity-maturation curve of ageing', it is simple to see that if groups are dependent, they then have low status. However, in a gerontocracy where power and age are interlinked, the elderly will have high status. Thus, inequality is not only about economic capital, but also due to the values of a society. This shows that status dictates one's position in society and thus is relative to that society. Age may be a factor that brings high or low status dependent on the key values of a society.

> **Activity**
>
> **Paul Spencer and the Samburu society**
>
> 1 Research the work of Paul Spencer and his time with the Samburu society to understand an example of a gerontocracy.
> 2 Why would this show that age inequality is a social construction?
> 3 How could this be used as an example of the 'activity theory' as an explanation of age inequality?

Interactionists: Labelling

All interactionists question the social construction of inequality. Negative labelling and stigmatisation of both the elderly and the young by the media and other agents of social control and socialisation could be said to create a self-fulfilling prophecy. If the elderly are labelled as 'useless, lonely, dependent and unable to learn' (Victor 1994), then perhaps those stereotypes become reality. Looking at the cases of supposed age discrimination in the media (as previously discussed in this chapter), perhaps media creators believe that the public think that the elderly are 'useless, lonely, dependent and unable to learn' and thus replace them with younger people, which of course, in turn causes the elderly to become 'useless, lonely, dependent and unable to learn'. Stan Cohen's (1972) work on moral panics would be a relevant explanation for the inequality that young people face in the media (see page 142).

> **Activity**
>
> **Representations of the elderly**
>
> 1 Complete a content analysis on adverts on the topic 'Both the young and the old suffer from negative media representation'. Consider how you will operationalise 'suffer from negative media representation'.
> 2 After conducting your research, write up a paragraph showing what you found. Are youth and the elderly always stereotyped negatively?

Evaluation of social action theories

As with all critiques of social action theories, there are some who believe that while these ideas attempt a micro approach, considering the effects of other factors such as wealth and ethnicity, they still fail to recognise the structural causes of inequality such as patriarchy and capitalism. Approaches such as activity theory are criticised for ignoring the institutional ageism that is at the basis of many laws and practices within a society, and structuralists would question what conclusions can be drawn from such ideas.

Postmodernist theories

Postmodernism is not a macro theory, so, like social action theories, the many various micro studies do not make one conclusion when it comes to explaining age inequality. Some postmodernists look at the disparity of experience of the elderly, while others actually refute that old age is a time of inequality, highlighting advantages of ageing in the modern world (examples of which will be discussed below). Discussions of inequality suffered by youth often blame the media for the creation of a 'youth culture', agreeing with Stan Cohen and his work on 'folk devils' (1972). Postmodernists such as Polemus (1997) focus on youth being a non-homogeneous group shopping at the 'supermarket of style'. Owing to this, there is not one single postmodernist explanation for the inequality offered by the young, but lots of micro studies exploring the issue.

Old age as a positive time of life

A critique of much of the social research on ageing is that it ignores many of the changes in the contemporary UK. While much research shows the older people get, the more they become invisible and marginalised, looking at consumer culture shows a different picture. Advertising acronyms such as SKIER (spending the kids' inheritance) and GRUMPY (grown-up urban professionals) show that stereotypes may be changing. The 'grey pound' is strong and thus advertisers are focusing on getting that money. Postmodernists Laczko and Phillipson (1991) researched early retirement and found that the inequality faced by some elderly people was due to wealth and not ageing itself. Their work, alongside that of Featherstone and Hepworth (1993), led to the idea that traditional explanations of age inequality focus too much on imaginary boundaries of age.

Discussions of the decision of many who are wealthy enough to retire early show that retirement can be a positive experience. Blaikie (1999) discusses the idea of positive ageing, which agrees with the idea of a fourth age filled with active but leisure-based pursuits.

Activity
Positive aspects of ageing

The University of the Third Age (U3A) movement is a unique and exciting organisation that provides, through its U3As, life-enhancing and life-changing opportunities. Retired and semi-retired people come together and learn together, not for qualifications but for its own reward: the sheer joy of discovery!

Members share their skills and life experiences; the learners teach and the teachers learn, and there is no distinction between them.

The U3A movement is supported by its national organisation, the Third Age Trust.

1 How does this university substantiate the work of Blaikie, Laczko and Phillipson, and Laslett?

The mask of old age

Discussions from postmodernists focus on the experience of ageing. J.B. Priestley, an author, stated that, for him, ageing was like someone had kidnapped him and made him old, yet behind his appearance he had the same thoughts as when he was younger (Powell 2001). These ideas have been seen as similar to wearing a mask: one thing on the outside, another on the inside. Such explanations suggest that the inequalities faced by the elderly are therefore more to do with labelling than ageing.

New technology and the fight against ageism

Not all people grow old gracefully; some fight it with the use of new technology and cosmetic surgery. Powell and Biggs (2000) wrote that this allows some to continually re-create themselves. While this may mean that age discrimination against the elderly is just based on the 'mask', it is impossible to tell, as those who can afford to re-create themselves may suffer less ageism due to other factors such as wealth.

Globalisation

Postmodernists recognise the importance of globalisation as a key cause of social change. As Britain becomes more multicultural, ageism changes. Some cultures are a gerontocracy where, instead of the elderly feeling marginalised and useless, their age brings them high status. In countries such as Kenya, where the elderly are still very much part of the family, their experience may be very different to that of a British person. This may mean that the cause of age inequality rests largely on culture. Similarly, the high status children have in the UK and its child-centred families can be counted with reference to cultures where a child has low status, or is expected to take on adult roles such as working or fighting in the army at a young age. These ideas show that it is not necessarily chronological age that causes some to suffer inequality but the norms and values within that society, such as retirement age.

Age is a complicated stratum for explaining inequality

While some believe that age can result in inequality that is an undeserved social construction based on labelling, others believe that it is directly related to what someone has to offer to society. What is clear is that the idea of homogeneous age groups all given the same high or low status ignores differences related to ethnicity, social class and gender.

Representations of different views

1 These were the statements you discussed at the beginning of this section. Now you should be able to identify which statement represents which view.

A. Society's pity and negative treatment of the elderly causes them to become dependent and helpless.

B. Old people should not be allowed to take jobs from young people as they are less able.

C. Old people are less important as they have no money to spend and are just a drain on society's resources.

D. You cannot judge someone by their age you need to look at factors such as wealth and market position to understand their life chances.

E. Young people should not get jobs when there is someone more experienced who could do it.

F. Young people have more energy and thus should get jobs over old people.

G. The elderly are not useless; their age and time of life just allows them to move on to other roles such as helping with childcare of grandchildren.

Section summary

Fill in the blanks, using the words given below.

Sociologists discuss inequality in several ways, but they can be grouped into three perspectives: _____, consensus or _____. Conflict perspectives include _____ and _____, which focus on inequality being the result of the needs of either capitalism or patriarchy. However, both can be criticised for treating age as _____, ignoring the differences that gender, class and culture make. Social action theorists consider inequality in a more micro way. _____ wrote that inequality is complex due to class, party and status, which can be applied to an understanding of age inequality. Others feel that age inequality is a media or social construction, whereas _____ consider age inequality as being more due to both the elderly and the young not having the skills and experience that others have. However, _____ believe that age inequality is too complex to explain in one way. They believe that there is a _____ of experience at every age.

conflict, disparity, feminist, functionalists, homogeneous, Marxism, postmodernists, social action, Weber

Practice questions

1 Outline ways in which female pensioners in the UK may suffer disadvantages. [20]

2 "Age discrimination has structural causes to benefit those in power". Discuss. [40]

Glossary

Age patriarchy The power which adults exert over children.

Ageism The offensive exercise of power through reference to age.

All singing all dancing superdads is a concept associated with a study undertaken by Warin et al. It describes the pressures that some men feel about the demands of juggling work and family roles.

Anomie A state of normlessness or uncertainty about how to behave in a situation where there is rapid change in society.

Anti-school subculture A group within a school that have their own norms and values usually in opposition to the dominant values of the school organisation.

Canalisation is a concept associated with feminist Ann Oakley and refers to a process in gender roles socialisation where children are channelled towards toys and activities seen as the norm for their sex.

Capitalist societies Societies based on the private ownership of wealth where production of goods and services is undertaken by workers working for wages and organised by capitalists investing wealth.

Capitalists Individuals who possess capital or wealth and who invest it in businesses in the hope of acquiring profits.

Catharsis is the process of releasing strong or repressed emotions thus providing relief. According to the theory of catharsis, media images of violence might release aggression and make deviant behaviour less likely.

Chronological age Age in years.

Class divisions Term describing how society is divided into groups based on economic and other inequalities, usually associated with divisions between different occupational groups.

Coding/decoding are terms within Stuart Hall's "Encoding-Decoding" model of communication, which states that the creator of a media message builds an intended meaning into that message and the audience interpret the message in a variety of different ways that accord with their social background.

Communist society A society where the means of production are shared between all members of the community and resources are used for the common good rather than private gain.

Concepts Terms used by sociologists to analyse and classify things which they observe in society. Concepts are the building blocks of sociological theories.

Concrete ceiling is similar to the concept of the glass ceiling but suggests that barriers to promotion in employment for women and minority groups are much tougher to break through than is proposed by the glass ceiling and that even promotion to middle management is restricted.

Conflict theories are ideas about society which regard society as being based on inequality rather than equality and consensus.

Consensus theories Theories in sociology which see society as based on shared values

Consumers are people who acquire goods or services to use or own. The term is increasingly used to emphasize the influence of products/services on an individual's identity rather than other social roles such as citizen, worker or homemaker.

Cosmeticisation Women are encouraged to improve their appearance.

Crisis in masculinity is a concept that proposes that changes in society such as de-industrialisation and feminisation of the labour have left some men feeling a sense of loss and confusion about their role and identity in society.

Cultural separation A widening gap between two groups and their norms and values e.g. between youth and the elderly.

Cultural view Blaming an individual or group's norms and / or values for any inequality they suffer.

Demographic timebomb A predicted potential crisis based on changes to the population e.g. ageing population

Desensitisation is the process by which people are repeatedly exposed to stimuli such as violent media images and, as a result, have a diminished emotional response to those stimuli.

Digital divide Commonly used to discuss financial divides born out of differential access to technology.

Digital generational gap A gap between the young and older generation based on abilities with technology.

Disengagement theory A functionalist view that the elderly are slowly withdrawn from responsibilities and roles such as work to help maintain social stability.

Disparity of experience Inconsistencies in life chances of a group/culture.

Dual labour market sees the labour market as divided into two segments; the primary labour market and the secondary labour market. The primary labour market is characterised by well paid, secure, skilled employment held by dominant groups in society such as white men. The secondary labour market is made up of insecure, low skilled and low waged jobs, mainly occupied by women and minority groups.

Ethnic inequalities Differences of wealth, power and status between ethnic groups.

Euthanasia Helping someone to die as an act of mercy.

False class consciousness is a concept in Marxist theory which refers to situations in which a working class adopt the perspective of the ruling class in society and do not, therefore, struggle against their oppression.

False consciousness A situation where subordinate groups in society are unable to see the reality of their exploited situation.

Femicide A crime involving the violent and deliberate killing of a woman.

Feminisation of the labour market refers to changes in the nature of employment that have resulted in the increased presence of women in the workplace. It is proposed that this change has been brought about by a number of factors including de-industrialisation, a shift to an economy with a larger tertiary (service) sector containing jobs that require 'soft skills' such as communication and the influence of feminism.

Feminism A political movement and group of sociological theories which sees women as unequal to men and which tries to liberate women from gender inequality.

Folk devil refers to a member of a deviant group who is seen as posing a threat to the social order.

Fragmented inequality Recognising inequality does not affect groups in a homogenous fashion, but is affected by many variables.

Fuel poverty Being unable to afford to heat your home, whereby paying for fuel means going without other necessities such as food.

Functionalism A sociological theory which focuses on the functions performed by different parts of society and the interrelationship between them.

Functions The job or purpose of an institution or part of society which expresses it contribution to the smooth running of the whole system.

Gender inequalities Ways in which men and women are unequal, for example in status, wealth and power

Gender-based marginalisation Social exclusion based on sex, usually female.

Geronticide Also known as senicide, it is the abandonment to death, suicide or killing of the elderly.

Gerontology The study of the biological, psychological and social process of ageing.

Glass ceiling is a concept that suggests that women and minority groups experience an unacknowledged, discriminatory barrier that prevents them from moving up the promotion ladder in employment to reach the higher positions.

Glass elevator effect explains that men are often promoted faster up the career ladder than women in female-dominated careers, such as teaching and nursing, because of gender stereotypes held by employers.

Globalisation The process by which societies are becoming increasingly interconnected.

Grey power Consumption habits and patterns of those over 65.

Hegemony is a term used by Marxists to describe a situation in which the ideas and world -view of the dominant class are presented in such a way that they are accepted by other classes as 'common sense' and the only sensible way of seeing the world. Any groups who present an alternative view are seen as deviant and, therefore, are marginalized in society.

Homogenous A group or society with individuals that are all the same, sharing the same norms and values.

Horizontal segregation is where the workforce of a specific sector of employment is mostly made up of one particular sex. Examples include the engineering industry, where men make up the majority of the workforce, and childcare occupations which are almost exclusively female.

Human Capital Theory puts forward the view that wage and role differences between employees can be explained by the level of skills, knowledge and personal attributes that each employee possesses rather than social inequality or discrimination.

Hybrid identities are formed from mixing aspects of two or more identities thereby creating a new identity. Such identities tend to be created within a society that is culturally diverse.

Identity How we see ourselves and how others see us.

Ideological state apparatus refers to agencies, such as education and the media, which spread the ideology of the ruling class and justify their dominance.

Ideology is a set of values, ideas and beliefs that represent the outlook of a social group. Ideological beliefs justify the social position of the upper classes and fail to accurately reflect the nature of society. It is a concept used by Marxists to describe the distorted viewpoint put across by the ruling class that results in a state of false class consciousness for the working class.

Ideology The dominant ideas in society which serve to legitimate the power of the ruling class or other dominant groups such as men.

Individualism The idea that people are individuals choosing their own identities rather than having their lives structured by membership of social groups e.g. genders, occupational groups or religious faiths

Institutionally marginalised Societies' institutions pushing some individuals/groups out of society e.g. compulsory redundancy.

Interpretivism An approach to sociology which focuses on the meanings and interpretations individuals and groups develop in understanding the social world.

Labelling The process by which groups categorise individuals, often negatively, based on certain social characteristics.

Legitimate To make something appear to be fair and justified.

Life course Age measured as a stage of life.

Macro theories Theories which focus on understanding society as a whole and the relationship between parts of society.

Male gaze derives from film theory and is used by feminists to refer to the tendency of media producers, such as film-makers, to assume the point of view of a heterosexual male, for example, in the way the camera lingers on a woman's body. As a result the female is seen as a passive object.

Malestream is a term that was created by feminists to be used in place of the word 'mainstream'. It suggests that in a male-dominated society most things are interpreted from a male perspective and this viewpoint then becomes seen as the norm.

Manipulation is a concept associated with feminist Ann Oakley and refers to a process in gender roles socialisation where parents/carers encourage gender-related forms of behaviour that are seen as the norm for a boy or girl and discourage behaviour seen as going against gender norms.

Marxism A sociological and political theory deriving from the ideas of Karl Marx which sees all societies developing through class struggles until the final emergence of communist society.

Master status A deviant status which comes to over-ride other characteristics of an individual and tends to define how they are treated by others.

Means of production Land, buildings, raw materials, machinery and other necessities used to produce goods and services required by members of society.

Meritocracy is a social system in which people receive rewards, such as higher pay or promotion on the basis of merit or ability.

Metanarratives Broad overarching theories which try to explain how society works and the nature of social change e.g. Marxism and functionalism.

Micro theories Theories which focus on looking in detail at individuals and small groups and how they interact within society.

Modernity A period in the development of human societies in which traditional ways of thinking began to be questioned and replaced by science and belief in progress. Modernity is also associated with the rise of machine technologies and mass production of goods.

Moral panic is a groundswell of public concern about an overstated or imaginary threat to society's norms and values. A moral panic is stimulated by sensationalised reporting in the media.

NEETs Young people who are not in education, employment or training.

Negatively privileged status groups Being kept out of high status groups through social segregation (usually used to discuss ethnic minorities).

Neo Marxists develop the ideas of Karl Marx, who stated that the economy shapes society, placing greater emphasis on the role of ideas in shaping society.

New Right thinkers are a group of academics, politicians and other public figures who believe traditional ideas are important and that the individual should take responsibility for themselves rather than the state. This set of ideas has had considerable influence on the media and policies.

Nomadic societies Culture where people live by travelling from place to place.

Occupational segregation is the division of labour in paid employment which results in dominant social groups, such as white men, occupying different jobs and roles from other groups, such as women and men from some ethnic minority groups.

Party is a concept associated with Max Weber that refers to a social division based on political power. It refers to levels of power and influence that may be achieved through membership of, or connections with, political parties.

Patriarchal terrorism is a term associated with Michael Johnson to describe a form of control of women by their male partners through fear and intimidation.

Patriarchy is a social system where men are in control and hold power and authority both in society and in personal relationships.

Pester power A child's ability to nag a parent insistently until the parent gives in to the child's request.

Political economy theory Inequality meets the needs of the economy.

Polygamous The practice or custom of having more than one wife or husband at the same time.

Postmodernity An era after modernity which some writers claim we are now moving into. Postmodern society is seen as diverse and moving in many directions simultaneously meaning the idea of society progressing in one direction is no longer relevant.

Poverty porn is any type of media that portrays the condition of the poor in an exploitative way to generate sympathy in order to sell newspapers or increase charitable donations or generate support for a 'good' cause.

Reciprocity-maturation curve of ageing Explains age stigmatization through exchange theory as an effect of declining ability to meet the expectation that people will respond to each other in similar ways leading to a lessening of status.

Reserve army of labour is a concept associated with Marxism. It refers to a segment of the labour force, usually associated with low skill occupations, which can be called into the work force when the need arises e.g. in times of economic prosperity and excluded when not needed e.g. when the economy is in recession. When not being used in the labour market, the reserve army are likely to be claiming unemployment benefit or engaged in domestic labour.

Self-fulfilling prophecy A process by which individuals are labelled in a manner predicting their future behaviour and because they come to see themselves as they have been labelled start to live up to the prediction.

Senicide Also known as geronticide: the abandonment to death, suicide or killing of the elderly.

Sensitising effect is the process of becoming increasingly aware of, or sensitive to, an image, film or other media product.

Silver surfers Those post 65 accessing and using digital technology.

Social action theories Theories which seek to understand the meanings individuals give to their actions and their subjective interpretations of the social world.

Social closure is a term first used by Max Weber to describe the way that groups maintain their power and resources by establishing boundaries based on shared norms, values and status that exclude others from membership of the group. shared norms, values, and status often stick together in order to maintain their advantage in society

Social competence A person's ability to get on with others.

Social inequalities Differences of wealth, status and power, for example based on social class, gender and ethnicity.

Social institutions Groups and organisation made up of individuals performing related roles, for example families, schools and companies.

Social order Term describing the idea that social life operates in regular predictable ways.

Social redundancy Being no longer useful to society.

Social solidarity A sense of unity and belonging in a group created by shared values and experiences.

State pension A regular payment made by the government to people of or above the official retirement age and to some widows and disabled people.

Status is a concept associated with Max Weber that refers to a social division based on social power. It refers to how highly-respected an individual or group is in society or in their community in terms of levels of honour and prestige that may be separate from economic position.

Stereotype is a simplified or generalised view of the characteristics of a social group. A stereotype does not allow for individual divergences between members of the group.

Strata A level or class to which people are assigned according to their social status, education, or income.

Structural theories Theories which see society as a structure which influences individuals to behave in orderly and patterned ways.

Supermarket of style Postmodernist idea youths can choose from different fashions, musical tastes and identities in the same way as supermarket shoppers are offered numerous choices.

Symbolic interactionism A sociological theory which focuses on how through social interactions individuals create meaningful interpretations of the social world.

The self An individual's sense of who they are, partly based on the expectations of others.

Theories Frameworks of ideas used by sociologists to organise and interpret their data and help understand the working of society in a systematic way.

Tokenism is the practice of doing something, such as giving a job to a person who belongs to a minority group, only to prevent criticism and give the impression that people are being treated fairly.

Toxic childhood According to Sue Palmer the idea that children are being damaged by a diet of junk food, excessive exposure to computer games and lack of love or discipline from parents forced to work long hours outside the home.

Vertical segregation refers to a division in the labour market where dominant social groups, such as white men are concentrated in the jobs that have more power, higher status and better pay.

Weberian theories Theories deriving from the ideas of the sociologist Max Weber.

Working class Usually seen as the lowest class in capitalist societies. Some sociologists use the term to describe just manual workers, while Marxists see all workers who work for wages as working class.

References

Abbott, P. (1990) 'A re-examination of "Three theses re-examined"', in Payne, G. and Abbott, P. (eds) *The Social Mobility of Women: Beyond Male Mobility Models*, London: Routledge, pp. 37–46.

Abrams, M. (1959) *The Teenage Consumer*, London: Press Exchange.

Abu-Harb, I. A. (2002) *A Brief Illustrated Guide to Understanding Islam* available at http://www.islam-guide. com/ch3-15.htm (accessed 2015).

Agencies (2013), '"Pester Power" costs parents £460 a year'', *Telegraph*, 17 October, available online at http:// www.telegraph.co.uk/finance/personalfinance/10385226/Pester-power-costs-parents-460-a-year.html (accessed 2015).

Alexander, C. (1996a) *The Art of Being Black*, Oxford: Oxford University Press.

Alexander, C. (1996b) 'The art of being black', *Times Higher Education*, 8 January, available online at www. timeshighereducation.co.uk/news/the-art-of-being-black/91969.article (accessed 10 May 2015).

Alexander, C. (2000) *The Asian Gang*, Oxford: Berg.

Allan, G. and Crow, G. (2001) *Families, Households and Society*, Basingstoke: Palgrave.

Althusser, L. (1971) *Lenin and Philosophy and Other Essays*, London: New Left Books.

Anderson, B. (1983) *Imagined Communities: Reflections on the Origins and Spread of Nationalism*, London: Verso.

Anderson, C.A., Berkowitz, L., Donnerstein, E., Rowell Huesmann, J.D., Johnson, J.D., Linz, D., Malamuth, N.M. and Wartella, E. (1994) 'The influence of media violence on youth', *Psychological Science in the Public Interest*, 4(3), 81–110, available online at http://rcgd.isr.umich.edu/aggr/articles/Huesmann/2003.Anderson_ etal.InfluenceofMediaViolenceonYouth.PsychologicalScienceinthePublicInterest.pdf (accessed 28 May 2015).

Ansley, F. (1976), quoted in Bernard, J. *The Future of Marriage*, Harmondsworth: Penguin, p. 233.

Arber, S., Dale, S. and Gilbert, N. (1986) 'The limitations of existing social class classification of women', in Jacoby, A. (ed.) *The Measurement of Social Class*, London: Social Research Association.

Archer, L. (2003) *Race, Masculinity and Schooling: Muslim Boys and Education*, Maidenhead: McGraw-Hill.

Archer, L. and Yamashita, H. (2003) 'Theorising inner-city masculinities: "race", class and gender in education', *Gender and Education*, 15(2), 115–32.

Archer, L., Halsall, A. and Hollingworth, S. (2007) 'Class, gender, (hetero)sexuality and schooling: paradoxes within working-class girls' engagement with education and post-16 aspirations', *British Journal of the Sociology of Education*, 28(2), 165–80.

Atkinson, A.B. (2013) *Wealth and Inheritance in Britain from 1896 to the Present*, CASEpaper 178, Centre for Analysis of Social Exclusion, London: London School of Economics, available online at http://sticerd.lse.ac.uk/ dps/case/cp/casepaper178.pdf (accessed 28 May 2015).

Atkinson, J.M. (1978) Discovering Suicide: Studies in the Social Organisation of Sudden Death. London: MacMillan.

Back, L. (1996) *New Ethnicities and Urban Culture: Racisms and Multiculture in Young Lives*, London: UCL Press.

Bagguley, P. and Hussain, Y. (2007) 'The role of higher education in providing opportunities for South Asian women' York: Joseph Rowntree Foundation.

Ballard, R. (1982) 'South Asian families', in Rapoport, R.N., Fogarty, M.P. and Rapoport, R. (eds) *Families in Britain*, London: Routledge & Kegan Paul.

Ballard, R. (1990) 'Marriage and kinship', in Clarke, C., Peach, C. and Vertovec, S. (eds) *South Asians Overseas: Migration and Ethnicity*, Cambridge: Cambridge University Press.

Bandura, A.; Ross, D.; Ross, S. A. (1961). "Transmission of aggression through the imitation of aggressive models". *Journal of Abnormal and Social Psychology* 63 (3): 575–582.

Bandura, A.; Ross, D.; Ross, S. A. (1963). "Imitation of film-mediated aggressive models".*Journal of Abnormal and Social Psychology* 66 (1): 3–11

Barker, C. (1999) *Television, Globalization and Cultural Identities*, Buckingham: Open University Press.

Barker, E. (1984) The Making of a Moonie: Brainwashing or Choice? Oxford: Blackwell.

Barn, R. with Ladino, C. and Rogers, B. (2006) *Parenting in Multi-Racial Britain*, London: National Children's Bureau.

Barron, G. and Norris, R. (1976) 'Sexual divisions and the dual labour market', in Barker, D.L. and Allen, S. (eds) *Dependence and Exploitation in Work and Marriage*, London: Longman.

Bartley, M. (2003) *Health Inequality: An Introduction to Theories, Concepts and Methods*, Cambridge: Polity Press.

Barwise, P. and Ehrenberg, A. (1988) *Television and Its Audience*, London: Sage.

Batchelor, S. (2001) 'The myth of girl gangs', *Criminal Justice Matters*, 43, 26–7, reprinted in Jewkes, Y. and Letherby, G. (eds) (2002) *Criminology: A Reader*, London: Sage.

Baudrillard, J. (1988) *Selected Writings*, Cambridge: Polity Press.

Baudrillard, J. (1994) *Simulacra and Simulation (The Body in Theory: Histories of Cultural Materialism)*, Michigan, MI: University of Michigan Press.

Bauman, Z. (2003) *Liquid Love: On the Frailty of Human Bonds*, Cambridge: Polity Press.

BBC Democracy Live (2013) 'Executive Pay and Remuneration Bill', *BBC Democracy Live* website, 31 January, available online at www.bbc.co.uk/democracylive/house-of-commons-21274226 (accessed 18 May 2015).

BBC Inside Out (2014) 'From rags to riches', *BBC Inside Out* website, 24 September, available online at www.bbc.co.uk/insideout/southeast/series4/rags_to_riches_entrepreneurs.shtml (accessed 18 May 2015).

BBC News (2012) 'Iain Duncan Smith promises to "champion" families and marriage', *BBC News* website, 13 March, available online at www.bbc.co.uk/news/uk-politics-17351353 (accessed 10 May 2015).

BBC News (2013) 'Huge survey reveals seven social classes in UK', *BBC News* website, 3 April, available online at www.bbc.co.uk/news/uk-22007058 (accessed 18 May 2015).

BBC News (2014a) 'Executive pay "180 times average", report finds', *BBC News* website, 14 July, available online at www.bbc.co.uk/news/28286264 (accessed 18 May 2015).

BBC News (2014b) 'Child poverty set to rise, says social mobility commission', *BBC News* website, 20 October, available online at www.bbc.co.uk/news/uk-politics-29686628 (accessed 18 May 2015).

Beaujouan, E. and Ní Bhrolcháin, M. (2011) 'Cohabitation and marriage in Britain since the 1970s', *Population Trends*, 145, 35–59, available online at www.palgrave-journals.com/pt/journal/v145/n1/pdf/pt201116a.pdf (accessed 27 May 2015).

Beck, U. (1992) *Risk Society: Towards a New Modernity*, London: Sage.

Beck, U. and Beck-Gernsheim, E. (1995) *The Normal Chaos of Love*, Cambridge: Polity Press.

Becker, A.E., Gilman, S.E. and Burwell, R.A. (2005) 'Changes in prevalence of overweight and in body image among Fijian women between 1989 and 1998', *Obesity Research*, 13(1), 110–7.

Becker, H. (1963) *Outsiders*, New York: The Free Press.

Becker, H. (1963) *Outsiders: Studies in the Sociology of Deviance*, London: Macmillan.

Benatar, D. (2012) *The Second Sexism*, Hoboken, NJ: John Wiley & Sons.

Bennett, A. (1999) 'Subcultures or neo-tribes? Rethinking the relationship between youth, style and musical taste', *Sociology*, 33(3).

Bennett, T., Wright, R. and Brookman, F. (2006) *A Qualitative Study of the Role of Violence in Street Crime*, London: Economic & Social Research Council.

Benston, M. (1972) 'The political economy of women's liberation', in Glazer-Malbin, N. and Waehrer, H.Y. (eds) *Woman in a Man-Made World*, Chicago, IL: Rand McNally, pp. 119–28.

Bernardes, J. (1997) *Family Studies: An Introduction*, London: Routledge.

Berthoud, R. (2001) *Family Formation in Multi-Cultural Britain: Three Patterns of Diversity*, ISER Working Paper 2000-34, Colchester: Institute for Social and Economic Research, University of Essex, available online at www.sociology.org.uk/as4fm1.pdf (accessed 27 May 2015).

Berthoud, R. and Beishon, S. (1997) 'People, families and households', in Modood, T. and Berthoud, R. (eds) *Ethnic Minorities in Britain: Diversity and Disadvantage*, London: Policy Studies Institute, pp. 18–59, available online at www.psi.org.uk/pdf/Ethnic%20Minorities%20In%20Britain_small_file.pdf (accessed 27 May 2015).

Bettelheim, B. (1969) *The Children of the Dream*, London: Macmillan.

Bhatti, G. (1999) *Asian Children at Home and at School: An Ethnographic Study*, London: Routledge.

Biggs, S. (1993) *Understanding Ageing*, Buckingham: Open University Press.

Blackman, S. (1998) 'The school: 'poxy Cupid!' An ethnographic and feminist account of a resistant female youth culture: the New Wave Girls', in Skelton, T. and Valentine, G. (eds) *Cool Places: Geographies of Youth Cultures*, London: Routledge.

Blaikie, A. (1999) *Ageing and Popular Culture*. Cambridge University Press, 1999.

Blanden, J. (2009) *How Much Can We Learn from International Comparisons of Intergenerational Mobility?*, Centre for the Economics of Education Discussion Paper III.

Blanden, J., Greg, P. and Machin, S. (2005) *Intergenerational Mobility in Europe and North America*, London: Centre for Economic Performance.

Bourdieu, P. (1973) 'Cultural reproduction and social reproduction', in Brown, R. (ed.) *Knowledge, Education and Cultural Change*, London: Tavistock

Bourdieu, P. (1984) *Distinction: A Social Critique of the Judgment of Taste*, Cambridge, MA: Harvard University Press.

Bourdieu, P. (1986) 'The forms of capital', in Richardson, J. (ed.) *Handbook of Theory and Research for the Sociology of Education*, London: Greenwood Press.

Bourgois, P. (1995) *In Search of Respect*, Cambridge: Cambridge University Press.

Bowers, S., Treanor, J., Walsh, F., Finch, J., Collinson, P. and Traynor, I. (2013) 'Bonuses: the essential guide', *Guardian*, 28 February, available online at www.theguardian.com/business/2013/feb/28/bonuses-the-essential-guide (accessed 10 May 2015).

Bowles, S. and Gintis, H. (1976) *Schooling in Capitalist America*, London: Routledge & Kegan Paul.

Bradley, H. (1996) *Fractured Identities: Changing Patterns of Inequality*, Cambridge: Polity Press.

Bradshaw, J., Middleton, S., Davis, A., Oldfield, N., Smith, N., Cusworth, L. and Williams J. (2008) *A Minimum Income Standard for Britain: What People Think*, York: Joseph Rowntree Foundation, available online at www.jrf.org.uk/sites/files/jrf/2226-income-poverty-standards.pdf (accessed 28 May 2015).

Brah, A. (1996) *Cartographies of Diaspora*, London: Routledge.

Brake, M. (1977) *Hippies and Skinheads: Sociological Aspects of Subcultures*, PhD thesis, London School of Economics.

Brake, M. (1980) *The Sociology of Youth Culture and Youth Subcultures*, London: Routledge.

Brake, M. (1985) *Comparative Youth Subculture: The Sociology of Youth Culture and Youth Subcultures in America, Britain and Canada*, London: Routledge.

Brannen, J. (2003) 'The age of beanpole families', *Sociology Review*.

Braverman, H. (1974) *Labour and Monopoly Capital*, New York: Monthly Press.

Brewer, J.D. (2000) Ethnography. Buckingham: Open University Press.

Briggs, A. and Cobley, P. (2002) *The Media: An Introduction*, Harlow: Pearson.

Brindle, D. (2000) 'The disappearance of Britishness: our lives are becoming hopelessly Americanised says professor', *Guardian*, 27 January, available online at www.theguardian.com/uk/2000/jan/27/davidbrindle (accessed 10 May 2015).

Bristol Fawcett Society (2008) REPRESENTATION/ MISREPRESENTATION/ NO REPRESENTATION OF WOMEN IN THE MEDIA, available online at www.rowitm.org.

British Library (n.d.) 'Timeline of the Women's Liberation Movement', available online at www.bl.uk/learning/histcitizen/sisterhood/timeline.html (accessed 20 May 2015).

British Sociological Association (BSA), available online at http://www.britsoc.co.uk/about/equality/statement-of-ethical-practice.aspx, Ethical Guidelines.

Brown, P. (1987) *Schooling Ordinary Kids*, London: Tavistock.

Brown, S. (2012) 'In what ways has criminology sought to understand the rave movement as organised deviance?', *Plymouth Law and Criminal Justice Review*, 2012(1), 152–61, available online at www.pbs.plymouth.ac.uk/plr/vol4/Brown,%20Steven%20-%20The%20Rave%20Movement%20as%20Organised%20Deviance%20%28FINAL%20DRAFT%29.pdf (accessed 27 May 2015).

Bruegel, I. (1979) 'Women as a reserve army of labour', *Feminist Review*, 3, 12–23.

Bryman, A. (1988) Quantity and Quality in Social Research .London: Allen & Unwin.

Buck, D. and Gregory, S. (2013) *Improving the Public's Health: A Resource for Local Authorities*, London: King's Fund, available online at www.kingsfund.org.uk/sites/files/kf/field/field_publication_file/improving-the-publics-health-kingsfund-dec13.pdf (accessed 28 May 2015).

Burdsey, D. (2004) 'One of the lads? Dual ethnicity and assimilated ethnicities in the careers of British professional footballers', *Ethnic and Racial Studies*, 27(5), 757–9.

Burman, M., Tisdall, K., Brown, J. and Batchelor, S. (2000) *A View from the Girls: Exploring Violence and Violent Behaviour: Research Findings*, Swindon: Economic & Social Research Council.

Burns, J. (2014) '"Deeply elitist UK locks out diversity at top"', *BBC News* website, 28 August, available online at www.bbc.co.uk/news/education-28953881 (accessed 18 May 2015).

Butler, C. (1995) 'Religion and gender: young Muslim women in Britain', *Sociology Review*, 4(3).

Calhoun, C. (1997) 'Family outlaws: rethinking the connections between feminism, lesbianism and the family', in Nelson, H.L. (ed.) *Feminism and Families*, London: Routledge.

Campbell, A. (1981) *Girl Delinquents*, Oxford: Blackwell.

Campbell, A. (1986) *The Girls in the Gang*, New York and Oxford: Blackwell.

Campbell, B. (1993) *Goliath: Britain's Dangerous Places*, London: Methuen.

Canaan, J. (1996) 'One thing leads to another: drinking, fighting and working-class masculinities', in Mac an Ghaill, M. (ed.) *Understanding Masculinities: Social Relations and Cultural Arenas*, Maidenhead: McGraw-Hill.

Carrigan, M. and Szmigin, I. (2000) 'Advertising in an ageing society', *Ageing and Society*, 20(1), 217–33.

Cashmore, E. (1997) *The Black Culture Industry*, London: Routledge.

Cashmore, E. and Troyna, B. (1990) *Introduction to Race Relations*, London: Falmer Press.

Centre for Social Justice (2006) *The State of the Nation Report: Fractured Families*, London: Centre for Social Justice, available online at www.centreforsocialjustice.org.uk/UserStorage/pdf/Pdf%20reports/BreakdownB_family_breakdown.pdf (accessed 27 May 2015).

Centre for Social Justice (2009) *Dying to Belong: An In-Depth Review of Street Gangs in Britain*, London: Centre for Social Justice, available online at www.centreforsocialjustice.org.uk/UserStorage/pdf/Pdf%20reports/DyingtoBelongFullReport.pdf (accessed 27 May 2015).

Centre for Social Justice (2012) *Time to Wake Up: Tackling Gangs One Year After the Riots*, London: Centre for Social Justice, available online at http://www.centreforsocialjustice.org.uk/UserStorage/pdf/Pdf%20reports/Gangs-Report.pdf (accessed 27 May 2015).

Centre for Social Justice (2014) *Girls and Gangs*, London: Centre for Social Justice, available online at www.centreforsocialjustice.org.uk/UserStorage/pdf/Pdf%20reports/Girls-and-Gangs-FINAL-VERSION.pdf (accessed 27 May 2015).

Chamberlain, M. (1999) 'Brothers, sisters, uncles and aunts: a lateral perspective on Caribbean families', in Silva, E.B. and Smart, C. (eds) *The New Family?*, London: Sage.

Chambers, D. (2001) *Representing the Family*, London: Sage.

Chambers, D. (2012) *A Sociology of Family Life: Change and Diversity in Intimate Relations*, Cambridge: Polity Press.

Chandler, D. (n.d.) 'Semiotics for beginners', *Visual Memory*, available online at http://visual-memory.co.uk/daniel/Documents/S4B/sem10.html (accessed 28 May 2015).

Channel 4 News (2013) 'Low-pay Britain: one in five Brits earning below living wage', *Channel 4 News* website, 4 September, available online at www.channel4.com/news/living-wage-uk-pay-poverty-workers-hospitality-retail (accessed 18 May 2015).

Chant, S. (2011), 'The links between gender and poverty are ver-simplified and under-problematised: a time of economic crisis is an opportune moment to rethink the "feminisation of poverty" and address the "feminisation of responsibility"', London: London School of Economics, available online at http://eprints.lse.ac.uk/33443/1/blogs.lse.ac.uk-The_links_between_gender_and_poverty_are_over-simplified_and_under-problematised-_a_time_of_economic_.pdf (accessed 19 May 2015).

Chapman, T. (2004) *Gender and Domestic Life: Changing Practices in Families and Households*, London: Palgrave Macmillan.

Charles, N. and Kerr, M. (1988) *Women, Food and Families*, Manchester: Manchester University Press.

Chester, R. (1985) 'The rise of the neo-conventional family', *New Society*, 9 May.

Cicourel, A. (1968) *The Social Organisation of Juvenile Justice*, New York: Wiley.

Clarke, J. (1976) 'The Skinheads and the magical recovery of community' in Hall, S. and Jefferson, T. (eds) *Resistance through Rituals*, London: Routledge, 99–102.

Cloward, R. and Ohlin, L. (1961) *Delinquency and Opportunity*, Glencoe, IL: The Free Press.

Cochrane, K. (2013) 'The fourth wave of feminism: meet the rebel women', *Guardian*, 10 December, available online at www.theguardian.com/world/2013/dec/10/fourth-wave-feminism-rebel-women (accessed 29 May 2015).

Cohen, A. (1955) *Delinquent Boys: The Culture of the Gang*, New York: The Free Press.

Cohen, P. (2003) 'Mods and shockers: youth cultural studies in Britain', in Bennett, A., Cieslik, M. and Miles, S. (eds) *Researching Youth: Issues, Controversies and Dilemmas*, London: Palgrave.

Cohen, S. (1972) *Folk Devils and Moral Panics: The Creation of the Mods and Rockers*, London: Paladin.

Cohen, S. (2002) *Folk Devils and Moral Panics: The Creation of the Mods and Rockers*, third edition, London: Routledge.

Collins, P.H. (1990) *Black Feminist Thought*, London: Hyman.

Connell, R. (1995) *Masculinities*, Cambridge: Polity Press.

Connell, R. (2014) 'King hits: young men, masculinity and violence', *The Conversation*, 21 January, available online at www.theconversation.com/king-hits-young-men-masculinity-and-violence-22247 (accessed 27 May 2015).

Connell, R.W. (1995) *Masculinities*, Cambridge: Polity Press.

Cooper, D. (1972) *The Death of the Family*, Harmondsworth: Penguin.

Cooper, N., Purcell, S. and Jackson, R. (2014) *Below the Breadline: The Relentless Rise of Food Poverty in Britain*, Salisbury: The Trussell Trust, available online at www.trusselltrust.org/resources/documents/foodbank/6323_Below_the_Breadline_web.pdf (accessed 29 May 2015).

Corner, L. (1999) 'Developing approaches to person-centred outcome measures for older people in rehabilitation settings', PhD thesis, cited in Bond, J. and Corner, L. (2004) *Quality of Life and Older People*, Maidenhead: McGraw-Hill.

Cowell, F., Karagiannaki, E., and McKnight, A. (2012) *Accounting for Cross-Country Differences in Wealth Inequality*, CASEpaper 168, Centre for Analysis of Social Exclusion, London: London School of Economics, available online at www.lisdatacenter.org/wps/lwswps/13.pdf (accessed 28 May 2015).

Cracknell, R. (2010) *The Ageing Population: Key Issues for the New Parliament 2010*, London: House of Commons Library Research, available online at www.parliament.uk/documents/commons/lib/research/key_issues/Key-Issues-The-ageing-population2007.pdf (accessed 27 May 2015).

Cribb, J., Hood, A., Joyce, R. and Phillips, D. (2013) *Living Standards, Poverty and Inequality in the UK: 2013*, London: Institute for Fiscal Studies, available online at www.ifs.org.uk/comms/r81.pdf (accessed 28 May 2015).

Crompton, R. (2005) *Class and the Family*, GeNet Working Paper No. 9, available online at www.genet.ac.uk/workpapers/GeNet2005p9.pdf (accessed 27 May 2015).

Crompton, S. (2008) 'Are you an over-protective parent?', *Times*, 26 July, available online at www.thetimes.co.uk/tto/life/families/article1757991.ece (accessed 10 May 2015).

Cuddy, A.J. and Fiske, S.T. (2004) 'Doddering, but dear: process, content, and function in stereotyping of older persons', in Nelson, T.D. (ed.) *Ageism: Stereotyping and Prejudice Against Older Persons*, Cambridge, MA: MIT Press, pp. 3–26.

Cunningham, H. (2007) 'Social constructions of childhood', *Sociology Review*.

Curran, J. and Gurevich, M. (1977) *Mass Communications and Society*, London: Hodder Education.

Dalla Costa, M. and James, S. (1972) *The Power of Women and the Subversion of the Community*, Bristol: Falling Wall Press.

Davis, K. and Moore, W.E. (1945) 'Some principles of social stratification', *American Sociological Review*, 10.

Dawney, L. (2008) *Racialisation of Central and East European Migrants in Hertfordshire*, Working Paper No. 53, University of Sussex, available online at www.sussex.ac.uk/webteam/gateway/file.php?name=mwp53.pdf&site=252 (accessed 26 May 2015).

Decker, S.H. and Van Winkle, B. (1996) *Life in the Gang: Family, Friends, and Violence*, Cambridge: Cambridge University Press.

Delphy, C. and Leonard, D. (1992) *Familiar Exploitation: A New Analysis of Marriage in Contemporary Western Societies*, Cambridge: Polity Press.

Delphy, C. and Leonard, D. (1992) *Familiar Exploitation: A New Analysis Of Marriage In Contemporary Western Societies*, Cambridge: Polity Press.

Dench, D., Ogg, J. and Thomson K. (1999) 'The role of grandparents', in Jowell, R., Curtis, J., Park, A. and Thomson, K. (eds) *British Social Attitudes: The 16th Report: Who Shares New Labour's Values?*, Farnham: Ashgate.

Dennis, N. and Erdos, G. (2000) *Families without Fatherhood*, London: Institute for the Study of Civil Society.

Denscombe, M. (2001) 'Critical incidents and the perception of health risks: the experiences of young people in relation to their use of alcohol and tobacco', *Health, Risk & Society*, 3(3), 293–306.

Department for Work and Pensions (2013) *Households Below Average Income: An Analysis of the Income Distribution 1994/95–2011/12*, London: Department for Work and Pensions, available online at www.gov.uk/government/uploads/system/uploads/attachment_data/file/206778/full_hbai13.pdf (accessed 27 May 2015).

Department for Work and Pensions (2014) *Households Below Average Income: An Analysis of the Income Distribution 1994/95–2012/13*, London: Department for Work and Pensions, available online at www.gov.uk/government/uploads/system/uploads/attachment_data/file/325416/households-below-average-income-1994-1995-2012-2013.pdf (accessed 27 May 2015).

Department of Work and Pensions (2013) 'Households below average income (HBAI)', available online at www.gov.uk/government/collections/households-below-average-income-hbai--2 (accessed 29 May 2015).

Dermott, E. (2003) 'The "intimate father": defining paternal involvement', *Sociological Research Online*, 8(4), available online at www.socresonline.org.uk/8/4/dermott.html (accessed 27 May 2015).

Derrington, C. and Kendall, S. (2004) *Gypsy Traveller Students in Secondary Schools: Cultures, Identity and Achievement*, Stoke-on-Trent: Trentham Books.

Devereux, E. (2008) *Understanding the Media*, London: Sage.

Dines, G. and Humez, J.M. (eds) (1995) *Gender, Race and Class in Media: A Text-Reader*, London: Sage.

Dodd, K. and Dodd, P. (1992) 'From the East End to *EastEnders*: representations of the working class, 1890 to 1990', in Strinati, D. and Wagg, S. (eds), *Come On Down? Popular Media Culture in Post-War Britain*, London: Routledge.

Dodd, V. (2012) 'Ethnic minority women face jobs crisis', *Guardian*, 7 December, available online at www.theguardian.com/world/2012/dec/07/ethnic-minority-women-jobs-crisis (accessed 20 May 2015).

Donovan, C.K. and Driskill, Q.-L. (n.d.) 'Why should I cut my dreads? What's wrong with a Mohawk?', *Make*, available online at www.makezine.enoughenough.org/mohawksdreads.htm (accessed 10 May 2015).

Dorling, D. (2012) *Fair Play*, Bristol: Policy Press.

Doughty, S. (2015) 'Senior judge says married couples who stay married should get a tax break – and those who divorce should be penalised', *Daily Mail*, 10 January, available online at www.dailymail.co.uk/news/article-2904096/Senior-judge-says-couples-stay-married-tax-break.html (accessed 10 May 2015).

Dransfield, S. (2014) *A Tale of Two Britains: Inequality in the UK*, Oxford: Oxfam, available online at http://policy-practice.oxfam.org.uk/publications/a-tale-of-two-britains-inequality-in-the-uk-314152 (accessed 28 May 2015).

Dugan, E. (2014) 'The food poverty scandal that shames Britain: nearly 1m people rely on handouts to eat – and benefit reforms may be to blame', *Independent*, 16 April, available online at www.independent.co.uk/news/uk/politics/churches-unite-to-act-on-food-poverty-600-leaders-from-all-denominations-demand-government-uturn-on-punitive-benefits-sanctions-9263035.html (accessed 10 May 2015).

Duncan, S. and Phillips, M. (2008) 'New families? Tradition and change in modern relationships', in Park, A., Curtice, J., Thompson, K., Phillips, M., Johnson, M. and Clery, E. (eds) *British Social Attitudes: The 24th Report*, London: Sage.

Duncombe, J. and Marsden, D. (1995) 'Women's "triple shift": paid employment, domestic labour and "emotion work"', *Sociology Review*, 4(4).

Dunne, G. (1997) *Lesbian Lifestyles: Women's Work and the Politics of Sexuality*, London: Macmillan.

Durkheim, E. (1897) Suicide: A Study in Sociology. London: Routledge & Kegan Paul, 1970.

Easthorpe, A. (1990) *What a Man's Gotta Do: The Masculine Myth in Popular Culture*, London: Routledge.

Easton, M. (2008) 'Births outside marriage – a real cause for concern', *BBC News* website, 24 September, available online at www.bbc.co.uk/blogs/legacy/thereporters/markeaston/2008/09/births_outside_marriage_a_real.html (accessed 10 May 2015).

Easton, M. (2011) 'Big nudge, no cash', *BBC News* website, 5 April, available online at www.bbc.co.uk/blogs/thereporters/markeaston/2011/04/big_nudge_no_cash.html (accessed 18 May 2015).

Eisenstadt, S.N. (1956) *From Generation to Generation: Age Groups and Social Structure*, New York: The Free Press.

Electoral Commission (2004) *Gender and Political Participation*, London: Electoral Commission, available online at www.electoralcommission.org.uk/__data/assets/electoral_commission_pdf_file/0019/16129/Final_report_270404_12488-9470__E__N__S__W__.pdf (accessed 29 May 2015).

Elliott, L. (2014) 'Britain's five richest families worth more than poorest 20%', *Guardian*, 17 March, available online at www.theguardian.com/business/2014/mar/17/oxfam-report-scale-britain-growing-financial-inequality (accessed 19 May 2015).

Engels, F. (1972) *The Origin of the Family, Private Property and the State*, New York: Pathfinder Press.

Equal Opportunities Commission (2007) *The State of the Modern Family*, Manchester: Equal Opportunities Commission, available online at www.fatherhoodinstitute.org/uploads/publications/283.pdf (accessed 29 May 2015).

Equality and Human Rights Commission (2011) *Sex and Power 2011*, Manchester: Equality and Human Rights Commission, available online at www.equalityhumanrights.com/sites/default/files/documents/sex+power/sex_and_power_2011_gb__2_.pdf (accessed 29 May 2015).

Equality Trust (n.d.a) 'The scale of economic inequality in the UK', available online at www.equalitytrust.org.uk/about-inequality/scale-and-trends/scale-economic-inequality-uk (accessed 18 May 2015).

Equality Trust (n.d.b) 'Social mobility', available online at www.equalitytrust.org.uk/research/social-mobility (accessed 18 May 2015).

Eurostat (2014) 'Marriage and divorce statistics', available online at http://ec.europa.eu/eurostat/statistics-explained/index.php/Marriage_and_divorce_statistics (accessed 27 May 2015).

Faludi, S. (1993) *Backlash: The Undeclared War Against American Women*, London: Vintage.

Faludi, S. (1999) *Stiffed: The Betrayal of the American Man*, London: Chatto & Windus.

Fantazia (n.d.) 'Rave new world: commercialisation of rave', available online at www.fantazia.org.uk/Scene/ravenewworld.htm (accessed 28 May 2015).

Farrell, W. (2013) 'Labor Day's glass cellars and women's wisdom', available online at http://warrenfarrell.com/labor-days-glass-cellars-and-womens-wisdom/ (accessed 29 May 2015).

Farrington, D.P. (1989) 'The origins of crime: the Cambridge Study in Delinquent Development', Home Office Research and Planning Unit, Research Bulletin No. 27, London: HMSO, pp. 29–33.

Fawbert, J. (2008) 'Hoodies: moral panic or justifiable concern?', Bedford Talks, public lecture, University of Bedfordshire.

Fawcett Society (2013) 'Equal pay', available online at www.fawcettsociety.org.uk/2013/11/equal-pay/ (accessed 29 May 2015).

Featherstone, M. and Hepworth, M. (2005) 'Images of ageing: cultural representations of later life', in Johnson, M. (ed.) *The Cambridge Handbook of Age and Ageism*, Cambridge: Cambridge University Press.

Feeley, D. (1972) 'Antoinette Konikow: Marxist and feminist', *International Socialist Review*, 33, 19–23.

Ferguson, M. (1983) *Forever Feminine: Women's Magazines and the Cult of Femininity*, London: Heinemann.

Feshbach, S. and Singer, R.D. (1971) *Television and Aggression: An Experimental Field Study*, San Francisco, CA: Jossey-Bass.

Fielding, N. (2001) 'Ethnography' in N. Gilbert (ed) Researching Social Life, 2nd edn. London: Sage.

Finch, J. (2007) 'Displaying families', Sociology, 41(1).

Fletcher, R. (1966) The Family and Marriage in Britain, Harmondsworth: Penguin.

Fox, K. (2004) Watching the English, London: Hodder & Stoughton.

Francis, B. and Archer, L. (2005) 'British-Chinese pupils' and parents' constructions of the value of education', British Educational Research Journal, 31(1), 89–107.

Frazer, E. (1987) 'Teenage girls reading Jackie', Media, Culture & Society, 9, 407–25.

Freyenberger, D. (2013) 'Amanda Knox: A Content Analysis of Media Framing in Newspapers Around the World', Electronic Theses and Dissertations. Paper 1117. http://dc.etsu.edu/etd/1117.

Friedrichs, D. (1996) Trusted Criminals: White-Collar Criminals in Contemporary Society, Belmont, CA: Wadsworth.

Furedi, F. (1994) 'A plague of moral panics', Living Marxism, 73.

Furedi, F. (2001) Paranoid Parenting, Harmondsworth: Penguin.

Gamson, W.A., Croteau, D., Hoynes, W. and Sasson, T. (1992) 'Media images and the social construction of reality', Annual Review of Sociology, 18, 373–93.

Gauntlett, D. (1995) Moving Experiences: Understanding Television's Influences and Effects, London: John Libbey.

Gauntlett, D. (2008) Media, Gender and Identity: An Introduction, London: Routledge.

Gay Left Collective (1980) Homosexuality: Power and Politics, London: Allison & Busby.

Gentleman, A. (2009) 'A day in the life of an old people's home', Guardian, 14 July, available online at www.theguardian.com/society/2009/jul/14/older-people-care-home (accessed 22 May 2015).

Gershuny, J. (1999) The Work/Leisure Balance and the New Political Economy of Time, paper presented at the lectures on Challenge of the New Millennium hosted by Tony Blair, available from Institute for Social and Economic Research, University of Essex.

Ghumann, P.A.S. (1999) Asian Adolescents in the West, Leicester: BPS Books.

Gibson, C. (1994) Dissolving Wedlock, London: Routledge.

Giddens, A. (1991) Modernity and Self-Identity: Self and Society in the Later Modern Age, Cambridge: Polity Press.

Giddens, A. (1992) The Transformation of Intimacy: Sexuality, Love and Eroticism in Modern Societies, Cambridge: Polity Press.

Giddens, A. (2006) Sociology, 5th edition. Cambridge: Polity Press.

Gill, C.J. (1997) 'Four types of integration in disability identity development', Journal of Vocational Rehabilitation, 9(1).

Gill, R. (2008) Discourse Analysis: Text, Narrative and Representation, Buckingham: Open University Press.

Gillbourn, D. (1990) 'Race', Ethnicity and Education, London: Unwin Hyman.

Gillies, V. (2005) 'Raising the meritocracy', Sociology, 39(5).

Gilroy, P. (1993) The Black Atlantic: Modernity and Double Consciousness, London: Verso.

Ginn, J., Arber, S., Brannen, J., Dale, A., Dex, S., Elais, P., Moss, P., Pahl, J., Roberts, C. and Rubery, J. (1996) 'Feminist fallacies: a reply to Hakim on women's employment', British Journal of Sociology, 47(1), 167–74.

Gittins, D. (1993) The Family in Question, Basingstoke: Macmillan.

Glascock, J. (2001) 'Gender roles on prime-time network television: demographics and behaviors', Journal of Broadcasting & Electronic Media, 45, 656–70.

Global Citizen (2014) 'Introduction to the challenges of achieving gender equality', available online at www.globalcitizen.org/en/content/introduction-to-the-challenges-of-achieving-gender/ (accessed 19 May 2015).

Golding, P. and Middleton, S. (1982) Images of Welfare: Press and Public Attitude to Poverty, Oxford: Blackwell.

Goldthorpe, J. (1980) Social Mobility and Class Structure in Modern Britain, Oxford: Clarendon Press.

Goldthorpe, J. (1983) 'Women and class analysis: in defence of the conventional view', Sociology, 14.

Goldthorpe, J. and Payne, C. (1986) 'Trends in intergenerational mobility in England and Wales 1979–83', Sociology, 20.

Goldthorpe, J. H., Lockwood, D., Bechhofer, F & Platt. J. (1969) The Affluent Worker in the Class Structure. Cambridge: Cambridge University Press.

Gomm, R. (2004) Social Research Methodology: A Critical Introduction. Basingstoke: Palgrave MacMillan.

Goode, E. and Ben-Yehuda, N. (1994) *Moral Panics: The Social Construction of Deviance*, Oxford: Blackwell.

Goode, W.J. (1963) *World Revolution and Family Patterns*, New York: The Free Press.

Gordon, D., Mack, J., Lansley, S., Main, G., Nandy, S., Patsios, D. and Pomati, M. (2013) *The Impoverishment of the UK: PSE UK First Results: Living Standards*, London: Economic & Social Research Council, available online at www.poverty.ac.uk/sites/default/files/attachments/The_Impoverishment_of_the_UK_PSE_UK_first_results_summary_report_March_28.pdf (accessed 28 May 2015).

Graham, J. and Bowling, B. (1995) *Young People and Crime*, Home Office Research Study No. 145, London: HMSO, available online at http://dera.ioe.ac.uk/17550/1/a3814uab.pdf (accessed 28 May 2015).

Gramsci, A. (1971) *Selections from the Prison Notebooks*, London: Lawrence & Wishart.

Grandparentsplus (2009) *Rethinking Family Life: Exploring the Role of Grandparents and the Wider Family*, London: Grandparentsplus, available online at www.grandparentsplus.org.uk/wp-content/uploads/2011/03/RethinkingFamilyLife.pdf (accessed 27 May 2015).

Gray, A. (2006) 'The time economy of parenting', *Sociological Research Online*, 11(3), available online at www.socresonline.org.uk/11/3/gray.html (accessed 27 May 2015).

Greer, G. (2000) *The Whole Woman*, London: Anchor.

Grundy, E. and Henretta, J.C. (2006) 'Between elderly parents and adult children: a new look at the intergenerational care provided by the "sandwich generation"', *Ageing and Society*, 26(5), 707–22, available from http://researchonline.lshtm.ac.uk/6347/1/ageing_and_society1.pdf (accessed 27 May 2015).

Guardian (2012) 'Occupy London: timeline of the St Paul's Cathedral protest camp', 18 January, available online at www.theguardian.com/uk/2012/jan/18/occupy-london-timeline-protest-camp (accessed 18 May 2015).

Guasp, A. (2010) *Different Families: The Experiences of Children with Lesbian and Gay Parents*, Cambridge: Centre for Family Research, University of Cambridge, available at www.stonewall.org.uk/documents/different_families_final_for_web.pdf (accessed 27 May 2015).

Hakim, C. (2000) *Work-Lifestyle Choices in the 21st Century: Preference Theory*, Oxford: Oxford University Press.

Hakim, C. (2004) *Key Issues in Women's Work: Female Diversity and the Polarisation of Women's Employment*, London: Glasshouse Press.

Hakim, C. (2010) '(How) can social policy and fiscal policy recognise unpaid family work?', *Renewal: A Journal of Social Democracy*, 18(1–2), 23–34, available online at www.lse.ac.uk/newsAndMedia/news/archives/2010/08/CatherineHakimRenewal.pdf (accessed 27 May 2015).

Hakim, Catherine (2006) Women, careers, and work-life preferences. *British Journal of Guidance and Counselling*, 34 (3). pp. 279-294.

Hall, P.C., West, J.H. and Hill, S. (2011) 'Sexualization in lyrics of popular music from 1959 to 2009: implications for sexuality educators', *Sexuality & Culture*, 16(2), 103–17.

Hall, R., Ogden, P.E. and Hill, C. (1999) 'Living alone: evidence from England and Wales and France for the last two decades', in McRae, S. (ed.) *Changing Britain: Families and Households in the 1990s*, Oxford: Oxford University Press.

Hall, S. (1973) *Encoding and Decoding in the Television Discourse*, Birmingham: Centre for Contemporary Cultural Studies.

Hall, S. (1981) 'The whites of their eyes: racist ideologies and the media', in Bridges, G. and Brunt, R. (eds), *Silver Linings: Some Strategies for the Eighties*, London: Lawrence & Wishart.

Hall, S. (1982) 'The rediscovery of "ideology": return of the repressed in media studies', in Gurevich, M., Bennett, T., Curran, J. and Woollacott, J. (eds) *Culture, Society and the Media*, London: Methuen, pp. 52–86.

Hall, S. (1991) 'The local and the global: globalization and ethnicity', in King, A. (ed.) *Culture, Globalization and the World-System: Contemporary Conditions for the Representation of Identity*, Basingstoke: Macmillan, pp. 19–39.

Hall, S. (1995) 'The whites of their eyes: racist ideologies and the media', in Dines, G. and Humez, J.M. (eds) *Gender, Race and Class in Media: A Text-Reader*, London: Sage, pp. 18–22.

Hall, S. and Jefferson, T. (eds) (1976) *Resistance through Rituals*, London: Routledge.

Hall, S., Critcher, C., Jefferson, T., Clarke, J. and Roberts, B. (1978) *Policing the Crisis: Mugging, the State and Law and Order*, London and Basingstoke: Macmillan.

Halloran, J. (1977) 'Mass media effects: a sociological approach' Mass Communication and Society Block 3, Milton Keynes: Open University Press.

Hardcastle, K., Hughes, K., Sharples, O. and Bellis, M. (2013) *Alcohol in Popular Music: Changes in the UK Music Charts 1981–2011*, Liverpool: Centre for Public Health, Liverpool John Moores University, available online at www.cph.org.uk/wp-content/uploads/2013/09/Hardcastle-Katie-Alcohol-in-popular-music-Changes-in-the-UK-music-charts-1981-2011.pdf (accessed 28 May 2015).

Hardill, I. (2002) *Gender, Migration and the Dual Career Household*, London: Routledge.

Hardill, I., Green, A., Dudlestone, A. and Owen, D.W. (1997) 'Who decides what? Decision making in dual career households', *Work, Employment & Society*, 11(2).

Harding, S. (2014) *The Street Casino: Survival in Violent Street Gangs*, London: Policy Press.

Harkness, S. (2008) 'The household division of labour: changes in families' allocation of paid and unpaid work', in Scott, J., Dex, S. and Joshi, H. (eds) *Women and Employment*, Cheltenham: Edward Elgar, pp. 234–67.

Harper, S. (2013) *Ageing Societies*, London: Routledge.

Harris, J. (1998) *The Nurture Assumption*, New York: The Free Press.

Hart, N. (1976) *When Marriage Ends: A Study in Status Passage*, London: Tavistock.

Haskey, J. and Lewis, J. (2006) 'Living-apart-together in Britain: context and meaning', *International Journal of Law in Context*, 2(1), 37–48.

Hatter, W., Vinter, L. and Williams, R. (2002) *Dads on Dads: Needs and Expectations at Home and at Work*, Manchester: Equal Opportunities Commission.

Heath, S. (2004) 'Transforming friendship: are housemates the new family?', *Sociology Review*.

Hebdige, D. (1976) 'Reggae, Rastas and Rudies', in Hall, S. and Jefferson, T. (eds) (1976) *Resistance through Rituals*, London: Routledge.

Hebdige, D. (1979) *Subculture: The Meaning of Style*, London: Methuen.

Hebdige, D. (1988) *Hiding in the Light: On Images and Things*, London: Routledge.

Heidensohn, F. (1985) *Women and Crime*, London: Macmillan.

Heidensohn, F. (1989) *Crime and Society*, Basingstoke: Macmillan.

Heintz-Knowles, K. (2002) *The Reflection on the Screen: Television's Image of Children*, Oakland, CA: Children Now.

Hewitt, R. (2005) *White Backlash and the Politics of Multiculturalism*, Cambridge: Cambridge University Press.

Hey, V. (1997) *The Company She Keeps: An Ethnography of Girls' Friendships*, Maidenhead: McGraw-Hill.

Higher Education Funding Council for England (HEFCE) (2014) 'Differences in degree outcomes: key findings', available online at www.hefce.ac.uk/pubs/year/2014/201403/ (accessed 29 May 2015).

Hills, J. (2013) 'The distribution of wealth: what we think, and how it is', *Discover Society*, 3, London: London School of Economics, available online at www.discoversociety.org/wp-content/uploads/2013/11/DSIssue3_Hills-3A.pdf (accessed 28 May 2015).

Hills, J., Bastagli, F., Cowell, F., Glennerster, H., Karagiannaki, E. and McKnight, E. (2013) *Wealth in the UK: Distribution, Accumulation and Policy*, Oxford: Oxford University Press.

Hochschild, A.R. (2003) *The Commercialisation of Intimate Life: Notes from Home and Work*, Oakland, CA: University of California Press.

Hockey, J. and James, A. (1993) *Growing Up and Growing Old: Ageing and Dependency in the Life Course*, London: Sage.

Holden, C. (1980) 'Identical twins reared apart', *Science*, 207(4437), 1323–8.

Hollands, R. and Chatterton, P. (2002) *Youth Cultures, Identities and the Consumption of Night-Life City Spaces*, Report to the Economic & Social Research Council, Newcastle: University of Newcastle.

Hollands, R.G. (1995) *Friday Night, Saturday Night: Youth Cultural Identification in the Post-Industrial City*, Newcastle: University of Newcastle, available online at http://research.ncl.ac.uk/youthnightlife/HOLLANDS.PDF (accessed 28 May 2015).

Hooks, B. (1981) *Ain't I a Woman: Black Women and Feminism*, Boston, MA: South End Press.

Hopkins, N. (2000) 'Tide of violence in the home: domestic attacks occur "every six seconds"', *Guardian*, 26 October, available online at www.theguardian.com/society/2000/oct/26/uknews (accessed 10 May 2015).

HSBC (2007) *The Future of Retirement: The New Old Age*, London: HSBC.

Hutnyk, J. (2000) *Critique of Exotica: Music, Politics and the Culture Industry*, London: Pluto Press.

Hutton, W. (1995) *The State We're In*, London: Vintage.

Ingram, N. (2009) 'Working-class boys, educational success and the misrecognition of working-class culture', *British Journal of the Sociology of Education*, 30: 4 pp421-434

Institute for Fiscal Studies (IFS) (2014) 'Inequality and poverty spreadsheet', available online at www.ifs.org.uk/bns/bn19figs.xlsx (accessed 18 May 2015).

Jackson, C. (2006) *Lads and Ladettes in School: Gender and the Fear of Failure*, Buckingham: Open University Press.

Jackson, C. (2006) *Lads and Ladettes in School: Gender and the Fear of Failure*, Maidenhead: Open University Press.

Jacobson, J. (1997) 'Religion and ethnicity: dual and alternative sources of identity among young British Pakistanis', *Ethnic and Racial Studies*, 20(2).

Jacobson, J., Bhardwa, B., Gyateng, T., Hunter, G. and Hough, M. (2010) *Punishing Disadvantage: A Profile of Children in Custody*, London: Prison Reform Trust, available online at www.prisonreformtrust.org.uk/portals/0/documents/punishingdisadvantage.pdf (accessed 28 May 2015).

James, O. (2003) *They F*** You Up: How to Survive Family Life*, London: Bloomsbury.

James, W. (1993) 'Migration, racism and identity formation', in James, W. and Harris, C. (eds) *Inside Babylon: The Caribbean Diaspora in Britain*, London: Verso.

Jamieson, L., Anderson, M., McCrone, D., Bechhofer, F., Stewart, R. and Li, Y. (2002) 'Cohabitation and commitment: partnership plans of young men and women', *The Sociological Review*, 50(3), 356–77.

Jefferson, T. (1976) 'Culture responses of the Teds', in Hall, S. and Jefferson, T. (eds) *Resistance through Rituals*. London: Routledge, pp. 81–86.

Johal, S. (1998) 'Brimful of Brasia', *Sociology Review*, 8(1).

Johnson, J., Bytheway, B. (1993) in Moore, S. *et al. Sociology for AS-Level*, London: Collins.

Johnson, M. P. (1995). 'Patriarchal terrorism and common couple violence: Two forms of violence against women'. *Journal of Marriage and the Family* 57: 283–294.

Jones, I., Leontowitsch, M. and Higgs, P. (2010) 'The experience of retirement in second modernity: generational habitus among retired senior managers', *Sociology*, 44(1), 103–20.

Jones, M. (2011) 'Grandparents: the new reserve army of labour?', *Sociology Review*.

Jones, O. (2012) *Chavs: The Demonization of the Working Class*, London: Verso.

Joseph Rowntree Foundation (2007) *Poverty and Ethnicity in the UK*, York: Joseph Rowntree Foundation, available online at www.jrf.org.uk/publications/poverty-and-ethnicity-uk (accessed 20 May 2015).

Joseph Rowntree Foundation (2008) *Women and Poverty*, York: Joseph Rowntree Foundation, available online at www.jrf.org.uk/system/files/2186-women-poverty-policy.pdf (accessed 29 May 2015).

Joseph Rowntree Foundation (2014) 'Proportion of people in poverty by ethnicity', available online at http://data.jrf.org.uk/data/poverty-rate-ethnicity/ (accessed 18 May 2015).

Joseph, S. (2010) 'Hijabi Barbie: growing up Muslim in a world of body image', *Emel*, 66, March, available online at www.emel.com/article.php?pageNum_show_comments=1&totalRows_show_comments=25&id=69&a_id=1913&c=73&return=jew& (accessed 21 May 2015).

Kagan, D. (1980) 'Activity and aging in a Colombian peasant village', in Fry, C. (ed.), *Aging in Culture and Society*, New York: Bergin.

Kan M.Y. (2008) 'Does gender trump money? Housework hours of husbands and wives in Britain', *Work, Employment & Society*, 22(1), 45–66.

Katz, E. and Lazarsfeld, P. (1955) *Personal Influence*, New York: The Free Press.

Katz, I., Corlyon, J., La Placa, V. and Hunter, S. (2007) *The Relationship between Parenting and Poverty*, York: Joseph Rowntree Foundation, available online at www.jrf.org.uk/sites/files/jrf/parenting-poverty.pdf (accessed 27 May 2015).

Kellner, P. and Wilby, P. (1980) 'The 1:2:4 rule of class in Britain', *Sunday Times*, 13 January.

Kelly, G. (2011) 'Social mobility has increased in past decades, but there has been no "revolution" in opportunity', *The London School of Economics and Political Science* website, 24 March, available online at http://blogs.lse.ac.uk/politicsandpolicy/social-mobility-recent-decades-uk/ (accessed 18 May 2015).

Khanum, S.M. (2001) 'The household patterns of a "Bangladeshi village" in England', *Journal of Ethnic and Migration Studies*, 27, 489–504.

Kingman, D. (2012) *Spending Power Across the Generations*, London: Intergenerational Foundation, available online at www.if.org.uk/wp-content/uploads/2013/01/Spending-Power-Across-the-Generations-Report.pdf (accessed 27 May 2015).

Kinsey, A. *et al.* (1948) *Sexual Behaviour in the Human Male*, Philadelphia, PA: W.B. Saunders.

Klapper, J. (1960) *The Effects of Mass Communication*, New York: The Free Press.

Klein, M.W. (1995) *The American Street Gang*, New York: Oxford University Press.

Klinenberg, E. (2013) *Going Solo: The Extraordinary Rise and Surprising Appeal of Living Alone*, Harmondsworth: Penguin.

Kumar, K. (2003) *The Making of English National Identity*, Cambridge: Cambridge University Press.

Lacey, C. (1970) *Hightown Grammar*, Manchester: Manchester University Press.

Lader, D., Short, S. and Gershuny, J. (2006) *The Time Use Survey 2005: How We Spend Our Time*, London: Office for National Statistics, available online at www.timeuse.org/sites/ctur/files/public/ctur_report/1905/lader_short_and_gershuny_2005_kight_diary.pdf (accessed 27 May 2015).

Landis, S. (2002) 'Module 5: Representations of Different Age Groups or Occupations', CI5472 Teaching Film, Television, and Media, University of Minnesota, available online at www.tc.umn.edu/~rbeach/teachingmedia/module5/9.htm (accessed 28 May 2015).

Langford, W. (1999) *Revolutions of the Heart*, London: Routledge.

Lauzen, M.M. (2014) *The Celluloid Ceiling: Behind-the-Scenes Employment of Women on the Top 250 Films of 2013*, San Diego, CA: Center for the Study of Women in Television and Film, San Diego State University, available online at http://womenintvfilm.sdsu.edu/files/2013_Celluloid_Ceiling_Report.pdf (accessed 28 May 2015).

Lea, J. and Young, J. (1993) *What Is to Be Done about Law and Order?*, London: Pluto Press.

Leach, E. (1967) *A Runaway World*, London: BBC Publications.

Lees, S. (1983) 'How boys slag off girls', *New Society*, 13 October 1983.

Lees, S. (1997) *Ruling Passions: Sexual Violence, Reputation and the Law*, Buckingham: Open University Press.

Levin, I. (2004) 'Living apart together: a new family form', *Current Sociology*, 52(2), 223–40.

Li, Y. and Devine, F. (2011) 'Is social mobility really declining? Intergenerational class mobility in Britain in the 1990s and the 2000s', *Sociological Research*, 16(3)4, available online at www.socresonline.org.uk/16/3/4.html (accessed 19 May 2015).

Li, Y. and Heath, A. (2014) *Addressing Ethnic Inequalities in Social Mobility*, Manchester: Economic & Social Research Council, available online at www.ethnicity.ac.uk/medialibrary/briefings/policy/code-social-mobility-briefing-Jun2014.pdf (accessed 29 May 2015).

Ligali (2006) *Ligali*, available online at www.ligali.org/index.php (accessed 28 May 2015).

Living Wage Foundation (n.d.) 'What is the living wage?', available online at www.livingwage.org.uk/what-living-wage (accessed 18 May 2015).

Low Pay Commission (2007) National Minimum Wage Low Pay Commission Report 2007, Figure 2.8, p32. http://www.lowpay.gov.uk/lowpay/report/pdf/6828-DTi-Low_Pay_Complete.pdf.

Lynch, J., Smith, G.D. and House, J.S. (2000) 'Income inequality and mortality: importance to health of individual income, psychosocial environment, or material conditions', *British Medical Journal*, 320(7243).

Lyotard, J.-F. (1984) *The Postmodern Condition: A Report on Knowledge*, Manchester: Manchester University Press.

Lyotard, J.F. (1992) *The Postmodern Condition*, Manchester: Manchester University Press.

Mac an Ghaill, M. (1988) *Young, Gifted and Black: Student–Teacher Relations in the Schooling of Black Youth*, Buckingham: Open University Press.

Mac an Ghaill, M. (1994) *The Making of Men: Masculinities, Sexualities and Schooling*, Buckingham: Open University Press.

MacDonald, R. (2008) 'Disconnected youth? Social exclusion, the "underclass" and economic marginality', *Social Work & Society*, 6(2), 236–48.

MacDonald, R. and Marsh, J. (2005) *Disconnected Youth? Growing Up in Britain's Poor Neighbourhoods*, Basingstoke: Palgrave Macmillan.

Mack, J. and Lansley, S. (1985) *Poor Britain*, London: Allen & Unwin.

Mackintosh, M. and Mooney, G. (2004) 'Identity, inequality and social class', in Woodward, K. (ed.) *Questioning Identity: Gender, Class, Ethnicity*, London: Routledge.

Maffesoli, M. (1996) *The Time of the Tribes: The Decline of Individualism in Mass Society*, London: Sage.

Maguire, K. (2014) 'Where do you rank in the official earnings list? Figures reveal huge pay gap between rich and poor', *Daily Mirror* (2014), 19 January available online at http://www.mirror.co.uk/news/uk-news/uk-average-salary-26500-figures-3002995 (accessed 2015).

Malik, S. (2002) 'Race and ethnicity', in Briggs, A. and Cobley, P. (eds) *The Media: An Introduction*, Harlow: Pearson.

Malik, S. (2002) *Representing Black Britain*, London: Sage.

Malik, S. (2008) 'Diversity knocks', *Guardian*, 17 July, available online at www.theguardian.com/commentisfree/2008/jul/17/television.race (accessed 28 May 2015).

Mann, R. (2009) *Evolving Family Structures, Roles and Relationships in Light of Ethnic and Social Change*, London: Futurelab, available online at www.beyondcurrenthorizons.org.uk/evolving-family-structures-roles-and-relationships-in-light-of-ethnic-and-social-change/ (accessed 27 May 2015).

Manzoor, S. (2011) 'Asian parents in care homes', *Guardian*, 26 February, available online at www.theguardian.com/lifeandstyle/2011/feb/26/asian-parents-care-homes-sarfraz-manzoor (accessed 10 May 2015).

Maplethorpe, N., Chanfreau, J., Philo, D. and Tait, C. (2010) *Families with Children in Britain: Findings from the 2008 Families and Children Study (FACS)*, London: Department for Work and Pensions, available online at www.gov.uk/government/uploads/system/uploads/attachment_data/file/214426/rrep656.pdf (accessed 27 May 2015).

Margo, J. and Dixon, M. (2006) 'Crisis of youth? Childhood, youth and the civic order', *Public Policy Research*, 13(1), 48–53.

Marmot, M., Allen, J., Goldblatt, P., Boyce, T., McNeish, D., Grady, M. and Geddes, I. (2010) *Fair Society, Healthy Lives: The Marmot Review*, London: Institute of Health Equity, available online at www.instituteofhealthequity.org/Content/FileManager/pdf/fairsocietyhealthylives.pdf (accessed 28 May 2015).

Marsh, I., Keating, M. (2006) *Sociology: Making Sense of Society*: 3rd Paperback. Harlow: Prentice Hall.

Marshall, G., Newby, H., Rose, D. and Vogler, C. (1988) *Social Class in Modern Britain*, London: Hutchinson.

Marshall, G., Rose, D., Newby, H. and Vogler, C. (1988) Social class in modern Britain, London: Unwin Hyman.

Marvasti, A.B. (2004) Qualitative Research in Sociology. London: Sage.

Marx, K. (1844) *Selected Writings*, 2000 edition, Oxford: Oxford University Press.

Marx, K. (Bottomore, T. and Rubel, M. (eds)) (1961) *Karl Marx: Selected Writings*, Harmondsworth: Penguin.

Marx, K. and Engels, F. (1848) *The Communist Manifesto*, 2002 edition, Harmondsworth: Penguin.

McIntosh, M. (1996) 'The homosexual role', in Siedman, S. (ed.) *Queer Theory/ Sociology*, Oxford: Blackwell.

McLuhan, M. (1964) *Understanding Media: The Extensions of Man*, London: Routledge & Kegan Paul.

McNeill, P. and Chapman, S. (2005) *Research Methods*, third edition, London: Routledge.

McQuail, D. (1972) *Sociology of Mass Communications: Selected Readings*, Harmondsworth: Penguin.

McQuail, D. (1987) *Mass Communication Theory: An Introduction*, London: Sage.

McRobbie, A. (1991) *Feminism and Youth Culture: From Jackie to Just Seventeen*, London: Macmillan.

McRobbie, A. (1994) *Postmodernism and Popular Culture*, London: Routledge.

McRobbie, A. (2005) *The Uses of Cultural Studies: A Textbook*, London: Sage.

McRobbie, A. and Garber, J. (1976) 'Girls and subcultures', in Hall, S. and Jefferson, T. (eds) *Resistance through Rituals*, London: Routledge.

McSmith, A. (2009) 'The Big Question: Why does the marriage rate continue to decline, and does the trend matter?', *Independent*, 13 February, available online at www.independent.co.uk/news/uk/this-britain/the-big-question-why-does-the-marriage-rate-continue-to-decline-and-does-the-trend-matter-1608177.html (accessed 10 May 2015).

McVeigh, T. and Finch, I. (2014) 'Fathers spend seven times more with their children than in the 1970s', *Observer*, 15 June, available online at www.theguardian.com/lifeandstyle/2014/jun/15/fathers-spend-more-time-with-children-than-in-1970s (accessed 10 May 2015).

Mead, G.H. (1934) Mind, Self and Society. Chicago: University of Chicago Press.

Mead, M. (1928) *Coming of Age in Samoa*, New York: William Morrow & Company.

Mead, M. (1935) *Sex and Temperament in Three Primitive Societies*, New York: William Morrow & Company.

Mercer, K. (1987) 'Black hair/style politics', in Gelder, K. and Thornton, S. (eds) (1997) *The Subcultures Reader*, London: Routledge.

Merton, R. (1938) 'Social structure and anomie', *American Sociological Review*, 3, 672–82.

Messerschmidt, J.W. (1993) *Masculinities and Crime: Critique and Reconceptualization of Theory*, Lanham, MD: Rowman & Littlefield.

Miliband, R. (1969) *The State in Capitalist Society*, London: Weidenfeld & Nicolson.

Miller, L., Neathey, F., Pollard, E. and Hill, D. (2004) *Occupational Segregation, Gender Gaps and Skill Gaps*, EOC Working Paper Series No. 15, Manchester: Equal Opportunities Commission.

Miller, W. (1958) 'Lower-class culture as a generating milieu of gang delinquency', *Journal of Social Issues*, 14.

Millett, K. (1970) *Sexual Politics*, Champaign, IL: University of Illinois Press.

Milner, C., Van Norman, K. and Milner, J. (2002) *The Media's Portrayal of Ageing*, available online at www.kayvannorman.com/wp-content/uploads/2012/05/chapter4-medias-portrayal-of-ageing.pdf (accessed 28 May 2015), 26.

Ministry of Justice (2013), *Transforming Youth Custody: Putting Education at the Heart of Detention*, London: HMSO, available online at https://consult.justice.gov.uk/digital-communications/transforming-youth-custody/supporting_documents/transformingyouthcustody.pdf (accessed 28 May 2015).

Mirza, H. (2009) *Race, Gender and Educational Desire: Why Black Women Succeed and Fail*, London: Routledge.

Modood, T. and Berthoud, R. (eds) (1997) *Ethnic Minorities in Britain: Diversity and Disadvantage*, London: Policy Studies Institute, available online at www.psi.org.uk/pdf/Ethnic%20Minorities%20In%20Britain_small_file.pdf (accessed 27 May 2015).

Moore, S., Aiken, D. and Chapman, S. (2005) *Sociology AS for OCR*, London: HarperCollins.

Morgan, D.H.J. (1996) *Family Connections*, Cambridge: Polity Press.

Morgan, P. (2000) *Marriage-Lite: The Rise of Cohabitation and Its Consequences*, London: Institute for the Study of Civil Society, available online at www.civitas.org.uk/pdf/cs04.pdf (accessed 27 May 2015).

Morrison, J. (2002) 'What kind of dad are you? Forceful? Useful? Or just plain embarrassing?', *Independent*, 20 October, available online at www.independent.co.uk/news/media/what-kind-of-dad-are-you-forceful-useful-or-just-plain-embarrassing-608240.html (accessed 10 May 2015).

Mulvey, L. (1975) 'Visual pleasure and narrative cinema', *Screen*, 16(3), 6–18, available online at http://imlportfolio.usc.edu/ctcs505/mulveyVisualPleasureNarrativeCinema.pdf (accessed 28 May 2015).

Muncie, J. (1999) *Youth and Crime: A Critical Introduction*, London: Sage.

Murdock, G.P. (1949) *Social Structure*, New York: Macmillan.

Murray, C. (1984) *Losing Ground: American Social Policy, 1950–1980*, New York: Basic Books.

Murray, C. (1989) 'Underclass', *Sunday Times* magazine, 26 November.

Murray, C. (1990) *The Emerging British Underclass*, London: Institute of Economic Affairs.

Murray, C. (1994) *Underclass: The Crisis Deepens*, London: Institute of Economic Affairs.

Murray, C. (2001) *Underclass +10: Charles Murray and the British Underclass 1990–2000*, London: Civitas, available online at www.civitas.org.uk/pdf/cs10.pdf (accessed 27 May 2015).

Murray, C. (2005), 'The advantages of social apartheid', *Sunday Times*, 3 April 2005.

Murugami, M. (2009) 'Disability and identity', *Disability Studies Quarterly*, 29(4).

Nahdi, F. (2003) 'Doublespeak: Islam and the media', *Open Democracy*, 3 April, available online at www.opendemocracy.net/faith-europe_islam/article_1119.jsp. (accessed 28 May 2015).

Nairn, T. (1988) *The Enchanted Glass: Britain and Its Monarchy*, London: Radius/Hutchinson.

Nayak, A. (2003) *Race, Place and Globalization: Youth Cultures in a Changing World*, Oxford: Berg.

Nazroo, J. Y. (1997). The Health of Britain's Ethnic Minorites: Findings From a National Survey. London: Policy Studies Institute.

Newman, D.M. (2006) *Sociology: Exploring the Architecture of Everyday Life*, London: Sage.

Newson, E. (1994) *Video Violence and the Protection of Children*, Report of the Home Affairs Committee, London: HMSO.

Ní Bhrolcháin, M. and Beaujouan, E. (2012) 'Fertility postponement is largely due to rising educational enrolment', *Population Studies: A Journal of Demography*, 66(3), 311–27, available online at www.tandfonline.com/doi/pdf/10.1080/00324728.2012.697569 (accessed 27 May 2015).

Nightingale, C. (1993) *On the Edge*, New York: Basic Books.

Noble, J. and Davies, P. (2009) 'Cultural capital as an explanation of variation in participation in higher education', *British Journal of the Sociology of Education*, 30(5), 591–605.

O'Donnell, K. and Sharpe, S. (2000) *Uncertain Masculinities*, London: Routledge.

Oakley, A. (1974) *House Wife*, London: Allen Lane.

Oakley, A. (1974) *The Sociology of Housework*, Oxford: Martin Robertson.

Oakley, A. (1981) *Subject Women*, Oxford: Martin Robertson.

Offe, C. (1985) 'New social movements: challenging the boundaries of institutional politics', *Social Research*, 52(4), 817–67.

Office for National Statistics (2010), 'Households and families', *Social Trends*, 40, 13–26, available online at www.palgrave-journals.com/st/journal/v40/n1/full/st20106a.html (accessed 27 May 2015).

Office for National Statistics (2011) 'Stepfamilies in 2011', available online at www.ons.gov.uk/ons/rel/family-demography/stepfamilies/2011/stepfamilies-rpt.html (accessed 27 May 2015).

Office for National Statistics (2012a) 'Short Report: Cohabitation in the UK, 2012', available online at www.ons.gov.uk/ons/rel/family-demography/families-and-households/2012/cohabitation-rpt.html (accessed 27 May 2015).

Office for National Statistics (2012b) 'Family size in 2012', available online at www.ons.gov.uk/ons/rel/family-demography/family-size/2012/family-size-rpt.html (accessed 27 May 2015).

Office for National Statistics (2012c) 'Births in England and Wales, 2012', available online at www.ons.gov.uk/ons/rel/vsob1/birth-summary-tables--england-and-wales/2012/stb-births-in-england-and-wales-2012.html#tab-Live-births--numbers-and-rates- (accessed 27 May 2015).

Office for National Statistics (2012d) '2011 Census: population estimates for the United Kingdom, 27 March 2011', available online at www.ons.gov.uk/ons/rel/census/2011-census/population-and-household-estimates-for-the-united-kingdom/stb-2011-census--population-estimates-for-the-united-kingdom.html#tab-The-structure-of-the-population-of-the-United-Kingdom (accessed 27 May 2015).

Office for National Statistics (2012e) 'Population ageing in the United Kingdom, its constituent countries and the European Union', available online at www.ons.gov.uk/ons/rel/mortality-ageing/focus-on-older-people/population-ageing-in-the-united-kingdom-and-europe/rpt-age-uk-eu.html#tab-Ageing-in-the-UK (accessed 27 May 2015).

Office for National Statistics (2013a) 'Families and households, 2013', available online at www.ons.gov.uk/ons/rel/family-demography/families-and-households/2013/stb-families.html#tab-Key-points (accessed 27 May 2015).

Office for National Statistics (2013b) 'Cohort fertility, England and Wales, 2012', available online at www.ons.gov.uk/ons/rel/fertility-analysis/cohort-fertility--england-and-wales/2012/index.html (accessed 27 May 2015).

Office for National Statistics (2013c) 'Childlessness at the age of 30', available online at www.ons.gov.uk/ons/rel/fertility-analysis/cohort-fertility--england-and-wales/2012/info-childlessness.html (accessed 10 May 2015).

Office for National Statistics (2014a) 'Divorces in England and Wales, 2012', available online at www.ons.gov.uk/ons/rel/vsob1/divorces-in-england-and-wales/2012/stb-divorces-2012.html#tab-Number-of-divorces (accessed 27 May 2015).

Office for National Statistics (2014b) 'Marriages in England and Wales (provisional), 2012', available online at www.ons.gov.uk/ons/rel/vsob1/marriages-in-england-and-wales--provisional-/2012/index.html (accessed 27 May 2015).

Office for National Statistics (2014c) 'National life tables, 2010–2012', available online at www.ons.gov.uk/ons/rel/lifetables/national-life-tables/2010---2012/index.html (accessed 27 May 2015).

Office for National Statistics (ONS) (2001) *Psychiatric Morbidity Among Adults Living in Private Households, 2000*, London: Office for National Statistics, available online at www.ons.gov.uk/ons/rel/psychiatric-morbidity/psychiatric-morbidity-among-adults-living-in-private-households/2000/psychiatric-morbidity-among-adults-living-in-private-households.pdf (accessed 29 May 2015).

Office for National Statistics (ONS) (2010) 'Child mortality statistics', available at http://www.poverty.org.uk/24/index.shtml (accessed 2015).

Office for National Statistics (ONS) (2011) '2011 Census of England and Wales', available online at www.ons.gov.uk/ons/guide-method/census/2011/index.html (accessed 18 May 2015).

Office for National Statistics (ONS) (2012a) 'Compare your pay to the national average in your job', available online at http://www.thisismoney.co.uk/money/article-2269520/Best-paid-jobs-2012-Official-figures-national-average-UK-salaries-400-occupations.html (accessed 2015).

Office for National Statistics (ONS) (2012b) 'Measuring national well-being – personal finance, 2012', available online at www.ons.gov.uk/ons/rel/wellbeing/measuring-national-well-being/personal-finance/art-personal-finance.html (accessed 18 May 2015).

Office for National Statistics (ONS) (2012c) *South East Has Biggest Share of the Wealthiest Households*, London: Office for National Statistics, available online at www.ons.gov.uk/ons/dcp171776_289407.pdf (accessed 18 May 2015).

Office for National Statistics (ONS) (2013), 'Women in the labour market', available online at www.ons.gov.uk/ons/rel/lmac/women-in-the-labour-market/2013/rpt---women-in-the-labour-market.html (accessed 19 May 2015).

Office for National Statistics (ONS) (2014) 'The effects of taxes and benefits on household income, 2012/13', available online at www.ons.gov.uk/ons/rel/household-income/the-effects-of-taxes-and-benefits-on-household-income/2012-13/index.html (accessed 18 May 2015).

Osgerby, B. (2002) 'The good, the bad and the ugly': media representations of youth since 1945', in Briggs, A. and Cobley, P. (eds), *The Media: An Introduction*, Harlow: Pearson.

Oxfam (2008) 'Policy and practice: GenderWorks', available online at http://policy-practice.oxfam.org.uk/our-work/poverty-in-the-uk/genderworks (accessed 29 May 2015).

Packard, V. (1957) *The Hidden Persuaders*, New York: David McKay Co., Inc.

Pahl, J. (1989) *Money and Marriage*, Basingstoke: Macmillan.

Pahl, J. (2005) 'Individualisation in couple finances: who pays for the children?', *Social Policy and Society*, 4(4), 381–91.

Pahl, J. (2008) 'Family finances, individualisation, spending patterns and access to credit', *The Journal of Socio-Economics*, 37(2), 577–91.

Pakulski, J. and Waters, M. (1996) *The Death of Class*, London: Sage.

Palmer, S. (2007) *Toxic Childhood: How Modern Life Is Damaging Our Children... and What We Can Do About It*, London: Orion.

Panico, L., Bartley, M., Kelly, Y., McMunn, A. and Sacker, A. (2010) 'Changes in family structure in early childhood in the Millennium Cohort Study', *Population Trends*, Winter(142), 75–89.

Park, A., Bryson, C., Clery, E., Curtice, J. and Phillips, M. (2013) *British Social Attitudes: The 30th Report*, London: Sage, available at http://bsa-30.natcen.ac.uk/read-the-report/personal-relationships/introduction.aspx (accessed 27 May 2015).

Park, S.M. (2014) *Mothering Queerly, Queering Motherhood: Resisting Monomaternalism in Adoptive, Lesbian, Blended, and Polygamous Families*, New York: State University of New York Press.

Parsons, T. (1942) 'Age and sex in the social structure of the United States', *American Sociological Review*, 7(5).

Parsons, T. (1951) *The Social System*, New York: The Free Press.

Parsons, T. (1962) 'Youth in the context of American society', *Daedalus*, 91(1), 97–123.

Parsons, T. and Bales, R.F. (1955) *Family, Socialization and Interaction Process*, Glencoe, IL: The Free Press.

Pearce, J.J. and Pitts, J.M. (2011) Youth gangs, sexual violence and sexual exploitation: a scoping exercise, The Office of the Children's Commissioner for England, Luton: University of Bedfordshire p.19.

Pearson, G. (1983) 'Victorian boys, we are here!', in Jewkes, Y. and Letherby, G. (eds) (2002) *Criminology: A Reader*, London: Sage.

Pettersson, P. (2012) *Does Unemployment Contribute to a Poor Self-Esteem, and Does Social Support, Coping and Perceived Control Have Any Effect During Unemployment?*, Sweden: University of Gävle, available online at www.diva-portal.org/smash/get/diva2:536319/FULLTEXT02 (accessed 18 May 2015).

Phillips, C. (2008) 'Negotiating identities: ethnicity and social relations in a young offenders' institution', *Theoretical Criminology*, 12(3), 313–31.

Philo, G., Bryant, E. and Donald, P. (2013) *Bad News for Refugees*, London: Pluto Press.

Pilcher, J. (1995) *Age and Generation in Modern Britain*. Oxford: Oxford University Press.

Platt, L. (2009) *Ethnicity and Family: Relationships Within and Between Ethnic Groups – An Analysis Using the Labour Force Survey*, London: Equality and Human Rights Commission, available online at www.equalityhumanrights.com/sites/default/files/documents/raceinbritain/ethnicity_and_family_report.pdf (accessed 27 May 2015).

Plummer, K. (1996) 'Symbolic interactionism and forms of homosexuality', in Siedman, S. (ed.) *Queer Theory/Sociology*, Oxford: Blackwell.

Polhemus, T. (1994) *Streetstyle*, London: Thames & Hudson.

Popenoe, D. (1996) 'Modern marriage: revising the cultural script', in Popenoe, D., Elshtain, J. and Blankenhorn, D. (eds) *Promises to Keep*, Lanham, MD: Rowman & Littlefield.

Postman, N. (1982) *The Disappearance of Childhood*, London: W.H. Allen.

Powell, J. (2001) *Aging & Social Theory: A Sociological Review*. Liverpool: Liverpool John Moores University available at http://homepages.uwp.edu/takata/dearhabermas/powell01bk.html (accessed 2015).

Powell, J; Biggs, S. (2000) 'Managing Old Age: The Disciplinary Web of Power, Surveillance and Normalization'. *Journal of Aging and Identity*, Vol. 5, No. 1, 2000.

Price, G. (2014) 'Decoding *Benefits Street*: how Britain was divided by a television show', *Guardian*, 22 February, available online at www.theguardian.com/commentisfree/2014/feb/22/benefits-street-tv-programme-divided-the-nation (accessed 28 May 2015).

Prince Cook, L. and Gash, V. (2010) 'Wives' part-time employment and marital stability in Great Britain, West Germany and the United States', *Sociology*, 44(6), 1091–108.

Prudential Insurance (2011) *Retirement Income Gender Gap Is £6500 a Year*, available online at www.pru.co.uk/pdf/presscentre/retirement_income_ge1.pdf (accessed 29 May 2015).

Quinn, D.M. (2001) *Same-Sex Dynamics among Nineteenth-Century Americans*, Champaign, IL: University of Illinois Press.

Quirk, A. & Lelliott, P. (2002) Acute wards: problems and solutions; A participant observation study of life on an acute psychiatric ward. Psychiatric Bulletin 26, pages 344-345.

Radford, L., Corral, S., Bradley, C., Fisher, H., Bassett, C., Howat, N. and Collishaw, S. (2011) *Child Abuse and Neglect in the UK Today*, London: NSPCC, available online at www.nspcc.org.uk/globalassets/documents/research-reports/child-abuse-neglect-uk-today-research-report.pdf (accessed 27 May 2015).

Rapoport, R., Rapoport, R. et al. (1982), *Families in Britain*, London: Routledge & Kegan Paul.

Rastogi, P.N. (2002) 'Knowledge management and intellectual capital as a paradigm of value creation', *Human Systems Management*, 21(4), 229–40.

Ratcliffe, R. (2013) 'Gender gap in university applications widens further after fees rise', *Guardian*, 13 December, available online at www.theguardian.com/education/2012/dec/13/gender-gap-university-applications-widens (accessed 29 May 2015).

Reay, D. (2009) 'Making sense of white working class educational underachievement', in Sveinsson, K.P. (ed.) *Who Cares about the White Working Class?*, London: Runnymede Trust, pp. 22–8, available online at www.runnymedetrust.org/uploads/publications/pdfs/WhoCaresAboutTheWhiteWorkingClass-2009.pdf (accessed 28 May 2015).

Reddington, H. (2003) 'Lady punks in bands: a subculturette?', in Muggleton, D. and Weinzierl, R. (eds) *The Post-Subcultures Reader*, Oxford: Berg.

Redhead, S. (1990) *The End of the Century Party: Youth and Pop Towards 2000*, Manchester: Manchester University Press.

Reiner, R. (2010) 'Media-made criminality: the representation of crime in the mass media', in Maguire, M., Morgan, R. and Reiner, R. (eds) *The Oxford Handbook of Criminality*, Oxford: Oxford University Press.

Reiss, A. (1961) 'The social integration of peers and queers', *Social Problems*, 102–20.

Reynolds, T. (2002) 'Re-analysing the Black family', in Carling, A., Duncan, S. and Edwards, R. (eds) *Analysing Families: Morality and Rationality in Policy and Practice*, London: Routledge.

Ribbens McCarthy, J., Edwards, R. and Gillies, V. (2003) *Making Families: Moral Tales of Parenting and Step-Parenting*, Durham: Sociology Press.

Rich, A. (1980) 'Compulsory heterosexuality and lesbian existence', in Jackson, S. and Scott, S. (eds) (1996) *Feminism and Sexuality*, New York: Columbia University Press.

Ridley, L. (2014) 'Does this article make you feel awkward?', *BBC News* website, 11 May, available online at www.bbc.co.uk/news/blogs-ouch-27338770 (accessed 10 May 2015).

Ripped-Off Britons (2014) 'Graphs at a glance: are the improving unemployment figures all they seem to be?', 3 August, available online at www.blog.rippedoffbritons.com/2014/08/graphs-at-glance-are-improving.html#.VVpimFJfjYh (accessed 18 May 2015).

Roberts, K. (2001) *Class in Modern Britain*, Basingstoke: Palgrave.

Roberts, K. (2011) *Class in Contemporary Britain*, second edition, Basingstoke: Palgrave Macmillan.

Rock, P. (1999) 'Participant observation' in Bryman, A. and Burgess, R. Qualitative Research. London: Sage.

Rodgers, B. and Pryor, J. (1998) *Divorce and Separation: The Outcomes for Children*, York: Joseph Rowntree Foundation, available online at www.jrf.org.uk/publications/divorce-and-separation-outcomes-children (accessed 27 May 2015).

Rosneil, S. and Budgeon, S. (2004) 'Cultures of intimacy and care beyond "the family": personal life and social change in the early 21st century', *Current Sociology*, 52(2), 135–59.

Rowlingson, K. (2012) *Wealth Inequality: Key Facts*, Birmingham: University of Birmingham, available online at www.birmingham.ac.uk/Documents/research/SocialSciences/Key-Facts-Background-Paper-BPCIV.pdf (accessed 28 May 2015).

Rowlingson, K. and McKay, S. (2013) *What Do the Public Think about the Wealth Gap?*, Birmingham: University of Birmingham, available online at www.birmingham.ac.uk/Documents/research/policycommission/BPCIV-Report-Summary---what-the-public-think.pdf (accessed 28 May 2015).

Rowlingson, K. and Mullineux, A. (2013) *Sharing Our Good Fortune: Understanding and Responding to Wealth Inequality*, Birmingham: University of Birmingham, available online at www.birmingham.ac.uk/Documents/research/policycommission/BPCIV-Distribution-of-wealthfull-report.pdf (accessed 28 May 2015).

Runnymede Trust (2010), *Ready for Retirement?*, London: Runnymede Trust, available online at www.runnymedetrust.org/uploads/publications/pdfs/ReadyForRetirement-2010.pdf (accessed 20 May 2015).

Sardar, Z. (2002) 'Nothing left to belong to?', *The New Statesman*, February.

Saunders, P. (1990) *Social Class and Stratification*, London: Routledge.

Saunders, P. (1996) *Unequal but Fair? A Study of Class Barriers in Britain*, London: Institute of Economic Affairs.

Savage, L. (2011) *Moving On Up? Social Mobility in the 1990s and 2000s*, London: Resolution Foundation.

Savage, L. (2011) *Snakes and Ladders: Who Climbs the Rungs of the Earnings Ladder*, London: Resolution Foundation, available online at www.resolutionfoundation.org/wp-content/uploads/2014/08/Snakes-and-Ladders-Final-Report.pdf (accessed 29 May 2015).

Savage, M. and Egerton, M. (1997) 'Social mobility, individual ability and the inheritance of class inequality', *Sociology*, 31(4).

Savage, M., Bagnall, G. and Longhurst, B. (2001) 'Ordinary, ambivalent and defensive: class identities in the northwest of England', Sociology, Vol. 35, no.4, pp.875-892.

Savage, M., Bagnall, G. and Longhurst, B. (2001) 'Ordinary, ambivalent and defensive: class identities in the north west of England', *Sociology*, 35(4).

Savage, M., Devine, F., Cunningham, M., Taylor, M., Li, Y., Hjellbrekke, J., Le Roux, B., Friedman, S. and Miles, A. (2013) 'A new model of social class: findings from the BBC's Great British Class Survey experiment', *Sociology*, available online at http://soc.sagepub.com/content/early/2013/03/12/0038038513481128 (accessed 28 May 2015).

Schlafly, P. (1977) *The Power of the Positive Woman*, New York: Crown Publishing.

Schlafly, P. (2003) *Feminist Fantasies*, Dallas, TX: Spence Publishing Company.

Sedghi, A. (2014) 'Ethnic minorities, employment and social mobility: see the research findings', *Guardian*, 12 June, available online at www.theguardian.com/news/datablog/2014/jun/12/ethnic-minorities-employment-and-social-mobility-see-the-research-findings (accessed 19 May 2015).

Sedghi, A. and Arnett, G. (2014) 'GCSE results 2014: the full breakdown', *Guardian*, 21 August, available online at www.theguardian.com/news/datablog/2014/aug/21/gcse-results-2014-the-full-breakdown (accessed 29 May 2015).

Sewell, T. (1997) *Black Masculinities and Schooling: How Black Boys Survive Modern Schooling*, Stoke-on-Trent: Trentham Books.

Sewell, T. (2000) *Black Masculinities and Schooling*, Stoke-on-Trent: Trentham Books.

Shakespeare, T. (1996) 'Disability, identity, difference', in Barnes, C. and Mercer, G. (eds) *Exploring the Divide: Illness and Disability*, Leeds: The Disability Press, pp. 94–113.

Sharpe, S. (1976) *'Just Like a Girl': How Girls Learn to Be Women*, Harmondsworth: Penguin.

Sharpe, S. (1994) *'Just Like a Girl': How Girls Learn to Be Women – from the Seventies to the Nineties*, Harmondsworth: Penguin.

Skeggs, B. (1997) *Formations of Class and Gender: Becoming Respectable*, London: Sage.

Skelton, C. and Francis, B. (2003) *Boys and Girls in the Primary Classroom*, Buckingham: Open University Press.

Sklair, L. (2003) 'Globalization, capitalism and power', in Holborn, M. (ed.) *Developments in Sociology*, Vol. 19, Ormskirk: Causeway Press.

Smart, C. (2007) *Personal Life*, Cambridge: Polity Press.

Smart, C. and Smart, B. (eds) (1978) *Women, Sexuality and Social Control*, London: Routledge & Kegan Paul.

Smith, A., Wasoff, F. and Jamieson, L. (2005) *Solo Living Across the Adult Lifecourse*, Edinburgh: Centre for Research on Families and Relationships, available online at www.era.lib.ed.ac.uk/bitstream/1842/2822/1/rb20.pdf (accessed 27 May 2015).

Smith, J. (2010) 'Mothers in the workplace: call this choice?', *Guardian*, 8 June, available online at www.theguardian.com/commentisfree/2010/jun/08/motherhood-work-sexist-suppression (accessed 10 May 2015).

Social Mobility and Child Poverty Commission (2014) 'State of the Nation 2014: Social Mobility and Child Poverty in Great Britain', The Stationary Office (formerly HMSO).

Somerville, J. (2000) *Feminism and the Family: Politics and Society in the UK and the USA*, Basingstoke: Macmillan.

Song, M. (1997) 'Children's labour in ethnic family businesses: the case of Chinese take-away businesses in Britain', *Ethnic and Racial Studies*, 20(4).

Spencer, N. (2005) 'Does material disadvantage explain the increased risk of adverse health, educational and behavioural outcomes among children in lone parent households in Britain? A cross sectional study', *Journal of Epidemiology and Community Health*, 59(?).

Spencer, S., Ruhs, M., Anderson, B. and Rogaly, B. (2007) *The Experiences of Central and East European Migrants in the UK*, York: Joseph Rowntree Foundation, available online at www.jrf.org.uk/publications/experiences-central-and-east-european-migrants-uk (accessed 26 May 2015).

Spiro, M.E. (1966) *Children of the Kibbutz*, New York: Schocken Books.

St John, G. (2003) 'Post-rave technotribalism and the carnival of protest', in Muggleton, D. and Weinzierl, R. (eds) *The Post-Subcultures Reader*, Oxford: Berg.

Stacey, J. (1993) 'Untangling feminist theory' in D. Richards and V. Robinson (eds) *Introducing Women's Studies*, MacMillan, London.

Stacey, J. (1996) *Rethinking the Family: Family Values in the Postmodern Age*, Boston, MA: Beacon Press.

Stanko, E.A. (1994) 'Challenging the problem of men's individual violence', in Newburn, T. and Stanko, E.A. (eds) *Just Boys Doing Business? Men, Masculinities and Crime*, London, Routledge.

Stanworth, M. (1984) 'Women and class analysis: a reply to John Goldthorpe', *Sociology*, 18(2).

Statham, J. (2011) *Grandparents Providing Child Care*, London: Childhood Wellbeing Research Centre, available online at www.gov.uk/government/uploads/system/uploads/attachment_data/file/181364/CWRC-00083-2011.pdf (accessed 22 May 2015).

Statham, J. (2011) *Grandparents Providing Childcare: Briefing Paper*, London: Childhood Wellbeing Research Centre, available online at www.gov.uk/government/uploads/system/uploads/attachment_data/file/181364/CWRC-00083-2011.pdf (accessed 27 May 2015).

Stone, L. (1990) *The Family, Sex and Marriage in England, 1500-1800*, Harmondsworth: Penguin.

Strand, S. and Winston, J. (2008) 'Educational aspirations in inner-city schools', *Educational Studies*, 34(4).

Strinati, D. (1995) *An Introduction to Theories of Popular Culture*, London: Routledge.

Sunday Times (2012) '*Sunday Times* Rich List', 29 April, available online at http://features.thesundaytimes.co.uk/richlist/2012/live (accessed 18 May 2015).

Sutherland, J. (2005) 'The ideas interview: Arlie Russell Hochschild', *Guardian*, 12 December, available online at www.theguardian.com/education/2005/dec/12/academicexperts.highereducation (accessed 10 May 2015).

Sutton Trust (2006) *The Educational Backgrounds of Leading Journalists*, available online at www.suttontrust.com/wp-content/uploads/2006/06/Journalists-backgrounds-final-report.pdf (accessed 28 May 2015).

Syal, R. (2013) 'British male identity crisis "spurring machismo and heartlessness"', *Guardian*, 14 May, available online at www.theguardian.com/politics/2013/may/14/male-identity-crisis-machismo-abbott (accessed 29 May 2015).

Taylor, L. (1971) *Deviance and Society*, London: Michael Joseph.

Taylor, Y. (2007) *Working-Class Lesbian Life: Classed Outsiders*, Basingstoke: Palgrave Macmillan.

The Economist (2014) 'End of the baby boom?', *The Economist*, 16 July, available online at www.economist.com/blogs/blighty/2014/07/britains-birth-rate (accessed 10 May 2015).

Thompson, M., Vinter, L. and Young, V. (2005) *Dads and Their Babies: Leave Arrangements in the First Year*, Manchester: Equal Opportunities Commission.

Thornton, S. (1995a) *Clubcultures: Music, Media and Subcultural Capital*, Cambridge: Polity Press.

Thornton, S. (1995b) 'The social logic of subcultural capital', in Gelder, K. and Thornton, S. (eds) (1997) *The Subcultures Reader*, London: Routledge.

Timmins, N. (2010) 'Social advantages still shape life chances', *Financial Times*, 27 January, available online at www.ft.com/cms/s/0/72110f9e-0ab1-11df-b35f-00144feabdc0.html#axzz3aVaUOqGe (accessed 18 May 2015).

Tinker, R. (2014) 'The truth behind the latest poverty statistics', *Fabian Society*, 2 July, available online at www.fabians.org.uk/the-truth-behind-the-latest-poverty-statistics/ (accessed 18 May 2015).

Townsend, P. (1957) The Family Life of Old People. London: Routledge & Kegan Paul; Harmondsworth: Pelican 1963.

Townsend, P. (1979) Poverty in the United Kingdom. Harmondsworth: Pelican.

Townsend, P. and Davidson N. (1982) *Inequalities in Health: The Black Report*, Harmondsworth: Penguin.

Tuchman, G. (1978) *Making News: A Study in the Construction of Reality*, New York: The Free Press.

Tumin, M. (1953) 'Some principles of stratification: a critical analysis', *American Sociological Review*, 18(4), 387–94.

Turkle, S. (1995) *Life on the Screen: Identity in the Age of the Internet*, New York: Touchstone.

Turner, B. (1989) 'Ageing, status politics and sociological theory', *British Journal of Sociology*, 40(4), 588–606.

UK Feminista (n.d.) 'Facts and statistics on gender inequality', available online at http://ukfeminista.org.uk/take-action/facts-and-statistics-on-gender-inequality/ (accessed 19 May 2015).

United Nations (2014) *The Millennium Development Goals Report 2014*, New York: United Nations, available online at www.un.org/millenniumgoals/2014%20MDG%20report/MDG%202014%20English%20web.pdf (accessed 29 May 2015).

Vale, V. and Juno, A. (eds) (1989) *Re/Search #12: Modern Primitives. An Investigation of Contemporary Adornment & Ritual*, San Francisco, CA: Re/Search Publications.

Van Dijk, T.A. (1991) *Racism and the Press*, London: Routledge.

Venkatesh, S. (2009) Gang Leader for a Day. London: Penguin.

Victor, C. (1994) Old Age in Modern Society. Dordrecht: Springer Science + Business Media.

Victor, C., Bowling, A., Bond, J. and Scambler, S. (2003) *Loneliness, Social Isolation and Living Alone in Later Life: Research Findings 17 from the Growing Older Programme*, Sheffield: Economic & Social Research Council Growing Older Programme, available online at www.growingolder.group.shef.ac.uk/ChristinaVic_F17.pdf (accessed 27 May 2015).

341

Waddington, P.A.J. (1999) 'Police (canteen) subculture: an appreciation', *British Journal of Criminology*, 39(2), 287–309.

Walby, S. (1990) *Theorizing Patriarchy*, Oxford: Blackwell.

Walby, S. (1997) *Gender Transformations*, London: Routledge.

Waldfogel, J. and Washbrook, E. (2008) *Early Years Policy Paper*, prepared for the Sutton Trust–Carnegie Summit: Social Mobility and Education Policy, 1–3 June, available online at www.bristol.ac.uk/media-library/sites/ifssoca/migrated/documents/waldfogeleyp.pdf (accessed 18 May 2015).

Wallerstein, J. and Lewis, J. (2004) 'The unexpected legacy of divorce: report of a 25-year study', *Psychoanalytic Psychology*, 21(3), 353–70, available online at www.fellowshipoftheparks.com/Documents%5CUnexpected_Legacy_of_Divorce.pdf (accessed 27 May 2015).

Walter, N. (2008) *Living Dolls: The Return of Sexism*, London: Virago Press.

War on Want (n.d.) 'Sweatshops in Bangladesh', available online at www.waronwant.org/overseas-work/sweatshops-and-plantations/sweatshops-in-bangladesh (accessed 19 May 2015).

Warin J., Solomon, Y., Lewis, C. and Langford, W. (1999) *Fathers, Work and Family Life*, London: Family Policy Studies Centre.

Wasoff, F., Jamieson, L., and Smith, A. (2005) 'Solo living, individual and family boundaries: findings from secondary analysis', in McKie, L. and Chunningham-Burley, S. (eds) *Families in Societies: Boundaries and Relationships*, Bristol: Policy Press.

Watson, N. (2002) '"Well, I know this is going to sound very strange to you, but I do not see myself as a disabled person"', *Disability and Society*, 17(5), 509–27.

Watson, T.J. (2008) 'Managing identity: identity work, personal predicaments and structural circumstances', *Organization*, 15, 121–43.

Wayne, M. (2007) 'The media and young people: hyping up the new folk devils', *Socialist Worker*, 18 September, available online at http://socialistworker.co.uk/art/12750/The+media+and+young+people+-+hyping+up+the+new+folk+devils (accessed 28 May 2015).

Weber, M. (1947) *The Theory of Economic and Social Organisations*, New York: The Free Press.

Weber, M. (1948) 'Class, status, party', in Gerth, H. and Mills, C.W. (eds) *From Max Weber*, London: Routledge.

Weeks, J. (1987) 'Questions of identity', in Caplan, P. (ed.) *The Cultural Construction of Sexuality*, London: Routledge, pp. 31–51.

Weeks, J. (1991) 'Sexual identification is a strange thing', in Lemert, C. (ed.) (1993) *Social Theory: The Multicultural and Classic Reading*, Oxford: Westview Press.

Weeks, J., Donovan, C. and Heaphy, B. (1999) 'Everyday experiments: narratives in non-heterosexual relationships', in Silva, E.B. and Smart, C. (eds) *The New Family*, London: Sage.

Westergaard, J. and Resler, H. (1976) *Class in a Capitalist Society*, Harmondsworth: Penguin.

Westwood, S. (1999) 'Girls just want to have fun: representing gender', *Sociology Review*.

Whale, J. (1980) *The Politics of the Media*, London: Fontana.

Whannel, G. (2002) *Media Sport Stars: Masculinities and Moralities*, London: Routledge.

Whelehan, I. (2000) *Overloaded*, London: Women's Press.

White, C. and Edgar, G. (2010) 'Inequalities in healthy life expectancy by social class and area type: England, 2001–03', *Health Statistics Quarterly*, 45(1), 28–56.

White, R. (2002) 'Understanding youth gangs', *Trends & Issues in Crime and Criminal Justice*, No. 237, Australian Institute of Criminology, available online at www.aic.gov.au/media_library/publications/tandi_pdf/tandi237.pdf (accessed 28 May 2015).

Whiting, S. (2012) *Socio-Demographic Comparison Between Those UK Families with up to Two Children and Those with Three or More*, London: Population Matters, available at http://populationmatters.org/documents/family_sizes.pdf (accessed 27 May 2015).

Whyte, W.F. (1955) Street Corner Society. Chicago: University of Chicago Press.

Wilkins, L.T. (1967) *Social Deviance: Social Policy, Action and Research*, London: Routledge.

Wilkinson, R. and Pickett, K. (2009) *The Spirit Level: Why Equality Is Better for Everyone*, Harmondsworth: Penguin.

Williams, K. (2010) *Get Me a Murder a Day!: A History of Media and Communication in Britain*, London: Bloomsbury Academic.

Willis, P. (1977) *Learning to Labour: How Working Class Kids Get Working Class Jobs*, Farnborough: Saxon House.

Willmott, P. (1988) 'Urban kinship past and present', *Social Studies Review*.

Wilson, E.O. (1975) *Sociobiology: The New Synthesis*, New York: Harvard University Press.

Wolf, N. (1991) *The Beauty Myth: How Images of Beauty Are Used Against Women*, London: Vintage.

Women in Journalism (2009) 'Hoodies or altar boys: what is media stereotyping doing to our British boys?', available online at http://womeninjournalism.co.uk/hoodies-or-altar-boys/ (accessed 28 May 2015).

Women's Budget Group (WBG) (2005) *Women's and Children's Poverty: Making the Links*, London: Women's Budget Group, available online at www.wbg.org.uk/documents/WBGWomensandchildrenspoverty.pdf (accessed 29 May 2015).

Wood, H. & Skeggs, B. (2011) Reality Television and Class. Basingstoke: Palgrave MacMillan.

Woods, R.I. and Smith, C.W. (1983) 'The decline of marital fertility in the late nineteenth century: the case of England and Wales', *Population Studies: A Journal of Demography*, 37, 207–26.

World Economic Forum (2014) 'The Global Gender Gap Report 2014', available online at http://reports.weforum.org/global-gender-gap-report-2014/ (accessed 29 May 2015).

World Health Organization (2014) *Global and Regional Estimates of Violence Against Women: Prevalence and Health Effects of Intimate Partner Violence and Non-Partner Sexual Violence*, Geneva: World Health Organization, available online at http://apps.who.int/iris/bitstream/10665/85239/1/9789241564625_eng.pdf (accessed 29 May 2015).

Wright Mills, C. The Sociological Imagination. Oxford: Oxford University Press.

WRVS (2011) *Gold Age Pensioners: Valuing the Socio-Economic Contribution of Older People in the UK*, Cardiff: WRVS, available online at www.royalvoluntaryservice.org.uk/Uploads/Documents/gold_age_report_2011.pdf (accessed 27 May 2015).

Young, J. (1971) 'The role of the police as amplifiers of deviancy, negotiators of reality and translators of fantasy', in Cohen, S. (ed.) *Images of Deviance*, Harmondsworth: Penguin.

Young, J. (2003) 'Merton with energy, Katz with structure: the sociology of vindictiveness and the criminology of transgression', *Theoretical Criminology*, 7(3), 389–414.

Young, J. (2003) *Constructing the Paradigm of Violence: Mass Media, Violence and Youth*, available online at http://www.ukobservatory.com/downloadfiles/Paradigm%20of%20Violence.pdf (accessed 28 May 2015).

Young, J. (2007) *The Vertigo of Late Modernity*, London: Sage.

Young, M. and Willmott, P. (1973) *The Symmetrical Family*, London: Routledge & Kegan Paul.

Zaretsky, E. (1976) *Capitalism, the Family and Personal Life*, London: Pluto Press.

Zola, I.K. (1982) *Missing Pieces: A Chronicle of Living with a Disability*, Philadelphia, PA: Temple University Press.

Index